lonely planet

Guatemala

Conner Gorry

LONELY PLANET PUBLICATIONS
Melbourne • Oakland • London • Paris

GUATEMALA

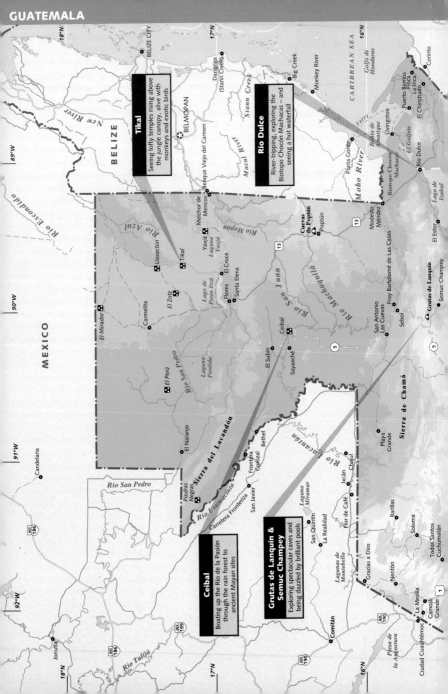

Tikal
Seeing lofty temples rising above the jungle canopy, alive with monkeys and exotic birds

Río Dulce
River-tripping, exploring the Biotopo Chocón Machacas – and seeing a hot waterfall

Ceibal
Boating up the Río de la Pasión through the rain forest to ancient Mayan sites

Grutas de Lanquín & Semuc Champey
Exploring spectacular caves and being dazzled by brilliant pools

CARIBBEAN SEA

Golfo de Honduras

MEXICO

BELIZE

BELIZE CITY

BELMOPAN

New River

Río Escondido

Río Azul

Río Mopán

Río San Juan

Río Machaquilá

Río San Pedro

Laguna Perdida

Sierra del Lacandón

Río Usumacinta

Carretera Frontera

Río Lacantún

Sierra de Chamá

Lagunas de Montebello

Río San Pedro

Río Tulijá

Presa de la Angostura

Lago de Izabal

Bahía de Amatique

Moho River

Monkey River

Big Creek

Dangriga (Stann Creek)

Stann Creek

Macal River

Melchor de Mencos

Benque Viejo del Carmen

Yaxhá

Laguna Yaxhá

Uaxactún

Tikal

El Zotz

El Cruce

Flores

Santa Elena

Lago de Petén Itzá

Carmelita

El Mirador

El Perú

El Naranjo

Piedras Negras

Bethel

Frontera Corozal

Flor de Café

San Javier

La Realidad

San Quintín

Laguna Miramar

Ixcán

Chajul

Playa Grande

Barillas

Soloma

Todos Santos Cuchumatán

La Mesilla

Camojá Grande

Ciudad Cuauhtémoc

Comitán

Nentón

Gracias a Dios

Candelaria

Ionoltá

Cuevas de Poptún

Poptún

Modesto Méndez

Fray Bartolomé de las Casas

San Antonio Las Cuevas

Sebol

Grutas de Lanquín

Semuc Champey

El Estor

El Golfete

Río Dulce

Macharía

Biotopo Chocón

Punta Gorda

Livingston

Puerto Barrios

Finca La Inca

El Chinchado

Corinto

Ceibal

El Subín

Sayaxché

13

13

5

5

186

190

190

199

186

1

18°N 17°N 16°N

92°W 91°W 90°W 89°W

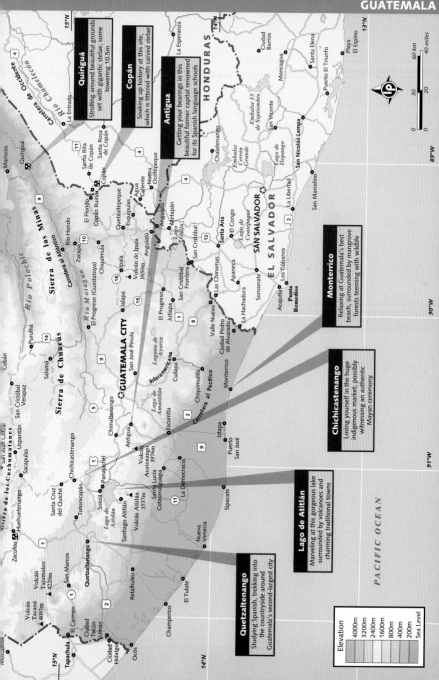

Guatemala
1st edition – January 2001

Published by
Lonely Planet Publications Pty Ltd A.C.N. 005 607 983
90 Maribyrnong St, Footscray, Victoria 3011, Australia

Lonely Planet Offices
Australia Locked Bag 1, Footscray, Victoria 3011, Australia
USA 150 Linden St, Oakland, CA 94607
UK 10a Spring Place, London NW5 3BH
France 1 rue du Dahomey, 75011 Paris

Photographs
All the images in this guide are available for licensing from
Lonely Planet Images.
email: lpi@lonelyplanet.com.au

Front cover photograph
Bus in Antigua (Tony Wheeler)

ISBN 0 86442 684 4

Printed by The Bookmaker International Ltd
Printed in China

Contents

THE HIGHLANDS 156

THE PACIFIC SLOPE 226

CENTRAL & EASTERN GUATEMALA 244

EL PETÉN 303

LANGUAGE 341

MENU TRANSLATOR 348

GLOSSARY 351

INDEX 359

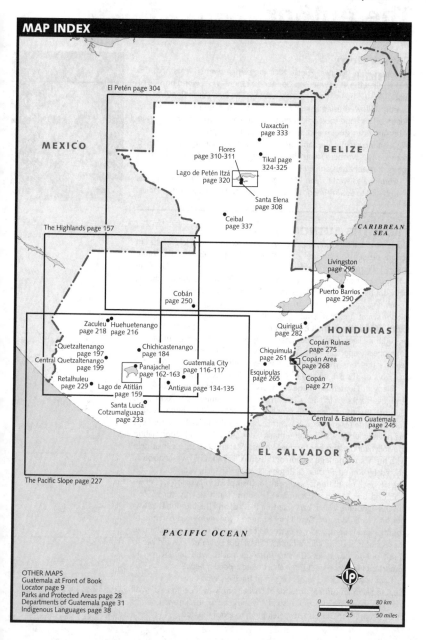

MAP INDEX

El Petén page 304

MEXICO

Uaxactún page 333

Flores page 310-311

Tikal page 324-325

Lago de Petén Itzá page 320

Santa Elena page 308

Ceibal page 337

BELIZE

CARIBBEAN SEA

The Highlands page 157

Cobán page 250

Livingston page 295

Puerto Barrios page 290

Zaculeu page 218

Huehuetenango page 216

Quetzaltenango page 197

Central Quetzaltenango page 199

Chichicastenango page 184

Panajachel page 162-163

Guatemala City page 116-117

Retalhuleu page 229

Lago de Atitlán page 159

Antigua page 134-135

Santa Lucia Cotzumalguapa page 233

Quiriguá page 282

HONDURAS

Copán Ruinas page 275

Chiquimula page 261

Copán Area page 268

Esquipulas page 265

Copán page 271

Central & Eastern Guatemala page 245

EL SALVADOR

The Pacific Slope page 227

PACIFIC OCEAN

OTHER MAPS
Guatemala at Front of Book
Locator page 9
Parks and Protected Areas page 28
Departments of Guatemala page 31
Indigenous Languages page 38

0   40   80 km
0   25   50 miles

The Author

Conner Gorry

It all started in Vieques, Puerto Rico more than twenty years ago. On that seminal trip, it dawned on Conner that there was a world outside of suburban strip malls and prepubescent pap. The Dominican Republic and Culebra followed (islands kick ass!), and it wasn't long before she was hooked. The habit took hold, and between adventures, she got a BA in Latin American studies and an MA in international policy.

Conner currently lives among all those dot commies in San Francisco (somebody save her!!) with her partner, Koch. Day by day the siren songs of Manhattan and Havana grow mightier.

Conner also wrote *Read This First: Central & South America* and has contributed to *South America on a shoestring* and other fabulous LP titles.

FROM THE AUTHOR

Guatemala is an incredible place, and this was an incredible project. I'm feeling blessed for this and other things right now. Topping the 'other things' list is my partner and travel king, Koch, who makes life so damn fun and fulfilling I laugh at myself for refusing his first date requests. Thanks, baby, for being you and always loving the sometimes intolerable me.

Writing and publishing an LP book is like giving birth (with pain, blood, sweat and tears), and there are scores of people working their butts off to make each title good. In Oaktown, making this guide stellar are editrix Elaine Merrill, designer Margaret Livingston, a team of cartographers (especially Annette Olsen), Michele Posner and Ben Greensfelder – the consummate editor. I am also indebted to Nancy Keller for her work on the 3rd edition of *Guatemala, Belize & Yucatán*.

Many in Guatemala made my work easier, groovier or healthier. In Antigua, thanks go to Nancy Hoffman and Luis Ramirez of Vision Travel; Gunther Blauth of Germany supplied good info on the 'jungle route.' Tom Lingenfelter in Xela was a terrific help. Dr Bill in Todos Santos kept me healthy in body and spirit – thanks, doc. Also, heartfelt appreciation to Molly Harlow and her teacher, Rosario Martin Chavez, for their help with the Mam language section of this book. In Momos, I was graciously hosted by Kermit Frazier & Rigoberto Itzep Chanchavac. Rosie & Bill Fogerty rock on all fronts, and being at their place in Jaibalito was ethereal. Christine & Aimee (Denmark) saved my sanity in Fray, for which I am truly grateful. Words can't capture the trial and the triumph that was our hike to El Mirador. Gerd Unni Rougnø (Norway) was a paragon of courage and insight, and the better half of the first female expedition to make that trip. Unni, you're fantastic. Last, but not least, I would like to shout out to our guide Calistro from Carmelita, who taught me an important life lesson with three short words: *poco a poco*.

I am very interested in hearing from travelers who have experienced Guatemala in an offbeat, intense or challenging way. Feel free to email me at connergo@ekno.com. Also, if anyone reading this knows Lourdes or Elyse (last seen in Monterey), tell them to email me, too.

This Book

This 1st edition of *Guatemala* was written by Conner Gorry. Some of the information, written by Nancy Keller and Tom Brosnahan, appeared previously in the 3rd edition of *Guatemala, Belize & Yucatán* and was reviewed and updated by Conner.

FROM THE PUBLISHER

Guatemala is the first book produced in LP's Oakland office to employ a new, streamlined production process. A diverse and talented team collaborated to make it happen, pooling their skills to wrestle the book through numerous complicated phases.

The book was edited by Elaine Merrill, with near-perfect proofing by Erin Corrigan. Susan Derby and Paul Sheridan also helped with the proofing. Michele Posner patiently and expertly oversaw every step as the new procedure unfolded. Ben Greensfelder served as the Latin America expert and all-around helpful guy, especially early in the book's life. Suki Gear was ever ready with answers to obscure editing questions, while Belinda Bennett-Gow kept a good chronicle of the project's progress. Kate Hoffman and Mariah Bear both generously gave their time to attend meetings and provide solutions to unforeseen problems. Jacqueline Volin prepared the brief. Ken DellaPenta indexed the book.

Ace lead cartographer Annette Olson, aided by Ed Turley, created *Guatemala*'s maps under the expert guidance of Tracey Croom and Alex Guilbert. Cartographers Heather Haskell, Kat Smith, Chris Gillis, Mary Hagemann and Patrick Phelan also pitched in.

Susan Rimerman oversaw the incomparable design team. Margaret Livingston designed the color pages and did an expert job on layout, with help from Shelley Firth. The irrepressible Beca Lafore designed the cover and coordinated the illustrations. Illustrations, ranging from the whimsical to the sublime, were made by Hugh D'Andrade, Hayden Foell, Rini Keagy, Beca Lafore, Justin Marler, Henia Miedzinski, Hannah Reineck, Jennifer Steffey and Lisa Summers. Special thanks for the Maximon candle illustration to Jacques VanKirk and Parney Bassett-VanKirk and their book, *Remarkable Remains of the Ancient Peoples of Guatemala* (University of Oklahoma, 1996).

Lastly, but certainly not least, the new process would never have come off without the unflagging enthusiasm of Conner Gorry.

Foreword

ABOUT LONELY PLANET GUIDEBOOKS

The story begins with a classic travel adventure: Tony and Maureen Wheeler's 1972 journey across Europe and Asia to Australia. Useful information about the overland trail did not exist at that time, so Tony and Maureen published the first Lonely Planet guidebook to meet a growing need.

From a kitchen table, then from a tiny office in Melbourne (Australia), Lonely Planet has become the largest independent travel publisher in the world, an international company with offices in Melbourne, Oakland (USA), London (UK) and Paris (France).

Today Lonely Planet guidebooks cover the globe. There is an ever-growing list of books, and there's information in a variety of forms and media. Some things haven't changed. The main aim is still to help make it possible for adventurous travelers to get out there – to explore and better understand the world.

At Lonely Planet we believe travelers can make a positive contribution to the countries they visit – if they respect their host communities and spend their money wisely. Since 1986 a percentage of the income from each book has been donated to aid projects and human-rights campaigns.

Updates Lonely Planet thoroughly updates each guidebook as often as possible. This usually means there are around two years between editions, although for more unusual or more stable destinations the gap can be longer. Check the imprint page (following the color map at the beginning of the book) for publication dates.

Between editions, up-to-date information is available in two free newsletters – the paper *Planet Talk* and email *Comet* (to subscribe, contact any Lonely Planet office) – and on our website at www.lonelyplanet.com. The *Upgrades* section of the website covers a number of important and volatile destinations and is regularly updated by Lonely Planet authors. *Scoop* covers news and current affairs relevant to travelers. And, lastly, the *Thorn Tree* bulletin board and *Postcards* section of the site carry unverified, but fascinating, reports from travelers.

Correspondence The process of creating new editions begins with the letters, postcards and emails received from travelers. This correspondence often includes suggestions, criticisms and comments about the current editions. Interesting excerpts are immediately passed on via newsletters and the website, and everything goes to our authors to be verified when they're researching on the road. We're keen to get more feedback from organizations or individuals who represent communities visited by travelers.

Lonely Planet gathers information for everyone who's curious about the planet – and especially for those who explore it firsthand. Through guidebooks, phrasebooks, activity guides, maps, literature, newsletters, image library, TV series and website, we act as an information exchange for a worldwide community of travelers.

Research Authors aim to gather sufficient practical information to enable travelers to make informed choices and to make the mechanics of a journey run smoothly. They also research historical and cultural background to help enrich the travel experience and allow travelers to understand and respond appropriately to cultural and environmental issues.

Authors don't stay in every hotel because that would mean spending a couple of months in each medium-size city and, no, they don't eat at every restaurant because that would mean stretching belts beyond capacity. They do visit hotels and restaurants to check standards and prices, but feedback based on readers' direct experiences can be very helpful.

Many of our authors work undercover; others aren't so secretive. None of them accept freebies in exchange for positive write-ups. And none of our guidebooks contain any advertising.

Production Authors submit their raw manuscripts and maps to offices in Australia, the USA, the UK or France. Editors and cartographers – all experienced travelers themselves – then begin the process of assembling the pieces. When the book finally hits the shops, some things are already out of date, we start getting feedback from readers and the process begins again....

WARNING & REQUEST

Things change – prices go up, schedules change, good places go bad and bad places go bankrupt – nothing stays the same. So, if you find things better or worse, recently opened or long since closed, please tell us and help make the next edition even more accurate and useful. We genuinely value all the feedback we receive. Julie Young coordinates a well-traveled team that reads and acknowledges every letter, postcard and email and ensures that every morsel of information finds its way to the appropriate authors, editors and cartographers for verification.

Everyone who writes to us will find their name in the next edition of the appropriate guidebook. They will also receive the latest issue of *Planet Talk*, our quarterly printed newsletter, or *Comet*, our monthly email newsletter. Subscriptions to both newsletters are free. The very best contributions will be rewarded with a free guidebook.

Excerpts from your correspondence may appear in new editions of Lonely Planet guidebooks, the Lonely Planet website, *Planet Talk* or *Comet*, so please let us know if you *don't* want your letter published or your name acknowledged.

Send all correspondence to the Lonely Planet office closest to you:

Australia: Locked Bag 1, Footscray, Victoria 3011, Australia
USA: 150 Linden St, Oakland, CA 94607
UK: 10A Spring Place, London NW5 3BH
France: 1 rue du Dahomey, 75011 Paris

Or email us at: talk2us@lonelyplanet.com.au

For news, views and updates, see our website: www.lonelyplanet.com

HOW TO USE A LONELY PLANET GUIDEBOOK

The best way to use a Lonely Planet guidebook is any way you choose. At Lonely Planet, we believe the most memorable travel experiences are often those that are unexpected, and the finest discoveries are those you make yourself. Guidebooks are not intended to be used as if they provided a detailed set of infallible instructions!

Contents All Lonely Planet guidebooks follow the same format. The Facts about the Country chapters or sections give background information ranging from history to weather. Facts for the Visitor gives practical information on issues like visas and health. Getting There & Away gives a brief starting point for researching travel to and from the destination. Getting Around gives an overview of the transport options available when you arrive.

The peculiar demands of each destination determine how subsequent chapters are broken up, but some things remain constant. We always start with background, then proceed to sights, places to stay, places to eat, entertainment, getting there and away, and getting around information – in that order.

Heading Hierarchy Lonely Planet headings are used in a strict hierarchical structure that can be visualized as a set of Russian dolls. Each heading (and its following text) is encompassed by any preceding heading that is higher on the hierarchical ladder.

Entry Points We do not assume guidebooks will be read from beginning to end, but that people will dip into them. The traditional entry points are the list of contents and the index. In addition, however, some books have a complete list of maps and an index map illustrating map coverage.

There may also be a color map that shows highlights. These highlights are dealt with in greater detail later in the book, along with planning questions and suggested itineraries. Each chapter covering a geographical region usually begins with a locator map and another list of highlights. Once you find something of interest in a list of highlights, turn to the index.

Maps Maps play a crucial role in Lonely Planet guidebooks and include a huge amount of information. A legend is printed on the back page. We seek to have complete consistency between maps and text, and to have every important place in the text captured on a map. Map key numbers usually start in the top left corner.

Although inclusion in a guidebook usually implies a recommendation, we cannot list every good place. Exclusion does not necessarily imply criticism. In fact, there are a number of reasons why we might exclude a place – sometimes it is simply inappropriate to encourage an influx of travelers.

Introduction

Guatemala is one of those rare destinations that rewards even the most jaded world travelers with revelatory experiences – a place where indigenous life perseveres much as it did when the Europeans first showed up, and where there are still pockets unsullied by the 'been there, done that' crowd. From the geography to the people to the ancient and extant culture, the country is a beautiful and complex amalgam of the best the Western Hemisphere has to offer. Perhaps most stunning is the fact that Guatemala has just recently emerged from 36 years of civil war, offering the mindful traveler the opportunity to witness the peace process first hand.

Few superlatives can accurately capture the grandeur of Guatemala's topography. With 30 volcanoes spread throughout the highlands, it seems there's always some cone – a few huffing with smoke and fire – looming over your shoulder. There's temperamental Volcán Pacaya (a popular day trip), Volcán Agua keeping watch over Antigua and no fewer than three volcanoes

ringing Lago de Atitlán, one of the most majestic spots on this spinning blue rock we call Earth.

All this stellar geography means travelers can hike, scuba dive, go white-water rafting, explore caves, mountain bike, kayak and play at outdoor and adventure activities ad infinitum. Save for snowboarding and other wintry fun stuff, chances are you can find a beautiful spot in Guatemala to pursue your outdoor interest. As the peace process gathers momentum and the tourist industry continues to grow, so too should the opportunities to explore Guatemala's natural gems.

Guatemala also boasts large tracts of primary rain forest in the northern Petén region, though the stands are shrinking too rapidly as oil, lumber and cattle interests move in. Couple these economic exploits with the internal migration of poor Guatemalans and returning war refugees searching for a new place to eke out a subsistence existence, and the future of the forest appears pretty bleak. Luckily, new

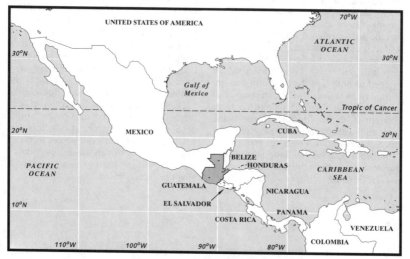

preservation efforts such as the creation of the Reserva de la Biosfera Maya along the Guatemalan-Mexican border are an encouraging first step in much needed programs to protect the rain forest.

Though birding and wildlife viewing are gaining popularity in the Petén, most travelers visit this region to explore the spectacular Mayan ruins spread across hundreds of kilometers of virgin rain forest. Guatemala is practically synonymous with Tikal, one of Mesoamerica's greatest Mayan cities and archaeological sites, made even more special by its sprawling layout and towering temples set within an incredible jungle tableau. Easy to get to, the ruins at Tikal are a must-see for any visitor. Still, difficult to reach sites such as El Mirador in the extreme jungle depths may be even more spectacular than Tikal, because getting there is an adventure in its own right – and not for the timid!

While the list of the Petén's remote archaeological sites is as intriguing as it is exotic, including places such as Ceibal, Nakbé, Yaxjá and Piedras Negras, visiting them is even more so.

Excavations are not limited to the Petén, however, and visitors will be well rewarded by checking out the various Mayan sites in the highlands, too. The stelae at Quiriguá, the mysterious influences at Abaj Takalik and the sedate ruins at Zaculeu are arresting facets of the Guatemalan landscape that offer insight into this ancient culture. Travelers intrigued by all things Mayan will be psyched to note that the beautiful and important ruins at Copán in Honduras are just over the border and easily visited from Guatemala. New discoveries are being made all the time, providing increasingly detailed insight into this complex civilization.

Studying Spanish has long served as a traveler's gateway to the intense, pervasive and refreshing culture that defines Guatemala, and language study increasingly rivals the ruins as the country's primary draw. Whether you prefer the international scene of Antigua, the cosmopolitan atmosphere of Quetzaltenango or the mountain seclusion of Todos Santos, odds are there's a Spanish school and setting for you. Many programs encourage volunteer stints and offer weekly outings and electives such as dancing or weaving. Students of Mayan culture can take advantage of many opportunities for learning indigenous dialects like Mam and Quiché as well. Most students opt to live with a Guatemalan family during their course of study to experience total immersion, both cultural and linguistic.

Perhaps the most striking feature of Guatemala is the people. A visit to the raucously colorful markets in towns like Chichicastenango or San Francisco El Alto will give you a feel for the living culture that typifies Guatemala's indigenous population. From the tortillas at breakfast to the *huipil* worn by the matron next to you on the bus, culture here is palpable and rich. The people really make traveling in Guatemala special, and their amicable and helpful demeanor is infectious. For this reason, it's a particularly great destination for solo travelers.

There are so many fascinating components of Guatemala that pages of accolades could make up this introduction, but since you've already got this book, you are on your way to discovering the beauty of traveling here yourself. The most important thing to keep in mind is that it is very easy (and highly encouraged!) to get off the beaten track in Guatemala. Hop on the back of a pickup to a small Mayan village or catch a bus to the end of the line, and you're off. Since peace was struck in 1996, travelers have had better and safer access to rarely visited corners of this beautiful country. Take advantage of that access and you won't be disappointed.

Facts about Guatemala

Guatemala is like an onion, with layer after layer growing more intense the longer you peel away at it, until finally you're faced with a reality infinitely more complex and hard to grasp than you ever imagined. Little is clear cut here, and the sometimes harmonious but often violent and bloody relations between the indigenous and ladino populations are deeply rooted in the country's history. Nowhere is this clash more evident than in the 36-year civil war, an armed conflict that pitted the national armed forces against guerrilla cadres in a tragic face-off that left hundreds of thousands dead, 'disappeared' or homeless.

The distinction between indigenous and 'European' blood, between traditional and 'modern' culture and commerce, has been a defining factor of Guatemalan society since the days of the conquistadors. Indeed, many of the social and economic patterns set in motion following the arrival of the Spaniards persist in modern Guatemala. Today, the distinction divides Guatemalan society in two, creating a polemic of 'haves' and 'have nots.' Unfortunately, the ladinos (the 'haves') hold fast to a political and economic power base that has a vested interest in keeping the indigenous population (the 'have nots') undereducated and misinformed. The powers that be perpetuate this cycle, flouting specific provisions in the Peace Accords of 1996 calling for equal rights for the country's indigenous people, including access to education and basic health care. Resistance by the elite to full and equal rights for Guatemala's 22 different ethnic groups, chronic as it is, will likely continue in the future.

But it seems the fiercely proud Maya of Guatemala understand who are the rightful caretakers of this land. Though they are reticent to assert it publicly or politically, the Maya who live in the highlands amid breathtaking mountain scenery guard jealously their ancient customs and way of life. Holidays and ceremonies are filled with ancient pageantry and animism, and the weekly markets are ablaze with the vivid colors of traditional handmade clothing, known as *traje*. Mayan women in particular are staunch torchbearers of indigenous culture and customs.

At the same time, the modern world is penetrating Mayan culture, bringing good things and bad. Money from tourism is helping some Maya to improve their quality of life, education and health, but it is also luring the younger generation away from their traditions and toward the rough and bustling cities. Even in the Guatemalan outback, it is becoming common for Mayan youth to speak Spanish instead of their indigenous language and to have a greater understanding of the latest Nintendo game than of the sacred Mayan calendar.

Traditional life and modern values also clash when local farmers and ranchers clear the rainforest to provide for their families. The need is for a livelihood; the method is the traditional one of slash-and-burn; the result is ecological disaster.

There is hope, however. New school curricula taught in indigenous dialects, conservation efforts spearheaded and run by local communities, and Mayan candidates in public office mean *poco a poco*, little by little, Guatemala's indigenous community is striking a balance for living traditionally in the modern age.

HISTORY

Scholars believe the ancient Maya may be descended from the first people to cross the Bering Strait, some 20,000 years before Christopher Columbus was even a gleam in his mother's eye. If this is true, nearly half of Guatemala's population today can count these prehistoric pioneers as ancestors. As a percent of the total population, Guatemala's indigenous community is one of the largest in the hemisphere. This is amazing considering the diseases introduced by the Europeans in the 16th century and the bloody conquest, both of which took a heavy toll on Mesoamerica's – indeed, the entire New World's – indigenous population.

Since discovery and independence, Guatemala's history has been one of rivalry and struggle between the indigenous Maya and colonizing Europeans. Modern history, however, has witnessed a more pronounced clash between the forces of left and right. The liberals have historically wanted to turn backward Guatemala into an enlightened republic of political, social and economic progress. The conservatives have hoped to preserve the traditional verities of colonial rule, with a strong church and an omnipotent government backed by an armed force partial to draconian tactics. Their motto might have been 'power must be held by those with merit, virtue and property.' Historically, both movements have benefited the social and economic elite and disenfranchised the people of the countryside, mostly Maya.

Were it only disenfranchisement, perhaps humanity could forgive, forget and move on. However, between 1960 and 1996, civil war raged throughout Guatemala, during which authorities estimate 200,000 people were killed, a million forced from their homes and countless thousands 'disappeared.'

Archaic Period (20,000–2000 BC)

The massive glaciers that blanketed northern Europe, Asia and North America in the Pleistocene Epoch sapped the oceans of colossal amounts of water, dramatically lowering the earth's sea level. The receding waters exposed enough land so that wandering bands of Asiatic men and women could find their way on dry land from Siberia to Alaska, and then southwards through the Western Hemisphere.

The wandering bands made this journey perhaps as early as 23,000 years ago and soon spread throughout every part of North and South America down to the Straits of Magellan. When the glaciers melted (about 7000 BC) and the sea level rose anew, the land bridge over which they crossed became submerged beneath what is now called the Bering Strait.

These early inhabitants hunted mammoths, fished and gathered wild foods. The Ice Age was followed by a hot, dry period in which the mammoths' natural pastureland disappeared and the wild nuts and berries became scarce. The primitive inhabitants had to find some other way to survive, so they sought out favorable microclimates and invented agriculture.

Then, like now, maize (corn) was king. The Maya successfully hybridized this native grass and planted it alongside beans, tomatoes, chili peppers and squash (marrow). Agriculture was clearly a more stable – and, at the time – sustainable way of life. Baskets were woven to carry in the harvest, and turkeys and dogs were domesticated for food. These early homebodies used crude stone tools and primitive pottery and shaped simple clay fertility figurines.

Early Preclassic Period (2000–800 BC)

The improvement in the food supply led to an increase in population, a higher standard of living and more leisure time to experiment with different agricultural techniques and artistic niceties. Decorative pots and healthier, fatter corn strains were produced during this time. Even at the beginning of the Early Preclassic period, people in Guatemala spoke an early form of the Mayan language. These early Maya also decided that living in caves and under palm fronds was passé, so they invented the *na*, or thatched Mayan hut. You won't have to travel extensively in Guatemala to observe that these huts are still used today, some 4000 years later, throughout much of the country. Where spring floods were a problem, a family would build its na on a mound of earth. Similar to other Native American burial practices, when a family member died, burial took place right there in the living room, after which the deceased attained the rank of honored ancestor.

The Copán Valley (in present-day Honduras) had its first proto-Mayan settlers by about 1100 BC, and a century later the settlements on the Guatemalan Pacific coast were developing a hierarchical society.

Timeline

The history of the Maya and their predecessors stretches back over 4000 years. The following timeline may help you to keep track of what was happening when and where. The division of historical periods for Mayan civilization is that used by Professor Michael D Coe (author of *The Maya*). Notes in parentheses highlight contemporary historical events in the Old World so you can compare developments.

20,000 to 2000 BC: Archaic Period People survive by hunting and gathering. After the end of the Ice Age (7500 BC), primitive agriculture begins.

2000 to 800 BC: Early Preclassic Period In a few Mayan regions, fishing and farming villages form and produce primitive crops. Early Olmec civilization flourishes (1200 to 900 BC) at San Lorenzo, Veracruz; Teotihuacán culture flourishes in central Mexico. (Old Testament times of Abraham, Isaac and Jacob; Israelites escape from Egypt and cross Jordan into the Promised Land; reigns of King David, King Solomon, Tutankhamen and Nefertiti.)

800 to 300 BC: Middle Preclassic Period There are larger towns; Olmec civilization reaches its height at La Venta, Tabasco. The Mayan population greatly increases. (Flowering of classical Hellenic culture and art around the Aegean Sea.)

300 BC to 250 AD: Late Preclassic Period Mayan cities have large but simple temples and pyramids; pottery and decoration become elaborate. (Alexander the Great's conquests; Ptolemy dynasty in Egypt; Roman republic and early empire; life of Jesus.)

250 to 600: Early Classic Period The Long Count calendar is in use. In the highlands of Guatemala and Chiapas, great temples are built around spacious plazas; Mayan art is technically excellent. (Founding of Constantinople and building of Hagia Sophia; Huns invade Europe; Vandals sack Rome, beginning of Middle (or Dark) Ages in Europe; Saxons invade Britain.)

600 to 900: Late Classic Period High Mayan civilization moves from the western highlands to the lowlands of Petén and Yucatán. Mayan art is at its most sensitive and refined. (Life of Mohammed; rise of the Arab Empire; Dome of the Rock built in Jerusalem; Harun al-Rashid sends an ambassador to the court of Charlemagne.)

900 to 1200: Early Postclassic Period Population growth, food shortages, decline in trade, military campaigns, revolutions and migrations cause the swift collapse of Classic Mayan culture. In central Mexico, Toltecs flourish at Tula, later abandon it and invade Yucatán, establishing their capital at Chichén Itzá. (Europe's Dark Ages continue; Norman invasion of Britain; Crusades.)

1200 to 1530: Late Postclassic Period Toltec civilization collapses mysteriously, and the Itzaes move from Campeche to El Petén, then to Belize, and finally dominate northern Yucatán. (Magna Carta; Mongol invasion of Eastern Europe under Genghis Khan; Gothic architecture; fall of Constantinople; reigns of Süleyman the Magnificent, Henry VIII, Charles V; European Renaissance; rise of the Inca Empire in Peru.)

1530 to 1821: Colonial Period Francisco de Montejo conquers Yucatán, and Pedro de Alvarado subdues Chiapas and Guatemala, but harsh colonial rule leads to frequent Mayan rebellions.

1821 to Present: Independence Period Yucatán declares independence from Spain and soon after joins the Mexican union. United Provinces of Central America proclaims independence, later divides into separate countries.

Middle Preclassic Period (800–300 BC)

By this time there were rich villages in Honduras' Copán Valley, and settlers had founded villages at what is known today as Tikal in the northern Petén region. Trade routes developed, with coastal peoples exchanging salt and seashells for highland tribes' tool-grade obsidian. A brisk trade in ceramic pots and vessels flourished throughout the region. With this exchange of wares came a concomitant exchange of ideas.

Late Preclassic Period (300 BC–250 AD)

As the Maya honed their agricultural techniques, including developing fertilizer and elevating fields to boost production, a rich, noble class emerged that indulged in such extravagances as resident scribes and artists. Among the luxuries in demand were temples, consisting of raised platforms of earth topped by a thatch-roofed shelter very much like a normal na. Pyramid E-VII-sub, of the Chicanel culture at Uaxactún, 23km north of Tikal, is a good example of this; others are found at Tikal and El Mirador, sites that flourished during this period. As with a na, the local potentate was buried beneath the shelter, thereby increasing the sacred power of the building and its site.

In the lowlands, where limestone was abundant, the Maya began to build platform temples from stone. As each succeeding local potentate had to have a bigger temple, subsequent, larger platforms were built over the existing platforms, forming huge step pyramids with a na-style shelter on top. The potentate was buried deep within the stack of platforms. Sometimes the pyramids were decorated with huge stylized masks. One of the grandest examples of this type of architecture is at El Mirador in

Chac, god of rain

the northernmost region of the Petén. At 18 stories high, archaeologists believe the El Tigre pyramid here is the largest ever built by the Maya. Recent discoveries at El Mirador (specifically, symbols and other precursors to the Mayan hieroglyphic writing system) are challenging long held theories of the Mayan timetable and how their culture developed and spread to neighboring areas.

More and more pyramids were built around large plazas, in much the same way that the common people clustered their thatched houses in family compounds facing a communal open space. The stage was set for the flowering of classic Mayan civilization.

Early Classic Period (250–600)

The great ceremonial and cultural centers at Copán, Tikal, Yaxchilán (just over the Guatemalan border in Mexico) and especially Kaminaljuyú (near present-day Guatemala City) flourished during this time. While Tikal began to assume a primary role in ancient and modern Guatemalan history around 250 AD, El Mirador was mysteriously abandoned. Some scholars believe a severe drought hastened this great city's demise. Mayan astronomers began using the elaborate Long Count calendar to date all of human history.

Late Classic Period (600-900)

At its height, the Mayan lands were ruled not as an empire but as a collection of independent but also interdependent city-states. Each city-state had its noble house, headed by a king who was the social, political and religious focus of the city's life. The king placated the gods by shedding his blood in ceremonies during which he pierced his tongue, penis or ears with a sharp object. He also led his soldiers into battle against rival cities, capturing prisoners for use in human sacrifices. Many a king perished in a battle he was too old to fight; but the king, as sacred head of the community, was required to lead in battle for religious as well as military reasons.

After foundering against rival cities and under their kings in the middle of the sixth century, Tikal rose to prominence around 700 under a resolute king named Moon Double Comb, also known as Ah Cacau (Lord Chocolate). Following several military successes during Moon Double Comb's reign from 682-734, Tikal was once again the focal point of Mayan civilization. By the end of the period, however, the great Mayan cities of Tikal, Yaxchilán, Copán, Quiriguá and Piedras Negras had reverted to little more than minor towns or even villages.

Early to Late Postclassic Period (900-1530)

The collapse of classic Mayan civilization was sudden. It seems as if the upper classes demanded ever more servants, acolytes and laborers, and, though the Mayan population was growing rapidly, it did not produce enough farmers to feed everyone. Nor were there inexhaustible plots of land on which to practice slash and burn agriculture – a rudimentary technique that requires letting the fields lie fallow for three or four years before planting them again. Water and wood shortages may have also contributed to the overall strain, particularly on natural resources. Funny how history *does* tend to repeat itself: If the Guatemalan population doubles by the year 2020 as experts estimate, the country will certainly face this same type of crisis. This cyclical nature of life is integral to the ancient and modern Mayan understanding of existence and is known as *cosmovisión*.

Ixtab, suicide goddess

In the early 13th century, the Itzáes, a race of people believed to be Mayan, were forced from their traditional homeland in Tabasco, Mexico. These people founded Tayasal on the shores of what came to be known as Lake Petén Itzá in Guatemala's Petén region, at modern day Flores. The Itzáes emphasized and strengthened the belief in sacred cenotes in this area (the natural limestone caves that provided the Maya with their water supply on the riverless plains of the northern Yucatán Peninsula); caves like these throughout Guatemala continue to be used in Mayan religious ceremonies today. In 1697, the Spanish finally conquered the Itzá capital, squashing what is believed to have been the last holdout of Mayan ceremonies and religious practices in the region.

The Coming of the Spaniards Entrenched in their conquest of Mexico and fueled by a maniacal quest for anything gold, it took the Spanish conquistadors some time to make it across the border to Guatemala. Prior to the foreigners' inauspicious arrival, several groups of Guatemalan highland Maya sent emissaries to ask Hernán Cortés, subjugator of the indigenous groups of Mexico, for his protection. In response, Cortés dispatched to Guatemala Pedro de Alvarado, one of his most brutal, loyal and tactless lieutenants.

By the time Alvarado stormed Guatemala's western province of Retalhuleu in 1524, the fatal effects of internecine warfare among several Mayan groups, and European diseases spread from Mexico had already begun to take their toll. Despite historical animosities, the powerful and savvy Quiché of the highlands attempted to forge an alliance between the disparate indigenous groups, most notably, the Cakchiquels and Tz'utuhils. The Cakchiquels

Hernán Cortés

dismissed the overture, preferring to ally with the Spanish rather than their traditional enemies. With the help of the Cakchiquels, Alvarado and company blazed a bloody trail through the highlands, capturing the Quiché capital at Utatlán and the important commercial city of Xelajú (Quetzaltenango).

The romance between the Spanish and the Cakchiquels soured when the latter couldn't meet the ever-increasing demands for gold, and Alvarado – not surprisingly – turned on them. Not long after he set up shop at the Cakchiquel capital at Iximché, near modern day Tecpán, he burned the capital to the ground and conquered its residents. And so it went throughout all of Guatemala as the megalomaniacal Alvarado set out to increase his wealth and renown by murdering and subjugating the Mayan population. The one notable exception was the Rabinals of present day Baja Verapaz, who successfully resisted the Spaniards and survived with their preconquest identity intact. To this day, the Rabinals remain one of Guatemala's most traditional groups, though influences of the Catholic Church have crept in over the years.

When Alvarado wasn't out killing, he was up to other mischief. In 1524 his mistress Luisa Xicotenga Tecubalsi, a Tlaxcalan princess whom he brought with him from Mexico, gave birth to the world's first child of mixed Spanish and Indian blood, and so the *mestizo* race was born. Alvarado may have been a lover and a fighter, but he was no urban planner: Ciudad Vieja, the capital he established in 1527, was destroyed by a flood and had to be relocated in 1543 to La Ciudad de Santiago de los Caballeros de Guatemala, known today as Antigua, Guatemala.

Colonial Period & the Rise of the Church (1540-1830)

There were few silver linings for the Guatemalan Maya once the Spaniards got hold of things. Greedy, ignoble Europeans began a land grab sanctioned by the Spanish Crown and (adding insult to injury) enslaved the heretofore landowners – most of them indigenous – to work these ill-gotten acres. This system of *encomiendas* (the land) and *repartimiento* (the labor) was among the greatest disgraces of the colonial period and was repeated throughout the hemisphere as it was colonized by the Spanish. Refusal to work the land meant death. With the most fertile land and a labor force to work it firmly in hand, the colonists believed themselves omnipotent and behaved accordingly. That is to say, badly.

Enter the Catholic Church and Dominican Friar Bartolomé de Las Casas. De Las Casas had been hanging around Latin America since shortly after Columbus arrived and had witnessed firsthand the near complete genocide of the indigenous populations of Cuba and Hispaniola. Convinced he could catch more flies with honey than vinegar and horrified at what he saw in the Indies, de Las Casas appealed to Charles V of Spain to stop the violence. De Las Casas described the fatal treatment of the population in his influential tract *A Very Brief Account of the Destruction of the Indians*. Charles V agreed with de Las Casas that the indigenous people should no longer be regarded as chattel and should be considered vassals of the King (in this way they could also pay taxes). Charles V immediately enacted the New Laws of 1542, which technically ended the *repartimiento* system. In reality, however, forced labor continued to exist.

There is no doubt that the Catholic Church contributed to the erosion of traditional ways in Guatemala. But thanks to de Las Casas, there were at least enough Maya still alive to pursue those traditions, however amended. With the killing all but stopped, de Las Casas and other Dominican, Franciscan and Augustinian friars went about converting the Maya to Christianity, which took on certain aspects of animism and ceremony particular to the indigenous belief system.

A large portion of the church's conversion 'success' can be attributed to the pacifism with which they approached Mayan communities, the relative respect they extended traditional beliefs (permitting syncretism between rites and idols, for example) and the education they provided in indigenous dialects. In short, the Catholic Church became extremely powerful in Guatemala quite quickly, and no clearer evidence existed than the 38 houses of worship (including a cathedral) built in the new capital, Antigua. Sophistication wasn't limited to religion and architecture, however; in 1676, the first university in Central America, the University of San Carlos, was established in Antigua and later moved to Guatemala City. After a devastating earthquake on July 29, 1773, razed most of Antigua, Guatemala City was chosen for the nation's new capital.

Independence Period

By the time thoughts of independence from the Spanish began stirring among Guatemalans, society was already rigidly stratified. At the very top of the colonial hierarchy were the European-born Spaniards; next were the creoles, people born in Guatemala of Spanish blood; below them were the ladinos or *mestizos*, people of mixed Spanish and Indian blood; and at the bottom were the Indians and blacks of pure race. (It is worth noting here that there is a black community of Garífunas on Guatemala's Caribbean coast.) Only the pure-blooded Spaniards born in Spain had any real power, but the creoles lauded their own might over the ladinos and, in turn, this group exploited the indigenous population who, as you read this, still remain on the bottom rung of the socio-economic ladder.

What really kicked off the move toward independence was the Crown's continued appointment of Spanish-born Guatemalans to important posts, at the expense of Guatemalans born in the New World. Perturbed at being passed over for advancement, Guatemalan creoles took advantage of a weakened Spanish Empire after Napoleon's invasion and in 1821 successfully rose in revolt. Unfortunately, independence changed little for the country's indigenous communities, who remained under the control of the church and the landowning elite.

Recently, independent Mexico urged the leaders of Yucatán, Chiapas and Central America to join it to form one large new state. At first only Guatemala accepted, but Yucatán and Chiapas later changed their minds. Once that was settled, Yucatán and Chiapas joined the Mexican union, and Guatemala led the formation of the United Provinces of Central America (July 1, 1823), along with El Salvador, Nicaragua, Honduras and Costa Rica. Their union, torn by civil strife from the start, lasted only until 1840 before breaking up into its constituent states.

Though this second round of independence brought prosperity to the creoles, it worsened the lot of the Guatemala Maya. The end of Spanish rule meant that the Crown's few liberal safeguards, which had afforded the Indians minimal protection from the most extreme forms of exploitation, were abandoned. Mayan claims to ancestral lands were largely ignored and huge plantations were created for the cultivation of tobacco, sugarcane and henequen (agave rope fiber). The Maya, though technically and legally free, were enslaved by debt peonage to the great landowners. From slaves to supplicants to serfs, the history of the Maya since the arrival of the Spaniards has been a cycle of physical, cultural and psychological oppression.

Morazán & the Liberals

Once the winds of independence started blowing, the lines were drawn. The liberals, the first to advocate independence, opposed the vested interests and status quo of the elite conservatives, who had the Catholic Church and the large landowners on their side.

During the short existence of the United Provinces of Central America, liberal president Francisco Morazán (1830-39) instituted reforms aimed at correcting three persistent problems: the great economic, political and social power of the church; the division of society into a Latino upper class and an indigenous lower class; and the region's impotence in world markets. This liberal program was echoed by Guatemalan chief of state Mariano Gálvez (1831-38).

But unpopular economic policies, heavy taxes and a cholera epidemic in 1837 led to an Indian uprising that brought a conservative pig farmer, Rafael Carrera, to power. Carrera held power until 1865 and undid much of what Morazán and Gálvez had achieved. The Carrera government naively allowed Great Britain to take control of Belize in exchange for construction of a road between Guatemala City and Belize City. The road called for in the treaty was never built, and Guatemala's claims for compensation were never resolved. This dispute between now independent Belize and Guatemala persists to this day and is revived every so often – usually when one or the other nation needs to distract its population from domestic policy and problems.

Liberal Reforms of Rufino Barrios

The liberals came to power again in the 1870s, first under Miguel García Granados, next under Justo Rufino Barrios, a rich young coffee *finca* (plantation) owner who held the title of president, but ruled as a dictator (1873-79). With Rufino Barrios at its head the country made great strides toward modernization, with construction of roads, railways, schools and a modern banking system. To boost the economy, everything possible was done to encourage and stimulate coffee production. Peasants in good coffee-growing areas (up to 1400m altitude on the Pacific Slope) were forced off their lands to make way for new coffee fincas, and those living above 1400m (mostly Maya) were forced to work on the fincas. This land appropriation and forced labor was not unlike what occurred on plantations during colonial times and created migrant labor patterns that still exist among some highland groups. Idealistic liberal policies, championed by the British and often meant to benefit the common people, ended up oppressing them. Ironically, most of the policies of the liberal reform movement benefited the finca owners and the traders in the cities.

Succeeding governments generally pursued the same policies. Economic control of the country was in the hands of a small group of land-owning and commercial families; foreign companies were given generous concessions; opponents of the government were censored, imprisoned or exiled by the extensive police force; and the government apparatus remained subservient to economic interests despite a liberal constitution.

Estrada Cabrera & Minerva

Manuel Estrada Cabrera ruled from 1898 to 1920, and his dictatorial style, while bringing progress in technical matters, placed a heavy burden on all but the ruling oligarchy. He fancied himself a bringer of light and culture to a backward land, styling himself the 'Teacher and Protector of Guatemalan Youth.'

He sponsored Fiestas de Minerva (Festivals of Minerva) in the cities, inspired by the Roman goddess of wisdom, invention and technology, and ordered construction of temples to Minerva, some of which still stand (as in Quetzaltenango). Guatemala was to become a 'tropical Athens.' At the same time, however, he looted the treasury, ignored the schools and spent extravagantly to beef up the armed forces. Estrada

Cabrera was also responsible for courting the United Fruit Company, a business of gross hegemonic proportions that set up shop in Guatemala in 1901.

Jorge Ubico

When Estrada Cabrera was overthrown in 1920, Guatemala entered a period of instability, which ended in 1931 with the election of General Jorge Ubico as president. Ubico had a Napoleon complex and ruled as Estrada Cabrera had, but more efficiently. Though his word was law, he insisted on honesty in government, and he modernized the country's health and social welfare infrastructure. Debt peonage was outlawed, releasing the Maya from this servitude, but a new bondage of compulsory labor contributions to the government road-building program was established in its place. Other public works projects included the construction of the vast presidential palace on the main plaza in Guatemala City.

During WWII, Ubico dispossessed and exiled the great German coffee finca owners and otherwise assumed a pro-Allied stance. But at the same time, he openly admired Spain's Generalissimo Francisco Franco. In 1944 he was forced to resign and go into exile.

Arévalo & Arbenz Guzmán

Just when it appeared that Guatemalan politics was doomed to become a succession of well-intentioned but harsh dictators, the elections of 1945 brought a philosopher – Juan José Arévalo – to the presidential palace. Arévalo, in power from 1945 to 1951, established the nation's social security system, a government bureau to look after Indian concerns, a modern public health system and liberal labor laws. During his six years as president there were 25 coup attempts by conservative military forces – almost one coup attempt every three months.

Arévalo was succeeded by Colonel Jacobo Arbenz Guzmán. Arbenz continued the policies of Arévalo, instituting an agrarian reform law that was meant to break up the large estates and foster high productivity on small, individually owned farms. He also expropriated vast lands conceded to the United Fruit Company during the Estrada Cabrera and Ubico years that were being held fallow. Compensation was paid at the value that the company had declared for tax purposes (which was far below its actual value), and Arbenz announced that the lands were to be redistributed to peasants and put into cultivation for food. But the expropriation, supported by the Guatemalan Communist Party, set off alarms in Washington, which (surprise! surprise!) supported the interests of United Fruit. In 1954, the US, in one of the first documented covert operations by the Central Intelligence Agency (CIA), orchestrated an invasion from Honduras led by two exiled Guatemalan military officers, and Arbenz was forced to step down. The land reform never took place.

After Arbenz, the country had a succession of military presidents elected with the support of the officers' corps, business leaders, compliant political parties and the Catholic Church. Violence became a staple of political life. Opponents of the government regularly turned up dead or didn't turn up at all. Land reform measures were reversed, voting was made dependent on literacy (which disenfranchised around 75% of the population), the secret police force was revived and military repression was common.

The poor majority was getting rightfully pissed off, and there was no way their grievances could be addressed within the system. In 1960 guerrilla groups began to form.

1960s & 1970s

During the 1960s and '70s, Guatemalan industry developed at a fast pace. Most profits from the boom flowed upwards, labor union organization put more stresses on the political fabric, and migration from the countryside to the cities, especially the capital, produced urban sprawl and slums.

As the pressures in society increased, so did the cyclical violence of protest and repression, which led to the total politicization of society. Everyone took sides; usually it was the poorer classes in the rural areas versus the power elite in the cities. By 1979, Amnesty International estimated that 50,000 to 60,000 people had been killed during the political violence of the 1970s alone.

A severe earthquake in 1976 killed about 22,000 people and left around a million people homeless. Most of the aid sent to help the people in need never reached them.

1980s

In the early 1980s, the military suppression of antigovernment elements in the countryside reached a peak, especially under the presidency of General José Efraín Ríos Montt, an evangelical Christian who came to power in a coup in March 1982. Alarming numbers of people, mostly indigenous men, were killed in the name of anti-insurgency, stabilization and anti-Communism.

The policy behind these killings was known as 'scorched earth;' Guatemalans refer to it as *la escoba*, the broom, because of the way the reign of terror swept over the country, taking everything in its wake. While officials did not know the identities of the rebels, they did know which areas were bases of rebel activity, so the government decided to exterminate the general populations of those areas to kill off the rebels. The government also hoped such tactics would dissuade the peasantry from joining or supporting the guerrillas. Over 400 villages were razed, and most of their inhabitants massacred (often tortured as well).

Survivors of the scorched earth policy were herded into remote, newly constructed 'model villages' surrounded by army encampments. It was later estimated that 15,000 civilian deaths occurred as a result of counter-insurgency operations during Ríos Montt's term of office alone, not to mention the estimated 100,000 refugees (again, mostly Maya) who fled over the border to Mexico during this period. Civil Defense Patrols, armed cadres of rural villagers, did most of the army's dirty work and were ultimately responsible for some of the worst human-rights abuses during Ríos Montt's

rule. Participation in the Civil Defense Patrols was mandatory for all men aged 18 to 60.

Despite these heavy-handed tactics, perhaps half a million people, mostly peasants in the western and central highlands and in the northern El Petén region, actively supported the guerrilla movement. In February 1982 four powerful guerrilla organizations united to form the URNG (Guatemalan National Revolutionary Unity).

As the civil war dragged on and atrocities were committed by both sides, the lines between them blurred. Many peasants and rural people did support the guerrilla movement but perhaps even more came to feel caught in the crossfire and between a rock and a hard place. They were damned if they supported the insurgents and damned if they didn't.

In August 1983 Ríos Montt was deposed by a coup led by General Oscar Humberto Mejía Victores, but the abuses continued. It was estimated that over 100 political assassinations and 40 abductions occurred each and every month under his rule. The bloodbath led to a cutoff of US military assistance to the Guatemalan government, which in turn resulted in the 1985 election of a civilian president, Marco Vinicio Cerezo Arévalo, the candidate of the Christian Democratic Party.

Before turning over power to the civilians, the military ensured that its earlier activities would not be examined or prosecuted, by establishing formal mechanisms for military control of the countryside. There was hope that Cerezo Arévalo's administration would temper the excesses of the power elite and the military and establish a basis for true democracy. When Cerezo Arévalo's term ended in 1990, however, many people wondered whether any real progress had been made.

Early 1990s

President Cerezo Arévalo was succeeded by Jorge Serrano Elías (1990-93), an evangelical Christian who ran as the candidate of the conservative Movimiento de Acción

Solidaria (Solidarity Action Movement). Serrano reopened a dialogue with the URNG, hoping to bring the decades-long civil war to an end. When the talks collapsed, the mediator from the Catholic Church blamed both sides for intransigence.

Massacres and other human-rights abuses continued during this period despite the country's return to democratic rule. In one dramatic case in 1990, Guatemalan anthropologist Myrna Mack was fatally stabbed dozens of times by a high ranking army official, ostensibly for her work documenting continued army violence against the rural Maya. Later that same year, the army massacred 13 Tz'utuhil Maya (including three children) in Santiago Atitlán. Outraged, the Tz'utuhils fought back, expelling the army and forcing the breakup of the local Civil Defense Patrol. Santiago was the first town to oust the army by popular demand. That unprecedented success, plus the ensuing demilitarization, was a watershed event for the Mayan and human-rights cause in Guatemala.

Meanwhile, Serrano's popularity began to wane and he came to depend more on the army for support. On May 25, 1993, Serrano carried out an *autogolpe* (autocoup), supported by the military. After a tense few days Serrano was forced to flee into exile. Congress elected Solicitor for Human Rights Ramiro de León Carpio, an outspoken critic of the army's strong-arm tactics, as the country's new president to complete Serrano's term, which was scheduled to end in January 1996.

In March 1995 the US announced it was suspending aid yet again, this time because of the government's failure to investigate the murder or disappearance of US citizens in Guatemala. These cases included the 1990 murder of Michael DeVine, who had operated Finca Ixobel in Poptún, and URNG leader Efraín Bámaca Velásquez, whose wife, US attorney Jennifer Harbury, had been conducting an internationally publicized protest since his disappearance in 1992. Eventually it was revealed that both had been murdered. Charges were made that the CIA had been instrumental in the murders (or at the very least had knowledge of them beforehand), but the US government investigated the claims and determined they were unfounded. For more on these killings, see the boxed text 'The Murder of Michael DeVine' in the El Petén chapter.

In the presidential elections held on November 12, 1995, no candidate won a majority, necessitating a runoff on January 7, 1996. The runoff was won by Álvaro Enrique Arzú Irigoyen of the middle-right PAN (Partido de Avanzada Nacional), who took office on January 14.

Negotiations continued between the government and the URNG, and finally, in December 1996, the two parties came to agreement and peace accords were signed.

Signing of the Peace Accords

'A Firm and Lasting Peace Agreement,' as the accords are called, was signed at the National Palace in Guatemala City on December 29, 1996, putting an end to the 36-year civil war. During that period, an estimated 200,000 Guatemalans had been killed, a million made homeless, and untold thousands had 'disappeared.' The accords contain provisions calling for accountability for the human-rights violations perpetrated by the armed forces during the war and the resettlement of Guatemala's one million displaced people. The accords also address the identity and rights of indigenous peoples, health care, education and other basic social services, women's rights, the abolition of obligatory military service and the incorporation of the ex-guerrillas into civilian life. Many of these provisions remain unfulfilled.

The greatest challenge to a lasting peace stems from great inequities in the basic social and economic power structure of Guatemalan society. It's estimated that 70% of cultivable land is owned by less than 3% of the population. According to a United Nations report, the top 20% of the population has an income 30 times (that's 3000%) greater than the bottom 20%. Discrimination against indigenous Guatemalans, which has been deeply ingrained in the society for five centuries, manifests itself in poverty and misery for most of the population. The dire need for improvement in economic and social conditions, basic social services, land reform and labor rights has been the motivation for much of the revolutionary movement. How these needs are addressed and met may be the most important factor in creating a true and lasting peace.

Both sides acknowledged that the signing of the peace accords was not a conclusion but a beginning. As one guerrilla representative stated, 'The peace accords will be signed on December 29. Our most challenging work will begin on December 30.'

Implementing the Peace Accords

The initial four-year implementation period stipulated by the accords has elapsed, and it's time to check the scorecards. Facilitating and overseeing the implementation of the accords is the United Nations Mission for the Verification of Human Rights (MINUGUA). Since 1994, MINUGUA has been documenting human-rights abuses, gathering information and working to build a peaceful, workable relationship between governmental and guerrilla factions. By most accounts, the UN presence in Guatemala has contributed to a decrease in systematic violence and abuses and made a small, but significant, dent in the fight against impunity.

On the down side, violence against critics of the ruling elite continues. In a particularly tragic flouting of peace and democracy, Bishop Juan Gerardi, coordinator of the Guatemalan Archbishop's Human Rights Office (ODHAG), was beaten to death outside his home. This was on April 26, 1998, only two days after Bishop Gerardi made public his findings concerning human-rights violations by the armed forces during the civil war. The blatant timing of this attack gives you an idea of the level of impunity and self-righteousness of the powers that be. Three suspects were finally arrested in January 2000 – one of the first proactive moves by the new, democratically elected government – an encouraging sign that the

unconscionable impunity defining Guatemalan government for the last four decades can be stemmed.

Impunity of the powerful was dealt another blow in late 1999 when convictions were meted out for the 1995 massacre of 11 newly returned refugees (including two women and two children) in Xamán, 65km north of Cobán. Some welcome home. Pitifully, most of the accused were later set free on appeal. Even though 10 of the guilty soldiers are serving 12 years behind bars for the massacre, this action falls well short of the justice ideal modern democracies (should) strive for.

Comprehensive implementation of the peace agreement was stalled in 1999 when the populace voted down a referendum for constitutional reforms decreed by the accords. These reforms aimed to institutionalize the peace process by formally legislating the rights of indigenous people, adding checks and balances to the executive office and retooling the national security apparatus. Prefaced by a flurry of propaganda and disinformation, the constitutional reform referendum was voted down by a margin of 49% to 43%. However, only 18% of registered voters turned out to vote, so this can hardly be considered a mandate from the Guatemalan people.

Several other hurdles remain before the peace process can be fully implemented. One of the most important terms of the agreement calls for disarmament by the URNG and a concomitant demobilization by the armed forces. The guerrillas lived up to their end of the bargain, but the armed forces have yet to fully comply. Some critics maintain that the astronomic rise in petty crime and violence in Guatemala since the signing of the accords is in part attributable to former soldiers who are still armed and dangerous. Safety and security were the linchpin issues in the 1999 presidential elections, as organized crime and freelance executions of known and suspected criminals reached near crisis levels.

On the political scene, there have been some triumphs and setbacks. One positive result of the peace process has been more

sophisticated political organization and mo-
bilization by the Maya. As indigenous groups
become more empowered to articulate and
demand their rights through the democratic
process, the balance of power in Guatemala
will shift to meet the needs of its diverse population more accurately and equitably. This is
the ideal, anyway; the reality is that the peace
process has a long way to go.

Guatemala Today

Guatemala's future hangs in the balance. In
November 1999, the country held its first
peacetime elections in nearly 40 years.
Several diverse candidates were fielded (including a woman and some erstwhile guerrillas), but by the time the elections rolled
around, just three front runners remained:
the former mayor of Guatemala City, Oscar
Berger of the incumbent Partido de Avanzada Nacional (PAN), conservative and ad-
mitted murderer Alfonso Portillo of the
Frente Republicano Guatemalteco (FRG,
colloquially known as the Blue Hand) and
leftist A'lvaro Colom of the Alianza Nueva
Nación (ANN). Although voter turnout was
53%, none of these candidates took the
simple majority needed to win, and a runoff
was scheduled for December 26 between
Portillo and Berger.

Portillo appealed to voters by promising
to be tough on criminals and cited his
murders as evidence. He claimed he killed
two men in self-defense, and said if he could
defend himself, he could defend his people
and his country. For many human-rights and
political observers, even more disturbing
than this muddy logic was the fact that
Efraín Ríos Montt (executor of the
'scorched earth' policy under which tens of
thousands indigenous people were killed)
was also running on the FRG ticket and advising Portillo. Unbelievably, Ríos Montt actually went on to win, and became the
leader of Congress. Although officials antic-
ipated high absenteeism in a vote held the
day after Christmas, 41% of the voters
turned out. They responded to Portillo's
anti-crime platform, handing the FRG candidate 68.3% of the vote to make him
Guatemala's new president.

GEOGRAPHY

Guatemala covers an area of 109,000 sq km
with mountainous forest highlands and
jungle plains. For those who care, relative to
US states, Guatemala is about the size of
Tennessee.

The western highlands, linked by the Interamericana, are the continuation of
Chiapas' Sierra Madre and include 30 volcanoes reaching heights of 3800m in the
Cuchumatanes range northwest of Huehuetenango. Directly south of the Cuchumatanes is Volcán Tajumulco, at 4220m the
tallest peak in Central America. Many of
the volcanoes are active, which signals that
Guatemala is an earthquake area as well.
Major quakes struck in 1773, 1917 and 1976.
Land that has not been cleared for Mayan
milpas (cornfields) is covered in ever-
shrinking pine forests.

The Pacific Slope of Guatemala is the
continuation of Chiapas' Soconusco, with
rich coffee, cacao, fruit and sugar plantations along the Carretera al Pacífico. Down
along the shore the volcanic slope meets the
sea, yielding vast beaches of black volcanic
sand in a sweltering climate that is difficult
to bear. Grass grows profusely in this
climate, and it's fed to cattle.

South and east along the Interamericana,
the altitude decreases to about 1500m at
Guatemala City. This part of Guatemala is
cut through by several valleys and is home
to the largest population centers.
Guatemala City sits under a ceiling of smog
most days in La Ermita valley (also known
as Valle de la Virgen), while Antigua sits
pretty in the Valle de Panchoy.

North of Guatemala City, the highlands
of Alta Verapaz gradually decline to the
lowland of El Petén, which is the continuation of southern Yucatán. The Petén's
climate and topography is like that of
Yucatán, hot and humid or hot and dry, depending upon the season. Central
America's largest tract of virgin rainforest
straddles the Guatemala-Mexico border in
the northern Petén. This last statement
may soon become untrue if conservation
efforts are not stepped up. To the southeast
of the Petén is the valley of the Río

Motagua, dry in some areas, moist in others. Bananas and sugarcane thrive in the Motagua Valley.

GEOLOGY

Guatemala is at the confluence of three tectonic plates. While the volcanoes created millennia ago when these plates shifted are stunningly beautiful, they can also be dangerous. In the southwest of the country is the Cocos plate, which is abutted by the North American plate. The most southern part of Guatemala lies on top of the Caribbean plate, and when any or all of these plates get frisky, earthquakes and volcanic eruptions ensue. Collapsed volcanic cones also contribute to the dynamic Guatemalan landscape by creating lakes such as Lago de Atitlán.

The unique geology of Guatemala also includes a tremendous system of aboveground and subterranean caves. Millions of years ago, when the sea level fell, exposing the landmass that now comprises Guatemala and the Yucatán, Cretaceous and Tertiary mollusks perished on the surface and eventually settled into limestone. For eons, water coursed over this limestone base, creating aquifers and conduits that eventually gave way to subterranean caves, rivers and sinkholes when the surface water drained into underground caverns and streams. This type of terrain (known as karst) is found throughout the Verapaces region and makes Guatemala a killer spelunking destination. In addition, there are surface-level caves, which have been used for ceremonies since ancient times, as the Maya believe caves serve as portals between our world and the underworld.

CLIMATE

Although Guatemala's official motto is the 'Land of Eternal Spring,' that only tells the warm and fuzzy part of the story. In fact, temperatures can get down to freezing at night in the highland mountains. Days can be dank and chill during the rainy season, but in the dry season from late October to May they're warm and delightful; hence the motto. Dry season nights are often cool.

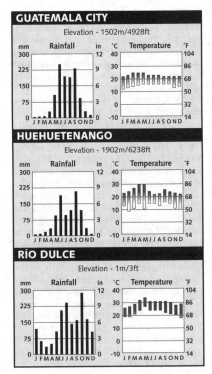

Guatemala's coasts are tropical, rainy, hot and humid, with temperatures often reaching 32°C to 38°C (90°F to 100°F) and dogged by pervasive high humidity, which abates only slightly in the dry season. While the rainy and dry seasons are distinct on the Pacific coast and in the Highlands, on the Caribbean side rain is possible anytime. Cobán has only about one month of strictly dry weather (in April), though you can catch some less wet spells between November and March as well.

The department of El Petén is almost entirely tropical lowland, meaning it's pretty much hot and humid all the time. In this case, hot means temperatures that hover around 30° to 35°C. The high humidity is perhaps worse than the sizzling temperatures: In this type of humidity, nothing ever dries, including your sweat. The rainy season stretches from May to November, with September and October being the wettest. It doesn't rain all day every day during the rainy season, but you can expect daily downpours at the very least. Depending on the location, the annual rainfall in El Petén measures between 100 and 240cm. Temperatures generally cool off in the rainy season, particularly at night. December and January are the coolest months; March and April are the hottest and can feel like hell on Earth.

ECOLOGY & ENVIRONMENT

Like (almost) everywhere else on the planet, deforestation is a problem in Guatemala. This is especially true in the Petén, where jungle is being felled at an alarming rate to make way for cattle ranches and oil pipelines. Colonization by Guatemalans migrating from more crowded areas and refugees returning from Mexico are also taxing the region's resources. Government estimates indicate that 600 sq miles of Guatemalan forest are felled annually – one of the world's worst deforestation rates. A few years ago, the government required anyone buying land in the Petén to clear part of it, presumably in the name of 'progress.'

Most of the Petén is now officially designated as a protected area; in addition to the 575-sq-km Tikal national park, there's the nearly two-million-hectare Maya Biosphere Reserve, which includes most of the northern Petén region. This biosphere recognizes that the many demands placed on the land require innovative preservation strategies. In this vein, the Maya Biosphere Reserve is split into three spheres. The first, known as the multiple use zone, is on the very fringe of the reserve and permits settlements and all types of agriculture, including the debilitative slash and burn. The second sphere is called the buffer zone and allows only minimal impact activities such as gathering forest products. The last and smallest sphere is deep in the center of the reserve and allows no human activity except ecotourism.

Unfortunately, these spheres function in theory only. In reality, the forest is still being ravaged by people illegally harvesting timber on a massive scale, looters desecrating Mayan tombs deep in the jungle and tourists (no matter how conscientious) negatively impacting the very fragile ecosystem the biospheres are trying to protect. Hope for the Guatemalan rainforest ultimately lies with the local communities that are gaining more awareness of the threat by participating in projects that generate income from alternative forest products. Guatemalan and international nongovernmental organizations are also spearheading aggressive policies to save the forest, including buying and preserving tracts of forest and promoting sustainable practices.

On the Pacific side of the country, where most of the population of Guatemala lives, the land is mostly agricultural or given over to industrial interests. The remaining forests in the Pacific coastal and highland areas are not long for this world, as local communities cut down the remaining trees to use for heating and cooking.

The following organizations in Guatemala City are good resources for finding out more about Guatemala's natural and protected areas:

Asociación Amigos del Bosque (☎ 238-3486), 9a Calle 2-23, Zona 1

Centro de Estudios Conservacionistas de la Universidad de San Carlos or CECON (☎ 331-0904, 334-6064, 334-7662), Avenida La Reforma 0-63, Zona 10

Comisión Nacional del Medio Ambiente or CONAMA (☎ 334-1708, 331-2723), 5a Avenida 8-07, Zona 10

Consejo Nacional de Areas Protegidas or CONAP (☎ 332-0465, 332-0464), Via 5 4-50, Edificio Maya, 4th Floor, Zona 4

Fundación Defensores de la Naturaleza (☎ 334-1885, fax 361-7011, ✉ defensores@pronet.net.gt), 14 Calle 6-49, Zona 9

Fundación para el Ecodesarrollo y la Conservación or FUNDAECO (☎ 472-4268), 7a Calle A 20-53, Zona 11, Colonia El Mirador

Fundación Solar (☎ 360-1172, 332-2548, fax 332-2548, ✉ funsolar@guate.net), 15a Avenida 18-78, Zona 13

For current information on conservation efforts in the Petén, you can drop in on some of the nongovernmental organizations concentrating solely on that region. The following are all in Flores:

Asociacíon Alianza Verde, (☎/fax 926-0718, 📧 alianzaverde@conservation.org.gt), north side of plaza

Centro de Información sobre la Naturaleza, Cultura y Artesanía de Petén or CINCAP, north side of plaza (There is no phone for this organization; also no street name for the passage along the north side of plaza.)

ProPetén (☎ 926-1370, fax 926-0495, 📧 propeten@ guate.net, www.conservation.org), Calle Central

Aside from deforestation, the biggest immediate environmental problem facing Guatemala is garbage and its disposal. Nasty, smelly, open dumps are common sites outside of towns and cities where garbage collection exists. Where it doesn't, people burn what they can, creating noxious fumes from the mountain of plastic fed to the fire. What can't be burned is thrown in rivers or along the road. Although there are some grassroots efforts, such as the annual cleanup of Lago de Atitlán organized by ATI Divers, there are no large-scale garbage collection and disposal programs in place. If this problem is ignored long enough, it will become a health as well as environmental issue.

FLORA & FAUNA
Flora

Guatemala has more than 8000 species of plants in 19 different ecosystems ranging from the mangrove forests on both coasts to the pine forests of the mountainous interior and the cloud forests at higher altitudes. In addition, the Petén region supports a variety of trees, including mahogany, cedar, ramón and sapodilla. The last was used to craft the door lintels on ancient Mayan temples.

The national flower, the *monja blanca* or white nun orchid, is said to have been picked so much that it's now rarely seen in the wild; nevertheless, with around 600 species of orchid (one-third of these species endemic to Guatemala), you shouldn't have any trouble finding some. If you're interested in orchids, make sure to visit Cobán

and check out the orchid nursery there. See the Cobán section of the Highlands chapter for more information.

Guatemala also holds the dubious honor of having the perfect climactic conditions for a plant called *xate* (sha-tay). Xate is a low growing fern that thrives in the Petén and is prized in the developed world (particularly the US) as filler in flower arrangements, of all ridiculous things. *Xateros* – the men who collect the plant – live in the jungle for months at a time harvesting xate and adversely effecting the endangered ecosystem there in the process. The same degradation is perpetuated by the *chicleros* in the Petén, men who harvest chicle from the sapodilla tree for chewing gum.

The demand for xate is so acute that sprawling plantations have been established on the gentle slopes of the Verapaces, smack in the middle of the traditional stomping/ breeding grounds of the quetzal, Guatemala's national bird. The quetzal no longer frequents the area and the denuded hills are covered in huge sheets of black plastic under which the xate thrives.

Fauna

With its 19 ecosystems, Guatemala also has an abundance of animals. So far, estimates point to 250 species of mammals, 600 species of birds, 200 species of reptiles and amphibians and many species of butterflies and other insects.

The national bird, the resplendent quetzal, is often used to symbolize Central America as well. (The national monetary unit, the quetzal, is named for the bird.) It's a small but exceptionally beautiful bird. The males sport a bright red breast, a brilliant blue-green neck, head, back and wings, a spot of bright white on the underside of the tail, and a blue-green tail several times as long as the bird's body, which stands only around six inches tall. The females, alas, have decidedly less wild plumage than their male counterparts.

Other interesting birds in Guatemala include toucans, macaws and parrots. If you visit Tikal, you can't miss the ocellated turkey, also called the Petén turkey, a large, impressive, multicolored bird reminiscent of a peacock, which struts its stuff around the park entrance. Tikal is a birding hot spot, with some 300 tropical and migratory species sighted to date. Several species of woodpeckers, nine types of hummingbirds, two oriole and four Trogon species are just the beginning. There are also large white herons, hawks, warblers, kingfishers, harpy eagles (rare) and a plethora of other resident and migratory birds. Some of the best areas for sighting waterfowl, including Jabirus, are near the Yaxhá site and Lake Petexbatún, both in the Petén. All together there are nearly 20 bird species endemic to Guatemala.

Although Guatemala's forests still host many types of mammal and reptile species, many will remain hidden from the casual observer. Still, visitors to Tikal will enjoy the antics of the omnipresent pizotes (technically known as coatimundis) and, with eyes peeled, can see both howler and spider monkeys. Deeper in the Petén forest, other resident mammals include the jaguar, ocelot, puma, two species of peccaries, agoutis, opossum, tapirs, kinkajous, pizotes, tepezcuintles, white-tailed and red brocket deer, and armadillos. There are also some very large rattlesnakes and plenty of weird bugs to make your skin crawl. Reptiles and

Pizote

amphibians in the rest of Guatemala include at least three species of sea turtles (the leatherback, the olive ridley and the *tortuga negra*) and at least two species of crocodile (one found in the Petén, the other in the Río Dulce). Manatees are also found in the waters of the Río Dulce, though they're notoriously low key and hard to spot.

Parks & Protected Areas

Guatemala has more than 30 protected areas, including *parques nacionales* (national parks) and *biotopos* (biological reserves). More than 40 more areas have been proposed for protection, though whether they ever become a reality remains to be seen. Many of the protected areas are remote and not accessible to the independent traveler; the ones mentioned here are some of the easiest to reach and the most interesting to visitors.

Reserva de la Biosfera Maya – Covering the northern half of the Petén region, this 1,844,900-hectare reserve is Guatemala's largest protected area. Within its boundaries are many important Mayan archaeological sites, including Tikal, Uaxactún, El Zotz, El Mirador and Río Azul. The last two comprise Parque Nacional El Mirador-Dos Lagunas-Río Azul. Tours and access information are available in Flores.

Reserva de la Biosfera de Sierra de las Minas – In the eastern part of the country, Guatemala's most important cloud forest reserve protects a mountainous area ranging in elevation from 150m to over 3000m above sea level. Before entering, visitors must obtain permission from the Fundación Defensores de la Naturaleza (see Ecology & Environment earlier in this chapter) in Guatemala City.

Parque Nacional Tikal – One of Guatemala's principal tourist attractions, this park within the larger Maya Biosphere Reserve contains the magnificent Tikal archaeological site as well as 57,600 hectares of pristine jungle. It's also one of the easiest places to observe wildlife in Guatemala.

Parque Nacional Ceibal – This site tucked into the jungle near Sayaxché is only accessible by boat for most of the year. Ceibal is noted for its carved stelae and several temples, including a rare circular temple. Tours are available from Flores or Sayaxché.

PARKS & PROTECTED AREAS

BIOSPHERE RESERVES
3 Reserva de la Biosfera Maya
15 Reserva de la Biosfera de
   Sierra de Las Minas

NATIONAL PARKS
1 Parque Nacional-Mirador-
   Dos Lagunas-Río Azul
5 Parque Nacional Tikal
6 Parque Nacional Sierra
   del Lacandón
8 Parque Nacional Ceibal
11 Parque Nacional Laguna Lachuá
12 Parque Nacional los
   Cuchumatanes
18 Parque Nacional Río Dulce

RESERVES
9 Reserva Aguateca-Dos Pilas
10 Reserva Machaquilá
13 Reserva Natural Cerro Bisís

BIOLOGICAL RESERVES
2 Biotopo Laguna del Tigre-
   Río Escondido
4 Biotopo San Miguel-
   La Pelotada-El Zotz
7 Biotopo Cerro Cahuí
14 Biotopo del Quetzal
   (Biotopo Mario Dary Rivera)
17 Biotopo Chocón Machacas
20 Biotopo Punta de Manabique
30 Biotopo Monterrico-Hawaii

VOLCANOES
21 Volcán Tacaná (4093m)
22 Volcán Tajumulco (4220m)
23 Volcán Santa María (3772m)
24 Volcán San Pedro (3020m)
25 Volcán Atitlán (3537m)
26 Volcán Acatenango (3976m)
27 Volcán Fuego (3763m)
28 Volcán Agua (3766m)
29 Volcán Pacaya (2552m)

WILDLIFE REFUGES
16 Bocas del Polochic
19 Cerro San Gil

Parque Nacional Río Dulce – In eastern Guatemala, between Lago de Izabal and the Caribbean, this 7200-hectare reserve protects the canyon of the Río Dulce, one of the country's most beautiful rivers. Boat trips on the river can be taken from either Lívingston or the town of Río Dulce.

Parque Nacional Laguna Lachuá – This 10,000-hectare park in the northeast of the department of Alta Verapaz contains a beautiful, circular, turquoise-colored lake that is only 5km in surface area but more than 220m deep, with a great abundance and variety of fish. Within the park are hiking trails, a camping area and visitors center.

Parque Nacional Sierra del Lacandón – In the western Petén region, this large park includes the southern portion of the Sierra del Lacandón mountains and abuts the Río Usumacinta, which forms part of the border between Guatemala and Mexico. It's accessible from El Naranjo or by boat along the Río Usumacinta.

Biological reserves *(biotopos protegidos)* include the following:

Biotopo del Quetzal – This 1000-hectare cloud forest reserve, also called the Biotopo Mario Dary Rivera, was established for the protection of quetzals. Well-maintained trails snake through a lush, cool forest of broad-leaf and coniferous trees, climbing plants, ferns, mosses, orchids and bromeliads. This is one of the easiest to access of all Guatemalan reserves and as a result, has very few (if any) quetzals in residence.

Biotopo Cerro Cahuí – On the northeast shore of Lago Petén Itzá, this well protected 650-hectare reserve has campgrounds and hiking trails with fine views. Over 300 species of birds have been documented here, including toucans, kingfishers, woodpeckers and herons.

Biotopo Chocón Machacas – This 7600-hectare reserve is within the Río Dulce national park on the north bank of the river. If you're going to be treated to a manatee sighting, it will likely be here.

Biotopo Punta de Manabique – This 50,000-hectare reserve is on the Caribbean. The only access is by boat, which can be arranged from the piers at either Puerto Barrios or Lívingston.

Biotopo San Miguel-La Pelotada-El Zotz – Part of the Maya Biosphere Reserve, this is west of and contiguous to Tikal national park. It protects a dense forest, bat caves *(zotz)* and the archaeological site El Zotz.

Biotopo Laguna del Tigre/Río Escondido – Situated within the Maya Biosphere Reserve in the northwest of the Petén, this 46,300-hectare reserve is one of Guatemala's most remote protected areas. It conserves the largest freshwater wetlands in Central America and is a refuge for countless bird species. Organized tours are available through EcoMaya and ProPetén in Flores. Boat trips can also be arranged at El Naranjo, where the administration office is situated, with prior permission from the Centro de Estudios Conservacionistas de la Universidad de San Carlos (CECON) in Guatemala City. For more information about contacting this agency, check out the Ecology & Environment section earlier in this chapter.

Wildlife refuges include the following:

Bocas del Polochic – On the western side of Lago de Izabal, the Río Polochic forms a marshy delta where it empties into the lake; this is Guatemala's second-largest freshwater wetland area. It's especially attractive for birders, with more than 300 species of birds, 40% of which are migratory. It's accessible only by water; boats are most easily arranged at El Estor.

Cerro San Gil – On the south side of El Golfete, east of Lago de Izabal, this refuge occupies the highest part of the Montañas del Mico, the continuation of the Sierra de las Minas. It has many endemic species and great biodiversity. Two parts of the refuge are open to the public; contact FUNDAECO in Guatemala City for access permission and information (see the Ecology & Environment section for contact details).

Natural and cultural monuments include the following:

Quiriguá – This Mayan archaeological site, 2km off the Carretera al Atlántico and easily accessible, is famous for its giant stelae, the tallest in the Maya world.

Iximché – Capital of the Cakchiquel Maya at the time of the Spanish conquest, this is one of the few archaeological sites with a documented history. Though you wouldn't know it by the dearth of visitors, this site is easily accessible from Tecpán, only 2km away.

Aguateca-Dos Pilas – This monument protects several important archaeological sites and the forest around them. This is actually a group of sites along the Río La Pasión, in the southwest of the Petén, in the municipality of Sayaxché. It's accessible from Sayaxché or by tour from Flores/ Santa Elena.

Yaxjá – On the shores of Lake Petexbatún in eastern Petén, archaeologists believe this site was a vacation getaway for the Mayan nobility and the Topoxté site in the middle of the lake was an observatory. Tours are available from Santa Elena.

Semuc Champey – On the Río Cahabón in the municipality of Lanquín, Alta Verapaz, Semuc Champey is a series of pristine pools surrounded by forest. It's accessible by 4WD vehicle, on foot or by tour from Cobán.

Grutas de Lanquín – 61km from Cobán and serviced by frequent buses, these caves are at least several kilometers long and have never been completely penetrated by spelunkers. The first few hundred meters of the caves are lit. You can camp just outside the entrance to the caves. Tours are also available from Cobán.

GOVERNMENT & POLITICS

Guatemala is a republic with 22 departments. Executive power is held by a president who is elected by direct universal adult suffrage to a term of four years. The president is assisted by a vice president and an appointed cabinet. The unicameral national congress consists of 80 members (64 departmental representatives and 16 national seats) also elected to four-year terms. Judicial power rests in a supreme court and associated courts.

Government in Guatemala has traditionally been one of beautiful theory and brutal reality. Always a constitutional democracy in form, Guatemala has been ruled by a succession of military strongmen ever since Pedro de Alvarado was sent by the Spanish to Guatemala and conquered the Maya in the 16th century. With a few notable exceptions, such as the administrations of Juan José Arévalo and Jacobo Arbenz Guzmán, Guatemala's government has been controlled for the benefit of the commercial, military, landowning and bureaucratic ruling classes of society. While the niceties of democracy are observed, real government often takes place by means of intimidation and secret military activities (see History earlier in this chapter for more on these base behaviors).

Now is a great time to put true democracy to the test. Guatemala recently emerged from civil war, and 1999 witnessed the election of the first peacetime president in several decades. As president, Alfonso Portillo's rhetoric is encouraging. He has vowed to clean up the judicial system, crack down on crime, tax the rich and respect human rights.

In March 2000, he invited the UN observers responsible for overseeing implementation of the peace accords to stay beyond their targeted December 2000 departure date. Portillo doesn't come off as a champion of the poor, however, and riots in April 2000 over price increases for public transportation (which often hit the poorest hardest) were troubling and didn't help his image. Still, it is action, not rhetoric, that makes history, and only time will tell if Portillo goes down in infamy or as a legend.

ECONOMY

The Guatemalan highlands are given over to agriculture, particularly corn, with some mining and light industry around the larger cities. The Pacific Slope has large coffee, citrus and sugarcane plantations worked by migrant labor from the highlands, and the Pacific coast has cattle ranches and some fishing villages. Coffee is the country's biggest export crop, followed by sugar, cotton, bananas and cardamom. Fruits, vegetables, natural rubber and flowers are also grown for export. Tourism is the second-largest hard currency earner after coffee, though repatriated dollars from Guatemalans working in the United States may be the greatest unofficial source of hard currency.

Guatemala City is the industrial and commercial center of the country, very similar in sprawl and bustle to Mexico City, its great sister to the north. Like Mexico City and many other Latin American urban centers, Guatemala City has problems of immigration, pollution, congestion and crime arising from its near-monopoly on the commercial life of the country.

Guatemala's Motagua Valley has some mining, but agriculture is most important

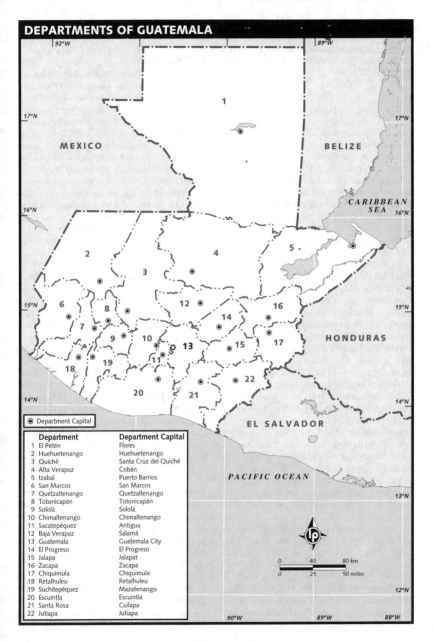

DEPARTMENTS OF GUATEMALA

MEXICO

BELIZE

CARIBBEAN SEA

HONDURAS

EL SALVADOR

PACIFIC OCEAN

⊚ Department Capital

	Department	Department Capital
1	El Petén	Flores
2	Huehuetenango	Huehuetenango
3	Quiché	Santa Cruz del Quiché
4	Alta Verapaz	Cobán
5	Izabal	Puerto Barrios
6	San Marcos	San Marcos
7	Quetzaltenango	Quetzaltenango
8	Totonicapán	Totonicapán
9	Sololá	Sololá
10	Chimaltenango	Chimaltenango
11	Sacatepéquez	Antigua
12	Baja Verapaz	Salamá
13	Guatemala	Guatemala City
14	El Progreso	El Progreso
15	Jalapa	Jalapat
16	Zacapa	Zacapa
17	Chiquimula	Chiquimula
18	Retalhuleu	Retalhuleu
19	Suchitepéquez	Mazatenango
20	Escuintla	Escuintla
21	Santa Rosa	Cuilapa
22	Jutiapa	Jutiapa

0   40   80 km
0   25   50 miles

here, with vast banana and sugarcane plantations. In the lush green hills of Alta Verapaz there are dairy farms, cardamom and coffee plantations and some small forests for timber.

El Petén depends upon tourism and farming for its livelihood. The rapid growth of agriculture and cattle farming is a serious threat to the ecology of the Petén, a threat that will have to be controlled if the forests of this vast jungle province are to survive. Tourism, on the other hand, is a mostly positive factor here, providing alternative sources of income in jobs that depend upon the preservation of the ecology for success. Still, not all tour outfits wearing the ecotourism label are promoting environmentally responsible adventures. Besides, in such a fragile environment, low impact tourism may be an oxymoron.

POPULATION & PEOPLE

According to estimates from July 1999, Guatemala has a population nearing 12.5 million people. Official census statistics show 56% of the population as mestizo or ladino and 44% as indigenous. In fact, the total Mayan population in Guatemala probably exceeds 50%, but this doesn't register in the census because that survey only defines 'indigenous' as those people still wearing traditional dress and speaking their Mayan dialect. Obviously, this excludes all people of indigenous ancestry who may be full-blooded (and self-identified) Maya, but who also speak Spanish and wear jeans – even Super-Maya Rigoberta Menchú has been known to sport polar fleece on occasion. There is also a very small population of non-Maya indigenous people called the Xinca living in the southeastern corner of the country.

About 40% of all Guatemalans live in cities, the biggest of which are Guatemala City, Quetzaltenango and Escuintla. The Izabal and El Petén regions are the most sparsely populated, though migration to both those areas is on the rise. On average, the country has a population density of 170 inhabitants per square kilometer. The Guatemalan population is due to double by the year 2020 if it continues to grow at its current rate of 2.68% annually.

EDUCATION

Education in Guatemala is free and compulsory between the ages of seven and 14. Primary education lasts for six years; it's generously estimated that 79% of children of this age are actually in school. Secondary education begins at age 13 and lasts for up to six years, with two cycles of three years each; it's estimated that only 23% of children of the relevant age group are in secondary school. Note that not all secondary education is free – an incredible deterrent for the average Guatemalan student. Guatemala has five universities. The University of San Carlos, founded in 1676 in Antigua (later moved to Guatemala City), was the first university in Central America.

Overall, adult literacy is around 65% in Guatemala. The average rate of adult illiteracy is 37% for males and 53% for females, the second highest rate in the Western Hemisphere. There's a big variation in literacy rates among different groups, however. A Guatemalan organization specializing in Mayan women's concerns estimates that 95% of rural women (who are mostly Mayan) are illiterate. Mayan children who do seasonal migrant work with their families are least likely to get an education, as the time the families go away to work – often migrating clear across the country – falls during the normal school year. Indigenous children, especially those living or working near urban centers, are increasingly turning to Spanish to get by and ahead in life.

ARTS

Various traditional handicrafts are still practiced in Guatemala. Most noticeable are the weaving, embroidery and other textile arts practiced by Mayan women, but others include basketry, ceramics and wood carving. A number of well-known Maya painters work in a distinctive primitivist style and depict daily life. This genre is typified by vibrant colors rendered with oil paints and is centered in San Pedro La Laguna and Santiago Atitlán on Lago Deti-

Faces of Guatemala

RICHARD I'ANSON

ERIC L WHEATER

ERIC L WHEATER

More faces of Guatemala

tlán. Known as Tz'utuhil Mayan oil painting, legend has it that one day Rafael Gonzalez y Gonzalez noticed some dye that had dripped and mixed with the sap of a tree; he made a paintbrush from his hair and began creating the type of canvases still popular today. Other accomplished artists of this style include Pedro Rafael Gonzalez Chavajay and Mariano Gonzalez Chavajay. For more on Mayan oil painting, visit the Arte Maya Web site at www.artemaya.com.

Music

Music is an important part of Guatemalan society, and it is no small source of pride that the marimba was probably invented in Guatemala. Although scholars cannot agree whether this xylophone-type instrument already existed in Africa before slaves brought it to Guatemala, or if the instrument was created and/or refined in the New World, marimba music can still be heard throughout the country. The very earliest marimbas used a succession of increasingly large gourds as the resonator pipes, but modern marimbas are more commonly outfitted with wooden pipes, though you may

see the former type in more traditional settings. The instrument is usually played by three men and has a carnival-like quality to its sound and traditional compositions.

Festivals are typically raucous and freewheeling in Guatemala and provide great opportunities for hearing traditional music. Instruments used during fiestas include the *chirimía*, a reed instrument of Moorish roots related to the oboe, cane flutes and square drums.

Literature

Another great source of national pride is the Nobel Prize for Literature that was bestowed on native Guatemalan Miguel Ángel Asturias in 1967. Best known for his thinly veiled vilification of Latin American dictators in *El Señor Presidente*, Asturias also wrote poetry (collected in the early volume *Sien de Alondra*, published in English as *Temple of the Lark)* and served in various diplomatic capacities for the Guatemalan government. Other celebrated Guatemalan authors include Luis Cardoza y Aragón, principally known for his poetry and for fighting in the revolutionary movement that deposed dictator Jorge Ubico in 1944, and short story master Augusto Monterroso, who was born in Honduras but raised in Guatemala.

ARCHITECTURE
Mayan

Mayan architecture is a mixed bag of incredible accomplishments and severe limitations. While the Maya of Guatemala erected awesome temples in sophisticated, urban centers like El Mirador and Tikal, they did it without beasts of burden (unless you include humans) or the luxury of the wheel. In addition, Mayan architecture was limited because architects of the day never devised an equivalent to Roman arches and Gothic-style vaulting. Instead, they used what is known as a corbeled (or false) arch, a set of stones set at an angle sloping inward – like two upside down staircases – and topped by another stone called a capstone. This creates a triangular rather than rounded arch and requires the structure be

Una marimba

long and narrow. In addition, buildings made with corbeled arches need an incredibly strong foundation and substructure because, unlike with the true arch, stones in a corbeled arch are not self-supporting. Once the structures were completed, experts hypothesize, the buildings were covered with stucco and painted red with a mixture of hematite and most probably water.

Although formal studies and excavations of Mayan sites in Guatemala have been ongoing for more than a century, much of the Mayan architectural how and why remains a mystery. For example, the purpose of *chultunes*, underground chambers carved from bedrock filled with offerings, continues to baffle scholars. Further, while we know that the Maya habitually built one temple on top of another as leaders fell in and out of favor, we have no idea how they actually erected these symbols of power. Without wheels or work animals, all the limestone used to erect the great Mayan cities had to be moved and set in place by hand – an engineering feat yet to be explained unequivocally, though all sci-

entists agree it took an astronomical amount of human labor. Try to imagine mining, shaping, transporting and hefting 2 million cubic meters of limestone blocks: This is the amount of rock scholars estimate was used in the construction of the Danta complex at El Mirador.

Archaeologists continue to probe the ancient Mayan cities in search of answers. Ongoing projects such as the excavation of the massive Temple V at Tikal and investigations into quarries such as the one at nearby Nakbé used by the ancient builders, will hopefully shed more light on the architectural processes used and refined by the Maya.

More recent discoveries, such as the cave at Naj Tunich with its rich and varied cave paintings and tombs built inside, are also augmenting our understanding of the function of these ceremonial centers in the religious and cultural life of the Maya. Unfortunately, looters usually uncover new sites before researchers get there, robbing archaeologists and the world of important new information regarding the Maya enigma. Indeed, Naj Tunich has been closed to visitors since 1989 following a particularly thorough plundering.

Colonial

Not surprisingly, architecture changed drastically with the arrival of the Spanish. Baroque flourishes were incorporated into facades, espe-

Miguel Ángel Asturias

cially on churches, which were built high and strong to protect the elite from lower classes in revolt. While the architectural concepts were European-inspired, the labor used to actualize them was strictly indigenous. Interestingly, Mayan embellishments can be found on many colonial buildings – such as the water lily blossoms and vegetable motifs that adorn Antigua's La Merced – serving as testament to the countless laborers forced to make the architectural dreams of Guatemala's newcomers a reality.

The architecture of Antigua is particularly striking, as new and improved styles and engineering techniques developed following each successive earthquake. Columns, for example, got lower and thicker to provide more stability, as the colonial period and cycle of earthquakes progressed. The Palacio de los Capitanes Generales on the central park even added a double-arch construction to strengthen it after the earthquake in 1717. With so many colonial buildings in different states of grandeur and decay, from nearly crumbled to completely restored, Antigua was designated a World Heritage Site by UNESCO in 1979.

Scholars divide the colonial styles into four periods ranging from 1650 to 1773. In the latter year, one of the most devastating earthquakes to date struck Guatemala, prompting the founding of a new capital at present-day Guatemala City. After the capital was relocated in 1776, the predominant architectural style, known as neoclassic, came to emphasize durability. Decorative focus was saved for the inside, with elaborate altars and furniture adorning churches and homes. By this time, Guatemalan architects were hell-bent to see their buildings still standing, no matter how powerful the next earthquake. Even though several serious quakes have hit Guatemala City since then, many colonial buildings (such as the Metropolitan Cathedral) have withstood the tremors. The same cannot be said for the humble abodes of Guatemala City's residents, who suffered terribly when the devastating quake of 1976 struck, reducing their homes to rubble.

SOCIETY & CONDUCT

Guatemalan society is divided between the ladino and Maya populations, both pursuing pathways that are sometimes convergent but often at odds. While the ladino culture is proceeding into the modern world, in many ways the Maya, who are the majority of Guatemala's population, are holding on tight to their traditional culture and identity despite five centuries of European domination and occupation of their land. Though customs such as head flattening and the ball game have gone out of style, traditional clothing, language and ceremonies endure.

Ancient Mayan Culture

Personal Beauty Spanish Franciscan priest and bishop of Yucatán Diego de Landa wrote that the Maya of the 16th century, just as in the Classic period, flattened their children's foreheads by tying boards tightly to them. This custom was practiced by many indigenous groups throughout the hemisphere, as a flat forehead was considered a mark of beauty. Crossed eyes were another desirable trait, and to encourage it parents tied a bead of wax so it dangled between the child's eyes. Young boys had scalding-hot cloths placed on their faces to discourage the growth of beards, which were considered ugly by the Maya. Whether or not this trait was genetically selected in later generations is up for debate. Nevertheless, modern Maya have little body hair.

Both men and women made cuts in their skin so as to promote much-desired scar markings, and both were enthusiastic about tattoos. Women sharpened their teeth to points, another mark of beauty, which, for all we know, may have helped them to keep their men in line. And both men and women dyed their bodies red, though women refrained from dyeing their faces.

Clothing As for preconquest clothing, the men wrapped long cloths around their loins, with the ends hanging in front and back; a square cape was worn on the shoulders, and leather sandals on the feet. Though this sort of clothing has long since disappeared, the men in many Guatemalan highland villages still wrap cloths around them to make a sort of skirt; they wear trousers underneath. Everybody still wears sandals (mostly of the ubiquitous plastic variety) or goes barefoot.

The women wore *huipiles*, longer versions of the embroidered dresses that are still worn by Mayan women throughout the country today. These shin-length, typically white, huipiles are still worn by women elders in small villages such as San Juan Ixcoy in the Cuchumatanes mountains.

Food & Drink De Landa describes how the Maya loved to give banquets for one another, offering roast meat, stews with vegetables, corn cakes (perhaps tortillas or tamales) and cocoa, not to mention lots of alcoholic beverages. The lords got so drunk at these banquets that their wives had to come and drag them home, a condition that still persists, though women are getting in on the action themselves nowadays. The 'banquets' today are cantinas, and the 'lords' are workmen, but the dragging remains the same.

Sport The recreation most favored by the Maya was hip-ball. Using a hard rubber ball on stone courts, players tried to stop the ball from hitting the ground, keeping it airborne by batting it with any part of their body other than their hands, head or feet. A wooden bat may have been used. In some regions, a team was victorious if one of its players hit the ball through stone rings with holes little larger than the ball itself.

The ball game was taken quite seriously and was often used to settle disputes between rival communities. On occasion, it is thought that the captain of the losing team was punished by the forfeiture of his life.

Surviving Mayan Culture

Dress Mayan culture expresses itself in many ways. Most awe-inspiring to visitors is the beautiful traditional clothing worn by Mayan women. In most parts of Guatemala, Mayan men now wear western clothing, but in some places, such as Sololá and Todos

Santos Cuchumatán, the men also still wear their traditional *traje*. Each village has its own unique style of dress, and within the village style there can be variations according to social status; when all of the different variations are taken into account, there are something like 500 distinctive forms of design, each with its own significance. Historians surmise that the colonists encouraged the development of distinct designs by separate villages so they could better track the movements of their Mayan charges. Popular belief holds that both the army and the guerrillas used the same strategy during the 36 years of civil war.

Some styles still in use go back to precolonial times. Among these (all worn by women) are the *huipil*, a long, sleeveless tunic; the *tzut* or *kaperraj*, a piece of all-purpose cloth used as a shawl, to carry babies or haul and cover produce; the *tocoyal*, a head-covering of woven material and decorated with colorful pompoms or tassels; and the *córte*, a long piece of material seven or 10 yards in length that is used as a wraparound skirt. The skirt is bound by a *paz* or *faja*, a long strip of woven material used as a belt. Blouses are colonial innovations. Mayan men's garments owe more to Spanish influence; nudity was discouraged by the church, so shirts, hats and *calzones*, long baggy shorts that eventually evolved into full-length pants in most regions, were introduced.

The most arresting feature of these costumes is their colorful embroidery. Often entire garments are covered in a multicolored web of stylized animal, human, plant and mythological shapes that can take months to complete. Each garment identifies the group and village from which its wearer hails. The *fajas*, waist sashes, which bind the garments and also hold what we would put in pockets, are also important in this respect.

Materials and techniques are changing, but the pre-Hispanic backstrap loom is still widely used. The warp (long) threads are stretched between two horizontal bars, one of which is fixed to a post or tree, while the other is attached to a strap that goes round the weaver's lower back. The weft (cross) threads are then woven in. All throughout the highlands you can see women weaving in this manner outside the entrance to their homes. Nowadays, some huipiles and fajas are machine made as it is faster and easier than on a loom.

Yarn is hand spun in many villages. For the well-to-do, silk threads are used to embroider bridal huipiles and other important garments. Vegetable dyes are not yet totally out of use, and natural indigo is employed in several areas. Red dye from cochineal insects and purple dye from sea snails are used by some groups. Modern luminescent dyes go down very well with the Maya, who are happily addicted to bright colors, as you will see.

The variety of techniques, materials, styles and designs is bewildering. For more on clothing and other handicrafts, see Shopping in the Facts for the Visitor chapter.

Language Mayan languages are still the way most Maya communicate, with 20 separate (and often mutually unintelligible) languages spoken in different regions of the country. In addition, there is a Pipil-based language spoken by the Xinca people in the southeast. Though not a Mayan language, it is often erroneously counted among the Mayan dialects. Traditional religion, firmly based in nature, is also still practiced by many Maya.

Today, the Maya are being pushed farther and farther into the background of society. Travelers, who often find the Maya and their traditions beautiful and intriguing, may be surprised to learn that in Guatemala the Maya (who are the majority of the population) are viciously and often violently discriminated against. While some Maya are going to universities, working in the business world and joining modern society, those continuing the traditional way of life are the poorest sector of Guatemalan society.

The plight of these people has attracted international attention. Many nongovernmental organizations from around the world are working to assist Guatemala's indigenous people. Travelers can help by volunteering with one of these organizations, patronizing Maya-owned businesses and buying traditional Mayan handicrafts. If the Maya can sell their wares to tourists and receive fair prices, it helps to make their craft an economically viable occupation. Also, to break the ice and bridge two worlds, try out a few Mayan words and phrases in your travels. For assistance, see the Modern Mayan section of the phrasebook at the end of this book.

Ceremonies Though visitors can observe traditional Mayan ceremonies in places such as the shrine to Pascual Abaj in Chichicastenango and the altars on the shore of Lake Chicabal outside Quetzaltenango, most traditional rites are off limits to foreigners. Fertility rites, healing ceremonies and sacred observances to ring in the New Year are still practiced with gusto in Guatemala. These types of ceremonies are directed or overseen by a Mayan *sacerdote* (priest) and involve burning *copal* (a natural incense from the bark of various tropical trees), making offerings to the gods and praying for whatever the desired outcome may be – a healthy harvest or a prosperous new year, for example. Some ceremonies involve chicken sacrifices as well.

Dos & Don'ts

Politeness is a very important aspect of social interaction in Guatemala, as it is everywhere in this part of the world. When beginning to talk to someone, even in such routine situations as in a store or on the bus, it's polite to preface your conversation with a greeting to the other person – a simple 'Buenos días' or 'Buenas tardes' and a smile, answered by a similar greeting on the other person's part, gets any conversation off to a positive start. The same holds true for when you enter a room, including public places such as a restaurant or waiting room; make a general greeting to everyone in the room – the requisite 'Buenos días' or 'Buenas tardes' will do. When leaving a restaurant, it is common to wish the other diners 'Buen provecho' (bon appétit) or

INDIGENOUS LANGUAGES

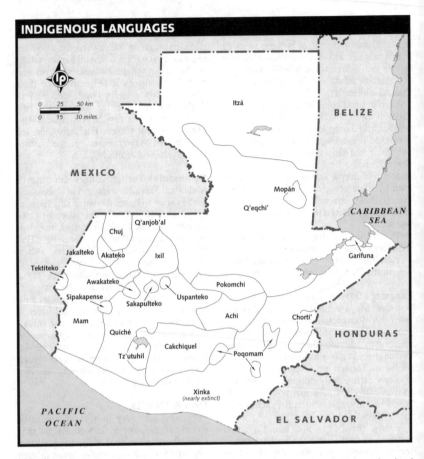

simply 'Provecho.' Handshakes are another friendly gesture and are used frequently.

Note that many Maya, especially the farther off the beaten track you venture, speak only their indigenous language. Where this is the case, it's futile to try to engage them in a conversation in Spanish, though sign and body language are always viable options.

In recent years, stories circulated throughout Guatemala that some foreign visitors (particularly white women) were kidnapping Mayan children, perhaps for the grisly purpose of selling their bodily organs.

An alternative twist on the tale maintained that foreigners were kidnapping Guatemalan children to raise them as their own. Do be aware that some people are extremely suspicious of foreigners who make friendly overtures toward children, *especially foreigners who photograph indigenous children*. Women traveling alone are treated most distrustfully in this regard, but in April 2000 two men (a Japanese tourist and his Guatemalan driver) were beaten to death by a mob in Todos Santos after the tourist started taking photos of children and a rumor circulated that he wanted to kidnap one of them. Photographing children was the same spark that inflamed a frenzied crowd to beat a female tourist into a coma in San Cristóbal Verapaz in 1994.

Portrait photography is a particularly sticky issue in Guatemala, where it's so tempting to photograph every Mayan family you meet; clearly too many people have done just that and many Maya are very touchy about having their photograph taken. Rather than giving in to temptation and just clicking off a few shots, always ask permission to take pictures first. Sometimes your request will be denied, often you'll be asked for a quetzal or two and maybe in a few special instances, you'll make new friends.

Many Mayan women prefer to avoid contact with foreign men; in their culture, talking with strange men is not something that a virtuous woman does. With this in mind, male travelers in need of directions or information should try to find another man or a child to approach.

Pay attention to your appearance when traveling. Latin Americans on the whole are very conscious of appearance, grooming and dress; it's difficult for them to understand why a foreign traveler, who is naturally assumed to be rich, would go around looking scruffy when even poor people in Latin America do their best to look neat. Try to be as clean and presentable as possible, especially if you're dealing with officialdom (police, border officials, immigration officers). In such cases it's a good idea to look not only clean, but also as conservative and respectable as possible.

Interestingly, Mayan women are extremely eager to sell their traditional clothing to foreign visitors, especially the beautiful embroidered huipiles (blouses), but, paradoxically, it is considered very bad form for a visitor to actually wear these items in Guatemala. Indeed, travelers sporting traje stick out like sore thumbs; better save them for home.

Standards of modesty in dress are becoming more relaxed in recent years; you may see women wearing mini-skirts in the largest cities, where just a few years ago this would have been unthinkable. Nevertheless, not all locals appreciate this type of dress. Take particular care not to offend with your attire.

Dress modestly when entering churches, as this shows respect for the people and their culture. Some churches in heavily touristed areas will post signs at the door asking that shorts and tank tops (singlets) not be worn in church, but in most places such knowledge is assumed. Shorts are usually worn by both sexes only at the beach and in coastal towns, or where there are plenty of foreign tourists. (See the Women Travelers section in the following chapter for further tips specifically for women travelers.)

Also think about safety in connection with your appearance. Particularly in the capital, locals will warn you against wearing even cheap imitation jewelry: You could be mugged for it. If you have any wealth, take care not to flaunt it. See the Dangers & Annoyances section in the Facts for the Visitor chapter for other basic rules of travel safety.

On the language front, travelers should be aware that using the term *indio* to refer to a Mayan person is derogatory and carries racist undertones. The preferred term is *indígena*.

Visitors checking out Mayan sites should show the proper respect for these ancient cities. Sitting on altars or touching stelae is completely taboo, and under no circumstances should you do this, no matter how sore your feet are from traipsing all around the ruins!

RELIGION

Roman Catholicism is the predominant religion in Guatemala, but it is not the only religion by any stretch of the imagination. Since the 1980s, evangelical Protestant sects, around 75% of them Pentecostal, have surged in popularity, and it is estimated that about 30% of Guatemalans now ascribe to this faith. These numbers are growing as evangelical Protestants blatantly swoop into an area after a natural disaster, distribute food, build houses and erect a church. After the dust settles and the flood waters recede, these altruists are rewarded with an instant congregation.

When Catholicism was imposed in Guatemala it did not wipe out the traditional Mayan religion, and it still has not today, as many aspects of Catholicism easily blend with Mayan beliefs. In fact, the Maya still worship at a number of places where they have worshipped since ancient times, bringing offerings and making sacrifices to gods that predate the arrival of the Spanish.

Various Catholic saints hold a double meaning for the Maya; often the Catholic identity of the saint was superimposed over a deity or saint the Maya people already worshipped when the Spanish arrived. This religious syncretism survives to this day. The Maya also have some of their own saints, which are quite independent of the Catholic Church: including Maximón (venerated in Santiago Atitlán), San Simón (venerated in Zunil) and Ry Laj Man (worshipped in San Jorge La Laguna). For more on this bizarre, but likeable deity, see the boxed text 'A God is a God is a God' in the Highlands chapter.

Ancient Mayan Religion
World-Tree & Xibalba For the Maya, the world, the heavens and the mysterious 'unseen world' or underworld called Xibalba (shee-bahl-bah) were all one great, unified structure that operated according to the laws of astrology and ancestor worship. The towering ceiba tree was considered sacred, for it symbolized the Whack Chan, or world-tree, which united the 13 heavens, the surface of the earth and the nine levels of the underworld of Xibalba. The world-tree had a sort of cruciform shape and was associated with the color blue-green. In the 16th century, when the Franciscan friars came bearing a cross and required the Indians to venerate it, the symbolism meshed easily with the established Maya belief in the ceiba or world-tree.

Points of the Compass In Mayan cosmology, each point of the compass had special religious significance. East was most important, as it was where the sun was

reborn each day; its color was red. West was black because it was where the sun disappeared. North was white and was the direction from which the all-important rains came, beginning in May. South was yellow because it was the 'sunniest' point of the compass.

Everything in the Mayan world was seen in relation to these cardinal points, with the world-tree at the center; but the cardinal points were only the starting point for the all-important astronomical and astrological observations that determined fate. See the Mayan Calendar System section later in this chapter for more on Mayan astrology.

Bloodletting & Human Sacrifice Humans had certain roles to play within this great system. Just as the great cosmic dragon shed its blood, which fell as rain to the earth, so humans had to shed blood to link themselves with Xibalba.

Bloodletting ceremonies were the most important religious ceremonies, and the blood of kings was seen as the most acceptable for these rituals. Mayan kings often initiated bloodletting rites to heighten the responsiveness of the gods. Thus, when the friars said that the blood of Jesus, the King of the Jews, had been spilled for the common people, the Maya could easily understand and embrace the symbolism – a nice coincidence for the friars.

Sacred Places Mayan ceremonies were performed in natural sacred places as well as their human-made equivalents. Mountains, caves, lakes, cenotes (natural limestone cavern pools), rivers and fields were all sacred and had special importance in the scheme of things. Natural sacred spots are still actively used in Guatemala. Pyramids and temples were thought of as stylized mountains; sometimes these had secret chambers within them, like the caves in a mountain. A cave was the mouth of the creature that represented Xibalba, and to enter it was to enter the spirit of the secret world. This is why some Mayan temples have doorways surrounded by huge masks:

As you enter the door of this 'cave' you are entering the mouth of Xibalba.

As these places were sacred, it made sense for succeeding Mayan kings to build new and ever grander temples directly over older temples, as this enhanced the sacred character of the spot. The temple being covered over was not seen as mere rubble to be exploited as building material, but as a sacred artifact to be preserved. Certain features of these older temples, such as the large masks on the facades, were carefully padded and protected before the new construction was placed over them. At some sites such as Copán, visitors can see these layers of construction via subterranean tunnels.

Ancestor worship and genealogy were very important to the Maya, and when they buried a king beneath a pyramid or a commoner beneath the floor or courtyard of a na, the sacredness of the location was increased.

The Mayan 'Bible' One of the most important Mayan texts, the *Popol Vuh*, survived as a transcription into the Latin alphabet of a Mayan narrative; that is, it was written in Quiché Maya, but in Latin characters, not hieroglyphs. The *Popol Vuh* was apparently written by the Quiché Maya of Guatemala who had learned both Spanish and the Latin alphabet from the Dominican friars. The authors showed their book to Francisco Ximénez, a Dominican who lived and worked in Chichicastenango from 1701 to 1703. Friar Ximénez copied the Quiché's book word for word, then translated it into Spanish. Both his copy and the Spanish translation survive, but the Maya original has been lost.

For a translation of the Spanish version into English, see *Popol Vuh: Ancient Stories of the Quiche Indians of Guatemala*, by Albertina Saravia E (Guatemala City: Editorial Piedra Santa, 1987), on sale in many book stores in Guatemala for about US$4. Any library worthy of the name will have a translation of this important text.

According to the *Popol Vuh*, the great god K'ucumatz created humankind first

from earth (mud), but these 'earthlings' were weak and dissolved in water. The god tried again, using wood. The wood people had no hearts or minds and could not praise their creator. These too were destroyed, all except the monkeys who live in the forest, who are the descendants of the wood people. The Creator tried once again, this time successfully, using substances recommended by four animals – the grey fox, the coyote, the parrot and the crow. The substance was white and yellow corn, ground into meal to form the flesh and stirred into water to make the blood.

After the devastating earthquake of 1976, the government rebuilding program included the printing and distribution of posters bearing a picture of an ear of corn and the words *Hombre de maíz, ¡levántate!* (Man of corn, arise!). A great source of pride and heritage, it is not uncommon to see references in Guatemala to men of corn. Indeed, when the first refugees streamed home from Mexico after the peace agreements, their caravans were draped in banners reading, 'Hombre de maíz, ¡levántate!'

Shamanism & Catholicism The ceiba tree's cruciform shape was not the only correspondence the Maya found between their animist beliefs and Christianity. Both traditional Mayan animism and Catholicism have rites of baptism and confession, days of fasting and other forms of abstinence, religious partaking of alcoholic beverages, burning of incense and the use of altars. In addition, the *Popol Vuh* includes descriptions of virgin birth and tells of sacrificial death that is then followed by a return to life.

Today, the Mayan practice of Catholicism is a fascinating fusion of shamanist-animist and Christian ritual. The traditional religious ways are so important that often a Maya will try to recover from a malady by seeking the advice of a religious shaman rather than a medical doctor. Use of folk remedies and herbal cures linked with animist tradition are widespread in Mayan areas.

MAYAN CALENDAR SYSTEM

In some ways, the ancient Mayan calendar is more accurate than the Gregorian calendar we use today. Without sophisticated technology, Mayan astronomers were able to ascertain the length of the solar year, the lunar month and the Venus year. Their calculations enabled them to pinpoint eclipses with uncanny accuracy; their lunar cycle was a mere seven minutes off today's sophisticated technological calculations, and their Venus cycle erred by only two hours for periods covering 500 years.

Time and the calendar, in fact, were the basis of the Mayan religion, which in some parts of the country has survived to the present day. In some respects the ancient cosmology resembles modern astrology. Astronomical observations played such a pivotal role in Mayan life that astronomy and religion were linked and the sun and moon were worshipped. The cycle of life and repeated patterns found in the universe were integral parts of the belief system. Most Mayan cities were constructed in strict accordance with celestial movements, and observatories were not uncommon.

How the Calendar Worked

Perhaps the best analogue to the Mayan calendar (which is still used in certain parts of Guatemala) is found in the gears of a mechanical watch, where small wheels mesh with larger wheels, which in turn mesh with other sets of wheels to record the passage of time.

Tonalamatl or Tzolkin The two smallest wheels in this Mayan calendar 'watch' were two cycles of 13 days and 20 days. Each of the 13 days bore a number from one to 13; each of the 20 days bore a name such as Imix, Ik, Akbal or Xan. As these two 'wheels' meshed, the passing days received unique names. For example, Day 1 of the 13-day cycle meshed with the day named Imix in the 20-day cycle to produce the day named 1 Imix. Next came 2 Ik, then 3 Akbal, 4 Xan etc. After 13 days, the first cycle began again at one, even though the 20-day name cycle still had seven days to

run, so the 14th day was 1 Ix, then 2 Men, 3 Cib etc. When the 20-day name cycle was finished, it began again with 8 Imix, 9 Ik, 10 Akbal, 11 Xan etc. The permutations continued for a total of 260 days, ending on 13 Ahau, before beginning again on 1 Imix.

The two small 'wheels' of 13 and 20 days thus created a larger 'wheel' of 260 days, called a *tonalamatl* or *tzolkin*. Let's leave the 13-day and 20-day 'wheels' and the larger 260-day wheel whirling to look at another set of gears in the watch.

Vague Year (Haab) Another set of wheels in the Mayan calendar watch comprised the 18 'months' of 20 days each, which formed the basis of the Mayan solar Vague Year calendar, or *haab*. Each month had a name – Pop, Uo, Zip, Zotz, Tzec etc, and each day had a number from zero (the first day, or 'seating', of the month) to 19, much as our Gregorian solar calendar does. There was 0 Pop (the 'seating' of the month Pop), 1 Pop, 2 Pop and so forth to 19 Pop, then 0 Uo, 1 Uo and so on.

Eighteen months, each of 20 days, equals 360 days; the Maya added a special omen-filled five-day period called the *uayeb* at the end of this cycle in order to produce a solar calendar of 365 days. Anthropologists today call this the Vague Year, its vagueness coming from the fact that the solar year is actually 365.24 days long. To account for this extra quarter-day, we add an extra day to our Gregorian calendars every four years in Leap Year. The Maya did not do this.

Calendar Round The huge wheels of the tzolkin and the haab also meshed, so that each day actually had two names and two numbers, a tzolkin name-number and a haab name-number, used together: 1 Imix 5 Pop, 2 Ik 6 Pop, 3 Akbal 7 Pop and so on. By the time the huge 260-day wheel of the tzolkin and 365-day wheel of the Vague Year had meshed completely, exhausting all the 18,980 day-name permutations, a period of 52 solar years had passed.

This bewilderingly complex meshing of the tzolkin and the haab is called the Calendar Round, and it was the dating system used throughout Mesoamerica by the Olmecs, the Aztecs, the Zapotecs and the Maya. In fact, it is still in use in some traditional mountain villages, but you can see why a special Mayan elder has to be designated to keep track of the days, significant and ordinary, to alert his community to important days in this complex system.

Though fascinating in its complexity, the Calendar Round has its limitations, the greatest being that it only goes for 52 years. After that, it starts again, and it provides no way for Maya ceremony planners (or modern historians) to distinguish a day named 1 Imix 5 Pop in this 52-year Calendar Round cycle from the identically named day in the next cycle, or in the cycle after that, or a dozen cycles later. Thus the need for the Long Count.

Long Count As Mayan civilization developed, Mayan scientists recognized the limits of a calendar system that could not run more than 52 solar years without starting over, so they developed the so-called Long Count or Great Cycle, a system of distinguishing the 52-year Calendar Round cycles from one another. The Long Count came into use during the Classic period of Mayan civilization.

The Long Count system modified the Vague Year solar mechanism, then added yet another set of wheels to the already complex mechanism of Mayan time.

In place of the Vague Year of 365 days, the Long Count uses the *tun*, the 18 months of 20 days each, and ignores the final five-day period. In Long Count terminology, a day was a *kin* (meaning 'sun'). A 20-kin 'month' is called a *uinal*, and 18 uinals make a tun. Thus the 360-day tun replaced the Vague Year in the Long Count system. The time wheels added by the Long Count were huge (see the Mayan Time Divisions table for the names of all the time divisions).

In practice, the gigantic units above baktun (pictun, calabtun etc) were not used except for grandiose effect, as when a very self-important king wanted to note exactly when his extremely important reign took place in the awesome expanse of time. The largest unit used in monument inscriptions was usually the baktun. There were 13 baktuns (1,872,000 days, or 5125 Gregorian solar years) in a Great Cycle.

When a Great Cycle was completed a new one would begin, but for the Maya of the Classic period this was unimportant as Classic Mayan civilization died out long before the end of the first Great Cycle. For them, the Great Cycle began on August 11, 3114 BC (some authorities say August 13), and it will end on December 23, 2012 AD. The end of a Great Cycle was a time fraught

Mayan Time Divisions

Unit	Same as	Days	Gregorian Years*
Kin	-	1	-
Uinal	20 kins	20	-
Tun	20 uinals	360	0.99
Katun	20 tuns	7200	19.7
Baktun	20 katuns	14,000	394
(Great Cycle)	13 baktuns	1.872 million	5125
Pictun	20 baktuns	2.88 million	7885
Calabtun	20 pictuns	57.6 million	157,705
Kinchiltun	20 calabtuns	1.152 billion	3,154,091
Alautun	20 kinchiltuns	23.04 billion	63,081,809
* Approximate			

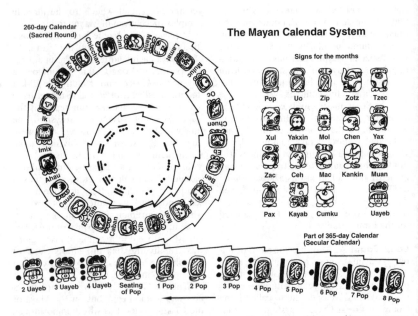

The Mayan Calendar System

260-day Calendar (Sacred Round)

Signs for the months

Pop Uo Zip Zotz Tzec

Xul Yakxin Mol Chen Yax

Zac Ceh Mac Kankin Muan

Pax Kayab Cumku Uayeb

Part of 365-day Calendar (Secular Calendar)

2 Uayeb 3 Uayeb 4 Uayeb Seating of Pop 1 Pop 2 Pop 3 Pop 4 Pop 5 Pop 6 Pop 7 Pop 8 Pop

with great significance – usually fearsome. Keep that date in mind, and keep on your toes as this Great Cycle finishes up!

Even the awesome alautun was not the largest unit used in the Long Count. In order to date everything in proper cosmic style, one date found at Cobá in Mexico is equivalent to 41,341,050,000,000,000,000,-000,000,000 of our years! (In comparison, the Big Bang that is said to have created our universe is estimated to be a mere 15,000,000,000 years ago.)

It's important to remember that to the Maya, time was not a continuum but a cycle, and even this incomprehensibly large cycle of years would be repeated, over and over, infinitely, in infinitely larger cycles. In effect, the Mayan 'watch' had an unlimited number of gear wheels, and they kept ticking around and around forever.

Mayan Counting System The Mayan counting system was elegantly simple: dots were used to count from one to four; a horizontal bar signified five; a bar with one dot

above it was six, with two dots was seven and so forth. Two bars signified 10, three bars 15. Nineteen, the highest common number, was three bars stacked up and topped by four dots.

To signify larger numbers the Maya used positional numbers, a fairly sophisticated system similar to the one we use today, and much more advanced than the crude additive numbers used in the Roman Empire.

In positional numbers, the position of a sign as well as the sign's value determine the number. For example, in our decimal system the number '23' is made up of two signs: a '2' in the 'tens' position and a '3' in the 'ones' position: two tens plus three ones equals 23.

The Maya used not a decimal system (base 10) but a vigesimal system, that is, a system with base 20; and positions of increasing value went not right to left (as ours do) but from bottom to top. So, the bottom position showed values from one to 19, the next position up showed values from 20 to 380. The bottom and upper positions together could show up to 19 twenties plus 19 ones (ie, 399). The third position up showed values from one 400 to 19 four hundreds (ie 7600). The three positions together could signify numbers up to 7999. By adding more positions one could count as high as needed.

Such positional numbers depend upon the concept of zero, a concept the Romans never developed but which the Maya did. The zero in Mayan numbering was represented by a stylized picture of a shell or some other object – anything except a bar or a dot.

The Mayan counting system was used by merchants and others who had to add up many things, but its most important use –

and the one you will encounter during your travels – was in writing calendar dates.

LANGUAGE

Spanish is the official national language, but in practice 23 different languages are spoken in Guatemala, including Spanish, Garífuna, 20 Mayan languages and a Pipil-based language spoken by the Xinca people. Many Maya speak Spanish, but you can't assume for sure that they do; many Mayan elders, women and children do not. Mayan children often start to learn Spanish only after they start school or drop out to start working.

KATUN
20 Years

BAKTUN
400 Years

PICTUN
8000 Years

CALABTUN
160,000 Years

KINCHILTUN
3,200,000 Years

ALAUTUN
64,000,000 Years

Facts for the Visitor

HIGHLIGHTS

Tikal is far and away the most frequented spot in Guatemala, and while it lives up to most (if not all) expectations, there are scads of other stellar natural, cultural and archaeological sites to explore. The following list suggests places and activities worth your travel time; getting off the beaten track in the departments of Huehuetenango and Alta and Baja Verapaz is wholeheartedly recommended as well.

Markets

Guatemala is renowned for its markets of both the tourist and local varieties. Chichicastenango has the greatest of the former, where the shopping is legendary and the market a near institution. Nebaj and Todos Santos both have mellower versions in spectacular settings. Shopping local style is best at Solalá, Rabinal or San Francisco El Alto, though almost all towns have some sort of colorful market to pique a traveler's interest.

Archaeological Sites

Tikal and Copán (just over the border in Honduras) are the biggest archaeological draws in this part of the world and are not to be missed for their grandeur. Still, other sites tucked beneath the jungle canopy and worth the trip for the setting alone (if not the actual ruins themselves) include El Mirador, Ceibal, Nakbé, El Zotz and Yaxjá. For pure artistry, visit the painted caves of Río Azul in the north or the giant stelae at Quiriguá. Adventure and river travel can be combined to visit the sites at Yaxchilán and Piedras Negras.

Mountains & Volcanoes

With 30 volcanoes and several challenging mountain peaks strewn throughout the country, there are many opportunities here for hardcore and recreational alpinists. Volcán Pacaya and Volcán San Pedro in the highlands are great for day trips; Pacaya is active and belches smoke and fire daily. Volcán Tajumulco is the highest peak in Central America and you make the summit in a two-day trip from Quetzaltenango. Other peaks worth a go include Santiaguito, Volcán Santa Mariá and Volcán Tacaná. The mountains within the Cordillera de los Cuchumatanes offers challenging hikes in a stunning landscape. For more information and details on upcoming mountaineering trips, visit the Asociación de Andinismo Web site at http://get.to/andinismo.

Festivals

The motley pageantry of Mayan culture commingling with the rites of Catholicism make for some awesome and effervescent festivals here. *Semana Santa,* or Easter Week, is celebrated with elaborate processions over carpets of rainbow-colored flower petals called *alfombras* in Antigua and San Cristóbal Verapaz. *Día de Todos los Santos* (All Saint's Day) is celebrated on November 1 with drunken horse races in Todos Santos and giant kite festivals in Sumpango and Santiago Sacatepéquez in the highlands. The Burning of the Devil is celebrated throughout the country on December 7 with huge bonfires and pyrotechnic displays. In fact, there are so many festivals in Guatemala you won't have too much trouble stumbling upon a few or working one into your itinerary (see Public Holidays & Special Events later in this chapter).

Natural Attractions

Semuc Champey is often called the most beautiful natural attraction in Guatemala, though others would argue the honor belongs to Lago de Atitlán or the Bocas de Polochic. Still, the caves at Lanquín, the temperate waterfalls at Finca El Paraíso, the beach and mangroves at Monterrico and the Río Dulce and Lívingston area are quite beautiful in their own right. Then there's the amazing Petén jungle, which some people feel is unparalleled for its drama, visual and otherwise.

Wildlife Viewing

Some of Guatemala's greatest wildlife viewing is deep in the Petén where chainsaws and televisions have yet to penetrate. Good opportunities to see animals exist in the Biotopo Laguna del Tigre-Río Escondido, Parque Nacional El Mirador-Rio Azul, the Biotopo San Miguel-La Pelotada-El Zotz and the El Perú area in the Maya Biosphere Reserve. There is exceptional birding around Río Polochic on Lake Izabal, in the mangroves of Monterrico and north of Cobán in Alta Verapaz; this last is one of the few remaining strongholds of the resplendent quetzal and is best visited during the mating season from March to June. Children especially will enjoy the Auto Safari Chapín, where scores of animals, including peccaries, deer, lions and rhinos, are raised in compassionate captivity.

Studying Spanish

This is such a popular pursuit in Guatemala it deserves mention here. Antigua is far and away the favorite place to study, with Quetzaltenango a distant second. Schools in Panajachel and San Pedro on Lago de Atitlán are for those wishing to study in a gorgeous, laid-back setting. In fact, from the mountains to the jungle, if you want to go to Spanish school in Guatemala, you can take your pick from various settings, speeds and flavors. For the total immersion experience, combine your studies with electives, volunteer opportunities or a homestay with a Guatemalan family. Many schools offer programs for children, an engaging alternative activity if you're traveling with kids.

SUGGESTED ITINERARIES

Whether you fly into Guatemala City or Flores, arrive overland into the Petén or cruise into Puerto Barrios by boat, there are certain sights you won't want to miss. One important detail to keep in mind while planning your trip is that Antigua and Guatemala City are only 45 minutes apart by bus. Since the former is so much more

pleasant, you can plan on launching or finishing your trip there, simply returning to the capital for your outbound flight. Also, Guatemala is a fairly small country, so speedy travel times mean many places can be squeezed into short itineraries. The following trip ideas are simply suggestions; ignore them completely and strike out on your own if you feel like it!

One Week

Assuming you arrive by air in Guatemala City, head straight to Antigua for a day of acclimatization and exploration of that singular colonial city. On day two, hop a bus to Lago de Atitlán, which deserves a two day stay, though undoubtedly you'll want to spend longer. Around the lake you can hike, kayak, scuba dive or shop. Some folks love Panajachel, others hate it, but check out other traditional towns around the lake regardless of your take on this classic Gringo Trail town. Santiago and Santa Catarina Palopó are two favorites. Day four can be spent at the market at Chichicastenango, before heading back to Guatemala City or Antigua for the very early morning flight to Flores the next day. Spend day five and six at Tikal and exploring Lake Petén Itzá before returning to Guatemala City and beyond.

Two Weeks

This is a decent amount of time to see the major sites, with some interesting bus rides thrown in. You can relax and catch your breath in several places, including Flores, Río Dulce or Poptún; this itinerary opts for the last. Alternatively, if you don't have the time or patience for the bus, you can fly to and from Flores, spending the resulting free time visiting Cobán, Semuc Champey and environs, only four hours by good road north of Guatemala City. This last option can also be rushed (or scrapped, though Semuc Champey is a life highlight) so you can include Quetzaltenango and around, also about four hours from Guatemala City. Travelers enthralled with Mayan culture and ruins should amend the following to include at least one day and night at Copán Ruinas in Honduras.

Day 1 – Guatemala City or (preferably) Antigua, arrive and find your hotel.

Day 2 – Explore Antigua or climb Volcán Pacaya; overnight.

Day 3 – To Panajachel and overnight.

Day 4 – Visit Santiago and San Pedro on Lago de Atitlán; overnight in either.

Day 5 – Relax for a day in San Marcos, Jaibalito or Santa Cruz; overnight.

Day 6 – Bus to the market at Chichicastenango; overnight.

Day 7 – To Guatemala City or Antigua and overnight

Day 8 – Fly to Flores, explore Tikal; overnight in Flores or El Remate.

Day 9 – Explore Tikal for another morning and get the afternoon bus to Uaxactún, overnight.

Day 10 – Bus to Poptún and spend two nights.

Day 11 – Kick back and relax in Poptún.

Day 12 – Bus to Río Dulce and overnight there or hop a boat to Lívingston and hang out there for a night.

Day 13 – Bus to Quiriguá and overnight there or down the road in Río Hondo.

Day 14 – Return to Guatemala City or Antigua and fly home.

Three Weeks

An itinerary of three weeks is a healthy chunk of time for visiting Guatemala and permits a bit of lingering in whatever places strike a chord. Follow all the suggestions for the two week itinerary, making a point of getting to Cobán and Semuc Champey and including a visit to the mangrove forests at Monterrico. Build time into this itinerary to explore Quetzaltenango (more often referred to by its abbreviated Mayan name, Xela, pronounced shay-la) and the very cool, traditional towns in the surrounding countryside. Inspiring day trips in this area include the Fuentes Georginas hot springs, Lake Chicabal, San Andrés Xequl, Momostenango and San Francisco El Alto, among others. If time permits, check out Huehuetenango and Todos Santos or Nebaj in the Cuchumatanes mountains.

Four Weeks

One month is more like it and will allow you to delve deeper into the physical and cultural landscape that makes Guatemala unique. If you like, follow the two week itinerary and supplement it with two weeks of one-on-one Spanish lessons while living with a Guatemalan family. Otherwise, follow the three week itinerary with some exploration off the beaten track: take the bus between Cobán and Poptún or Cobán and Huehuetenango; travel overland from Flores to Sayaxché, visiting some archaeological ruins in the jungle there before taking a bus or hitching a ride to Cobán; or visit some Mayan towns in the mountain vastness of the Cuchumatanes mountains and the Ixil Triangle (Nebaj, Chajul and Cotzal).

One to Three Months

Three months is not too long for Guatemala (otherwise, why would immigration make that the maximum allowable stay?!). If you have this much time, do all of the above including studying Spanish, and throw in a visit to Palenque in Mexico via the Río San Pedro, a trip to the world's tallest Mayan temple at El Mirador, and a camping stint or two in some of the lesser visited parks in Guatemala like Laguna Lachuá or the Biosfera Sierra de las Minas. Altruistic folk may want to investigate volunteer opportunities, of which Guatemala has no shortage (see Volunteer Work in the Work section later in this chapter).

PLANNING
When to Go

There is really no bad time for visiting Guatemala, though the rains will limit access to certain areas. In the lowland jungles of the Petén, for example, the rainy season is technically from May to late October (meaning it drags into November or even December!) and the mud at this time will be a bummer, guaranteed. The rainy season can also be very cold and damp in the highlands, especially at night. The dry season is from about November to April and this means sweltering heat in the Petén, possible rain in the Caribbean and comfortably warm days in the highlands. Take note however, that altitude effects climate and while it may be warm in the highlands during the dry season, it is not hot; sweaters or jackets are usually necessary at night.

The height of the tourist season is from the end of December to the beginning of April, becoming acute around Christmas, New Year's and Easter; a secondary high season lasts from June to August when throngs of Westerners descend on Guatemala to study Spanish and travel about. At these times negotiating prices for rooms and the like may be tough. At other times of the year, try bargaining. It is not uncommon during the high season for the best affordable rooms in popular spots like Antigua and Xela to fill up by early afternoon, especially on weekends.

What Kind of Trip

Guatemala has something for everyone, save for beaches, so if you're looking to loll around a tropical paradise, look elsewhere. However, if culture is what you crave, there's no better place. From markets held beneath towering volcanoes to ancient temples tucked into the jungle, the culture of Guatemala resonates through the ages. Travel times by bus are very reasonable, so you can see a decent portion of the country even in a short amount of time. Solo women travelers will be pleasantly surprised at the amount and tenor of help extended by locals; most Guatemalans will go out of their way to help with baggage, offer advice and steer you in the right direction – even if they haven't a clue which direction is right!

Thematic trips with a focus such as birding, archaeological sites, spelunking or learning Spanish are all possible here. Even a general tour of this beautiful and friendly country will stick in your mind and heart long after you've returned home or wherever 'real life' may deposit you.

Maps

International Travel Maps, a division of ITMB Publishing Ltd, (☎ 360-371-2012), PO Box 2290, Vancouver, BC V6B 3W5, Canada, publishes a series of Traveler's Reference Maps. The *Guatemala-El Salvador* (1:500,000) map is very good and covers neighboring portions of Chiapas, Tabasco, Belize and Honduras.

These maps are also available from many travel book and map stores, including World Wide Books & Maps (☎ 604-687-3320, fax 687-5925), 736A Granville St, Vancouver, BC V6Z 1G3, Canada. In Australia you can try The Travel Bookshop (☎ 02- 9241 3554), 20 Bridge St, Sydney, NSW 2001, or Mapland (☎ 03-9670 4383), 372 Little Bourke St, Melbourne, Vic 3000. In New York, The Map & Travel Store of Rand McNally should have them (212-758-7488, www.randmcnallystore.com), 150 East 52nd St, New York, NY 10022, and in London try Stanfords Map Centre (☎ 020-7836 1321), 12-14 Long Acre, London WC2E 9LP.

A letter to the Instituto Guatemalteco de Turismo (INGUAT), 7 Avenida 1-17, Zona 4, Guatemala City, Centro America, sent well in advance of your departure, will yield a useful map of the country with city street plans, but the scale is fairly small. The same map, called the *Mapa Vial Turístico*, may be bought in Guatemala at shops or from street vendors for a few dollars (you can bargain with vendors). This map is also available over the Internet from Latin American Travel Consultants at www.amerispan.com/lata/. One of the best organizations for travelers to Latin America, the South American Explorers (☎ 607-277-0488, fax 607-277-6122) also sells a good map to Guatemala. Maps can be ordered from their Web site at www .samexplo.org.

In Guatemala, the Instituto Geográfico Militar (☎ 332-2611), Avenida Las Américas 5-76, Zona 13, Guatemala City, publishes and sells a number of mostly useless, dated maps of various cities. However, this is the storehouse for topographical maps, so mountaineers may find it worth their time to head over there.

What to Bring

Many a traveler has fallen into the hot and sunny frame of mind when preparing for their Guatemalan trip, when in fact, the country can be downright cold. You'll want at least a sweater and light jacket to keep out the chill of the highland evenings and a pair of fairly warm pants, something akin to denim will prove comfortable. If you are visiting during the rainy season or plan to spend time in the mountains, bring a heavier jacket – fleece works particularly well here – and dress in layers.

On the topic of shorts, tank tops and other hot weather wear, bring a change or two and leave it at that – you won't need more. Not only are there few beaches, but you'll stick out big time wearing shorts anywhere but the most laid-back places; locals certainly aren't exposing this much skin. A bathing suit is useful for the hot springs, rivers or lakes you may visit.

If you're heading to the hot jungle region of the Petén, long, light clothing is preferable to anything that exposes your skin to sun and insects. In this region always wear a hat, sunglasses and sunblock cream. If your complexion is particularly fair or if you burn easily, consider wearing light cotton shirts with long sleeves and light cotton pants.

Visitors going to Guatemala during the rainy season should bring a poncho or similar rain gear and have a strategy for keeping their pack dry: buy or fashion a pack cover, carry an umbrella, line the inside with plastic bags or get a poncho big enough to cover you and your pack.

After mosquito nets it seems that shoes and sleeping bags are probably the most confounding packing issues for travelers. Since Guatemala can get very cold at night and because the $3 room won't always be so spotless, bring a sleeping bag to keep you warm and distanced from any dicey linens. As for shoes, you'll want something water resistant if it's the rainy season and of the hiking boot variety if you'll be heading to the mountains. For the general traveler, however, one of those hybrid sneaker/ walking/hiking shoes should do the trick. Also bring a pair of sandals or flip flops for the shower.

Toiletries such as shampoo, soap, toothpaste, toilet paper, razors and shaving cream are readily available in all but the smallest villages. You should bring your own contact lens solution, tampons, contraceptives and deodorant.

Don't forget the all-important insect repellent containing DEET (see the Health section), which may be easier to find at home. Besides, if you buy it before you leave home, you'll have it when you need it. Even if you only plan to visit Tikal, pack it; you'll want and need it.

To bring or not to bring the mosquito net? While the highlands are refreshingly mosquito-free, if you are traveling on a super strict budget or plan an extended jungle adventure, it's better to have your own net. Most of the cheapest rooms won't have screens on the windows, let alone nets. With your own, you can sleep in the cheapest rooms and hammocks without getting eaten alive. Travelers planning on living with Guatemalan families in the lowland regions might consider bringing a net as well, especially if you're the type to be bothered by insects buzzing about your head. Being snug and bug free beneath your net while your host family feigns sleep and slaps irritatingly at the pests can be awkward, however.

Other items you might find useful are a flashlight (torch) for exploring caves, pyramids and your hotel room when the electricity fails, disposable lighter (for the same reasons), pocket knife, alarm clock (for catching the very early bus), two to three meters of cord, fishing equipment, a small sewing kit, money belt or pouch, lip balm and a small dictionary with sections in Spanish and your native language.

RESPONSIBLE TOURISM

Tourism and the intrusion that goes with it is a fairly sensitive subject in a country just emerging from 36 years of civil war. The Mayan population (traditionally a very private people) has suffered terribly during this period and travelers should refrain from probing into wartime tragedies and atrocities. Don't dig for information, let your hosts offer it. Almost everyone has a war experience, most of them awful, and once you get to know someone, they may be willing to share their story. In highland towns hit very hard by the war, tourists are requested to refrain from furtive movements and let local people pass first rather than trying to muscle through.

New areas have opened for tourism since the end of the war and many companies, both local and foreign, peg Guatemala as the next Costa Rica or ecotourism haven. While some outfits are running real environmentally friendly tours, others are simply exploiting the enthusiasm for low impact travel and are harming the environment more than helping it.

Just the presence of people in ecologically sensitive areas can disrupt the natural balance. This is a growing problem with some Petén jungle tours, for example, especially those visiting very remote areas. The garbage created on these trips is supposed to be packed out, but rarely makes it and the mules used on multi-day tours eat the leaves of the sapodilla tree, deforesting the precise area ecotourism is designed to protect. Consider these issues when you set up a tour; research your guides and their techniques and insist garbage is packed out. Of course, independent travelers should also take out all trash they create. For more ideas on responsible travel, see that section in the Petén chapter.

There is also a trend toward serving 'exotic' fare at some restaurants and this may include endangered or threatened species. On certain menus you'll find anything from turtle soup to *tepescuintle*. Don't contribute to the demise of Guatemalan fauna by ordering these dishes.

TOURIST OFFICES
Local Tourist Offices
The main office of the Instituto Guatemalteco de Turismo (INGUAT), the national tourist office, is in the Centro Cívico of Guatemala City. There is also a satellite office in Zone 9 of the capital. Branch offices are in Antigua, Panajachel, Quetzaltenango and at the international airports in Guatemala City and Flores/Santa Elena. A

second Petén office on the Parque Central in Flores is quite helpful.

Tourist Offices Abroad
INGUAT (toll free in the US ☎ 888-464-8281, @ inguat@guate.net) has a Web site, www.travel-guatemala.org.gt, which is utilitarian for the most basic travel queries. Try a Guatemalan consulate or embassy for general information if the site proves inadequate or there isn't a tourist office near you. The following INGUAT offices should be able to help with travel-related questions:

Canada (☎ 613-233-7188, 233-7237), Guatemalan Embassy, 130 Albert St, Suite 1010, Ottawa, ON K1P 5G4

France (☎ 33 14 227 7863, fax 33 14 754 0206), Guatemalan Embassy, 73 rue de Courcelles, 75008 Paris

Germany (☎ 49 228 351 579, fax 49 228 328 627), Guatemalan Embassy, Ziethen Strasse 16, 53173 Bonn; Guatemalan Consulate in Hamburg (☎ 49 40 430 6051, fax 49 40 430 4274), Fruchtalle 17, 2059; Guatemalan Consulate in Munich (☎ 49 89 406 214), Grafinger Strasse 2, 81671

Italy (☎ 39 6 5091 274), Viale Prassilla 152, 00124 Rome

Mexico (☎ 52 5 540 7520, 520 9249, fax 52 5 202 1142), Guatemalan Embassy, Avenida Explanada 1025, Lomas Chapultepec 11000, Mexico 4, Mexico City

Spain (☎ 34 91 344 1417, fax 34 91 458 7894), Guatemalan Embassy, Rafael Salgado, No 3, 40 Izquierda, 28036 Madrid

UK (☎ 44 20 7349 0346, fax 44 20 7376 5708, @ 101740.3655@compuserve.com), Guatemalan Embassy, 13 Fawcett St, London SW10 9HN

US (☎ 202-745-3873, fax 202-745-1908), Guatemalan Embassy, 2220 R St NW, Washington, DC 20008; Guatemalan Tourist Commission in Florida (☎ 305-443-0343, fax 305-443-0699), 300 Sevilla Ave Suite 210-A, Coral Gables, FL 33134

VISAS & DOCUMENTS
The Guatemalan government changed its visa requirements in 1999 and is moving toward revising others (especially extensions), so you should check with the nearest Guatemalan embassy or consulate before heading off. If you are traveling overland by

private car, you will need motor vehicle insurance and a valid import permit. See Vehicle Documents later in this chapter for details.

Passport

To be permitted entry into Guatemala, your passport must be valid for three months *beyond* your intended stay. Don't cut things too close by only having four months left on your passport before you hit the road. If your passport is that near the expiration date, replace it. Guatemala is one of those destinations where a three week holiday can turn into a three year odyssey. If the opportunity or desire to stay on arises during your travels, you don't want to be caught short with an expired passport.

Visas

Most travelers can enter Guatemala without a visa. If you need a visa and arrive at the border without one, however, you will be turned back; if you're flying into Guatemala, you probably won't be allowed to board the plane without having the visa you need for entry.

As of early 2000, citizens of the following countries need no visa or tourist card and receive 90 days in Guatemala upon arrival: Andorra, Argentina, Australia, Austria, Belgium, Brazil, Canada, Chile, Costa Rica, Denmark, El Salvador, Finland, France, Germany, Greece, Honduras, Ireland, Israel, Italy, Japan, Liechtenstein, Luxembourg, Mexico, Monaco, New Zealand, Nicaragua, Norway, the Netherlands, Panama, Paraguay, Spain, Sweden, Switzerland, Taiwan, the UK, Uruguay, Venezuela and the US. Officials don't always give you the 90 day maximum; ask for the maximum stay or you may end up with only a 30-day stamp.

Citizens of the following countries do not need a visa or tourist card and receive 30 days in Guatemala upon arrival: Belize, Portugal, San Marino and the Vatican.

Citizens of the following countries can enter either with a visa or a tourist card, which can be obtained at the time of entry: Bahrain, Czech Republic, Iceland, Kuwait, the Philippines, Poland, Saudi Arabia, Slovakia and South Africa.

Citizens of all other countries must obtain a visa from a Guatemalan consulate.

If you want to cross into Honduras on a day (or two) pass to visit Copán, the Guatemalan Migración official will usually allow you to return to Guatemala and continue your journey without interrupting your original entry stamp. For information on this, refer to the section on Copán.

Minors Traveling Alone Solo travelers under 18 years of age are (technically) required to have a letter of permission signed by both parents and witnessed by a Guatemalan consular official in order to enter Guatemala. On occasion border officials will flex their muscle and ask for this permission slip if you're under 18.

Visa Extensions Guatemala had a visa extension system that old hands called the '90-90-3.' This meant you received an initial 90 day stamp and could extend your stay for another 90 days. When that extension expired, you could leave the country for a three day respite (usually crossing into Mexico or Honduras for the duration) and return to Guatemala to start the process all over again. Some foreigners have been repeating this cycle for years and Guatemalan immigration wants it to stop. The new regulations stipulate that foreigners can receive a maximum total of 180 days – the original 90 and an extension for another 90 – but cannot leave for three days to start the process anew. The crackdown may or may not have begun by the time you arrive.

Extensions must be applied for in person at the Dirección General de Migración (☎ 634-8476/7/8), 7a Avenida 1-17, Piso 2, INGUAT office, Zona 4, Guatemala City. There are very welcome plans to establish a second immigration office in Antigua to handle extension requests. You can check on this with the INGUAT office in Antigua when you arrive. To apply for an extension you'll need your passport, a recent photo, proof of funds and an onward ticket. A 90-day extension costs

US$13. Companies specializing in private immigration services can be hired to expedite this process, attending to all of the paperwork for you. INGUAT maintains a list of recommended companies.

Onward Tickets

Technically, Guatemala requires all visitors to show proof of funds and an onward ticket before they're permitted entry to the country. Very rarely will you be asked to produce either, though if your visa or extension depends upon it, you can usually present a credit card as proof of funds and an international bus ticket as proof of onward passage.

Travel Insurance

A travel insurance policy to cover theft, loss and medical problems is a wise idea. Travel agencies sell them; STA Travel and other student travel organizations usually offer good value. Certain policies provide a lost baggage per diem, which could come in handy in this part of the world.

Some policies specifically exclude 'dangerous activities,' which can include scuba diving, motorcycling, even trekking. If such activities are on your agenda, you don't want that sort of policy. If you have a policy that requires you to pay medical expenses up front, save all your original receipts and documentation, as photocopies are not usually accepted. With any policy, check the small print.

Driver's License & Permits

Travelers planning on renting a car in Guatemala or driving their own vehicle into the country need to carry their driver's license. Even if you don't anticipate driving, a license serves as good secondary identification and can be useful if you hook up with other travelers with a car. Make doubly sure that your license won't expire during your trip and keep a photocopy in a safe place (see Copies later in this section).

International Driving Permit Guatemala requires an International Driving Permit (IDP) and you should get one before setting off if you plan on driving during your trip. IDPs are issued by the automobile association in your home country and are valid for a year. There is a nominal fee charged to obtain the permit and you'll have to fill out an application and provide two passport size photos.

Vehicle Documents While the mountain of paperwork and liability involved with driving a car into Guatemala deters most travelers, some folks do successfully and enjoyably drive their own vehicles here. If you wish to make this kind of trip, do your research beforehand and be prepared to exercise amazing amounts of patience, especially if all your paperwork is not consistent and clear. Oftentimes border officials will try to extort money from travelers, especially those arriving with cars. Known as *la mordida* or 'the bite,' it can be very effective in greasing the squeaky wheels of officialdom; depending on your philosophy and budget, you may consider paving your way with these less than legit 'fees.' See the section on land travel in the Getting There & Away chapter for more information on la mordida.

You will need the following documents to enter Guatemala with a car: current and valid registration; proof of ownership (if you don't own the car, you'll need a notarized letter of authorization from the owner that you are allowed to take it); your driver's license, current and valid; and a temporary import permit typically available free at the border and good for 30 days. Insurance from foreign countries is not recognized by Guatemala, forcing you to purchase a policy locally. Most border posts and nearby towns have offices selling liability policies.

Guatemala has strict rules about leaving with your vehicle. To deter foreigners from selling cars in Guatemala, the authorities make you exit the country with the vehicle you used to enter it. Do not be the designated driver when crossing borders if you don't own the car, because all the permits will be registered on your documentation and if you split from your companions, you will not be allowed to leave Guatemala until you produce the car.

Copies

Getting photocopies of your documentation is one of the least exciting parts of preparing for a trip, but it's also among the most important. Before you leave, get two photocopies of the following paperwork: the front page of your passport and any visas, credit and debit cards (with the expiration date crossed out), plane tickets, travel insurance card and a list of traveler's checks serial numbers. Leave one set at home with someone trustworthy and take the other set with you, separate from the originals. Stash an emergency US$50 cash or so with your spare set.

It's also a good idea to store details of your vital travel documents in Lonely Planet's free online Travel Vault in case you lose the photocopies or can't be bothered with them. Your password-protected Travel Vault is accessible online anywhere in the world – you can create it on line at www.ekno.lonelyplanet.com.

EMBASSIES & CONSULATES
Guatemalan Embassies & Consulates Abroad

Some of the consulates mentioned here are actually honorary consuls or consular agencies. These posts can issue visas, but they refer more complicated matters to the nearest full consulate or to the embassy's consular section. All the listings are for embassies unless noted.

Australia – Guatemala does not maintain an embassy in Australia; contact the Guatemalan Embassy in Tokyo

Belize (☎ 2-33024, 32999, fax 2-33032) Mile 3, North Western Hwy, Hotel Belize Pilsmore Plaza, Room 146, Belize City

Canada (☎ 613-224-4322, fax 613-237-0492) 294 Albert St, Suite 500, Ottawa, Ontario K1P 5G4; Consulates in Vancouver and Montreal

Costa Rica (☎ 314074, fax 316645) Avenida Primera, Calles 24 y 28, No 2493, San Jose

El Salvador (☎ 271-2225, fax 271-3019) 15 Avenida Norte 135, San Salvador

France (☎ 01-42-27-78-63, fax 01-47-54-02-06) 73 rue de Courcelles, 75008 Paris; Consulates in Ajaccio, Bordeaux, Le Havre, Strasbourg and Marseilles

Germany (☎ 228-35-15-79, fax 228-35-49-40) Zietenstrasse 16, 53173 Bonn; Consulates in Dusseldorf, Hamburg, Munich and Stuttgart

Honduras (☎ 32-9704, 32-1543, fax 32-1580) 4a Calle & Avenida Juan Lindo, No 2421, Colonia Las Minitas, Tegucigalpa; Consulate (☎ 53-3560, fax 55-7748) 8a Calle between 14a & 15a Avenida No 148 B, Barrio Los Andes, San Pedro Sula

Japan (☎ 3-3400-1830, fax 3-3400-1820) 38 Kowa Bldg, Room 905, 4-12-24 Nichi-Azabu, Tokyo 106; Consulate in Osaka

Mexico (☎ 5-540-7520, fax 5-202-1142) Avenida Explanada 1025, Lomas de Chapultepec, 11000 México 4, DF; Consulate (☎ 9-832-30-45) Retorno Número 4, Casa 8, Fraccionamiento Bahía, Chetumal, Q Roo; Consulate (☎ 962-8-01-84, fax 962-8-01-93) Avenida Central Norte, No 12, Ciudad Hidalgo, Chiapas; Consulate (☎ 963-2-26-69) Avenida 2 Pte Sur at Calle 1 Sur Pte, No 28, Comitán, Chiapas; Consulate (☎ 36-11-15-03, fax 36-10-12-46) Callejon de Los Claveles, No 127, Colonia de Buganvillas, Guadalajara; Consulate (☎ 8-375-7248) Belisario Dominguez 2005, Colonia Obispado, Monterrey; Consulate (☎ 962-6-12-52) 2 Calle Oriente No 33, Tapachula, Chiapas

Netherlands (☎ 55-55-74-21, fax 55-21-17-68) 2e Beukelaan 3, 7313 Apeldoorn

New Zealand Guatemala does not maintain an embassy in New Zealand; contact the Guatemalan Embassy in Tokyo

Nicaragua (☎ 279-697, fax 279-478) Km 11.5, Carretera a Masaya, Managua; Consulate in León

Panama (☎ 769-3475, fax 723-1922) Edificio ADIR, Piso 6, Apartamento 6B, El Cangrejo, Panama City

UK (☎ 020-7351-3042, fax 020-7376-5708) 13 Fawcett St, London SW 10

US (☎ 202-745-4952, fax 202-745-1908) 2220 R St NW, Washington DC; Consulates in Atlanta, Baltimore, Chicago, Houston, Fort Lauderdale, Leavenworth, Los Angeles, Memphis, Miami, Minneapolis, Montgomery, New Orleans, New York, Philadelphia, Pittsburgh, Providence, San Antonio, San Diego, San Francisco and Seattle

Embassies & Consulates in Guatemala

All of the following are in Guatemala City unless otherwise noted.

Belize (☎ 334-5531, 331-1137, fax 334-5536) Avenida La Reforma 1-50, Zona 9, Edificio El Reformador, Office 803

Canada (☎ 333-6102, fax 363-4208) 13a Calle 8-44, Zona 10, Edificio Plaza Edyma (8th Floor)

Costa Rica (☎ 331-9604, ☎/fax 332-0531) Avenida La Reforma 8-60, Zona 9, Edificio Galerías Reforma, Office 702

El Salvador (☎ 366-2240, fax 366-7960) 4a Avenida 13-60, Zona 10

France (☎ 337-3639, 337-3180) 16a Calle 4-53, Zona 10, Edificio Marbella, 11th Floor

Germany (☎ 337-0028) 20a Calle 6-20, Edificio Plaza Marítima, Zona 10

Honduras (☎ 335-3281, 338-2068, fax 338-2073) 12a Calle 1-25, Edificio Géminis, 12th Floor, Zona 10; Consulate (☎ 943-2027, 943-1547, fax 943-1371), 2a Avenida in the Hotel Payaquí, Esquipulas

Japan (☎ 367-2244, fax 367-2245) Avenida la Reforma 16-85, 10th Floor, Zona 10

Mexico (☎ 333-7254 to 333-7258) 15a Calle 3-20, Edificio Centro Ejecutivo, 7th Floor, Zona 10; Consulates (☎ 331-8165, 331-9573) 13a Calle 7-30, Zona 9; 5a Avenida 4-11, Zona 1, Huehuetenango; (☎ 763-1312/3/4/5) 9a Avenida 6-19, Zona 1, Quetzaltenango

Netherlands (☎ 367-4761, fax 367-5024, contact @ nlgovgua@infovia.com.gt) 16a Calle 0-55, Torre Internacional, 13th Floor, Zona 10

Nicaragua (☎ 368-0785, fax 337-4264) 10a Avenida 14-72, Zona 10

Panama (☎ 333-7182/3, 337-2495, fax 337-2445) 5a Avenida 15-45, Edificio Centro Empresarial, Torre II, Offices 702, Zona 10

UK (☎ 367-5425/6/7/8/9, fax 367-5430, @ embassy@ infovia.com.gt) 16a Calle 0-55, Torre Internacional, 11th Floor, Zona 10

US (☎ 331-1541 to 331-1555) Avenida La Reforma 7-01, Zona 10

CUSTOMS

Customs officers only get angry and excited about a few things: drugs and paraphernalia, weapons, large amounts of currency, and automobiles and other expensive items that might be sold while you're in the country. Don't take illegal drugs or any sort of firearm into (or out of) Guatemala. It is also illegal to bring fruit, vegetables or plants through the international airports at Guatemala City and Flores.

Normally customs officers won't look seriously in your luggage and may not look at all. At some border points the amount of search is inversely proportional to the amount of 'tip' you have provided: big tip no search, no tip big search. (See the section on Border Crossings in the Getting There & Away chapter for more information.)

Whatever you do, keep it formal. Anger, hostility or impoliteness can get you thrown out of the country or into jail, or worse.

MONEY
Currency

The Guatemalan quetzal (Q) is named for the country's gorgeous but rare national bird. The quetzal is divided into 100 centavos. There are coins of one (useless), five, 10 and 25 centavos and bills (notes) of 50 centavos, one, five, 10, 20, 50 and 100 quetzals. In late 1999 the government introduced new coins in denominations of one and 50 centavos and one quetzal. The coins were so wildly unpopular, they may not even be in circulation when you get there.

Exchange Rates

Currency exchange rates at the time of writing were:

country	unit	Guatemala	Honduras
Australia	A$1	Q5.18	L9.58
Belize	BZ$1	Q4.00	L7.31
Canada	C$1	Q5.40	L9.99
euro	€1	Q8.13	L15.00
Germany	DM1	Q4.16	L7.70
El Salvador	ES¢1	Q0.90	L1.66
France	FF1	Q1.24	L2.30
Japan	¥100	Q7.46	L13.74
Mexico	N$10	Q8.28	L15.26
Netherlands	fl	Q3.70	L6.82
New Zealand	NZ$1	Q4.10	L7.53
Spain	pta1	Q4.89	L9.01
UK	UK£1	Q13.00	L24.00
US	US$1	Q7.77	L14.6

Exchanging Money

Cash US dollars are the currency to bring to Guatemala. Any other currency – even the currencies of neighboring Honduras, El Salvador and Mexico – will probably prove impossible to exchange. The bank exchange desks at the airports in Guatemala City and Flores/Santa Elena are among the few places that exchange other currencies. Going to the bank can be a long, drawn out affair, so set aside ample time to exchange money.

Many establishments accept cash dollars instead of quetzals, usually at the bank exchange rate, but sometimes worse. Even so, you'll need quetzals because shopkeepers, restaurateurs and hotel desk clerks may not want to deplete their supplies of ready quetzals and take on dollars, which they must then take to the bank. Many towns, even those of a decent size, suffer from change shortages, in which case paying for lunch becomes a time-consuming exercise in high finance. To avoid this fate, carry a stash of small bills regularly.

Traveler's Checks Traveler's checks are usually easy to exchange, though some banks make a policy of not changing them. Complicating matters, most banks in small or very far off towns don't change traveler's checks either. American Express checks are the most common and will present the fewest hassles at the bank. The rate for traveler's checks is sometimes slightly lower than the rate for cash.

ATMs Automated teller machines *(cajeros automáticos)* are up and running in the biggest cities and most popular tourist towns. There are also two ATMs (one for Visa, the other for MasterCard) at the international airport in Guatemala City. Esso gas stations and Super 24 stores often have ATMs as well. ATM instructions are usually in Spanish only, and the machines issue local currency debited against your home cashcard account or credit card. ATMs are a great resource when banks are closed.

Many banks give cash advances on Visa cards, fewer on MasterCard. Credomatic branches in Guatemala City and Quetzaltenango give cash advances on both.

Don't depend on ATMs to supply all your local-cash needs. Have traveler's checks, a bit of cash and/or a credit card for backup.

Credit & Debit Cards The majority of ATMs in Guatemala are on the Visa/Plus system and your life will be a whole lot easier if you have one of these cards. MasterCard is completely useless in most of Guatemala and some banks impose a 500 quetzal ($65) daily withdrawal limit on MasterCards; if you have the choice, travel with a Visa card. Guatemalan ATMs will only accept personal identification numbers (PINs) of four digits, so contact your bank before you leave home to get a compatible PIN.

Visa and MasterCard are accepted for pricier items such as airline tickets and car rentals and at the larger hotels and restaurants. American Express cards are often accepted at the fancier places and at some humbler ones too.

Black Market There's a healthy unofficial exchange market for dollars, but it pays about the same as the bank rate and so is of little benefit to travelers. The national hotbed of this activity is around the main post office in Guatemala City. At border crossing points without banking facilities, you may find yourself buying quetzals unofficially; at the airports, the bank exchange desks are open only during certain hours, but there are also ATMs.

Security

As pickpockets and robbers are not unheard of in Guatemala, it's important to carry your money, passport and other valuables in a pouch or belt underneath your clothing. For daily expenses, it's recommended you carry a small change purse or wallet in a front or side pocket with a zipper or button.

There are different schools of thought on where and how to conceal your big money and important documents; some people prefer a neck pouch worn under the clothing, even though the strap is never fully concealed by crew neck shirts. A belt worn around the waist can be utilitarian, but for some is uncomfortable and never fully functional because it requires digging around under clothing. Lamentable is the new trend toward Velcro closures on money pouches, for no matter how slick your moves, you'll never be able to disguise the sound of ripping open a Velcro-sealed pouch. Some shrewd travelers of the fairer sex suggest stashing large amounts of cash in a sanitary pad, slit open to accommodate the wad.

If your hotel has a safe or lock box for valuables, use it. Throw the pouch in the safe, get a receipt for all the things therein and travel about carefree. Otherwise, you can hide it somewhere clever in your hotel room proper, but be aware this can backfire. Suggestions for room concealment include: behind framed art or a mirror; in a plastic bag in the toilet tank; or thumb tacked behind a piece of wooden furniture. It's a personal decision whether to undertake day trips and short adventures with all your money and documentation on you – do what makes you most comfortable.

Costs

Prices in Guatemala are among the best in Central America. Beds in little pensions may cost US$3 per person in a double, and camping can be even cheaper. Markets sell fruits and snacks for pennies, cheap eateries called *comedores* offer one-plate meals for about US$2 and bus trips cost less than US$1 per hour. It's completely realistic to spend less than US$15 a day in Guatemala without too much hardship. If you want a bit more comfort, you can readily move up to rooms with private showers and meals in nicer restaurants and still pay only US$25 per day for a room and two – or even three – meals.

Unfortunately, there are few bargains here for solo travelers, as there isn't much price difference between a single and double room. If it's practical, hook up with some other folks to defray room costs. Prices for everything are higher around Tikal.

Tipping & Bargaining

A 10% tip is expected at restaurants. In small *comedores* tipping is optional, but follow the local practice of leaving some spare change. Tour guides are generally tipped, especially on longer trips. Figure on tipping guides around 10%, more if the tour was truly outstanding.

Bargaining is essential in some situations and not done in others. Bargaining is standard practice at handicrafts markets or any other time you're buying handicrafts; the first price you're told will often be double or triple what the seller really expects. Remember that bargaining is not a fight to the death. The object is to arrive at a price agreeable to both you and the seller, thereby creating a win-win situation. Be friendly about it, keep your sense of humor and deal with patience and mirth.

You can sometimes bargain for better rates at hotels and pensions, especially at times when business is slow. Often you can get a discount if you take the room for a few days or a week; ask about this when you check in.

Taxes

Guatemala's IVA is 10%, and there's also a 10% tax on hotel rooms to pay for the activities of the Guatemala Tourist Commission (INGUAT), so a total tax of 20% will be added to your hotel bill. All prices in this book include tax. The very cheapest places usually charge no tax.

A departure tax of US$20 is levied on travelers leaving Guatemala by air.

POST & COMMUNICATIONS
Post

The Guatemalan postal service was privatized in 1999. Though it is infinitely more reliable now, it's not infallible; mail sent from the farthest outposts may take a long time to arrive at its destination, while other letters are forever missing in action. Generally, however, letters take a week to travel to the US and Canada and about twice that to reach Europe. Almost every city and town (but not villages) has a post office where you can buy stamps and send mail. Privatization means more reliable service but also higher prices: A letter sent to North America costs around US$0.40 and to everywhere else in the world around US$0.50.

The Guatemalan mail system no longer holds post restante or general delivery mail. The easiest and most reliable way to receive mail is through a private address. American Express will hold mail for card members and people using their traveler's checks, and some travel agencies in Antigua will hold mail for clients. It is important to address mail clearly; the last lines should read Guatemala – Centro America and all correspondence should be marked 'por avión.'

Telephone

The Guatemalan phone system, now known as Telgua, was also recently privatized and has experienced a jump in reliability, technology and price. Coin operated phones used to be everywhere, but are going the way of the typewriter – and new-fangled public phones will only accept cards. Phone cards are available in denominations of 20, 30 and 50 quetzals and are sold (so they say) wherever the phones are found.

The following cities support these type of phones from which you can make local, long distance and international calls: Guatemala City (including the airport), Antigua, Panajachel, Esquipulas and Xela. A local call costs about US$0.12 a minute; long distance is twice that. Using the phones is very straightforward as you just dial direct. In cities and towns without these phones, you have to go to the Telgua office to make calls. In the very smallest towns where there is no Telgua office, there will likely be a *teléfono comunitario* (community telephone) that you can use to place calls. Look for these wherever public phones are few and far between. Guatemala's country code is 502. There are no area codes.

International Calls The best way to call internationally is through agencies offering phone services. These are common in cities and tourist towns and typically charge around US$0.75 a minute to the US and US$1.50 to Europe. Using a card in the public phones is slightly more expensive, but if you use an

agency, you can have your party call you back. Dear for them, but dirt cheap for you!

Unless it's an emergency, don't use the black phones placed strategically in tourist towns that say 'Press 2 to call the United States free!' This is a bait and switch scam; the operator quotes you a price (or no operator comes on at all), you put the call on your credit card and return home to find the calls cost between US$8 and $20 per minute.

Also, avoid going to Telgua offices to make international calls as they charge a US$4 connect fee to anywhere in the world and exorbitant per-minute rates thereafter. Telgua does allow you to make free collect calls, but only to Central America, Mexico, the US, Canada, Japan, Italy, Spain and Switzerland. Be forewarned that collect calls are also billed at usurious rates – around US$2.50 a minute to the US.

In an effort to enhance their competitiveness, Telgua now has a plan featuring reduced rates to the US and Europe. From a private phone, dial ☎ 147 before the international prefix '00' (zero zero), country code, area or city code, and local number to receive a rate of US$0.40 a minute to the US and US$0.95 to Europe. A similar program is offered by Telered to the US: Dial ☎ 133 at the beginning of the call. Sprint, MCI and AT&T have similar deals: Preface the numbers listed below with ☎ 99-99 to receive the reduced rate.

There are also numerous 'direct line' services, such as AT&T's *USADirect*: Dial ☎ 190 and you will be connected with an AT&T operator in the US who will complete your collect or credit card call. Below are the direct line numbers.

Intercity Long Distance Calls	☎ 121
Directory Assistance	☎ 124
International Calls (by operator)	☎ 171
MCI Call USA	☎ 189
USADirect (AT&T)	☎ 190
España Directo	☎ 191
Italia Directo	☎ 193
Sprint Express	☎ 195
Costa Rica Directo	☎ 196
Canada Direct	☎ 198

There's a wide range of international phone cards. Lonely Planet's eKno Communication Card is aimed specifically at independent travelers and provides budget international calls, a range of messaging services, free email and travel information. Check it out at www.ekno.lonelyplanet.com to join, or for access numbers from other countries and updates on new features. Or, in the US, call toll-free ☎ 800-707-0031.

Cellular Phones Travelers planning a lengthy stay in Guatemala may want to consider leasing a cellular phone. There are many companies offering the equipment and service, but it's important to read the fine print on any cell phone contract before signing on. One company to try is Cellular Rent (☎/fax 331-6251), 6a Avenida 6-45, Zona 10 in Guatemala City.

Fax

Again, you can send faxes with Telgua, but it will be much cheaper with an agency catering to the communication needs of tourists. Outgoing faxes may be charged by the minute or the page. Incoming are always charged by the page.

Email & Internet Access

Travelers will have little problem getting their email fix in Guatemala. All cities and most larger towns have some type of (surprisingly reliable) Internet capabilities. Access is often slow, however, and many places have Spanish keyboards only, which can be frustrating if you're unfamiliar with them. Prices for Internet access range from US$1.50 an hour in Antigua to an incredible US$7.75 an hour in Cobán.

Cybercafés are far and away the most popular places to get online, but some hotels have email services for their guests. Most cybercafés already have pulldown menus on their computers for major internet service providers such as AOL, Yahoo and Hotmail. Another option for collecting mail through cybercafés is to open a free eKno Web-based email account online at www.ekno.lonelyplanet.com. You can then access your mail from anywhere in the world from any net-connected machine running a standard Web browser.

You need to think long and hard before taking your own computer to Guatemala. While it's not impossible to hook up, it's tricky and unless you know what you're doing, it's fraught with potential problems. Only the most expensive hotel rooms have telephones in the rooms, so unless you're sporting a completely wireless system, you'll have to hunt down a phone jack to plug into.

There are several issues you need to consider if you want to travel with a laptop. First is the actual plug; Guatemala is on a 110 volts, two-pronged, flat plug system like that found in the US. Second is the telephone jack; Guatemalan jacks are square, with a little tab similar to the ones in the United States. Plug and telephone jack adapters and information about hooking up in foreign countries are available from Austin House (☎ 800-268-5157, contact @ travelessentials@austinhouse.com), 2880 Portland Dr, Oakville, Ontario L6H 5W8, Canada . Also, your modem may or may not work once you leave your home country – and you won't know until you try. The safest option is to buy a reputable 'global' modem before you leave home. For more information on traveling with a portable computer, see www.teleadapt.com or www.warrior.com.

Having said all that, if you *still* want to travel with a laptop, consider using a local ISP. Going the local route has its own problems, but few international ISPs have bps nodes (access numbers) in Guatemala. America Online, with a GlobalNet node in Guatemala City (modem 230-0931), is one exception.

Your best bet for a Guatemalan ISP is Conexion (☎ 832-3768, fax 832-0082, users@conexion.com, www.conexion.com) in Antigua. The multilingual owner, Ludwig (Luis) Deutsch, speaks English, German and Spanish and knows his computers. In Guatemala City, Telered (☎ 336-3599), Avenida La Reforma 6-64, No 302, Zona 9, has also been well recommended.

INTERNET RESOURCES

The World Wide Web is a rich resource for travelers. You can research your trip, hunt down bargain air fares, book hotels, check on weather conditions or chat with locals and other travelers about the best places to visit (or avoid!).

There's no better place to start your Web explorations than the Lonely Planet Web site (www.lonelyplanet.com). Here you'll find succinct summaries on traveling to most places on earth, postcards from other travelers and the Thorn Tree bulletin board, where you can ask questions before you go or dispense advice when you get back. You can also find travel news and updates to many of our most popular guidebooks, and the subWWWay section links you to the most useful travel resources elsewhere on the Web.

Among the comprehensive Web sites that will keep you excited with your research is the Guatemalan Web Page Directory, http://mars.cropsoil.uga.edu/trop-ag/guatem.htm, which stands out for its indepth cultural information and terrific page for kids. Also try the Guatemala Web at www.guatemalaweb.com. The University of Texas is known for its Latin American expertise, and its Guatemala resource page at

Online Services

The following are some Web sites that you might find helpful.

Useful Organizations

AmeriSpan Guatemala www.amerispan.com
American Association of Retired Persons www.aarp.org
Arenal Lesbigay Homepage www.indiana.edu/~arenal/ingles.html
Asociacion De Andinismo http://get.to/andinismo
Foreign and Commonwealth Office Travel Advice www.fco.gov.uk/travel/
INGUAT www.travel-guatemala.org.gt
La Ruta Maya Online www.larutamayaonline.com
Mobility International www.miusa.org
Mundo Maya Organization www.wotw.com/mundomaya
National Information Communication Awareness Network www.nican.com.au
Royal Association for Disability & Rehabilitation www.radar.org.
Society for the Advancement of Travelers with Handicaps www.sath.org/index.html
South American Explorers www.samexplo.org
United Nations Mission for the Verification of Human Rights – MINUGUA www.un.org/Depts/minugua/
US Department of Health, Centers for Disease Control & Prevention www.cdc.gov/travel/travel.html
US Department of State, Bureau of Consular Affairs http://travel.state.gov

Transportation

Air Courier Association www.aircourier.org
Air Courier International www.aircourierintl.com
Council Travel www.ciee.org
eXito Latin America Travel www.wonderlink.com
Explore Worldwide Ltd www.explore.co.uk
Flight Centre www.flightcentre.com.au
Grupo Taca www.grupotaca.com

http://lanic.utexas.edu/la/ca/guatemala will show you why.

Check out La Ruta Maya Online, www.larutamayaonline.com, a great source for information on all things Mayan in Guatemala and neighboring countries. This is a good place to start if you're interested in exploring and participating in Mayan culture during your travels.

Several cities and regions support their own Web sites, which are a rich vein for detailed information. One of the best is the Quetzaltenango Pages, www.xelapages.com, which has information on everything from job openings to where to find an English speaking lawyer while in Xela. Similar pages are available for Antigua at www.theantiguajournal.com; Lake Atitlán at www.atitlan.com; and the Río Dulce area at www.mayaparadise.com.

If you're visiting Guatemala to study Spanish, check out the Learn Spanish Web site, www.studyspanish.com, for a list of schools. Volunteer opportunities can be found on the WWWanderer CA Volunteer guide, www.tmn.com/wwwanderer/Volguide /projects.html. Travelers interested in Mayan ceremonial life and the sacred calendar are encouraged to visit www.geocities .com/RainForest/Jungle/9089/.

Online Services

International Association of Air Travel Couriers www.courier.org
Journey Latin America www.journeylatinamerica.co.uk
Latin American Travel Consultants www.amerispan.com/lata/
Nouvelles Frontières www.nouvelles-frontieres.com
OTU Voyages www.otu.fr
SSR Voyages www.ssr.ch
STA Travel www.statravel.com
Tica Bus www.ticabus.com
Travel CUTS www.travelcuts.com
Usit Campus www.usitcampus.com

General
Access-Able Travel Source www.access-able.com
Accessible Journeys www.disabilitytravel.com
Antigua Pages www.theantiguajournal.com
Arte Maya www.artemaya.com
Central American Report www.worldcom.nl/inforpress
Fiestas of Guatemala www.mayaparadise.com/fiestas/fiestas.htm
Guatemala Travel www.guatemala.travel.com.gt
Guatemala Web www.guatemalaweb.com
Guatemala Weekly www.pronet.net.gt/gweekly/
Lake Atitlán Pages www.atitlan.com
Learn Spanish www.studyspanish.com
Momostenango Pages www.geocities.com/RainForest/Jungle/9089
Quetzaltenango Pages www.xelapages.com
Revue www.revue.conexion.com
Río Dulce Pages www.mayaparadise.com
The Siglo News www.sigloxxi.com
University of Texas Guatemala Resource Page http://lanic.utexas.edu/la/ca/guatemala
WWWanderer CA Volunteer guide www.tmn.com/wwwanderer/Volguide/projects.html

BOOKS

The catalog of books on Guatemala is long and varied. Many titles deal with the tragedies of the 36-year civil war; any of these selections, along with the Nobel prize-winning testimony by Rigoberta Menchú, are definitely worth your while to read. Plant and animal lovers should be sated with the myriad Guatemalan titles out there and history buffs won't be disappointed either.

Most books are published in different editions by different publishers in different countries. As a result, a book might be a hardcover rarity in one country but readily available in paperback in another.

Lonely Planet

Guatemala, Belize & Yucatán: La Ruta Maya is the guide to get for a trip through the Mayan world. *Central America on a shoestring* is the superlative choice if you're traveling through the rest of the region on a tight budget. Anyone linguistically challenged should check out the pocket-sized *Latin American Spanish Phrasebook*, and if you've never before traveled to this part of the world and need to know the ins and

Rigoberta Menchú Tum

Rigoberta Menchú was born in 1959 in Guatemala's southern highlands and lived the life of a typical young Mayan woman until the early 1980s, when the country's internal turmoil affected her tragically. By 1981 she had lost her father, mother and brother, who were killed in the course of the rampages carried out by the Guatemalan military in the name of 'pacification' of the countryside and the repression of guerrilla movements.

Menchú fled to exile in Mexico, where she wrote her story, *I, Rigoberta Menchú*, which was translated and published throughout the world. While in Mexico and after returning to Guatemala, she worked tirelessly in defense of the rights of indigenous peoples throughout Latin America.

In 1992, Rigoberta Menchú was awarded the Nobel Prize for Peace, which provided her and her cause with international stature and support.

Guatemalans were proud that one of their own had been recognized by the Nobel committee. In the circles of power, however, Menchú's renown was unwelcome, as she was seen as a troublemaker. But among most of the indigenous people of Guatemala. she is the hero who brought worldwide recognition to their plight.

In December 1999, Menchú was thrust into the international spotlight anew when she formally accused several former military leaders and dictators – including General Oscar Humberto Mejía Victores (1983-86) and Efraín Ríos Montt (1982-83), now a Guatemalan congressman – of genocide. Menchú brought the case before a Spanish court, where she pressed for extradition proceedings. This was akin to the strategy pursued by the accusers of former Chilean dictator Augusto Pinochet. Not so fast, said the the Guatemalan henchmen, who filed their own case in Guatemala leveling treason charges against Menchú. With that move, the legal battle had officially begun. As of July 2000, the suit was still unfolding, and Menchú was prohibited from entering Guatemala upon threat of immediate arrest for treason. Menchú has considered applying for temporary exile due to the antagonism that defines her relationship with the Guatemalan ruling elite and prohibits safe repatriation.

outs, see *Read this First: Central and South America.* A good on-the-road read is *Green Dreams: Travels in Central America* by Stephen Benz.

In *Green Dreams: Travels in Central America* (Lonely Planet Journeys), Stephen Benz explores the myths and realities of ecotourism, focusing on the Ruta Maya tourist route and its effect on the Maya of Guatemala.

Guidebooks

There are many terrific thematic books dealing with Guatemala, and you may want a more in-depth guide exploring your particular area of interest. Here is just a partial list of what is out there.

The very readable *Tikal: A Handbook of the Ancient Maya Ruins* by William R Coe (not to be confused with Michael Coe, cited under Mayan Life & Culture), is available at Tikal but may be cheaper if you buy it at home before you leave. If you expect to spend several days exploring Tikal, you'll want this excellent guide and the superlative map that comes with it. Another option is *Tikal National Park: A Visitors Guide* by Thor Janson, sold throughout Guatemala. Both these books are available in several different foreign language editions.

Books on other archaeological sites include *Images from the Underworld: Naj Tunich and the Mayan Tradition of Cave Painting* by Andrea J Stone and *Río Azul: An Ancient Mayan City* by eminent Mayan scholar Richard E W Adams.

Backpacking in Central America by Tim Burford (Bradt Publications, 1996) is a fine book with maps and descriptions for hikes both short and long in all the Central American countries except Belize.

Orchids of Guatemala and Belize by Oakes Ames and Stewart Donovan (Dover Publications, 1985) remains one of the best handbooks on orchids available internationally. *Birds of Guatemala* by Hugh C Land (Livingston, 1970) is a field guide to birdwatching in Guatemala. *The Birds of Tikal: An Annotated Checklist for Tikal National Park and Petén, Guatemala* by Randell A Beavers is a must-have for birders.

Travel

The often quoted and highly revered *Incidents of Travel in Central America, Chiapas and Yucatan,* in two volumes (1969 and later reprints of the original 1841 edition) by John L Stephens and illustrated by Frederick Catherwood explores parts of Guatemala. More than just travelogues, their discoveries and painstaking explorations produced the first extensive and serious look at many Mayan archaeological sites. Their detailed descriptions and drawings are the only evidence for some features of sites that have been lost, destroyed or stolen. This tome is a laborious, but interesting, read.

Contemporary writers have also found Guatemala inspiring. *Sweet Waist of America* by Anthony Daniels (Arrow/ Hutchinson, 1990) is a fine book telling about the author's travels, mostly in Guatemala but also in Honduras, El Salvador and Nicaragua. *Guatemalan Journey* by Stephen Benz casts an honest and funny traveler's eye on modern Guatemala. This book makes for good on the road reading.

Around the Edge, otherwise entitled *Tekkin a Waalk* (Viking Penguin, 1991; Flamingo, 1993), is by Peter Ford, who traveled by foot and boat along the Caribbean coast from Belize to Panama.

Time Among the Maya: Travels in Belize, Guatemala, and Mexico by Ronald Wright is a thoughtful account of numerous journeys made in recent years among the descendants of the ancient Maya and will certainly help you to 'feel' Mayan culture as you travel the region.

Bird of Life, Bird of Death by Jonathan Evan Maslow, subtitled 'A naturalist's journey through a land of political turmoil,' tells of the author's travels in Guatemala, where he went to see the resplendent quetzal (the 'bird of life'). What he found was the quetzal becoming increasingly endangered, while the *zopilote* (vulture), the 'bird of death,' was flourishing.

Mayan Life & Culture

This genre is so flooded with titles, you're encouraged to choose those that interest you. Among the recognized best works are *Maya: The Riddle and Rediscovery of a Lost Civilization* by Charles Gallenkamp; the more scholarly *The Maya* by the eminent Mayanist Michael D Coe; and *A Forest of Kings: The Untold Story of the Ancient Maya* by Linda Schele and David Freidel (Morrow, 1990). The out-of-print *The Two Crosses of Todos Santos: Survivals of Mayan Religious Ritual* by Maud Oakes is a fascinating read on that area of Guatemala.

If you have access to back issues of *National Geographic*, see 'La Ruta Maya,' Volume 176, No 4 (October 1989), pp 424-505, for a short introduction to Guatemala and La Ruta Maya. Reprints are widely sold in Guatemala and are theoretically free at INGUAT offices. Other *National Geographic* articles worth reading are 'Jade, Stone of Heaven' and 'Exploring a Vast Maya City, El Mirador,' Volume 172, No 3 (September 1987), pp 282-339. Try to get hold of this volume if you have any interest in going to El Mirador, as articles on this site are few and far between and this piece is rich.

History

Guatemala in the Spanish Colonial Period by Oakah L Jones Jr is a comprehensive assessment of 300 years of Spanish dominance. Where this book leaves off, Paul . Dosal's *Doing Business with the Dictators: A Political History of United Fruit in Guatemala, 1899-1944* takes over. *Bitter Fruit: The Story of the American Coup in Guatemala* by Stephen Schlesinger et al is a readable policy analysis of US dirty business and meddling.

Modern Guatemalan histories oftentimes refer to the civil war years. *I, Rigoberta Menchú: An Indian Woman in Guatemala*, by 1992 Nobel Peace Prize laureate Rigoberta Menchú, is a case in point. This book tells the story of Menchú's life among the highland Maya and the birth of her social consciousness during this period. Almost single-handedly, Menchú brought the plight of Guatemala's indigenous population to the attention of the world. In

Guatemala, where the position of the Maya in society is a continuing, contentious issue, both she and the book, which clearly conveys the point of view of a highland Quiché Maya, are controversial. Highly recommended. Her follow up attempt *Crossing Borders* was published in 1998.

David Stoll shocked the world with the 1999 publication of *Rigoberta Menchú and the Story of All Poor Guatemalans*, in which he contests the autobiographical veracity of Menchú's first book. Stoll's thesis is still hotly debated – you may want to read it to see what's what for yourself.

Jennifer Harbury's *Searching for Everardo: A Story of Love, War and the CIA in Guatemala* tells how she attracted the attention of the world when she conducted three hunger strikes, two in front of Guatemala's National Palace and one in front of the White House in Washington, DC, asking for information on her husband, a URNG commander, who disappeared mysteriously in 1992. Her earlier book, *Bridge of Courage: Life Stories of the Guatemalan Compañeros and Compañeras* (Common Courage Press) focuses on a number of people who fought in the Guatemalan guerrilla movement.

A fascinating account of the war's aftermath is presented in *Return of Guatemala's Refugees: Reweaving the Torn* by Taylor Clark. In this same vein is the unequivocal condemnation of human rights abuses *Guatemala: Never Again!* by the Archdiocese of Guatemala. This will prove to difficult to secure outside of Guatemala, but look for it in your travels or visit a library on the road to read this disturbing chronicle of human atrocities.

Stunning visuals of the period just before and after the Peace Accords are provided by Thomas Hoepker in his book of photographs *Return of the Maya: Guatemala – A Tale of Survival*. Another worthwhile photography book is *A Mayan Struggle: Portrait of a Guatemalan People in Danger* by Vince Heptig, with an introduction by Rigoberta Menchú. Linda Green tackles the brutality of the war head-on with *Fear As a Way of Life: Mayan Widows in Rural Guatemala*.

Colorful, delicious, delightful markets

TONY WHEELER

TONY WHEELER

RICHARD I'ANSON

TONY WHEELER

TONY WHEELER

TONY WHEELER

TONY WHEELER

Architecture – old and new – is colorful and varied.

Unfinished Conquest: The Guatemalan Tragedy by Victor Perera explores the current situation of the Maya in their homeland and the long history preceding it. *Guatemala: A Guide to the People, Politics and Culture* by Trish O'Kane is a well-written book on modern Guatemala. Tom Barry's *Guatemala: A Country Guide* provides a useful overall look at the country, but you may have to hunt for this one, as it's out of print. *Time and the Highland Maya* by Barbara Tedlock is an anthropological book about Momostenango and the Quiché Maya who live there.

General

To get a handle on shamanism around Lago de Atitlán, check out *Scandals in the House of Birds: Shamans and Priests on Lake Atitlán* by Nathaniel Tarn or one of several books by Martin Prechtel. The most recent is *Long Life, Honey in the Heart: A Story of Initiation and Eloquence from the Shores of a Mayan Lake*. A good companion read to either of these would be *Mayan Folktales: Folklore from Lake Atitlán, Guatemala*, translated by James D Sexton.

The basic text of Mayan religion is the *Popol Vuh,* which recounts the Mayan creation myths. A version easily available in Guatemala is *Popol Vuh: Ancient Stories of the Quiché Indians of Guatemala* by Albertina Saravia E.

The Blood of Kings: Dynasty & Ritual in Maya Art by Linda Schele and Mary Ellen Miller is a heavily illustrated guide to the art and culture of the Mayan period with particular emphasis on sacrifices, bloodletting, torture of captives, the ball game and other macabre aspects of Mayan culture. The illustrated analyses of Mayan art are fascinating, and Schele, who passed away in 1998, was one of the world's eminent Mayanists. Anything written by her will prove illuminating.

The Maya Textile Tradition, edited by Margot Blum Schevill with pictures by Jeffrey Jay Foxx, is a superbly written and beautifully photographed tome on Maya weaving. Anyone interested in this living art will be well rewarded with this book.

Guatemala boasts its own stable of world renowned authors and poets, including Miguel Ángel Asturias, Luis Cardoza y Aragón and Augusto Monterroso (for more information, see the Arts section in the Facts About Guatemala chapter).

FILMS

Though there are few Guatemala-specific films, what exists is poignant and of high quality. *El Silencio de Neto* is a coming of age story set in 1954 that traces the development of a young boy as the coup of Jacobo Arbenz Guzmán unfolds. *La Hija del Puma* is a powerful drama about the displacement, torture and genocide suffered by the Guatemalan Maya during the civil war. This film is available in Spanish with English, Swedish or Danish subtitles.

Several documentaries have been made about Guatemala and hopefully more are on the way. In the meantime, check out *Dirty Secrets: Jennifer Everardo & the CIA in Guatemala,* which is the abbreviated story of Jennifer Harbury and her disappeared husband during the civil war. *The Devil's Dream* is a very moving account of the plight of the highland Maya in the late 1980s. There is also a great documentary called *Todos Santos,* which tells the story of that mountain town, though it is very difficult to find outside of Guatemala; keep your eyes peeled. *Tikal* is a film with some accomplished aerial cinematography and is sold in Flores for US$15.

NEWSPAPERS & MAGAZINES

Guatemala has many daily newspapers, ranging from serious to farcical, including *La Prensa Libre, El Gráfico, La República, Siglo Veintiuno, El Periódico* and *Al Día. La Prensa Libre* is the most widely respected and read. There's also a weekly paper, *El Regional,* written in both Spanish and Maya languages; it's read by many Maya people. *La Cuerda,* a well-written newspaper dedicated to Guatemalan women's issues and perspectives, is a monthly insert in El Periódico and El Regional. Look for it.

Some major US newspapers such as *USA Today,* the *Miami Herald* and the *Los*

Angeles Times are sold in a few luxury-hotel newsstands and big-city and airport bookstores in the region. *Newsweek* and *Time* magazines are also sometimes available, along with *The New York Times* and the *Wall Street Journal*. When desperate, you can hit up Peace Corp volunteers for their old complimentary copies of mainstream news magazines.

Newspapers in English include the *Guatemala Weekly* and *The Siglo News*, both free weekly papers published in Guatemala City and distributed in major hotels and tourist spots around the country. The *Revue* is Guatemala's English-language magazine, published monthly. Subscriptions are available by mail and over the Internet. Contact:

Guatemala Weekly (☎ 337-1061, fax 337-1076, ✉ gweekly@pronet.net.gt), 14 Calle 3-27, Zona 10, Local 8, Guatemala City; in the US, PO Box 591999-F-69, Miami, FL 33159-1999

Revue (☎/fax 832-4619, ✉ revue@mail.com, www.revue.conexion.com), 4a Calle Oriente No 23, Antigua, Guatemala

The Siglo News (☎ 332-8101/2/3, fax 332-8119, ✉ sales@sigloxxi.com, www.sigloxxi.com/news), 11 Calle 0-65, Zona 10, Edificio Vizcaya, 4th Floor, Guatemala City; in the US (☎ 888-287-4921), NotiNET SA, Worldbox Gu-0147, PO Box 379012, Miami, FL 33137-9012

Several other publications focus on making news about Guatemala available internationally.

CERIGUA is an independent Guatemalan news agency providing alternative news and analysis about Guatemala in English and Spanish. In English, it produces the *Weekly Briefs,* comprehensive news and analysis covering human rights, labor, politics, popular organizing, the economy, the environment and more. For subscriptions to the *Weekly Briefs* contact ANI, PO Box 578191, Chicago, IL 60657-8191. For services in English and Spanish, in Guatemala City contact ☎/fax 232-5519, ✉ cerigua@guate.net, 9a Calle A 3-49, Zona 1.

Central America Report is the English-language publication of Inforpress Cen-

troamericana, providing a weekly news analysis of the Central America region, with the greatest emphasis on Guatemala. In Guatemala City, you can find them at 7a Avenida 2-05, Zona 1 (☎ 221-0301, ☎/fax 232-9034, ✉ inforpre@guate.net, www.worldcom.nl/inforpress). Foreign correspondence or checks should be sent to Inforpress Centroamericana, Section 23, PO Box 52-7270, Miami, FL 33152-7270.

The Guatemala News and Information Bureau (GNIB) puts out *Report On Guatemala,* the quarterly publication of the Network in Solidarity with the People of Guatemala (NISGUA). Contact GNIB (☎/fax 415-826-3593, ✉ gnib@igc.org), 3181 Mission St, Box 12, San Francisco, CA 94110.

RADIO & TV

Guatemala has 11 radio stations and five TV stations. The radio waves are flooded with Latin American pop and evangelical crusaders. Because you'll probably get enough of that on the bus, consider bringing a short-wave radio. Even a low-end unit will grab signals for the well-recommended Radio Canada International (www.rcinet.ca/), the BBC World Service (www.bbc.co.uk/worldservice/tuning/) or Voice of America (www.voa.gov/allsked.html). Other broadcasts in every language from Arabic to Russian can also be heard. Short-waves are a great way to stay in touch and entertained.

TV stations in Guatemala leave something to be desired, and almost everyone with a television also has cable, as this is the only way to ensure reception. Whenever a hotel boasts televisions in the rooms, assume it includes cable. A number of stations from the US, including CNN news, come in by cable. Movies and sports in both English and Spanish are shown on cable stations as well.

PHOTOGRAPHY

In theory, you are allowed to bring no more than one camera and 12 rolls of film into Guatemala, though this is rarely, if ever, enforced. Ubiquitous film stores and pharmacies sell film. Prices for film are slightly lower than in the US and Europe, though always check the expiration date.

Print film, both B&W and color, is easily found, though you may not find the brand you like without a bit of a hunt. Processing is not particularly expensive and can be done in a day or two, even quicker in the large cities. Quality varies widely, however.

Slide (transparency) film may be more difficult to find, but not impossible. Special Fuji, Kodak and Agfa stores will likely have anything you need from new lithium batteries to camera parts to film.

Photographing People

Photography is a sensitive subject in Guatemala. You should always ask permission before taking portraits, especially of Mayan women and children. Don't be surprised if your request is denied. Indigenous children make a habit of requesting payment in return for posing. This is usually about the equivalent of US$0.15. In certain places, like the church of Santo Tomás in Chichicastenango, photography is forbidden. Mayan ceremonies (should you be so lucky to witness one) are off limits for photography unless you are given explicit permission to take pictures. If local people make any sign of being offended, you should put your camera away and apologize immediately, both out of decency and for your own safety. Never take photos of army installations, men with guns or other sensitive military subjects. For more on photo etiquette, see the Dos & Don'ts section in the Facts about Guatemala chapter.

TIME

North American Central Standard Time (GMT/UTC minus six hours) is the basis of time in Guatemala. Daylight saving (or 'summer') time is not used. The 24-hour clock (military time) is often used in Guatemala, so 1 pm is written as 13. Here's the time in some other cities when it's noon in Guatemala:

city	summer	winter
Paris, Rome	8 pm	7 pm
London	7 pm	6 pm
GMT/UTC	6 pm	6 pm
New York, Toronto	2 pm	1 pm
Chicago	1 pm	noon
San Francisco, LA	11 am	10 am
Perth, Hong Kong	3 am*	2 am*
Sydney, Melbourne	5 am*	4 am*
Auckland	6 am*	7 am*

*next day

ELECTRICITY

Electrical current, flat-pronged plugs and sockets (points) are the same as in the US and Canada: 115 to 125 V, 60 Hz.

WEIGHTS & MEASURES

Guatemala uses the metric system. For conversion information, see the inside back cover of this book. Because of the great commercial influence from the US, you may find that ounces (onzas), pounds (libras), feet (pies), miles (millas) and US gallons (galones) are used informally – at village markets, for instance. Gas is sold in gallons. Officially, however, everything is metric.

LAUNDRY

Laundries are everywhere in Guatemala, offering wash, dry and fold service for around US$2 per load. Often you can drop it off and pick it up a few hours later. To ensure that everything you drop off gets returned, make a list of the clothes and check it when you pick up your laundry. In some regions such as the Caribbean coast, clothes dryers (secadoras) are rare, so if you drop off your laundry on a cloudy day, you may be returned a soggy, smelly mass.

Cheaper lodgings often have a lavadero or pila where you can wash your clothes by hand. These sinks are usually divided into three sections: two shallow basins with drains where you scrub the clothes and a deep middle section filled with water. A small plastic scoop or bowl will be floating in the water-filled basin. Use the scoop to pour water into the shallow basins, but never allow soap to get into the middle trough as this may serve as a potable water source and for multiple tasks, not just washing clothes. Clothes are hung on a line to dry, so wait for a sunny day to do laundry.

TOILETS

The most important thing to know about Guatemalan toilets is that you cannot throw anything into them, including toilet paper. For this reason, bathrooms are equipped with some sort of receptacle (usually a small wastebasket) into which you throw soiled paper. This system functions well most of the time, although you can imagine the humorous and gross scatological experiences that have beset many a traveler here. Toilet paper is rarely provided, so always carry your own stash.

In a hot climate, where your body loses lots of moisture through perspiration, you have less frequent need of toilets. This is good in one sense, as public toilets are few and far between. Use the ones in cafés, restaurants, your hotel and at archaeological sites. Bus stations usually have *sanitarios*, but use them at your own risk. You're better off going into the office of a bus company and using one there. This privilege costs US$0.15.

Long bus trips can be particularly uncomfortable as few buses have toilets. While men alight and relieve themselves whenever and wherever the feeling strikes, this is a problem for the fairer sex. If you're headed for a long ride, use the toilet before getting on the bus and go easy on the fluids. If you really need a bathroom en route, you'll rarely be refused at a private home if you ask politely.

HEALTH

Travel health depends on your predeparture preparations, your daily health care while traveling and how you handle any medical problem that does develop. Don't let the following long section on potential health problems freak you out; the majority of travelers in Guatemala, under all types of circumstances and taking all sorts of risks, do not get sick. Or at least they don't get really sick – maybe one bout of diarrhea or projectile vomiting per odyssey. You'll probably meet other travelers who will frighten and delight you with personal tales of malaria or dengue fever, so while illness does happen, it probably won't befall you.

Immunizations

Specific immunizations are not required for travel anywhere in Guatemala. Still, you may want to peruse the recommended immunizations described below. Plan ahead for getting your vaccinations: Some of them require more than one injection, and some vaccinations should not be given together. Note that some immunizations should not be given during pregnancy or to people with allergies – discuss these with your doctor.

It is recommended that you seek medical advice at least six weeks before travel. Be aware that children and pregnant women are often at greater than normal risk for contracting diseases.

Discuss your requirements with a doctor, but vaccinations worth considering for a Guatemalan trip include the following (for niggling details about the diseases themselves, see the individual disease entries later in this section).

Diphtheria & Tetanus Vaccinations for these two diseases are usually combined (called a dip-tet) and are recommended for everyone. After an initial course of three injections (usually given in childhood), boosters are necessary every 10 years.

Polio Everyone should keep up to date with this vaccination, which is normally given in childhood. A booster every 10 years maintains immunity.

Hepatitis A This vaccine (eg, Avaxim, Havrix 1440 or VAQTA) provides long-term immunity (possibly more than 10 years) after an initial injection and a booster at six to 12 months.

Alternatively, an injection of gamma globulin can provide short-term protection against hepatitis A – two to six months –

depending on the dose given. It is not a vaccine, it is a ready-made antibody collected from blood donations. It is reasonably effective and, unlike the vaccine, it is protective immediately. However, because it is a blood product, there are currently concerns about its long-term safety.

Hepatitis A vaccine is also available as Twinrix, a form that is combined with hepatitis B vaccine. Three injections over a six-month period are required, the first two providing substantial protection against Hepatitis A.

Hepatitis B Travelers who should consider vaccination against hepatitis B include those embarking on a long trip, as well as those anticipating sexual contact, needle sharing or other exposure to possibly contaminated blood. Health workers or doctors especially should investigate this immunization. Vaccination involves three injections, with a booster at 12 months. More rapid courses are available if necessary.

Typhoid Vaccination against typhoid is not required for Guatemala, but is recommended if you are traveling for more than a couple of weeks. It is now available as either an injection or capsules that are taken orally.

Yellow Fever You only need a yellow fever certificate to enter the country if, within the last six months, you have been to a country where yellow fever is present. You may have to go to a special yellow fever vaccination center for this injection.

Rabies Vaccination for rabies should be considered by those who will spend a month or longer in Guatemala, especially if they will be cycling, handling animals, caving or traveling to remote areas, and for children (who may not report a bite). Pretravel rabies vaccination involves three injections over 21 to 28 days. If someone who has been vaccinated is bitten or scratched by an infected animal, they will require two booster injections of vaccine; those not vaccinated require more (ouch!).

Medical Kit Check List

Following is a list of items you should consider including in your medical kit – consult your pharmacist for brands available in your country.

- ❏ **Aspirin or paracetamol** (acetaminophen in the USA) – for pain or fever
- ❏ **Antihistamine** – for allergies, eg, hay fever; to ease the itch from insect bites or stings; and to prevent motion sickness
- ❏ **Cold and flu tablets, throat lozenges and nasal decongestant**
- ❏ **Multivitamins** – consider for long trips, when dietary vitamin intake may be inadequate
- ❏ **Antibiotics** – consider including these if you're traveling well off the beaten track; see your doctor, as they must be prescribed, and carry the prescription with you
- ❏ **Loperamide or diphenoxylate** –'blockers' for diarrhea
- ❏ **Prochlorperazine or metaclopramide** – for nausea and vomiting
- ❏ **Rehydration mixture** – to prevent dehydration, which may occur, for example, during bouts of diarrhea; particularly important when traveling with children
- ❏ **Insect repellent, sunscreen, lip balm and eye drops**
- ❏ **Calamine lotion, sting relief spray or aloe vera** – to ease irritation from sunburn and insect bites or stings
- ❏ **Antifungal cream or powder** – for fungal skin infections and thrush
- ❏ **Antiseptic (such as povidone-iodine)** – for cuts and grazes
- ❏ **Bandages, Band-Aids (plasters) and other wound dressings**
- ❏ **Water purification tablets or iodine**
- ❏ **Scissors, tweezers and a thermometer** – note that mercury thermometers are prohibited by airlines
- ❏ **Sterile kit** – in case you need injections in a country with medical hygiene problems; discuss with your doctor

Malaria Medication Antimalaerial drugs do not prevent you from becoming infected, but they do kill the malaria parasites during a stage in their development and significantly reduce your risk of becoming very ill or dying. Expert advice on medication should be sought, as there are many factors to consider, including the area to be visited, the risk of exposure to malaria-carrying mosquitoes, the side effects of medication, your medical history and whether you are pregnant. Travelers to isolated areas may want to carry a treatment dose of medication to use if symptoms occur.

Health Insurance
Make sure that you have adequate health insurance. See Travel Insurance under the Visas & Documents section earlier in this chapter for details.

Travel Health Guides
Lonely Planet's *Healthy Travel Central & South America* is conveniently pocket-sized and packed with useful information, including pretrip planning, emergency first aid, immunization and disease information as well as what to do if you get sick on the road. *Travel with Children*, from Lonely Planet, includes advice on travel health for younger adventurers. Travelers committed to the Guatemalan long haul should invest in a copy of *Where There is No Doctor: A Village Health Care Handbook* by David Werner et al. Not for the casual visitor, this book gives advice on treating medical problems most likely to afflict people living under local conditions for extended periods of time.

There are also a number of excellent travel health sites on the Internet. From the Lonely Planet home page, www.lonelyplanet .com/weblinks/w1heal.htm, there are links to the World Health Organization (WHO) and the US Centers for Disease Control & Prevention, among others.

Other Preparations
Ideally, you should make sure you're healthy before you set off. If you're going for more than a couple of weeks, make sure your teeth are OK; Guatemala is not a fun place to visit the dentist. An effective, albeit temporary, elixir for infected teeth or gums is one teaspoon salt dissolved in eight ounces of water; rinse with this several times daily. If you wear glasses, take a spare pair and your prescription.

If you require a particular medication, take an adequate supply, as it may not be available locally. Take part of the packaging showing the generic name rather than the brand name: this will make getting replacements easier. To avoid any problems, it's a good idea to have a legible prescription or letter from your doctor to show that you legally use the medication.

If you take herbal or homeopathic supplements such as echinacea, acidophilus, St John's wort, melatonin (good for jet lag) or grapefruit seed extract (good for mild intestinal problems), bring them with you. These are available in the biggest Guatemalan towns, but they're not cheap.

Basic Rules
Food Food can be contaminated by bacteria, viruses and/or parasites when it is harvested, shipped, handled, washed (if the water is contaminated) or prepared. Vegetables and fruit should be washed with purified water or (better still) peeled when possible. It's generally a good idea to steer clear of lettuce, which is difficult to purify effectively. Beware of ice cream sold on the street or anywhere it might have been melted and refrozen. Shellfish such as mussels, oysters and clams should be avoided, as should undercooked meat. Ceviche, a savory dish of raw, marinated fish, is also guilty of causing many a gastrointestinal illness.

If a place looks clean and well run and the vendor also looks clean and healthy, the food is probably safe. This goes for restaurants and food stalls in the market. In general, places that are packed with travelers or locals are fine. The food in busy restaurants is cooked and eaten quickly, with little standing around, and it is probably not reheated.

Nutrition

If your diet is poor or limited in variety, if you're traveling hard and fast and therefore missing meals or if you simply lose your appetite, you can soon start to lose weight and place your health at risk.

Make sure your diet is well balanced. Cooked eggs, tofu, beans, lentils (dhal in India) and nuts are all safe ways to get protein. Fruit you can peel (bananas, oranges or mandarins, for example) is usually safe and a good source of vitamins. Melons can harbor bacteria in their flesh and are best avoided. Try to eat plenty of grains (including rice) and bread. Remember that although food is generally safer if it is cooked well, overcooked food loses much of its nutritional value. If your diet isn't well balanced or if your food intake is insufficient, it's a good idea to take vitamin and iron pills.

In hot climates make sure you drink enough – don't rely on feeling thirsty to indicate when you should drink. Not needing to urinate or voiding small amounts of very dark yellow urine is a danger sign. Always carry a water bottle with you on long trips. Excessive sweating can lead to loss of salt and therefore muscle cramping. Salt tablets are not a good idea as a preventative, but in places where salt is not used much, adding salt to food can help.

Water Don't trust any water except that which has been boiled for 20 minutes, treated with purifiers or comes in an unopened bottle labeled *agua purificada*. Make sure bottles of water have a serrated seal before you buy them, as some miscreants refill the bottles with tap water and sell them to unsuspecting foreigners. Hotels sometimes have large jugs of purified water from which you can fill your canteen – take advantage of them when you can! Guatemala City boasts that its purified tap water is safe to drink. This is a dubious assertion – bottled water is the way to go, even in the capital.

Use only pure water for drinking, washing food and making ice. Tea, coffee and other hot beverages should be made with boiled water. Most establishments that you'll find in tried-and-true tourist spots such as Antigua only make juices and drinks with purified water. Still, it doesn't hurt to ask.

On the tooth brushing issue, some travelers aver that using that little bit of tap water each day slowly accustoms their system to the bacteria in foreign water. Over time, the theory goes, they build an immunity and are less likely to get sick from food and other slightly contaminated sources. If you're on a lengthy trip and want to test this hypothesis, go for it. If you've only a short stint in Guatemala, however, it's not worth the risk

of being laid up; brush with bottled water and enjoy.

The simplest way to purify water is to boil it thoroughly. Twenty minutes of vigorous boiling should be satisfactory to kill germs and parasites; however, water boils at a lower temperature at high altitude, so germs are less likely to be killed. Boil your water for at least 10 minutes longer in these environments.

Consider purchasing a water filter for a long trip. There are two main types of filter. Total filters remove all parasites, bacteria and viruses and make water safe to drink. They are often expensive, but they can be more cost effective (and environmentally friendly) than buying bottled water. Simple filters (which can even be a nylon mesh bag) remove dirt and larger foreign bodies from the water so that chemical solutions work much more effectively; if water is dirty, chemical solutions may not work at all. When you're buying a filter, it's very important to read the specifications, so that you know exactly what it removes from the water and what it leaves behind.

Simple filtering does not remove all dangerous organisms, so if you cannot boil water, you should treat it chemically. Chlorine tablets (such as Potable-Agua in the US) kill many pathogens but not some nasty parasites such as giardia and amoebic cysts. These treatments are available in

Guatemala: Ask for *gotas* (drops) or *pastillas* (tablets) *para purificar agua*, sold in pharmacies and supermarkets.

Iodine is more effective than chlorine in purifying water and is available in tablet form. Follow the directions carefully, and remember that too much iodine can be harmful. Tincture of iodine 2% (called *yodo*) is sold in pharmacies. To treat a liter of water, add about seven drops; strain cloudy water through a clean cloth first, then add 14 drops of iodine per liter.

Medical Problems & Treatment

Self-diagnosis and treatment can be risky, so you should always seek medical help if you fall ill. Your embassy or consulate can usually recommend a local doctor who can treat you in your native language. Upscale hotels may also be able to refer you to a doctor. Once you see a doctor, don't be afraid to get a second opinion. Although drug dosages are offered in this section, they are for emergency use only. Correct diagnosis is vital. In this section, the generic names for medications are used – check with a pharmacist for brands available locally.

Note that antibiotics should ideally be administered only under medical supervision. Take only the recommended dose at the prescribed intervals and use the whole course, even if the illness seems to be cured earlier. Stop immediately if there are any serious reactions, and don't use the antibiotic at all if you are unsure that you have the correct one. Do not drink alcohol while taking antibiotics. Some people are allergic to commonly prescribed antibiotics such as penicillin; carry this information (eg, on a bracelet) while traveling.

Environmental Hazards

Heat Dehydration and salt deficiency can cause heat exhaustion. Take time to acclimatize to high temperatures, drink sufficient liquids and do not tackle anything too physically demanding. Don't just drink when you're thirsty, make it a habit to drink frequently whether you're thirsty or not. Alcohol, coffee and tea are diuretics – they make you urinate and lose fluids. They are not a cure for dehydration, they're part of the problem. Drink pure water, fruit juices and soft drinks instead; go easy on the beer.

Salt deficiency is characterized by fatigue, lethargy, headaches, giddiness and muscle cramps; salt tablets may help, but adding extra salt to your food is better.

Anhydrotic heat exhaustion is a rare form of heat exhaustion that is caused by an inability to sweat. It tends to affect people who have been in a hot climate some time rather than newcomers. It can progress to heat stroke. Treatment involves removal to a cooler climate.

Heat stroke, a condition that is serious and occasionally fatal, can occur if the body's heat-regulating mechanism breaks down and body temperature rises to dangerous levels. Long, continuous periods of exposure to high temperatures and insufficient fluids can leave you vulnerable to heat stroke, especially in the jungle lowlands.

The symptoms are feeling unwell, not sweating very much (or at all) and a high body temperature (39° to 41°C or 102° to 106°F). Where sweating has ceased, the skin becomes flushed and red. Severe, throbbing headaches and lack of coordination can occur, and the sufferer may be confused or aggressive. Eventually the victim becomes delirious or convulses. Hospitalization is essential, but in the interim, get victims out of the sun, remove their clothing, cover them with a wet sheet or towel and fan them continually. Give fluids if they are conscious.

Sun In the tropics, the desert or at high altitude, you can get sunburned surprisingly quickly, even through clouds. Wear sunscreen, a hat and lip balm. Calamine lotion and commercial after-sun preparations are good for mild sunburn, as is aloe vera. Protect your eyes with good quality sunglasses, particularly near water. Light, cotton clothing that completely covers your arms and legs is also good protection against the sun.

Infectious Diseases

Diarrhea Seemingly simple things such as a change in diet, water or climate can all cause a mild bout of diarrhea, but a few rushed toilet trips with no other symptoms are not indicative of a major problem. In fact, this is par for the course!

Dehydration is the main danger with any diarrhea, particularly for children or the elderly, because dehydration can occur quickly. Under all circumstances, *fluid replacement* (at least equal to the volume lost) is the most important thing to remember. Weak black tea with a little sugar, soda water or soft drinks allowed to go flat and diluted 50% with purified water are all good. With severe diarrhea (or vomiting), using a rehydrating solution is recommended to replace lost minerals and salts. Commercially available oral rehydration salts (ORS) are very useful; add them to boiled or bottled water. In an emergency, you can make up a solution of 6 teaspoons of sugar and a half teaspoon of salt to a liter of purified water. You need to drink at least the same volume of fluid that you are losing in bowel movements and/or vomit. Urine is the best guide to the adequacy of replacement – if you have small amounts of concentrated urine, you need to drink more and should keep drinking small amounts often. Stick to a bland diet as you recover – white rice, crackers and broth, for example.

Gut-paralyzing drugs such as loperamide or diphenoxylate can be used to bring relief from symptoms, although they do not actually cure the problem. Only use these drugs if you do not have access to toilets, eg, if you *must* travel. Note that these drugs are not recommended for children younger than 12 years old.

To stem mild bouts of diarrhea, eat a banana or two. This is usually effective almost immediately. Veteran Guatemalan travelers also recommend eating two pieces of Milan dark chocolate, made by Gallito and sold in even the smallest stores. Grapefruit seed extract (sold in health food stores) can also cure not-too-serious cases of diarrhea. Dilute five drops of the bitter liquid in 12oz of water or better yet, soda allowed to go flat.

In certain situations, antibiotics may be required. Indications are diarrhea with blood or mucus (dysentery), any diarrhea with fever, profuse watery diarrhea, persistent diarrhea that doesn't improve after 48 hours and severe diarrhea. These suggest a more serious cause of diarrhea, and in these situations, gut-paralyzing drugs should be avoided. A stool test (widely available and affordable in Guatemala) may be necessary to diagnose what is causing your diarrhea, so you can seek medical help. When this is not possible, the recommended drugs for bacterial diarrhea (the most likely cause of severe diarrhea in travelers) are norfloxacin 400mg twice daily for three days or ciprofloxacin 500mg twice daily for five days. These are not recommended for children or pregnant women. The drug of choice for children is co-trimoxazole, with dosage dependent on weight. A five-day course is given. Ampicillin or amoxycillin may be taken in pregnancy, but medical supervision and care is necessary.

Two other causes of persistent diarrhea in travelers are giardiasis and amoebic dysentery. **Giardiasis** is caused by a common but nasty parasite, *giardia lamblia*. Symptoms include stomach cramps, nausea, a bloated stomach, watery, foul-smelling diarrhea and frequent gas. Giardiasis can appear several weeks after exposure to the parasite and is sometimes misdiagnosed. The symptoms may disappear for a few days and then return; this can go on for several weeks.

Amoebic dysentery, caused by the protozoan *Entamoeba histolytica*, is characterized by a gradual onset of low-grade diarrhea, often with blood or mucous. Cramping, abdominal pain and vomiting are less likely than in other types of diarrhea, and fever may not be present. It will persist until treated and can recur and cause other health problems.

You should seek medical advice if you think you have giardiasis or amoebic dysentery, but when this is not a possible option, tinidazole or metronidazole are the recommended drugs. Standard treatment is a 2g single dose of tinidazole or 250mg of metronidazole three times daily for five to 10 days.

Fungal Infections These infections commonly occur in hot weather and are usually found on the scalp, between the toes (athlete's foot) or fingers, in the groin and on the body (ringworm). You get ringworm (which is a fungal infection, not a worm) from infected animals or people. Moisture encourages these infections.

To prevent fungal infections, wear loose, comfortable clothes, avoid artificial fibers, wash frequently and dry yourself carefully. A pair of thongs or flip flops specifically for the shower will go a long way to protect you from athlete's foot. If you do get an infection, wash the infected area at least daily with a disinfectant or medicated soap and water, and rinse and dry meticulously well. Apply an antifungal cream or powder such as tolnaftate. Try to expose the infected area to air or sunlight as much as possible; wash all towels and underwear in hot water, change them often and let them dry in the sun.

Hepatitis Hepatitis is a general term for inflammation of the liver. It is a common disease worldwide. Several different viruses cause hepatitis, and they differ in the way that they are transmitted. Symptoms are similar in all forms of the illness and include fever, chills, headache, fatigue, feelings of weakness and aches and pains, followed by loss of appetite, nausea, vomiting, abdominal pain, dark urine, light-colored feces, jaundiced (yellow) skin and yellowing of the whites of the eyes. People who have had hepatitis should avoid alcohol for some time after the illness, as the liver needs time to recover.

Hepatitis A is transmitted by contaminated food and drinking water. You should seek medical advice, but there is not much you can do apart from resting, drinking lots of fluids, eating lightly and avoiding fatty foods. **Hepatitis E** is transmitted in the same way as hepatitis A; it can be particularly serious in pregnant women.

There are almost 300 million chronic carriers of **hepatitis B** in the world. It is spread through contact with infected blood, blood products or body fluids (for example,

through sexual contact, unsterilized needles and blood transfusions, or contact with blood via small breaks in the skin). Other risk situations include getting a shave, tattoo or body piercing (increasingly popular in Guatemala) with contaminated equipment. Symptoms of hepatitis B may be more severe than those of type A, and the disease can lead to long-term problems such as liver damage, liver cancer or a long-term carrier state. **Hepatitis C** and **D** are spread in the same way as hepatitis B and can also lead to long-term complications.

There are vaccines against hepatitis A and B (see Immunizations), but there are currently no vaccines against the other types of hepatitis. Following the basic rules about food and water (hepatitis A and E) and avoiding risk situations (hepatitis B, C and D) are important preventative measures.

HIV & AIDS Infection with the human immunodeficiency virus (HIV) may lead to acquired immune deficiency syndrome (AIDS), which is a fatal disease. Any exposure to blood, blood products or body fluids may put you at risk. The disease is often transmitted through sexual contact or dirty needles – vaccinations, acupuncture, tattooing and body piercing can be as potentially dangerous as intravenous drug use. If you do need an injection, ask to see the syringe unwrapped in front of you, or take a needle and syringe pack with you. HIV/AIDS can also be spread through blood transfusions; Guatemala generally doesn't screen the blood used for transfusions.

Fear of HIV infection should never preclude treatment for serious medical conditions.

Schistosomiasis Also known as bilharzia, this disease is transmitted by minute worms. They infect certain varieties of freshwater snails found in rivers, streams, lakes and behind dams in particular. The worms multiply and are eventually discharged into the water. Transmission occurs when an individual's skin comes into contact with infected water during activities such as swimming, washing or paddling. Snails usually live on weeds and stones near the surface of water – but not exclusively. Currents can also spread the flukes to areas well away from the contaminated water.

The worm enters through the skin and attaches itself to your intestines or bladder. Initial infection is often asymptomatic but itching can occur at the site of entry. The first symptom may be a general unwell feeling or tingling and sometimes a light rash around the area where the worm entered. Weeks later, a high fever may develop. After the disease is established, other signs are abdominal pain and blood in the urine. The infection often isn't noticed until the disease is well established (several months to years after exposure) and damage to the bladder, kidneys, bowel or liver irreversible.

The main method of preventing the disease is to (surprise!) avoid swimming or bathing in fresh water where bilharzia is present and to avoid drinking contaminated water. It is hard to tell if the water has these nasties; even deep water can be infected. If you do get wet, dry off yourself and your clothes quickly.

Sexually Transmitted Diseases HIV/AIDS and hepatitis B can be transmitted through sexual contact – see those sections, earlier in this chapter, for more details. Other sexually transmitted diseases include gonorrhea, herpes (incurable) and syphilis; sores, blisters or rashes around the genitals and discharges or pain when urinating are common symptoms and bad signs. With some sexually transmitted diseases, such as wart virus or chlamydia, symptoms may be less marked or not observed at all, especially in women. Chlamydia infection can cause infertility in men and women before any symptoms are noticed. Syphilis symptoms eventually disappear completely, but the disease continues and can cause severe problems down the line. Although abstinence from sexual contact is the only 100% effective prevention, using condoms reduces the risk. All of the various sexually transmitted diseases require their own specific antibiotics.

Typhoid Medical help must be sought for this dangerous gut infection, which is caused by contaminated water and food.

In its early stages, sufferers may feel they're coming down with a bad cold or flu, as initial symptoms are a headache, body aches and a fever that rises a little each day until it's around 40°C (104°F) or more. The victim's pulse is often slow relative to the degree of fever present – unlike a normal fever, in which the pulse increases. There may also be vomiting, abdominal pain, diarrhea or constipation.

In the second week, the high fever and slow pulse continue and a few pink spots may appear on the body; trembling, delirium, weakness, weight loss and dehydration may occur. Complications such as pneumonia, perforated bowel or meningitis may result.

Insect-Borne Diseases

Chagas' disease, filariasis and typhus are all insect-borne diseases, but they don't pose a great risk to travelers. For more information on them, see Less Common Diseases at the end of the Health section.

Malaria This serious and potentially fatal disease is spread by mosquitoes. If you are traveling in endemic areas (especially the farthest reaches of the Petén), it is extremely important to avoid mosquito bites, and you may also consider taking tablets to prevent this disease. Some travelers opt not to take preventative malaria medicine for a variety of reasons, including adverse side effects, inconsistent protection results and cost. Whether or not you take malaria pills is up to you, but make an informed decision: Visit a qualified tropical disease medical practitioner and avail yourself of all the facts about malaria and the prevention strategies prior to choosing a course of action. Malaria-carrying mosquitoes tend to be more prevalent during the rainy season (May to October). Symptoms range from fever, chills and sweating, headache, diarrhea and abdominal pains to a vague feeling of ill health. Seek medical help immediately if malaria is suspected. Without treatment, malaria can rapidly become more serious and cause death.

If medical care is not available, you can use malaria tablets for treatment. You need to use a tablet that is different from the one you were taking when you contracted malaria, however. The standard treatment dose of mefloquine is two 250mg tablets, followed by another two six hours later. For Fansidar, it's a single dose of three tablets. If you were previously taking mefloquine and cannot obtain Fansidar, other alternatives are Malarone (atovaquone-proguanil; four tablets once daily for three days), halofantrine (three doses of two 250mg tablets every six hours) or quinine sulphate (600mg every six hours). There is a greater risk of side effects with these dosages than in normal use if used with mefloquine, so medical advice is preferable. Be aware, too, that halofantrine is no longer recommended by the WHO as emergency standby treatment because of side effects, and it should be used only if no other drugs are available.

Travelers are advised to prevent mosquito bites at all times. The main messages are as follows:

• Wear light-colored clothing.
• Wear long pants and long-sleeved shirts.
• Try to remain indoors at dusk and dawn, when malarial mosquitoes are most active.
• Use mosquito repellents containing the compound DEET on exposed areas (some people are very sensitive to this agent and prolonged use of DEET may be harmful, especially to children, but its use is considered preferable to being bitten by disease-transmitting mosquitoes).
• Avoid perfumes and aftershaves.
• Use a mosquito net impregnated with repellent (permethrin) – it may be worth taking your own.
• Impregnate clothes with permethrin to deter mosquitoes and other insects.
• In hotel rooms, kill all the mosquitoes you find. The *anopheles* mosquito is the one carrying malaria; you can recognize her by how she rests against the wall on her head, with her tail section in the air.

Dengue Fever This viral disease is transmitted by mosquitoes and is fast becoming one of the top public health problems in the tropical world, including Guatemala. Unlike the malaria mosquito, the *Aedes aegypti* mosquito, which transmits the dengue virus, is most active during the day, and it is found mainly in urban areas, in and around human dwellings.

Signs and symptoms include a sudden onset of high fever, headache, joint and muscle pains (hence its old name, 'breakbone fever'), nausea and vomiting. A rash of small red spots sometimes appears three to four days after the onset of fever. In the early phases, dengue may be mistaken for other infectious diseases, including malaria and influenza. Minor bleeding such as nosebleeds may occur in the course of the illness, but this does not necessarily mean that you have progressed to the potentially fatal dengue hemorrhagic fever (DHF). This is a severe illness, characterized by heavy bleeding that is thought to be a result of second infection due to a different strain (there are four major strains), and usually it affects local residents rather than travelers. Recovery from even simple dengue fever may be prolonged, with tiredness lasting for several weeks.

You should seek medical attention as soon as possible if you think you may be infected. A blood test can exclude malaria and indicate the possibility of dengue fever. There is no specific treatment for dengue. Aspirin should be avoided, as it increases the risk of hemorrhaging. Also, there is no vaccine against dengue fever. The best prevention is to avoid mosquito bites at all times by covering up and using insect nets and insect repellents containing the compound DEET – see the above Malaria section for more advice on avoiding mosquito bites.

Bedbugs, Lice & Scabies Bedbugs live in various places, but particularly in dirty mattresses and bedding. They may be evidenced by spots of blood on bedclothes or on the wall. Bedbugs leave itchy bites in neat rows. Calamine lotion, a sting relief spray or Tiger Balm may help. Fleas can also be a problem in bedding.

All lice cause itching and discomfort. They make themselves at home in your hair (head lice), clothing (body lice) or pubic hair (crabs). You catch lice through direct contact with infected people or by sharing combs, clothing and other personal items. Infected areas can be shaven or treated with a powder or shampoo available at pharmacies. Scratch where you have 'em and the pharmacist should be able to produce the cure. Infected clothing and bedding should be washed in very hot (preferably boiling), soapy water and left in the sun to dry.

The same advice holds for scabies, a mite that burrows beneath the skin's surface and causes intense itching. They like certain areas on the body: between the fingers and toes, around the wrists and chest and under the arms are the most popular. It's very important to treat your clothing to prevent reinfection. Guatemalan pharmacists are well acquainted with these nasties and can sell you the correct treatment.

Bites & Stings Bee and wasp stings are usually painful rather than dangerous. However, people who are allergic may experience severe breathing difficulties and require urgent medical care. Calamine lotion or a sting relief spray will help the itch, and ice packs will reduce the pain and swelling. There are some spiders with dangerous bites, but antivenins are usually available. Scorpion stings are notoriously painful and sometimes fatal. Scorpions lurk in shoes or clothing, so shaking out clothes and shoes before donning them is good standard operating procedure.

Women's Health

Antibiotic use, synthetic underwear, sweating and contraceptive pills can lead to fungal vaginal infections, especially in hot climates. Fungal infections are characterized by a rash, itch and discharge and can be treated with a vinegar or lemon-juice douche or with yogurt. Acidophilus has also proven effective in treating vaginal infections. Nystatin, miconazole or clotrimazole suppositories or vaginal cream are the usual chemical treatments. Maintaining good personal hygiene and wearing loose-fitting clothes and cotton underwear are good form and also may help prevent these infections.

Sexually transmitted diseases are a major cause of vaginal problems. Symptoms include a smelly discharge, painful intercourse and sometimes a burning sensation when urinating. Medical attention should be sought and male sexual partners need to be treated as well. For more details, see the section on Sexually Transmitted Diseases, earlier. Besides abstinence, the best thing is to practice safer sex using condoms.

It is not advisable to travel to some places while pregnant, as some vaccinations normally used to prevent serious diseases carry risk when administered to pregnant women (eg, yellow fever, though this vaccination is not required for travel to Guatemala). In addition, some diseases, such as malaria, are much more serious for a pregnant woman and may increase the risk of a stillborn child.

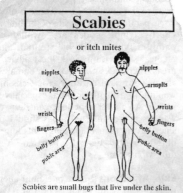

Scabies

or itch mites

nipples · nipples · armpits · armpits · wrists · wrists · fingers · fingers · belly button · belly button · pubic area · pubic area

Scabies are small bugs that live under the skin. They cause an itchy rash from the neck down.

The rash is usually on the:

fingers
wrists
armpits
nipples
belly button
pubic area

Most miscarriages occur during the first three months of pregnancy. Miscarriage is not uncommon and can occasionally lead to severe bleeding. The last trimester of a pregnancy should be spent within reasonable distance of good medical care. A baby born as early as 24 weeks stands a chance of survival, but only in a good, modern hospital. Pregnant women should avoid all unnecessary medication, although vaccinations and malarial prophylactics should still be taken when needed. Additional care should be taken to prevent illness, and particular attention should be paid to diet and nutrition. Alcohol and nicotine, for example, should be avoided.

Less Common Diseases

The following diseases pose a small risk to travelers and so are mentioned in passing. Seek medical advice if you think you may have one of these diseases.

Chagas' Disease In remote rural areas of Central and South America, this parasitic disease is transmitted by a bug that hides in crevices. This bug likes the walls and thatched roofs of mud huts and the creases of palm fronds. It bites at night and a hard, violet-colored swelling appears in about a week. Chagas' disease can be treated in its early stages, but can lead to death if untreated. Without offending their hosts, travelers in a remote homestay situation should try to plug holes in thatch roofs and mud walls.

Cholera This is the worst of the watery diarrheas, and medical help should be sought. Outbreaks of cholera are generally widely reported, so avoid problem areas. *Fluid replacement is the most vital treatment* – the risk of dehydration is severe, as you may lose up to 20 liters a day. If there is a delay in getting to a hospital, begin taking tetracycline. The adult dose is 250mg four times daily. It is not recommended for children under nine years old, nor for pregnant women. Tetracycline may help shorten the illness, but adequate fluids are required to prevent death.

Filariasis This mosquito-transmitted parasitic infection is found in many parts of Central America. Possible symptoms include fever, pain, swelling of the lymph glands, inflammation of lymph drainage areas, swelling of a limb or the scrotum, skin rashes and blindness. Treatment is available to eliminate the parasites from the body, but some of the damage already caused may be irreversible. Medical advice should be obtained promptly if infection is suspected.

Rabies This fatal viral infection is present in Guatemala. Many animals can be infected (such as dogs, cats, bats and monkeys), and it is their saliva that is infectious. Any bite, scratch or even lick from an animal should be cleaned immediately and thoroughly. Scrub with soap and running water and then apply alcohol or iodine solution. If exposed, seek medical help to initiate a course of injections to prevent the onset of symptoms and death.

Typhus This disease is spread by ticks, mites and lice. It begins with fever, chills, headache and muscle pains, followed by a body rash a few days later. There is often a large, painful sore at the site of the bite, and nearby lymph nodes are swollen and painful. Typhus can be treated under medical supervision. Seek local advice on areas where ticks pose a danger and always check your skin carefully for ticks after walking in a high risk area, especially the jungle. An insect repellent can help, and walkers in tick-infested areas should consider having their boots and pants impregnated with benzyl benzoate and dibutylphthalate.

Skin Afflictions Insect bites and allergic reactions to plants such as poison ivy can lead to painful itching and oozing sores. Scratching can cause the bite to burst and get infected – a very unwelcome circumstance, especially in the jungle where sores are slow to close and heal. Antihistamines can alleviate some of the discomfort. Anti-itch preparations and oatmeal or baking soda baths can also provide temporary relief. If the itching becomes unbearable and you'll try anything for relief, some travelers recommend swabbing the effected area with your own urine.

WOMEN TRAVELERS

Women should encounter no special problems traveling in Guatemala. In fact, solo women will be pleasantly surprised by how gracious and helpful most locals are. The primary thing you can do to make it easy for yourself while traveling here is to dress modestly; most Guatemalan women do. Modesty in dress is highly regarded, and if you practice it you will usually be treated with respect.

Specifically, shorts should be worn only at the beach, not in town, and especially not in the highlands. Skirts should be at or below the knee. Be sure to wear a bra, as going braless is considered provocative. Many local women swim with T-shirts over their swimming suits; in places where they do this, you may want to follow suit, to avoid stares.

Women traveling alone can expect plenty of attempts by men to chat them up. Often they are just curious and not out for a foreign conquest. It's up to you how to respond, but there's no need to be intimidated. Consider the situation and circumstances (on a bus is one thing, on a barstool another) and stay confident. Try to sit next to women or children on the bus if that makes you more comfortable. Local women rarely initiate conversations, but usually have lots of interesting things to say once the ball is rolling.

The catcalls, hisses and howls that are so frequently directed at women in some other parts of the region are less common in Guatemala. Still, it can happen, the sad reality being that this is how some men behave when they see a female. Do what the local women do – ignore it completely.

Nasty rumors about Western women kidnapping Guatemalan children for a variety of sordid ends not limited to organ harvesting have all but died down. Still, women travelers should be cautious around children, especially indigenous kids in the Cobán and Huehuetenango regions.

While there's no need to be paranoid, you must be aware that the possibility of rape and assault does exist. It happens more in some places than others. Use your normal traveler's caution – avoid walking alone in isolated places or through city streets late at night, skip hitchhiking, don't camp alone. Taking a self-defense class specifically for women is a good way to prepare for your trip and bolster your confidence and awareness.

See the Society & Conduct section in the Facts about Guatemala chapter for more on behavior that can help to smooth your way while you travel here.

GAY & LESBIAN TRAVELERS

Few places in Latin America are outwardly gay-friendly, and Guatemala is no different. Technically, homosexuality is legal for persons 18 years and older, but the reality can be another story, with harassment and violence against gays too often poisoning the plot. Don't even consider testing the tolerance for homosexual public displays of affection here.

Though Antigua has a palatable – but subdued – scene, affection and action are still kept behind closeted doors; the exception is La Casbah near the Santa Catalina arch, which is so hopping on Thursday nights that it has become more of a mixed than a gay crowd. In Guatemala City, Pandora's Box and Eclipso are the current faves. In large part though, gays traveling in Guatemala will find themselves keeping it low key and pushing the twin beds together, a tired but workable compromise if all else fails.

Toto Tours (☎ 800-565-1241, 773-274-8686, fax 773-274-8695, ✉ info@tototours.com, www.tototours.com), 1326 West Albion Ave, Chicago, IL 60626, runs all-gay-men adventure trips to Guatemala and other parts of Central America.

The International Gay & Lesbian Travel Association (☎ 800-448-8550, ✉ IGLTA@iglta.org, www.IGLTA.org), Box 4974, Key West, FL 33041, USA can locate travel agents familiar with gay and gay-friendly tours and lodgings.

The Arenal Spanish Lesbigay home page (www.indiana.edu/~arenal/ingles.html) has some terrific information on homosexuality laws and norms throughout Latin America, plus reports from the gay political front and updates on human rights.

DISABLED TRAVELERS

Guatemala is not the easiest country to negotiate with a disability; there are no provisions made for the hearing or sight impaired, and wheelchair-bound travelers will be faced with formidable challenges. Although many sidewalks in Antigua have ramps and cute little inlaid tiles depicting a wheelchair, the streets are cobblestone, so the ramps are anything but smooth and the streets worse!

Many hotels in Guatemala are old converted houses with rooms around a courtyard that are wheelchair accessible. The most expensive hotels have facilities such as ramps, elevators and accessible toilets. Transportation will be the biggest hurdle for disabled travelers, though locals will usually lend a hand. Travelers in a wheelchair may consider renting a car and driver as the buses will prove especially challenging (but not impossible) due to lack of space. If you want to go by bus, arrive early for the best spot.

There are several Internet sites which may be of use to travelers with a disability. For general information, consult the Access-Able Travel Source homepage at www.access-able.com. The Accessible Journeys Web site, www.disabilitytravel.com, has great advice, resources and trips for disabled travelers as well.

The following organizations devoted to disabled travelers are based in the US: Mobility International USA (☎ 541-343-1284, www.miusa.org), PO Box 10767, Eugene, OR 97440; Access Foundation (☎ 516-887-5798), PO Box 356, Malverne, NY 11565; and the Society for the Advancement of Travelers with Handicaps or SATH (☎ 718-858-5483, www.sath.org/index.html), 26 Court St, Brooklyn, NY 11242.

In Australia and New Zealand, try the National Information Communication Awareness Network or NICAN (☎ 02-6285 3713; fax 6285 3714, www.nican.com.au), PO Box 407, Curtin, ACT 2605. In the UK, there is the Royal Association for Disability & Rehabilitation or RADAR (☎ 020-7250 3222; fax 250 0212, www.radar.org.uk), 12 City Forum, 250 City Rd, London EC1V 8AF.

Transitions/Guatemala (☎ 832-4261, ✉ transitions@guate.net), Colonia Candelaría, No 80 in Antigua, is an organization aiming to increase awareness and access for disabled persons in Guatemala.

SENIOR TRAVELERS

Senior travelers should consult their doctor before venturing to Guatemala and take particular care with food and drink while there. While no tour outfits exist specifically for seniors going to Guatemala, there are several organizations that can help with general travel plans and advice. These include the American Association of Retired Persons or AARP (☎ 800-424-3410, www.aarp.org), 601 E St NW, Washington, DC 20049, which is for people 50 years and over (non-US residents can get one-year memberships for $10).

Grand Circle Travel (☎ 617-350-7500, 800-350-7500), 347 Congress St, Boston, MA 02210, offers a useful free booklet, *Going Abroad: 101 Tips for Mature Travelers,* and the US's National Council of Senior Citizens (☎ 301-578-8800), 8403 Colesville Road, Silver Spring, MD 20910, provides discount information and travel-related advice.

TRAVEL WITH CHILDREN

Children are highly regarded in Guatemala and can often break down barriers and open the doors to local hospitality. Logistically, traveling here with children is not a problem. However, Guatemala is so culturally dense, with such an emphasis on history and archaeology, that children can get easily bored. Parents will have to be creative and make a point of visiting some of the more kid-friendly sites like the Auto Safari Chapín south of the capital. Water parks, recreation centers (called *turicentros)* with pools and games, playgrounds and hands-on activities such as weaving are all available in Guatemala. Most Spanish courses are open to kids, too.

For a wealth of good ideas, pick up a copy of Lonely Planet's *Travel with Children* by Maureen Wheeler (1995).

USEFUL ORGANIZATIONS

The South American Explorers (☎ 607-277-0488, fax 607-277-6122, contact ✉ explorer@ samexplo.org, www.samexplo.org), 126 Indian Creek Road, Ithaca, NY 14850 USA, has mountains of information and advice on traveling in Latin America, from on-the-road updates from fellow adventure seekers to discount travel agents. Individual annual membership costs US$40 and includes a subscription to the *South American Explorer* magazine, access to clubhouses in Peru and Ecuador and discounts on books and other materials. Advice on trip planning is also available.

AmeriSpan (☎ 215-751-1100, toll free in the US 800-879-6640, fax 215-751-1986, ✉ info@amerispan.com, www.amerispan .com), PO Box 40007, Philadelphia, PA 19106, offers detailed recommendations for volunteer opportunities and Spanish programs in Guatemala. They have an office in Antigua; see the Information section of that chapter for details.

DANGERS & ANNOYANCES
Safety

Guatemala is not as dangerous as some would have you think, though travelers are advised to be alert and do their research. Up-to-date travel advisories are available from the US Department of State's Web site (http://travel.state.gov/travel_warnings.html). US citizens can telephone the Department of State's Citizens Emergency Center (☎ 202-647-5225). Less alarmist is the UK's Foreign and Commonwealth Office Travel Advice Web site (www.fco.gov.uk/travel/). British subjects can contact them at (☎ 020-7270-3000).

The 36-year-long civil war is kaput, but this violent struggle has been replaced by a precipitous rise in the general crime rate. There have been incidents of rape, robbery,

carjacking and even murder of foreign tourists. These incidents are unpredictable and occur at random.

Your best defenses against trouble are having up-to-date information and exercising reasonable caution. You should take the time to contact your government, inquire about current conditions and trouble spots and follow the advice offered.

If you plan to travel by road in the highlands or El Petén, you should ask as many other travelers as possible about current conditions. Don't rely on local newspapers, government officials or businesspeople as your sole sources of information, as they often cover up 'unpleasant' incidents that might result in the loss of tourist revenues.

In past years there have been a few bizarre incidents in which foreign visitors have been unjustly suspected of kidnapping Guatemalan children in order to use their organs in transplant operations. One woman taking photographs of children in a town near Cobán was nearly murdered by a hysterical crowd. Be careful not to put yourself in any situation that might be thus misinterpreted. Crowds, especially of the drunken variety, can be very volatile.

The very popular hike up Volcán Pacaya can be dangerous. This is an active volcano, and tourists have been injured by flaming rocks and debris issuing forth from the cone. In January 2000 this volcano was upgraded to orange alert status, meaning eruption was more likely and hazardous. Keep abreast of developments before you head up here.

Robbery & Theft

Robbery is a danger in Guatemala City, Antigua and Chichicastenango. Theft, particularly pocket picking and purse snatching, is also not unusual on the bus. Foreign tourists are particularly singled out for thefts, as they are presumed to be 'wealthy' and to be carrying valuables.

To protect yourself, take these common-sense precautions:

Unless you have immediate need of them, leave most of your cash, traveler's checks, passport, jewelry, airline tickets, credit cards, expensive watch (and perhaps your camera) in a sealed, signed envelope in your hotel's safe; obtain a receipt for the envelope. Virtually all hotels except the very cheapest provide safekeeping for guests' valuables. You may have to provide the envelope (available at a *papelería*, or stationer's shop). Your signature on the envelope and a receipt from the hotel clerk will help prevent pilfering.

Leaving valuable items in a locked suitcase in your hotel room is often safer than carrying them with you on the streets of Guatemala City. Hiding valuables behind a mirror, tacked to the back of some furniture or in a toilet tank are some other options when a safe is unavailable.

Have a money belt or a pouch on a string around your neck, place your remaining valuables in it and wear it underneath your clothing. You can carry a small amount of ready money in a pocket or bag.

Be aware that any purse or bag in plain sight may be slashed or grabbed. Often two thieves work together, one cutting the strap, the other grabbing the bag in a lunge past you, even as you walk along a street or stand at a bus stop. At ticket counters in airports and bus stations, keep your bag between your feet, particularly when you're busy talking to a ticket agent.

Do not wander alone in empty city streets or isolated areas, particularly at night.

Do not leave any valuables visible in your vehicle when you park, unless it is in a guarded parking lot.

Do not camp overnight in lonely places unless you can be sure it's safe.

Reporting a Robbery or Theft There's little point in going to the police after a robbery unless you're insured, in which case you'll need a statement from the police for your insurance company. You'll probably have to communicate with the police in Spanish, so if your own is poor take a more fluent speaker along. Say, *Yo quisiera poner una acta de un robo* (I'd like to report a robbery). This should make it clear that you merely want a piece of paper and aren't going to ask the police to do anything proactive like actually look for the thieves or attempt to recover your goods. With luck you should get the required piece of paper without too much trouble. You may have to write it up your-

self, then present it for official stamp and signature.

There are several numbers you can call collect (reverse charges) to report lost or stolen traveler's checks or credit cards:

American Express: ☎ 801-968-8300; in Guatemala call ☎ 334-0040

MasterCard: ☎ 212-974-5696; in Guatemala call ☎ 331-8027

VISA: ☎ 415-574-7111

Thomas Cooke: in Guatemala ☎ 331-4155

EMERGENCIES

To reach the Tourism Police arm of the National Police, dial ☎ 110; the Police can also be reached at ☎ 120. The fire department can be reached on ☎ 122 or 123, and ambulances are on ☎ 125 or 128. The Red Cross *(Cruz Roja)* is on ☎ 125, and the official time can be had by dialing ☎ 126.

LEGAL MATTERS

Police officers in Guatemala are sometimes part of the problem rather than the solution. The less you have to do with the law, the better.

Whatever you do, *don't* get involved in any way with illegal drugs: don't buy or sell, use or carry, or associate with people who do – even if the locals seem to do so freely. As a foreigner, you are at a distinct disadvantage, and may be set up by others. Drug laws in Guatemala are strict, and though enforcement may be uneven, penalties are severe. If you do get caught buying, selling, holding or using drugs, you're best first defense may be to suggest you and the officer 'work things out.' This intimation usually gets the point across that you'd like to give a little cash donation to the officer for overlooking your offense.

BUSINESS HOURS

Guatemalan businesses are generally open daily from 8 am to noon and from 2 to 6 pm. A two hour siesta is the norm, especially in smaller towns, and hours may be curtailed on Sundays or completely discretionary. Government offices keep shorter hours; usually they are open weekdays from 8 am to 4 pm. Official business is always better conducted in the morning.

PUBLIC HOLIDAYS & SPECIAL EVENTS

Guatemala's big national holidays fall according to the Roman Catholic Church calendar. Christmas and Holy Week (Semana Santa), leading up to Easter, are the most important, though these festivities have distinct Mayan shamanist flavors and twists. Hotels and buses are packed during Holy Week, especially in towns that have elaborate and colorful celebrations, such as Antigua.

Visitors interested in the Mayan life cycle might want to head to one of the towns still observing the traditional Mayan calendar (eg, Momostenango or Todos Santos) for Wajshakib Batz, the sacred Mayan New Year. It falls on the following dates: November 5, 2000, July 23, 2001, April 9, 2002, December 25, 2002, September 11, 2003, and May 28, 2004. Outsiders are not necessarily invited to join in the ceremonies as they tend to be sacred affairs, but it's still a good time to be in one of these traditional towns.

Every town has one day a year slotted for a blowout party with dancing, parades and fireworks. Oftentimes the fiesta will last a week or longer and usually falls on the saint's day for which that town was named, especially in the highlands. Consult the Fiestas of Guatemala Web site at www.mayaparadise.com/fiestas/fiestas.htm to find out where and when the most happening fiestas are on.

Any and all occasions are celebrated with fireworks in Guatemala – the more the better seems to be the feeling – and you will definitely be treated to some sort of pyrotechnic antics if you're visiting during a festival or holiday. At festival time, it's not unusual to see children as young as six wandering around with a string of firecrackers clutched in one hand, a book of matches in the other and a gleam in their eye. Some of the most intriguing fiestas are noted below.

January

January 1 – New Year's Day is a legal holiday in Guatemala.

January 15 – El Cristo de Esquipulas is a super devout holiday in Esquipulas, with pilgrims coming from all over Central America to catch a glimpse of the Black Jesus housed in the Basilica here.

January 19 to 25 – Rabinal's annual fiesta has some of the most traditional dancing and costuming anywhere in Guatemala. Festivities peak on January 21.

February

Religious Holidays – Pre-Easter celebrations get under way around the country. Once Lent starts, things quiet down considerably until Semana Santa kicks off in April.

April

The rainy season may start by late April. The few weeks preceding the rains are often the hottest of the year. Everyone and everything swelters in the lowlands, while up in the mountains pleasant weather prevails.

Religious Holidays – During Semana Santa, or Holy Week, the week before Easter Sunday, things are abuzz, particularly in the highlands. Holy Week begins on Palm Sunday, the Sunday before Easter. Holy Thursday, Good Friday, Holy Saturday and Easter Sunday are official holidays.

Good Friday – the Huelga de Dolores, a century-old parade during which political figures and issues of the day are hilariously and creatively lampooned, makes it's way through the streets of Guatemala City, ending at the National Palace.

May

The rainy season begins in earnest, with heavy rains during the first few weeks after the season begins. No place escapes the rains, though they are heaviest in the highlands.

May 1 – Labor Day is a legal holiday in Guatemala.

June

Heavy rains may continue during June.

June 30 – Army Day and commemoration of the revolution of 1871 is a legal holiday.

July

Rains are less bothersome, and the summer tourist season is in full swing. The hurricane season officially begins in July, though historically there are few storms this month.

Last Week in July – Cobán celebrates its annual fiesta. This is followed by the national Folkloric Festival of Rabin Ajau (see August), one of the largest and most spectacular indigenous festivals in the country. Momostenango also celebrates its annual fiesta from July 21 to August 1. The wildest day is July 25; traditional folkloric dances are a highlight.

August

The summer tourist season peaks, and rooms in some places may be difficult to find. Hurricane season comes to the Caribbean; this is one of the most active months for tropical storms.

First Week in August – The Folkloric Festival of Rabin Ajau in Cobán reaches a fevered pitch with marimba concerts, art exhibits, parades and the election of the Tezulutlán Princess.

August 11 to 16 – Fiesta de la Virgen de la Asunción is celebrated with folk dances and parades in Tactic, Sololá, Guatemala City and Jocotenango.

August 15 – Festival of Guatemala takes place in Guatemala City; offices and shops close for the day.

August 29 – It's the Postal Workers' Holiday; all post offices closed.

September

The summer crowds start to thin out, but it's still quite hot and humid.

September 15 – Independence Day is a legal holiday in Guatemala.

October

The rains stop sometime during October or shortly thereafter, though they can extend into November in the jungle lowlands. The number of visitors drops off, facilities are less crowded and there are many bargains to be had. It's a great time to travel here.

October 1 to 7 – Fiesta de San Francisco de Asis is observed with La Danza de Conquista and La Danza de los Monos in San Francisco El Alto and with massive drinking and fireworks in Panajachel.

October 20 – The revolution of 1944 is commemorated.

October 28 – The Birthday of Ry Laj Man, also known as Maximón or San Simón, is celebrated with an all-out pagan party in San Andrés Iztapa, near Antigua, and a festival in Zunil.

October 31 – On the eve of Todos los Santos (All Saints' Day), religious processions and alfombras (carpets made from flower petals and colored sawdust) liven up the streets of Antigua and San Cristóbal Verapaz.

November

The low season arrives. Expect empty hotels, quiet restaurants, an unhurried pace and discount prices. Hurricane season officially comes to an end and the lightning storms begin. Lago de Atitlán and the Río Dulce areas get particularly dramatic shows between now and February.

November 1 – Día de Todos los Santos or All Saints' Day is celebrated with giant kite festivals in Santiago Sacatepéquez and Sumpango in the highlands and with the spectacularly renowned drunken horse races in Todos Santos. San José on Lago de Petén Itzá observes the day with a sundown procession featuring a human skull on a velvet pillow, followed by feasts at predetermined houses visited by the skull.

December

Until the Christmas rush begins, December is an excellent month to visit, with little rain, good temperatures and low prices. The crowds begin to arrive – and prices rise substantially – after December 15. The national orchid show comes to Cobán every December as well.

December 7 – Quema del Diablo, Burning of the Devil, starts at around 6 pm throughout the country when everyone takes to the streets with their old garbage, physical and psychic, to stoke huge bonfires of trash. This is followed by an impressive fireworks display.

December 8 – The Feast of the Immaculate Conception takes place in many towns. The festivities in Chichicastenango on this and the preceding day are particularly lively.

December 13 to 21 – On the Feast of Saint Thomas in Chichicastenango, parades, dances (including the elaborate Baile de Conquista) and drinking culminate on the 21st with the *palo volador* or flying pole extravaganza. This must be seen to be believed.

December 24 to 25 – Christmas Eve and Christmas Day are holidays.

December 31 – New Year's Eve afternoon is a holiday.

ACTIVITIES

While Mayan culture, art and archaeology are of great interest and very accessible to most travelers, Guatemala has more going for it than just ruins. As the country improves its infrastructure and tourism facilities, expect to see more adventure and outdoor activities on offer.

Archaeology

If archaeology is what you're after, Guatemala is the place. Tikal is in a lush jungle setting with many wildlife viewing opportunities. Copán in Honduras, Abaj Takalik on the Pacific Slope and Quiriguá are all important sites.

Challenging jungle treks to El Mirador, Yaxjá and Río Azul are among the greatest adventures to be had here. River trips can be made to El Ceibal, Dos Pilas and Piedras Negras in El Petén, or try a multi-day excursion to the El Zotz or El Perú sites.

Travels to the Far Side

Some of the most intriguing aspects of Guatemala are the mysticism, shamanism and alternative healing practices that have taken hold and flourished.

The curing and divining powers of shamans have long been important to Mayan culture, and these traditions are still going strong in Momostenango near Xela and Santiago on Lago de Atitlán, among other places. Part of the tradition's continued strength undoubtedly comes from the general prohibition against foreigners participating in or observing ceremonies. However, there are many places travelers can go in Guatemala to explore the farther side of reality, whether it be through healing, massage, meditation or tarot. Here are some suggestions:

Casa de los Nahuales, 3a Avenida Sur No 6, Antigua, offers a variety of services within one complex, including Mayan horoscopes, massages, cleansings, crystal healings and movement therapy.

Centro de Masajes El Original (☎ 762-2223), Calles los Arboles, Panajachel, is highly recommended for Thai and Swedish massage administered by Jennifer Martin. She also does reflexology and Reiki and will make house/hotel calls by appointment.

Cinco Ajpuu (☎/fax 832-1628), 5a Avenida Sur No 1, Antigua, sells healing stones, Tibetan meditation objects, pyramids, crystals, incense and New Age music. You can arrange for Tarot readings here or have a wholesome vegetarian meal in their courtyard.

Fraternidad Naturista Antigua (☎ 832-2443), Calle Real No 80, Jocotenango, offers massage, sauna, colonic and chiropractic services. They also sell an amazing variety of herbs. A 45-minute massage and unlimited sauna time costs US$7; there are separate (very clean) facilities for men and women, including lockers, showers and beverage service. The massages are very strenuous, some say rough, and men should be especially careful here as the masseurs are wicked strong. Hours are Sunday to Thursday from 7 am to 6 pm and Friday from 7 am to 1 pm.

Las Pirámides (☎ 205-7302, 205-7151), San Marcos La Laguna, Lago de Atitlán, has an integrated program of meditation, massage, channeling and spiritual guidance. See the Highlands chapter for more information.

Takiliben May Wajshakib Batz', 3a Avenida A No 6-85, Zona 3, Momostenango, offers Mayan cleansing ceremonies and a tuj (sweat lodge) under the direction of Mayan sacerdote Rigoberto Iztep Chanchavac. For prices, reservations and information, see the Web site at www.geocities.com/RainForest/Jungle/9089/Ceremonies.htm/.

Tarot Readings by Udi (☎ 332-5546, ✉ benbjorn@hotmail.com) offers comprehensive readings in English or Spanish by an accomplished tarot reader with nearly 20 years of experience. A one-hour session, available by appointment in Guatemala City or Antigua, is US$25.

Mountaineering

Guatemala is a climber's paradise, with lots of peaks and breathtaking scenery. There are very few facilities and services, so you'll need to be self-sufficient or guided. The Cuchumatanes range has quality climbs in quantity, Volcán Tacaná (4093m) is considered one of the most challenging ascents around, and Volcán Tajumulco (4220m) is the highest peak in Central America. Several outfitters specialize in these and other climbs. Popular day trips include hiking the very active Volcán Pacaya or the dormant but stunning Volcán San Pedro on Lago de Atitlán.

Cycling

There's probably no better way to experience the Guatemalan highlands than by bicycle. The topography and roads are tailor-made for mountain biking (some of it extreme), and tour operators and independent travelers are beginning to realize the cycling potential here. Antigua, Panajachel and Xela are the best launch points, and several agencies in these cities offer trips and/or equipment; see the Antigua chapter and the Panajachel and Quetzaltenango sections in The Highlands chapter for more details.

Spelunking

A caving mecca, Guatemala attracts spelunkers from the world over. The Verapaces are particularly conducive to the pursuit, as this whole part of the country is karst and riddled with caves. While the caves of Lanquín and Poptún have long been popular, new cave discoveries such as the Gruta Rey Marcos, the Chicoy Cave and the caves at Candelaria are broadening the spelunking opportunities here. All these sites can be reached on a day trip from Cobán.

Wildlife Viewing & Bird-Watching

National parks and biospheres here have few tourist facilities, but compensate with lots of wildlife and bird-watching. Sites such as Tikal, El Mirador and the Biotopo Cerro Cahuí in the Petén have an abundance of wildlife; birding is especially rich at Tikal. The Bocas de Polochic on Lake Izabal and the mangrove swamps near Monterrico are among the best places to see a variety of birds. Even day trips to Lake Chicabal near Xela or the Atitlán Nature Reserve in Panajachel can reward visitors with rich wildlife viewing.

White-Water Rafting

From placid Class II to raging Class IV rapids, Guatemala has some excellent rafting in the most majestic settings. The Cahabón River can be run year-round, while the Esclavos, Motagua and Naranjo are rushing from June to October. Quality equipment and guides are available. White-water kayaking is another possibility on several rivers throughout the country, including the Ríos Lanquín, Cahabón and Sauce.

For more on the water sports front, scuba enthusiasts can hop over to Belize for superlative diving along the world's second-largest barrier reef or head north to the Yucatán Peninsula to dive the turquoise waters there.

LANGUAGE COURSES

Spanish-language courses are wildly popular in Antigua and Quetzaltenango; together those cities boast more than 100 Spanish schools. Students wanting something a little more off the beaten track will have no problem finding a school and situation in Guatemala to suit their taste. San Pedro La Laguna and Panajachel on Lago de Atitlán, Todos Santos in the Cuchumatanes mountains, Cobán in Alta Verapaz, Copán in Honduras, on the Río Tatín near Lívingston and San Andrés and San José on Lago de Petén Itzá all support schools of different tenors. Whatever the locale, schools typically provide one-on-one instruction, homestays with Guatemalan families, electives such as dancing or weaving and volunteer or social action opportunities. Some highland schools also offer instruction in Mayan languages such as Mam and Quiché.

WORK

Guatemala is an extremely poor country, and work is hard to come by. You might find work teaching English, but don't count on it. Service jobs are probably easier to land because hotels, bars and restaurants catering to travelers are always on the lookout for worldly employees. Xela, Antigua, Monterrico and Panajachel are likely spots to find service jobs, at least temporarily. Skilled tour guides such as alpinists will have an easier time getting work as the tourism industry continues to blossom. Even if you do find work, however, wages will be low; expect to cover your expenses and that's about it.

Volunteer Work

If you really want to get to the heart of Guatemalan matters and you've altruistic leanings, consider volunteering for a piece. Volunteering is rewarding and exposes foreigners to the rich and varied local culture typically out of reach for the average traveler. Opportunities abound, from caring for abandoned animals and kids to tending fields. Travelers with specific skills such as nurses, doctors or educators are particularly encouraged to investigate volunteering in Guatemala.

To learn more about Guatemalan volunteer positions, visit the AmeriSpan volunteer Web site (www.amerispan.com/volunteer/default.htm) or the WWWanderer CA Volunteer Guide (www.tmn.com/wwwanderer/Volguide/projects.html). Volunteer opportunities available in Xela can be perused on the Xela Pages Web site at www.xelapages.com/Volt.htm.

Most volunteer posts require basic or better Spanish skills and a minimum time commitment. Depending on the position and the organization, volunteers may have to pay for room and board for the duration of their stay. Before making a commitment, you may want to talk to past volunteers and also read the fine print associated with the position. What follows are some well established organizations in search of volunteers.

ARCAS (Asociación de Rescate y Conservación de Vida Silvestre, the Wildlife Rescue and Conservation Association) operates two wildlife stations. One is a wildlife rescue center near Flores; the other is a sea turtle hatchery east of Monterrico. See the Monterrico section in the Pacific Slope chapter and the Flores section in the Petén chapter for details. ARCAS also has volunteer projects in other fields, including education and health. Contact ARCAS (☎ /fax 591-4731,✆ arcas@pronet.net.gt), 1a Calle 50-37, Zona 11, Colonia Molino de las Flores, Guatemala City. The mailing address in the US is ARCAS, Section 717, PO Box 52-7270, Miami, FL 33152-7270.

Asociación Hogar Nuevos Horizontes (☎ 761-2608, fax 761-4328), 3a Calle 6-51, Zona 2, Quetzaltenango. This nongovernmental organization is dedicated to putting an end to domestic violence. It runs a battered women's shelter, legal clinic, medical clinic and child care center. They also administer classes, seminars and programs for women and children. Men are encouraged to apply. A minimum one-month commitment is required.

Casa Alianza (☎ 253-2965, 251-2569, fax 253-3003, ✆ guatemala@casa-alianza.org), 3a Avenida 11-28, 5th floor, Zona 1, Guatemala City. Casa Alianza runs a shelter for street children in Guatemala City. Volunteers can work in the shelter or administrative offices. Working in the shelter requires at least a six-month commitment.

Casa Guatemala (☎ 232-5517, ✆ casaguatemal@guate.net, www.mayaparadise.com/casaguae.htm), 14a Calle 10-63, Zona 1, Guatemala City. Casa Guatemala helps abandoned, orphaned and malnourished children. A second facility and the main administrative offices (☎/fax 331-9408) are at 5a Avenida 7-22, Zona 10. In Guatemala City it has a clinic, food distribution program and temporary home for teenage orphans and pregnant teens. Casa Guatemala also has an orphanage on the Río Dulce (☎ 902-0612, 208-1779, fax 902-0612) in eastern Guatemala. Short-term opportunities are available.

Escuela de la Calle (☎ 761-1521, fax 763-2104, ✆ edelac@usa.net, http://beef.brownrice.com/streetschool/home.htm), Diagonal 15, 7-61, Zona 5, Quetzaltenango. In the US, contact Michael Shorr (☎ 505-820-0114, mhshorr@earthlink.net), 2003 Hopi Road, Santa Fe, NM 87505-2401. Information is also available at Quetzaltrekkers (☎ 761-2470, ✆ quetzaltrekkers@hotmail.com),

Diagonal 12 8-37, Zona 1, Quetzaltenango, who donate all their proceeds to the Escuela. This organization has a variety of programs designed to help at-risk children in Xela, including a school and dorm. A two-month commitment is required.

Kuinik Ta'ik Volunteer Program (contact Coordinator Kermit Frazier at ✆ momostenango@conexion.com.gt, www.GeoCities.com/RainForest/Jungle/9089) This program offers opportunities in and around Momostenango for teachers, medical personnel and agricultural specialists. Minimum commitment of three months is required except for medical personnel, who need only commit to a month. Homestays are available.

Proyecto Ak' Tenamit (✆/fax 254-1560), 11a Avenida A 9-39, Zona 2 Guatemala City, or in Río Dulce (✆ 902-0608). In the US, contact the Guatemalan Tomorrow Fund (✆ 407-747-9790, fax 407-747-0901), PO Box 3636, Tequesta, FL 33469. The Proyecto works with the Q'eqchi' Maya people of eastern Guatemala near Río Dulce. They have a medical volunteer project, a dental clinic, a school, potable water projects and a women's cooperative. A year's commitment is preferred.

Red International (contact Volunteer Coordinator Alex Morales at ✆ redidh@yahoo.com) Information about the Red International is also available from Quetzaltrekkers (✆ 761-2470), Diagonal 12 8-37, Zona 1, Quetzaltenango. This organization sends human rights observers for a minimum of three weeks to small villages in the state of Chiapas, Mexico. Observers conduct interviews with villagers and file reports about the human rights situation in Chiapas.

ACCOMMODATIONS

Accommodations range from luxury hotels to budget hotels to very cheap *pensiones* (pensions), hostels with shared dorm rooms and hammock space. In the cheaper places, beds are often short, saggy, lumpy or a combination of these undesirable characteristics. Pillows in Guatemala are big, leaden and better for propping open doors than for laying down your head.

Camping

Camping can be a hit-or-miss affair in Guatemala, as there are few designated campgrounds and safety is never guaranteed. Where campsites are available,

though, expect to pay from US$3 to US$5 per night, depending upon the facilities and the choiceness of the location. National parks are a particularly good place to camp, especially at the Tikal ruins. Expect more camping opportunities as Guatemala's popularity as an adventure destination grows.

Hostels

Guatemala does not have youth hostels on the European system. However, some tourist towns now have hostels that offer cheap dormitory accommodation where you get a bunk bed in a room shared with other travelers. A night in one of these places usually runs about US$3.

Hotels, Motels & Pensions

The luxury resort hotels are mainly found in Guatemala City. They are all expensive, but most offer excellent value for what you get compared to similar establishments at home. Double room rates start at about US$80 per night and go beyond US$250.

In the middle range are comfortable hotels and motels, some with appealing colonial ambiance, others quite modern with lawns, tropical flowers and swimming pools shaded by palm trees; still others are urban high-rise buildings with many services and comforts. These range in price from US$25 to US$80 or so for a double, the higher prices being charged in the major cities.

Budget lodgings, those costing from US$4 to US$25 a double, come in many varieties and degrees of comfort and cleanliness. Pensiones offer the cheapest rooms around, sometimes for as little as US$1.20 a person.

Homestays

Travelers attending Spanish school have the option of living with a Guatemalan family in situations of varying degrees of comfort and authenticity. This is usually a pretty good bargain – expect to pay between US$50 and US$70 a week for room and board. It's important to find a homestay that jibes with your needs and goals. For example, some families host as many as seven foreign students at a time, creating more of an international hotel atmosphere than a family environment.

Hammocks

Hanging your own hammock is definitely the cheapest (though not always the most comfortable) way to go. Lugging a hammock and mosquito net around may not be part of your plan, but you can rent a hammock, net and a place to hang them (usually under a thatched roof outside a small hotel or a family's hut) for less than US$3 in most places. It's easy enough to buy hammocks in Guatemala, but look for the Mexican variety as they are usually the best quality.

FOOD

While not entirely disappointing, Guatemalan food is very basic. Try to develop a taste for corn *tortillas* before your trip because you'll be seeing stacks of them at breakfast *(el desayuno)*, lunch *(el almuerzo)* and dinner *(la cena)*. Maintaining a vegetarian diet will be challenging here, but if you request a meatless meal, you'll probably get some rice and steamed vegetables at the very least.

Tortillas are thin round patties of pressed corn (maize) dough cooked on a griddle called a *comal*. Fresh handmade tortillas can be very delicious or not – some women have the touch, others don't. Tortillas are the exclusive domain of women and you'll see and hear women making them in every corner of the country. A woman feeding a family of eight (not unusual in Guatemala) will make about 170 tortillas a day. Fresh machine-made ones can be bought at a *tortillería*. What you usually get in a restaurant or *cafetería* are fairly fresh ones kept warm in a hot, moist cloth. These are all right, but they take on a rubbery quality. Worst are old tortillas; their edges curl and dry out while the center could be used to patch a tire. But don't confuse old tortillas with toasted, thoroughly dried, crisp tortillas, which are another thing altogether, and very good. Meals come with unlimited tortillas; if you run out, just ask for more.

Frijoles are beans, to be eaten boiled, fried, refried, in soups, spread on tortillas or with eggs. Frijoles may come in a bowl swimming in their own dark sauce, as a runny mass on a plate, or as a thick and almost black paste. No matter how they come, they can be delicious and are always nutritious. The only bad ones are refried beans that have been fried using too much or low-quality fat.

You'll be eating a lot of *huevos*: Eggs can come at breakfast or dinner, along with beans, fried plantains and *crema*, which is like a sweet sour cream. There is always some type of hot sauce on hand, either bottled or homemade, and the extra kick it provides can make the difference between a blah and a tasty meal.

Other foods you will encounter include *bistec* (tough grilled or fried beef), *pollo asado* (grilled chicken), and lighter fare such as *hamburguesas* (hamburgers) or *refacciones* – a catch-all phrase for snacks like tostadas and tacos.

Chinese restaurants are ubiquitous in this and other Latin American countries where Chinese labor was imported on a massive scale following the abolition of slavery. Chinese food is a cheap, filling alternative to the omnipresent beans, eggs and tortillas and is a good bet for vegetarians.

For full lists of menu items with translations, see the Menu Translator at the back of this book.

Breakfast

This can be either continental, US-style or what's called *desayuno chapín*. A light, continental-style breakfast can be made of sweet rolls or toast and coffee.

US-style breakfasts are available in tourist towns, but rarely off the beaten track. These can include bacon or sausage and eggs, *panqueques* (pancakes), cold cereal such as corn flakes or hot cereal such as oatmeal or cream of wheat, fruit juice and coffee. You may order eggs in a variety of ways (see the Menu Translator).

Desayuno chapín, or Guatemalan breakfast (chapín is a local term for Guatemalans), is a huge affair involving eggs, beans, fried plantains, tortillas and coffee. Sometimes this is augmented with mosh, an oats and hot milk concoction with a disturbingly phlegmatic texture. Scrambled eggs are often made with chopped tomatoes and onions thrown in.

Lunch

This is the biggest meal of the day and is served about 1 or 2 pm. A fixed-price meal of several courses called an *almuerzo* (the bargain or daily special meal) is usually offered, and may include from one to five or six courses; choices and price are often displayed near the front door of the restaurant. Otherwise, just ask what the almuerzo is for the day. Simple almuerzos may consist of a soup or pasta, a main course featuring a meat and starch such as rice or potatoes, coffee and dessert; more expensive versions may have a fancy soup or ceviche, a choice main course such as steak or fish, salad, dessert and coffee.

Supper

La cena is a lighter version of lunch, served about 7 pm. In local and village eateries, supper is the same as breakfast: eggs, beans and plantains. Sometimes pollo or bistec will be on offer as well. In restaurants catering to tourists, supper can be anything from chicken cordon bleu to penne in Bolognese sauce.

Bus Food

Bus snacks are an important part of the traveler's diet, as long bus rides with early morning departures are not uncommon. Bus food is often regional (keep your eyes out for the blue corn tortillas around Cobán), but always cheap and filling. Women and girls come on the bus proclaiming *hay comida* (loosely translated as 'food here'). This is usually a small meal consisting of tortillas smeared with beans, accompanied by a piece of chicken or a hard boiled egg. Other snacks include fried plantains, ice cream, peanuts, *chocobananos* (chocolate covered bananas), *hocotes* (a tropical fruit eaten with salt, lime and nutmeg) and *chuchitos* (corn dough filled

with meat and wrapped in corn husk, not unlike tamales). *Elotes* are grilled ears of corn on the cob eaten with salt and lime.

DRINKS
Water & Soft Drinks

Bottled or purified water is widely available in hotels and shops (see Water in the Health section earlier in this chapter). You can also order safe-to-drink bottled carbonated water by saying 'soda;' Shangri-La is a tasty brand.

Besides the easily recognizable and internationally known brands of *aguas* (sodas) such as Orange Crush (far and away the most widely available), Coca-Cola, Pepsi and Seven-Up, you will find interesting local flavors. La India Indígena brand of soda, for example, comes in super-sugary orange and lime varieties and is available in the department of Quiché.

Coffee, Tea & Cocoa

While Guatemala grows some of the world's richest coffee, it's rarely available because most of the highest quality beans are cultivated for export; drinking instant coffee day after day in light of this is frustrating. In the tourist towns you can find deliciously brewed coffee, but everywhere else, coffee is of the weak and overly sweet instant variety. If you like milk in your coffee, ask for *café con leche*.

Black tea *(té negro)*, usually made from bags (often locally produced Lipton), tends to disappoint devoted tea drinkers. It's best to bring your own supply of loose tea and a tea infuser or bags, then just order *una taza de agua caliente* (a cup of hot water) and brew your own. The hot water is often free.

Herbal teas are much better. Chamomile tea *(té de manzanilla)*, a common item on restaurant and café menus, is a specific remedy for queasy stomach and grippy gut. Hibiscus tea *(té de rosa de jamaica)* is another tasty herbal found throughout Guatemala. Again, you can bring your own supply of bags and order hot water to save money.

Hot chocolate or cocoa was the royal stimulant during the Classic period of

Mayan civilization, being drunk on ceremonial occasions by the kings and nobility. Their version was unsweetened and dreadfully bitter. Today it's sweetened and, if not authentic, at least more palatable. Hot chocolate can be ordered *simple* (with water) or *con leche* (with milk).

Juices

Fresh fruit and vegetable juices *(jugos)* and milkshakes *(licuados)* are wildly popular and with good reason: they rock. Almost every village market and bus terminal has a stand with a battalion of blenders used to make juice or licuados. All of the fruits and a few of the squeezable vegetables are used either individually (as in jugos) or in some combination (as in licuados).

The basic licuado is a blend of fruit or juice with water and sugar. Other items can be added or substituted: raw egg, milk, ice, flavorings such as vanilla or nutmeg. The combinations are practically limitless.

Limonadas are delicious and addicting drinks made with lime juice, water and sugar. Try a *limonada con soda,* which adds a fizzy dimension to the typical limonada – and you may have a new drink of choice. *Naranjadas* are the same thing made with orange juice. *Jamaica* (pronounced hah-my-cah) is a refreshing juice made from hibiscus flowers.

Alcoholic Drinks

Breweries were first established in Guatemala by German immigrants in the late 19th century. European techniques and technology have been used ever since the beginning, but don't expect near European quality in local suds.

Guatemala's two nationally distributed beers are Gallo (gah-yoh, rooster) and Cabro (goat). The distribution prize goes to Gallo – you'll find it everywhere – but Cabro is darker and more flavorful. Moza is the darkest local beer, but its distribution is limited. Imported beers are available in only the largest cities and most popular Gringo trailheads.

In restaurants and bars unaccustomed to tourists, beer is sometimes served at room temperature. If you want to be sure of getting a cold beer, ask for *una cerveza fría.* Sometimes the waiter or bartender will hand you the bottle and let you feel it for proper coldness. This usually means it's not very cold, and your choice is then warm beer or no beer.

Wine drinkers will be sorely disappointed in Guatemala. Local wines are no thrill to drink and imported wines are fairly expensive, but at least they're available (sometimes). In all but the best places you may have to specify that you want your red wine at room temperature and your white wine chilled.

Rum is one of the favorite strong drinks in Guatemala, and though most is cheap in price and taste, some local products are exceptionally fine. Zacapa Centenario is a smooth, aged Guatemalan rum made in Zacapa. It should be sipped slowly and neat, like fine cognac. *Ron Botrán Añejo,* another dark rum, is also good. Cheaper rums like Venado are often mixed with soft drinks to make potent but cooling drinks such as the *Cuba libre* of rum and Coke. On the coast you'll find *cocos locos,* green coconuts with the top sliced off into which rum is poured to mingle with the coconut water.

Aguardiente is a sugarcane firewater that flows in cantinas and on the streets and gets you drunk hard and fast. Look for the signs advertising *Quetzalteca Especial.* This is the aguardiente of choice.

The town of Salcajá, outside Xela, is renowned for its alcoholic brews including *caldo de frutas* (literally, fruit stew). This is a mélange of apples, peaches, pears and other fruits that is set in bottles to ferment for several years. The result is a very potent potable, not unlike sangría in taste, but with a much bigger punch. Salcajá brewmeisters also make a yellow egg liquor called *rompopo.*

ENTERTAINMENT

Slim pickings are the operative words for entertainment in Guatemala. There are some nightclubs in Guatemala City and a couple of discos in Antigua and Panajachel, but that's about it. Awards go to Guatemala City for a burgeoning, hip youth scene that supports coffee houses, open mike performances, poetry readings and live music.

Traditional cinemas and movie houses showing multiple titles on several big screen televisions are common in the biggest towns and cities. The theater companies in Guatemala City and Xela put up consistently good productions; international dance and drama companies sometimes swing through Guatemala with stops either in the capital or, more rarely, Antigua. Soccer games are a popular local diversion – seats range from US$3 to US$7.

SHOPPING
Textiles
Guatemala's brilliantly colored weavings and textiles are world-famous. Weaving is a traditional and thriving art of the Mayan people here. Wall hangings, clothing (especially the beautiful embroidered *huipiles* (blouses) and the *cortes* (skirts) of the Mayan women), purses, belts, sashes, friendship bracelets, tablecloths, bedspreads and many other woven items are ubiquitous and good values. A recent trend toward adapting traditional weavings into tourist items such as hacky sacks, backpacks and pot holders has taken hold.

The largest markets are the Thursday and Sunday markets in Chichicastenango and the permanent market in Panajachel, where there are many wholesalers. Some believe the former has gotten too touristy and has the inflated prices to show for it. If you're serious about buying handicrafts, though, it's worth a trip to one of these places. Many fine textiles of an infinite variety are also available in Antigua, but at higher prices.

Each village also has market days, often the best place to buy textiles directly from the weaver. Or you can go directly to a town whose designs you admire. Todos Santos is famed for vibrant red *traje* (traditional woven cloth). Sololá and Santa Catarina Palopó on Lago de Atitlán are other great smaller towns in which to buy typical textiles. Momostenango is justly famed for

thick, woolen blankets, which are coveted in many a cold clime, including Guatemala.

When buying textiles, it's normal practice to bargain until buyer and seller arrive at a mutually agreeable price. (See Tipping & Bargaining in the Money section earlier in this chapter for more about bargaining.)

Leather Goods
Guatemala has some terrific leather goods, which is not surprising given that much of the arable land is devoted to cattle and the cowboy culture that goes with it. Fine briefcases, duffel bags, backpacks and belts are sold in most handicrafts markets. Cowboy boots and hats are a specialty in some areas and custom work is welcome. The prices and craftsmanship are usually phenomenal.

Wooden Masks
Ceremonial masks are fascinating, eye-catching and still in regular use. You'll see them in the markets in Panajachel, Chichicastenango, Sololá and Antigua. In some towns, including Chichicastenango, you can visit the artists in their *morerías* (workshops) and watch as they create the masks.

Coffee
Although most of the finest beans are earmarked for export, some are (thankfully) held back for the tourist trade. While almost every tourist shop in the country sells pounds of coffee in cute bags made of traditional cloth, these are woefully overpriced and the freshness and quality of the beans suspect. Some is even sold already ground – java blasphemy! To ensure you're getting the finest, freshest coffee beans available, visit one of the several farms and/or roasters and buy from them directly. Cobán and Antigua produce some of the world's greatest coffee and both towns support growers and roasters. There are also roasters in Quetzaltenango and Panajachel; see those sections in The Highlands chapter for details.

Jade
In 1958 an ancient Mayan jade quarry near Nebaj, Guatemala, was rediscovered (see

the Nebaj section in The Highlands chapter for more on this area). When it was shown to yield true jadeite equal in quality to Chinese stone, the mine was reopened. Today it produces jade (pronounced hah-deh) both for gemstone use and for carving.

Jade is sold at markets in Antigua, Panajachel, Chichicastenango and elsewhere. Beautiful well-carved stones can cost US$100 or much more. Look for translucency, purity and intensity of color and absence of flaws. Ask the merchant if you can scratch the stone with a pocket knife; if it scratches, it's not true jadeite but an inferior stone. Many travelers have fallen for the false stone scam; don't join their ranks.

Shipping

Although it's possible to ship packages through the Guatemalan post, it's better to use an international shipping service if you want to ensure a relatively safe, timely arrival of your goods. International companies like DHL and Federal Express are definitely more secure ways to send your packages home. DHL has drop off locations in Guatemala City, Antigua, Xela and Solalá and can ship packages up to 50 kilograms door-to-door. Businesses specializing in international shipping (including really big parcels), such as International Bonded Couriers in Guatemala City and Antigua, will pack and ship door-to-door to over 200 countries worldwide.

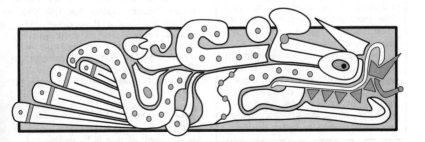

Getting There & Away

While most travelers zip into Guatemala by air, there are those who prefer to travel overland by bus, car or motorcycle and still others who come in under sail. Private sailboats and their crew (known in travel lingo as 'yachties') are ubiquitous on the Caribbean coast near Lívingston and Río Dulce, as sailors moor here for a respite before heading down through the Panama Canal. Though there is no regular ferry service between the US and Guatemala, travelers can arrive by ferry or motorboat from Belize or Honduras. The major highways linking Guatemala to Honduras, Belize, Mexico and El Salvador are smooth, paved and serviced by regularly scheduled buses.

AIR
Airports & Airlines
Guatemala's two major international airports are in Guatemala City (Aeropuerto Internacional La Aurora) and Flores, near Tikal in El Petén. Limited international service is also provided at the airports in Puerto Barrios and Quetzaltenango.

As there are few direct flights from anywhere to Guatemala, travelers arriving by air will likely have to pass through one of the major 'hub' cities: Atlanta, Dallas/Fort Worth, Houston, Los Angeles, Miami, Mexico City or San Salvador. This may involve a plane change or a layover.

Of the big US carriers, Continental, Delta, Northwest, American and United Airlines offer the most flights to Guatemala. Aeroméxico, Aeronica, Aeroquetzal, Aerovías, Aviateca, COPA, LACSA, Mexicana and TACA are the Latin American airlines with flights to the US and Central American cities.

Atlanta – Delta has daily flights.

Belize City – TACA has four flights a week via El Salvador. Tikal Jets flies five days a week via Flores. Aerovías flies three times a week via Flores.

Cancún – Aerocaribe, Aviateca, TACA and Tikal Jets have daily flights.

Chetumal (Mexico) – Aeroméxico has flights four times weekly via Flores.

Copán (Honduras) – Aereo Ruta Maya/Jungle Flying Tours flies to a strip on the Guatemala-Honduras border, from where a bus takes you to the Copán ruins.

Flores, El Petén (for Tikal) – Mayan World has three flights daily. Tikal Jets Racsa, TACA, and Aviateca have daily flights. All are direct flights.

Havana – Aviateca has direct flights twice a week. Cubana Air has three flights a week.

Houston – Continental has two direct flights daily. Aviateca has three direct flights per week. TACA has daily flights via El Salvador and Belize City.

Huatulco – Mexicana has direct flights three times a week.

Los Angeles – Aviateca, United and TACA all have daily direct flights. Mexicana has daily flights via Mexico City.

Madrid – Iberia has daily flights via Miami.

Managua – TACA and COPA both have two daily flights via San Salvador.

Mexico City – Mexicana, United and Aviateca have daily nonstop flights.

Mérida – Aviateca has a morning flight three days per week.

Miami – American has three daily flights. Aviateca and Iberia each have one direct flight a day. TACA has daily flights via El Salvador.

New Orleans – TACA has flights four times weekly via El Salvador.

New York – TACA has flights daily via Washington DC. Delta and American have one daily flight.

Palenque – Tikal Jets has daily flights from Flores.

Panama City – COPA has three flights daily; two are via San José Costa Rica.

San José (Costa Rica) – Both United and COPA have direct flights every day. TACA, Aviateca and LACSA have daily flights, making one stop on the way. Avianca has a flight going Guatemala City-San José-San Andrés Island-Bogotá.

San Francisco (California, USA) – United and Continental have daily flights via Houston. TACA has direct flights four times weekly.

San Pedro Sula (Honduras) – TACA and COPA have daily flights.

San Salvador – TACA, COPA and Aviateca fly several daily nonstops..

Tapachula (Mexico) – Tikal Jets has daily flights from Guatemala City; some connect through Quetzaltenango. Racsa has flights on Friday and Sunday.

Washington DC – TACA and American have daily flights.

Here is how to contact the airlines in Guatemala City:

Aereo Ruta Maya/Jungle Flying Tours (☎ 360-4917/20, fax 331-4995, ✉ jungleflying@guate.net), Avenida Hincapie and18a Calle, Hangar F1, Zona 13

Aerocaribe – see Mexicana

Aerolíneas Argentinas (☎ 331-1567, Web site www.aerolineas.com.ar), 10a Calle 3-17, Zona 10

Aeroméxico – see Mexicana

Aerovías (☎ 332-7470, 361-5703, fax 334-7935), La Aurora International Airport

Alitalia (☎ 331-1276, www.alitalia.com/english/index.html), 10a Calle 3-17, Zona 10

American Airlines (☎ 334-7379, Web site www.americanair.com), Hotel El Dorado, 7a Avenida 15-45, Zona 9

Avianca (☎ 334-6801/2/9, ☎/fax 334-6797, www.avianca.com.co), Avenida La Reforma 13-89, Local 1, Zona 10

Aviateca – see TACA

British Airways (☎ 332-7402/3/4, fax 332-7401, www.british-airways.com), 1a Avenida 10-81, Zona 10, Edificio Inexsa, 6th floor

Continental Airlines (☎ 335-3341, 366-9985, fax 335-3444, www.continental.com), 12a Calle 1-25, Zona 10, Edificio Géminis 10, Torre Norte, 12th floor; the office is located at 1210; La Aurora International Airport (☎ 331-2051/2/3/4, fax 331-2055)

COPA (Compañía Panameña de Aviación, ☎ 361-1567/1607, fax 331-8314, www.copaair.com), 1a Avenida 10-17, Zona 10

Delta Airlines (☎ 337-0642/70, fax 337-0588), 15a Calle 3-20, Zona 10, 2nd floor

El Al (☎ 334-3314, www.elal.com), 10a Calle 6-21A, Zona 9, 3rd floor

Iberia (☎ 334-3816/17, fax 334-3715, www.iberia.com), Avenida La Reforma 8-60, Zona 9, Edificio Galerías Reforma, Local 204; La Aurora International Airport (☎ 332-5517/8, fax 332-3634)

LACSA (Líneas Aéreas Costarricenses) – see TACA

Ladeco (☎ 331-8564, 334-6238), Avenida La Reforma 12-81, Zona 10

Lufthansa German Airlines (☎ 336-5526, fax 339-2995, www.lufthansa.com), Diagonal 6 10-01, Zona 10, Centro Gerencial Las Margaritas, Torre II, 8th floor

LTU International Airways (☎ 337-0107/8, fax 337-0109), 6a Avenida 20-25, Zona 10

Mayan World (☎ 334-2067, 339-1519), 7a Avenida 6-53, Zona 4, Edificio El Triángulo, 2nd floor

Mexicana (☎ 333-6048, www.mexicana.com), 13a Calle 8-44, Zona 10; La Aurora International Airport (☎ 332-1924, 331-3291)

Nica – see TACA

SAM – see Avianca

TACA – reservations ☎ 334-7722; main office (☎ 331-8222, fax 334-2775), Avenida Hincapié 12-22, Zona 13; Centro de Servicio (☎ 332-2360/4640), 7 Avenida 14-35, Zona 9; Hotel Ritz Continental (☎ 238-1415, 238-1479), 6a Avenida A 10-13, Zona 1; La Aurora International Airport (☎ 331-8222); Plaza Biltmore (☎ 331-2520, 337-3462), 14 Calle 0-20, Zona 10

Tapsa – La Aurora International Airport (☎ 331-4860/9180, fax 334-5572)

Tikal Jets (☎ 334-5631, 334-5568, fax 361-3343, www.tikaljets.centroamerica.com), La Aurora International Airport

United Airlines (☎ 332-2995, fax 332-3903, www.ual.com), Avenida La Reforma 1-50, Zona 9; Edificio El Reformador, 2nd floor, La Aurora International Airport (☎ 332-1994/5, fax 332-2795)

Varig (☎ 331-1952, fax 332-0286, www.varig .com.bra), Avenida La Reforma 9-00, Zona 9, Edificio Plaza Panamericana, 8th floor

Buying Tickets

For most travelers, airfare to Guatemala will be the wallet buster, but you can reduce your costs by finding discounted fares. Stiff competition has resulted in widespread discounting – welcome news for travelers! The only folks likely to pay full fare these days are those flying in 1st or business class. For the rest of us, stuck in economy class, there is usually some sort of discount to be had. To get the lowest fare, you'll need to get informed and be flexible about fares and dates.

Long-term travelers will find a host of discount tickets valid for 12 months, permitting multiple stopovers with open dates. It gets a little trickier for shorter trips, but cheaper fares are available by traveling midweek, staying over a Saturday night or taking advantage of quickie promotional offers.

When looking for bargain airfares, head to a travel agent rather than directly to the airline. While airlines do have special offers from time to time, travel agents regularly buy blocks of seats at a discount and pass the savings on to travelers. If possible, track down a travel agent that specializes in Latin America, and you're bound to get a deal.

One exception to the above is buying tickets directly from the airline over the Internet. Many airlines offer super deals on their Web sites, either via auction or simply by slashing prices to reflect the reduced cost of e-business. Online ticket sales work well if you are doing a simple one-way or return trip on specified days. However, online speed demon fare generators are no substitute for a talented travel agent who knows all about special deals, has strategies for avoiding layovers and can offer advice on everything from which airline has the tastiest vegetarian food to the best travel insurance to bundle with your ticket. Many travel agents have Web sites, which can make the Internet a quick and easy way to comparison shop and give you a heads-up on what tickets to Guatemala may cost.

The days when nefarious travel agents fleeced travelers by running off with their money are (happily) all but over. Paying by credit card generally offers protection, as most card issuers provide refunds if you can prove you didn't get what you paid for. Agents who accept only cash should hand over the tickets then and there and not tell you to 'come back tomorrow.' After you've made a reservation or paid your deposit through an agent, call the airline and confirm that the reservation was indeed made. It's never a good idea to send money (even checks) through the mail unless the agent is very well established, as some travelers have reported being ripped off by fly-by-night mail-order ticket agents.

You may feel more comfortable paying more than the rock-bottom fare by opting for the safety of a better-known travel agent. Firms such as STA Travel, with offices worldwide, Council Travel in the US and Usit Campus (formerly Campus Travel) in the UK are not going to disappear overnight, and they do offer competitive prices to most destinations.

If you buy a ticket through an agent and later want to make changes in dates or routes or get a refund, you need to contact the original travel agent. Airlines only issue refunds to the purchaser of a ticket – usually the travel agent who bought it on your behalf. Many travelers change their routes halfway through their trips, so think carefully before you buy a ticket that is not easily refundable.

Regional Air Passes Regional airlines, including Aviateca, COPA, LACSA, NICA and TACA, have formed a marketing

Air Travel Glossary

Cancellation Penalties If you have to cancel or change a discounted ticket, there are often heavy penalties involved; insurance can sometimes be taken out against these penalties. Some airlines impose penalties on regular tickets as well, particularly against 'no-show' passengers.

Courier Fares Businesses often need to send urgent documents or freight securely and quickly. Courier companies hire people to accompany the package through customs and, in return, offer a discount ticket which is sometimes a phenomenal bargain. However, you may have to surrender all your baggage allowance and take only carry-on luggage.

Full Fares Airlines traditionally offer 1st class (coded F), business class (coded J) and economy class (coded Y) tickets. These days there are so many promotional and discounted fares available that few passengers pay full economy fare.

Lost Tickets If you lose your airline ticket an airline will usually treat it like a travelers check and, after inquiries, issue you with another one. Legally, however, an airline is entitled to treat it like cash and if you lose it then it's gone forever. Take good care of your tickets.

Onward Tickets An entry requirement for many countries is that you have a ticket out of the country. If you're unsure of your next move, the easiest solution is to buy the cheapest onward ticket to a neighboring country or a ticket from a reliable airline, which can later be refunded if you do not use it.

Open-Jaw Tickets These are return tickets where you fly out to one place but return from another. If available, this can save you backtracking to your arrival point.

Overbooking Since every flight has some passengers who fail to show up, airlines often book more passengers than they have seats. Usually excess passengers make up for the no-shows, but occasionally somebody gets 'bumped' onto the next available flight. Guess who it is most likely to be? The passengers who check in late.

Promotional Fares These are officially discounted fares, available from travel agencies or direct from the airline.

Reconfirmation If you don't reconfirm your flight at least 72 hours prior to departure, the airline may delete your name from the passenger list. Ring to find out if your airline requires reconfirmation.

Restrictions Discounted tickets often have various restrictions on them – such as needing to be paid for in advance and incurring a penalty to be altered. Others are restrictions on the minimum and maximum period you must be away.

Round-the-World Tickets RTW tickets give you a limited period (usually a year) in which to circumnavigate the globe. You can go anywhere the carrying airlines go, as long as you don't backtrack. The number of stopovers or total number of separate flights is decided before you set off, and they usually cost a bit more than a basic return flight.

Transferred Tickets Airline tickets cannot be transferred from one person to another. Travelers sometimes try to sell the return half of their ticket, but officials can ask you to prove that you are the person named on the ticket. On an international flight, tickets are compared with passports.

Travel Periods Ticket prices vary with the time of year. There is a low (off-peak) season and a high (peak) season, and often a low-shoulder season and a high-shoulder season as well. Usually the fare depends on your outward flight – if you depart in the high season and return in the low season, you pay the high-season fare.

organization named America Central Corporation. Through this consortium you can buy a Mayan Airpass or a Central American Airpass, allowing you to fly from a US gateway (usually Miami, New Orleans or Houston) and visit as few as four regional cities (two in the case of the Central American Airpass) and as many as eight for a very competitive fare. For more information on these passes, contact eXito Latin America Travel (☎ 800-655-4053, fax 510-655-2154, ✆ exito@wonderlink.com), 1212 Broadway, Suite 910, Oakland, CA 94612. Their useful website (www.wonderlink .com) has a calculator that spits out a fare after you enter the destination cities of your choice.

Aerocaribe also offers a Mayan airpass; visit their website at www.aerocaribe.com .mx/english/mayapass.html for more information.

Student & Youth Fares Full-time students and travelers younger than 26 have access to better deals than the rest of us. The deals may not always be cheaper fares but can include more flexibility and/or routes. You have to show documentation proving your date of birth or a valid International Student Identity Card (ISIC) when buying your ticket and boarding the plane. The world abounds with places to get fake student cards, but if you're busted using one, your plane ticket may be confiscated.

Courier Flights Courier flights are the bargain of all bargains if you're lucky enough to find one that works for you. Airfreight companies need to ship cargo, sometimes urgently, so they send it with passengers on normal, commercial flights as their baggage allowance. As the 'courier,' you get the seat on the plane, but you can't check any baggage; one carry-on bag is all you're permitted. In return, you get a deeply discounted ticket.

Before you rush out to become a courier, you should know there are other restrictions: Courier tickets are sold for fixed dates, so changes can be difficult to make. If you buy a round-trip ticket, your schedule will be even more rigid. Before you fly, clarify what restrictions apply to your ticket, and don't expect a refund once payment is made.

Reserving a courier ticket takes some effort. Courier tickets are not always readily available and arrangements may have to be finalized as much as a month or more in advance. You won't find courier flights on all routes either. Guatemala, after all, can hardly be considered a commercial hub. Still, once you're in the courier loop, you'll discover it's so dirt cheap to fly to the different destinations they serve, it's hard to resist just packing a carry-on and hitting the road. Some courier companies even allow you to keep the frequent flier miles you accrue.

Most courier organizations require that you become a member and pay an annual fee before you'll be given access to flight information. Be aware also that becoming a member of any of these organizations does not guarantee that you will get a flight through them. Some of the larger outfits include the Air Courier Association (☎ 800-822-0888 in the US); for enrollment information visit their Web site at www .aircourier.org. Air Courier International (☎ 800-682-9470 in the US) also has a Web site at www.aircourierintl.com. Another possibility (at least for US residents) is the International Association of Air Travel Couriers or IAATC (☎ 561-582-8320 in the US, www.courier.org). The US$45 membership fee gets participants a bimonthly update of air-courier offerings, access to a special fax-on-demand service with daily updates on last minute bargains and the bimonthly newsletter *Shoestring Traveler*.

Ticketless Travel Ticketless travel, whereby your reservation details are contained within an airline computer, is becoming more common. On simple round-trip flights, the absence of a ticket can be a benefit – it's one less thing to worry about. However, if you are planning a complicated itinerary that you may wish to amend en route, there is no substitute for the good old paper version.

Travelers with Special Needs

If you have any dietary restrictions, unusually large baggage (eg, a surfboard), are traveling with infants, have a disability or fear of flying, contact the airline well before your departure date (one month prior is a good benchmark) to discuss special arrangements. The airline should provide you with information and alternatives to make your flight easier and more enjoyable. For example, special meals for those observing a vegetarian or Kosher diet can be ordered and a seat assignment to accommodate especially tall people could be arranged. As your departure date approaches, confirm and reconfirm any special arrangements with the airline; try to call 48 hours prior to your flight.

Airlines usually allow babies up to two years of age to fly for 10% of the adult fare, although a few may allow them free of charge. For children between the ages of two and 12, the fare on international flights is usually 50% of the regular fare or 67% of a discounted fare.

Departure Tax

There is a US$30 departure tax on all international flights from Guatemala. Some airlines include this tax in the price of the ticket, though many do not. You'll be well served to be informed on this point.

The US

Discount travel agents in the US are known as consolidators. San Francisco is the ticket consolidator capital of the US, though good deals can also be had in Los Angeles, New York and other big cities. Consolidators can be found through the Yellow Pages, major daily newspapers and cosmopolitan weeklies such as the *Village Voice* and *SF Weekly*. Weekly travel sections with consolidator ads are in *The New York Times*, the *Los Angeles Times*, the *Chicago Tribune* and the *San Francisco Examiner* – although if you are in Los Angeles or San Francisco you should double check, since at the time of this writing these two major daily newspapers in those cities were in the process of being sold.

Council travel, the US's largest student travel organization, has about 60 offices around the country; its head office (☎ 800-226-8624) is at 205 E 42nd St, New York, NY 10017. Call for the office nearest you or visit the Web site at www.ciee.org. STA Travel (☎ 800-777-0112) has offices in Boston, Chicago, Miami, New York, San Francisco and other major cities. Call for office locations or visit the Web site at www.statravel.com.

There are dozens of airfares that apply to any given route. They vary with each company, class of service, season of the year, length of stay, dates of travel, date of purchase and reservation. Your ticket may cost more or less depending upon the flexibility you are allowed in changing your plans. The price of the ticket is even affected by how and when you buy it and from whom.

Fares from the US are relevant if you are coming from Africa, since you will go through Europe and/or the US; if your trip originates in Asia your flight will go through Los Angeles.

Here are some sample fixed-date round-trip fares (also called excursion fares) from various US cities to Guatemala City. Keep in mind that these are close to the worse case scenario as prices go – with a little research and flexibility, you can probably get a cheaper flight.

Chicago	US$419
Dallas/Fort Worth	US$446
Los Angeles	US$578
Miami	US$385
New York	US$478

Canada

Canadian discount air ticket sellers are also known as consolidators, and their airfares tend to be about 10% higher than those in the US. The *Globe & Mail*, the *Toronto Star*, the *Montreal Gazette* and the *Vancouver Sun* carry travel agents' ads and are good places to look for cheap fares. Note that there are no direct flights from Canada to Guatemala; travelers originating in Canada must connect in a US city.

Travel CUTS (☎ 800-667-2887) is Canada's national student travel agency, with offices in all major cities. Its Web address is www.travelcuts.com.

Mexico, Caribbean, Central & South America

Council Travel has affiliate offices in Mexico and Costa Rica. In Costa Rica, contact SIN-LIMITES (☎ 506-280-5182), 200m east of Pollos Kentucky, Los Yoses, Apdo 1, San José. In Mexico, visit SETEJ (☎ 52-5-211-07-43), Hamburgo 305, Colonia Juarez, Mexico City for discount tickets and other deals.

Venezuela has some of the cheapest air-links to Central America. In Caracas, IVI Tours (☎ 02-993 60 82), residencia La Hacienda, Piso Bajo, Local 1-4-T, Final Avenida Principal de las Mercedes, is the agent for STA Travel in Venezuela and often has a range of good deals.

There are no shortage of travel agents in Rio de Janeiro. The Student Travel Bureau (☎ 021-259 0023), an affiliate of STA Travel, is at Rua Visconde de Piraja 550, Ipanema.

In Buenos Aires, deals are to be had at ASATEJ (☎ 011-4315 14570), Argentina's nonprofit student travel agency and the agent for STA Travel. The offices are at Florida 835, 3rd floor, Oficina 319-B, Buenos Aires.

America Central Corporation airlines (Aviateca, COPA, LACSA, NICA and TACA) predominate in the region, though Tikal Jets and Aerocaribe serve destinations in Mexico, and the latter flies to Havana, Cuba as well. If you're interested in flying among several different regional destinations, consider purchasing a Mayan Airpass or a Central American Airpass (see the Mayan Route Tickets section, earlier in this chapter). Otherwise, you can pick up a ticket between your desired destinations, though these can be expensive. Here are some sample fares, though the more research you do and flexibility you enjoy, the cheaper your flight will be. All the following round-trip fares are to Guatemala City unless otherwise noted.

Belize City (Flores)	US$160
Caracas	US$496
Cozumel	US$250
Havana	US$478
Mexico City	US$365
Quito	US$492
Palenque (Flores)	US$130
Rio de Janeiro	US$1099
San José	US$150
San Pedro Sula	US$110
San Salvador	US$156

Australia

There are a lot of competing airlines and a wide variety of fares from Australia to Guatemala, but no direct flights. Cheap flights from Australia generally go via Japan, Mexico City, Hawaii, Los Angeles or other US hub cities. Discount returns from Sydney to Los Angeles cost from A$1599. Cheap flights from the US to Guatemala are hard to find in Australia. The cheapest Los Angeles-Guatemala City fares are A$586 return (see The US section). A Sydney-Guatemala City return ticket via Los Angeles at the time of writing was A$2288.

Another option is Round-the-World (RTW) tickets, which are often the real bargains. Since getting to Latin America requires you fly halfway around the world anyway, it is oftentimes cheaper to just keep on going and circumnavigate the globe on a RTW than to do a U-turn on a round-trip ticket. A RTW fare originating in Australia and taking in Guatemala was A$2599 at the time of writing.

Quite a few Australian travel offices specialize in discount air tickets. Some travel agents, particularly smaller ones, advertise bargain fares in the travel sections of weekend newspapers, such as the *Age* in Melbourne and the *Sydney Morning Herald*.

Two well-known agents for cheap fares are STA Travel and Flight Centre. STA Travel (☎ 03-9349 2411) has its main office at 224 Faraday St, Carlton, VIC 3053, and offices in all major cities and on many university campuses. Call ☎ 131 776 Australia-wide for the location of your nearest branch or visit the Web site at www.statravel.com.au. Flight Centre (☎ 131 600 Australia-wide, www.flightcentre.com.au) has a central office at 82 Elizabeth St, Sydney and dozens of offices throughout Australia.

New Zealand

Again, Round-the-World (RTW) and Circle Pacific fares for travel from New Zealand are usually the best value, especially if you want to head down to South America after Guatemala. Depending on the carrier, you may have optional (and free) stopovers in Honolulu or Los Angeles, Australia or one of the Pacific Islands.

The *New Zealand Herald* has a travel section in which travel agents advertise fares. Flight Centre (☎ 09-309 6171) has a central office in Auckland at National Bank Towers (corner of Queen and Darby Sts) and many branches throughout the country. STA Travel (☎ 09-309 0458) has its main office at 10 High St, Auckland, and other offices in Auckland, Hamilton, Palmerston North, Wellington, Christchurch and Dunedin. Check out their internet site at www.statravel.com.au.

The published return fare from Auckland to Guatemala City via Los Angeles and Mexico City at the time of writing was NZ$2832. Tickets such as these allow you at least one free stopover (and sometimes as many as three), with additional stopovers available for a NZ$115 charge.

A fixed-date return fare from Auckland, New Zealand, to South America stopping in Los Angeles, Guatemala City and Lima is around NZ$4634. A far better price can be had for a RTW ticket originating in New Zealand and taking in Guatemala; at the time of writing the fare was NZ$2999.

The UK

Airline discounters in the UK are known as bucketshops. Discount air travel is big business in London, and it's here that you'll find the cheapest flights from Europe to Guatemala. Advertisements for many travel agents appear in the travel pages of the weekend broadsheets, such as the *Independent* on Saturday and the Sunday *Times*. Free magazines such as *TNT* are also a good resource for cheap fares; these are widely available in London, particularly near the main railway and underground stations.

A typical fixed-date return (excursion) fare from London to Guatemala City at the time of writing was UK£630.

For students or travelers under 26, popular travel agencies in the UK include STA Travel (☎ 020-7361 6161), which has an office at 86 Old Brompton Rd, London SW7 3LQ, and other offices in London and Manchester. Visit their Web site at www.statravel.co.uk. Usit Campus (☎ 020-7730 3402) has branches throughout the UK. The Web address is www.usitcampus.com. Both agencies sell tickets to all travelers but cater especially to young people and students. Charter flights work out as a cheaper alternative to scheduled flights, particularly if you are not a traveler of the student or under-26 variety.

Other recommended travel agencies include the following:

Bridge the World (☎ 020-7734 7447), 4 Regent Place, London W1R 5FB

Flightbookers (☎ 020-7757 2000), 177-178 Tottenham Court Rd, London W1P 9LF

Journey Latin America (☎ 44 208 747 3108, ✉ flights@journeylatinamerica.co.uk), 12 & 13 Heathfield Terrace, Chiswick London W4 4JE. There is another office in northern England (☎ 44 161 832 1441, fax: 44 161 832 1551, www.journeylatinamerica.co.uk), 2nd Floor Barton Arcade, 51 – 63 Deansgate, Manchester M3 2BH

Trailfinders (☎ 020-7938 3939)

Continental Europe

Though London is the discount travel capital of Europe, there are several other cities in which to find good deals. Generally however, don't expect much variation in fares for departures from the main European cities. All the major airlines are usually offering some sort of deal and travel agents generally have bargains available, so it pays to shop around.

Across Europe, many travel agencies have ties to STA Travel, where cheap tickets can be bought. Outlets in major cities include the following:

France

Voyages Wasteels (☎ 08 03 88 70 04 – this number can only be dialed from within France, fax 01 43 25 46 25), 11 rue Dupuytren, 756006 Paris

Germany

STA Travel (☎ 030-311 0950, fax 313 0948), Goethestrasse 73, 10625 Berlin

Greece

ISYTS (☎ 01-322 1267, fax 323 3767), 11 Nikis St, Upper floor, Syntagma Square, Athens

Italy

Passaggi (☎ 06-474 0923, fax 482 7436), Stazione Termini FS, Gelleria Di Tesla, Rome

France has a network of student travel agencies that sells discount tickets to travelers of all ages. OTU Voyages (☎ 01 44 41 38 50, www.otu.fr) has a central Parisian office at 39 ave Georges Bernanos (5e) and 42 offices around the country. Acceuil des Jeunes en France (☎ 01 42 77 87 80), 119 rue Saint Martin (4e), is another popular discount travel agency.

General agencies in Paris that offer some of the best services and deals includes Nouvelles Frontières (☎ 08 03 33 33 33, www .nouvelles-frontieres.com), 5 Ave de l'Opèra (1er); and Voyageurs du Monde (☎ 01 42 86 16 00), 55 rue Sainte Anne (2e).

Belgium, Switzerland and the Netherlands are also good places for buying discount air tickets. In Belgium, Acotra Student Travel Agency (☎ 02-512 86 07), at rue de la Madeline, Brussels, and WATS Reizen (☎ 03-226 16 26), at de Keyserlei 44, Antwerp, are both well-known agencies. In Switzerland, SSR Voyages (☎ 01-297 11 11, www.ssr.ch) specializes in student, youth and budget fares. In Zurich, there is a branch of SSR Voyages at Leonhardstrasse 10, and there are others in most major Swiss cities.

In the Netherlands, NBBS Reizen is the official student travel agency. The Amsterdam office (☎ 020-624 09 89) is at Rokin 66 and there are several other agencies around the city. Another recommended agency in Amsterdam is Malibu Travel (☎ 020-626 32 30), at Prinsengracht 230.

Here are some typical fixed-date return (excursion) fares to Guatemala City valid at the time of writing:

Amsterdam	f 2039
Brussels	BF 28,500
Frankfurt	DM 1557
Paris	FFr 4637
Rome	Lit 1384
Zurich	SwF 1340

LAND
Border Crossings

If you're departing from North America, you can travel overland through Mexico to Guatemala. Brownsville, Texas is the farthest point south in the United States before you hit the Mexican border. From here it is another 1500km to Guatemala. You can make this trip either by bus or private car (see Car & Motorcycle later in this chapter for details).

Real off-the-beaten-track border crossings from Guatemala to neighboring countries are largely a thing of the past; even the so-called 'jungle route' from eastern Guatemala to Honduras and heretofore obscure river crossings between the Petén and Mexico are becoming well trodden as of late. Courtesy is the rule when crossing borders. Travelers with all their paperwork in order should have no troubles at Guatemalan immigration.

Immigration officials sometimes request unofficial 'fees' from travelers crossing borders. Typically la mordida, the 'bite', is put on you in an official tone of voice: The officer will jot something on your tourist card or in a ledger, stamp your passport or do some other insignificant action, then say 'veinte quetzales' (20 quetzals) or something similar. If you're unlucky, surly or otherwise uncooperative, the officials on both sides of the border may play this game, causing you to part with a quantity of cash before you're finally through the formalities. Although some border fees are legitimate, the following advice will help you discern whether you're paying the real thing or being bilked.

When border officials demand money, ask for a receipt, *un recibo*. If the fee is legitimate, you'll be given an official-looking receipt; often officials will show you the ledger when they make the request, to prove to you that the fee is legitimate. If you don't get a receipt or the immigration official protests, you're experiencing the *mordida*, a tip or bribe.

Some travelers have had success completely ignoring officials' fee requests by just drifting away in a self-absorbed fog. If it's a legitimate fee, you'll be stopped, if not, you'll walk away without paying a cent. Still others have offered to pay the fee in an odd currency, Japanese yen or Norwegian krone for example, and been waved off by baffled officials who were not familiar with the funny money. When in doubt, try to observe what other travelers, both local and foreign, are paying (or not, as the case may be) before it's your turn.

Travelers have reported incidences of la mordida at the international airport in Flores; visitors arriving by air never have to pay a border fee here, so don't fall for this one.

Bus

If you are traveling overland from North America, you will have to change buses at the US-Mexican border; plans for buses from the interior of the US to the interior of Mexico that would preclude a change at the border have yet to be implemented. Note that buses within Mexico are way more efficient and expensive than their Guatemalan counterparts.

There are several international bus routes connecting Guatemala to Mexico and Guatemala to Belize, Honduras, El Salvador and points south. Tica Bus (see San Salvador in the following list) has daily service from Guatemala City to San Salvador, from where the bus continues to Tegucigalpa, Managua, San José and Panama City. When traveling between Guatemala and neighboring countries, you will often have the choice of a direct, 1st-class bus or a series of chicken buses. The latter option usually takes longer, but is always cheaper and infinitely more interesting. As you plan, refer to the following international bus routes originating in Guatemala City:

Belize City – US$55, 12 hours, 684km. Autopullman Línea Dorada (☎ 232-9658, 220-7990, *@* lineadorada@intelnet.net.gt), 16a Calle 10-55, Zona 1, has Thursday and Sunday departures at 8 pm. They return on Fridays and Mondays at 4 pm.

El Carmen/Talismán (Mexican border) – US$6, 5 to 6 hours, 275km. Transportes Galgos (☎ 232-3661, 253-4868), 7a Avenida 19-44, Zona 1, runs direct buses to this border-crossing point at 5:30 and 10 am, 1:30 and 3:30 pm. They also operate buses going all the way to Tapachula (Mexico); see Tapachula.

El Florido/Copán (Honduras) – US$3.50, 6 hours, 227km to El Florido. Has daily departures every 30 minutes to Chiquimula, where you change buses to continue on to the border at El Florido. See the Getting Around chapter for details on buses to El Florido.

La Mesilla/Ciudad Cuauhtémoc (Mexican border) – US$4.50, 7 hours, 345km. Transportes Velásquez, 20a Calle and 2a Avenida, Zona 1, has hourly buses from 8 am to 4 pm.

Managua – US$25, 14 hours, 667km. Very crowded, chicken bus leaves from 9a Avenida 15-10, Zona 1 daily at 1 pm. Get there at least 3 hours early.

Melchor de Mencos (Belize border) – 10 to 12 hours, 588km. Transportes Rosita buses leave from 15a Calle 9-58, Zona 1, at 3, 5 and 8 pm (US$8). Autopullman Línea Dorada has 1st-class buses departing daily from their terminal in Guatemala City at 8 pm to Melchor de Mencos via Santa Elena (US$30). They make the return trip every day at 6 pm.

San Salvador (El Salvador) – US$6.45, 5 hours, 268km. Melva Internacional (☎ 331-0874), 3a Avenida 1-38, Zona 9, runs buses via Cuilapa, Oratorio and Jalpatagua to the Salvadoran border at Valle Nuevo and onward to San Salvador hourly from 5 am to 4 pm. Tica Bus (☎ 261-1773, 331-4279, *@* ticabus@ticabus.com, www.ticabus.com), 11a Calle 2-72, Zona 9, has a daily departure at 1 pm (US$8.50 one-way, US$17 round-trip). From San Salvador, buses continue to all the other Central American capitals except Belize City. Confort Lines (☎ 332-6702), Avenida Las Américas and 2a Calle Zona 13, Edificio El Obelisco, Nivel 1, has luxury buses daily at 8 am and 2 pm (US$15 one-way, US$25 round-trip). Transportes King Quality (☎ 331-1761), 7a Avenida 14-44, Zona 9, Edificio La Galería, luxury buses depart at 6:30 am and 3:30 pm (US$20 one-way, US$35 round-trip), with connections to Tegucigalpa. Pulmantur (☎ 332-9797) has two daily luxury bus departures at 6:15 am and 3:15 pm from the Radisson Suites Villa Magna Hotel, 1a Avenida 12-43, Zona 10 (US$23 one way, US$45 round-trip).

Tapachula (Mexico) – US$22, 7 hours, 291km. Transportes Galgos, (☎ 253-4868, 232-3661), 7a Avenida 19-44, Zona 1, has direct buses at 7:30 am and 1:30 pm. (From Tapachula they depart for Guatemala City at 9:30 am and 1:30 pm.) These buses cross the border at El Carmen/Talismán and go into Mexico as far as Tapachula, where they connect with Mexican buses.

Tecún Umán/Ciudad Hidalgo (Mexican border) – US$4.50, 5 hours, 248km. Transportes Fortaleza (☎ 232-3643, 251-7994), 19 Calle 8-70, Zona 1, has 30 daily departures from 1:30 am to 7:15 pm.

Car & Motorcycle

For some travelers, driving to Guatemala via the US and/or Mexico is an attractive option. If you have plenty of time, patience and good humor, driving may be for you. It's good to be somewhat savvy as to the mechanics of your car or bike, and keeping an emergency cash stash for the unforeseen breakdown, mishap or bribe request is recommended. There is a lot of paperwork involved with driving into Guatemala, and it's a good idea to know what you're getting into before committing to this type of adventure (for more details on cars and paperwork, see Vehicle Documents in the Visas & Documents section of the Facts for the Visitor chapter).

Parts will likely be hard to find in Guatemala; spiffy, new-ish vehicles with sophisticated electronics and emissions-control systems will be a challenge to repair here. Old Toyota pickups are ubiquitous, though, and may be the best make to drive into Guatemala, as parts and mechanics will be more widely available.

Shuttle Minibus

Shuttle minibuses are becoming increasingly popular as Guatemala begins to attract independent travelers with more money on their hands than time. International routes served include Antigua to Copán in Honduras, Flores to Belize City, Flores to Chetumal in Mexico, Flores to Palenque and Panajachel to La Mesilla or Tecún Umán, both on the Mexican border. You can arrange international shuttle transport easiest in Antigua, Panajachel or Flores.

Though tourist minibuses are fast, they are comparatively expensive and are an armed-bandit magnet with their 'tourists on board' stickers.

SEA

Aside from sailing your own boat, few ocean approaches exist to Guatemala. There are daily departures from Punta Gorda in Belize to Puerto Barrios on the Caribbean coast and two regularly scheduled boats a week between Punta Gorda and Lívingston. Passage from Omoa in Honduras to Lívingston is also possible twice a week, though it may be difficult to arrange in the low season. Generally, it is easiest to arrange sea passage to and from Puerto Barrios, as this is an active transit point.

If arriving or departing by sea, make sure you get your exit and entry stamps at the appropriate immigration offices in both countries. Sometimes, if you're caught up in your travel experience, it's easy to forget you're crossing national boundaries when they're underwater.

RIVER

There are three river crossings from Chiapas in Mexico to the Petén in Guatemala. These are good, adventurous alternatives for travelers wishing to visit the ruins of Palenque and Tikal in one trip. All three options involve a not-too-arduous bus and boat combination, though prepare for the unexpected whenever your Guatemalan itinerary calls for river travel. Tour operators in Palenque and Flores offer these trips at a cost. See the El Petén chapter for the full scoop on these trips.

One popular route is via La Palma (Mexico) and the Río San Pedro to El Naranjo in Guatemala. The predawn bus from Tenosique drops you in La Palma, where there is an immigration post and many *lancheros* (the people who pilot the boats) waiting to take passengers up the Río San Pedro to El Naranjo (US$20 per person, two hours). Buses to Flores depart regularly from El Naranjo, so it is possible to make it from Palenque to Flores in one long day.

If you start early and make smooth connections, the quickest river route is via Frontera Corozal (Mexico) to Cooperativa Bethel in Guatemala. This route takes you up the well-traveled Usumacinta River and can get you from Palenque to Flores in a day as well. From Frontera Corozal it's a half hour trip upriver to Bethel from where there are regularly scheduled buses to Santa Elena/Flores.

The least trodden river route is via Benemérito in Mexico to Sayaxché on the Río de la Pasión; passage may be hard to arrange for solo travelers or during the off season when there isn't much traffic. From Benemérito there are cargo boats that make the eight hour trip up the Río de la Pasión when enough people and goods need to go. The Guatemalan border post is at Pipiles on the river; don't forget to get your passport stamped.

ORGANIZED TOURS

While there are many well-regarded organized tour operators within Guatemala (see the Getting Around chapter for details), travelers with limited time or experience may want to arrange a tour from home. These will almost always be more expensive than a similar package arranged in Guatemala, however.

Travelers in search of a thematic trip (for example, archaeology or birding) led by experts, may be interested in organized tours as well. Whatever your reasoning for taking an organized trip, tour operators should be available to answer any questions

or concerns you have well before departure and be willing to provide a detailed itinerary upon request. Read the fine print and be aware of exactly what the tour price includes. The following operators offer tours to Guatemala:

Ceiba Adventures (☎ 800-217-1060, 520-527-0171, fax 520-527-8127, ☻ ceiba@primenet.com), PO Box 2274, Flagstaff, AZ 86003 USA. This company offers white-water rafting trips to some of the most inaccessible Mayan ruins in the Petén.

Guatemala Unlimited (☎ 800-733-3350, 510-496-0631, 510-496-0632, ☻ guatemala1@aol.com, hometown.aol.com/guatemala1/html/guatunl.htm), 1212 Broadway, Suite 910, Oakland, CA 94612 USA. This company offers general and deep-sea fishing tours, plus interesting trips to archaeological sites (including Yaxjá and Mixco Viejo) not visited by many tour groups.

Highland Guatemala Tours (☎ 503-236-5849, contact ☻ info@shamanictours.com, www.shamanictours.com), PO Box 71641, Eugene, OR 97401 USA. This company specializes in shaman tours and Mayan cosmology.

Journey Latin America (☎ 44 208 747 8315, fax 44 208 742 1312, ☻ tours@journeylatinamerica.co.uk, www.journeylatinamerica.co.uk), 12 & 13 Heathfield Terrace, Chiswick, London W4 4JEU K. A second office (☎ 44 161 832 1441, fax 44 161 832 1551, ☻ man@journeylatinamerica.co.uk) is at 2nd Floor Barton Arcade, 51-63 Deansgate, Manchester M3 2BH UK. This company arranges individual or group itineraries, from the adventurous to luxurious.

Lost World Adventures (☎ 800-999-0558, or contact ☻ info@lostworldadventures.com, www.lostworldadventures.com), 112 Church St, Decatur, GA 30030 USA. This outfit arranges tours of the highlands, Petén and similar destinations of interest to the general traveler.

Offbeat Adventures (☎ 905 509 4494, fax 905 509 0444, contact ☻ offbeat@sympatico.ca, www.offbeatadventures.com), 284 Lancrest St, Pickering Ontario, Canada L1V 6N3. This company offers tours to ruins, beaches and volcanoes with scuba certification and snorkeling options.

Yax Pac Tours (☎/fax 41-01 432 62 92,☻webmaster@yaxpactours.com, www.yaxpactours.com), in Switzerland, contact Susette Isenschmied, Grimselstrasse 28, 8048 Zürich. This company runs tours long on adventure, short on comfort; recommended for backpackers who want a little structure.

There are many more tour operators than it is possible to list here. For further ideas about organized tours, it may be worth a visit to the Guatemalan Resource Page at the helpful Web site at www.gorp.com \gorp\location\latamer\guatemal.htm.

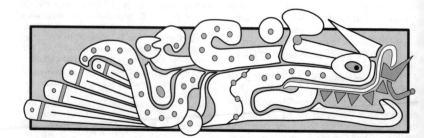

Getting Around

Buses are the cheapest and most accessible way to get around Guatemala. Though bus travel gives you the best feel for local life, not everyone has the time or patience to ride cheek by jowl with the masses and their produce (vegetable *and* animal). Luckily, domestic air travel is on the rise with new routes and airports – or at least serviceable strips – permitting speedy access to farther-off destinations.

Rental cars are expensive, and navigating very narrow roads alongside hell-bent drivers is no treat. In most cases you cannot drive a rental car across the border, which will be a consideration for folks wishing to visit Copán in Honduras. To do so, you'll need permission in writing from the car rental company.

AIR

Guatemala claims several active airports, though not all of them are operable year round. If you're traveling during the high season (December and January, Easter and June through August), however, flights should be available.

In addition to the international airports in Guatemala City and Santa Elena/Flores, there are airports in the following cities: Coatepeque, Cobán, Huehuetenango, Playa Grande, Puerto Barrios, Quetzaltenango, Quiché, Retalhuleu and Río Dulce. You can also fly into a strip near Copán in Honduras with Aereo Ruta Maya/Jungle Flying Tours (see the Getting There & Away chapter for details). Aircraft servicing these destinations will most likely be small, two-propeller passenger planes. Most of these planes have a per-passenger baggage limit of 20 pounds; you must pay extra for anything over the limit. Also, there is a US$0.65 domestic departure tax levied on domestic flights.

You can avoid some laborious, time-consuming trips by flying between points. The following chart shows some popular routes and one-way fares.

Guatemala City-Copán	US$96
Guatemala City-Flores (Tikal)	US$50-85
Guatemala City-Huehuetenango	US$55
Guatemala City-Puerto Barrios	US$50
Guatemala City-Quetzaltenango	US$40
Puerto Barrios-Flores	US$65

For schedules, see the individual regional sections.

BUS

The prevalent means of transport is bus. Guatemalan buses are something to behold, as the majority of them are ancient, resurrected school buses from the US and Canada. It is not unusual for a local family of five to squeeze into seats designed for two child-sized butts. These vehicles are known as chicken buses after the live cargo accompanying many passengers. Chicken buses are frequent and cheap. Expect to pay US$1 (or less!) for an hour of travel on these buses.

Chicken buses will stop anywhere, for anyone, if there is even a remote chance of wedging them in someplace. When you approach a bus, helpers will yell '*hay lugares!*' (eye loo-gar-ays), which literally means 'there are spaces.' This is clearly subjective, as the space to which they refer may be a sliver of air and light between hundreds of locals mashed against one another. These same helpers will also yell the destination of their bus in voices of varying hilarity and cadence; just listen for the song of your town. Tall travelers will be especially challenged on these buses. To catch a chicken bus, simply stand by the side of the road in the direction you're heading with your arm extended out parallel to the ground.

Popular routes, especially between big cities, are serviced by more luxurious Pullman or *especial* buses. These may have bathrooms, televisions and in some cases, food service. Pullmans are the most expensive option, but not all are worth the extra money as they can be as crowded as chicken buses. Some bus companies are infamous for standing-room-only Pullman coaches.

In general, you'll find more bus departures in the morning (some leave as early as 3 am) than in the afternoon. Bus traffic drops off precipitously after about 4 pm; night buses are rare indeed and not recommended regardless. The exception is the overnight Pullman from Guatemala City to Flores, which used to be considered dangerous, but has not experienced any trouble of note in several years. The farther off the beaten track you veer, the earlier bus services start and stop.

Remote towns and villages may or may not have bus services. If not, pickup trucks serve as de facto buses; you hail them and pay them as if they were the genuine article. Often buses from far off villages are a means for locals to transport goods to market in larger towns. In this case, buses depart from the village wicked early in the morning and return from the market town by mid-afternoon. If you want to visit such a village, you may have to take an afternoon bus and stay the night or hitch a ride back on a pickup, though reverse traffic on market day can be slow.

There are several important crossroads, called *cruces* or *tronques*, from where you can change buses or hail pickups to all different parts of the country. Chimaltenango is the closest junction to Antigua; Los Encuentros and Cuatros Caminos are important for getting to points farther north. In Alta Verapaz, Sebol or San Antonio are the crossroads for rides into the Petén. Finally, La Ruidosa is where the Río Dulce and Puerto Barrios roads meet.

Though cheap and chock-full of blithe Guatemalan families, buses (and pickups) can be dangerous. At least a couple of times a month, a bus plunges over a cliff or rounds a blind bend into a head-on collision. Newspapers are full of gory details and diagrams of the latest wreck, which doesn't foster endearing feelings toward Guatemalan public transportation.

Guatemala City has no central bus terminal, though if you ask, locals will probably refer you to the Terminal de Autobuses in Zona 4. Ticket offices and departure points are different for each company. Many are near the huge, chaotic market in Zona 4. If the bus you want is one of these, go to the market and ask until you find it; this is a snap, as men working for the bus companies actively recruit passengers and will probably find you before you find the bus. The following Guatemala City bus in-

Chicken buses will stop anywhere for anyone.

formation should get you most places you want to go:

Amatitlán – US$0.30, 30 minutes, 25km; 30 buses depart from 20a Calle & 2a Avenida, Zona 1, every half-hour from 7 am to 7 pm. Also see Puerto San José.

Antigua – US$0.50, 1 hour, 45km; Transportes Unidos (☎ 232-4949, 253-6929), 15 Calle 3-65, Zona 1, makes the trip every half-hour from 7 am to 7 pm, stopping in San Lucas Sacatepéquez. Other buses depart more frequently, every 15 minutes from around 4 am to 7 pm, from the lot at 18a Calle and 4a Avenida, Zona 1.

Autosafari Chapín – US$1, 1½ hours, 88km; Delta y Tropical, 1a Calle & 2a Avenida, Zona 4, runs buses every 30 minutes via Escuintla.

Biotopo del Quetzal – US$2.20, 3 hours, 156km; Escobar y Monja Blanca, 8a Avenida 15-16, Zona 1, has hourly buses, 4 am to 5 pm via El Rancho and Purulhá.

Chichicastenango – US$1.45, 3½ hours, 144km; Veloz Quichelense, Terminal de Buses, Zona 4, runs buses every half-hour from 5 am to 6 pm, stopping in San Lucas, Chimaltenango and Los Encuentros. Many go to Quiché and Nebaj.

Chiquimula – US$3, 3 hours, 169km; Rutas Orientales (☎ 253-7282, 251-2160), 19 Calle 8-18, Zona 1, runs buses via El Rancho, Río Hondo and Zacapa to Chiquimula every 30 minutes from 5 am to 6 pm. Next door, Transportes Guerra has five daily departures (US$2.30). If you're heading for Copán, Honduras, change buses at Chiquimula to continue to the border.

Cobán – US$3.60, 4 hours, 213km; Escobar Monja Blanca (☎ 251-1878), 8a Avenida 15-16, Zona 1, has buses hourly from 4 am to 5 pm, stopping at El Rancho, the Biotopo del Quetzal, Purulhá, Tactic and San Cristóbal. Pullman and regular service buses are also available.

El Estor – US$7.75, 4 hours, 216km; Fuentes del Norte (☎ 238-3894, 251-3817), 17a Calle 8-46, Zona 1, has one daily departure at 10 am.

Escuintla – US$1.15, 1 hour, 57km; see Autosafari Chapín, La Democracia, Monterrico, Puerto San José and Tecún Umán.

Esquipulas – US$3.10, 4 hours, 222km; Rutas Orientales (☎ 253-7282, 251-2160), 19a Calle 8-18, Zona 1, has buses departing every half-hour from 5 am to 6 pm, with stops at El Rancho, Río Hondo, Zacapa and Chiquimula.

Flores (Petén) – US$10.30, 12 hours, 488km; Fuentes del Norte (☎ 238-3894, 251-3817), 17a Calle 8-46, Zona 1, runs over a dozen daily buses departing from the capital and stopping at Río Dulce and Poptún. Their Maya del Oro service (US$19.50) departs at 8 pm daily. Máxima (☎ 232-2495, 238-4032), 9a Avenida 17-28, Zona 1, has buses departing at 4, 6 and 8 pm. Autopullman Línea Dorada (☎ 232-9658, 220-7990, ✉ lineadorada@intelnet.net.gt), 16a Calle 10-55, Zona 1, has three luxury buses daily at 9 am and 8 and 9 pm (US$30, eight hours). Buses stop at Río Dulce and Poptún. Buses usually leave Guatemala City and Santa Elena full; anyone getting on midway stands. Transportes Rosita, 15a Calle 9-58, Zona 1, has chicken bus departures at 3, 5 and 8 pm (US$6.45, 12 hours).

Huehuetenango – US$3.75, 5 hours, 266km; Los Halcones, 7a Avenida 15-27, Zona 1, runs three buses a day (7 am and 2 and 5 pm) up the Interamericana to Huehue, stopping at Chimaltenango, Patzicía, Tecpán, Los Encuentros, San Cristóbal and Totonicapán. Buses to La Mesilla also stop here; see La Mesilla.

Jalapa – US$1.30, 3 hours, 81km; Transportes Unidos Jalapanecos (☎ 238-3418), 22a Calle 1-20, Zona 1, has departures every half-hour from 4 am to 6 pm.

La Democracia – US$1, 2 hours, 92km; Chatla Gomerana, Muelle Central, Terminal de Autobuses, Zona 4, has buses every half-hour from 6 am to 4:30 pm, stopping at Escuintla, Siquinalá (change for Santa Lucía Cotzumalguapa), La Democracia, La Gomera and Sipacate.

La Mesilla/Ciudad Cuauhtémoc (Mexican border) – US$4.50, 7 hours, 345km; Transportes Velásquez, 20a Calle & 2a Avenida, Zona 1, has buses going to La Mesilla, on the Interamericana at the border with Mexico, hourly from 8 am to 4 pm. Stops are at Los Encuentros, Totonicapán and Huehuetenango.

Livingston – see Puerto Barrios.

Monterrico – US$1.50, 4 hours, 124km; Transportes Cubanita, Muelle Central, Terminal de Buses, Zona 4, has buses departing at 10:30 am, 12:30 and 2:30 pm, stopping at Escuintla, Taxisco and La Avellana.

Nebaj – 7½ hours, 235 km; see Chichicastenango

Panajachel – US$1.70, 3 hours, 148km; Transportes Rébuli (☎ 251-3521), 21a Calle 1-34, Zona 1, departs for Lago de Atitlán and Panajachel hourly from 7 am to 4 pm, stopping at Chimaltenango, Patzicía, Tecpán Guatemala (for the ruins at Iximché), Los Encuentros and Sololá. They also have one daily Pullman departure from Antigua (US$3.20, two hours, 146km).

Poptún – see Flores.

Puerto Barrios – US$5.15, 5 hours, 295km; Transportes Litegua (☎ 232-7578, 253-8169), 15a Calle 10-40, Zona 1, has *especial* buses at 6, 6:30, 7:30, 10, 10:30, 11:30 am, 12:30, 2, 2:30, 4, 4:30 and 5 pm, with stops at El Rancho, Teculután, Río Hondo, Los Amates and Quiriguá. There are also a dozen regular buses (US$3.85) a day. Boats run from Puerto Barrios to Lívingston until about 5 pm.

Puerto San José – 2 hours, 106km; Transportes Esmeralda (☎ 471-0327), Trebol, Zona 12, operates buses every 10 minutes from 5 am to 8 pm, stopping at Amatitlán, Palín and Escuintla.

Quetzaltenango – US$3.60, 4 hours, 206km; Transportes Alamo (☎ 253-0219), 21a Calle 1-14, Zona 1, has buses at 8 and 10 am, 12:45, 3 and 5:45 pm. Líneas América (☎ 232-1432), 2a Avenida 18-47, Zona 1, has buses departing at 5:15 and 9:15 am, noon, 3:15, 4:40 and 7:30 pm. Transportes Galgos (☎ 253-6312, 232-3661), 7a Avenida 19-44, Zona 1, makes this run at 5:30, 8:30 and 11 am, and 12:30, 2:30, 5 and 7 pm. These buses stop at Chimaltenango, Los Encuentros and San Cristóbal.

Quiché – 3 hours, 163km; see Chichicastenango.

Quiriguá – see Puerto Barrios.

Retalhuleu – US$3.65, 3 hours, 186km; see El Carmen and Tecún Umán.

Río Dulce – US$4.50, 5 hours, 274km; Transportes Litegua (☎ 232-7578, 253-8169), 15a Calle 10-40, Zona 1, daily at 6 and 9 am and 1 pm; see Flores.

Río Hondo – see Chiquimula, Esquipulas and Puerto Barrios.

San Pedro La Laguna, on Lago de Atitlán – US$2.65, 3 to 4 hours, 170km; Ruta Méndez, 21a Calle & 5a Avenida, Zona 1, operates buses at 10 and 11 am, noon and 1 pm.

Santa Elena – see Flores.

Santa Lucía Cotzumalguapa – see La Democracia and Tecún Umán.

Sayaxché – US$9, 11 hours, 397km; Fuentes del Norte (☎ 238-3894, 251-3817), 17a Calle 8-46, Zona 1, has one daily departure at 4:30 pm.

Tecún Umán/Ciudad Hidalgo (Mexican border) – US$4.50, 5 hours, 248km; Transportes Fortaleza (☎ 232-3643, 251-7994), 19 Calle 8-70, Zona 1, hourly from 1:30 am to 7:15 pm, stopping at Escuintla (change for Santa Lucía Cotzumalguapa), Mazatenango, Retalhuleu and Coatepeque.

Tikal – see Flores.

Distances & Travel Times

It's possible to get from almost any point in Guatemala to almost any other point by bus. What follows is a summary of distances and travel times.

The following distances and approximate travel times are from Guatemala City.

destination	distance	time
Antigua	45km	1 hour
Monterrico	124km	4 hours
Copán Ruinas	240km	7.5 hours
Puerto Barrios	295km	5 hours
Cobán	213km	4 hours
Flores	488km	12 hours
Huehuetenango	266km	5 hours
Chichicastenango	144km	3.5 hours
Quetzaltenango	206km	4 hours
Ciudad Tecún Umán	248km	5 hours

A few distances and approximate travel times from Flores follow.

destination	distance	time
Bethel	127km	4 hours
El Naranjo	131km	5 hours
Tikal	71km	1 hour
Melchor de Mencos	100km	2 hours
Poptún	113km	2 hours

Below are distances and approximate travel times between various destinations within Guatemala.

from/to	distance	time
Río Dulce-Poptún	95km	3 hours
Poptún-Fray BLC	100km	5 hours
Fray BLC-Cobán	101km	5 hours
Huehuetenango-La Mesilla	79km	2 hours
Quetzaltenango-El Carmen	69km	2 hours

CAR & MOTORCYCLE

Driving a car or motorcycle in Guatemala means you can travel where you want, when you want. For some, a van is even more attractive, as it negates the need for hotels night in and night out. The major issues to consider are whether you can make repairs, how you'll secure your vehicle in big cities and how comfortable you are driving in a foreign country with different and screwy road rules. Wannabe bikers should take into account the rainy season and likelihood of inclement weather before donning the leathers and zooming off into the sunset. The bureaucracy involved with importing private vehicles is substantial. See the Getting There & Away chapter to familiarize yourself with the paperwork rigmarole before committing to this type of trip.

There are three types of fuel available in Guatemala. Regular (87 octane) costs around US$1.75 a gallon; premium or super (91 octane) costs US$1.90 a gallon. Diesel fuel is widely available and costs about US$1.25 a gallon.

Road Rules

Local driving etiquette may be very different from what you're used to back home: passing on blind curves, ceding the right of way to cars coming uphill on narrow passes and deafening honking for no apparent reason are just the start. Expect no road signs in Guatemala. They are very rare, but a pleasant surprise when they pop up and are actually accurate. A tree branch or other foreign matter in the middle of the road means trouble up ahead – a breakdown or rock slide perhaps – and you should slow down and drive carefully in this situation. A vehicle coming uphill always has the right of way. *Tumulos* are speed bumps which are generously (sometimes oddly) placed throughout the country, usually on the main drag through a town.

Speaking Spanish will go a long way toward making a driving trip a more enjoyable trip. At least learn some car and directional lingo before you set off. Driving at night is a bad idea for many reasons, not the least of which are armed bandits, drunk drivers and decreased visibility.

Rental

Rental cars are expensive: Expect to pay around US$50 to US$75 a day, not including gas. Trucks, minivans and 4WD vehicles are also available. Insurance policies accompanying rental cars may not protect you from loss or theft, in which case you can be liable

for US$600 to US$1500 or more in damages. Be careful where you park, especially in Guatemala City and at night. Motorcycles can be rented in Antigua and Panajachel. Although not required by law, safety gear such as a helmet and gloves are recommended for motorcyclists.

To rent a car or motorcycle you need to show your passport, driver's license and a major credit card. Usually, the person renting the vehicle must be 25 years or older. If you are not the holder of a valid credit card, you may be able to leave a large cash deposit. Obviously, an official receipt would be needed in this event. Guatemala has both international and local rental car companies. If you want to rent a car before your arrival, try one of the following companies at their toll-free number in the US or visit their Web sites:

Avis	☎ 800-230-4898
Budget	☎ 800-527-0700
Dollar	☎ 800-800-4000
Hertz	☎ 800-654-3131
National	☎ 888-227-7368
Thrifty	☎ 800-367-2277

BICYCLE

Cycling is coming into its own in Guatemala: Not only can you rent bikes in several cities, you can also take mountain-bike tours or hit the hills independently (see Cycling in the Activities section of the Facts for the Visitor chapter). Bikes can be rented in Antigua (probably the least attractive place for cycling around town, as all the streets are cobblestone), Flores, Panajachel and Quetzaltenango.

Long-distance road cycling can be dangerous, as few drivers are accustomed to sharing the roads with bikes; be aware at all times and equip your bike with the proper mirrors and safety equipment such as reflectors.

HITCHHIKING

Hitchhiking in the strict sense of the word is not practiced in Guatemala because it is not safe. However, where the bus services are sporadic or nonexistent, pickup trucks and other vehicles serve as supplemental forms of public transport. If you stand by the side of the road with your arm out, someone will stop. You are expected to pay the drivers as if it were a bus and the fares will be similar. This is a safe and reliable system used by locals and travelers, and the only inconvenience you're likely to encounter is full to overflowing vehicles – get used to it.

Your best bet for free rides is with other foreign tourists who have their own vehicles. Occasionally, Guatemalans will give you a free lift, but don't assume this to be the case: Always offer to pay.

BOAT

Speedy motorboats called *lanchas* are becoming the transport of choice on Lago de Atitlán and between Puerto Barrios and Lívingston. Bigger, slower and cheaper ferries run sporadically on these routes, but have been largely discontinued in favor of the faster but more dangerous motorboats. Lívingston and Río Dulce are also serviced by lanchas. Río Dulce is the perfect place to learn how to paddle a traditional dugout canoe while exploring the area.

Dugout canoes and motorboats are also used on Lago Petén Itzá near Flores and within the mangrove forests near Monterrico. A few of Guatemala's natural parks and reserves (eg, Bocas de Polochic) and archaeological sites (eg, Ceibal) are accessible only – or preferably – by water (see Parks & Protected Areas in the Facts about Guatemala chapter).

There is boat service connecting Punta Gorda, in southern Belize, with Lívingston and Puerto Barrios, and Omoa in Honduras. The three border crossings between the Petén and Palenque in Mexico also involve boat travel. Also, the only way to get to the Carribean coast town of Lívingston is by boat. The trip from Puerto Barrios takes about an hour.

LOCAL TRANSPORTATION
Bus

Local buses are crowded and cheap. In Guatemala City there are two types of local buses, the sort-of dilapidated and the super dilapidated. The first type are called *servicio preferencial*, are usually bright red and cost US$0.15. Worse are buses of the latter type; they are very cramped and ratty, but cost a mere US$0.10. In many places the buses are insufficient to meet demand, and thus tend to be packed. Guatemalan buses run on diesel, which causes them to belch noxious smoke and pollution at every turn.

Shuttle Minibus

Shuttle minibuses (typically minivans) run between many popular tourist destinations. The shuttle routes you're most likely to use are from La Aurora International Airport-Antigua, Antigua-Panajachel and Flores-Tikal. Tourist shuttles are not for budget travelers; it is always cheaper to travel by chicken bus. For example, from Antigua to Panajachel on local buses it's US$2.45; on a shuttle it is US$9.

Taxi

Few Guatemalan taxis are metered and fares are quite expensive. Determine the price of the trip before setting out, writing it on a slip of paper as proof, if necessary. Rates are set, but drivers will often quote a higher price, especially at the airport. If you don't like the price quoted, walk away. There's usually another cab to be found.

Boat

Lakeside villages on Lago de Atitlán and Lago de Petén Itzá use boats for local transport. For pennies you can hop a boat from Flores to Santa Elena or San Benito, and to San Andrés or San José for not much more. Even the smallest towns around Lago de Atitlán will have some kind of makeshift pier at which to dock.

Horse

Riding is more for pleasure than transport, though many in the mountains still rely on their beasts of burden, and longer trips into remote regions of the Petén utilize horses or mules. Horses can be hired in Antigua and some of the villages near Lago de

Atitlán; in San Pedro La Laguna horses are popular for the trek up Volcán San Pedro.

ORGANIZED TOURS

Guatemala is becoming a travel hot spot, and the quantity of locally organized tours reflect this growing popularity. White-water rafting trips to archaeological sites or simply a general tour of the country are most easily arranged from Guatemala City, Antigua or Flores. Local tours can be cheap or expensive depending on the tour's breadth, the guide, accommodations and type of transport. Here is a selection of local, recommended tour operators:

Area Verde Expeditions (☎/fax 719-583-8929, ✉ guatemala@areaverde.com, www.adventure sports.com/kayak/areaverd/welcome.htm), 1a Avenida Sur No 15, Antigua, offers white-water rafting and kayaking trips, plus general tours.

Aventuras Turísticas (☎ 951-4213, ☎/fax 951-4214), 3a Calle 2-38, Zona 3, Cobán, has a host of tours in the Verapaces and El Petén, plus they will customize tours.

Aventuras Vacacionales (☎/fax 832-3352, ✉ sailing@conexion.com, www.sailing.conexion .com), 1a Avenida Sur No 11B, Antigua, arranges seven-day sailing tours to the Belizean reef from Río Dulce on the catamaran *Las Sirenas*.

AVINSA Tikal Travel (☎ 926-0808, fax 926-0807, ✉ info@tikaltravel.com, www.tikaltravel.com), 4a Calle, Santa Elena, has trips with horseback, hiking and camping to remote sites in the Petén including Yaxjá and Nakum. They can also arrange sailing trips that go from Río Dulce to Belize.

Clark Tours (☎ 339-2888, fax 339-2909, ✉ clark@ guate.net, www.clarktours.com.gt), Centro Gerencial Las Maragritas, Diagonal 6 10-01, Torre II, Zona 10, Guatemala City, is the oldest tour operator in the country and offers high-end luxury trips to the most popular destinations.

Ecotourism & Adventure Specialists (☎ 361-3104, fax 334-0453, ✉ info@ecotourism-adventure .com), Avenida La Reforma 8-60, Zona 9, Guatemala City, offers extreme sports tours and ecologically sensitive jungle adventures to rarely visited sites. They have expert guides and can co-ordinate trips with their satellite offices in Belize, Mexico and Honduras. English, Spanish and Hebrew are spoken, and their Web site, www.ecotourism-adventure.com, has a Japanese version.

EcoMaya (☎ 926-1363, 926-3321, fax 926-3322, ✉ ecomaya@guate.net, www.ecomaya.com), Calle 30 de Junio, Flores, runs hardcore adventure trips to the jungle areas and archaeological sites of El Mirador, El Perú, El Zotz and Tikal.

Guatemalan Birding Resource Center (☎ 767-7339, contact ✉ birdguatemala@latinmail.com, www. xelapages.com/gbrc), 7a Calle 15-18, Zona 1, Quetzaltenango – in the US contact Anne M Berry (☎ 317-842-1494), 7361 Hawthorne Ln, Indianapolis, IN 46250 – offers birding tours to the Pacific coast and the Highlands.

Maya Expeditions (☎ 363-4955/65, ☎/fax 337-4666, ✉ mayaexp@guate.net), 15a Calle 1-91, Zona 10, Local 104, Guatemala City, runs one- to five-day rafting trips. In Antigua, contact Sin Fronteras (☎ 832-1017, ☎/fax 832-2674), 3a Calle Poniente No 12.

Monkey Eco Tours (☎ 201-0759, fax 926-0807; in the US fax 978-945-6486, ✉ nitun@nitun.com, www.nitun.com), run by the Ni'tun Ecolodge, San Andrés, Petén. This company has luxury adventure jungle trips with specialist guides including archaeologists, biologists and ecologists.

Old Town Outfitters (☎ 832-4243, ✉ trvlnlite@ hotmail.com, www.bikeguatemala.com), 6a Calle Poniente No 7, Antigua, specializes in mountain biking, hiking and volcano tours – 'we summit any volcano' is their motto.

Proyecto EcoQuetzal (☎/fax 952-1047, ✉ bidaspeq@guate.net, www.granjaguar.com/ peq), 2a Calle 14-36, Zona 1, Cobán, arranges full-immersion ethnotourism trips to Q'eqchi' villages and builds quetzal-viewing platforms 10m from nesting birds; available from March to June, one month prior reservation is required for the viewing platforms.

Quetzalventures (☎ 761-2470, contact ✉ info@ quetzalventures.com, www.quetzalventures .com), Diagonal 12 8-37, Zona 1, Quetzaltenango, offers three types of tours: traditional, adventure and budget adventure, including diving, rafting, bungee jumping and Spanish classes. All profits go to the Xela nonprofit Escuela de la Calle.

Unicornio Azul (☎ 205-9328, fax 764-2098), Chancol, Huehuetenango, offers horseback riding and camping trips in the Cuchumatanes.

Vision Travel & Information Services (☎ 832-3293, 832-1962, fax 832-1955, contact ✉ vision@ guatemalainfo.com, www.guatemalainfo.com), 3a Avenida Norte No 3, Antigua, offers all manner of tours to the Highlands, Tikal, Copán and Lago de Atitlán. They offer special tours for Día de los Todos Santos and Easter.

Guatemala City

• **pop 2 million** • **elevation 1500m**

Guatemala's capital city, the largest urban agglomeration in Central America, spreads across a flattened mountain range run through by deep ravines. It's not a pretty site.

Initially, the sprawl and smog may remind you of Mexico City, that mighty Latin megalopolis to the north. But Guatemala City (or Guate as it's referred to locally) has a distinct flavor. There's the huge and chaotic market, bursting with

enough sounds, colors and odors to stun even the well-initiated. There are the rickety urban buses chugging along in clouds of diesel, trolling for ever more passengers. And there are the street urchin orphans and poverty-stricken outlying areas: shantytowns overflowing with displaced war victims who fled the countryside while the army and guerrillas battled it out, leveling their hometowns in the process.

There are few colonial buildings sprucing up Guate, a fairly young city. The colonial buildings and ruins are all in nearby Antigua, the former capital. Little architecture in Guatemala City is stunning or notable, but at least most of the buildings are only five or six stories high, allowing light to flood the narrow streets – a small consolation for travelers finding themselves here.

The few interesting sights in Guatemala City may be seen in a day or two. Many travelers skip the city altogether, preferring to make Antigua their base. Still, you may need to get acquainted with the capital because this is the hub of the country, where all transportation lines meet and all services are available.

HISTORY

Sitting on top of three tectonic plates, Guatemala has suffered its fair share of earthquakes, and Guatemala City is all too well acquainted with Mother Nature in this regard; the devastating *temblor* of July 29, 1773 resulted in its founding. Prior to that, the Spanish capital of Central America was at La Ciudad de Santiago de los Caballeros de Guatemala, known today as Antigua Guatemala (or simply Antigua), in the Panchoy valley. The 1773 earthquake razed much of the colonial capital, and the government decided to move its headquarters to La Ermita valley, the present site of Guatemala City, hoping to escape any such further terrible destruction. On September 27, 1775, King

114

Carlos III of Spain signed a royal charter for the founding of La Nueva Guatemala de la Asunción, and Guatemala City was officially born.

Unfortunately, the colonial powers didn't move the capital far enough or fast enough, for earthquakes in 1917, 1918 and 1976 rocked the capital and beyond, reducing buildings to rubble. The 1976 quake killed nearly 23,000, injured another 75,000 and left an estimated one million homeless. The city's comparatively recent founding and its history of earthquakes have left little to see in the way of colonial churches, palaces or quaint old neighborhoods.

ORIENTATION
Streets
Guatemala City, like (almost) all Guatemalan towns, is laid out on a street grid that is logical and easy to use. Avenidas run north-south; calles run east-west. Streets are usually numbered from north and west (lowest) to south and east (highest); building numbers run in the same directions, with odd numbers on the left-hand side and even on the right as you head south or east. However, Guatemala City is divided into 15 *zonas*; each zona has its own separate version of this grid system. Thus 14a Calle in Zona 10 is a completely different street several miles distant from 14a Calle in Zona 1, though major thoroughfares such as 6a Avenida and 7a Avenida cross through several zones while maintaining the same name.

In smaller Guatemalan cities and towns this street grid system allows you to pinpoint destinations effortlessly. However, in villages and some small towns (Lívingston and San Pedro La Laguna, for example), street names are not used at all.

Addresses are given in this form: '9a Avenida 15-12, Zona 1,' which means '9th Avenue above 15th Street, No 12, in Zone 1.' The building you're looking for (in this case the Hotel Excel), will be on 9th Avenue between 15th and 16th Streets, on the right-hand side as you walk south. Beware, though, of Guatemala City's street grid anomalies, such as diagonal streets called

rutas and *vías* and wandering boulevards called *diagonales*.

Short streets may be numbered 'A,' as in 14a Calle A, a short street running between 14a Calle and 15a Calle.

Landmarks
The ceremonial center of Guatemala City is the Plaza Mayor (sometimes called the Parque Central) at the heart of Zona 1, surrounded by the Palacio Nacional, the Catedral Metropolitana and the Portal del Comercio. Beside the Plaza Mayor to the west is the large Parque Centenario, the city's central park. Zona 1 is also the retail commercial district, with shops selling clothing, crafts, film and myriad other items of varying utility. The Mercado Central, a market selling lots of crafts, is behind the cathedral. Most of the city's good, cheap and middle-range hotels are in Zona 1. Major thoroughfares connecting Zona 1 to the rest of the city include 6a Avenida running south and 7a Avenida running north.

On and to the immediate north of the border of Zona 4 and Zona 1 is the modern Centro Cívico (Civic Center) with several government buildings, including the main office of the national tourist bureau. In southwestern Zona 4 is the city's major market district and chaotic bus terminals.

Zona 9 (west of Avenida La Reforma) and Zona 10 (east of Avenida La Reforma) are both south of Zona 4; Avenida La Reforma is the southerly extension of 10a Avenida. These are the tony residential areas of the city, which also boast several of the most interesting small museums. Zona 10 is the poshest, with its Zona Viva (Lively Zone) arrayed around the deluxe Camino Real Guatemala and Guatemala Fiesta hotels. Many of the city's fancier restaurants and nightclubs are in the Zona Viva. In Zona 9, convenient landmarks are the mini-Eiffel Tower called the Torre del Reformador at 7a Avenida and 2a Calle, and the Plazuela España traffic roundabout at 7a Avenida and 12a Calle.

Zona 13, just south of Zona 9, has the large Parque Aurora, several museums and the Aeropuerto Internacional La Aurora.

GUATEMALA CITY

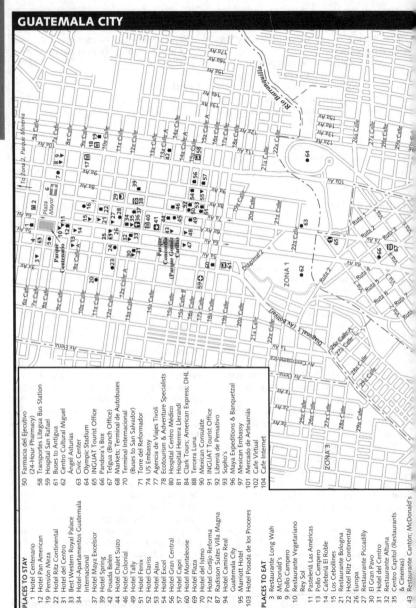

PLACES TO STAY
1 Hotel Centenario
12 Hotel Pan American
19 Pensión Meza
22 Hotel Ritz Continental
31 Hotel del Centro
33 Best Western Royal Palace
34 Hotel-Apartamentos Guatemala
   Internacional
37 Hotel Maya Excelsior
39 Hotel Spring
42 Posada Belén
44 Hotel Chalet Suizo
46 Hotel Colonial
49 Hotel Tally
51 Hotel Fenix
52 Hotel Clariss
53 Hotel Ajau
54 Hotel Excel
56 Hotel Gran Central
57 Hotel Capri
60 Hotel Monteleone
69 Hotel Plaza
70 Hotel del Istmo
72 Hotel Cortijo Reforma
87 Radisson Suites Villa Magna
94 Hotel Camino Real
   Guatemala City
95 Marriott Hotel
103 Hotel Posada de los Proceres

PLACES TO EAT
3 Restaurante Long Wah
8 McDonald's
9 Pollo Campero
10 Restaurante Vegetariano
   Rey Sol
11 Pastelería Las Américas
13 Pollo Campero
14 Cafetería El Roble
15 Los Cebollines
21 Restaurante Bologna
22 Hotel Ritz Continental
26 Europa
27 Restaurante Piccadilly
30 El Gran Pavo
31 Hotel del Centro
32 Restaurante Altuna
35 Centro Capitol (Restaurants
   & Cinemas)
43 Restaurante Cantón; McDonald's

50 Farmacia del Ejecutivo
   (24-Hour Pharmacy)
58 Transportes Litegua Bus Station
59 Hospital San Rafael
61 Buses to Antigua
62 Centro Cultural Miguel
   Ángel Asturias
63 Civic Center
64 Olympic Stadium
65 INGUAT Tourist Office
66 Pandora's Box
67 Telgua (Branch Office)
68 Markets; Terminal de Autobuses
70 Terminal Internacional
   (Buses to San Salvador)
71 Torre del Reformador
74 US Embassy
77 Agencia de Viajes Tivoli
78 Ecotourism & Adventure Specialists
80 Hospital Centro Médico
81 Hospital Herrera Llerandi
84 Clark Tours; American Express; DHL
88 Tercera Luna
90 Mexican Consulate
91 INGUAT Tourist Office
92 Librería de Pensativo
93 Sopho's
96 Maya Expeditions & Banquetzal
97 Mexican Embassy
101 Mercado de Artesanías
102 Cafe Virtual
104 Cafe Internet

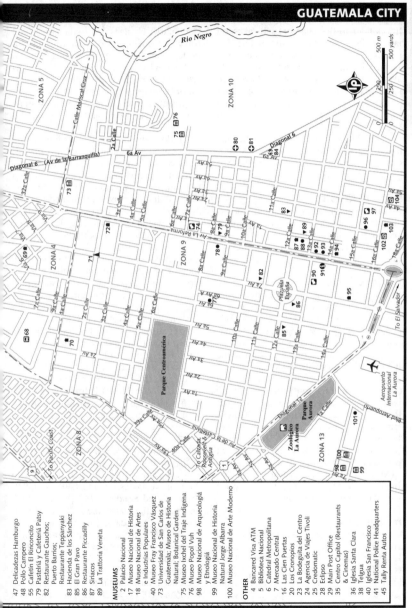

GUATEMALA CITY

47 Delicadezas Hamburgo
48 Pollo Campero
55 Cafetín El Rinconcito
79 Pastelería y Cafetería Patsy
82 Restaurante Gauchos;
    Puerto Barrios;
    Restaurante Teppanyaki
83 Hacienda de los Sánchez
85 El Gran Pavo
86 Restaurante Piccadilly
87 Siriacos
89 La Trattoria Veneta

MUSEUMS

2   Palacio Nacional
17 Museo Nacional de Historia
18 Museo Nacional de Artes
    e Industrias Populares
40 Museo Fray Francisco Vásquez
73 Universidad de San Carlos de
    Guatemala; Museo de Historia
    Natural; Botanical Garden
75 Museo Ixchel del Traje Indígena
76 Museo Popol Vuh
98 Museo Nacional de Arqueología
    y Etnología
99 Museo Nacional de Historia
    Natural Jorge Albarra
100 Museo Nacional de Arte Moderno

OTHER

4   Bancared Visa ATM
5   Biblioteca Nacional
6   Catedral Metropolitana
7   Mercado Central
16 Las Cien Puertas
20 Los Cronopios
23 La Bodeguita del Centro
24 Agencia de Viajes Tivoli
25 Credomatic
28 Eclipso
29 Main Post Office
35 Centro Capitol (Restaurants
    & Cinemas)
36 Iglesia Santa Clara
38 Telgua
40 Iglesia San Francisco
41 National Police Headquarters
45 Tally Renta Autos

Maps

The INGUAT tourist office (see Tourist Offices later in this chapter) sells a useful map for US$1, with the country on one side and several cities and towns on the other. This map has an inset of greater Guatemala City, as well as a close-up of the downtown area. The Librería de Pensativo (see Bookstores) sells the exceptional Guatemala map produced by International Travel Maps.

Detailed topographical maps can be purchased at the Instituto Geográfico Militar (see Maps in the Facts for the Visitor chapter for details).

INFORMATION

Official tourist publications and bureaucrats will tell you the tap water in Guatemala City is safe to drink. Unless you're very determined to test their assertions, stick to bottled water.

Tourist Offices

The tourist office is in the lobby of the INGUAT headquarters (Guatemalan Tourist Commission; ☎ 331-1333, fax 331-8893, 331-4416, ✆ inguat@guate.net, www.travel.guatemala.com.gt), 7a Avenida 1-17, Centro Cívico, Zona 4. Look for the blue-and-white sign with the letter 'i' on the east side of the street, next to a flight of stairs a few meters south of the railway viaduct that crosses above 7a Avenida. Hours are Monday to Friday from 8 am to 4 pm, Saturday 8 am to 1 pm, closed Sunday. Staff members are friendly and helpful. There is a second INGUAT office at Avenida La Reforma 13-70, Zona 9.

INGUAT's office at La Aurora international airport (☎ 331-4256, ext 294) is open every day from 6 am to 9 pm.

Immigration

If you need to extend your visa or tourist card for a longer stay, contact the Dirección General de Migración (☎ 634-8476/7/8), 7a Avenida 1-17, Piso 2, INGUAT office, Zona 4. The office is open weekdays from 9 am to 3 pm.

Money

Banco del Agro, on the south side of Parque Centenario, changes US dollars cash and traveler's checks; it's open Monday to Friday from 9 am to 8 pm, Saturday 10 am to 2 pm. ATMs are popping up all over: At last count there are more than 100 ATM locations throughout the city, with the majority accepting cards on the Visa/Plus system. Find a Bancared sign and you've found a Visa ATM.

Credomatic in the tall building at the corner of 5a Avenida and 11a Calle, Zona 1, gives cash advances on Visa and Master-Card. It's open Monday to Friday from 8 am to 7 pm, Saturday 9 am to 1 pm. Inside, you can withdraw a maximum of US$500; the 24-hour ATM gives a maximum of US$100 per transaction, but there's no limit to the number of transactions permitted.

The airport terminal office of Banco del Quetzal is open Monday to Friday from 7 am to 8 pm, Saturday and Sunday 8 am to 6 pm. Here you can change US dollars cash or traveler's checks into quetzals, change European currencies into US dollars and buy US-dollar traveler's checks. There is a MasterCard ATM at this location. The Banco Industrial on the arrivals level at the airport has a Visa ATM.

American Express (☎ 339-2877, fax 339-2882) is in the Centro Gerencial Las Margaritas, Diagonal 6 10-01, Torre II, Zona 10, with Clark Tours. It's open Monday to Friday, 8:30 am to 5 pm.

Post

The city's main post office is at 7a Avenida 12-11, Zona 1, in the huge pink building – you can't miss it. It's open from 8 am to 7 pm on weekdays, 8 am to 4:30 pm on Saturday, closed Sunday. EMS (Express Mail Service), in the rear of the post office building, is open weekdays, 9 am to 5 pm.

At La Aurora international airport there's a post office open Monday to Friday from 7 am to 3 pm.

There is a DHL drop off at Centro Gerencial Las Margaritas, Diagonal 6 10-01, Zona 10, Local 202-B. They are open

Monday to Friday, 8:30 am to 7 pm and Saturday from 8:30 am to noon.

Telephone & Fax

Telgua's central office is on 7a Avenida, between 12a and 13a Calles, Zona 1, near the main post office. Services are available every day from 7 am to midnight. Several smaller Telgua branches are found around the city. There is also a Telgua branch at the airport, open every day, 7 am to 7 pm. You can fax to or from Telgua offices; outgoing faxes may be charged by the minute or the page, while incoming are charged by the page.

Consider buying a phone card if you anticipate making many calls, as most pay phones in Guatemala City operate using the card technology only.

Email & Internet Access

Although the Internet is gaining a toehold here, services in Guatemala City are largely limited to expensive cybercafés in Zona 10. One exception is the Hotel Ajau, 8a Avenida 15-62, Zona 1, where visitors (including nonguests) can get on line for US$3 a half-hour.

In Zona 10, try Cafe Virtual, on the corner of 16a Calle and 2a Avenida at the entrance to the Los Proceres shopping center. They are open Monday to Saturday from 8 am to 9 pm and Sundays 10 am to 8 pm; US$5.15 gets you an hour of Internet access and a complimentary beverage. Cafe Internet, 5a Avenida 16-11, Zona 10, has email for US$3.85 an hour. They are open Monday to Saturday from 9 am to 9 pm and Sundays from 10 am to 7 pm.

Travel Agencies

Agencia de Viajes Tivoli has two convenient locations. The Zona 9 office (☎ 339-2260/1/2, fax 334-3297, ✉ viajes@tivoli.com.gt) is at 6a Avenida 8-41. There is also an office in Zona 1 (☎ 238-4771/2/3, fax 220-4744, ✉ centro@tivoli.com.gt), 12a Calle 4-55, Edificio Herrera. The Edificio Herrera houses many other travel agencies; take your pick. SERVISA (☎/fax 332-7526), Avenida La Reforma 8-33, Zona 10, is another travel

agency and authorized representative of many international and regional airlines.

Bookstores

The Arnel bookstore is at No 108 in the Edificio El Centro, at the corner of 9a Calle and 7a Avenida, Zona 1, a block from Parque Central. It has a variety of books in English and French, including general fiction, Latin American literature in translation, travel guides, books about the region, Maya civilization and Spanish language learning.

Sopho's at Avenida La Reforma 13-89, El Portal No 1, Zona 10, has a good selection of books and magazines in English. This is a relaxed place to have a coffee and read while in the Zona Viva. Librería de Pensativo (☎ 332-5055), Avenida La Reforma 13-01, Zona 9, has a selection of Lonely Planet guidebooks and a good choice of titles about Guatemala in English at fair prices. They also sell maps. The Europa bar/restaurant (see Places to Eat later in this chapter) has a shelf of used books in English for sale or trade.

Geminis Bookstore (☎ 366-1031), in the Casa Alta at 3a Avenida 17-05, Zona 14, has a good selection of books in English, but it's rather far from the center of things. It's open weekdays from 9 am to 1 pm and 3 to 6 pm and Saturday 9 am to 1 pm. There's also Vista Hermosa Book Shop (☎ 269-1003) at 2a Calle 18-50, Zona 15.

Libraries

The Biblioteca Nacional (National Library; ☎ 232-2443), on the west side of Parque Centenario, is open Monday to Friday, 9 am to 6 pm.

Laundry

There are laundries throughout the city. In Zona 1, try the Lavandería Internacional on 18a Calle between 11a and 12a Avenidas. There are also laundry facilities at many hotels, including the Spring Hotel (see Places to Stay).

Whether you have a catastrophe or simply run short and need to buy some

GUATEMALA CITY

cheap, new clothes, you can find it all from underwear to overalls on 6a Avenida between 8a and 13a Calles. Every day this stretch of 6a Avenida is choked with vendors hawking their wares.

Medical Services

Guatemala City has many private hospitals and clinics. One is the Hospital Centro Médico (☎ 332-3555, 334-2157) at 6a Avenida 3-47, Zona 10. Another is Hospital Herrera Llerandi (☎ 334-5959, emergencies 334-5955), which is also called Amedesgua, at 6a Avenida 8-71, Zona 10. Both of these hospitals should have English-speaking doctors on duty.

Public hospitals and clinics are strung along 2a Avenida between 12a and 17a Calles in Zona 1. The Hospital San Rafael (☎ 230-5048, 232-5352), 16a Calle 2-42, is recommended and cheap, though don't count on finding a doctor who speaks anything but Spanish. The Guatemalan Red Cross (☎ 125) is at 3a Calle 8-40, Zona 1.

Guatemala City uses a duty-chemist *(farmacia de turno)* system with designated pharmacies remaining open at night and weekends. Ask at your hotel for the nearest farmacia de turno, or consult the farmacia de turno sign in the window of the closest chemist/pharmacy. The Farmacia del Ejecutivo, on 7a Avenida at the corner of 15a Calle, Zona 1, is open 24 hours; it accepts Visa and MasterCard.

Emergency

Emergency telephone numbers are:

Ambulance	☎ 125, 128
Fire	☎ 122, 123
Police	☎ 120, 137, 138

Dangers & Annoyances

Guatemala City is not an extraordinarily safe place to begin with, and street crime is increasing. Use normal urban caution (behaving as you would in say, Manhattan or Rome): Don't walk down the street with your wallet bulging out of your back pocket, and avoid walking downtown late at night. It's safe to walk downtown in early evening,

as long as you stick to streets with plenty of lighting and people. Stay alert and leave your valuables in your hotel. Don't flaunt anything of value, and be aware that women and children swell the ranks of thieves here.

The area around 18a Calle in Zona 1 has many bus stations and hosts the lowlifes and hustlers that tend to lurk around them. This part of town (also renowned as a red light district) is notoriously dangerous at night; if you are arriving by bus at night or must go someplace on 18a Calle at night, take a taxi.

The more affluent sections of the city – Zona 9 and Zona 10, for example – are much safer. Still, even in these sections, traveling in pairs is better than alone, and you should leave your documents and the bulk of your cash in the hotel safe before venturing out.

All buses, but especially those of the local variety, are the turf of adroit pickpockets. You wouldn't be the first traveler to discover your wallet missing hours after the fact; they are that slick. Stay on the ball and try to take the more expensive, red *preferencial* buses plying local routes in the capital.

ZONA 1
Plaza Mayor

Most of the city's notable sights are in Zona 1 near the Plaza Mayor, which is bounded by 6a and 8a Calles and 6a and 7a Avenidas.

According to the standard colonial urban-planning scheme, every town in the New World had to have a large plaza for military exercises, reviews and ceremonies. On the north side of the plaza was the *palacio de gobierno* or colonial government headquarters. On another side, preferably the east, there was a church (if the town was large enough to merit a bishop, it was a cathedral). On the other sides of the square there could be additional civic buildings or the large and imposing mansions of wealthy citizens. Guatemala's Plaza Mayor is a good example of the classic town plan.

To appreciate the Plaza Mayor, visit on a Sunday when the citizenry come out in their best to stroll, lick ice cream cones, play in the fountains, take the air, gossip, make out on a bench and groove to *salsa* music on boom boxes. If you can't make it on a Sunday, try for lunchtime or late afternoon. You'll be besieged by shoeshine boys and purveyors of kitsch and knickknacks; ignore or indulge them as is your wont.

Palacio Nacional

On the north side of the Plaza Mayor is the magnificent Palacio Nacional, built during the dictatorial presidency of General Jorge Ubico (1931-44) at enormous cost, both in dollar and human terms. It's the third palace to stand here.

The Palacio Nacional is being restored and eventually will house a museum of the history of Guatemala.

Free tours are given Monday to Friday from 9 am to 5:30 pm, Saturday and Sunday 8 am to 3 pm. The tour takes you through a labyrinth of gleaming brass, polished wood, carved stone and frescoed arches painted by Alberto Gálvez Suárez. Notable features include the two-ton gold, bronze and Bohemian-crystal chandelier in the reception salon and the two Arabic-style inner courtyards.

Catedral Metropolitana

Built between 1782 and 1809 (the towers were finished in 1867), the Catedral Metropolitana has survived earthquake and fire much better than the site of the Palacio Nacional, though the quake of 1917 did substantial damage and the one in 1976 did even more. Despite being completely restored, it's not a particularly beautiful building, inside or out. Heavy proportions and sparse ornamentation make it look severe, though it does have a certain stateliness and the altars are worth a look. The cathedral is supposedly open every day from 8 am to 7 pm, but you may find it closed, especially at siesta time.

Mercado Central

Until it was destroyed by the quake of 1976, the Mercado Central on 9a Avenida between 6a and 8a Calles behind the cathedral was the place locals shopped for food and other necessities. Reconstructed in the late 1970s, the new central market specializes in tourist-oriented items such as cloth (hand-woven and machine-woven), carved wood, worked leather and metal, basketry and other handicrafts. Vegetables and other daily needs have been moved aside to the streets surrounding the market. When you visit the Plaza Mayor you may feel like browsing, though there are better places to buy crafts. Market hours are 7 am to 6 pm Monday to Saturday, 6 am to noon Sunday.

The city's true 'central' food market is in Zona 4, near the bus terminals.

Museums

Museums in Zona 1 include the **Museo Fray Francisco Vasquez** (☎ 232-3625), Iglesia San Francisco, at the corner of 6a Avenida and 13a Calle. It houses the belongings of this Franciscan friar. The museum is open every day, 9 am to noon and 3 to 6 pm.

The **Museo Nacional de Artes e Industrias Populares** (☎ 238-0334), 10a Avenida 10-72, is the national popular arts museum, with paintings, ceramics, masks, musical instruments, metalwork and gourds. It's open Monday to Friday, 9 am to 5 pm.

The collection of the **Museo Nacional de Historia** (☎ 253-6149), 9a Calle 9-70, on the corner of 10a Avenida, is a jumble of historical relics with a strong emphasis on photography. It's open Tuesday to Friday 9 am to 4 pm and weekends from 9 am to noon and 2 to 4 pm. Entrance is US$1.25. This museum may be moved to the Palacio Nacional after it's restored.

ZONA 2
Parque Minerva

Zona 2 is north of Zona 1. Though mostly a middle-class residential district, its northern end holds the large Parque Minerva, itself surrounded by golf courses, sports grounds and the buildings of the Universidad Mariano Gálvez.

Minerva, goddess of wisdom, technical skill and invention, was a favorite of President Manuel Estrada Cabrera (1898-1920; see the History section in the Facts about Guatemala chapter).

The Parque Minerva is a placid place, good for relaxing, walking among the eucalyptus trees and sipping a cool drink. However, be on your guard for pickpockets, purse-snatchers and other such ne'er-do-wells who look especially for tourists as marks.

The prime sight in Zona 2 is the Relief Map of Guatemala, called simply the **Mapa En Relieve** in Parque Minerva. Constructed in 1904 under the direction of Francisco Vela, the map shows the country at a scale of 1:10,000, but the height of the mountainous terrain has been exaggerated to 1:2000 for dramatic effect. The Mapa was fully restored and repainted in late 1999, so it's in fine shape these days. Little signs indicate major towns and topographical features. Viewing towers afford a panoramic view. This is an odd but fun place, and costs US$2 for admission; hours are 9 am to 5 pm every day. Nearby are carnival rides and games for children.

The Mapa En Relieve and Parque Minerva are 2km north of the Plaza Mayor along 6a Avenida, but that street is one-way heading south. Catch a northbound bus (No 1, 45 or 46) on 5a Avenida in Zona 1 and take it to the end of the line.

ZONA 4

Pride of Zona 4, just on the border of Zona 1, is the Centro Cívico, constructed during the 1950s and '60s. (The complex of buildings actually stretches into Zona 1 and Zona 5.) Here you'll find the Palace of Justice, the headquarters of the Guatemalan Institute of Social Security (IGSS), the Banco del Quetzal, city hall and the headquarters of INGUAT. The Banco del Quetzal building bears high-relief murals by Dagoberto Vásquez depicting the history of his homeland; in the city hall is a huge mosaic by Carlos Mérida completed in 1959.

Behind INGUAT, in the adjacent Zona 5, is the Ciudad Olímpica sports grounds, and on a hilltop across the street from the Centro Cívico, is the Centro Cultural Miguel Ángel Asturias, which houses the national theater, chamber theater, open-air theater and a small museum of old armaments.

Zona 4 is known mostly for its markets and its bus stations, all thrown together in the frenetic southwestern corner of the zone near the railway.

ZONA 10

East of Avenida La Reforma, Zona 10 is the upscale district of posh villas, luxury hotels, embassies and two of the city's most important museums.

The **Museo Ixchel del Traje Indígena** (☎ 331-3634/8) is named for Ixchel, wife of Mayan sky god Itzamná and goddess of the moon, women, reproduction and textiles (among other fantastic things!). Photographs and exhibits of Indian costumes, textiles and other village crafts show the incredible richness of traditional arts in Guatemala's highland towns. If you enjoy seeing Guatemalan textiles at all, you must make a visit to this museum. It's open weekdays from 8 am to 5:50 pm and Saturdays from 9 am to 12:50 pm.

Behind this is the **Museo Popol Vuh** (☎/fax 361-2301), where well-chosen polychrome pottery, figurines, incense burners, burial urns, carved wooden masks and traditional textiles fill several exhibit rooms. Others hold colonial paintings and gilded wood and silver objects. A faithful copy of the Dresden Codex, one of the precious 'painted books' of the Maya, is among the most interesting pieces. This is an important collection, especially for its precolonial holdings. The Museo Popol Vuh is open Monday to Friday from 9 am to 5 pm, Saturday 9 am to 1 pm.

Both museums are in large, new buildings at the Universidad Francisco Marroquín, on the east end of 6a Calle in Zona 10, about six blocks east of Avenida La Reforma. Admission to either is US$1.95.

The biology department at the Universidad de San Carlos de Guatemala (☎ 476-2010) at Calle Mariscal Cruz 1-56 has a **natural history museum** and a large **botanical garden** open to the public Monday to Friday from 8 am to 3 pm. Admission is US$1.25.

ZONA 13

The major attraction in the southern reaches of the city is the Parque Aurora, with its zoo, children's playground, fairgrounds and several museums.

The Moorish-looking **Museo Nacional de Arqueología y Etnología** (☎ 472-0478) has a collection of Mayan artifacts from all over Guatemala, including stone carvings, jade, ceramics, statues, stelae, a tomb and models of the ruins at Tikal and Zaculeu. Exhibits in the ethnology section show the distribution of all the various indigenous peoples and languages throughout Guatemala, with exhibits on their traditional costumes, dances and implements of daily life. The museum is open Tuesday to Friday 9 am to 4 pm, Saturday 9 am to noon and 2 to 4 pm. Admission is a stiff (for Guatemala) US$3.85.

Facing the Museo Nacional de Arqueología y Etnología is the **Museo Nacional de Arte Moderno** (☎ 472-0467), with a collection of 20th-century Guatemalan art that is especially strong on painting and sculpture. The museum is open Tuesday to Friday from 9 am to 4 pm, Saturday and Sunday from 9 am to noon and 2 to 4 pm. Admission is US$1.25. Nearby is the Museo Nacional de Historia Natural Jorge Albarra (☎ 472-0468), which claims fame for its large collection of dissected animals. The museum is open Tuesday to Friday from 9 am to 4 pm and weekends from 9 am to noon and 2 to 4 pm; admission is US$1.30.

Several hundred meters east of these museums is the city's official handicrafts market, the **Mercado de Artesanías** (☎ 472-0208), on 11a Avenida just off the access road to the airport. Like most official handicrafts markets, it's a sleepy place in which shopkeepers display the same items available in hotel gift shops. It's open 8 am to 6 pm Monday to Saturday, 8:30 am to 2 pm Sunday.

The city zoo, the pleasant **Zoológico La Aurora** (☎ 472-0507), is open Tuesday to Sunday from 9 am to 5 pm. The admission cost is US$1 for adults and half price for children.

KAMINALJUYÚ

Several kilometers west of the center are the extensive ruins of Kaminaljuyú (☎ 253-1570, 232-5948), a Late Preclassic/Early Classic Mayan site displaying both Mexican and Mayan influences.

Unfortunately, much of Kaminaljuyú, located in Colonia Kaminaljuyú, Zona 7, has been covered by urban sprawl. Though you can visit from 9 am to 4 pm daily and pay US$1.25 for the privilege, your time would be better spent looking at the artifacts recovered here that are on display in the city's museums. Buses Nos 35 and 37 come here from 4a Avenida, Zona 1.

PLACES TO STAY

As you would expect from a capital city, Guatemala City has all sorts of accommodations for every budget. The very cheapest rooms, as well as the most expensive, tend to fill up fast, but there are usually plenty to be had at prices in-between. Prices are higher here than anywhere else in the country, save for perhaps Tikal.

Budget

For a good selection of budget hotels, head about four blocks south of the Plaza Mayor near the Policia Nacional (National Police Headquarters) and the Correos (Post Office), within the area bounded by 6a Avenida A and 9a Avenida and 12a and 16a Calles. Here you'll find at least a dozen decent hotels and several convenient and cheap little restaurants as well. It's important to keep street noise in mind as you look for a room; this is a city, after all, and the ambient noise can be disrupting. All the places listed below are in Zona 1, except for the Hotel del Istmo.

Hotel Spring (☎ 230-2858, 230-2958, fax 232-0107, 8a Avenida 12-65) is a clean and comfortable old hotel that's often *completo* (full) because the location is good, the 43 rooms presentable, the courtyard sunny and the price decent. Singles/doubles/triples with shared, hot bath are US$10/14/20, rooms with private bath and color cable TV are US$14/20/24, and fancier rooms in the new *anexo* are US$22/28/34. Some of the annex rooms are wheelchair accessible. A cafeteria serves meals from 6:30 am to 1:30 pm. You can do laundry here and store luggage and valuables.

Hotel Ajau (☎ 232-0488, 251-3008, fax 251-8097, ❷ hotajaugua.gbm.net, 8a Avenida 15-62) is fairly clean, somewhat cheaper and quite a bit quieter than many hotels on the 8a Avenida strip. It's a favorite with Central Americans in transit. Singles/doubles/triples are US$7/8/10 with shared bath, US$12/13/15 with private bath. All rooms come with color cable TV. Laundry service and coffee are available. Email (for guests and nonguests) is US$3 a half-hour.

Hotel Chalet Suizo (☎ 251-3786, fax 232-0429, 14a Calle 6-82) has been a travelers' favorite for decades. The 47 rooms around plant-filled courtyards are comfortable and exceptionally clean. Rates are US$12/16 a single/double with shared bath, or US$24/28 with private bath. They have a safe and luggage storage. Book in advance.

Hotel Excel (☎ 253-2709, 230-0140, fax 238-4071, 9a Avenida 15-12) is a bright, modern place with 17 rooms on three levels around an L-shaped courtyard used as a car park. It has a cafeteria. Rooms with bath and cable TV are US$20/23/27 a single/double/triple. Across the street is the super budget *Hotel Gran Central* (☎ 232-9514) where cleanish, very basic, dark rooms in the sprawling three-story building are US$4/5/6. They claim to have hot water. Have some earplugs handy, as this place can get as loud as Grand Central. Popular with

GUATEMALA 1988
P348124
CENTRO AMERICA

TONY WHEELER

Guatemalan businesspeople and families is the nearby *Hotel Capri* (☎ 232-8191, 251-3737, 9a Avenida 15-63), where a single with shared bath is US$7 and singles/doubles with private bath and cable TV are US$12/16. They have a safe for valuables and parking.

There are several hotels that have long been popular with savvy travelers, including the *Pensión Meza* (☎ 232-3777, 10a Calle 10-17). This place has forgettable rooms but is busy with international budget travelers who like the sunny courtyard, the camaraderie, the helpful proprietor and the low prices. With shared bath, rooms are US$7/8 with one bed, US$9 with two beds, or US$4.50 per person in a dormitory. The restaurant serves cheap meals. They have a book swap with a large selection here.

The *Hotel Fenix* (☎ 251-6625, 7a Avenida 15-81) has been a budget standby for years thanks to the friendly family atmosphere and clean rooms. This is one of the best budget bets in town and is secure despite the somewhat dodgy locale. Basic rooms with shared, hot-water bath are US$5.50 for one or two people; triples/quadruples are US$10/11. There is a cafeteria and spacious communal hangout areas.

If you're arriving by bus from San Salvador, the *Hotel del Istmo* (☎ 332-4389, 3a Avenida 1-38, Zona 9) at the Terminal Internacional bus terminal, is clean, comfortable and convenient. Rooms with private hot bath are US$11/13/16 a single/double/triple, and there's an inexpensive cafeteria. If you're arriving late from Cobán, try the *Hotel Clariss* (☎ 232-1113, 232-3466, 8a Avenida 15-14) next to the bus depot. Here singles/double/triples with private hot bath and cable TV are US$11/13/16. What with the cheap carpet and pink walls, the emphasis here is not on interior decorating, but it is a reasonably friendly place that is all right for a night. The hotel has parking.

The *Hotel Monteleone* (☎ 238-2600, fax 253-9205, 18a Calle 4-63) is very conveniently located across from the Antigua bus lot and has a good reputation. Clean rooms in a friendly atmosphere are US$7.50 for one or two people with shared bath and US$12 for a double with private bath.

Mid-Range

Guatemala City's mid-range lodgings are good values. All are comfortable and some are even charming. All these places are in Zona 1, except for the Hotel Plaza and the Hotel Posada de los Proceres.

Posada Belén (☎ 232-9226, 253-4530, fax 251-3478, ✉ pbelen@guatemalaweb.com, 13a Calle A 10-30) is on a quiet side street. A converted colonial home, the Belén is a quaint hostelry with 11 rooms with bath, a dining room serving all meals and laundry service. Rooms accommodate one (US$36), two (US$43), three (US$48) or four (US$53) people.

Hotel Pan American (☎ 232-6807/8/9, fax 251-8749, ✉ panamhot@infovia.com.gt, 9a Calle 5-63) was this city's luxury hotel before WWII. It still attracts many faithful return visitors who like its faded charm. The 55 rooms, all Art Deco and Biedermeier, are pleasant and comfortable, with cable TV, telephone, private bath (with tub) and fan. Avoid rooms facing the noisy street. Rates are US$41/43/46/48 a single/double/triple/quadruple; rooms with six beds are US$53, so could be affordable for a group. There's a restaurant serving all meals, and guests have access to email services.

Hotel del Centro (☎ 232-5980, 238-1519, fax 230-0208, ✉ hotelcentro@guate.net, 13a Calle 4-55) is a good, solid hotel, dependable for decades. The 55 large, comfortable rooms come with shiny baths, color cable TV and often with two double beds; there's a bit of street noise in some. Singles/doubles/triples are US$42/48/54. There's also a restaurant, a bar with music on Friday nights and a rooftop terrace garden.

Hotel Colonial (☎ 232-6722, 232-2955, fax 232-8671, ✉ colonial@infovia.com.gt, 7a Avenida 14-19) is a large old house converted to a hotel with heavy, dark colonial decor. The covered interior court is welcoming and the 42 rooms clean. Singles/doubles in four rooms with general bath are US$18/24; the rest, all with private bath, are US$24/32/41 a single/double/triple. The at-

tached restaurant serves meals from 6:30 am to 2 pm.

Hotel-Apartamentos Guatemala Internacional (☎ 238-4441/2, fax 232-4350, 6a Avenida 12-21) offers 27 furnished units, attractive for long stays or families, as the location is convenient and the prices are good. All apartments have TV, telephone and fully equipped kitchens, except for the studios, which lack the last. Studios are US$18/20 for singles/doubles; larger one- or two-bedroom apartments are US$24/27 single, US$30/33 double and US$36/40 triple or quad. Some larger apartments sleep six.

Hotel Centenario (☎ 230-4005/07, fax 238-2039, 6a Calle 5-33), on the north side of the Parque Centenario, has 42 rooms, many with a double and a single bed, plus well-worn but clean showers. Prices for this central location are US$25/32/40/45 a single/double/triple/quad.

Hotel Maya Excelsior (☎ 238-2761/2/3/4/5, fax 250-0707, 7a Avenida 12-46) is a cavernous, hushed place where *The Shining* could have been filmed: Eerie back-lighting illuminates dark hallways, through which the seemingly friendly staff wander before disappearing around corners. Each of the 80 rooms is different; some are carpeted, others have linoleum and a few rooms facing the street have views. Some units are wheelchair accessible. All rooms have cable TV, private hot bath and ample closets. Singles/doubles/triples are US$20/25/35. Large apartments with sitting room, bedroom and fully equipped kitchen are rented by the month for US$275 for one or two people, including all utilities. Some rooms haven't seen the light of day lately, so avoid getting stuck in musty and stale digs by looking before you (s)leap.

Hotel Tally (☎ 232-9845, 251-7082, fax 253-1749, 7a Avenida 15-24) is one of the capital's best new mid-range places. The rooms are sparkling, it's conveniently located and its sister business is Tally Renta Autos (see Getting There & Away at the end of this chapter), which can be very handy if you want to rent a car. All rooms have private hot bath, cable TV and air con.

Singles/doubles/triples/quads are US$23/29/33/37. This place is often full, so reservations are recommended.

The brand-spanking-new *Best Western Royal Palace* (☎ 232-5125/6/7, fax 238-3715, *6a Avenida 12-66*) is an old colonial hotel that's had a major face lift. This place has all the amenities of a luxury, chain hotel, with the character of a smaller, family-owned outfit. Each huge room is unique and carpeted, with a small balcony, private bathroom, fan and cable TV. Facilities include a restaurant, bar, gym and sauna. Singles/doubles/triples, all of which are wheelchair accessible, are US$65/70/75.

Hotel Plaza (☎ 331-6173, 331-0396, fax 331-6824, Vía 7, No 6-16, Zona 4), with colonial appointments, is 1km south of the Centro Cívico and a 15-minute walk east of the market and bus station area. The 64 ample rooms, each with private bath, telephone and color cable TV, go for US$55/61 per single/double.

Hotel Posada de los Proceres (☎ /fax 363-0744, 363-4423, fax 368-1405, **@** posadazv@guate.net, 16a Calle 2-40) is in a tranquil residential district in the upmarket Zona 10 near Los Proceres shopping center. Singles/doubles/triples are US$49/59/69. Most other hotels in this district are much more expensive; this one is a find.

Top End

Most luxurious of this city's hotels is the *Camino Real Guatemala City* (☎ 333-4633, fax 337-4313, in the US 800-937-8461, **@** caminor@guate.net, Avenida La Reforma at 14a Calle, Zona 10), in the heart of the Zona Viva. This is part of the Westin chain and is the capital's international-class hotel, with 400 rooms and five-star comforts, including swimming pools and lush gardens. Rates are US$168/192 for standard/deluxe rooms – the only difference is deluxe rooms are more attractively located. Hertz and American Express have offices in the lobby.

Another excellent luxury hotel in the Zona Viva is the four-star, 100-suite *Radisson Suites Villa Magna* (☎ 332-9797, fax 332-9772, in the US 800-333-3333, contact **@** radisson@gold.guate.net, 1a Avenida 12-46,

Zona 10). The one-bedroom upper-floor suites have beautiful views from full-wall windows for US$169. Junior suites have one big room for US$139. A buffet breakfast is included. The Banco Industrial ATM at the entrance accepts Visa cards.

The modern, five-star *Marriott Hotel* (☎ 331-7777, fax 332-1877, in the US or Canada 800-228-9290, 7a Avenida 15-45, Zona 9) has 385 rooms for US$114 for two or three people, including breakfast. Facilities include a pool, spa, gym and every other perk befitting a luxury hotel.

Several hundred meters north of the Zona Viva stands the *Hotel Cortijo Reforma* (☎ 332-0712, fax 331-8876, Avenida La Reforma 2-18, Zona 9). The 120 suites feature a bedroom, living room, minibar, tiled bathroom with tub and shower, a kitchenette and a tiny balcony. Singles/doubles/triples are a good value at US$72/78/84.

Downtown, the four-star *Hotel Ritz Continental* (☎ 238-1671/5, fax 238-1527, **@** hotritz@medianet.com.gt, 6a Avenida A 10-13, Zona 1) has recently been renovated. Junior suites are US$96, master suites are US$120, including breakfast; there's a swimming pool. The location, three blocks south of the Plaza Mayor, is quiet and convenient. The Ritz offers deals from their desk on the lower level of the airport and free transfers to the hotel.

You can't help but gawk at the *Tikal Futura* (☎ 440-1234, fax 440-4050, Calzada Roosevelt 22-43, Zona 11), with its towering glass architecture and sprawling layout. This is Hyatt's contribution to the Guatemalan hotel scene, offering double rooms with views, satellite TV, minibar and continental breakfast for US$135. The complex also has a shopping mall, ten cinemas and a bowling alley.

Near the Airport

There are a couple of serviceable budget hotels near the airport, of which *Dos Lunas* (☎/fax 334-5264, **@** lorena@pronet.gt, www.xelapages.com/doslunas, 21a Calle 10-92, Zona 13, Aurora II) is far and away the current favorite. Clean, secure and quiet rooms are US$10 per person, including free airport transfer and breakfast. This place is so popular, reservations are required. Another option near the airport is *Economy Dorms* (☎ 331-8029, 8a Avenida 17-74, Zona 13, Aurora I), which has rooms for US$10, including breakfast and airport shuttle.

For mid-range accommodation near the airport, try the recommended *Hotel El Aeropuerto Guest House* (☎ 332-3086, fax 362-1264, ✉ hotairpt@guate.net, 15a Calle A 7-32, Zona 13), which has doubles for US$25/US$30 with shared/private hot bath, breakfast and airport transfers. The *Hotel Hincapié* (☎ 332-7721, contact ✉ aruedap@infovia.com.gt, Avenida Hincapié 18-77, Zona 13) is another alternative, with doubles for US$25 including breakfast and airport transfers.

About a mile from the airport is the five-star *Crowne Plaza Las Américas* (☎ 339-0676, fax 339-0690, in the US 800-227-6963, Avenida Las Américas 9-08, Zona 13). Operated by Holiday Inn, this hotel has newly renovated singles/doubles for US$108/132.

PLACES TO EAT
Budget
Cheap eats are not hard to find, as fast-food and snack shops are plentiful in Guatemala. But if you're really strapped for cash, head for Parque Concordia, bound by 5a and 6a Avenidas and 14a and 15a Calles in Zona 1. The west side of the park is lined with little open-air food stalls serving sandwiches and snacks at rock-bottom prices from early morning to late evening. A meal for US$2 is the rule here.

Delicadezas Hamburgo (15a Calle 5-34, Zona 1), on the south side of Parque Concordia, features a long list of sandwiches at lunch and dinner. It's open from 7 am to 9:30 pm every day.

Restaurante Cantón (☎ 251-6331, 6a Avenida 14-29, Zona 1), on the east side of this park, is the place to go for Chinese food, at US$5 to US$8 per platter; it's open every day from 9 am to 9:30 pm. The soups here are just the ticket if you're suffering from stomach problems.

There are numerous other Chinese restaurants near the corner of 6a Avenida and 14a Calle, Zona 1. The city's other rich concentration of Chinese restaurants is in the blocks west of the Parque Centenario along 6a Calle, where you'll find the *Restaurante Long Wah* (☎ 232-6611, 6a Calle 3-70, Zona 1), along with several other places such as the *Palacio Real, Palacio Dorado* and the *Jou Jou*.

There are dozens of restaurants and fast-food shops of all types at 6a Avenida between 10a and 15a Calles: hamburgers, pizzas, pasta, Chinese, fried chicken. Around here you'll have no trouble eating well for US$3 to US$4. The *Pastelería Las Américas* (6a Avenida 8-52), half a block south of the Plaza Mayor, is a pleasant place to stop for a coffee and a European-style pastry or cake while you're out sightseeing.

In the midst of the cheap hotel area, 9a Avenida between 15a and 16a Calles has several good little restaurants. There's the *Cafetín El Rinconcito* (9a Avenida 15-74), which faces the Hotel Capri and is good for tacos and sandwiches, where breakfast, lunch and dinner each cost around US$1.50 to US$2. The restaurant in the Hotel Capri itself (9a Avenida 15-63, Zona 1), serves more substantial meals.

You might also want to try the *Cafetería El Roble* (9a Calle 5-46, Zona 1), facing the entrance to the Hotel Pan American. This clean little café is very popular with local office workers for lunch (US$1.65) as well as for breakfast and dinner (US$1.15).

Europa (☎ 253-4929, 11a Calle 5-16, Zona 1), next door to Credomatic, is a comfortable restaurant, bar and gathering place for locals and foreigners alike. A sign on the door says 'English spoken, but not understood.' It has international cable TV, a book exchange and good, inexpensive food; it's open Monday to Saturday, 8 am to 1 am. A block and a half north is *Los Cebollines* (6a Avenida 9-75, Zona 1), a casual, well-recommended place for Mexican food.

Pastelería y Cafetería Patsy, on the corner of 8a Calle and Avenida La Reforma in Zona 10, is a bustling place popular with the working crowd. The chicken, pasta, sandwiches and other light meals here are especially cheap for the Zona Viva.

For coffee in Zona 10, head over to **Tercera Luna** (☎ 362-5030, 1a Avenida 12-70), where the java is jumping and art exhibits and poetry readings are often going on. **Sopho's** (Avenida La Reforma 13-89, El Portal No 1, Zona 10) is primarily a bookstore, but has a nice outdoor café too.

Pollo Campero is the name of Guatemala's KFC clone. You can find branches of the chain on the corner of 9a Calle and 5a Avenida, at 6a Avenida and 15a Calle and at 8a Calle 9-29, all in Zona 1. Two pieces of chicken, french fries (chips) and a soft drink or coffee costs US$2.50.

Many branches of American fast-food chains like **McDonald's, Wendy's, Burger King** and **Pizza Hut** are sprinkled liberally throughout the city. They're open long hours, often from 7 am to 10 pm. Pizza Hut offers free delivery (☎ 230-3490 in Zona 1, 332-0939 in Zona 9).

The **Restaurante Vegetariano Rey Sol** (8a Calle 5-36), on the south side of Parque Centenario, has a long cafeteria line with a good selection where you can walk along and order what you like: whole grain breads and baked goods, sandwiches, soya products, fruit and vegetable salads, hot foods and more. It's open Monday to Saturday, 7:15 am to 8:45 pm.

Restaurante Piccadilly (☎ 230-2866, 253-9223, 6a Avenida 11-01, Zona 1) is among the capital's most popular eateries, with a multinational menu heavy on the Italian fare. Most main courses cost US$3 or less. There's another branch of the Piccadilly on the Plazuela España, 7a Avenida 12-00, Zona 9. Down the block, the Centro Capitol is a mall popular with teens who like hanging about the myriad casual restaurants and multiscreen cinema here.

Mid-Range

Most middle-range hotels in Zona 1 offer excellent set-price lunches for US$6 to US$10. Try the **Hotel Del Centro, Hotel Pan American** and **Hotel Ritz Continental**. Many travelers favor the **Pan American** (9a Calle 5-63, Zona 10) for ambiance, though

the waitstaff wandering around in full traditional regalia seems a bit put on.

Restaurante Altuna (☎ 232-0669, 251-7185, 5a Avenida 12-31, Zona 1) is a large restaurant with the atmosphere of a private club, located just a few steps north of the Hotel del Centro. Specialties are seafood and Spanish dishes, with meals running about US$7 to US$14 per person. It's open Tuesday to Saturday from noon to 11 pm, Sunday from noon to 4:30 pm, closed Monday.

Restaurante Bologna (☎ 251-1167, 10a Calle 6-20, Zona 1), just around the corner from the Hotel Ritz Continental, is very small but attractive, serving tasty pizza and pasta dishes for US$3 to US$4 per plate. It's open every day but Tuesday, 10 am to 9:30 pm.

Several other good restaurants have their main establishments in Zona 1 and their branches in Zona 9 or 10.

El Gran Pavo (☎ 232-9912, 13a Calle 4-41, Zona 1) is a big place just to the left (west) of the Hotel del Centro's entrance. The menu seems to include every Mexican dish imaginable. The birria, a spicy-hot soup of meat, onions, peppers and cilantro, served with tortillas, is a meal in itself for US$3.75. El Gran Pavo is open seven days a week from 10 am to midnight, with mariachi music on Friday and Saturday nights starting around 10 pm. There's another branch (☎ 331-3976) at 12a Calle 5-54, Zona 9, and a few others around town.

Top End

Guatemala City's most elegant dining is in the Zona Viva, in the area around the Hotel Camino Real Guatemala.

La Trattoria Veneta (☎ 331-0612, 334-3718, 13a Calle 1-55, Zona 10) is the place to go for good Italian specialties. Service is attentive. Expect to spend US$12 to US$15 per person for dinner, with wine.

Hacienda de los Sánchez (☎ 331-6240, 334-8448, 12a Calle 2-25, Zona 10) is where Guatemalan meat-eaters come to pig out. The ambiance is aggressively *ranchero*. Steaks and ribs are priced at about US$11 to US$12.50. The parking lot is full of shiny

Volcán Fuego rises above Antigua.

Ruins of the Iglesia y Convento de Santa Clara – Antigua

LEANNE WALKER & ANDREW MARSHALL

La Merced church – Antigua

TONY WHEELER

Iglesia y Convento de la Recolección – Antigua

American pickup trucks. It's open every day from noon to midnight.

Puerto Barrios (☎ 334-1302, 7a Avenida 10-65, Zona 9) is awash in nautical themes: waiters in knee breeches and frogged coats, oil paintings of buccaneers, portholes for windows and a big compass by the door. You can easily spend US$16 to US$30 per person here. It's open daily from 11 am to 3 pm or 7 to 11 pm.

In the same little complex, and open the same hours, are **Restaurante Gauchos** (☎ 334-1302), an Argentinean steak-and-seafood restaurant, and **Restaurante Teppanyaki** (☎ 332-4646), with Japanese cuisine.

Siriacos (☎ 334-6316, 1a Avenida 12-12, Zona 10), very near the Radisson Suites Villa Magna, is flashy but informal, with a sunken dining room and bar, a skylighted patio courtyard and a menu of continental specialties. Expect to spend US$15 or so per person for dinner. It's open for lunch Monday to Friday, dinner Monday to Saturday, closed Sunday.

ENTERTAINMENT

Wining and dining the night away in the Zona Viva is what many visitors do. If that's beyond your budget, take in a movie at one of the cinemas along 6a Avenida between the Plaza Mayor and Parque Concordia. Tickets sell for about US$1.50. Or check out the cultural events at the Centro Cultural Miguel Ángel Asturias (☎ 232-4041/2/3/4/5, 253-1743) in Zona 4.

There is a hopping, creative scene in Guatemala City, and visitors are encouraged to check out some of the bars and clubs listed below for a little urban/youth culture.

Bars

La Bodeguita del Centro (☎ 230-2976, 12a Calle 3-55, Zona 1) is a huge, bi-level, bohemian hangout with live music, poetry readings and performances. Hundreds of posters featuring the likes of Ché, Silvio Rodriguez, Van Gogh, Bob Marley and Pablo Neruda cover the walls from floor to ceiling, giving the place a gallery feel. Pick up a

schedule for upcoming events. Lunch and dinner are served.

Las Cien Puertas, in Zona 1 on Pasaje Aycincena running between 6a and 7a Avenidas and 9a Calle, has to be one of the coolest bars in Guatemala. This super-hip (but not studiously so) bar is a gathering place for all manner of local creative types who may be debating politics, strumming a guitar or drawing a portrait when you show up. The alley has a hundred doors (hence the name) and is sometimes closed off for live bands. They serve drinks and tasty bar snacks such as tacos and quesadillas. Similar is **Los Cronopios**, on the corner of 11a Calle and 3a Avenida in Zona 1. This bar has a healthy dose of young *chapines* hanging out for the live music, poetry readings and open microphone performances.

Gay Venues

Guatemala City is not a hot spot for gay action, so don't get too excited about this heading. However, there are a couple of places worthy of mention. **Pandora's Box**, at the intersection of Vía 3 and Ruta 4 in Zona 4, is the old standby that has been hosting Guatemala's gay crowd for years. There are other gay clubs in Zona 4, but it isn't the best section of the city, so don't go a-wandering unaccompanied or late at night. **Eclipso** (12a Calle 6-61, Zona 1) is a bit edgier, with dark rooms, sex toys for sale and a (supposedly) palatable S&M scene.

GETTING THERE & AWAY
Air

International air routes to Guatemala arrive and depart from the Aeropuerto Internacional La Aurora in Guatemala City and from the international airport at Flores/Santa Elena, near Tikal. Regional routes are also served by many regional carriers (for more details, see the Getting There & Away chapter).

There are many domestic flights which may serve your purposes if you want to save time getting around within Guatemala. For more information, see the Air section of the Getting Around chapter.

Bus

It is possible to travel overland by bus between Guatemala and the rest of Central America and Mexico. See the Getting There & Away chapter for more information on traveling by international bus, including schedules and details for Copán in Honduras.

Shuttle Minibus

Shuttle minibuses serve the most popular international routes frequented by tourists. See the Shuttle Minibus section of the Getting There & Away chapter for detailed information.

Car

Major international rental companies have offices both at La Aurora international airport and in the city center (see Rental in the Getting Around chapter for information on rental cars). Rental offices in Guatemala City include:

Ahorrent (☎ 361-5661, fax 361-5621), Boulevard Liberación 4-83, Zona 9; Hotel Cortijo Reforma, Avenida La Reforma 2-18, Zona 9 (☎ 332-0712, ext 180); La Aurora international airport (☎ 362-8921/2)

Avis (☎ 332-7744/7, fax 332-7448, @ avis@ guate.net), 6a Avenida 11-24, Zona 9; La Aurora international airport (☎ 331-0017, 361-5645)

Budget (☎ 332-2491), Avenida Hincapié 11-01, Zona 13; La Aurora international airport (☎ 331-0273, 360-8639)

Dollar (☎ 232-3446, fax 238-1046), Hotel Ritz Continental, 6a Avenida A 10-13, Zona 1; La Aurora international airport (☎ 331-7185, fax 362-5393)

Guatemala Rent (☎ 473-1330, contact @ rentautos@ centroamerica.com), 19a Calle 16-91 at Avenida Petapa, Zona 12; La Aurora international airport (☎ 362-0205/06)

Hertz (☎ 334-2540/41, fax 331-7924, @ rentauto@ guate.net), 7a Avenida 14-76, Zona 9; Hotel Camino Real (☎ 368-0107); La Aurora international airport (☎ 331-1711)

National (Interrent-Europcar-Tilden) (☎ 360-3963, 332-4702, fax 360-1404, @ national@ pronet.net.gt), 12a Calle 7-69, Zona 9; La Aurora international airport (☎ 331-8365, 361-5618)

Tabarini (☎ 332-2161, 334-5907, fax 334-1925), 2a Calle A 7-30, Zona 10; La Aurora international airport (☎ 331-4755)

Tally Renta Autos (☎ 232-0421/3327, fax 253-1749), 7a Avenida 14-60, Zona 1; La Aurora international airport (☎ 332-6063, fax 334-5925)

Thrifty (☎ 332-1130/1220, fax 332-1207), Avenida La Reforma 8-33, Zona 10; La Aurora international airport (☎ 332-1265)

Tikal (☎ 332-4721, 361-0247), 2a Calle 6-56, Zona 10

GETTING AROUND
To/From the Airport

Aeropuerto Internacional La Aurora (☎ 334-7680, 331-7241/3, 334-7689) is in Zona 13, in the southern part of the city, 10 to 15 minutes from Zona 1 by taxi, half an hour by bus. Car rental offices and taxi ranks are outside the arrivals level.

For the city bus, go upstairs to the departures level and walk across the airport parking lot to the bus stop. Bus No 83 comes by every 15 minutes, 6 am to 9 pm, costs US$0.15 and will take you through Zonas 9 and 4 to Zona 1. Coming from town to the airport, No 83 goes south through Zona 1 on 10a Avenida, through Zona 9 on 6a Avenida, passes by the zoo and the museums on 7a Avenida and stops right in front of the international terminal.

Taxi fares to various points in the center are supposedly set but are actually negotiable, though quite high: US$5 from the airport to Zona 9 or 10; to Zona 1, US$7. A tip is expected. Be sure to establish the destination and price before getting into the taxi (see also Taxi, at the end of this chapter).

Many companies offer direct shuttle service between the airport and Antigua, with door-to-door service on the Antigua end. They depart from the airport every hour or so, take an hour to reach Antigua and cost US$7. You may be able to negotiate a deal if you ask to be dropped at the Central Park in Antigua rather than a specific hotel. These shuttles usually do not run after 8 pm or so. A taxi to Antigua costs around US$20; bargain hard and hook up with other travelers to cut costs.

One cheap trick if you're destined for Antigua but don't feel up to negotiating Guatemala City's hectic bus terminals is to take a taxi from in front of the airport to the Tikal Futura (Hyatt) Hotel on Calzada Roosevelt, Zona 11. This costs around US$3 and takes 15 minutes. Cross the street and wait for the scores of Antigua-bound buses to pass (US$0.20, 30 minutes). This is a safe and easy way to get from the airport to Antigua at the fraction of the shuttle or taxi price.

Bus & Jitney

Guatemala City buses are cheap, frequent and, though often very crowded, useful. They are, however, not always safe. Theft and robbery are not unusual; there have even been incidents of rape. *Preferencial* buses are newer, safer, not as crowded and more expensive at about US$0.15 per ride. Ordinary buses cost US$0.10 per ride.

There are loads of buses traversing the city on 6a Avenida (southbound) and 7a Avenida (northbound) in Zona 9; in Zona 1 these buses tend to swing away from the commercial district and travel along 4a, 5a, 9a and 10a Avenidas. The most useful north-south routes are buses Nos 2, 5 and 14. Note that modified numbers (such as 2A or 5-Bolívar) follow different routes and may not get you where you expect to go. Any bus with 'Terminal' in the front window stops at the Terminal de Autobuses in Zona 4.

To get between Zona 1 and Zona 10, take bus Nos 82 or 101. You can catch these on the corner of 10a Avenida between 8a and 12a Calles, after which these buses swing over to 8a Avenida. The 82 bus passes the Centro Cívico before turning on to Avenida La Reforma; this one is good for getting to INGUAT and several embassies.

City buses stop running at about 9 pm, and *ruteleros* (jitneys) begin to run up and down the main avenues. The jitneys run all night, until the buses resume their rattling rides at 5 am. Hold up your hand as the signal to stop a jitney or bus.

Taxi

Outside of Zona 1, you will rarely see taxis cruising. Rather you'll probably have to phone for one. Taxi Amarilla (☎ 332-1515) charges about half the price of most of the other taxi companies, and their taxis are metered.

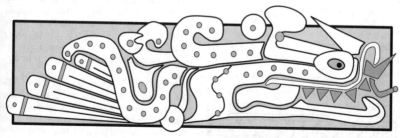

Antigua

• **pop 30,000** • **elevation 1530m**

Antigua Guatemala is one of the oldest and most beautiful cities in the Americas. Its setting is majestic, nestled between three dramatic volcanoes: Agua, Fuego and Acatenango. Fuego (Fire) is easily recognizable by its plume of smoke and – at night – by the red glow it projects against the sky. The cobblestone streets, sprays of bougainvillea bursting from crumbling ruins, pastel façades under terra cotta roofs and, of course, the volcanoes, make Antigua a stunning town even the most worldly can appreciate.

Highlights

- Visiting the museums and ruins strewn about town; favorites are Casa K'ojom and the convent ruins of La Merced
- Studying Spanish while living with a Guatemalan family
- Summiting Volcán Pacaya on a day trip
- Hiking or horseback riding to the Cerro de la Cruz vista point
- Shopping, either in Antigua proper or the famed weaving town of San Antonio Aguas Calientes, 14km from Antigua

Seasoned Guatemala travelers spend as little time in Guatemala City as possible, preferring to make Antigua their base, though many of these same veterans will gripe about Antigua's lack of authenticity – 'too many tourists,' they complain. At last check, few of these folks were making the miraculous transformation into Guatemalans, but hey, that's just a detail.

The major reason for Antigua's pan-international feel is that it's among the most popular Latin American cities in which to study Spanish, boasting more than 75 schools. It's true there are throngs of gringos in Antigua (especially from June through August), and you can dine on sushi or watch your football team on satellite television or sip a latte in the park. Whether you find this influence of western culture repulsive or attractive, it doesn't change the fact that Antigua is gorgeous and, in its own way, Guatemalan. Check out market days (Monday, Thursday and Saturday) or go for a sunrise stroll through the sleepy streets and you'll see.

Perhaps the most exciting time to visit Antigua is during Semana Santa or Holy Week (especially on Good Friday). If you have the opportunity to go then, seize it. It takes some advance planning, however (make your hotel reservations at least four months prior), as this is the busiest week of the year for tourism. Other busy tourist months are July and August and from November to April; May/June and September/October are quieter, but not drastically so. Antigua is cold after sunset, especially between September and March, so bring warm clothes; you might even consider packing a sleeping bag or buying a blanket or two, particularly if you're doing a homestay.

Antigua residents are known by the nickname *panza verde* (green belly), as they are said to eat lots of avocados, which grow abundantly here. Antigua is one of the more kid-friendly Guatemalan cities, with playgrounds, Spanish classes for children and food for the finicky.

HISTORY

Antigua was founded on March 10, 1543 as La muy Noble y muy Leal Ciudad de Santiago de los Caballeros de Goathemala, after the 1541 flooding of the previous capital, which was at present-day Ciudad Vieja on the flanks of Volcán Agua (see Around Antigua later in this chapter). The capital was moved to Antigua's current site in the Valle de Panchoy in 1543 and remained here for 233 years. In 1776, after the great earthquake of July 29, 1773 destroyed Antigua (which had already suffered considerable damage from earlier quakes), the capital was transferred again, this time to Guatemala City.

After the 1773 earthquake, Antigua was repopulated, very slowly, without losing its traditional character, architecture and cobblestone streets. In 1799 the city was renamed La Antigua Guatemala (Old Guatemala), though today everyone simply calls it Antigua. In 1944 the Legislative Assembly declared Antigua a national monument, and in 1979 UNESCO named the town a World Heritage Site.

Most of Antigua's buildings were constructed during the 17th and 18th centuries, when the city was a rich Spanish colonial capital and the Catholic Church was ascending to power. It seems no expense was spared in the city's magnificent architecture, and at the height of the Church's power Antigua had no fewer than 38 churches, including a cathedral. Many handsome, sturdy colonial buildings remain, and several impressive ruins have been preserved and are open to the public.

ORIENTATION

Volcán Agua is southeast of the city and visible from most points within it; Volcán Fuego is southwest and Volcán Acatenango is to the west. These three volcanoes (which appear on the city's coat of arms) provide easy reference points.

Antigua's street grid uses a modified version of the Guatemala City numbering system. (For details on that system, see Orientation in the Guatemala City chapter). In Antigua, compass points are added to the calles. The central point is the northeast corner of the city's main plaza, the Parque Central. Calles run east-west, so 4a Calle west of the Parque Central is 4a Calle Poniente.

The old headquarters of the Spanish colonial government, called the Palacio de los Capitanes, is on the south side of the plaza; you'll know it by its double (two-story) arcade. On the east side is the cathedral, on the north side is the Palacio del Ayuntamiento (Town Hall) and on the west side are banks and shops.

The Arco de Santa Catarina, spanning 5a Avenida Norte between 1a Calle and 2a Calle, is another famous Antigua landmark and is one of the few buildings that withstood the 1773 earthquake.

Buses arrive at the Terminal de Buses, a large open lot just west of the market, four blocks west of the Parque Central along 4a Calle Poniente. Buses serving towns and villages in the vicinity leave from the terminal as well, or from other nearby points around the market.

INFORMATION
Tourist Offices

Antigua's INGUAT tourist office (☎ 832-0763) is on the southeast corner of the Parque Central, next to the Palacio de los Capitanes. It's open from 8 am to 5 pm, seven days a week. They have free city maps, bus information and a schedule of Semana Santa events here.

There is an office of the newly formed Tourist Police (☎ 832-4131) on the corner of 4a Calle Oriente and 4a Avenida Norte. They offer free escorted tours to heretofore dangerous spots including the cemetery and the Cerro de la Cruz at 8:30 and 11 am and 3 pm daily. Anyone having the misfortune of being robbed should head here first, as the Tourist Police are reportedly very helpful in these situations.

Travelers interested in volunteering are encouraged to check out El Arco, 5a Avenida Norte No 25B, which distributes

ANTIGUA

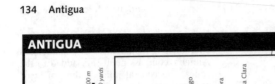

ANTIGUA

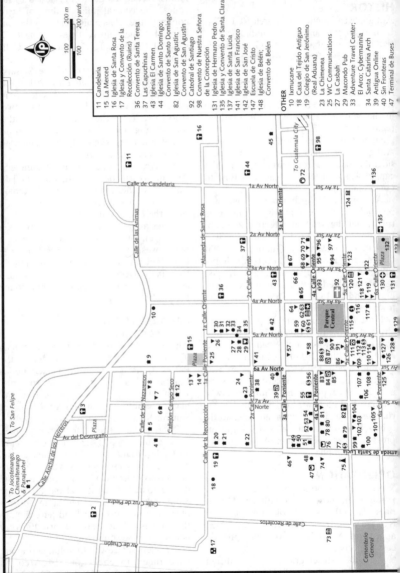

11 Candelaria
15 La Merced
16 Iglesia de Santa Rosa
17 Iglesia y Convento de la
   Recolección (Ruins)
36 Convento de Santa Teresa
37 Las Capuchinas
43 Iglesia El Carmen
44 Iglesia de Santo Domingo;
   Convento de Santo Domingo
82 Iglesia de San Agustín;
   Convento de San Agustín
92 Catedral de Santiago
98 Convento de Nuestra Señora
   de la Concepción
131 Iglesia de Hermano Pedro
135 Iglesia y Convento de Santa Clara
137 Iglesia de Santa Lucía
141 Iglesia de San Francisco
142 Iglesia de San José
147 Escuela de Cristo
148 Iglesia de Belén;
   Convento de Belén

OTHER
10 Ixmucane
18 Casa del Tejido Antiguo
19 Colegio de San Jerónimo
   (Real Aduana)
23 La Chimenea
25 WC Communications
27 La Casbah
29 Macondo Pub
33 Adventure Travel Center;
   El Arco; Cybermanía
34 Santa Catarina Arch
39 Antigua Online
40 Sin Fronteras
47 Terminal de Buses

ANTIGUA

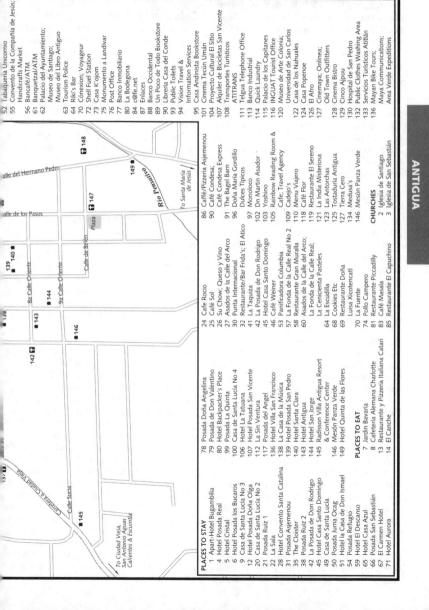

52 Tabaquería Unicornio
55 Convento de la Compañía de Jesús;
    Handicrafts Market
56 Bancafé/ATM
61 Banquetzal/ATM
62 Palacio del Ayuntamiento;
    Museo de Santiago;
    Museo del Libro Antiguo
63 Tourism Police
64 Riki's Bar
70 Conexion; Voyageur
72 Shell Fuel Station
73 Casa K'ojom
75 Monumento a Landivar
76 Post Office
77 Banco Inmobiliario
80 La Bodegona
84 c@fe.net
87 Enlaces
88 Banco Occidental
89 Un Poco de Todo Bookstore
90 Librería Casa del Conde
93 Public Toilets
94 Vision Travel &
    Information Services
95 Casa Andinista Bookstore
101 Cinema Tecún Umán
104 Proyecto Cultural El Sitio
107 Alquiler de Bicicletas San Vicente
108 Transportes Turísticos
    ATITRANS
111 Telgua Telephone Office
113 Banco Industrial
114 Quick Laundry
115 Palacio de los Capitanes
116 INGUAT Tourist Office
120 Museo de Arte Colonial;
    Universidad de San Carlos
122 Casa de los Nahuales
124 Casa Popenoe
126 El Afro
127 Cinemaya; Onlinea;
    Old Town Outfitters
128 Cinema Bistro
129 Cinco Aipnu
130 Hospital de San Pedro
132 Public Clothes Washing Area
133 Servicios Turísticos Atitlán
136 Mayan Bike Tours;
    Maya Communications;
    Area Verde Expeditions

PLACES TO STAY
1   Apart-Hotel Bugambilia
4   Hotel Posada Real
5   Hotel Cristal
6   Hotel Posada los Bucaros
9   Casa de Santa Lucia No 3
12 Hotel Posada Doña Olga
20 Casa de Santa Lucia No 2
21 Posada Ruiz 1
22 La Sala
28 Hotel Convento Santa Catalina
31 Posada Asjemenou
35 The Cloister
38 Posada Ruiz 2
42 La Posada de Don Rodrigo
45 Hotel Casa Santo Domingo
49 Casa de Santa Lucia
50 Posada Juma Ocag
51 Hotel la Casa de Don Ismael
54 Posada Refugio
59 Hotel El Descanso
65 Hotel Casa Azul
66 Posada San Sebastián
67 El Carmen Hotel
71 Hotel Aurora
78 Posada Doña Angelina
79 Posada de Don Valentino
80 Hotel Backpacker's Place
99 Posada La Quinta
100 Casa de Santa Lucia No 4
106 Hotel La Tatuana
107 Hotel Posada San Vicente
112 La Sin Ventura
117 Posada del Angel
136 Hotel Villa San Francisco
138 La Casa de la Música
139 Hotel Posada San Pedro
140 Hotel Santa Clara
143 Hotel Antigua
144 Hotel San Jorge
145 Radisson Villa Antigua Resort
    & Conference Center
146 Mesón Panza Verde
149 Hotel Quinta de las Flores

PLACES TO EAT
7   Jardin Bavaria
8   Cafetería Alemana Charlotte
13 Restaurante y Pizzería Italiana Catari
14 El Canche
24 Café Rocio
25 Café Sol
26 Su Chow; Queso y Vino
27 Asados de la Calle del Arco
30 Punta Internacional
32 Restaurante/Bar Frida's; El Atico
41 La Taquiza
42 La Posada de Don Rodrigo
45 Hotel Casa Santo Domingo
46 Café Weiner
53 Panificadora Columbia
57 La Fonda de la Calle Real No 2
58 Restaurante Gran Muralla
60 Asados de la Calle del Arco;
    La Fonda de la Calle Real;
    La Cenicienta Pasteles
64 La Escudilla
68 Cookies Etc
69 Restaurante Doña
    Luisa Xicotencatl
70 La Fonda
74 Pollo Campero
81 Restaurante Piccadilly
83 Café Masala
85 Restaurante El Capuchino
86 Caffé/Pizzeria Asjemenou
90 Café Condesa;
    Café Condesa Express
91 The Bagel Barn
96 Doña Maria Gordillo
    Dulces Típicos
97 Monoloco
102 Dn Martin Asador
103 Yoshino
105 Rainbow Reading Room &
    Cafe; Travel Agency
109 Cadejo's
110 Menu Viajero
118 Café Flor
119 Restaurante El Sereno
121 La India Misteriosa
123 Las Antorchas
125 Tostaduría Antigua
127 Tierra Cero
134 Medusa's
146 Mesón Panza Verde

CHURCHES
2   Iglesia de Santiago
3   Iglesia de San Sebastián

information and connects volunteers with opportunities. AmeriSpan Guatemala (☎ 832-0164, 832-4846, fax 832-1896, ✉ amerispan@guate.net), 6a Avenida Norte No 40A, is another option for researching volunteer prospects.

Visitors should look for the informative little book *Antigua Guatemala: An illustrated history of the city and its monuments* by Elizabeth Bell and Trevor Long.

Other useful sources of information are the *Revue* monthly magazine, the *Guatemala Weekly* newspaper and the bulletin boards at the Doña Luisa Xicotencatl restaurant, the Rainbow Reading Room & Cafe and the Casa Andinista bookstore, all described later in this chapter.

Money

Several banks around Parque Central change US dollars cash and traveler's checks. Banco Occidental, on 4a Calle Poniente just off the northwest corner of the plaza, changes both and also gives cash advances on Visa cards; it's open weekdays from 8:30 am to 7 pm, Saturday 9 am to 2 pm. Banco Industrial, on 5a Avenida Sur next to the Telgua office, just off the plaza, is open weekdays from 8 am to 7 pm, Saturday 8 am to 5 pm, and has a Visa ATM. Bancafé, 4a Calle Poniente No 22, also has a Visa ATM. Banquetzal was giving the best rate for dollars at the time of writing; their branch on the northwest corner of the park has a MasterCard ATM.

Post

The post office is at 4a Calle Poniente and Alameda de Santa Lucía, west of the Parque Central near the market.

If you want to ship packages, try DHL (☎ 832-3718, ☎/fax 832-3732) at 6a Avenida Sur No 16. This office is open Monday to Friday from 8 am to 6 pm and Saturday from 8 am to noon. An alternative is International Bonded Couriers (☎/fax 832-1696), 6a Avenida Sur No 12. They'll pick up, pack and deliver whatever you're shipping door-to-door. Envios is yet another shipping company, with locations at 3a Avenida Norte No 26 (☎ 832-1212, ✉ milagro@

conexion.com) and 3a Avenida Norte No 3 (☎ 832-0955).

Telephone & Fax

The Telgua telephone office is just off the southwest corner of the Parque Central, at the intersection of 5a Calle Poniente and 5a Avenida Sur. It's open every day and offers fax service, but you're better off phoning or faxing from one of the businesses catering to the communication needs of international tourists (see Email & Internet Access).

Don't use the phones spread throughout Antigua imploring you to call the US for free; they charge usurious rates to your credit card – up to US$20 a minute in some cases!

Email & Internet Access

Antigua is awash in businesses supplying reliable, affordable Internet services. One of the oldest is Conexion (☎ 832-3768, fax 832-0082, ✉ users@conexion.com), at 4a Calle Oriente No 14 inside La Fuente courtyard, where you can send and/or receive phone, fax, electronic mail and telex messages. Prices for sending and receiving are reasonable. Conexion also offers local dial-up access. They're open every day from 8:30 am to 7 pm. International telephone and fax services are also available at WC Communications (☎ 832-5666, contact ✉ wwcall@infovia.com), 1a Calle Poniente No 9, opposite La Merced church, and at Maya Communications in the Hotel Villa San Francisco, 1a Avenida Sur No 15, which claims it offers 24-hour access, seven days a week.

Enlaces (☎ 832-0216, contact ✉ enlace@pobox.com), 6a Avenida Norte No 1, has competitively priced email, phone and fax services and scores of computers and pay phones, so you rarely have to wait. They're open Monday to Saturday from 8 am to 7:30 pm and Sundays from 8 am to 1 pm. Other places to use the Internet include Onlinea at 6a Calle Poniente No 7; c@fe.net at 6a Avenida Norte No 14; Antigua Online at 3a Calle Poniente No 12; and Cybermannia at 5a Avenida Norte No 25B.

Travel Agencies

Everywhere you turn in Antigua, you'll see travel agencies offering tours to interesting sites in Guatemala, international flights, shuttle buses to the airport and the most popular tourist destinations, and more. Reputable agencies include, but are not limited to, the following:

Adventure Travel Center (☎/fax 832-0162, contact ✉ viareal@guate.net), 5a Avenida Norte No 25B, near the arch

Agencia de Viajes Tivoli (☎ 832-1370, 832-4274, fax 832-5690, ✉ antigua@tivoli.com), 4a Calle Oriente No 10, local 3

Gran Jaguar Travel Agency (☎ 832-2712), 4a Calle Poniente No 30; Alameda de Santa Lucia Sur No 3 (☎ 832-3149, 832-3107, evenings); has the cheapest tours to Volcán Pacaya

Monarcas Travel (☎ 832-4779), 7a Avenida Norte No 15A and 6a Avenida Norte No 60A (☎ 832-4305); does trips to Mayan sites and shuttles to Copán

Rainbow Travel Center (☎ 832-4202/3/4/5/6/7, fax 832-4206, ✉ myers@gua.gbm.net), 7a Avenida Sur No 8; English, French, German, Italian and Spanish spoken here

Servicios Turísticos Atitlán (☎/fax 832-1493, contact ✉ turisticosatitlan@yahoo.com, www .atitlan.com), 2a Avenida Sur No 4A

Sin Fronteras (☎ 832-1017, 832-1226, ☎/fax 832-2674, ✉ sinfront@sinfront.com), 3a Calle Poniente No 12; the Antigua representative for Maya Expeditions rafting tours; feature many tour packages to Cuba

Transportes Turísticos ATITRANS (☎ 832-1381, 832-1297, ☎/fax 832-0644, 832-3371 after 8 pm, ✉ atitrans@quick.guate.com), 6a Avenida Sur No 7 & 8

TURANSA (☎/fax 832-2928), Calle Sucia and Carretera a Ciudad Vieja, in the Hotel Radisson Villa Antigua; 5a Calle Poniente No 11B (☎/fax 832-3316)

Vision Travel and Information Services (☎ 832-3293, 832-1962/4, fax 832-1955, ✉ vision@ guatemalainfo.com, www.guatemalainfo.com), 3a Avenida Norte No 3 (behind the Cathedral); tours, information, guidebook library, shuttles and phone calls are offered here; also will hold mail and recycle/refill water bottles for cheap (well-recommended)

Voyageur (☎ 832-4237/8, fax 832-4247, ✉ info@ travel.net.gt), 4a Calle Oriente No 14, inside La Fuente courtyard

Warning: Several reports have alleged unprofessional behavior by the Eco Aventuras travel agency. There are many highly recommended agencies in Antigua, so you may be better off sticking with one of those.

Bookstores & Libraries

The Rainbow Reading Room & Cafe, at the corner of 7a Avenida Sur and 6a Calle Poniente, has thousands of used books in English and Spanish for sale, rent or trade.

Un Poco de Todo and the Librería Casa del Conde, both on the west side of Parque Central, and the Casa Andinista at 4a Calle Oriente No 5, opposite the Doña Luisa Xicotencatl restaurant, are other excellent bookstores. All carry both new and used books in several languages, and are open every day.

Hamlin y White at 4a Calle Oriente No 12A, inside Jade SA, boasts over 65 magazine titles and a Lonely Planet Travel Guide Center, with many regional guides that will interest travelers sallying forth from Guatemala. One of the best collections of used books for sale or swap is at Monoloco (see Place to Eat later in this chapter).

La Biblioteca Internacional de Antigua (The International Library of Antigua), 5a Calle Poniente No 15 in the Proyecto Cultural El Sitio building, has a good collection of books, with temporary or long-term memberships available.

Laundry

Laundries are everywhere. The block of 6a Calle Poniente between 5a Avenida and 7a Avenida Sur is jammed with them. Quick Laundry (☎ 832-1976), 6a Calle Poniente No 14, is fast and reliable. It's open Monday to Saturday 9 am to 6 pm. The going rate is about US$0.80 a pound for wash and dry.

Toilets

Public toilets are on 4a Calle Oriente near the corner of 4a Avenida Norte, just off the northeast corner of Parque Central.

Medical Services

Hospital de San Pedro (☎ 832-0301) is at 3a Avenida Sur and 6a Calle Oriente.

ANTIGUA

Ixmucane (☎ 832-5539, ✉ houston@ conexion.com.gt), 4a Avenida Norte No 32, provides a complete range of gynecological and obstetrical services, from dispensing birth control to delivering babies. Herbal supplements, treatment and information are available here as well; German, English and Spanish are spoken.

Emergency
The National Police can be reached at ☎ 832-0251; the Tourism Police are on ☎ 832-4131. The voluntary fire department is at ☎ 832-0234, and the municipal fire department can be reached at ☎ 832-1075.

Dangers & Annoyances
Antigua seems like such a mellow town that you wouldn't think any misfortune could ever befall you. Think again. Though you probably will never have a problem, be wary when walking the deserted streets late at night, as robberies have taken place. Armed robberies (and even murder) have also occurred on Cerro de la Cruz and on Volcán Pacaya (see Around Antigua later in this chapter, for details).

The cemetery has been the scene of many robberies, some armed, and is considered off limits by most, unless you are escorted by the Tourist Police. Crime against tourists has dropped precipitously in Antigua since the formation of this agency; they will accompany you to the Cerro or the cemetery, free of charge (see Tourist Offices earlier in this section).

PARQUE CENTRAL
This plaza is the gathering place for citizens and foreign visitors alike. On most days the periphery is lined with villagers who have brought their handicrafts to sell to tourists; on Sunday it's mobbed with marketers, and the streets on the east and west sides of the park are closed to traffic in order to give them room. The best prices are to be had late on Sunday afternoon, when the market is winding down. In the early evenings, children desperately trying to meet their daily quota of items sold will approach you offering insanely low prices for their handicrafts.

The plaza's famous fountain was built in 1738. On most weekend nights you can hear mariachi or marimba bands playing in the park.

Palacio de los Capitanes
Built in 1543, the Palacio de los Capitanes has a stately double arcade on its façade, which marches proudly across the southern extent of the park. Most of the façade is original, but the rest of the building was reconstructed a century ago. From 1543 to 1773 this building was the governmental center of all Central America, in command of Chiapas, Guatemala, Honduras and Nicaragua.

Catedral de Santiago
The Catedral de Santiago, on the east side of the park, was founded in 1542, repeatedly damaged by earthquakes, badly ruined in 1773, and only partially rebuilt between 1780 and 1820. In the 16th and early 17th centuries, Antigua's churches had lavish baroque interiors, but most lost this richness when they were rebuilt after the earthquakes. The present cathedral, stripped of its expensive decoration, occupies what was the narthex of the original edifice. In a crypt lie the bones of Bernal Díaz del Castillo, historian of the Spanish conquest, who died in 1581. Restoration work is being carried out on other parts of the cathedral, but it will never regain its former grandeur. If the front entrance is not open, you can enter from other entrances in the rear of the building and on the south side. This building is particularly striking at night when it is tastefully lit.

Palacio del Ayuntamiento
On the north side of the park stands the Palacio del Ayuntamiento, Antigua's town hall, which dates mostly from 1743. In addition to town offices, it houses the **Museo de Santiago**, which exhibits a collection of colonial furnishings, artifacts and weapons. Hours are 9 am to 4 pm Tuesday to Friday, and 9 am to noon and 2 to 4 pm on Saturday and Sunday (closed Monday); admission costs US$1.25.

Next door (and with the same hours and admission price) is the **Museo del Libro Antiguo** (Old Book Museum), which has exhibits of colonial printing and binding, and the colonial prison.

Universidad de San Carlos

The Universidad de San Carlos was founded in 1676; its main building (built in 1763), 5a Calle Oriente No 5 half a block east of the park, now houses the **Museo de Arte Colonial** (☎ 832-0429), keeping the same hours as the Museo de Santiago.

CASA K'OJOM

In 1984, Samuel Franco Arce began photographing Mayan ceremonies and festivals and recording their music on audiotape, and we are all the luckier for it. By 1987 he had enough to found Casa K'ojom ('House of Music'), a museum dedicated to Mayan music and the ceremonies in which it figures prominently.

The museum (☎ 832-3087) is at Calle de Recoletos No 55, a block west of the bus station. It's open Monday to Friday from 9:30 am to 12:30 pm and 2 to 5 pm (till 4 pm on Saturday), and is closed on Sunday. Admission costs US$0.65, including a superlative audiovisual show and a live demonstration of the instruments in the collection. The gift shop sells instruments and compact discs and is intriguing in its own right.

Some visitors to Guatemalan towns and villages are fortuitous enough to witness a parade of the *cofradías*, or some other age-old ceremony. But everyone can experience some of this fascinating culture in a visit to Casa K'ojom. Besides the fine collection of photographs, Franco has amassed musical instruments, tools, masks and figures. Though relatively small, the collection is cleverly displayed in two parts: The first room features traditional instruments in use before the Spanish arrived and the second has instruments that either evolved or survived after colonialism. Recordings of the music play softly in the background. Be sure to see the exhibit featuring Maximón, the evil folk-god venerated by the people of several highland towns.

CHURCHES

Once glorious in their gilded baroque finery, Antigua's churches have suffered indignities from both nature and humankind. Rebuilding after earthquakes gave the churches thicker walls, lower towers and belfries and unembellished interiors, and moving the capital to Guatemala City deprived Antigua of the population needed to maintain the churches in their traditional richness. Still, they are impressive. Most are open daily 9 am to 5 pm; entrance costs under US$2. In addition to those churches noted below, you'll find many others scattered around town in various states of decay.

La Merced

From the park, walk three long blocks up 5a Avenida Norte, passing beneath the Arco de Santa Catarina, built in 1694 and rebuilt in the 19th century. At the northern end of 5a Avenida is the Iglesia y Convento de Nuestra Señora de La Merced, known simply as La Merced – Antigua's most striking colonial church.

La Merced's construction began in 1548. Improvements continued to be made until 1717, when the church was ruined by earthquakes. Reconstruction was completed in 1767, but in 1773 earthquake struck again and the convent was destroyed. Repairs to the church were made from 1850 to 1855; its baroque façade dates from this period. Inside the ruins of the convent is a fountain 27m in diameter, which is said to be the largest in Central America. Notice the water lily blossoms (traditionally a symbol of power for Mayan lords) on this fountain and the one at the entrance to the Church, suggesting the influence of indigenous laborers used to construct La Merced. There are pretty views from the upper level. Entering the convent costs US$0.25 and is well worth it.

San Francisco

The next most notable church is the Iglesia de San Francisco at 7a Calle Oriente and 1a Avenida Sur. It dates from the mid-16th century, but little of the original building remains. Rebuilding and restoration over the centuries have produced a handsome structure; reinforced concrete added in 1961 protected the church from suffering serious damage in the 1976 earthquake. All that remains of the original church is the Chapel of Hermano Pedro (not to be confused with the Iglesia de Hermano Pedro on 3a Avenida Sur), resting place of Hermano Pedro de San José Betancourt, a Franciscan monk who founded a hospital for the poor and earned the gratitude of generations. He died here in 1667; his intercession is still sought by the ill, who pray fervently by where his casket once stood.

Las Capuchinas

The Iglesia y Convento de Nuestra Señora del Pilar de Zaragoza, usually called simply Las Capuchinas, 2a Avenida Norte and 2a Calle Oriente, was a convent founded in 1736 by nuns from Madrid. Destroyed repeatedly by earthquakes, it is now a museum featuring exhibits of the religious life in colonial times. The building has many unusual features, including a circular building of 18 nuns' cells built around a circular patio. Guided tours are available.

La Recolección

The Iglesia y Convento de la Recolección, a massive ruin at the west end of 1a Calle Poniente, is among Antigua's most impressive monuments. Built between 1701 and 1708, the church was inaugurated in 1717, but suffered considerable damage from an earthquake that same year. The buildings were destroyed in the earthquake of 1773.

Colegio de San Jerónimo (Real Aduana)

Near La Recolección, at the corner of Alameda de Santa Lucía and 1a Calle Poniente, this church was built in 1757 by friars of the Merced order. However, because it did not have royal authorization, it was taken over by Spain's Carlos III in 1761. In 1765 it was designated for use as the Real Aduana (Royal Customs House) but was destroyed in the earthquake of 1773. The construction includes the hermitage of San Jerónimo. The ruins are open daily from 9 am to 5 pm; admission is US$1.25.

Santa Clara

The Iglesia y Convento de Santa Clara, 2a Avenida Sur No 27, at the corner of 6a Calle Oriente, was built in 1715 and destroyed by earthquake two years later. The present construction was inaugurated in 1734 but was destroyed by the earthquake of 1773. The dome of the church, which survived the 1773 quake, was destroyed by another in 1874.

In front of the church is a small rectangular plaza and a public clothes washing area, where women still come today to do their wash, spreading their laundry out on the lawn to dry.

CASA POPENOE

At the corner of 5a Calle Oriente and 1a Avenida Sur stands this beautiful mansion built in 1636 by Don Luis de las Infantas Mendoza y Venegas. Ruined by the earthquake of 1773, the house stood desolate for 1½ centuries until it was bought in 1931 by Dr and Mrs Popenoe. The Popenoes' painstaking and authentic restoration yields a fascinating glimpse of how the family of a royal official (Don Luis) lived in Antigua in the 17th century. The house is open Monday to Saturday from 2 to 4 pm; a self-guided tour costs US$0.85.

MONUMENT TO LANDÍVAR

At the western end of 5a Calle Poniente is the Monumento a Landívar, a structure of five colonial-style arches set in a pristine little park. Rafael Landívar, an 18th-century Jesuit priest and poet, lived and wrote in Antigua for some time. Landívar's poetry is esteemed as the best of the colonial period, even though much of it was written in Italy after the Jesuits were expelled from Guatemala. Landívar's Antigua house was nearby on 5a Calle Poniente.

MARKET

At the west end of 4a Calle Oriente, on the west side of Alameda de Santa Lucía, sprawls Antigua's market – chaotic, colorful and always busy. Morning, when all the village people from the vicinity are actively buying and selling, is the best time to come. Official market days are Monday, Thursday and Saturday (see also Shopping later in this chapter).

CEMETERY

Antigua's Cementerio General west of the market and bus terminal is a beautiful conglomeration of tombs and mausoleums, all decked out with wreaths, exotic flowers and other recent signs of mourning. Unfortunately, it's also considered dangerous because thieves often lie in wait for tourists to come strolling by. If you want to check out the cemetery, go with a Tourist Police escort (see Tourist Offices for details) or in a group, though even large groups have been robbed here.

HORSEBACK RIDING

Several stables in Antigua rent horses and arrange day or overnight tours into the countryside. Establo Santiago has a solid reputation; contact them through the Adventure Travel Center (see Travel Agencies earlier in this chapter for detailed information).

Several readers have recommended the Ravenscroft Riding Stables (☎ 832-6229, afternoons), 2a Avenida Sur No 3 in San Juan del Obispo, 3.2km south of Antigua, on the road to Santa María de Jesús (buses leave every half-hour from the bus station behind the market). They offer English-style riding, with scenic rides of three, four or five hours in the valleys and hills around Antigua. Reservations and information are available through the Hotel San Jorge (☎ 832-3132), 4a Avenida Sur No 13.

Another option is La Ronda Stables (☎ 832-1224), which has tours from two to six hours and for every level of experience. Reservations and information are also available at the Bagel Barn (see Places to Eat later in this chapter).

BICYCLING

Bicycles can be rented at several places in Antigua, including Alquiler de Bicicletas

San Vicente (☎/fax 832-3311), 6a Avenida Sur No 6 in the Hotel Posada San Vicente and Aviatur (☎/fax 832-2642), 5a Avenida Norte No 35, just north of the arch. Prices are around US$1.35 an hour, US$4.15 a half-day, US$6 to US$8.35 a day, US$25 a week or US$35 for two weeks. Prices and equipment vary, so it pays to shop around.

Mayan Bike Tours (☎ 832-3383, 832-6506, ✉ mayanbikeone@conexion.com.gt, www .mayanbike.com), 1a Avenida Sur No 15, rents bikes and offers several area mountain bike tours. The tours include all gear and cost US$19 for a half day, US$39 for a full day with lunch. They also do hike-and-bike tours to Acatenango volcano (US$49, 12 hours) and Lago de Atitlán (US$175, two days/one night).

Old Town Outfitters (☎ 832-4243, ✉ trvlnlite@hotmail.com), 6a Calle Poniente No 7, rents high quality equipment. A standard bike is US$7 a day and a premium unit is US$14. They also offer a two day/one night peddle and paddle tour (bike and kayak) to Lago de Atitlán for US$125. You can rent camping gear here as well. See their Web site at www.bikeguatemala.com for more information.

WHITE-WATER RAFTING

Area Verde Expeditions (☎/fax 832-3383, in the US ☎/fax 719-583-8929, ✉ mayanbike@ guate.net) is housed with Mayan Bike Tours at 1a Avenida Sur No 15 in the Villa San Francisco. They offer a variety of whitewater rafting tours lasting from one to five days. Different rivers are rafted at different times of year, making it possible to raft all year round.

Maya Expeditions, represented in Antigua by Sin Fronteras (☎ 832-1017, ☎/fax 832-2674), 3a Calle Poniente No 12, also has a variety of full and multiday tours on several rivers throughout Guatemala.

LANGUAGE COURSES

Antigua is famous for its Spanish language schools, which attract students from around the world. There are many schools from which to choose – over 75 at last count.

Price, quality of teaching and satisfaction of students vary greatly from one school to another. Often the quality of the instruction depends upon the particular teacher, and thus may vary even within a single school. Visit several schools before you choose one. If possible, ask for references and talk to someone who has studied recently at your school of choice – you'll have no trouble running into lots of Spanish students in Antigua. The INGUAT tourist office also has a list of reputable schools. They include:

Academia de Español Guatemala (☎ 832-5057/60, fax 832-5058, contact @ aegnow@guate.net, www .travellog.com/guatemala/antigua/acadespanol/ school.html), 7a Calle Oriente No 15

Academia de Español Sevilla (☎/fax 832-0442), 1a Avenida Sur No 8

Academia de Español Tecún Umán (☎/fax 832-2792, contact @ etecun@centramerica.com, www.centralamerica.com/tecunuman), 6a Calle Poniente No 34

AmeriSpan Guatemala, 6a Avenida Norte No 40A (☎ 832-0164, 832-4846, fax 832-1896; @ info@amerispan.com, at www.amerispan .com); in the US, AmeriSpan USA, PO Box 40007, Philadelphia, PA 19106 (☎ 215-751-1100, fax 751-1986, 800-879-6640); not a school, but does maintain current lists of the most highly recommended Spanish institutions

Centro de Español Don Pedro de Alvarado (☎/fax 832-4180), 1a Calle Poniente No 24

Centro Lingüístico La Unión (☎/fax 832-7337, contact @ launion@conexion.com, www.launion .conexion.com), 1a Avenida Sur No 21; has a loyal following

Centro Lingüístico Maya (☎ 832-1342, @ clmmaya@guate.net), 5a Calle Poniente No 20

Christian Spanish Academy (CSA) (☎ 832-3922, fax 832-3760, @ chspanac@infovia.com.gt), 6a Avenida Norte No 15

Don Quijote Spanish Academy (☎ 832-2868, @ infocentral@donquijote.org, www.donquijote .org), Portal del Ayuntamiento No 6, in the Museo del Libro Antiguo, on the north side of Parque Central

Escuela de Español San José el Viejo (☎ 832-3028, fax 832-3029, @ spanish@guate.net, www.guate .net/spanish; in the US 800-562-6274), 5a Avenida Sur No 34; in the US write Section 544, P.O. Box 02-5289, Miami, FL 33102

Proyecto Lingüístico Francisco Marroquín (☎/fax 832-2886, @ info@langlink.com) has four locations in Antigua; main office at 7a Calle Poniente No 31

Classes start every Monday at most schools, though you can usually be placed with a teacher any day of the week. Cost for four hours of classes daily, five days a week, ranges from around US$75 to US$100 per week for one-on-one instruction; you can also enroll for up to seven hours a day of instruction. Most schools offer to arrange room and board with local families for around US$40 to US$60 per week.

Homestays are supposed to promote the 'total immersion' concept of language learning, but too often there are several foreigners staying with a local family at once. In this case, it's more like a hotel than a family atmosphere. Also, often there are separate mealtimes for students and the family. Make a point of inquiring after such homestay details if you really want to be totally immersed. Occasionally there have been problems with host families not receiving payments from the schools, even though the students already paid the school for the homestay. Ask if you can pay your host family directly if you have any doubts.

Antigua is not for everyone who wants to study Spanish; there are so many foreigners about, it takes some real discipline to converse in Spanish rather than your native tongue. If you think this will bother you, consider studying in Xela or the Petén where there are fewer foreign students and more opportunities to dive headfirst into learning Spanish.

ORGANIZED TOURS

One of the most popular organized tours from Antigua is the day hike to the summit of Volcán Pacaya. Though most agencies in Antigua offer this trip, many are subcontracted by Gran Jaguar Travel Agency, which actually provides the transportation, guide and security for the hike (see Around Antigua later in this chapter). Booking the trip directly with Gran Jaguar costs around US$5, whereas it can be double or even triple that elsewhere.

Elizabeth Bell, author of books on Antigua, offers cultural tours of the town (in English and/or Spanish) on Tuesdays, Wednesdays, Fridays and Saturdays at 9:30 am. On Mondays and Thursdays, the tours are led by her colleague Roberto Spillari and start at 2 pm. The walking tours take two hours and cost US$18. Reservations are suggested and can be made at Antigua Tours (☎ 832-0140, ext. 341, contact ✉ elizbell@guate.net), in the lobby of the Casa Santo Domingo, 3a Calle Oriente No 28. (See Entertainment later in this chapter, for information on her weekly slide shows.)

A variety of tours take you farther afield. The Adventure Travel Center offers an interesting three-hour Villages & Farm Tour for US$25. Vision Travel has a recommended Guatemala City museum tour for US$25.

Numerous travel agencies offer tours to many farther flung places, including Tikal, Copán, Quiriguá, Río Dulce, Monterrico, Chichicastenango and Panajachel.

SPECIAL EVENTS
Semana Santa
By far the most interesting time to be in Antigua is during the Semana Santa (Holy Week) celebrations, when hundreds of people dress in deep purple robes to accompany daily religious processions in remembrance of the Crucifixion. Dense clouds of incense envelop the parade. Streets are covered in breathtakingly elaborate and colorful *alfombras* (carpets) of colored sawdust and flower petals. These beautiful but fragile works of art are destroyed as the processions shuffle through them, but are recreated the next morning for another day of parades.

Traditionally, the most interesting days are Palm Sunday, when a procession departs from La Merced (see Churches) in mid-afternoon; Holy Thursday, when a late afternoon procession departs from the Iglesia de San Francisco; and Good Friday, when an early morning procession departs from La Merced, and a late afternoon one leaves from the Escuela de Cristo. Have ironclad hotel reservations well in advance of these dates, or plan to stay in Guatemala City or another town and commute to the festivities.

The booklet *Lent and Easter Week in Antigua* by Elizabeth Bell gives explanations and a day-by-day schedule of processions, *velaciones* (vigils) and other events taking place throughout the Lenten season, the 40 days before Easter.

On a secular note, beware of pickpockets. It seems that Guatemala City's entire population of pickpockets (numbering perhaps in the hundreds) decamps to Antigua for Semana Santa. In the press of the emotion-filled crowds lining the processional routes, they target foreign tourists especially.

PLACES TO STAY
Travelers should be aware that the climate in Antigua, combined with the plaster and cement used in building construction, means hotel rooms can be damp, musty and even moldy; this holds true for hotels in all price ranges, not just the budget places. Rooms on the ground floor and/or with carpet seem to fare worse, so avoid the mildew funk by going for an upstairs room, preferably with wood, tile or linoleum floors.

Budget
When checking a pension or budget hotel, look at several rooms, as some are much better than others. Where hot water is indicated, expect an electric unit taped to the shower head; feel especially blessed if there's actually a separate hot water tap.

Posada Refugio (4a Calle Poniente No 30) is the cheapie du jour among savvy travelers. It's a huge place with basic singles/doubles/triples without bath for US$3/3/4. Singles/doubles/triples with private bath are US$4/8/10. Don't expect anything fancy, and check out a few rooms to find one you like, as they vary widely. Another hopping budget option is *La Sala (☎ 832-6483)*, on the corner of Alameda de Santa Lucía and 2a Calle Poniente, which has dorm beds for US$2.30 per person. There's a restaurant here, too.

Posada Ruiz 2 (2a Calle Poniente No 25), is a good deal for the price, with small singles/doubles for US$3/4, all with shared bath, opening onto a central courtyard. Lots of young international travelers stay here, congregating in the courtyard in the evening. Not as nice is *Posada Ruiz 1* *(Alameda de Santa Lucía No 17)*, charging US$3.85 per person.

Less attractive, but acceptable for the price, *Posada La Quinta (5a Calle Poniente No 19)* near the bus station, is a basic place charging US$5/8 per person for rooms with shared/private bath. The nearby *Posada Doña Angelina (☎ 832-5173, 4a Calle Poniente No 33)*, has singles/doubles for US$4/7 with shared bath, US$8/11/18 for singles/ doubles/triples with private bath.

The new *Hotel Backpacker's Place (☎ 832-5023, 4a Calle Poniente No 27)* is conveniently located and though the dècor is generic, the beds are comfortable and the rooms spacious. Singles/doubles with shared bath are US$7/8; with private bath they are US$8/10. Try to get a room facing south for killer views of Volcán Agua.

Posada Juma Ocag (☎ 832-3109, Alameda de Santa Lucía No 13) is everything you could want in a budget hotel. The four spotless, comfortable rooms all have the highest quality mattresses (even a king!) and traditional appointments. Each room has a private hot bath; there's also a rooftop patio and small but well-tended garden. Service is attentive and touches like reading lamps and drinking water make this a great value with doubles/triples for US$11/13. It's very peaceful, despite the location across from the market and bus terminal. Unfortunately, they don't accept reservations.

Another terrific value is *Hotel la Casa de Don Ismael (3a Calle Poniente No 6)*, down the nameless alley off 3a Calle Poniente, between 7a Avenida and Alameda de Santa Lucía. Clean, comfortable singles/doubles with shared hot bath are US$6/8. This is a safe, friendly place that fills up fast; try to get an upstairs room off the terrace. There's a compact, lush courtyard and free coffee or tea for guests. Nearby is the *Hospedaje Primavera*, which has clean but musty singles/ doubles with shared bath for US$5/7 and doubles with private bath for US$8.

The *Hotel Cristal (☎ 832-4177, Avenida del Desengaño No 25)*, is great for the price, with 10 clean rooms around a beautiful central garden. Singles/doubles/triples are US$7/9/12 with shared bath, US$9/12/13 with private bath. Students receive a 10% discount. Meals are available. Another good option in this part of town is the *Hotel Posada Doña Olga (☎ 514-5323, Callejón Campo Seco No 3C)*. Quiet and safe rooms (some dark) are US$9 for one or two people.

Hotel Villa San Francisco (☎ 832-3383, @ mayanbikeone@conexion.com.gt, 1a Avenida Sur No 15), at the corner of 6a Calle Oriente, has rundown singles/doubles for US$10/13 with private bath. There are also cheaper rooms with general bath. An upstairs terrace, a courtyard garden, a telephone and fax service and bicycle rental are all here.

With four locations, Antigua has a burgeoning hotel chain in the *Casas de Santa Lucía*. All charge US$10.25 for doubles with private bath and none have signs. The original at Alameda de Santa Lucía No 9, between 5a and 6a Calles Poniente, has dark rooms with pseudo-colonial atmosphere, but was being remodeled at the time of writing and may offer better digs by the time you get there; ring the bell to the left of the door. There's parking.

More attractive are the three newer establishments. They are the *Casa de Santa Lucía No 2 (Alameda de Santa Lucía Norte No 21)*, *Casa de Santa Lucía No 3 (6a Avenida Norte No 43A)* and *Casa de Santa Lucía No 4 (Alameda de Santa Lucía No 5)*. All have clean, pleasant, attractive rooms with private hot bath and rooftop terraces with views. Nos 2 and 3 have parking. The architecture of No 4 makes it very loud – don't be surprised if you're serenaded by slamming doors and boisterous guests at odd hours.

Hotel La Tatuana (☎ 832-1223, 7a Avenida Sur No 3) has good, clean rooms with private bath for US$13/15 a single/ double. You may have success bargaining during the off-season here. Similar in price is *Hotel Posada San Vicente (☎ /fax 832-*

3311, 6a Avenida Sur No 6), which has doubles with private bath for US$13. Upstairs rooms are better; there's a pool table here and they rent bicycles.

A step up in quality, **Posada de Don Valentino** (☎ *832-0384, 5a Calle Poniente No 28)* has a nice patio and garden, with bright and clean rooms for US$12/20/25 a single/double/triple with private bath. They have a parking lot one block away.

Apart-Hotel Bugambilia (☎ */fax 832-2732, Calle Ancha de los Herreros No 27)* has 10 apartments, each with fully equipped kitchen, two or three double beds, cable TV and private hot bath. Daily rates are US$15/19/23 for one, two or three people. Discounts are offered for weekly and monthly stays. It has sitting areas, a beautiful patio garden, a fountain and a rooftop terrace.

Avoid the **Arizona Hotel** *(2a Calle Poniente No 29A)*, which has an unsavory reputation.

Mid-Range

Antigua's mid-range hotels allow you to wallow in the city's colonial charms for a very moderate outlay of cash.

Posada Asjemenou (☎ *832-2670, 5a Avenida Norte No 31)*, just north of the arch, is a beautifully renovated house built around a grassy courtyard with a fountain. It charges US$20/33 for single/double rooms with shared bath, US$26/40 with private bath. There are discounts for stays of a week or more.

The very friendly **Hotel Posada San Pedro** (☎ *832-3594, 3a Avenida Sur No 15)* comes highly recommended. The 10 rooms are super clean and nicely appointed; upstairs units have views and there is a communal kitchen, hangout space and roof patio. This is a good choice at US$20/25 for a single/double.

Hotel El Descanso (☎ *832-0142, 5a Avenida Norte No 9)*, '50 steps from the central plaza,' is friendly, clean and convenient. Its five rooms are US$24/30 for singles/doubles with private bath. There's a terrace upstairs in the rear. Also in this price range is the **Hotel Posada Los Bucaros** (☎ */fax*

832-2346, 7a Avenida Norte No 94), with gleaming singles/doubles/triples with private hot bath and cable TV for US$25/30/35. Guests have access to the kitchen and there are laundry and telephone services available.

Hotel Santa Clara (☎ */fax 832-0342, 2a Avenida Sur No 20)* is quiet, proper and clean, with a pleasant garden and some large rooms with two double beds. Singles/doubles with terrific hot water bath are US$21/25. In the low season rooms are a very reasonable US$13/16.

La Sin Ventura (☎ *832-0581, contact* ✉ *frontdesk@lasinventura.com, www.lasin-ventura.com, 5a Avenida Sur No 8)* has a great location just off the park; sparkling singles/doubles are US$19/30.

Hotel Posada Real (☎ *832-3396, Avenida del Desengaño No 24)* is a beautiful colonial hotel. Its nine rooms and suites, all with private hot bath and cable TV, are lovely, and many have fireplaces. Singles/doubles/triples are US$25/35/45. Rooms can be noisy, however.

Hotel San Jorge (☎ */fax 832-3132, 4a Avenida Sur No 13)* is in a modern building where all 14 rooms have fireplace, cable TV and private bath with tub. Parking and laundry are also here, and the guests (mostly older couples from the US) may use the swimming pool and room service facilities of the posh Hotel Antigua nearby. Rooms are US$30/35/40 a single/double/triple, with possible discounts in low season for students or stays of a month or more. Credit cards are accepted.

The **Posada San Sebastián** (☎ */fax 832-2621, 3a Avenida Norte No 4)* is like a museum where you get to spend the night. Each of the eight rooms is packed with Guatemalan antiques and laid with terra cotta tile, giving this place an historic, quirky ambiance. The rich, unique rooms, all with private hot bath and cable TV are US$36/46/56 for singles/doubles/triples. Guests have use of the kitchen and the rooftop terrace.

El Carmen Hotel (☎ *832-3850/1/2/3, fax 832-3847, 3a Avenida Norte No 9)* is very tidy and quiet despite its location only 1½

ANTIGUA

blocks from the square. Twelve pleasant rooms with cable TV, telephone, private bath and continental breakfast are US$44/50/60 for one to three beds, and there's a courtyard sitting area, a Jacuzzi and a rooftop terrace with a fine view.

La Casa de la Música (☎ 832-0335, fax 832-3690, contact ✉ ginger@guate.net, www.lacasadelamusica.centramerica.com, 7a Calle Poniente No 3) is a charming B&B with patios, fountains, gardens and a roof terrace. The five rooms and one suite range from US$125 to US$264 per week, including a fabulous breakfast. A one-week minimum stay is required. This place has a swing set in the yard and is very kid friendly.

The beautiful *Hotel Aurora* (☎ 832-0217, 4a Calle Oriente No 16) has a grassy courtyard graced by a fountain and many flowers. Its 17 old-fashioned rooms with bath are US$40/50/60 for singles/doubles/triples, including continental breakfast. There's a private car park.

Hotel Convento Santa Catalina (☎ 832-3080, fax 832-3079, 5a Avenida Norte No 28), just south of the arch, is a nicely renovated convent around a courtyard. Large singles/doubles/triples with bath, cable TV and telephone are US$50/72/82, though you may be paying more for the history than the comfort at this price.

Top End

The stunning *Mesón Panza Verde* (☎ 832-2925, fax 832-1745, ✉ mpv@infovia.com.gt, 5a Avenida Sur No 19), four blocks south of the park, is an elegant American-owned guesthouse with six comfy, quiet rooms, each with its own private garden, for US$58 and suites with fireplace for US$100. Price includes continental breakfast. The atmosphere and restaurant here are among the best in Antigua.

The *Hotel Quinta de las Flores* (☎ 832-3721, fax 832-3726, Calle del Hermano Pedro No 6) is a very special place. The spacious grounds have beautiful gardens and fountains, a children's play area, swimming pool, sitting areas and a restaurant. The eight large, luxurious rooms, most with fireplace, are US$54/66 for singles/doubles. Five

houses, each with two bedrooms, two stories, a kitchen and living room, are US$120 for five people. Considerable discounts are offered if you stay by the week.

The new *Hotel Casa Azul* (☎ 832-0961/2, fax 832-0944, 4a Avenida Norte No 5) is a designer's gem, with communal spaces, courtyard, garden and rooms all working together in seamless harmony. The upstairs units are spectacular, with sweeping views, luxurious baths, telephones and minibars. Some have fireplaces. The downstairs rooms are just as impressive, but have no views. Still, from downstairs you have better access to the pool, Jacuzzi and sauna. For two people, upstairs rooms are US$90, downstairs are US$78, including breakfast. This is a good spot for honeymooners.

Another romantic option is *The Cloister* (☎ /fax 832-0712, ✉ cloister@mailzone.com, www.thecloister.com, 5a Avenida Norte No 23 – in the US write A-0026, PO Box 669004, Miami Springs, Fl 33266), a renovated cloister from the 16th century and one of the most exclusive hotels in Antigua. Bubbling fountains highlight the horticultural triumph that is The Cloister's garden courtyard, and guests will likely spend a lot of time relaxing here. All rooms have antique furniture, bath, fireplace and library and cost US$90; suites for one/two/three people are US$110/115/120. All prices include breakfast.

Hotel Casa Santo Domingo (☎ 832-0140, 832-2628, fax 832-0102, 3a Calle Oriente No 28) is a wonderful luxury hotel set in the partially restored convent of Santo Domingo (1642), which takes up an entire city block. Rooms are of an international five-star standard, but the public spaces are wonderfully colonial and include a swimming pool. The Dominican friars never had it so good. Weekday rates are US$108 for one or two people and US$136 for three; on the weekends the rates rise to US$125/146.

Hotel Antigua (☎ 832-2801/2/3/4, fax 832-0807, ✉ hainfo@hotelant.com.gt, 8a Calle Poniente No 1) is a large Spanish colonial country club. The 60 rooms have private baths and fireplaces, and many have two double beds. Rates are US$102/114/126 a single/double/triple. Rates are higher during Semana Santa and New Year's.

The five-star **Radisson Villa Antigua Resort & Conference Center** (☎ 832-0011, fax 832-0237, in the US 800-333-3333, **❻** radisson@infovia.com.gt, www.radisson .com, Calle Sucia and Carretera a Ciudad Vieja) is the largest and most modern hotel in town, with 139 rooms and 45 suites. Rooms have balconies, fireplaces, modern baths, and the complex has every amenity. Rooms range from US$90 to US$180 depending on room size and location, time of year and whether meals are included.

La Posada de Don Rodrigo (☎ 832-0291, 832-0387, **❻** chotelera@c.net.gt, 5a Avenida Norte No 17) is a maze of rooms and restaurants around colonial courtyards. The restaurant/bar is the scene of free marimba concerts every afternoon and evening. Some of the 35 rooms are charming, if old-fashioned; others are just drab. A few have fireplaces. Rooms with bath are US$66/81/92 a single/double/triple, which is too much for what you get. The hotel's restaurants and public areas are much better than its rooms.

Since President Clinton bedded down there in 1999, Antigua's most notorious B&B is **Posada del Angel** (☎ 832-5303, ☎/ fax 832-0260, **❻** elangel@IBM.net, www .travellog.com/guatemala/antigua/posadangel, 4a Avenida Sur No 24A – in the US ☎ 800-934-0065 or write A-006, P.O. Box 669004, Miami Springs, Fl 33266). The three rooms and one suite all have private baths (some with tubs), fireplaces, fresh flowers and distinctive furnishings. Rooms are US$121, the suite US$165, including breakfast. Any need imaginable can be met here, including apparently, super-tight security.

PLACES TO EAT
Budget
Eating inexpensively is easy, even in tourist-plagued Antigua.

Probably the cheapest food in town is the good, clean, tasty food served from stands set up on 4a Calle Poniente a block west of the park from 11:30 am to 7:30 pm. You can also eat cheaply and well at the market.

Restaurante Gran Muralla (4a Calle Poniente No 18) is a simple, inexpensive place serving a Guatemalan highland version of Chinese food. Perhaps better for Chinese food is **La Estrella** across the street, which has some of the most efficient and friendly service anywhere.

Antigua's best known restaurant is probably the **Restaurante Doña Luisa Xicotencatl** (4a Calle Oriente No 12), 1½ blocks east of Parque Central. A small central courtyard is set with tables, with more on the upper level. The menu lists a dozen sandwiches made with bread baked on the premises, as well as yogurt, chili, burgers, stuffed potatoes, cakes and pies, all priced under US$4. Alcohol is served, as is excellent Antiguan coffee. The restaurant is open every day, 7 am to 9:30 pm, and it is usually busy. The bakery here sells many kinds of breads, including whole grain. Check out the hot-from-the-oven banana bread daily at around 4 pm.

Rainbow Reading Room & Cafe at 7a Avenida Sur and 6a Calle Poniente, is a lending library, bookstore, travelers' club and restaurant all in one. Healthy vegetarian dishes are a specialty, as is close camaraderie. The café is open every day from 9 am to 11 pm.

Café Condesa, in an opulent courtyard on the west side of the plaza (walk through the Librería Case del Conde bookstore to the courtyard in the rear), is a beautiful restaurant in the patio of an opulent Spanish mansion built in 1549, which is open every day. On the menu are excellent breakfasts, coffee, light meals and snacks. The Sunday buffet from 10 am to 2 pm, a lavish spread for US$6, is an Antigua institution. For a quick java fix, hit the **Café Condesa Express** next door to the Café proper; it's open daily from 6:45 am to 7:45 pm.

La Fuente (4a Calle Oriente No 14) is another beautiful restaurant, in the courtyard of an old Spanish home. It has lots of vegetarian selections, good coffee and desserts. It's open every day 7 am to 7 pm. The **Café Sol** (1a Calle Poniente No 9), opposite La Merced church at the corner of 6a

Avenida Norte, is a smaller, simpler, inexpensive patio restaurant with decent breakfasts and coffee.

Asados de la Calle del Arco, just off the Parque Central on the right-hand side of the street, has a simple but beautiful atmosphere, with candlelight in the evening and tables both inside and in the rear patio. It serves grilled meats and Tex-Mex food, though portions are small. It's open every day, 7 am to 10 pm. They have a second outpost next to the Hotel Convento Santa Catalina, which is on 5a Avenida Norte, north of Parque Central.

La Fonda de la Calle Real (*5a Avenida Norte No 5*) appears to have no room for diners, but that's because all the tables are upstairs. The menu is good and varied. The house specialty is *caldo real*, a hearty chicken soup that for US$3.50 makes a good meal. Grilled meats, *queso fundido* (melted cheese), *chiles rellenos* (stuffed peppers) and nachos are priced from US$3 to US$8. It's open every day, 7 am to 10 pm. Around the corner, *La Fonda de la Calle Real No 2* (*3a Calle Poniente No 7*) has the same menu and is open every day from noon to 10 pm.

La Cenicienta Pasteles (*5a Avenida Norte No 7*) serves mostly cakes, pastries, pies and coffee, but the blackboard menu often features quiche lorraine and quiche chapín (Guatemalan-style), yogurt and fruit as well. A slice of something and a hot beverage cost less than US$2. It's open every day. *Cookies Etc* (*3a Avenida Norte at 4a Calle Oriente*) is another good place for a sweet; it's open daily from 8 am and treats breakfast diners to bottomless cups of coffee. *The Bagel Barn*, on 5a Calle Poniente just off the Parque Central, is popular for bagels, soups, candies and coffee.

Also on 5a Avenida Norte, at No 29 near the arch, *Restaurante/Bar Frida's* (☎ *832-0504*) serves good Mexican fare and is jumping most evenings, sometimes with live music. They're open daily from 12:30 to midnight. Nearby at No 35, the *Punto Internacional* has been recommended by readers, as has *Su Chow* (*5a Avenida Norte*

No 36), which is a Chinese place open late night. Also on this strip at No 32 is *Queso y Vino*, a good choice for Italian food.

The best place in Antigua for breakfast is *Restaurante El Capuchino* (*6a Avenida Norte No 10*), where everything is US$1.70. Check out the omelet made with real cheese, olive oil and bell peppers, served with a side of bacon and homemade rolls. To top it off, they have an all you can drink coffee policy. They're open daily except Monday, from 7 am to 10 pm; they also serve lunch and dinner. Staying out on that 'best of' limb, the best coffee is at the *Tostaduría Antigua* (*6a Avenida Sur No 12A*). There's zero atmosphere, but Antonio, the ex-pat who owns the place, knows his coffee and is quite the conversationalist.

Cheap breakfast Guatemalan-style can be had along 4a Calle Poniente. The *Comedor Antigua* just down from Hotel Backpacker's Place has good, typical fare, or try the breakfast at the Posada Refugio (see Places to Stay). Both will run you around US$1.50.

Also on 4a Calle Poniente is an outlet of *Restaurante Piccadilly* (*4a Calle Poniente No 17*), serving up the three p's: pasta, pollo and pizza. Just around the corner at 6a Avenida Sur No 1A is *Cadejo's*, a popular place for pizza and a beer; occasionally there's live music. Also serving pizza is *Caffé/Pizzeria Asjemenou* (*5a Calle Poniente No 4*). Some opine that they have the best pies in town. It's open daily from 7 am to 10 pm.

One of the current favorites for food and fraternizing is *La Escudilla* (*4a Avenida Norte No 4*). This place features simple, well-prepared pasta and meat dishes and a set dinner special for under US$3. Also here is Riki's Bar (see Entertainment). Another leader in the popularity contest is *Menu Viajero* (*6a Calle Poniente No 14A*), which serves big plates of stir-fry or noodles, vegetarian or carnivore style, for as little as US$2.

Café Flor (*4a Avenida Sur No 1*) features huge portions of delicious food including Thai, Indonesian, Chinese and Indian dishes, each for around US$5, which can easily feed two people. They also offer take-out. It's open daily except Monday from 11 am to 11 pm; weekends until midnight. The *Café Masala (6a Avenida Norte No 14)*, near the corner of 4a Calle Poniente, has been reader recommended for its Thai and Japanese food. It's open every day except Wednesday from noon to 10 pm. Along the same pan-Asian gastronomic lines is *Cafe Rocio (6a Avenida Norte No 34)*, which has a romantic garden area. It's open daily from 7:30 am to 9:30 pm.

La Taquiza (☎ 832-1560, 6a Avenida Norte No 19) serves fresh, satisfying meals combining Mexican and Guatemalan flavors. The atmosphere is very relaxed and the service friendly. If you fancy a German meal, you can try *Café Weiner (Alameda de Santa Lucía Portal No 8)*, which boasts Antigua's only 'super schnitzel,' has decent breakfasts and a patio upstairs. *Cafetería Alemana Charlotte (Callejón de los Nazarenos No 9C)* has breakfasts, light meals and German newspapers. There's also *Jardin Bavaria (7a Avenida Norte No 49)* for food and drink. It's open daily from 8 am to 11 pm.

To satisfy a craving for Japanese food, head straight to *Yoshino (☎ 832-6766, 5a Calle Poniente No 17A)* where both the atmosphere and food are authentic. Choose from sushi, tempura, teriyaki and more; the daily special includes soup, salad, appetizer and a main dish for US$4. It's open Tuesday to Saturday from 12:30 to 4:30 pm and 6 to 9:30 pm and Sunday from 12:30 to 3:30 pm.

Tierra Cero (6a Calle Poniente No 7) is a casual place set around a courtyard, with good salads and other veggie options. Also here are a cinema, book exchange, internet café and bike rentals. *La India Misteriosa (3a Avenida Sur No 4)* is a well recommended place for vegetarian fare.

For Italian food there's the *Restaurante y Pizzería Italiana Catari (6a Avenida Norte No 52)*, opposite La Merced church, run by well-known chef Martedino Castrovinci. From noon to 4 pm the enormous lunch special including beverage is US$3. It's open daily. Two doors south (without a sign)

is *El Canche*. Walk straight through the tienda to the long tables in the back for some tried-and-true Guatemalan eats. You can watch three generations of women cooking up a storm as you eat. They're open daily except Sunday for lunch only, from around 1 pm to 3:30.

Monoloco, a restaurant/bar upstairs at 2a Avenida Norte No 6B between 4a and 5a Calle Oriente, serves tasty hamburgers, burritos and similar bar food for around US$3.50. The bar is a popular gathering place, with microbrews on tap and two satellite televisions showing the likes of the rugby World Cup and the baseball World Series. There's a great book swap, too.

There are two *Pollo Campero* outlets in Antigua, both serving (what else!) fried chicken. The one on Alameda de Santa Lucía by the bus terminal has a playground and is a favorite with kids.

The *Panificadora Columbia (4a Calle Poniente No 34)* is good for breads, coffee and breakfast before the 7 am pullman bus to Panajachel (see Getting There & Away later in this chapter). Across the street, *La Bodegona* is a full-blown mega-market selling everything from diapers to bottled water.

Mid-Range

The dining room in the *Posada de Don Rodrigo (☎ 832-0291, 832-0387, 5a Avenida Norte No 17)* is one of the city's most charming and popular places for lunch or dinner. Order the house favorite, the Plato Chapín, a platter of Guatemalan specialties for US$11. A marimba band plays every day from noon to 4 pm and 7 to 9 pm.

Mesón Panza Verde (☎ 832-2925, 5a Avenida Sur No 19) provides excellent Continental cuisine in an appealing Antiguan atmosphere. The chef is from Switzerland, the food is divine and the prices are moderate – about US$18 per person for a full dinner. *Café Terraza* is also here and recommended for those who don't have the budget for a full meal, but want to check out the great ambiance.

The owners of the perennial favorite Frida's have recently opened *Medusa's*

(☎ 832-6951, 2a Avenida Sur No 12), a ceviche and sushi palace. A bit spendy, but loaded with atmosphere, this place is warm, comfortable and does good seafood and snacks. There's a daily happy hour from 7 to 10 pm featuring free appetizers with each drink purchase.

Doña María Gordillo Dulces Típicos (4a Calle Oriente No 11), across the street from the Hotel Aurora, is filled with traditional Guatemalan sweets for take-out, and there's often a crowd of Antigüeños lined up to do just that. Local handicrafts are sold here as well.

Top End

El Sereno (☎ 832-0501, 4a Avenida Sur No 9) is Antigua's most exclusive restaurant. A colonial home has been nicely restored and modernized somewhat to provide a traditional wooden bar, plant-filled court and several small dining rooms hung with oil paintings. Cuisine is international, leaning heavily on French dishes; the menu changes every week. The short wine list is good but expensive. Expect to pay US$17 to US$30 per person for dinner; reservations are recommended. It's open noon to 3 pm and 6:30 to 10 pm every day.

For steaks, head straight to *Las Antorchas (☎ 832-0806, 3a Avenida Sur No1),* which has a beautiful courtyard to go with its mouth-watering beef. It's open daily for breakfast, lunch and dinner. Carnivores may also want to try *Dn Martin Asador (☎ 832-1668, 5a Calle Poniente No 15C),* where they specialize in grilled meats and seafood, prepared in a variety of unique ways. There is a rooftop terrace with decent views. It's open daily from noon to 10 pm.

The restaurant at the luxurious *Hotel Casa Santo Domingo* (see Places to Stay earlier in this chapter) is another beautiful spot for a splurge, with tables inside and out in the garden.

ENTERTAINMENT

There is no shortage of nightlife here, but weekends can be a bit crazed, as revelers pour in from Guatemala City for some action Antigua style. In many cases, the bar with the most economical happy hour is the most popular; cocktail fans will have no trouble getting a bargain buzz here.

Bars & Discos

Probably the hottest spot in Antigua (at the time of this writing) is *Riki's Bar (4a Avenida Norte No 4),* which attracts a hip, mixed crowd of locals, travelers and students. The big courtyard, decent food and low-key *Paris Bar Exclusivo* in the rear all make for a good night out. Another popular spot for students, Peace Corp types and good beer is *Monoloco* (see Places to Eat).

La Chimenea on the corner of 7a Avenida Norte and 2a Calle Poniente is a traveler's hang out with a decent happy hour from 6 to 9 pm. Down the block, *Latinos* is rougher around the edges, which may be just what you're looking for if you've been in Antigua awhile.

El Atico is upstairs from Frida's at 5a Avenida Norte No 29. This is a laid-back bar with a quality pool table. Happy hour is from 6 to 8 pm. Across the street, the *Macondo Pub* can be bustling or empty depending on when you turn up.

For dancing, try *La Casbah (5a Avenida Norte No 30),* near the Santa Catalina arch. It's open Wednesday to Saturday from 7 pm to 1 am. This disco is quite a party most nights, but Thursday is gay night and (not surprisingly), the best time to drop in and boogie. *El Afro (6a Calle Poniente No 9)* is the place to go salsa dancing. It's open Tuesday to Sunday from 6 pm to 1 am, but things don't heat up until around 10 pm.

Movies & Slide Shows

One of Antigua's most stimulating forms of entertainment is watching movies at cinema houses, where you can see a wide variety of international films. Places to try include the following:

Cine Café, 7a Calle Poniente No 22

Cinema Bistro, 5a Avenida Sur No 14

Cinema Tecún Umán, 6a Calle Poniente No 34A

Cinemaya, 6a Calle Poniente No 7

Proyecto Cultural El Sitio, 5a Calle Poniente No 15

Most show several films a day, with the titles changing daily; admission is around US$1.50. Check schedules posted at the door, or look for flyers advertising schedules around town. Some places have a frequent viewer program in which you can pay to see five films and view the sixth for free. Others offer bargain dinner and movie packages. All proceeds from Cine Café go to Vaso de Agua, an organization that feeds the homeless.

Proyecto Cultural El Sitio (☎ *832-3037, 5a Calle Poniente No 15)* presents a variety of cultural events including live theater, concerts, video films and art exhibitions. Stop by to check the schedule, or look in the *Revue* monthly magazine for shows at this and other venues.

Elizabeth Bell gives a fascinating slide show about Antigua called *Behind the Walls* on Tuesdays from 6 to 7 pm at the Christian Spanish Academy (see Language Courses); admission is US$2.50.

SHOPPING

Lots of vendors flood Antigua to satisfy tourists' desires for colorful Guatemalan woven goods and other handicrafts. Wherever there is an open space to spread their wares, you'll find villagers selling. The sleepy **Mercado de Artesanías**, on the west side of town by the bus station, has plenty of variety. Don't be afraid to bargain. A number of shops are on 4a Calle Poniente, in the blocks between the Parque Central and the market. Also look for outdoor markets at the corner of 6a Calle Oriente and 2a Avenida Sur, and at 4a Calle Poniente near 7a Avenida Norte. Vendors will also approach you in the Parque Central, while you take a coffee in a café or at the breakfast table in casual dining places.

Be aware that prices for handicrafts tend to be much higher in Antigua than elsewhere in Guatemala. If you will be traveling to other regions, you might want to wait for a better selection at cheaper prices; try the markets in Chichicastenango, Panajachel and even Guatemala City. When buying handicrafts, be sure to bargain for a decent price.

Antigua has several shops specializing in jade including La Casa de Jade, 4a Calle Oriente No 3, Jades, SA, 4a Calle Oriente

No 34 and the Jade Kingdom, 4a Avenida Norte No 10. At these places you can take a free tour of the jade factories in the rear of the showrooms. Jades, SA has interesting exhibits about jade. They are open every day.

Galería El Sitio, 5a Calle Poniente No 15 at the Proyecto Cultural El Sitio, specializes in paintings by modern Guatemalan artists. Ring the bell on the gate for admission. A number of other interesting galleries are along 4a Calle Oriente, in the blocks east of the Parque Central.

Nim Po't, 5a Avenida Norte No 29, boasts 'the world's largest retail collection of Maya dress,' a claim it would be hard to refute. This sprawling space is packed with traditional huipiles, córtes, fajas and more, all arranged according to region, so it makes for a fascinating visit whether you're in the market or not. If you're pressed for time, this is a great place for one-stop shopping. It's open daily from 9 am to 9 pm. Another intriguing place to buy textiles is the Casa del Tejido Antiguo, 1a Calle Poniente No 51, which is like a museum, market and workshop rolled into one. It's open every day from 8 am to 5 pm; admission is US$0.65.

For coffee, head over to the Tostaduría Antigua, 6a Avenida Sur No 12A, where a pound of beans, freshly roasted to your specifications, will run about US$3. Add a bag made from traditional material scraps for US$1. Alternatively, you can pick up coffee straight from the growers at Finca los Nietos (see Around Antigua later in this chapter).

Tabaquería Unicornio, 4a Calle Poniente No 38, sells a variety of the best Cuban cigars and tobacco from all over the world, including Drum and American Spirit brands.

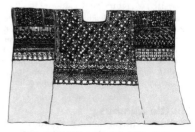

Colorful huipiles abound at Nim Po't.

GETTING THERE & AROUND
Bus

Buses arrive and depart from a large open lot to the west of the market, on the western edge of town. Bus connections with Guatemala City are insanely frequent, and there's one direct bus daily to Panajachel. To reach other highland towns such as Chichicastenango, Quetzaltenango and Huehuetenango, or Panajachel at any other time of day, take one of the frequent buses to Chimaltenango, on the Interamericana, and catch an onward bus from there. Or take a bus heading toward Guatemala City, get off at San Lucas Sacatepéquez and change buses there – this takes a little more time, but it's a good road and since you'll be boarding the bus closer to the capital you're more likely to get a seat (important if you want to avoid the possibility of standing for several hours).

Buses to outlying villages such as Santa María de Jesús (US$0.25, 30 minutes) and San Antonio Aguas Calientes (US$0.20, 25 minutes) depart from the bus area behind the market. It's best to make your outward trip early in the morning and your return trip by midafternoon, as bus services drop off dramatically as late afternoon approaches.

Chimaltenango – US$0.30, one hour, 19km; buses every 15 minutes, 6 am to 6 pm. Buses from here connect to many destinations including Chichi, Pana, Huehuetenango, Xela and San Andrés Itzapa.

Escuintla – US$0.65, 2½ hours, 102km; two buses daily, 7 am and 1 pm

Guatemala City – US$0.50, one hour, 45km; buses every 15 minutes, 4 am to 7 pm, stopping in San Lucas Sacatepéquez

Panajachel – US$3.25, 2½ hours, 146km; one pullman bus daily, 7 am, departs from Hotel Backpacker's Place. Or, take a chicken bus to Chimaltenango and change there for a bus bound for Los Encuentros, Sololá or Panajachel. One of these buses passes every 20 minutes or so. The entire trip costs US$2.45 and takes longer, but is more interesting than the pullman.

Shuttle Minibus

Numerous travel agencies and tourist minibus operators offer frequent and convenient shuttle services to places tourists go, including Guatemala City, Aeropuerto Internacional La Aurora, Panajachel and Chichicastenango. They also go less frequently (usually on weekends) to places further afield such as Río Dulce, Copán Ruinas (Honduras) and Monterrico. These services cost a lot more than ordinary buses (for example, from US$5 to US$10 to Guatemala City, as opposed to US$0.50 on a chicken bus), but they are comfortable and convenient, with door-to-door service on both ends.

There are dozens of these agencies in Antigua; you certainly won't have any trouble finding one. For recommendations, see Travel Agencies earlier in this chapter.

Car & Motorcycle

Rental companies in Antigua include:

Ahorrent (☎ 832-0968, ✆ ahorrent@infovia .com.gt, www.infovia.com.gt/ahorrent), 5a Calle Oriente No 11B

Moto Servicio Antigua (☎ 511-8932), Carretera a Ciudad Vieja No 90; rents motorcycles only

Sears Motorcycle Rental (☎ 832-6203), 3a Avenida Norte No 3

Tabarini (☎/fax 832-3091, contact ✆ tabarini@ centramerica.com, www.centramerica.com/ tabarini), 2a Calle Poniente No19A; in the Hotel Radisson Villa Antigua, Calle Sucia and Carretera a Ciudad Vieja (☎/fax 832-7450)

Taxi

Taxi stands are at the bus station and on the east side of Parque Central. A ride in town costs around US$1.65.

Bicycle

Several shops rent bicycles. There are also companies that offer biking tours (see Activities earlier in this chapter).

AROUND ANTIGUA
Cerro de la Cruz

Overlooking Antigua on the northeast side of town is Cerro de la Cruz (Hill of the Cross). You can get a fine view over town looking south toward Volcán Agua. However, it's dicey to go up there without a

Tourism Police escort (see Tourist Offices), as this hill is famous for muggers waiting to pounce on unsuspecting visitors. The Tourism Police was formed precisely because armed robberies on Cerro de la Cruz have been so numerous – numerous until the Tourism Police was founded, that is.

Jocotenango

This suburb of Antigua gives you a real taste of local life. Storefronts are occupied by tailors at their sewing machines, kids buying candy and women lingering over their purchases to gossip. Buses come and go and truck drivers stop for some roadside ceviche or tamales – by the red light over the door will you know where tamales are sold. The **church** dominating the central square is a marvel of crumbling pink stucco where they still hold services. Nearby is the **Fraternidad Naturista Antigua** if your body aches (see the boxed text 'Travels to the Far Side' in the Facts for the Visitor chapter).

If you're up for a short jaunt, take a left before the public washing area in front of the church and follow the signs to the **Mariposario Antigua** (☎ 203-3190, fax 220-6542). It takes about 10 minutes to walk to this lush butterfly farm on the edge of town. Scores of butterfly species are raised here and it makes for an interesting and educational side trip. The Mariposario is open daily from 9 am to 3 pm, but the butterflies only like to frolic when it's sunny, so plan accordingly; admission is US$2 for adults and US$1.25 for children.

You can walk to Jocotenango from Antigua in about a half an hour: Take Avenida del Desengaño or 6a Avenida Norte until you hit Calle Ancha de los Herreros; make a left on Calle Ancha de los Herreros and walk until you see the main square and church of Jocotenango. Buses leave from behind the market in Antigua every 15 minutes.

Ciudad Vieja & San Antonio Aguas Calientes

Six and a half km southwest of Antigua along the Escuintla road (the one that passes the Radisson Villa Antigua Resort) is Ciudad Vieja (Old City), site of the first capital of the Captaincy General of Guatemala. Founded in 1527, it was destroyed in 1541 when the aptly named Volcán Agua loosed a flood of water penned up in its crater. Cascading down the steep volcano's side, the water carried tons of rock and mud over the city, leaving only a few ruins of the Church of La Concepción.

Java junkies in this neck of the woods will want to check out the **Finca los Nietos** (☎ 831-5438) coffee plantation for a tour and a taste. The hour-long tour isn't cheap at US$5, but it will answer all your nitty gritty coffee questions, from how seedlings are propagated to how beans are roasted. The price of admission includes a bag of coffee. With a prior appointment, you can roast your own beans (minimum five pounds). To get to the finca, head out from Antigua on the Escuintla road and take a right at the crossroads before the textile shop called Carolina's (bus drivers know this intersection). Walk three blocks toward the volcano until you come to a white wall with bougainvillea. Ring the bell and you're in.

Just before San Miguel Dueñas is the **Valhalla Experimental Station** (☎ 831-5799, ✉ exstval@infovia.com.gt), a working macadamia farm that raises 300 species of that delicious nut. You can tour this organic, sustainable agriculture project and sample nuts, oils and cosmetics made from the harvest. Bring a picnic and save some room for the stellar, hand-dipped chocolate covered macadamia nuts for sale at the shop here. The station is open daily from 8 am to 4:30 pm.

Past Ciudad Vieja, turn right at a large cemetery on the right-hand side; the unmarked road takes you through San Miguel Dueñas to San Antonio Aguas Calientes. In San Miguel Dueñas, take the first street on the right – between two houses – after coming to the concrete-block paving; this, too, is unmarked. If you come to the Texaco station in the center of San Miguel, you've missed the road.

The road winds through coffee fincas, little fields of vegetables and hamlets of farmers to San Antonio Aguas Calientes,

14km from Antigua. As you enter San Antonio's plaza, you will see why the village is noted for its weaving. Market stalls in the plaza sell local woven and embroidered goods, as do shops on side streets (walk to the left of the church to find them). Bargaining is expected. Buses leave for San Miguel Dueñas (the bus placards will simply say 'Dueñas') every 15 minutes from behind the market in Antigua.

Volcanoes

Climbing the volcanoes around Antigua used to be tempting fate, as armed robbers repeatedly intercepted groups of foreigners, relieving them of everything, (including clothing). There were even incidents of rape and murder. Because Pacaya is the only active volcano near Antigua, it's the one that attracts the most tourists and in times past, the most bandits.

The situation on Pacaya is improving, however, since steps have been taken to guard the safety of tourists making the hike. For example, former thieves now have the alternative of making an honest living maintaining trails and latrines and creating lookout points along the way. Also, every group climbing Pacaya is now accompanied by a security guard (little comfort when the guard turns out to be a toothless geezer with a machete or a child with a stick!). Still, these efforts have been successful so far, and travelers these days are more likely to be hurt by flaming rocks and sulfurous fog than criminals.

Pacaya is very temperamental, and travelers have suffered serious (even fatal) injuries when the volcano erupted unexpectedly while they were near the summit. In early 2000, Pacaya started getting *really* uppity, necessitating an escalation to Orange Alert status. Violent eruptions and sulfur gases at the peak can be very dangerous, though there is little that can be done to prepare for them.

Get reliable advice about safety before you climb. Check with your embassy in Guatemala City, or with the INGUAT office in Antigua, or with some of Antigua's esteemed tourist and travel agencies. If you do decide to go, make sure you go with reputable guides, through an established agency.

Take sensible precautions. Wear adequate footwear (volcanic rock can be very rough on shoes), warm clothing (it's very cold up there) and, in the rainy season, some sort of rain gear. Carry a flashlight, partly because you may be climbing down after dark, and also in case the weather changes; it can get as dark as night when it rains on the mountain – though this is not a fun hike in the rainy season. Don't neglect to take water and snacks.

Various agencies operate tours up **Volcán Pacaya** (from US$5 to US$10 per person), including a 1½-hour bus ride to the trailhead followed by a fairly demanding two-hour trek to the summit. Gran Jaguar usually coordinates these tours, and you probably will get a cheaper tour if you book with them directly (see Travel Agencies earlier in this chapter).

The volcanoes nearer Antigua (Agua, Fuego and Acatenango) are not active, so they attract fewer tourists. Climbing one of these won't let you see the glow, but the volcanoes are still very impressive and offer magnificent views. **Volcán Agua** is the large volcano looming over Antigua, on the south side of town. To get there, follow 2a Avenida Sur or Calle de los Pasos south toward El Calvario (2km), then continue via San Juan del Obispo (another 3km) to Santa María de Jesús, 9km south of Antigua. This is the jumping-off point for treks up the slopes of Volcán Agua (3766m), which rises dramatically right behind the village.

Santa María (population 11,000, 2080m) is a village of unpaved streets and bamboo fences. The main plaza is also the bus terminal. *Comedor & Hospedaje El Oasis*, a tidy little pension, offers a meal or a bed for the night.

Various outfitters in Antigua can furnish details about the Volcán Agua climb.

You could also climb the other two volcanoes near Antigua, **Volcán Acatenango** and **Volcán Fuego**. Various companies offer guided tours on Acatenango; Mayan Bike Tours (see the Activities section earlier in this chapter) does hike/bike tours on Acatenango, and Old Town Outfitters will take you to the summit of any volcano.

Santiago Sacatepéquez & Sumpango Sacatepéquez

Throughout Latin America, All Saints' Day (November 1) is a spectacle worth catching. In Guatemala they celebrate with the *Feria del Barrilete Gigante* or the Giant Kite Festival. The two biggest parties occur in Santiago and Sumpango Sacatepéquez, about 15km and 25km from Antigua respectively. These kites are truly giant: Made from tissue paper, wood or bamboo braces and with guide ropes as thick as a man's arm, most measure more than 13m in diameter and have intricate, colorful designs. They're flown over the cemetery to speak with the souls of the dead. Judges rank the kites according to size, design, color, originality and elevation. Part of the fun is watching the crowd flee when a giant kite takes a nose dive.

Unfortunately, the wind is sometimes insufficient to lift these giant kites, which makes for an anticlimactic festival, despite the plethora of fantastic street food. *Fiambre*, a traditional dish made from meat, seafood and vegetables served cold in a vinaigrette, is typically eaten on this day. It's a labor of love to make a decent fiambre, and women take pride in their prowess at preparing it. It is, however, an acquired taste.

Many agencies run day trips from Antigua to Santiago Sacatepéquez on All Saints' Day for around US$7 per person, though you can easily get there on your own by taking any Guatemala City bound bus (US$0.25) and getting off with the throngs at the junction for Santiago. From here, you can hitch a ride or take one of the scores of buses covering the last few kilometers to Santiago. The fastest way to get to Sumpango is to take a bus to Chimaltenango and backtrack to Sumpango; in this way you will bypass all of the Santiago bound traffic, which is bumper to bumper on fair day.

Chimaltenango

The road westward from Antigua makes its way 17km up to the ridge of the Continental Divide, where it meets the Interamericana at Chimaltenango, capital of the department of Chimaltenango. This was an old town to the Cakchiquel Maya when the conquistadors arrived in 1526; today, it's mostly just a place to change buses, with little to detain you. Making bus connections here is easy, as many friendly folks will jump to your aid as you alight from one bus looking for another. Be alert here and don't leave your pack unattended, as bag slashing isn't unheard of in Chimal.

ANTIGUA

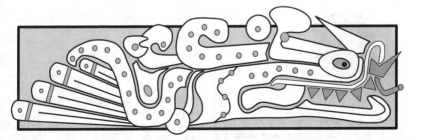

The Highlands

The Highlands, Guatemala's most frequently visited region, stretches from Antigua to the Mexican border northwest of Huehuetenango and offers the country's most dramatic scenery. Still, the rugged topography keeps certain places tucked away and off the beaten track. No doubt this is where you'll find some of your greatest adventures. The verdant hills are thick with emerald-green grass, fields of maize (corn) and towering stands of pine. All of this lushness comes from the abundant rain that falls between May and October. If you visit during the rainy season, be prepared for some dreary, chilly, damp days. But when the sun comes out, this land is stunning to behold.

Every town and village in the Highlands has a story to tell, which usually begins more than a thousand years ago. Most towns here were already populated by the Maya when the Spanish arrived. History turned bloody and inhumane with the beginning of the civil war in 1960, when the Highlands were targeted heavily by guerrillas and the army alike. During the 36-year war, merciless death squads killed with impunity, villages were razed and tens of thousands of refugees fled over the border to Mexico. Refugee resettlement programs are ongoing, and keen visitors can see the effects of war in the bombed-out craters and airstrips that mar this area.

The traditional values and customs of Guatemala's indigenous groups are strongest in the Highlands. Mayan dialects are the first language, Spanish a distant second. The age-old culture based on maize is still alive and well; a sturdy cottage set in the midst of a thriving *milpa* (field of maize) is a common sight, one as old as Maya culture itself. On every road you'll see men, women and children carrying burdensome loads of *leña* (firewood) to be used for heating and cooking.

Each highland town has its own market and festival days. Life in a highland town can be *muy triste* (sad, boring) when there's not a market or festival going on, so you should try to visit on those ebullient days. Still, there's no better way to maximize your experience with local people and their way of life than by showing up in a village and staying for awhile.

If you have only three or four days to spend in the Highlands, spend them in

HIGHLIGHTS

- Hiking, shopping, scuba diving, horseback riding, kayaking or plain chilling out on Lago de Atitlán, arguably the most majestic place you'll find

- Shopping at the notoriously grand market in Chichicastenango

- Visiting the hot springs, steam baths, volcanic lakes and traditional towns near Quetzaltenango

- Hiking and exploring around the Cuchumatanes, especially Todos Santos, Nebaj or towns farther afield

- Taking the rugged, beautiful and relatively untrodden Huehuetenango to Cobán route

HIGHLANDS

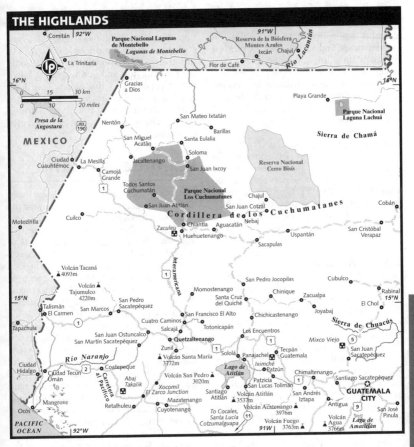

THE HIGHLANDS

Antigua, Panajachel and Chichicastenango. With more time you can make your way to Quetzaltenango and the sights in its vicinity, such as Zunil, Fuentes Georginas, San Francisco El Alto, Momostenango and Totonicapán.

Huehuetenango and the ruins nearby at Zaculeu are worth a visit only if you're passing through or if you have lots of time. Still, if you do have lots of traveling time, the towns and villages high in the Cuchumatanes mountains north of Huehuetenango offer stellar scenery and challenging opportunities for intrepid travelers.

Studying Spanish in this part of the country is increasingly popular. There are schools in Huehuetenango, Todos Santos, Xela and on Lago de Atitlán.

Warning

Though most visitors never experience any trouble, there have been incidents of robbery, rape and murder of tourists in the Highlands. These have occurred on trails up the volcanoes, on the outskirts of Antigua and Chichicastenango and at lonely spots along country roads. Attacks happen at random. If you use caution and common sense and don't do much roaming or driving at night, you should have a fine time in this beautiful region. Traveling local style – on chicken buses and in the back of pickups instead of in plush tourist shuttles – will make you less of a target. Never take photos of Mayan individuals without first asking permission. For more details on the dangers of uninvited photography, see the Dos and Don'ts section of the Facts about Guatemala chapter.

Before traveling in the Highlands, contact your embassy or consulate in Guatemala City for information on the current situation and advice on how and where to travel. Don't rely on local authorities for safety advice, as they may downplay the dangers. For a list of phone numbers, see Embassies in the Facts for the Visitor chapter.

Getting Around

Guatemala City and the Guatemalan/ Mexican border station at La Mesilla are connected by the Interamericana, which is also known as Centroamérica 1 (CA-1). It's a curvy mountain road, which must be traveled slowly and carefully in many places. Driving the 266km between Guatemala City and Huehuetenango can take five hours, but the time slips by effortlessly amid the beautiful scenery. (The Carretera al Pacífico (CA-2) via Escuintla and Retalhuleu is straighter and faster, and it's the better route to take if your goal is to reach Mexico as quickly as possible.)

The highway is thick with bus traffic; for scheduling information, refer to specific destinations in the Getting There & Away chapter. As most of the places you'll want to reach are some distance off the Interamericana, you may find yourself waiting at major highway junctions such as Los Encuentros and Cuatro Caminos to connect with the right bus or a pickup truck. These transfers are usually seamless, with not-too-frustrating waiting times, and there are always helpful locals lending a hand to travelers trying to negotiate the buses.

Travel is easiest on market days and in the morning. By mid- or late afternoon,

buses may be difficult to find, and all short-distance local traffic stops by dinner time. You should follow suit. To hail a bus, stick your arm out more or less parallel to the ground. Occasionally, people assume the bus will stop and don't signal it, while the driver assumes this means you don't need a ride. On more remote routes farther off the beaten track, you'll probably be relying more on trucks than buses for transport.

Lago de Atitlán

Westward 32km along the highway from Chimaltenango, you pass the turnoff for the back road to Lago de Atitlán via Patzicía and Patzún. The area around these two towns has been notable for high levels of guerrilla activity in the past and robberies very recently. Since the road is often in poor condition anyway, it's advisable to stay on the Interamericana to Tecpán Guatemala, the starting point for a visit to the ruined Cakchiquel capital city of Iximché.

If you travel another 40km westward along the Interamericana from Tecpán, you come to the highway junction of **Los Encuentros**. There is an ersatz town here, based on the presence of throngs of people waiting to catch buses. The road to the right heads north to Chichicastenango and Santa Cruz del Quiché. From the Interamericana a road to the left descends 12km to Sololá, capital of the department of the same name, and then 8km more to Panajachel, on the shores of Lago de Atitlán.

If you are not on a direct bus to these places, you can always get off at Los Encuentros and catch another bus or minibus, or even hitch a ride, from here down to Panajachel or up to Chichicastenango; it's a half-hour ride to either place.

The road from Sololá descends more than 500m through pine forests in its 8km course to Panajachel. Sit on the right-hand side of the bus for views.

Along the way, the road passes Sololá's colorful cemetery and a Guatemalan army base. The guard post by the main gate is in

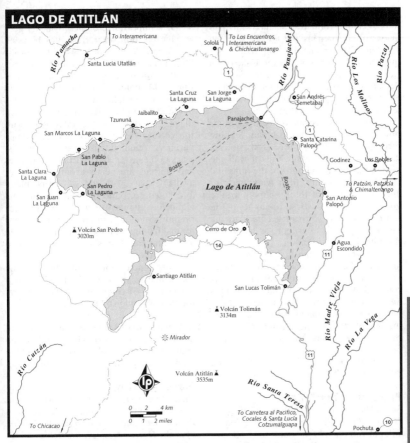

LAGO DE ATITLÁN

the shape of a huge helmet resting upon a pair of soldier's boots. Leaving the camp behind, the road soon begins its sinuous descent to the lakeshore, offering breathtaking views of the lake and its surrounding volcanoes.

TECPÁN GUATEMALA

Founded as the Spanish military headquarters during the conquest, Tecpán Guatemala today is a somewhat dusty little town with two small hotels and, not far away, the ruins of the Cakchiquel Maya capital of Iximché (pronounced eesh-im-chay).

Tecpán's market day is Thursday. The annual festival in honor of the town's patron saint, Francis of Assisi, is held in the first week of October.

Iximché

Iximché is set on a flat promontory surrounded by steep cliffs. This city was founded in the late 15th century and was well sited to be the capital city of the Cakchiquel Maya. During that time, the Cakchiquel were at war with the Quiché Maya, and the city's natural defenses served them well.

When the conquistadors arrived in 1524, the Cakchiquel formed an alliance with them against their enemies, the Quiché and the Tz'utuhils. The Spaniards set up their headquarters right next door to the Cakchiquel capital at Tecpán Guatemala, but Spanish demands for gold and other loot soon put an end to the alliance; the Cakchiquel were defeated in the ensuing battles.

As you enter Tecpán you will see signs pointing to an unpaved road leading through fields and pine forests to Iximché, less than 6km to the south. You can walk the distance in about an hour, see the ruins and rest (another hour), then walk back to Tecpán – a total of three hours. If you're going to walk, it's best to do it in the morning so that you can get back to the highway by early afternoon, as bus traffic dwindles by late afternoon.

After you enter the archaeological site and pass the small museum on the right, you come to four ceremonial plazas surrounded by grass-covered temple structures and ball courts. Some of the structures have been cleaned and maintained; on a few the original plaster coating is still in place, and there are even some traces of the original paint.

The site is open daily from 9 am to 4 pm; admission is US$3.25.

Places to Stay & Eat

Should you need to stay the night in Tecpán, *Hotel Iximché (1a Avenida 1-38, Zona 2)* will put you up in basic rooms for US$3 per person, as will the *Pensión Doña Ester (2a Calle 1-09, Zona 3)*. There are various small eateries.

Getting There & Away

Transportes Poaquileña runs buses to Guatemala City (1½ hours, 87km) every half hour from 3 am to 5 pm. From Guatemala City to Tecpán, buses run from 5 am to 7:30 pm just as frequently.

SOLOLÁ

• pop 9000 • elevation 2110m

Though the Spaniards founded Sololá in 1547, there was a Cakchiquel town (called Tzoloyá) here long before they showed up. Sololá's importance comes from its geographic position on trade routes between the *tierra caliente* (hot lands of the Pacific Slope) and *tierra fría* (the chilly highlands). All the traders meet here, and Sololá's terrific Friday market is one of the most authentic in the Highlands.

On market days (Tuesdays and Fridays) the plaza next to the cathedral is ablaze with the colorful costumes of people from a dozen surrounding villages and towns. Displays of meat, vegetables, fruit, housewares and clothing are neatly arranged in every available space, with tides of buyers ebbing and flowing around the vendors. Several elaborate stands are well stocked with brightly colored yarn and sewing notions for making the traditional costumes you see all around you. This is a local rather than a tourist market.

Every Sunday morning the officers of the traditional religious brotherhoods *(cofradías)* parade ceremoniously to the cathedral for their devotions. On other days, Sololá sleeps.

You can make a very pleasant walk from Sololá down to the lake, whether taking the highway to Panajachel (9km) or the walking track to Santa Cruz La Laguna (10km).

Places to Stay

Virtually everyone stays in Panajachel, but if you need a bed in Sololá, try the six-room *Posada del Viajero (7a Avenida 10-45, Zona 2)* or the *Hotel y Restaurante Belén* (☎ 762-3105, 10a Calle 4-36, Zona 1)* at the entrance to town. The Belén has eight rooms with shared hot-water bath for US$4/7/11; there's parking and a restaurant. *Hotel Santa Ana*, 150m uphill from the church tower on the road that comes into town from Los Encuentros, is a very simple pension.

PANAJACHEL

• pop 5000 • elevation 1560m

Nicknamed Gringotenango (Place of the Foreigners) by locals and visitors alike, Pana is one of Guatemala's oldest tourist hangouts. In the hippie heyday of the 1960s and

Family in front of thatched roof – Todos Santos

A village in the Highlands

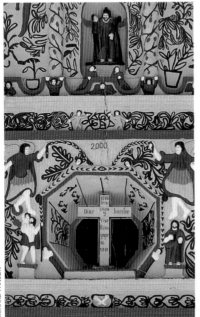
Church detail in San Andrés Xecul

Boats in Lago de Atitlán

'70s, it was crowded with laid-back travelers in semipermanent exile. When the civil war of the late '70s and early '80s made Panajachel a dangerous – or at least unpleasant – place to be, many moved on. But the town's tourist industry is booming again and has even spread to several lakeside villages.

There is no notable architecture in this town, which is a small and not particularly attractive place that has developed haphazardly according to the demands of the tourist trade. But you need only to head down to the shores of the lake to understand why Pana attracts so many visitors. Simply put, Lago de Atitlán is one of the world's most spectacular locales, period. Diamond splatters dance across the water, fertile hills dot the landscape with color, and over everything loom the powerful volcanoes, permeating the entire lake with a mysterious beauty. The place never looks the same way twice, offering a distinct face and feeling from different vantage points.

Lago de Atitlán is often placid and beautiful early in the day, which is the best time for swimming, though Pana's shores aren't the cleanest. By noon the Xocomil, a southeasterly wind, may have risen to ruffle the water's surface, sometimes violently, making it a tough crossing for small motorboats plying between the shores. This is particularly true between November and February, a time known as the windy season in these parts. As elsewhere in Guatemala, it's always good to get your traveling done in the morning if possible, when weather conditions are better and there is more traffic.

Note that the lake is a caldera (collapsed volcanic cone), more than 320m deep, with an area of 128 square km. The land drops off sharply very near the shore. Surrounding the lake are three volcanoes: Volcán Tolimán (3158m), due south of Panajachel; Volcán Atitlán (3537m), also to the south; and Volcán San Pedro (3020m), to the southwest. The water level of Lago de Atitlán fluctuates curiously from year to year.

Several different cultures mingle on the dusty streets of Panajachel: Ladinos and gringos control the tourist industry. The Cakchiquel and Tz'utuhil Maya from surrounding villages come to sell their handicrafts to tourists. The lakeside villa owners drive up on weekends from Guatemala City. Groups of tourists descend on the town from buses for a few hours, a day or an overnight. And always there are the 'traditional' hippies, with long hair, bare feet, local dress and Volkswagen minibuses.

Orientation

As you near the bottom of the long hill descending from Sololá, a road on the right leads to the Hotel Visión Azul, Hotel Atitlán, the Reserva Natural Atitlán and those ghastly white high-rise buildings. Lore varies as to the origin and possible demise of the last, but the latest scuttlebutt at this writing was that a foreign consortium has bought the beasts and is converting them into condominiums; stay tuned. The main road then bears left and becomes the Calle Real (also called Calle Principal), Panajachel's main street. Businesses don't typically use street addresses in Pananjachel, but street numbers have been provided for the few that do.

The geographic center of town, and the closest thing it has to a bus station, is the intersection of Calle Real and Calle Santander, where you will see the Banco Agrícola Mercantil (BAM). Calle Santander is the main road to the beach. All kinds of tourist services line Calle Santander in the few blocks running from the bus stop and the bank at the top of the street on down to the lake.

Northeast along Calle Real are more hotels, restaurants and shops; finally, at the northeastern end of town you come to the town's civic center, where you will find the telephone office, church, town hall, police station and market (busiest on Sunday and Thursday, but with some activity on other days, from 9 am to noon). Calle Rancho Grande is the other main road to the beach; it's parallel to, and east of, Calle Santander.

A beautiful green park stretches along the lakeside between Calle Santander and Calle Rancho Grande (Calle Rancho Grande is called Calle del Balneario for the

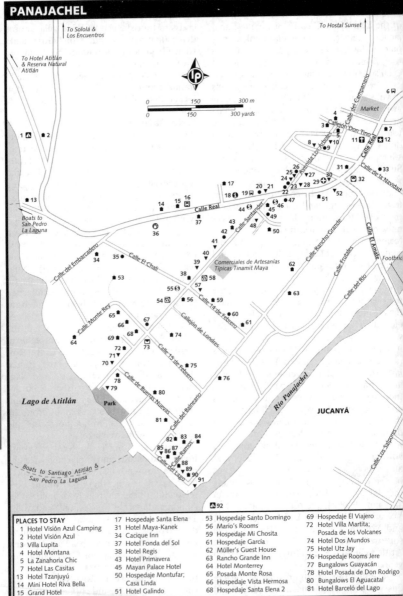

PANAJACHEL

To Sololá & Los Encuentros

To Hostal Sunset

To Hotel Atitlán & Reserva Natural Atitlán

Market

Calle del Campanario

Calle Real

Calle de la Navidad

Calle Rancho Grande

Calle El Amate

Footbridge

Callejón Don Tino

Avenida Los Árboles

Calle Santander

Calle El Chalí

Calle del Embarcadero

Calle Monte Rey

Calle 14 de Febrero

Callejón de Londres

Calle 15 de Febrero

Calle de Buenas Nuevas

Calle del Río

Calle Frutales

Calle del Balneario

Calle Ramos

Calle del Lago

Río Panajachel

JUCANYÁ

Calle Los Salpores

Boats to San Pedro La Laguna

Lago de Atitlán

Park

Boats to Santiago Atitlán & San Pedro La Laguna

Comerciales de Artesanías Típicas Tinamit Maya

HIGHLANDS

PLACES TO STAY

1 Hotel Visión Azul Camping	
2 Hotel Visión Azul	
3 Villa Lupita	
4 Hotel Montana	
5 La Zanahoria Chic	
7 Hotel Las Casitas	
13 Hotel Tzanjuyú	
14 Mini Hotel Riva Bella	
15 Grand Hotel	

17 Hospedaje Santa Elena
31 Hotel Maya-Kanek
34 Cacique Inn
37 Hotel Fonda del Sol
38 Hotel Regis
43 Hotel Primavera
45 Mayan Palace Hotel
50 Hospedaje Montufar; Casa Linda
51 Hotel Galindo

53 Hospedaje Santo Domingo
56 Mario's Rooms
59 Hospedaje Mi Chosita
61 Hospedaje García
62 Müller's Guest House
63 Rancho Grande Inn
64 Hotel Monterrey
65 Posada Monte Rosa
66 Hospedaje Vista Hermosa
68 Hospedaje Santa Elena 2

69 Hospedaje El Viajero
72 Hotel Villa Martita; Posada de los Volcanes
74 Hotel Dos Mundos
75 Hotel Utz Jay
76 Hospedaje Rooms Jere
77 Bungalows Guayacán
78 Hotel Posada de Don Rodrigo
80 Bungalows El Aguacatal
81 Hotel Barceló del Lago

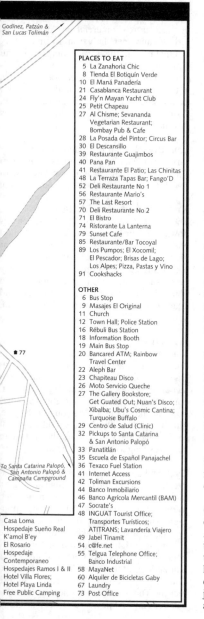

four blocks closest to the beach). It's a wonderful place for strolling, day and night.

The area east of the Río Panajachel is known as Jucanyá (Across the River); Panajachel itself is often referred to as simply 'Pana.'

Information

Tourist Offices The INGUAT tourist office (☎ 762-1392) is in the Edificio Rincón Sai on Calle Santander. It's supposedly open every day from 8 am to 1 pm and from 2 to 5 pm, but actual hours seem to vary. There is also a tourist information booth very near the bus stop; it has maps of Pana and rudimentary hotel information.

Money Banco Industrial on Calle Santander changes US dollars cash and traveler's checks, gives cash advances on Visa cards and has a 24-hour ATM. Banco Inmobiliario on the corner of Calle Santander and Calle Real also changes money, and it's open longer hours. BAM, on the same corner, changes money and is an agent for Western Union. There is a Bancared ATM which accepts Visa cards at Calle Real 0-78.

Apart from the banks, several other businesses offer financial services. You can change cash and traveler's checks at the INGUAT tourist office and at the Hotel Regis, both on Calle Santander. Cash advances on Visa and MasterCard are available from the Hotel Regis and from Servicios Turísticos Atitlán, both on Calle Santander, for a 10% commission.

Post & Communications The post office is on the corner of Calles Santander and 15 de Febrero.

An outfit named Get Guated Out (☎ 762-0595, fax 762-2015, ✉ gguated@ quetzal.net), in the Centro Comercial on Avenida Los Árboles, can ship your important letters and parcels by air freight or international courier. They will also buy handicrafts for you and ship them for export – handy if you can't come to Panajachel yourself. Internet and email services are also available here.

HIGHLANDS

DHL has a drop-off location in Panajachel on Calle Santander in the Rincón Sai complex with INGUAT. It's open Monday to Friday from 9 am to 6 pm and Saturday from 9 am to 1 pm.

The Telgua telephone office on Calle Santander is open every day. Many other places along Calle Santander offer the same services at better prices. Check the ubiquitous travel agencies for phone, fax and email services.

As you would expect from Panajachel's hip, international tenor, there are many places to surf the Web and send email. Stiff competition among businesses means Internet access in Pana is among the cheapest in Guatemala; expect to pay around US$1.50 an hour. MayaNet on Calle Santander, across from the Hotel Regis, is open Monday to Saturday, from 9 am to 9 pm, Sunday from 2:30 to 8 pm. Just down the block and adjacent to the Telgua office is c@fe.net. It's open daily from 9 am to 9 pm. Another option is Internet Access in the El Patio complex on Calle Santander.

Travel Agencies There are many full-service travel agencies along Calle Santander, offering trips, tours and shuttle bus services to other places around Guatemala. The following is just a partial list of what you'll find:

Rainbow Travel Center (☎ 762-1301/2/3, @ myers@gua.gbm.net), Calle Santander, opposite the BAM bank

Toliman Excursions (☎/fax 762-2455, contact @ globalnet@guate.net), Calle Santander 1-77

Transportes Turísticos ATITRANS (☎ 762-2336, 762-0146), Calle Santander, next to INGUAT

Travel Agency San Nicolas (☎ 762-0382, fax 762-0391), Calle Santander, next to Hotel Dos Mundos

Bookstores Owner/author Jake Horsley vows to make Xibalba the best used bookstore in Central America, and he's damn close. Horsley is selective about the books he'll swap (no Steele or L'Amour here), and specializes in the classics. There's also a lending library heavy on the lunatic fringe

and otherworldly topics; patio tables and coffee make it a fun place to kick back. It's in the Centro Comercial on Avenida Los Árboles and open daily from 10 am to 7 pm.

Upstairs in the same complex is the Gallery Bookstore (☎ 762-0595, fax 762-2015). It offers new and used books for sale, a telephone/fax service and travel and ticket sales. There's also Librería Agua Azul, at Comercial El Pueblito, Calle Los Árboles 3 Av.

Laundry There are a handful of laundry services in Pana. The Lavandería Viajero on Calle Santander in the complex with INGUAT is open daily from 8 am to 6 pm.

Reserva Natural Atitlán

The Reserva Natural Atitlán (☎ 762-2565) is down the spur leading to the Hotel Atitlán and is a good goal for a day trip on foot or bicycle. This private reserve is well designed, with trails, an interpretive center, butterfly farm, suspension bridges, a small coffee plantation, troops of resident monkeys and an aviary. It's open daily from 8 am to 5 pm; admission is US$3.

Activities

Various lakeside villages, reachable on foot, bike, bus or passenger boat, make for intriguing visits. You can walk from Panajachel to Santa Catarina in about an hour, continuing to San Antonio in about another hour; it takes only half as long on bicycle, but the road is hilly. Or take a bike by boat to Santiago, San Pedro or another village to start a cycling tour around the lake.

Cycling Lago de Atitlán is a cycling wonderland, with hill and dale spread amongst a fantastic setting; enthusiasts are encouraged to rent or bring their own bikes here. Equipment varies, so check out a bike before renting it: Test the brakes and tires, make sure it's the right height and that it's fairly comfortable. Several places along Calle Santander rent bicycles, as do Moto Servicio Queche (see Car & Motorcycle in the Getting There & Away section later in this chapter) and Alquiler de Bicicletas Gaby on Calle 14 de Febrero between Calle Santander and Calle Rancho Grande. Rentals start at around US$2.50 for a half day.

Scuba Diving ATI Divers (☎ 762-2646, ✉ santacruz@guate.net) has an office on Calle Santander near INGUAT and leads dive trips from Santa Cruz La Laguna (see that section later in this chapter). PADI beginning certification is a four-day affair and costs US$160. ATI also offers advanced certification, specialty courses and fun dives (US$25 for one, US$45 for two). Lago de Atitlán is an interesting dive site because it's a collapsed volcanic cone with bizarre geological formations, but there is not much marine flora or fauna here. During the rainy season the water clouds up, so the best time to dive is between May and October.

The folks at ATI Divers also organize the annual garbage cleanup of the lake, during which several tons of trash are collected (scary, but true). This event, typically held in September, is a great opportunity to give something back to the community and make some new friends, both local and foreign. ATI Divers also runs dive trips from Río Dulce to the Belizean reef (see the Río Dulce section of the Central & Eastern Guatemala chapter).

Boat Tours Travelers pressed for time are encouraged to take a boat tour of the lake, visiting various towns. To arrange a tour, head down to the pier at the foot of Calle Santander and start bargaining. A typical tour lasts nearly an entire day and visits San Pedro (one hour), Santiago (1½ hours) and San Antonio (one hour) for about US$7, depending on how many people are on the boat.

Most travel agencies (see Travel Agencies earlier in this chapter) also arrange boat tours, which may include weaving demonstrations and visits to coffee plantations or to the shrine of Maximón in Santiago.

Language Courses
Panajachel is carving out a niche in the Spanish school economy with several places offering courses. Panatitlán (☎ 762-0319,

✉ panatitlan@yahoo.com), Calle de la Navidad 0-40, Zona 1, will send the teacher to you, so you can stay and study in the lakeside village of your choice; the Escuela de Español Panajachel (☎ 762-2637, fax 762-0092, ✉ nicholas_tr@latinmail.com) is on Calle El Chali; and then there is the current favorite, Jabel Tinamit (☎ 762-0238, contact ✉ spanishschool@hotmail.com), just off Calle Santander near INGUAT. Six hours of one-on-one study five days a week, including a homestay with a local family, will cost around US$130 a week at any of these schools.

Places to Stay
Budget There's a *free public campground* on the beach on the east side of the Río Panajachel's mouth in Jucanyá. Safety can be a problem here, and it's more like a dirt patch than a campground. A safer and prettier (but more expensive) alternative is the *campground* on the spacious lakeside lawn at the Hotel Visión Azul (☎ 762-1426, ☎/fax 762-1419), on the western outskirts of town. This place has electrical and water hookups for campers and caravans; cost is US$1.30 per person, plus US$5 per tent and US$2.50 per vehicle.

Even better for price, location and vibe is *Campaña Campground* (☎ 762-2479), on the road to Santa Catarina Palopó. For US$2 you can pitch a tent and use the kitchen. There's a book exchange and luggage storage here and they'll pick you up from Pana if you call ahead.

Low-budget travelers will rejoice in Panajachel, as there are many little family-run hospedajes (pensions) here. They're as simple as they come – perhaps two rough beds, a small table and a light bulb in a room of bare boards – but cheap. Most provide clean-enough toilets, and some have hot showers.

One place to look for hospedajes is along Calle Santander midway between Calle Real and the beach. Follow signs along the main street for the various hospedajes down narrow side streets and alleys.

Hospedaje Santa Elena 2 (Calle 15 de Febrero 3-06), off Calle Santander on the

HIGHLANDS

road to the Hotel Monterrey, is tidy and typical of Pana's hospedajes. Singles/doubles with shared bath are US$3/5. The original **Hospedaje Santa Elena** is down a pathway off Calle Real, farther from the lake; it's a simple family-run place, where rooms sharing cold showers go for US$2/3/6.

Hospedaje Vista Hermosa (Calle 15 de Febrero 3-55) is a friendly place with simple rooms on two levels around a small courtyard. There are hot showers in the daytime only, with very little water at night. Serviceable cells with shared bath are US$2 per person. Better are the doubles with private bath for US$6. Next door, **Posada Monte Rosa** (☎ 762-0055) is a pleasant new hotel with five comfortable double rooms for US$14.

Cross Calle Santander and continue down Calle 15 de Febrero for 100m to the standout **Hotel Utz Jay** (☎ /fax 762-1358, @ utzjay@atitlan.com). Four beautifully furnished rooms in adobe casitas have tile floors, traditional fabrics and nice touches like candles and drinking water. Each has a private hot bath; the cost is US$13/16/18/21 for one, two, three or four people. There are great open spaces here, gardens, hammocks, a communal kitchen and a traditional Mayan sauna called a *chuj*. The owners speak Spanish, French and English and run hiking and camping trips around the lake.

For a great value, head to the family-run **Villa Lupita** off Calle de Campanario near the church. Clean, secure rooms with bedside tables and lamps, reading material and comfortable beds are US$3.20. There's a shared hot water bath.

For a place more removed from town, try the **Hostal Sunset**, perched high on a hillside with amazing views of Panajachel and beyond. From Calle Real, follow the signs north, along Avenida de los Árboles to Calle del Campanario, which eventually turns into a dirt track and graduated steps leading up to the hostal. It's about a ten minute walk from town and not for those with weak knees. Rooms with bunk beds are US$8/10 for two beds with private bath, though you may be able to bargain.

Hospedaje Santo Domingo (☎ 762-0236) is an amicable place with a variety of cheap rooms; take the road toward the Hotel Monterrey, then follow signs along a shady path. It's removed from the bustle of Calle Santander. Very basic wood-plank rooms with general bath are US$2/3.50, or US$6.45 for more attractive doubles upstairs. Singles/doubles with private bath are US$7/11. There's a grassy hangout area here that makes this place.

Mario's Rooms (☎ 762-2370, 762-1313) on Calle Santander is popular with young, adventurous travelers. Singles/doubles/triples with shared hot bath are US$5/6/8; with private cold bath they are US$8/11/14. The restaurant at Mario's serves economical meals. **Hospedaje Mi Chosita**, on Calle 14 de Febrero (turn at Mario's Rooms), is tidy, quiet and costs US$4/5/6 for a single/double/triple with shared bath. Similarly priced is the clean **Hospedaje García** (☎ 762-2187, 14a Calle 2-24, Zona 2), farther east along the same street toward Calle Rancho Grande. This place has nice, meticulously maintained grounds and is also the home to Stereo Pentacostes, the local Pentecostal radio broadcast.

Hotel Villa Martita, on Calle Santander half a block from the lake, is a friendly family-run place with singles/doubles with shared hot bath for US$6/8/10. The secure rooms are around a quiet courtyard, set back from the street. Next door, the more upmarket **Posada de los Volcanes** (☎ 762-0244, ☎/fax 762-2367, @ posadavolcanes@atitlan.com, www.atitlan.com/volcanes.htm, Calle Santander 5-51) is a beautiful place where all the rooms have private bath and cable TV; rooms are US$20/25.

Next door again, **Hospedaje El Viajero** (☎ 762-0128) is one of the best values for the money in town. It's a welcoming, clean place with just five rooms with private hot bath set about 40m back from the street. It's quiet and peaceful, yet you're near everything. Upstairs rooms have more air and light. Singles/doubles are US$7/10, and there's laundry service and parking.

Another clean, nice place with a pleasant courtyard is the **Hospedaje Montufar**

(☎ 762-0406), down a pathway off Calle Santander. Serene singles/doubles with shared bath are US$6/8. Next door is the *Casa Linda*, which is not as good at US$4/8 for singles/doubles.

The new *Hotel Primavera* (☎ /fax 762-2052, ✉ primavera@atitlan.com) on Calle Santander is a recommended, German-owned hotel. Upstairs rooms with private bath overlook a lush garden and are US$13/16 for singles/doubles in the high season and US$7/13 in low season.

La Zanahoria Chic (☎ 762-1249, fax 762-2138, Avenida Los Árboles 0-46) has seven clean rooms opening onto a communal upstairs sitting area with two shared baths. The rooms are simple but comfortable, and the whole place has a cozy, lived-in feeling. Downstairs is the La Zanahoria Chic videocafé. Singles/doubles/triples are US$4/8/12.

There are two good places on the southern stretch of Calle Rancho Grande (Calle de Balneario). *Hospedaje Rooms Jere* has clean, simple rooms for US$3/4. *Casa Loma* (☎ 762-1447) has good, firm beds in airy singles/doubles overlooking a big garden for US$6/8 with shared bath; US$7/11 with private bath. Rooms Jere also has several new, fully equipped apartments for two people, which rent for US$51.50 per day or US$500 by the month.

Prices rise the closer you get to the beach, but there is still some good value here. Walking parallel to the shore on Calle del Lago, the first place you come to is the *El Rosario* (☎ 762-1491), which has decent rooms for US$7.75 per person.

From Calle del Lago, hook a left up the alley called Calle Ramos to the *Hospedajes Ramos I & II* (☎ 762-0413) for basic rooms with private bath for US$5/8. They claim to have hot water. Fifty meters farther back along the alley is the *Hospedaje Contemporaneo* (☎ 762-2214), a hospitable place with simple but clean rooms with private bath for US$7/10. The upstairs rooms have partial lake views. Just beyond the Contemporaneo is the new and recommended *Hospedaje Sueño Real* (☎ 762-0608), which has tasteful, clean singles/doubles with shared bath for US$6/11; rooms with private bath

are US$7/12. They have international phone services, rent bicycles and offer a taxi service. Continuing even farther back on Calle Ramos, you'll come to the *K'amol B'ey* (☎ 762-0215), a motel-style place with parking, which is popular with vacationing Guatemalan families. New, clean singles/doubles with cable TV and private hot bath are US$9/16. This motel abuts several onion fields, which emit a powerful aroma.

Back on Calle del Lago along the shore is the *Hotel Villa Flores* (☎ 762-2193), next door to the Hotel Playa Linda. The singles/doubles/triples here are nothing to get excited about for US$7/12/18.

Moving up in comfort, *Hotel Las Casitas* (☎ 762-1224, fax 762-1069, ✉ lcasitas@quetzal.net, members.tripod.com/lcasitas), opposite the market near the church and town hall, rents little brick bungalows with private baths and tile roofs for US$7/12/17 for a single/double/triple. It has international phone and fax services and a luggage storage.

Hotel Fonda del Sol (☎ 762-1162, Calle Real 1-74, Zona 2) is a two-story building on the main street, west of the intersection with Calle Santander. The 25 simple rooms on the upper floor are well used but fairly decently kept; they cost US$10/13/16 with private bath. Larger, nicer rooms are more expensive, at US$12/20/23 for a single/double/triple. There is a restaurant downstairs.

Grand Hotel (☎ 762-2940/1, contact ✉ granhotel@infovia.com.gt) is the big, bright place at the Rebulí bus stop. Though it's not as attractive inside as out, the rooms are spacious and have decent beds. Singles/doubles/triples/quadruples are quoted as US$9/13/20/26, but you can bargain. There's a pool, restaurant and expansive grounds here, so it's a good place to stay if you're traveling with kids.

Also in the bus area, at the intersection of Calles Santander and Real, is the *Mayan Palace Hotel* (☎ 762-1028), with clean but bland rooms with private hot bath for US$10/11/14. There are better values to be had in Pana, but this will do in a pinch.

Hotel Maya-Kanek (☎ 762-1104, fax 762-0084), on Calle Real just down from the church, is a motel-style hostelry. Rooms face a cobbled court with a small garden; the court doubles as a secure car park. The 20 rooms, though simple, are a bit more comfortable than at a hospedaje, and they cost US$8/12/20 with private hot bath. It's quiet here.

Hotel Galindo (☎ /fax 762-1168), on Calle Real northeast of the Banco Agrícola Mercantil (BAM), has a surprisingly lush garden surrounded by modest rooms with private hot bath that rent for US$9/11 for smaller singles/doubles, US$13/15 for larger rooms (some with fireplace) or US$18 for triple rooms with fireplace. Look at the room before you rent.

Down an alleyway in front of the church, the *Hotel Montana* (☎ 762-1326, ☎/fax 762-2180) has 15 clean, bright, single/double/triple rooms with private bath and cable TV for US$16/21/26. Parking is available.

Mid-Range Mid-range lodgings are busiest on weekends. From Sunday to Thursday you may get a discount. All of these lodgings provide private hot showers in their rooms.

Rancho Grande Inn (☎ 762-1554, 762-2255, fax 762-2247, contact ❷ hranchog@quetzal.net), on Calle Rancho Grande, has 12 perfectly maintained German country-style villas in a tropical Guatemalan setting amid bright green lawns. The inn has some bungalows that sleep up to five people and also a few with fireplaces. Marlita Hannstein, who is the congenial proprietor, charges a very reasonable US$30/40 to US$60 for a single/double, including tax and a full delicious breakfast. This is perhaps Pana's best place to stay. It's a good idea to reserve in advance.

Several meters north on Calle Rancho Grande is *Müller's Guest House* (☎ 762-2442, 762-2392, fax 363-1306), which has three nicely appointed, if dampish, rooms with bath around well-tended gardens for US$45 for two or three people. There is plenty of comfortable communal space here, and the fact that a group can pool resources and rent the whole place is especially cool.

Bungalows El Aguacatal (☎ 762-1482, in Guatemala City 476-1582), on Calle de Buenas Nuevas, is aimed at weekenders from the capital. Each modern bungalow has two bedrooms, equipped kitchen, bath and salon, and costs US$46 for one to four people Sunday to Thursday, US$52 on Friday and Saturday. Bungalows without kitchens are cheaper, at US$10 per person Sunday to Thursday, US$45 for up to four people on weekends.

Mini Hotel Riva Bella (☎ 762-1348, 762-1177, fax 762-1353), on Calle Real, is a collection of neat two-room bungalows, each with its own parking place, set around expansive gardens. The location is convenient, and the price is US$27/32 for a single/double. The same owners also operate *Bungalows Guayacán*, just across the river, with six apartments, each with kitchenette, one bedroom, living room and garden, for US$42 for up to three people.

Hotel Dos Mundos (☎ 762-2078, 762-2140, fax 762-0127, ❷ dosmundos@atitlan.com, Calle Santander 4-72) is an attractive place with 16 bungalows, all with cable TV and nice decor, in a walled compound of tropical gardens for US$45/55/65 for a single/double/triple. This hotel is set well back from the street. Also here are a swimming pool and a good Italian restaurant.

Hotel Regis (☎ 762-1149, fax 762-1152, ❷ regis@atitlan.com), on Calle Santander, is a group of colonial-style villas set back from the street across a lush, palm shaded lawn. The 25 comfortable guestrooms are grouped around the ample grounds, which have a small swimming pool, a children's playground and an open-air mineral hot springs for guests only. Rooms are US$60/70/80 for a single/double/triple in the high season and US$27/40/50 in low.

Hotel Monterrey (☎ /fax 762-1126), on Calle Monte Rey, an unpaved road going west from Calle Santander (look for the sign), is a blue-and-white, two-story motel-style building facing the lake across lawns and gardens that extend down to the beach. The Monterrey offers 29 clean and cheerful single/double rooms opening onto a terrace with a beautiful lake view for US$25/35.

Hotel Playa Linda (☎ /fax 762-1159, ✉ akennedy@gua.gbm.net), facing the beach at Calle del Lago 0-70, has an assortment of rooms, a few with nice views of the lake and some that are wheelchair accessible. Rooms 1 to 5 have large private balconies with tables, chairs and wonderful lake views, rooms 6 to 15 do not; all have private bath, all but two have fireplaces and some have satellite TV. Doubles are US$54 with balcony and view, US$40 without.

Cacique Inn (☎ /fax 762-1205), on Calle del Embarcadero, off Calle Real at the western edge of town, is an assemblage of pseudorustic red-tile-roofed buildings arranged around verdant gardens and a swimming pool. The 34 large, comfortable rooms have double beds, fireplaces and locally made blankets. Rates are US$52/60/67 for a single/double/triple. Try bargaining here.

Hotel Visión Azul (☎ 762-1426, ☎/fax 762-1419), on the Hotel Atitlán road, is built into a hillside in a quiet location looking toward the lake through a grove of trees. The big, bright rooms in the main building have spacious terraces festooned with bougainvillea and ivy. Modern bungalows a few steps away provide more privacy for families. There's a swimming pool. Prices are US$39/44/49/52 for a single/double/triple/quad.

Along the same road, *Hotel Tzanjuyú* (☎ /fax 762-1318) has large garden grounds and a private beach on a beautiful cove. All the rooms open onto small balconies with a superb lake view and are US$31/35/39/43 for a single/double/triple/quad. There's a swimming pool and restaurant.

Top End The nicest hotel in town is the *Hotel Atitlán* (☎ /fax 762-1416/29/41, ✉ hotinsa@infovia.com.gt, in Guatemala City 360-8405, fax 334-0640), on the lakeshore 2km west of the town center. Spacious gardens surround this rambling three-story colonial-style hotel. Inside are gleaming tile floors, antique wood carvings and exquisite handicraft decorations. The patio has views across the heated swimming

pools to the lake. The 65 rooms with private bath and lake-view balconies are US$84/96/118 for a single/double/triple. There is also a fully equipped spa with gym, sauna and massages available.

At the lake end of Calle Santander, *Hotel Posada de Don Rodrigo* (☎ 762-2326/29, ✉ chotelera@c.net.gt) is another beautiful luxury hotel, with a lakeside swimming pool, terrace and many other amenities. Rooms are US$84/93/102 for a single/double/triple.

Hotel Barceló del Lago (☎ /fax 762-1555 to 1560, fax 762-1562, in Guatemala City ☎ 361-9683, fax 361-9667, contact ✉ barcelo@infovia.com.gt), at the beach end of Calle Rancho Grande, is a modern six-story building that seems out of place in low-rise, laid-back Panajachel. Besides the beach, the hotel has two swimming pools (one for children) set in nice gardens. All of its 100 rooms have two double beds and cost US$100 for a double in low season and US$182 in high, including all meals.

Places to Eat

Budget The cheapest places to eat are down by the beach at the mouth of the Río Panajachel. Right on the shore are cookshacks with rock bottom prices. The food stalls around the parking lot cost not much more. There are also little restaurants across the street, including *Los Pumpos, El Xocomil, El Pescador, Brisas de Lago* and *Los Alpes*. At US$4 for a fill-up, there are cheaper places to eat, but the lake view is priceless. *Pizza, Pastas y Vino* along here is open 24 hours.

At the lake end of Calle Santander, the open-air *Sunset Cafe* has a great lake vista. Meat or vegetarian meals are US$3 to US$5, snacks are less, and there's a bar and live music on weekends. It's open every day from 11 am to 10 pm.

Nearby, on Calle Santander, the *Deli Restaurante 2* is a tranquil garden restaurant serving a good variety of healthy, inexpensive foods to the strains of soft classical music. It's open every day except Tuesday from 7 am to 5:45 pm; breakfast is served all day. *Deli Restaurante No 1*, on Calle Real next to the Hotel Galindo, has the same menu and hours; it's closed on Thursday.

El Bistro, on Calle Santander half a block from the lake, is another lovely, relaxing restaurant with tables both inside and out in the garden. There's candlelight in the evening and live music some nights. It's open every day from 7 am to 10 pm.

Las Chinitas, on Calle Santander in the El Patio complex, has unbelievably delicious, inexpensive food with an Asian flavor. Ling, the friendly owner, is from Malaysia via New York and has been in Panajachel for many years. Down the block, *Restaurante Mario's*, beside Mario's Rooms, is another good spot for economical meals.

Nearby on Calle Santander is the popular *Restaurante Guajimbos*, which has scores of menu items, but is most notable for it's bottomless cup of coffee. Grab some whole wheat bread and pastries at *Pana Pan*, next door, to go with the all-you-can-drink joe.

The Last Resort restaurant/bar, just off Calle Santander on 14 de Febrero, is small, amicable and famous for its good, inexpensive food. A buffet breakfast is served for US$2; a good variety of meals, all served with soup, salad, bread and coffee, are US$3.35 to US$5. Alcohol is served, there's table tennis in the rear, and on cool evenings the fireplace is a welcome treat. It's open every day.

Al Chisme, on Avenida Los Árboles, is a favorite with locals and foreign Pana regulars, with its shady streetside patio. Breakfasts of English muffins, Belgian waffles and omelets cost US$2 to US$4. For lunch and dinner, Al Chisme offers a variety of meat and vegetarian dishes, including Tex-Mex specialties and 'death by chocolate.' It's open every day except Wednesday.

Next door, in the Centro Comercial complex on Los Árboles, is *Sevananda Vegetarian Restaurant*, offering sandwiches and vegetable plates for US$2 to US$4. It's open daily except Sunday. Adjacent to this complex is a second Centro Comercial housing the *Bombay Pub and Cafe*, which serves all vegetarian burritos, pastas and stir fry in a pretty courtyard setting.

La Posada del Pintor and its *Circus Bar*, on Avenida Los Árboles, is a restaurant, pizzería and bar with walls hung with old circus posters and a vast selection of items on the menu. The prices seem fair until you see the portions, which are pathetically small (think airplane meal). There's live music every night from 8 pm on; it's open every day, noon to midnight. If you're still hungry after dining at the Circus Bar, head across the street to *Petit Chapeau*. This casual place is recommended for its cheap, hearty snacks and meals with authentic Mexican flavors.

At the *Fly'n Mayan Yacht Club*, near the intersection of Calle Real and Calle Santander, the pizzas (US$3.50 to US$6.50) have a good reputation. It's open daily except Thursday.

Restaurante/Bar Tocoyal, near the Hotel Barceló del Lago at the beach end of Calle Rancho Grande, is a tidy, modern thatch-roofed place serving good, moderately priced meals (including seafood) for about US$8.

El Descansillo, at the junction of Calles Real and El Amate, is a relaxing place to have breakfast or a light meal thanks to the garden courtyard and art exhibits. The bread is homemade, the coffee rich and you'll find the menu selection interesting and varied. There are plenty of (safe) salads to choose from. It's open daily from 7:30 to 6 pm.

For do-it-yourself types, there's *El Maná Panadería* on Avenida Los Árboles near La Zanahoria Chic, with a terrific selection of fresh breads sold by the loaf, including carrot, banana and peanut. Across the street, *Tienda el Botiquín Verde* (*contact* @ *naturalfoodpana@hotmail.com*) sells organic vegetables, free-range eggs, tofu, tempeh, nut oils, juice and breads. You can also get vitamins and herbal remedies here. It's open weekdays from 9 am to 3 pm and Saturdays from 9 am to 1 pm.

Fango'D on Calle Santander in the complex with INGUAT, is a coffee roaster serving some of Pana's best coffee. It's open daily from 6 am to 5 pm, and you can buy beans by the pound.

Mid-Range *Ristorante La Lanterna* at the Hotel Dos Mundos, set back from the street on Calle Santander, is a good, authentic Italian restaurant with both inside and garden tables; you're welcome to use the swimming pool if you eat here. It's open every day, 7 am to 3 pm and 6 to 10 pm.

Upstairs in the same building as the INGUAT tourist office, *La Terraza Tapas Bar* (☎ 762-0041) is a lovely, upmarket open-air restaurant/bar that's open every day; locals regularly say this is one of Pana's best restaurants. *Restaurant El Patio*, also on Calle Santander, is another good but more expensive option, as is the *Casablanca Restaurant* (☎ 762-1015), at the intersection of Calle Santander and Calle Real. At this last place, however, some consider the food pedestrian in light of the hefty prices.

The luxury *Hotel Barceló del Lago* offers lavish Sunday breakfast and dinner buffets when the hotel is fully occupied, which usually happens on weekends and holidays. The breakfast/dinner buffets cost US$7/13.

The even more luxurious *Hotel Atitlán* (☎ 762-1416/29/41) has a beautiful restaurant with tables inside and out on the patio and magnificent lake views. If you come to eat here, you can use the swimming pool, gardens, beach and so on, all for free. Lunch or dinner buffets (US$11) are offered when occupancy is high and usually on Thursday afternoons; call ahead. Otherwise, there's an ample four-course set meal for the same price, as well as other selections on the menu.

Entertainment

Strolling along the path at the lakeside park, greeting the dawn or watching the sun set behind the volcanoes are unsurpassable entertainment. The colors of the lake, the sky, the volcanoes and knolls constantly change from dawn to sunset, and at night the sky over the lake is alive with stars.

Live music is happening at *La Posada del Pintor/Circus Bar*, *Sunset Cafe* and *El Bistro* (see Places to Eat). The recommended *Aleph Bar* on Avenida Los Árboles jumps with live music six nights a week.

Pana has two discos, the *Chapiteau* and *Nuan's*, both on Avenida Los Árboles. The former opens around 9 or 10 pm and the latter has an early evening happy hour. *Ubu's Cosmic Cantina*, in the Centro Comercial with Nuan's, has a pool table, giant screen TV and couches where you can kick back while sipping cocktails. Where Calle Real and Avenida Los Árboles meet is *Socrate's*, a cavernous bar with thumping music that is hugely popular with Guatemalan youth running wild in Pana.

Video films in English are shown at the *Turquoise Buffalo* on Avenida Los Árboles next to Al Chisme; it shows several films nightly and has schedules posted out front. At *La Zanahoria Chic* video café on Avenida Los Árboles, you can choose from a list of more than one hundred films.

Shopping

Set along Calle Santander, Comerciales de Artesanías Típicas Tinamit Maya is one of Guatemala's most extensive handicrafts markets, with dozens of stalls and an impressive variety of goods on offer. You can get good buys here if you bargain and take your time. Wholesale orders can be filled here, too. The market is open every day from 7 am to 7 pm.

Back in the day, industrious bohemians used to come to Pana to get loads of textiles cheap, carry or ship them back to the US or Europe and turn a nice profit on the resale. The loose infrastructure that developed around this trade still exists, and you can shop to your heart's content here and have the goods shipped to your door back home. There are even companies that will do the shopping and shipping for you. There are also wholesalers in Pana if you want to buy in bulk, and there is plenty of variety.

Calle Santander is lined with booths, stores and complexes that sell (among other things) traditional clothing, jade, leather items and wood carvings. Freelance vendors and artisans also set up tables or blankets to display their wares here, especially on the weekends when Pana feels a bit like a Guatemalan Grateful Dead tour. The approach to the beach at the end of Calle

HIGHLANDS

Traditional Clothing

Anyone visiting the Highlands can delight in the beautiful *traje indígena* (traditional clothing) of the local people. The styles, patterns and colors used by each village are unique, and each garment is the creation of its weaver, with subtle differences from the others.

The basic elements of the traditional wardrobe are the *tocoyal* (head-covering), *huipil* (blouse), *córte* or *refago* (skirt), *calzones* (trousers), *tzut* or *kaperraj* (cloth), *paz* or *faja* (sash) and *caítes* or *xajáp* (sandals).

Women's head coverings are beautiful and elaborate bands of cloth up to several meters in length, wound about the head and decorated with tassels, pom-poms and silver ornaments. In recent years they have been worn only on ceremonial occasions and for tourist photos.

Women's huipiles, however, are worn proudly every day. Though some machine-made fabrics are now being used, most huipiles are made completely by hand. The white blouse is woven on a backstrap loom, then decorated with appliqué and embroidery designs and motifs common to the weaver's village. Many of the motifs are traditional symbols. No doubt all had religious or historical significance at one time, though today that meaning may be lost to memory.

Córtes (refajos) are pieces of cloth seven to 10 yards long that are wrapped around the body. Traditionally, girls wear theirs above the knee, married women at the knee and old women below the knee, though the style can differ markedly from region to region.

Both men and women wear fajas, long strips of backloom-woven cloth wrapped around the midriff as belts. Wrapped with folds upward like a cummerbund, the folds serve as pockets.

Tzutes (male) or kaperraj (female) are the all-purpose cloths carried by local people and used as head coverings, baby slings, produce sacks, basket covers and shawls. There are also shawls for women called *perraj*, probably a contraction of kaperraj.

Before the coming of the Spaniards, it was most common for simple leather thong sandals (caítes, xajáp) to be worn only by men. Even today, many Highland women and children go barefoot, while others have thongs, more elaborate huarache-style sandals or modern shoes.

Rancho Grande is also lined with booths. Some travelers prefer the Pana shopping scene over the well-known market at Chichi because the atmosphere is low key and you're not bumping into tour groups with video cameras at every turn.

Getting There & Away

Bus The town's main bus stop is where Calle Santander meets Calle Real, across from the Mayan Palace Hotel. Rébuli buses depart from the Rébuli bus station on Calle Real (see Panajachel map).

Antigua – US$3.25, 2½ hours, 146km. Rébuli runs one direct pullman bus every day *except Sunday* at 11 am. Or take the 10 am Rébuli pullman (US$1.95) to Chimlatenango and change there. You can also take any bus headed to Guatemala City and change at Chimaltenango.

Chichicastenango – US$1.65, 1½ hours, 37km. Mendoza has nine buses daily, 6:45 am to 4 pm. Rébuli buses (US$1.30) leave at 6:45 am Thursday and Sunday, Chichi's market days. Or take any bus heading to Los Encuentros and change buses there.

Cocales (Carretera al Pacífico) – US$1, 2½ hours, 56km. Eight buses daily from 6:30 am to 3 pm.

El Carmen/Talismán (Mexican border) – via the Pacific route (231km). Take a bus to Cocales and change there. Via the highland route (255km), bus to Quetzaltenango and change there.

Guatemala City – US$2.60, 3½ hours, 148km. Rébuli has buses departing from its office on Calle Real 10 times daily, 5:30 am to 3 pm. Or take a bus to Los Encuentros and change there.

Huehuetenango – 3½ hours, 159km. Bus to Los Encuentros and wait there for a bus bound for Huehue or La Mesilla (see the Getting Around chapter for a schedule). Or catch a bus heading to Quetzaltenango, alight at Cuatro Caminos and change buses there. There are hourly buses from these junctions.

La Mesilla (Mexican border) – seven hours, 241km. See Huehuetenango.

Los Encuentros – US$0.50, 35 minutes, 20km. Take any bus heading toward Guatemala City, Chichicastenango, Quetzaltenango or the Interamericana.

Quetzaltenango – US$1.55, 2½ hours, 99km. There are six buses daily, at 5:30, 6:15, 7:30, 10 and 11:30 am and 2 pm. Or take a bus to Los Encuentros and change there.

San Antonio Palopó – US$0.40, 45 minutes, 9km. There are daily buses, via Santa Catarina Palopó, or grab one of the many pickups leaving from the corner of Calles Real and El Amate.

San Lucas Tolimán – US$1, 1½ hours, 24km. There are two buses daily, 6:45 am and 4 pm. Or take any bus heading for Cocales, get off at the crossroads to San Lucas and walk about 1km into town.

Santa Catarina Palopó – US$0.25, 20 minutes, 4km. Buses run daily, or get a pickup at the corner of Calles Real and El Amate.

Sololá – US$0.15, 10 minutes, 8km. There are frequent direct local buses. Or take any bus heading to Guatemala City, Chichicastenango, Quetzaltenango or Los Encuentros.

Shuttle Minibus Tourist shuttle buses are much faster than local buses; in most cases, they take half the time. A number of travel agencies on Calle Santander (see Travel Agencies earlier in this section) offer convenient but pricey shuttles to the following popular destinations:

Antigua	US$10
Chichicastenango	US$7
Guatemala City	US$20
La Mesilla	US$35
Quetzaltenango	US$15
Tecún Umán	US$35

Car & Motorcycle Dalton Rent A Car (☎/fax 762-1275, 762-2251) has an office on Avenida Los Árboles. Moto Servicio Queche (☎ 762-2089), just past the intersection of Avenida Los Árboles and Calle Real, rents bicycles and off-road motorcycles.

Boat Passenger boats depart from the public beach at the foot of Calle Rancho Grande in Panajachel. Head down there to grab a boat; you won't wait long, as they typically leave when six passengers are ready to go. While there used to be big, slow, scheduled ferries making the trip around the lake, these have largely been discontinued in favor of fast, frequent motor boats called *lanchas*. Lanchas may be efficient, but they can also be deadly: In 1999 a boy was mowed down by one of these boats while swimming. Some residents are concerned about the hasty, inexperienced boat drivers and are trying to get ferry service reinstated – so they may be running again by the time you get to Pana.

Be aware that the *lancheros*, men who drive the boats, and their agents, try to chisel money out of every gringo that comes along. One-way passage *anywhere* on Lago de Atitlán costs US$0.65, but the lancheros typically quote a price quadruple that. Generally, visitors end up paying around US$1.30, which is accepted by most as the going foreigner rate. Still, you can try and hold out for the US$0.65 fare – some people do it successfully – but you may have to let a few boats go before one agrees to take you for the lower fare.

The trip to Santiago Atitlán takes less than an hour, depending upon the winds. Another boat route stops in Santa Catarina Palopó, San Antonio Palopó and San Lucas Tolimán, though it's cheaper to go by bus to these nearby towns.

The last route goes counterclockwise around the lake, stopping in Santa Cruz La Laguna (15 minutes), Jaibalito, Tzununá, San Marcos La Laguna (30 minutes), San Juan La Laguna and San Pedro La Laguna (40 minutes). Boats depart Panajachel from the Calle Rancho Grande docks and then stop at another dock at the foot of Calle del Embarcadero before heading out of town (vice versa, when arriving at Pana). Boats stop running around 6 pm.

AROUND PANAJACHEL
Four kilometers east of Pana along a winding road lies the village of Santa Catarina

HIGHLANDS

Palopó. This is a picturesque, traditional town where narrow streets are paved in stone blocks, adobe houses have roofs of thatch or corrugated tin, and the gleaming white church commands the center of attention. Chickens cackle, dogs bark and the villagers go about their daily life dressed in their beautiful clothing. Except for exploring village life and enjoying views of the lake and the volcanoes, there's little in the way of sightseeing. Still, this is one of the best places to buy the luminescent indigo huipiles you see all around Lago de Atitlán. Young vendors usually line the path to the shore with their wares, or you can step into the simple wooden storefronts hung thick with the bright cloth. For refreshments, there are several little comedores on the main plaza, or try one of the reasonably priced meals at the open air *Restaurante Laguna Azul* on the lakeshore. Take the path past the Villa Santa Catarina toward the water to get there.

If your budget allows, a drink or a meal at the village's best hotel is a treat. The *Villa Santa Catarina* (☎ 762-1291, in Guatemala City 334-8136 to 39, fax 334-8134) has 30 comfortable rooms with bath and views of the lake. Rooms 24, 25, 26 and 27 (partly) face west and have fine views of Volcán San Pedro; all overlook the swimming pool and pretty grounds right on the shore. The dining room provides moderately priced table d'hôte meals. Accommodations cost US$60/68/72 for a single/double/triple, US$84 for a suite. Children under 12 stay free. High on the hill is *Hospedaje 5 Ajpu*, a more affordable option with lake views.

The road continues past Santa Catarina 5km to San Antonio Palopó, a larger but similar village where entire families clean mountains of scallions by the lakeshore and tend their terraced fields in bursts of color provided by their traditional dress. Three kilometers along the way, you pass the *Hotel Bella Vista* (☎ 762-1566, in Guatemala City 473-7594), 8km from Panajachel. Fourteen little bungalows, each with TV, private bath and lake view, share gardens with a swimming pool and a restaurant. The bungalows are US$54/63/71 a single/double/triple. In San Antonio there's also the *Hotel Terrazas del Lago* (☎ 762-1566, fax 762-0157), a beautiful place with a lovely lake view and singles/doubles/triples for US$24/31/36.

Getting There & Away

See the Panajachel section for details on buses, pickups and passenger or tour boats. From Panajachel, you can also walk to Santa Catarina in about an hour, continuing to San Antonio in about another hour. Bicycling is another option, but the road climbs and dips.

SAN LUCAS TOLIMÁN

Farther around the lake from San Antonio, and reached by a different road, San Lucas Tolimán is busier and more commercial than most lakeside villages. Set at the foot of the dramatic Volcán Tolimán, San Lucas is a coffee-growing town and a transport point on the route between the Interamericana and the Carretera al Pacífico. Market days are Monday, Tuesday, Thursday and Friday. From San Lucas, a newly paved road goes west around Volcán Tolimán to Santiago Atitlán, then around Volcán San Pedro to San Pedro La Laguna. On the lakeshore is the expensive, new *Pak'ok Marina & Resort* (☎ 206-7561, 334-6076, fax 334-6075, ✉ sonya@infovia.com.gt), which has 25 rooms arranged around a pool and lush gardens.

See Getting There & Away under Panajachel for details on buses and passenger boats.

SANTIAGO ATITLÁN

South across the lake from Panajachel, on the shore of a lagoon squeezed between the towering volcanoes of Tolimán and San Pedro, lies the town of Santiago Atitlán. Though it is the most-visited village outside Panajachel, it clings to the traditional lifestyle of the Tz'utuhil Maya. The women of the town still weave and wear huipiles with brilliantly colored flocks of birds and bouquets of flowers embroidered on them. The best day to visit is a market day (Friday and Sunday, with a lesser market on

Tuesday), but in fact any day will do. There's a burgeoning art and gallery scene here, featuring local oil painters who churn out canvasses depicting typical highland life.

Santiago is also a curiosity because of its reverence for Maximón (mah-shee-mohn). Maximón is paraded about triumphantly during Semana Santa processions (see Public Holidays & Special Events in the Facts for the Visitor chapter), which is a good excuse to head this way during Easter. The rest of the year, Maximón resides with a caretaker, receiving offerings of candles, beer and rum. Local children will offer to take you to see him for a small tip. See the boxed text 'A God is a God is a God' for more on this unique figure.

Also, Santiago was the site of a massacre in 1990 during which 13 Tz'utuhil villagers were killed by the army. Unwilling to take any more violence, the community banded together and ousted the army and forced the brutal Civil Defense Patrol to disband.

Children from Santiago greet you as you disembark at the dock, selling clay whistles and little embroidered strips of cloth. For a tip they will act as guides, find you a taxi or lead you to a hotel. Agree on the price beforehand or, as one sage traveler put it, you'll 'be amazed at the command of bad language some charming little girls can haul out.'

Orientation & Information
Walk to the left from the dock along the shore to reach the street into town, which is the main commercial street. Every tourist walks up and down it between the dock and the town, so it's lined with shops selling woven cloth and other typical handicrafts and souvenirs.

Near the dock is the office of the Grupo Guías de Turismo Rilaj Maam, a tourist guide cooperative offering trips to many nearby places, including the Atitlán, Tolimán and San Pedro volcanoes, the Chutinamit archaeological site and other places. The office is open every day from 8 am to 5 pm. Martin Tzina is a recommended guide out of Santiago for the hike up Volcán San Pedro; guides charge around

US$13 for two people for the six hour round trip.

Santiago has a post office, a Telgua telephone/fax office and a bank where you can change US dollars cash and traveler's checks.

Things to See
At the top of the slope is the main square, with the town office and huge **church**, which dates from the time, several centuries ago, when Santiago was an important commercial town. Tz'utuhil mythology considers the church site sacred, calling it 'the navel of the world.' Within the stark, echoing church are some surprising sights. Along the walls are wooden statues of the saints, each of whom gets new clothes made by local women every year. On the carved wooden pulpit, note the figures of corn (from which humans were formed, according to Mayan religion), of a quetzal bird reading a book and of Yum-Kax, the Mayan god of corn. There is similar carving on the back of the priest's chair.

On the walls of the church are paintings, now covered by a thin layer of plaster. A memorial plaque at the back of the church commemorates Father Stanley Francis Rother, a missionary priest from Oklahoma: Beloved by the local people, he was despised by ultrarightist 'death squads,' who murdered him right here in the church during the troubled year of 1981.

When grandfather of Tz'utuhil oil painting and Santiago native Juan Sisay took first place in an international art exhibition in 1969, there was an explosion of painters and their apprentices working in his style, and the legacy lives on. Many local painters support themselves by selling their art from **galleries** lining Santiago's main street. The bright, almost primitive style is distinctly Mayan and has been the theme of shows the world over. Although many canvasses can look similar, works by Pedro Rafael González Chavajay (from San Pedro) and occasionally those by Pedro Miguel Reanda Petzey exude a special energy generally not found in the pieces cranked out for the tourist trade (see the Arts section in the

HIGHLANDS

A God Is a God Is a God

The Spanish called him San Simón, the ladinos named him Maximón and the Maya knew him as Ry Laj Man (pronounced rhee-la-**mawn**). By any name, he's the revered deity found throughout the Guatemalan Highlands. Assumed to be a combination of Maya gods, Pedro de Alvarado (the fierce conquistador of Guatemala) and the biblical Judas, San Simón is an effigy to which Guatemalans of every stripe go and make offerings and ask for blessings. The effigy is usually cared for and housed by a *cofradía* member (town elder). The name, shape and ceremonies associated with this deity vary from town to town, but a visit will be memorable no matter where you encounter him. For a small fee, photography is usually permitted, and offerings of cigarettes, liquor or candles are always appreciated.

In Santiago Atitlán, Maximón is a wooden figure draped in colorful scarves and smoking a fat cigar. Locals worship him, singing and managing the offerings made to him. His favorite gifts are Payaso cigarettes and Venado rum, but he often has to settle for the cheaper firewater Quetzalteca Especial. Each year, Maximón is moved to a new home, a custom anthropologists believe was established to periodically redistribute the balance of power.

In Nahualá, between Los Encuentros and Quetzaltenango, the effigy is also called Maximón. Instead of scarves and a human face, however, this is an effigy à la Picasso: Here the deity is a simple wooden box with a cigarette protruding out of it. Still, the same offerings are made and simple blessings asked for, such as a good harvest and healthy days. In Zunil, near Xela, the deity is known as San Simón, but is similar to Santiago's Maximón in custom and form.

San Jorge La Laguna on Lake Atitlán is a very spiritual place for the Maya; here they worship Ry Laj Man. It is possible that the first effigy was made near here, carved from the *palo de pito* tree that spoke to the ancient shamans and told them to preserve their culture, language and traditions by carving Ry Laj Man. It should be noted that the flowers of the palo de pito can be smoked to induce hallucinations. The effigy in San Jorge looks like a joker, with a a an absurdly long tongue.

In San Andrés Itzapa near Antigua, they also worship Ry Laj Man. Here, instead of moving each year, he has a permanent home, and is brought out on October 28 and paraded about in an unparalleled pagan festival. This is an all-night, hedonistic party where cosmic dancers grab the staff of Ry Laj Man to harness his power and receive magical visions. San Andrés is less than 10km due south of Chimaltenango, so you can easily make the party from a base in Antigua.

Pilgrims offer colored candles to Maximon asking for his help in different areas of their lives: red for love, green for business, blue for work, pink for illness, black for enemies, light blue for money, purple for personal vices, yellow for an adult's protection, white paraffin for a child's protection, white sheep fat for protection against witches.

Facts about Guatemala chapter for more on Tz'utuhil oil painters).

Activities

Recommended **Spanish classes** are offered by sisters Cecilia and Rosa Archila (☎ 703-2562, fax 762-2466, or in the US write to PO Box 520972, Miami, FL 33152-0972). Follow signs from the dock or ask at the Grupo Guías office for more information.

In addition to climbing volcanoes, there are several rewarding, less strenuous **hikes** around Santiago. You can walk to San Pedro in about four hours by taking the path that veers right just beyond the Posada de Santiago and continuing around and over the San Pedro volcano saddle; get the last lancha back in the early afternoon. Alternatively you can catch a pickup to the small village of **Cerro de Oro**, about halfway between Santiago and San Lucas Tolimán. The climb to the top of the hill here yields great views, and there's a pretty church in town; this was once a seat of the Tz'utuhil kingdom. Pickups leave from in front of the Hotel Chi-Nim-Yá. One of the eager children hanging about can help with arrangements.

There's also a challenging 10km round-trip hike to the **mirador**, south of Santiago. This takes you through cloud forest populated with many birds, including parakeets, curassows, swifts, boat-tailed grackles and tucanets and on to the lookout point where there are beautiful views all the way to the coast. The path starts a kilometer beyond the Posada de Santiago, where it veers left at the fork. The trip takes about five hours round-trip, but start early, as the clouds tend to roll in by the afternoon. A guide costs US$13.

Dolores Ratzan Pablo is an accomplished guide specializing in **Mayan ceremonies**. This charming, funny Tz'utuhil woman can introduce you to the wonders of birthing and healing ceremonies, which are an integral part of the Mayan life cycle, or take you around to weaving demonstrations and art galleries. Dolores speaks English, Spanish, Cakchiquel and of course, Tz'utuhil. Tours typically last between one and

three hours and cost US$15 an hour. Contact the Posada de Santiago (☎ 721-7167) for more information on these tours or trips to the island bird refuge just north of Santiago.

Places to Stay & Eat

Near the dock, the *Hotel Chi-Nim-Yá* (☎ 721-7131) is a simple hotel with 22 rooms around a central courtyard. Clean singles/doubles with shared bath are US$3/4; with private bath they're US$7/8. The nicest room in the place is No 106, large and airy, with lots of windows and excellent lake views. Nearby, the *Restaurante Regiomontano* is open every day from 6:30 or 7 am to 7 pm.

Hotel y Restaurante Tzutuhil (☎ 721-7174), about three blocks uphill on the road coming from the dock, is a modern five-story building, an anomaly in this little town. Many of the rooms have large windows with decent views, and some have cable TV. Rooms vary widely so look before committing. Clean rooms are US$2 per person with shared hot bath, US$3.25 per person with private bath. It's a good place and a great deal for the price. Go up on the rooftop for great sunsets. The restaurant here is open every day from 6 am to 10:30 pm.

Along the eastern shore (left from the dock) is the *Hotel-Restaurant Bambú* (☎ 416-2122, ✉ bambu@virtualguatemala .com), a new, comfortable place with singles/doubles/triples/quads in free-standing cabañas with private hot bath for US$30/35/40/45. The grounds are pretty and some rooms have views. There are discounts for longer stays.

Restaurant Santa Rita, a few steps from the northeast corner of the plaza past Distribuidor El Buen Precio, boasts *deliciosos pays* (delicious pies).

One of the most charming hotels around the lake is the *Posada de Santiago* (☎ 721-7167, ✉ posdesantiago@guate.net). Half a dozen free-standing bungalows and two suites, all with stone walls, fireplaces, porches and hammocks, are set around beautiful gardens stretching up the hill from

HIGHLANDS

the lake. Rates are US$30/40/50/60/70 for a single/double/triple/quad/suite. It's 1km from the town center; to get there, walk out of town on the road past the Hospedaje Rosita, and keep walking along the lakeside road. Again, bunches of children will offer to assist you.

The restaurant at the Posada de Santiago is special, too, with well-prepared food and a very cozy ambiance.

Getting There & Away
Boats between Santiago and San Pedro La Laguna take about 20 minutes to make the crossing.

SAN PEDRO LA LAGUNA
The next most popular lakeside town to visit, after Santiago, is San Pedro La Laguna. Being (slightly) less touristy means that fewer flocks of young touts will swirl around you as you stroll the narrow cobblestone streets and wander to the outskirts for a dip in the lake. This town has been heavily populated by foreign bohemian travelers who liked it here so much they stayed on.

Coffee is grown in San Pedro. You'll see coffee being picked and spread out to dry on wide platforms at the beginning of the dry season. Marijuana is another widely cultivated crop in San Pedro. The 'we sell rolling papers' sign at Restaurante Nick's is a tip-off, but before long you will also smell the telltale blue smoke and have fielded pleas to purchase.

Accommodation in San Pedro is among the cheapest in Guatemala. Negotiate deals for longer stays and during the off season.

Orientation & Information
San Pedro has two docks. The one on the south side of town serves boats going to and from Santiago Atitlán. Another dock, around on the east side of town, serves boats going to and from Panajachel. At either dock, walk straight ahead a few blocks on the road leading uphill to reach the center of town. Alternatively, coming from the Santiago dock you can take your first right past the Ti Kaaj and follow the

beaten path for about 15 minutes to the other side of town. Along this path are several hospedajes and simple eateries. To take this route coming from the Panajachel dock, take your first left and then a right into the little alley across from the Hospedaje Casa Elena, a sign painted on the wall says 'to El Balneario.'

San Pedro has a post office, a Telgua telephone/fax office and a Banrural where you can change US dollars cash and traveler's checks. At the top of the hill in the center of town, the Banrural is also a Western Union agent. The folks at Thermal Waters (see that section, below) offer email services, but no Internet access.

Most of the hotels, restaurants and other businesses here don't have private telephones. To reach them, you can phone the community telephone at Telgua (☎ 762-2486) and give them a time when you'll call back; if all goes well, the business will send someone over to receive your return call.

For longer stays, it's also possible to rent a room or an entire house in town. Ask around.

Volcán San Pedro
When you arrive by boat from Panajachel, boys will greet you, asking if you want a guide to ascend the San Pedro volcano by hiking or horseback. It's worth it to go with a guide; cost is US$3 per person for the whole trip by hiking, or slightly more on horseback. The hike through fields of maize, beans and squash, followed by primary cloud forest, takes around four hours. Bring water and snacks, and bargain when contracting with a guide. If you prefer to ascend on horseback, make sure the horses are relatively healthy and beware of the wooden saddles used in these parts, as these will make for a very sore ass. In this case, a stint at Thermal Waters may be in order.

Thermal Waters
Thermal Waters (☎ 206-9658), right on the lakeshore between the two docks, has individual open-air solar-heated pools with a terrific view. A reservation is a good idea, as it's a popular spot. Cost is US$2.60 per

person. Antonio from California, the eccentric horticulturist inventor who built and operates Thermal Waters, also has an organic vegetarian restaurant here and a sweat lodge.

Walking

There are several walks between San Pedro and neighboring villages that make for good day trips. You can walk west to San Juan La Laguna (30 minutes), San Pablo La Laguna (1½ hours), San Marcos (three hours), Jaibalito (five hours) and finally, Santa Cruz (all day). From the last three you can easily hail a lancha back to San Pedro until around 3 pm. Walking southeast over and around the saddle of Volcán San Pedro, you can make it to Santiago Atitlán in around four hours.

Language Courses

Casa Rosario, a Spanish-language school, is operated by Professor Samuel Cumes, a well-known San Pedro teacher. It's more economical than most Spanish schools in Guatemala at US$55 per week for instruction and lodging (food not available). You can arrange weaving classes here as well. Another option on the path between the two docks is the San Pedro Spanish School; the way to both these places is well sign-posted. Some travelers have had success contracting private teachers not affiliated with either of the schools. Ask around town or at the Hospedaje Villa Sol for qualified instructors.

Places to Stay & Eat

When you arrive at the dock serving boats to and from Panajachel, head up the main street and make your first right, walking along the trash-strewn path for about 75m to reach the *Hotel & Restaurante Valle Azul* (☎ 207-7292). This four-story cement behemoth has seen better days; even the hammocks on the balconies with a great view across the lake fail to make it very appealing. Small, basic rooms with shared bath are US$1.95 per person (plus US$0.50 for shower privileges). As a saving grace, the restaurant nearby is a great, inexpensive

little place; it's open every day, 7 am to 10 pm.

Continue walking on the path past the Hotel Valle Azul and through the small cornfield for about five minutes to get to *Café Luna Azul*; you can see it from the dock, and most boatmen will drop you there en route if you ask. In-the-know travelers say this place has Guatemala's best three-egg omelet and hash brown breakfast for under US$2. They also serve lunch.

There are several other restaurants near here, including the *Restaurante El Viajero*, right beside the dock, and the *Restaurante El Fondeadero* to the right of it. You can't miss *Restaurante Nick's*, as this place is the vortex of the foreign traveler scene. Nick's has food and drink and hosts free movies nightly; there is also the occasional rager party here, usually around the full moon. Upstairs, *D'Noz* is another restaurant catering to western backpackers.

Make a left just beyond Nick's to reach *Hospedaje Casa Elena*, a popular, simple, family-run pension; singles/doubles with shared bath are US$3/4. Across the street is the *Hotel Bella Vista* and *Tony's Bar*, with a satellite TV showing big games from the US and Europe. Several meters farther on is a very simple, thatched restaurant called *El Paisaje*. If you take a right there, you'll see the *Hospedaje Xocomil*, which has quiet rooms around a cement courtyard for US$1.30 per person.

Continue through the alley opposite Hospedaje Casa Elena to reach several more pensions on the way to the Santiago dock. The route is not always abundantly clear, so follow the signs for the Casa Rosario Spanish school or ask along the way. Make your first left and then the following left to reach the *Hospedaje Posada Xetawal* and the *Posada Casa Domingo*; both have rooms for about US$1 a night. If you keep going straight instead, toward the Santiago dock, you come to *Restaurant Pinocchio*, which serves good, homemade pastas and cakes; the breakfast here is decent value. *Thermal Waters* is a few minutes walk more from here. Check out their very good bakery or, better yet, the

HIGHLANDS

organic restaurant. Choose from the extensive menu, and Antonio will run out to the garden to gather the ingredients. The campsites here are also winners, with awesome lake views in a secure, beautiful setting.

Next is the **Hotelito El Amanecer Sak'-cari**, which has recommended singles/doubles with private hot bath for US$5/9. Just past here the path takes a left and then a quick right to the friendly **Comedor Mata Hari**, a basic eatery serving wholesome, cheap food. Next door, the **Restaurante Brenda** is popular with locals.

Finally, you'll reach the **Ti Kaaj**, a popular, inexpensive place, with hammocks around the gardens and basic single/double/triple rooms with shared bath for US$2/3/4. There is a restaurant with great coffee and simple pasta dishes, a disco and bar, and kayaks available for rent. From the Santiago dock, make your first right to get here.

Along and just off the road leading uphill from the Santiago dock are several more good places to stay. **Hospedaje Villa Sol**, with 45 simple rooms around a grassy courtyard, charges US$4/6 per room with shared/private bath. Next door, **Hotel San Pedro** has rooms for US$2 per person with shared bath or US$4 with private bath. The police headquarters are also here, so it's (presumably) secure.

Just up this road and to the left is **Hospedaje San Francisco**, a favorite new place up on the hill. Rooms with shared bath are US$3.25 per person, and have hammocks in the garden and a great view of the lake from their tiny patios. Just beyond this is **Hotel San Francisco**, owned by the same family and offering similar rooms at the same price. Both of these hotels fill up fast. Nearby, **Hospedaje El Balneario** is among the cheapest places in town, with 14 charmless rooms, each with a lake view; single/double rooms with shared bath are US$2/4.

Heading left from the Santiago dock, you'll find the very laid-back **Las Milpas** (✉ lasmilpas@atitlan.com). It offers a variety of lodgings, including private bungalows for one/two people for US$7/8; rooms with

shared bath for US$10/14 or simpler versions for US$6.45 per person; and doubles/triples with private bath for US$20/24. You can also camp here and there's a kitchen. There's a hot tub, sauna and gardens available for guests' relaxation and enjoyment. You can arrange tours and boat passage here too.

Cafe Arte, on the road leading uphill from the Santiago dock, is a good, inexpensive café serving meat, fish and vegetarian dishes. It's operated by the family of internationally known primitivist artist Pedro Rafael González Chavajay. His paintings and those of many of his students are exhibited at the café. It's open every day from 7 am to 11 pm.

For good, basic food in a friendly atmosphere, keep going up the hill and bear right to **Rosalinda**.

Shopping

A few doors farther uphill from Cafe Arte is **Caza Sueños**, a leather shop owned by brothers Fernando and Pedro González. Here, they handcraft custom leather goods, including vests, shoes, boots, bags and whatever else you may want in hide. After taking an outline of your foot, for an incredibly reasonable US$35 the brothers will craft a pair of shoes, allowing you to specify your choice of color, fringe, trim and lace style; allow at least four days. Caza Sueños is open daily from 9 am to 1 pm and 3 to 5 pm.

Getting There & Away

The paved road from San Lucas Tolimán to Santiago Atitlán continues 18km to San Pedro, making its way around the lagoon and the back side of Volcán San Pedro.

A newly paved road connects San Pedro with the Interamericana; the turnoff is at Km 148. The road meets the lake at Santa Clara La Laguna and turns right to San Pedro, left to San Marcos. From San Pedro it continues to Santiago Atitlán and San Lucas Tolimán. From San Marcos it continues to Tzununá, but beyond that it's a walking trail only, which continues to Jaibalito and Santa Cruz La Laguna. Buses to Guatemala City depart from San Pedro at 3, 3:30 4, 4:30 and 5 am; see the Getting Around chapter for return buses. The trip takes three to four hours and costs US$2.65.

Unless you want to bring a vehicle, it's easier to reach San Pedro by boat. Passenger boats come here from Panajachel and Santiago (see those sections for details).

SAN MARCOS LA LAGUNA

San Marcos is a very peaceful place, with houses set among shady coffee plants near the shore. Lago de Atitlán is beautiful and clean here, with several little docks you can swim from. Between here and Santa Cruz are some of the most majestic views imaginable. In step with the tranquil surroundings, there are a handful of places here to pamper your body; look for flyers advertising massage, shiatsu and Reiki on hotel bulletin boards, or ask around.

San Marcos' greatest claim to fame is **Las Pirámides** meditation center (☎ 205-7302, 205-7151), on the path heading inland from Posada Schumann. A one-month spiritual course called the Curso Lunar de Meditación (lunar meditation course, for spiritual and human development) begins every full moon. It covers four elements of human development (physical, mental, emotional and spiritual), with one week dedicated to each. The last week of the course is a retreat requiring fasting and silence by participants and so is not recommended for novice spiritualists. Channeling sessions are held with those participating in the month-long course. If you can stay for a month to do the whole course, come in time for full moon. Most sessions are held in English, though occasionally they'll be translated from Spanish.

Other activities available here include yoga, aura work, massage (US$13 an hour), Tarot readings and regression. Nonguests can come for meditation or Hatha yoga sessions Monday through Saturday for US$3.90.

Every structure on the property is built in the shape of pyramids and oriented to the four cardinal points, including the two temples where sessions are held. Accommo-

dations are available in little pyramid-shaped houses for US$10/9/8 per day by the day/week/month. Included in this price is the meditation course, use of the sauna, and access to a fascinating library with books in several languages. There is also a great vegetarian restaurant here and room to wander about in the medicinal herb garden. The best chance to get a space here comes just prior to the full moon when the meditation program is finishing. Las Pirámides has a private dock; all the lancheros know it, so you can be dropped right here.

Places to Stay & Eat

Alighting at the public dock, you'll see loads of signs advertising accommodations in San Marcos. Just to the left of the dock is the **Hotel & Restaurante Arco Iris** (☎ 306-5039, ✉ arcoiris@atitlan.com). This is a comfortable hotel with good beds in clean rooms around neat, manicured grounds for US$5.15 per person. Overlooking the lake are hammocks to relax in and a restaurant serving delicious espresso. Italian, English, French and German are spoken here.

To get to the rest of the hotels on foot, you have to walk along the inland street running parallel to the lake for a few hundred meters. A left turn at the signs for Posada Schumann and others takes you down a dirt path where you'll find the rest of San Marcos' hotels.

The first place you come to is **Hotel Paco Real** (fax 762-1196), with beautiful gardens and rooms that are simple but tastefully decorated; all in all it's got a very artistic feel. Charming bungalows with loft beds, porches and shared bath are US$10.50 for two people. Clean rooms with tiled floors and shared bath are US$5/11/15 for a single/double/triple. Some rooms are musty, so check out several before choosing. Also here is a decent restaurant run by a French chef, open every day from 7 am to 9 pm.

Next on the strip is the very mellow **Hotel La Paz** (☎ 702-9168), with basic little bungalows on rambling grounds with organic gardens, a vegetarian restaurant and a traditional Mayan sauna. The bungalows sleep five dorm-style and are US$3.20 per

HIGHLANDS

person. To have one of these to yourself costs US$13. There's one private double for US$9. Camping is allowed, and there's a common room above the restaurant with musical instruments and books. Bartering is encouraged here.

Unicornio Rooms is another attractive place, with lovely gardens, a sauna and a communal kitchen (but no electricity). Three small, thatch-roofed A-frame bungalows with shared cold bath are US$3/6 for a single/double. There's also one large two-story bungalow with private kitchen and bath.

Right on the lakeside, *Posada Schumann* (☎ 202-2216, in Guatemala City 360-4049, 339-2683, fax 473-1326) has three stone bungalows, each with kitchen and private bath; there's also a restaurant and sauna. The bungalows for one/two people are US$12/24. You can save by renting weekly or monthly. There are also cheaper single/double rooms for US$8/16. The Posada Schumann has a private pier, negating the few-hundred-meter trek through town if you're arriving by lancha.

Hotel San Marcos is another option here, though it's not as beautiful as the other places. Rooms with shared cold bath are US$3 per person.

Getting There & Away

You can drive to San Marcos from the Interamericana, where there's a turnoff at Km 148. See San Pedro, earlier in this chapter. The walk or drive between Santa Clara La Laguna and San Marcos is breathtaking, as is the walk to towns farther east.

See the Panajachel section for information on passenger boats.

JAIBALITO

This tiny town is only accessible by boat or on foot, but visitors will be well rewarded once they arrive. There are picturesque hikes to San Marcos (three hours) and Santa Cruz (one hour) and you can hail lanchas to visit other lakeside towns.

Perched on a cliff facing the three volcanoes is the secluded *La Casa del Mundo Hotel & Cafe* (☎ 204-5558, fax 762-1092,

@ casamundo@yahoo.com), Guatemala's most magical hotel. Designed and built by husband and wife team Bill and Rosie Fogarty, this place has beautiful gardens and swimming holes, a 15m cliff jump into a pristine pool and a hot tub overhanging the lake. Rooms with private solar-heated bath are US$16.75 a double. Room No 1 has two balconies and panoramic lake views; No 3, above, is smaller, but seems to be floating on the water, as no land is visible beneath. Other nearly as spectacular rooms with shared hot bath are US$6.50 per person. Every room has privacy and views and is impeccably outfitted with comfortable beds, typical Guatemalan fabrics and fresh flowers. The restaurant is open to the public; dinner is a prix fixe affair (US$7) with four courses of seriously tasty food. You can rent kayaks or bikes here for exploring the lake. Hotel reservations are advisable.

Also in Jaibalito is the Norwegian-owned *Vulcano Lodge* (fax 762-0092, contact @ vulcanolodge@hotmail.com). This new place is set in a pretty stand of banana and coffee plants and has spotless singles/doubles with private hot bath for US$14/18. The bottom half of a whitewashed house is available for US$25 for two people, or you can rent the family suite upstairs for US$50. There are hammocks, a verandah and a reasonably priced restaurant.

Jaibalito has no roads, but you can walk on the path skirting the ridge from Santa Cruz La Laguna in about an hour and from San Marcos in two to three hours. Otherwise, it's a 20 minute lancha ride from Panajachel or San Pedro. The boatmen know the Casa del Mundo, which has a private pier. Sometimes this is underwater, however, in which case you'll need to be dropped at the public dock. From here, head to your right on a small path that traces the shore to get to the steps leading to Casa del Mundo. To get to the Vulcano Lodge, walk straight ahead and follow the signs.

SANTA CRUZ LA LAGUNA

Santa Cruz La Laguna is another serene little village beside the lake. The vibe here is somewhere between the international party scene of San Pedro and the therapeutic, spiritual feel of San Marcos. The main part of the village is up the hill from the dock; the hotels are on the lakeside, right beside the dock.

ATI Divers (fax 762-1196, ☻ santacruz@guate.net, in Pana 762-2646) operates a diving school and does underwater archaeology dives and special projects. A four-day PADI open-water diving certification course costs US$160; they also offer a PADI high-altitude advanced diving course and fun dives. It's based at La Iguana Perdida hotel, where you can also make arrangements to water ski.

You can take some good walks starting at Santa Cruz. A beautiful option is the lakeside walking track between Santa Cruz and San Marcos; it takes about four hours one way. You can stop for a beer and a meal at La Casa del Mundo en route (see above). Or you can walk up the hill to Sololá, a three- to 3½-hour walk one-way.

Places to Stay & Eat

Three welcoming lakeside hotels, all right near the dock, provide accommodations and meals. While there's electricity up the hill in town, there's none at the hotels. In the evening guests eat by candlelight and lantern-light.

None of these hotels has a telephone, but you can fax them at 762-1196 or contact them by email. It can take a few days to hear back from them.

Arca de Noé (☻ thearca@yahoo.com) is recommended for its excellent food and beautiful views of the lake from the dense, colorful gardens. They have a variety of rooms ranging from singles/doubles with shared bath for US$6/10 to plush singles/doubles with private bath for US$20/22. Dorm beds are also available for US$3.50.

Popular with the backpacking set, *La Iguana Perdida* (☻ santacruz@guate.net) also has a restaurant and a variety of accommodations. The cost is US$2.35 per person for a dorm bed, US$6/8 for a private single/double, or US$8/10 for one/two people in small cabañas with shared bath. Meals are served family-style, with every-one eating together; a three course dinner is US$4.50. You always have a vegetarian choice, and everything here is on the honor system; you keep tabs in a notebook of everything you do, eat and drink and it's totaled when you check out. There's also a sauna. The friendly managers, Deedle Denman (from the UK) and Mike Kiersgard (from Greenland), also operate ATI Divers.

The *Posada Abaj Hotel* (☻ abaj@atitlan.com), on the lakefront somewhat removed from the action of the other hotels, is a nice, quiet place that also has a restaurant. Rooms with shared bath are US$5 per person; bungalows with private bath are US$16.75 for two people. Spanish classes are offered here and there's a sauna amid very nicely maintained grounds.

See the Panajachel section earlier in this chapter for details on taking a passenger boat to Santa Cruz La Laguna.

Quiché

The Departamento del Quiché is famous mostly for the town of Chichicastenango, with its bustling markets on Thursday and Sunday. Beyond Chichi to the north is Santa Cruz del Quiché, the capital of the department. On its outskirts lie the ruins of K'umarcaaj (or Gumarcaah), also called Utatlán, the last capital city of the Quiché Maya.

The road to Quiché leaves the Interamericana at Los Encuentros, winding its way down through pine forests and cornfields into a steep valley and up the other side. Women sit in front of their little roadside cottages weaving gorgeous pieces of cloth on their simple backstrap looms. From Los Encuentros, it takes half an hour to travel to Chichicastenango, 17km to the north.

CHICHICASTENANGO
• pop 8000 • elevation 2030m
Surrounded by valleys, with nearby mountains looming overhead, Chichicastenango seems isolated in time and space from the rest of Guatemala. When its narrow cobbled

HIGHLANDS

CHICHICASTENANGO

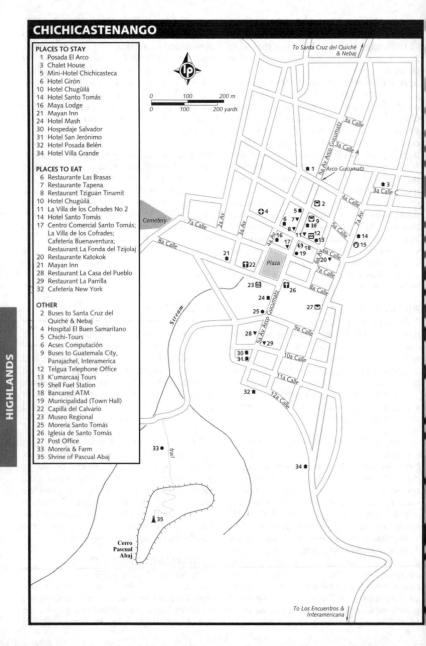

PLACES TO STAY
1 Posada El Arco
3 Chalet House
5 Mini-Hotel Chichicasteca
6 Hotel Girón
10 Hotel Chugüilá
14 Hotel Santo Tomás
16 Maya Lodge
21 Mayan Inn
24 Hotel Mash
30 Hospedaje Salvador
31 Hotel San Jerónimo
32 Hotel Posada Belén
34 Hotel Villa Grande

PLACES TO EAT
6 Restaurante Las Brasas
7 Restaurante Tapena
8 Restaurant Tziguan Tinamit
10 Hotel Chugüilá
11 La Villa de los Cofrades No 2
14 Hotel Santo Tomás
17 Centro Comercial Santo Tomás;
    La Villa de los Cofrades;
    Cafetería Buenaventura;
    Restaurant La Fonda del Tzijolaj
20 Restaurante Katokok
21 Mayan Inn
28 Restaurant La Casa del Pueblo
29 Restaurant La Parrilla
32 Cafetería New York

OTHER
2 Buses to Santa Cruz del
   Quiché & Nebaj
4 Hospital El Buen Samaritano
5 Chichi-Tours
6 Acses Computación
9 Buses to Guatemala City,
   Panajachel, Interamerica
12 Telgua Telephone Office
13 K'umarcaaj Tours
15 Shell Fuel Station
18 Bancared ATM
19 Municipalidad (Town Hall)
22 Capilla del Calvario
23 Museo Regional
25 Morería Santo Tomás
26 Iglesia de Santo Tomás
27 Post Office
33 Morería & Farm
35 Shrine of Pascual Abaj

To Santa Cruz del Quiché & Nebaj

0   100   200 m
0   100   200 yards

3a Calle
3a Av Arco Gucumatz
3a Calle A
1 Arco Gucumatz
1a Av Arco Gucumatz
3 3a Calle C
4a Calle
2
4a Av
5
6 7
8
9 10
11 12
13
14
15
16
17
4a Av
18 20
19
21
22 Plaza
23
26
24
27
25
28
29
5a Av Arco Gucumatz
30
31
10a Calle
32
11a Calle
12a Calle
8a Calle
9a Calle

Cemetery
7a Calle
2a Av
3a Av
8a Calle

Stream
trail

33

34

35
Cerro
Pascual
Abaj

To Los Encuentros &
Interamericana

streets and red-tiled roofs are enveloped in mist, as they often are, it can seem magical. Chichi is a beautiful, interesting place, with lots of shamanistic and ceremonial overtones, in spite of the shiny tour buses parked near the market and gaggles of camera-toting tour groups. If you have a choice of days, come for the Sunday market rather than the Thursday one, as the cofradías (religious brotherhoods) often hold processions on Sunday.

Though isolated, Chichi has always been an important market town. Villagers from throughout the region would walk for many hours carrying their wares to participate in the commerce here – and that was in the days before decent roads.

Today, though many traders come by bus, others still arrive on foot. When they reach Chichi's main square on the night before the market, they lay down their loads, spread out a blanket and go to sleep in one of the arcades that surround the square. At dawn on Thursday and Sunday they spread out their vegetables, fruits, chunks of chalk (ground to a powder, mixed with water and used to soften dried maize), balls of wax, handmade harnesses and other wares and wait for customers.

Many ladino business types also set up fairly touristy stalls in the Sunday and Thursday markets. Somehow they end up adding to the color and fascination, rather than detracting from it.

Besides the fabulous market, Masheños (citizens of Chichicastenango) are famous for their adherence to pre-Christian religious beliefs and ceremonies. You can readily see versions of these old rites in and around the church of Santo Tomás and at the shrine of Pascual Abaj on the outskirts of town.

Chichi has two religious and governmental establishments. The Catholic Church and the Republic of Guatemala appoint priests and town officials to manage their particular interests, but the local people elect their own religious and civil officers to deal with local matters.

The Indian town government has its own council, mayor and deputy mayor, and it has a court that decides cases involving local indigenous people exclusively. This system of government predates the arrival of the Spanish.

Once called Chaviar, this was an important Cakchiquel trading town long before the Spanish conquest. Just prior to the arrival of the conquistadors, the Cakchiquel and the Quiché (based at K'umarcaaj near present-day Santa Cruz del Quiché, 20km

Cofradías

Chichi's religious life is centered in traditional religious brotherhoods known as cofradías. Membership in the brotherhood is an honorable civic duty; leadership is the greatest honor. Leaders are elected periodically, and the man who receives the honor of being elected must provide banquets and pay for festivities for the cofradía throughout his term. Though it is very expensive, a *cofrade* (member of the brotherhood) happily accepts the burden, even going into debt if necessary.

Each of Chichi's 14 cofradías has a patron saint. Most notable is the cofradía of Santo Tomás, Chichicastenango's patron saint. The cofradías march in procession to church every Sunday morning and during religious festivals, with the officers dressed in costumes showing their rank. Before them is carried a ceremonial staff topped by a silver crucifix or sun-badge that signifies the cofradía's patron saint. An Indian drum and a flute, and perhaps a few more modern instruments such as a trumpet, may accompany the procession, as do fireworks.

During major church festivals, effigies of the saints are brought out and carried in grand processions, and richly costumed dancers wearing the traditional carved wooden masks act out legends of the ancient Maya and of the Spanish conquest. For the rest of the year, these masks and costumes are kept in storehouses called *morerías*; you'll see them, marked by signs, around the town.

north) went to war. The Cakchiquel abandoned Chaviar and moved their headquarters to Iximché, which was easier to defend. The conquistadors came and conquered K'umarcaaj, and many of its residents fled to Chaviar, which they renamed Chugüilá (Above the Nettles) and Tziguan Tinamit (Surrounded by Canyons). These are the names still used by the Quiché Maya, although everyone else calls the place Chichicastenango, a foreign name given by the conquistadors' Mexican allies. Like many unwieldy town names here, it's often shortened to just Chichi.

Information

Though supposedly laid out as a typical Spanish colonial street grid, Chichi's hilly topography defeats the logic of the plan, and the lack of street signs often keeps you wondering where you are. Use our map, identify some landmarks, and you should have little trouble, as Chichi is fairly small.

There is no official tourist information office in Chichi. Ask your questions at the museum on the main plaza or at one of the hotels. The staff at the Mayan Inn is perhaps the most helpful and best informed.

Since Sunday is Chichi's biggest day of commerce, all the banks here are open, taking their day off on some other day of the week (the day varies from bank to bank, so you can always find some bank open). Most banks change US dollars cash and traveler's checks. Bancafé, on 5a Avenida between 6a and 7a Calle, gives cash advances on Visa cards, and there's a Bancared ATM. This stretch of 5a Avenida is lined with banks, so take your pick. The Hotel Santo Tomás (see Places to Stay) will change traveler's checks for guests and nonguests alike, at a slightly worse rate than the banks.

The post office is at 7a Avenida 8-47, 3½ blocks south of the Hotel Santo Tomás on the road into town. The Telgua telephone office is on 6a Calle between 5a and 6a Avenida.

Acses Computación, on 6a Calle in the same complex as the Hotel Girón (see Places to Stay) has email and Internet access when their network is up and running.

The cemetery on the western edge of town is a decidedly unsavory place to wander and explore, even in groups. There have been several reports of tourists being robbed at gunpoint, so a solo visit here is not recommended.

When you get off the bus in Chichi, you'll likely be besieged by touts offering guide services and assistance in finding a hotel. Showing up at a hotel with a tout in tow means you'll be quoted a higher price for a room, as the hotel gives them a kickback – and this on top of your tip! In fact, you don't need their 'help,' because they are always taking foreigners to the same few hotels: places that have been around for years and that you'll already know about through this book. In fact, there are hotels these touts *won't* take you to because the owners refuse to provide kickbacks, and (wouldn't you know it) these are some of the best values in town.

Crowded markets are the favorite haunts of pickpockets, so be alert while you browse, wander and shop in the labyrinth of stalls here.

Market

Years ago, intrepid travelers made their way to this mountain fastness to witness Chichi's main plaza packed with Mayan traders attending one of Guatemala's largest indigenous markets. Today the market has stalls aimed directly at tourists, as well as those for locals.

On Wednesday and Saturday evenings you'll see men carrying bundles of long poles up the narrow cobbled streets to the square, then stacking them out of the way. In the evening the arcades around the square are alive with families cooking supper and arranging their bedding for a night's sleep out of doors. This sight is much less inspiring in the rainy season when the whole square is covered in black plastic tarps, severely limiting visibility.

Between dawn and about 8 or 9 am on Sunday and Thursday, the stacks of poles are erected into stalls, hung with cloth, furnished with tables and piled with goods for sale. In general, the tourist-oriented stalls selling carved wooden masks, lengths of embroidered cloth and garments are around the outer edges of the market in the most visible areas. Behind them, the center of the square is devoted to things that the villagers want and need: vegetables and fruit, baked goods, macaroni, soap, clothing, spices, sewing notions and toys. Cheap cookshops provide lunch for buyers and sellers alike.

Most of the stalls are taken down by late afternoon. Prices are best just before the market breaks up, as traders would rather sell than carry goods away with them.

Arriving in town the day before the market to pin down a room and a bed is highly recommended. In this way, too, you'll be up early for the day's festivities. One traveler wrote to say it's worth being here on Saturday night to attend Saturday night mass. Otherwise, you can always come by bus on market day itself, or by shuttle bus: Market-day shuttle buses come from Antigua, Panajachel and Guatemala City, returning in early afternoon. The market starts winding down around 3 or 4 pm.

Iglesia de Santo Tomás

Though dedicated to Catholic rites, this simple church dating from about 1540 is more often the scene of rituals that are only slightly Catholic and more distinctly Mayan. The front steps of the church serve much the same purpose as did the great flights of stairs leading up to Mayan pyramids. For much of the day (especially on Sunday), the steps smolder with incense of copal resin, while indigenous prayer leaders called *chuchkajaues* (mother-fathers) swing censers (usually tin cans poked with holes) containing *estoraque* incense and chant magic words in honor of the ancient Maya calendar and of their ancestors.

It's customary for the front steps and door of the church to be used only by important church officials and by the chuchkajaues, so you should go around to the right and enter by the side door.

Inside, the floor of the church may be spread with pine boughs and dotted with of-ferings of maize kernels, bouquets of flowers, bottles of liquor wrapped in corn husks, and candles – candles everywhere. Many local families can trace their lineage back centuries, some even to the ancient kings of Quiché. The candles and offerings on the floor are in remembrance of those ancestors, many of whom are buried beneath the church floor just as Maya kings were buried beneath pyramids. Photography is not permitted in this church.

On the west side of the plaza is another little whitewashed church, the Capilla del Calvario, which is similar in form and function to Santo Tomás, but smaller.

Museo Regional

In the arcade facing the south side of the square is the Museo Regional. Inside, you can see ancient clay pots and figurines, arrowheads and spearheads of flint and obsidian, copper ax-heads, and *metates* (grindstones for maize).

The museum also holds the Rossbach jade collection, with several beautiful necklaces, figurines and other objects. Ildefonso Rossbach served as Chichi's Catholic priest for many years until his death in 1944.

The museum is open every day but Tuesday, from 8 am to noon and 2 to 5 pm.

Shrine of Pascual Abaj

Before you have been in Chichi very long, some village lad will offer to guide you (for a tip) to a hilltop on the outskirts to have a look at Pascual Abaj (Sacrifice Stone), which is the local shrine to Huyup Tak'ah (Mountain Plain), the Mayan Earth god. Said to be hundreds – perhaps thousands – of years old, the stone-faced idol has suffered numerous indignities at the hands of outsiders, but local people still revere it. Chuchkajaues come here regularly to offer incense, food, cigarettes, flowers, liquor and Coca-Cola to the Earth god, and perhaps even to sacrifice a chicken. The offerings are in thanks and hope for the Earth's continuing fertility.

Sacrifices do not take place at regular hours. If you're in luck, you can witness one. The worshipers will not mind if you watch, and some (but not all) won't mind if you take photographs, though they may ask if you want to make an offering (of a few quetzals) yourself. Request permission to take photos and don't assume it will be granted. If there is no ceremony, you can still see the idol and enjoy the walk up to the pine-clad hilltop and the views of the town and valley.

There have been some incidents of robbery of tourists walking to visit Pascual Abaj, so the best plan is to join with others and go in a large group.

You don't really need a guide to find Pascual Abaj. Walk down the hill on 5a Avenida from the Santo Tomás church, turn right onto 9a Calle and continue downhill along this unpaved road, which bends to the left. At the bottom of the hill, when the road turns sharply to the right, bear left and follow a path through the cornfields, keeping the stream on your left. Signs mark the way. Walk to the buildings just ahead, which include a farmhouse and a *morería*, a workshop where masks are made. Greet the family here. If the children are not in school, you may be invited to see them perform a local dance in full costume on your return from Pascual Abaj (a tip is expected).

Walk through the farm buildings to the hill behind, and follow the switchback path to the top and along the ridge of the hill, called Turukaj, to a clearing in which you will see the idol in its rocky shrine. The idol looks like something from Easter Island. The squat stone crosses near it have many levels of significance for the Maya, only one of which pertains to Christ. The area of the shrine is littered with past offerings; the bark of nearby pines has been stripped away in places to be used as fuel in the incense fires.

Special Events

The traditional ceremonial atmosphere of Chichi means holidays and special events offer a more intriguing experience than the usual dancing, drinking and fireworks typical to all other Guatemalan fiestas. December 7 is *Quema del Diablo*, the Burning of the Devil, when residents burn their garbage in the streets and usher a statue of the Virgin Mary to the steps of the Iglesia de Santo Tomás. There's lots of incense and candles, a 12-piece marimba band and an ingenious and daring fireworks display that has observers running for cover. The following day is the Feast of the Immaculate Conception; don't miss the early morning dance of the giant, drunken cartoon characters in the plaza.

The Feast of Santo Tomás starts on December 13 and culminates on December 21 when pairs of brave (some would say maniacal) men fly about at high speeds suspended from a pole in the *palo volador* or flying pole extravaganza. Traditional dances and parades are also featured.

Places to Stay

Chichi does not have a lot of accommodations, and many places are in the higher price range. As rooms are scarce, it's a good idea to arrive early on Wednesday or Saturday if you want to secure a room for the Thursday and Sunday markets. Safe car parking is available in the courtyard of most hotels.

Budget *Hotel Girón* (☎ 756-1156, fax 756-1226, 6a Calle 4-52) is a clean hotel around a courtyard/carpark, and is an OK value for the money. Singles/doubles are US$6/8 with shared cold bath, US$13/16 with private hot bath.

Mini-Hotel Chichicasteca (☎ 756-1008, 5a Calle 4-42) is a good budget choice popular with locals. Rooms with shared bath are US$3.90 per person.

Of the cheap hotels, *Hospedaje Salvador* (☎ 756-1329, 5a Avenida 10-09), two blocks southwest of the Santo Tomás church, is the biggest. This large, mazelike, white-and-yellow building has 48 rooms on three floors. Fairly unattractive singles/doubles/triples are US$4/7/9 with shared bath, or US$9.65 for a double with private bath. Bargain hard here. Next door is the more expensive, appealing *Hotel San Jerónimo*.

Hotel Mash is a classic cheapie on 5a Avenida before you get to the Hospedaje Salvador. Enter through the black door under the Tienda El Tzijhola sign and walk through the alley, past the simple residences to the staircase with the potted plants. Big, wood-plank rooms with shared bath are US$4 a night. This is about as close as you get to authentic Guatemalan living short of a homestay.

Hotel Posada Belén (☎ /fax 756-1244, 12a Calle 5-55) is up on a hill away from the chaos of the market. Clean, comfortable rooms are US$5/8 for a single/double with shared bath, US$7/11 with private bath. The showers aren't the greatest, but this is offset by the friendly owners and killer views. You can pay US$1.65 more to get cable TV, and there's a laundry service.

Posada El Arco (☎ 756-1255, 4a Calle 4-36), near the Arco Gucumatz, is a winner guesthouse and the best accommodation for the price in Chichi. Here you can sit in the lawn chairs in the rear garden and enjoy a great northward view of the mountains of Quiché. All the rooms are spacious and spotless, with attractive decor and private hot bath. The upstairs rooms, with fireplaces, are US$15.50 for one or two people; downstairs, the rooms are larger but have no fireplaces, and are US$13.15 for one or two people. The friendly owners, Emilsa and Pedro Macario, speak English and Spanish. Reservations are a good idea.

Another charming, recommended place owned by a friendly husband and wife team is the *Chalet House* (☎ 756-1360, 3a Calle 'C' 7-44). Cozy rooms with good beds and nice touches are US$10.30 a double in low season, US$14.15 in high. Breakfast is available here and there's the occasional homemade pizza party.

Mid-Range *Hotel Chugüilá* (☎ 756-1134, fax 756-1279, 5a Avenida 5-24) is pretty and a decent value. All of the 36 colonial-style rooms have private bath, some have a fireplace, and there are even a few two-room suites and a restaurant. For what you get, the price is reasonable – US$31/36/40. Certain rooms are noticeably better than others, as mildew has beset some. Check out a few units before settling in for the night.

Maya Lodge (☎ /fax 756-1167), in the main plaza, has 10 rooms (some with fireplace) with clean add-on showers, all in the very midst of the market. Fairly plain despite some colonial touches, it is comfortable nonetheless. Rooms with private hot bath are US$25/31/39. There is parking and a restaurant here.

Top End The best hotel in town is the lovely old *Mayan Inn* (☎ 756-1176, fax 756-1212, 8a Calle A and 3a Avenida), on a quiet street one long block southwest of the plaza. Founded in 1932 by Alfred S Clark of Clark Tours, it has grown to include several restored colonial houses, their courtyards planted with exuberant tropical flora and their walls covered with brilliantly colored indigenous textiles. Not all of the 30 rooms are equally charming, so look before choosing. Each unit has a fireplace and antique furnishings including carved wooden bedsteads, headboards painted with country scenes, heavily carved armoires and rough-hewn tables. The private bathrooms (many with tubs) may be old-fashioned, but they are decently maintained. A staff member in traditional costume is assigned to help you carry your bags, answer any questions and even serve at your table in the dining room, as well as to look after your room – there are no door locks. Rates are US$90/98/108 for a single/double/triple.

Hotel Santo Tomás (☎ 756-1316, fax 756-1306, 7a Avenida 5-32), two blocks east of the plaza, is colonial in architecture and decoration but modern in construction and facilities, and it is thus a favorite with bus-tour operators. Each of the 43 rooms has private bath (with tub) and fireplace; all the rooms are grouped around pretty courtyards with colonial fountains. There's a swimming pool, Jacuzzi and a good bar and dining room. Rates are US$66/78/96 for a single/double/triple. There's a good selection of books for sale in the lobby.

Hotel Villa Grande (☎ 756-1053, 756-1236, fax 756-1140, ℮ infos@villasdeguatemala .com), 1km south of Chichi's main square along the road into town, is a resort and convention center with 75 modern rooms and suites in low tile-roofed buildings set into a hillside. The 10 minute walk from the hotel to town can make for a nice stroll, though it might not be the safest at night. The Villa Grande has fine views, a swimming pool and a restaurant. The regular rooms are rather stark, but the suites all have patios with a view and fireplaces. Singles/doubles/triples are US$65/75/85 for the regular rooms, US$97/107/117 for the suites. For special deals, be sure to visit their annoyingly animated Web site, found at www.villasdeguatemala.com/.

Places to Eat

Budget On Sunday and Thursday, eat where the marketers do – at the cook shacks set up in the center of the market. Don't be deterred by all the fried food stalls on the fringe – just dive into the center for more wholesome fare. Here you'll find the cheapest eats in town. On other days, look for the little comedores near the post office on the road into town (7a Avenida).

Restaurant La Fonda del Tzijolaj, upstairs in the Centro Comercial Santo Tomás on the north side of the plaza, has everything: good views, nice decor, decent food and reasonable prices – US$2 to US$3 for breakfast, twice that for lunch or dinner. It's closed Tuesday. There are several other restaurants with portico tables in the Centro Comercial. At *La Villa de los Cofrades* you can while away the hours with checkers (draughts), backgammon and the best coffee in town. It's a popular place, with breakfast for around US$2.50, lunch or dinner around US$4.

The inner courtyard of the Centro Comercial Santo Tomás is a vegetable market on market days and a basketball court the rest of the time. Upstairs inside the courtyard, overlooking the vegetable market, *Cafetería Buenaventura* is clean, with decent meals, and is one of the most economical places in town.

La Villa de los Cofrades No 2, upstairs overlooking the street at the corner of 6a Calle and 5a Avenida (enter from 6a Calle), has tables inside and out on the balcony, overlooking the market street. It's run by the same owners as the original La Villa de los Cofrades, has the same good coffee and serves delicious food. An ample lunch or dinner with several courses and big portions costs around US$4 to US$6; simpler meals are less. Down the block is the similar *Restaurante Katokok*, where pasta and meat dishes cost between US$4 and US$7. The coffee here is also potable.

Restaurant Tziguan Tinamit, at the corner of 6a Calle and 5a Avenida, takes its name from the Quiché Maya name for Chichicastenango. It's popular with locals and foreigners for pizza, pasta and meat dishes and is open every day.

On 6a Calle, upstairs from the Hotel Girón, is the *Restaurante Las Brasas*, serving meat dishes at reasonable prices. The breakfast here is a good deal, and they're open earlier than other places in Chichi.

Restaurante Tapena, on 5a Avenida across the street from the Hotel Chugüilá, is a lively, family-owned place with huge portions of tasty food for cheap. Sometimes there is live music in the back and the service is very attentive.

Restaurant La Parrilla, at the corner of 5a Avenida Arco Gucumatz and 10a Calle, catty-corner from Hospedaje Salvador, is a good restaurant for the thrifty, specializing in charcoal-grilled meats. Hearty meals of your choice of meat, served with rice, salad, soup and bread or tortillas, are US$3 to US$5; breakfasts are cheaper. Half a block away, *Restaurant La Casa del Pueblo* (*5a Avenida Arco Gucumatz 9-81*) is another popular little restaurant.

Nearby, the *Cafetería New York* is upstairs from the Hotel Posada Belén; the owner is a Guatemalan who spent 14 years in New York and speaks English.

Hotel Chugüilá (see Places to Stay) is one of the most inviting places to eat, and there you'll always find a few other travelers to talk with about life on the road. Main-course plates are priced at US$5.

Mid-Range The three dining rooms at the *Mayan Inn* (*8a Calle A and 3a Avenida*), one long block southwest of the plaza, have pale yellow walls, beamed ceilings, red-tiled floors, colonial-style tables and chairs and decorations of colorful local cloth. Waiters wear traditional costumes, which evolved from the dress of Spanish farmers of the colonial era: colorful headdress, sash, black tunic with colored embroidery, half-length trousers and squeaky leather sandals called *caïtes*. The food may not be as stellar as the costuming, however. The daily set-price meals are the most economical way to order here; they cost US$6 for breakfast and US$12 for lunch or dinner, plus drinks and tip.

The *Hotel Santo Tomás* (7a Avenida 5-32), two blocks east of the plaza, has a good dining room, but it's often crowded with tour groups. Try to get one of the courtyard tables, where you can enjoy the sun and the marimba band that plays at lunchtime on market days.

Getting There & Away

Chichi has no bus station. Buses heading south to Guatemala City, Panajachel, Quetzaltenango and all other points reached from the Interamericana arrive and depart from 5a Calle at the corner of 5a Avenida Arco Gucumatz, one block south of the arch. Buses heading north to Santa Cruz del Quiché and Nebaj arrive and depart from around the corner on 5a Avenida Arco Gucumatz. Any bus heading south can drop you at Los Encuentros, where you can catch a bus to your final destination.

Antigua – 3½ hours, 108km. Take any bus heading for Guatemala City and change buses at Chimaltenango.

Guatemala City – US$1.45, 3½ hours, 144km. Buses run every 20 minutes, 3:30 am to 6 pm.

Los Encuentros – US$0.35, 30 minutes, 17km. Take any bus heading south for Guatemala City, Panajachel, Quetzaltenango and so on.

Nebaj – US$2.50, 4½ hours, 103km. Two buses run daily, or take a bus to Santa Cruz del Quiché and change there.

Panajachel – US$1.65, 1½ hours, 37km. There are 11 buses daily (approximately hourly), 4:30 am to 2:30 pm; or take any bus heading south and change buses at Los Encuentros.

Quetzaltenango – US$1.50, three hours, 94km. Seven buses run daily, mostly in the morning; or take any bus heading south and change at Los Encuentros.

Santa Cruz del Quiché – US$0.50, 30 minutes, 19km. There are buses every 20 minutes, 6 am to 9 pm.

On market days, shuttle buses arrive en masse, bringing tourists from Pana, Antigua, Guatemala City and Xela. The shuttles arrive around midmorning, park in front of the Hotel Santo Tomás and depart for the return trip around 2 pm. If you're looking to leave Chichi, you can usually catch a ride out on one of these.

Two companies in Chichi offer shuttle bus services to these same places: Chichi-Tours (☎ 756-1134, 756-1008), at the corner of 5a Calle and 5a Avenida Arco Gucumatz, in the Mini-Hotel Chichicasteca and K'umarcaaj Tours (☎/fax 756-1226), 6a Calle 5-70, Local 1. With a minimum of three passengers (or an equivalent payment), Chichi-Tours will make trips to anyplace else you have in mind, including the ruins at K'umarcaaj (near Santa Cruz del Quiché).

SANTA CRUZ DEL QUICHÉ
• pop 13,000 • elevation 2020m

The capital of the department of Quiché is 19km north of Chichicastenango. As you leave Chichi heading north along 5a Avenida, you'll pass beneath Arco Gucumatz, an arched bridge built in 1932 and named for the founder of K'umarcaaj.

Without the attraction of the big market and the attendant tourism, Santa Cruz – which is usually called 'El Quiché' or simply 'Quiché' – is quieter and more typical of the Guatemalan countryside than is Chichi. The town is small, dusty and abustle with locals going about their business. There are few tourists here (probably because there's not much to see), but those who do come are treated well; the locals are friendly and will direct you anywhere you need to go.

Travelers who come to Quiché usually do so as a side trip from Chichi, or to change buses on their way to or from even more remote places in the Highlands (such as Nebaj or the remote mountain route between

Huehuetenango and Cobán), or to visit the ruins of K'umarcaaj (Utatlán). A visit to the ruins is best done early in the morning, as you may have to walk to the ruins and back (or you can take a taxi from town).

Market day is Saturday, making things only slightly more interesting, but way more crowded.

Information

Everything you need is within a few short blocks of the church, which is on the east side of the central plaza, called Parque Central. The bus station is about five blocks south and two blocks east of the church. The open-air market is one block east of the church.

On the northwest corner of the plaza, Banco Industrial changes US dollars traveler's checks and cash and gives advances on Visa and MasterCard.

K'umarcaaj

The ruins of the ancient Quiché Maya capital are 3km west of El Quiché along an unpaved road. Start out of town along 10a Calle and ask the way frequently. No signs mark the route and there is no regular transport, unless you hire a taxi in town. There's a taxi stand at the bus terminal; round-trip passage plus waiting time while you explore the ruins costs around US$6.50. Consider yourself very lucky if you succeed in hitching a ride with other travelers who have their own vehicle. Admission to the site is a few pennies.

The kingdom of Quiché was established in Late Postclassic times (about the 14th century) and was a mixture of indigenous people and Mexican invaders. Around 1400, King Gucumatz founded his capital at K'umarcaaj and conquered many neighboring cities. During the long reign of his successor Q'uikab (1425-75), the kingdom of Quiché extended its borders to Huehuetenango, Sacapulas, Rabinal and Cobán, even coming to influence the peoples of the Soconusco region in Mexico.

The Cakchiquel, a vassal people who once fought alongside the Quiché, broke away from their former overlords and es-

tablished their capital at Iximché during the 15th century.

Pedro de Alvarado led his Spanish conquistadors into Guatemala in 1524, and it was the Quiché, under their king, Tecún Umán, who organized the defense of the territory. In the decisive battle fought near Quetzaltenango on February 12, 1524, Alvarado and Tecún locked in mortal combat. Alvarado won. The defeated Quiché invited the victorious Alvarado to visit their capital, where they secretly planned to kill him. Smelling a rat, Alvarado enlisted the aid of his Mexican auxiliaries and the anti-Quiché Cakchiquel, and together they captured the Quiché leaders, burnt them alive and destroyed K'umarcaaj (called Utatlán by Alvarado's Mexican allies).

The history is more interesting than the ruined city, of which little remains but a few grass-covered mounds. Of the hundred or so large structures identified by archaeologists, only half a dozen are somewhat recognizable, and these are uninspiring. The site itself is a beautiful place for a picnic, however, shaded by tall trees and surrounded by ravines, which failed as a defense for the city against the conquista-

Don Pedro de Alvarado

dors. Local prayer-men keep the fires of ancient Quiché burning, so to speak, by using ruined K'umarcaaj as a ritual site. A long *cueva* (tunnel) beneath the plaza is a favorite spot for prayers and ritual chicken sacrifices.

Places to Stay & Eat

Hotel San Pascual (☎ 755-1107, 7a Calle 0-43), a block south of the church, is a clean hotel run by a dynamo señora who also administers a typing school for local children in a room off the lobby. It's a friendly place, with guests gathering to watch TV in the evening. Rooms are US$6/7/9 for singles/doubles/triples with private hot bath.

The *Hotel Rey K'iche* (☎ 755-0824, 8a Calle 0-39, Zona 5) is between the bus station and the plaza, about two blocks from each. This is a clean, modern place with singles/doubles with shared bath for US$6/8; rooms with private bath (some with color TV) are US$9/13. There's a decent restaurant here open daily until 9 pm.

The *Hospedaje Tropical*, a block from the bus terminal, is a classic dive, with basic rooms sharing a bath for a mere US$1.95 per person.

Comedor Fliper (1a Avenida 7-31), 1½ blocks south of the church, is inexpensive, small, clean and friendly. Guests from the Hotel San Pascual often walk around the corner to eat here. It's open every day, 7 am to 9 pm.

Restaurante El Torito Steak House, on 4a Calle half a block west of the plaza, serves breakfast for US$2; burgers or sandwiches are the same. The house specialty, filet mignon, is US$4.50 for breakfast, US$6 for a full dinner with soup and more. It's open every day. *La Casona*, on 2a Calle between 4a and 5a Avenidas, a few blocks northwest of the church, is another popular restaurant.

Getting There & Away

There are daily flights from Guatemala City US$55, 25 minutes) at 8:50 am, with an additional 2:25 pm departure on Thursdays and Sundays. The morning flight continues to Huehuetenango. Daily flights return to

Guatemala City at 10:15 am (originating in Huehue), with an additional 3 pm flight on Thursdays and Sundays.

Many buses from Guatemala City to Chichicastenango continue to El Quiché (look for 'El Quiché' or just 'Quiché' on the signboard). The last bus from El Quiché headed south to Chichicastenango and Los Encuentros leaves mid-afternoon, so don't tarry too long here unless you want to spend the night.

El Quiché is the transport point for the sparsely populated and somewhat remote reaches of northern Quiché, which extends all the way to the Mexican border.

The bus station is about five blocks south and two blocks east of the plaza. Buses include:

Chichicastenango – US$0.50, 30 minutes, 19km. Take any bus heading for Guatemala City.

Guatemala City – US$1.65, 3½ hours, 163km. Buses run every 20 minutes, 3 am to 4 pm.

Nebaj – US$1.30, four hours, 84km. There are buses at 8 and 10 am, 12:30, 1 and 3:30 pm. Or take a bus to Sacapulas and change there.

Sacapulas – US$1, 1½ hours, 50km. There are hourly buses, 9 am to 4 pm; or take any bus heading for Nebaj or Uspantán.

Uspantán – US$2, six hours, 90km. Buses depart at 10 and 11 am, noon and 1 pm. Or take a bus to Sacapulas and change there; there's only one proper bus a day leaving Sacapulas for Uspantán at 10 or 11 am (it varies), but you may be able to connect with a pickup.

NEBAJ
• pop 9000

High among the Cuchumatanes is the Ixil Maya village of Nebaj and the neighboring hamlets of Chajul and Cotzal. The scenery is breathtakingly beautiful, and the local people, adequately removed from the cultural influences of TV and modern urbanity, proudly preserve their ancient way of life. Nebaj women wear and weave very beautiful huipiles, and they make excellent handicrafts, especially textiles.

Nebaj's location in this mountain fastness has been both a blessing and a curse. The Spaniards found it difficult to conquer and laid waste to the inhabitants when they did.

HIGHLANDS

In recent years guerrilla forces made the area a base of operations, and the army took merciless measures to dislodge them, particularly during the short, but brutal, reign of Ríos Montt. According to a report compiled by the International Center for Human Rights Research, armed incursions into Nebaj and the Ixil Triangle resulted in the total destruction of more than two dozen villages. For the complete horrifying report and analysis of massacres in and around Nebaj, see the Web site hrdata.aaas.org/ciidh/dts/nebaj.html. The few surviving inhabitants of these villages were either herded into 'strategic hamlets,' as in the Vietnam War, or they fled across the border into Mexico. Refugees are still making their way back to what's left of their Guatemalan homeland here.

Travelers come to Nebaj for the scenery, local culture, excellent handicrafts (especially the detailed crocheted work), market (Thursday and Sunday) and, during the second week in August, the annual festival. There's also decent hiking here through forests, valleys and local villages.

The Nebaj branch of Bancafé is on 2a Avenida No 46; here you can change dollars and traveler's checks. The post office is on 4a Calle and is open weekdays from 8:30 am to 5:50 pm. Not all mail posted from Nebaj arrives at its destination, through no fault of the friendly folks working there, to be sure.

Things to See & Do

There are several beautiful and not too taxing **walks** you can take from Nebaj. After walking 10 or 15 minutes on the road heading toward Chajul, you'll reach a bridge over a small river. Just before the bridge, turn left onto a gravel road and follow the river. Walking downriver for 45 minutes to an hour, you'll pass several small waterfalls before reaching a larger **waterfall** about 25m high.

To reach a **mirador** and ceremonial **altar** overlooking Nebaj, follow 6a Avenida past the Hospedaje La Esperanza for a block, until you see a dirt road bearing left and down a steep hill. Follow this down and then up, bearing left until it turns into a more

proper road. Continue this way for about 10 minutes, when you'll see a well-maintained wooden fence. Go left here and take the stairs leading up to the mirador. At the top there is a *bruja,* or witch, altar where ceremonies are performed.

You can also take **guided hikes** to places farther afield. Gaspar Terraza Ramos is a recommended local guide who knows the area and its history well. He's had a tragic life: He lost his parents in the war and lived many years in a refugee camp in Mexico, where he learned Spanish. He can take you to see towns destroyed by the war, new villages where former refugees struggle to resume normal lives and nooks and crannies of the beautiful countryside around Nebaj. The hikes start at around US$3 an hour and you'll be asked to make a donation to area refugee programs championed by Gaspar, who's very dedicated to that cause. Gaspar is usually at the bus station or the plaza trying to drum up business.

Places to Stay & Eat

Pensión Las Tres Hermanas was once a Nebaj institution run by three little old ladies, but the days when they could maintain a pensión are long gone, so now there's but one pretty shabby room for US$1 There's no sign, but local children will bring you here from the bus. The *Hospedaje de la Esperanza,* on the corner of 6a Avenida and 3a Calle, is a better setup, with basic clean rooms for US$3.25 per person, but they also charge extra for bathroom tissue and hot water. The upper rooms are somewhat more attractive, as they provide more light and air.

The new *Posada de Don Pablo* (6a Avenida 5-15) is the most comfortable place in town; singles/doubles/triples with private hot bath are US$7/9/10. There's parking here, too. The current budget favorite is the friendly *Hotel Ixel,* where simple, clean rooms with shared bath are set around two courtyards. Each single/double/triple is different and costs US$3/4/6. For something a bit more upscale, ask about their nearby *anexo,* where rooms with private warm bath are US$4.80 per person.

Pasabien, at the bus terminal, has garnered rave reviews from inveterate travelers for its great food, ample portions and low prices. It's open for dinner only. Near the plaza, the *Comedor Irene* has filling, nutritious dinners in carnivore and vegetarian versions for just over US$1. *Maya-Inca* is another comedor on the plaza serving reasonably priced Guatemalan and Peruvian dishes.

A burgeoning cottage industry has developed around local women cooking typical Guatemalan meals for tourists. This is a great opportunity to be welcomed into homes and meet families, albeit briefly. One reader had a terrific meal made by Juana 'Big Mama' Marcos; you may try to track her down, or simply ask at your hotel if they know of any good cooks.

Getting There & Away

Buses come to Nebaj from Santa Cruz del Quiché, Huehuetenango, Sacapulas and Cobán. More frequent pickup trucks provide transport at a fare equivalent to that of the bus. Traffic is extremely light by late afternoon, and the earlier you're up and at 'em in this part of Guatemala, the better.

Coming from the Cobán side, you have to change buses several times, and it is nearly impossible to make Nebaj from Cobán in one day (see the Huehuetenango to Cobán section later in this chapter for details). It takes about 4½ hours from Cobán to Uspantán, three hours from Uspantán to Sacapulas, and two hours from Sacapulas to Nebaj. It's easier to reach Nebaj from Huehuetenango or from Santa Cruz del Quiché via Sacapulas, as buses are more frequent.

Leaving Nebaj, there are three daily buses to Quiché via Sacapulas (US$1.35) at 5 and 11:30 am and 2 pm. You must be on that first one to have any chance of making the connection in Sacapulas for Uspantán that same day.

Western Highlands

The departments of Quetzaltenango, Totonicapán and Huehuetenango are more mountainous and less frequented by tourists than regions closer to Guatemala City. The scenery here is incredibly beautiful, and the indigenous culture vibrant, colorful and fascinating. Most travelers going to and from the border post at La Mesilla will find these towns make welcome breaks from long hours of travel, and there are some interesting possibilities for excursions as well.

Highlights of a visit to this area include Quetzaltenango, Guatemala's second-largest city; the pretty nearby town of Zunil, with its Fuentes Georginas hot springs; Totonicapán, a department capital noted for its handicrafts; the Friday market at San Francisco El Alto; the blanket-makers of Momostenango; and the restored Mayan city of Zaculeu near Huehuetenango. Quetzaltenango is achieving a reputation for its Spanish-language schools, which attract students from around the world.

CUATRO CAMINOS

Following the Interamericana westward from Los Encuentros, the road twists and turns ever higher into the mountains, bringing still more dramatic scenery and cooler temperatures. After 59km you come to another important highway junction known as Cuatro Caminos (Four Roads). You'll know the place by the mountains of fruit artfully arranged for peaked travelers. The road east leads to Totonicapán (12km), west to Quetzaltenango (13km) and north (straight on) to Huehuetenango (77km). Buses pass through Cuatro Caminos, shuttling to/from Totonicapán and Quetzaltenango, about every half hour from 6 am to 6 pm.

TOTONICAPÁN

• pop 9000 • elevation 2500m

If you want to visit a laid-back, pretty Guatemalan highland town with few other tourists in sight, San Miguel Totonicapán is the place to go. There are buses between Totonicapán and Quetzaltenango (passing through Cuatro Caminos) frequently throughout the day. Placards in the bus window say 'Toto.'

HIGHLANDS

The ride from Cuatro Caminos is along a beautiful pine-studded valley. As you approach the town you pass a large hospital on the left, turn around the enormous Minerva fountain and enter town along 17a Avenida.

Totonicapán's main plaza has the requisite large colonial church as well as a wonderful municipal theater, built in 1924 in the neoclassical style and recently restored. Buses go directly to the parque (as the plaza is called) and drop you there.

Market days are Tuesday and Saturday; it's a locals' market, not a tourist affair, and it winds down by late morning.

Two kilometers from the park are the Agua Caliente hot springs, a popular bathing place for locals.

Casa de la Cultura Totonicapense

This interesting cultural center (☎/fax 766-1575, contact ✉ kiche78@hotmail.com, http://larutamayaonline.com/aventura.html), 8a Avenida 2-17, to the left of the Hospedaje San Miguel, has displays of indigenous culture and crafts. The museum administers a wonderful 'Meet the Artisans' program to introduce tourists to artisans and local families.

In 1991, artisans of the local Quiché community proposed to Sr Carlos Umberto Molino, director of the Casa de la Cultura Totonicapense, a program to interest tourists in visiting local handicrafts workshops. The program is now the most interesting activity in town. Starting at 10 am and lasting till about 4 pm, you meet local artisans, toy makers, potters, carvers of wooden masks and musical instruments, weavers and musicians. You watch them work, listen to their music, see their dances, experience their living conditions and eat a home-cooked lunch. Cost for the program depends on the number of people in the group, with prices ranging from US$42 per person for four people to US$20 per person for 15 to 20 people. The money goes directly to the artisans and musicians involved. An extended program includes a one-night stay with a local family for an additional US$15 per person including meals.

The Casa de la Cultura also offers other less expensive but equally interesting and worthwhile programs, including a tour of Totonicapán town (US$5 to US$13 per person), which visits workshops, community projects, schools and Mayan ceremonial sites, with permission. Other guided hikes to hot springs and altars (with permission) in the surrounding countryside are offered here as well. Reservations are requested; all tours are conducted in Spanish.

Special Events

Totonicapán celebrates the Fiesta de Esquipulas on January 15 in Cantón Chotacaj 3km from the park.

The festival of the Apparition of the Archangel Michael is on May 8, with fireworks and traditional dances. More dances follow on the last Sunday in June, with the Festival of Traditional Dance held in the Plaza Central from 9 am to 2 pm. There' also the Feria Titular de San Miguel Arcángel (Name-Day Festival of the Archange Saint Michael) from September 24 to 30 The principal celebration is held on the 29th

Places to Stay & Eat

On the way into town, one block before the park, the *Hospedaje San Miguel* (☎ 766 1452) is on the left at 3a Calle 7-49. It's a tidy place – not what you'd call Swiss-clean but good for the price. Singles/doubles are US$4/8 with shared bath, or US$6/10 with private bath. The rooms with private bath tend to be larger, with three beds. Flash heaters provide the hot water, which is thus fairly dependable. Next door, the *Cafe and Comedor Alex* is a clean and friendly place serving a hearty lunch for around US$1.30 Continue on 3a Calle for a block toward the park to the *Restaurante La Hacienda* i steaks are what you crave.

QUETZALTENANGO

• pop 101,000 • elevation 2335m

Quetzaltenango is called Xelajú or simpl Xela (shay-lah) by almost everyone, includ ing its Quiché Maya citizens, who still us this original Quiché name for the site wher the Spanish conquistadors built their town

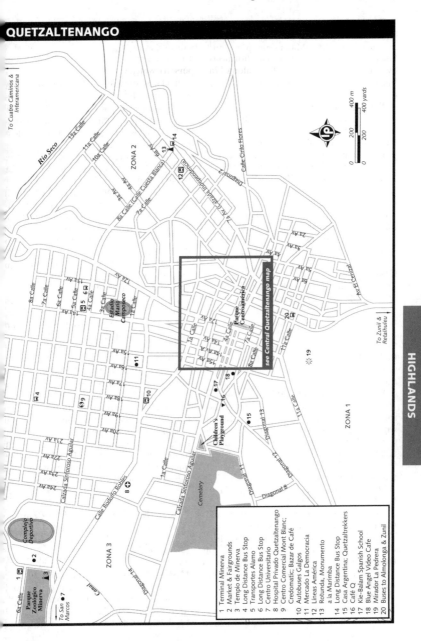

QUETZALTENANGO

To Cuatro Caminos & Interamericana

Río Seco

13a Calle

11a Calle

10a Calle

ZONA 2

Calle Cuesta Blanca

8a Calle

7a Calle

4a Av

5a Av

6a Av

13 ▼

14 📍

12 📍

4a Av (Cuarta Independencia)

Diagonal 2

Calle Cinto Flores

2a Av

3a Av

4a Av

see Central Quetzaltenango map

Parque Centroamérica

To Zunil & Retalhuleu

8a Calle

7a Calle

6a Calle

13a Av

12a Av

11a Av

📍 5   6 📍

4a Av

1a Calle

Estadio Mario Camposeco

📍 11

📍 10

📍 4

🅟 9

8 ➕

Calle Rodolfo Robles

Calzada Sinforoso Aguilar

21a Av

22a Av

23a Av

24a Av

15a Av

16a Av

17a Av

19a Av

20a Av

1a Calle

Children's Playground

📍 17

18 📍

16 ▼

📍 15

19 ☼

Diagonal 13

Diagonal 11

11a Calle

ZONA 1

20

Av El Central

2a Av

3a Av

4a Av

Complejo Deportivo

📍 2

🅟 7

🏨 3

📍 1

6a Calle

Parque Zoológico Minerva

To San Marcos

Cemetery

Calzada Sinforoso Aguilar

Diagonal 8

ZONA 3

Diagonal 4

Canal

0   200   400 m
0   200   400 yards

HIGHLANDS

1   Terminal Minerva
2   Market & Fairgrounds
3   Templo de Minerva
4   Long Distance Bus Stop
5   Transportes Alamo
6   Long Distance Bus Stop
7   Centro Universitario
8   Hospital Privado Quetzaltenango
9   Centro Comercial Mont Blanc;
    Credomatic; Bazar de Café
10 Autobuses Galgos
11 Mercado La Democracia
12 Líneas América
13 Rotunda, Monumento
    a la Marimba
14 Long Distance Bus Stop
15 Casa Argentina; Quetzaltrekkers
16 Café Q
17 Kie-Balam Spanish School
18 Blue Angel Video Cafe
19 Mirador La Pedrera
20 Buses to Almolonga & Zunil

Quetzaltenango is the commercial center of southwestern Guatemala. It is the center of the Quiché Maya people, and Guatemala's second-largest city. Towering over the city to the south is the 3772m Santa María volcano, with the active 2488m Santiaguito volcano on its southwestern flank.

Xela's good selection of hotels in all price ranges makes it an excellent base for several inspiring day trips to hot springs, lakes and traditional villages. In recent years, Xela has built a good, worldwide reputation for its Spanish-language schools. Many students prefer the Spanish schools in Xela over Antigua because the environment here more closely approaches the total immersion ideal of language study. Xela is a big, but surprisingly manageable and tidy city, probably because the bus terminals are removed from the center.

History

Quetzaltenango came under the sway of the Quiché Maya of K'umarcaaj when they began their great expansion in the 14th century. Before that it had been a Mam Maya town. For the story of Tecún Umán, the powerful leader of the Quiché, and Pedro de Alvarado, see the K'umarcaaj section of Santa Cruz del Quiché, earlier in this chapter.

When the Federation of Central America was founded in the mid-19th century, Quetzaltenango initially decided on federation with Chiapas and Mexico instead of with Central America. Later, the city switched alliances and joined the Central American Federation, becoming an integral part of Guatemala in 1840.

With the late 19th-century coffee boom, Quetzaltenango's wealth increased. Finca owners came to the city to buy supplies, and the coffee brokers opened warehouses. Things went along fine, the city getting richer and richer, until a dual calamity – an earthquake and a volcanic eruption – brought mass destruction and the boom went bust.

Still, the city's position at the intersection of the roads to the Pacific Slope, Mexico and Guatemala City guaranteed it some degree of prosperity. Today it's again busy with commerce, of the indigenous, foreign and ladino varieties.

Orientation

The heart of Xela is the Parque Centroamérica, shaded by old trees, graced with neoclassical monuments and surrounded by the town's important buildings. Most of Xela's lodging places are within a couple of blocks of the park.

Quetzaltenango has several bus stations. The largest and busiest is the 2nd-class Terminal Minerva, on the western outskirts near the Parque Minerva on 6a Calle in Zona 3, next to the market. City buses Nos 2, 6 and 10 run between the terminal and Parque Centroamérica – look for 'Terminal' and 'Parque' signs in the front windows of the buses.

First-class bus lines have their own terminals. For locations, see Getting There & Away, later in this section.

INGUAT has free maps of Xela. Alfa Internacional (see Post & Communications) open Monday to Saturday, sells decent maps of the country.

Information

Tourist Offices The INGUAT tourist office (☎/fax 761-4931) is in the right-hand wing of the Casa de la Cultura (also called the Museo de Historia Natural), at the lower (southern) end of the Parque Centroamérica. It's open Monday to Friday from 8 am to 1 pm and 2 to 5 pm, Saturday 8 am to noon (closed Sunday). It offers free maps and sorely limited information about the town and the area, in Spanish and English.

Consulates There's a Mexican Consulate (☎ 763-1312/3/4/5) at 9a Avenida 6-19, Zona 1. It's open Monday to Friday from 8 to 11 am and 2 to 3 pm.

Money Parque Centroamérica is the place to go if you're looking for banks. Banco de Occidente, in the beautiful building on the north side of the plaza, and Construbanco on the east side of the plaza, both change

CENTRAL QUETZALTENANGO

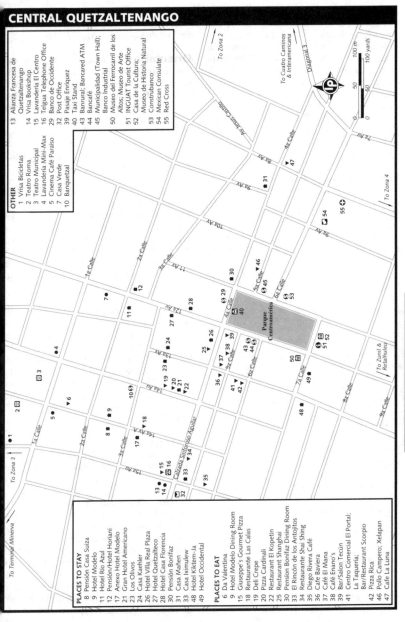

OTHER
1 Vrisa Bicicletas
2 Teatro Roma
3 Teatro Municipal
4 Lavandería Mini-Max
5 Cinema Café Paraíso
7 Casa Verde
10 Banquetzal
13 Alianza Francesa de Quetzaltenango
14 Vrisa Bookshop
15 Lavandería El Centro
16 Telgua Telephone Office
29 Banco de Occidente
32 Post Office
39 Pasaje Enríquez
40 Taxi Stand
43 Banrural; Bancared ATM
44 Bancafé
45 Municipalidad (Town Hall); Banco Industrial
50 Museo del Ferrocarril de los Altos; Museo de Arte
51 INGUAT Tourist Office
52 Casa de la Cultura; Museo de Historia Natural
53 Construbanco
54 Mexican Consulate
55 Red Cross

PLACES TO STAY
8 Pensión Casa Suiza
9 Hotel Modelo
11 Hotel Río Azul
12 Pensión/Hotel Horiani
17 Anexo Hotel Modelo
21 Gran Hotel Americano
23 Los Olivos
24 Casa Kaehler
26 Hotel Villa Real Plaza
27 Hotel Quetzalteco
28 Hotel Casa Florencia
30 Pensión Bonifaz
31 Casa Mañen
33 Casa Ixmulew
48 Hotel Kiktem-Ja
49 Hotel Occidental

PLACES TO EAT
6 Da Valentina
9 Hotel Modelo Dining Room
15 Giuseppe's Gourmet Pizza
18 Restaurante Las Calas
19 Deli Crepe
20 Pizza Cardinali
22 Restaurant El Kopetín
25 Restaurant Shanghai
30 Pensión Bonifaz Dining Room
33 El Rincón de los Antojitos
34 Restaurante Shai Shing
35 Diego Rivera Café
36 Café Baviera
37 Café El Maná
38 Café Enano's
39 Bar/Salon Tecún
41 Centro Comercial El Portal; La Taquería; Bar/Restaurant Scorpio
42 Pizza Rica
46 Pollo Campero; Xelapan
47 Cafe La Luna

US dollars cash and traveler's checks and give cash advances on Visa cards. Banco Industrial, on the east side of the plaza, has a 24-hour ATM machine which accepts Visa cards. There is also a Bancared ATM connected to the Banrural on 12a Avenida facing the park that accepts Visa cards. Banquetzal, on 14a Avenida, usually has the best exchange rate for US dollars.

Credomatic (☎ 763-5722), in the Centro Comercial Mont Blanc, 4a Calle 18-01, Zona 3, gives cash advances on both Visa and MasterCard.

Post & Communications The post office is at 4a Calle 15-07, Zona 1. The Telgua telephone office is nearby, upstairs in the little shopping center at the corner of 15a Avenida and 4a Calle. It's open daily. For shipping packages, there's an outlet of International Bonded Couriers at 8a Avenida 6-23, Zona 1.

Several other places offer international telephone and fax services as well as email and Internet connections. Email access here is some of the cheapest in Guatemala at around US$1.30 an hour. These services are available at:

Alfa Internacional, 15a Avenida 3-51, Zona 1; open Monday to Saturday, from 9 am to 6 pm; scanning, printing and shipping services also available here

Alternativos, 16a Avenida 3-35, Parque Benito Juárez, Zona 3

Arytex, below Casa de la Cultura, Parque Centroamérica, Zona 1

Casa Verde, 12a Avenida 1-40, Zona 1

International Speed Calls, 15a Avenida 5-22, Zona 1

Marketing Communications, on 4a Calle next to the post office; open daily 9 am to 10 pm

Maya Communications, Bar/Salon Tecún, Pasaje Enríquez, just off Parque Centroamérica, Zona 1; open daily 8 am to midnight

Travel Agencies You can make plane reservations, reconfirm flights and attend to other niggling travel details at Viajes SAB (☎ 765-0965, 763-6402), 1a Calle 12-35, Zona 1. There's also an office of Viajes

Tivoli (☎ 763-5792, fax 761-1447, ✉ xela@ tivoli.com.gt) at 4a Calle 18-01, Zona 3, in the Centro Comercial Mont Blanc.

Bookstores & Libraries Check out the Vrisa Bookshop, 15a Avenida 3-64, Zona 1, which has a large selection of quality used books in English. The Blue Angel Video Cafe (see Places to Eat) sells international books, magazines and postcards. Alfa Internacional, 15a Avenida 3-51, Zona 1, also sells magazines in Spanish and English.

The library on 7a Calle next to the Casa de la Cultura is open to the public.

Laundry Lavandería Mini-Max, 14a Avenida C47 at 1a Calle, faces the neoclassical Teatro Municipal. Lavandería El Centro is at 15a Avenida 3-51, Zona 1; it's open Monday to Friday, from 9 am to 6 pm and Saturday from 9 am to 5 pm. Or there's Lavandería Pronto, 7a Calle 13-25A, Zona 1. One load costs US$1 to wash and US$1 to dry at any of these places.

Medical Services Hospital San Rafael (☎ 761-4414, 761-2956, fax 765-1087), 9a Calle 10-41, has 24-hour emergency service; Dr Oscar Rolando de León there speaks English. Hospital Privado Quetzaltenango (☎ 761-4381, fax 763-0135), Calle Rodolfo Robles 23-51, Zona 1, is another option. There's an outpost of the Red Cross, *Cruz Roja* (☎/fax 761-2746) at 8a Avenida 6-62, Zona 1.

Emergency The National Police can be reached at ☎ 761-2569, the Municipal Police at ☎ 761-5805. For the fire department, *bomberos*, dial ☎ 761-2002.

Parque Centroamérica

The park and the buildings surrounding it are pretty much what there is to see in Xela. Start your tour at the southern (lower) end and walk around the square counterclockwise. The Casa de la Cultura holds the **Museo de Historia Natural**, which has exhibits on the Maya, the liberal revolution in Central American politics and the Estado de Los Altos, of which Quetzaltenango was the capital. Marimbas, the weaving industry, stuffed birds and animals and other local artifacts also claim places here. It's fascinating because it's funky. It's open Monday to Friday, from 8 am to noon and 2 to 6 pm, Saturday from 9 am to 1 pm; admission is US$1.

The once-crumbling **cathedral** has been rebuilt in the last few decades and was still being renovated at the time of writing. The facade of the colonial building has been preserved, and a modern sanctuary built behind it.

The city's **Municipalidad** (Town Hall), next to Pensión Bonifaz at the northeastern end of the park, which was rebuilt after a big earthquake in 1902, follows the grandiose neoclassical style so favored as a symbol of culture and refinement in this wild mountain country.

On the west side of the park between 4a and 5a Calles is the palatial **Pasaje Enríquez**, built to be lined with elegant shops – but, as Quetzaltenango has few elegant shoppers, it has suffered a decline.

At the southwest corner of the park, at 12a Avenida and 7a Calle, is the **Museo del Ferrocarril de los Altos**, which focuses on the railroad that once connected Xela and Retalhuleu. Upstairs is the **Museo de Arte**, exhibiting mostly modern art, along with schools of art, dance and marimba. Hours and admission are the same as at the Museo de Historia Natural.

Other Sights

Walk north on 14a Avenida to 1a Calle to see the impressive neoclassical **Teatro Municipal**, which holds regular, recommended performances. Inside are three tiers of seating, the lower two of which have private boxes for prominent families; each is equipped with a vanity.

Mercado La Democracia, in Zona 3, is about 10 blocks northwest of the Parque Centroamérica. To get there, walk along 14a Avenida to the Teatro Municipal, turn left on 1a Calle, turn right onto 16a Avenida, cross the major street called Calle Rodolfo Robles, and the market is on your right. It's an authentic Guatemalan city market with fresh produce and meat, foodstuffs and necessities for city dweller and villager alike.

Less than a kilometer west of the Parque Centroamérica, near the Terminal Minerva, is the **Parque Minerva** which hosts the neoclassical Templo de Minerva, built to honor the Roman goddess of education and to inspire Guatemalan youth to new heights of learning.

Near the Templo de Minerva is the Parque Zoológico Minerva, a zoo with a children's playground and carnival rides; it's open Tuesday to Sunday, 9 am to 5 pm. A large outdoor market is also nearby.

The Mirador La Pedrera, a 15-minute walk southwest from the center, offers a fine view over the city. A round-trip taxi ride should cost around US$4. At the top there's a *tienda* where you can buy snacks and drinks.

Activities

Xela has several social organizations that work with the local Quiché Maya people and need volunteers. The Asociación Hogar Nuevos Horizontes, La Escuela de la Calle and Red International are all based in Quetzaltenango. See the Volunteer Work section in the Facts for the Visitor chapter for contact details and position requirements. The Hogar de Esperanza, Diagonal 11 7-38, Zona 1, works with street children. Many of the Spanish-language schools also work with volunteer programs.

Salsa and merengue lessons are popular in Xela, and there are two recommended places offering one-on-one instruction. Latin Dance Lessons (☎ 763-0271) is at the Casa Verde, 12a Avenida 1-46, Zona 1. Classes are held Mondays, Wednesdays and Fridays and cost US$2 an hour. Latin Rhythm Dance Studio (☎ 761-2707, evenings call ☎ 767-2104, ✉ latinrhythm@latinmail.com) is inside the Diego Rivera Café, 15a Avenida 5-31, Zona 1. Classes are held Monday through Saturday from 9 am to noon and 3 to 7 pm. An hour of instruction is US$4.50; slightly more for couples or groups.

Volcán Tajumulco (4220m) is the highest point in Central America and a challenging

HIGHLANDS

two-day hike from Xela. Volcán Santiaguito (2488m) and Volcán Santa María (3772m) can also be ascended from Xela. Quetzaltrekkers (☎ 761-2470, ✉ quetzaltrekkers@ hotmail.com, http://beef.brownrice.com/ streetschool), Diagonal 12 8-37, Zona 1, is a professional, recommended outfit specializing in these ascents. They also offer a three-day trekking and camping trip to Lago de Atitlán. The Tajumulco trek is US$35 and the Lago de Atitlán trip is US$50. All profits go to the nonprofit Escuela de la Calle, which works with street children in Xela (see Volunteer Work in the Facts for the Visitor chapter).

There are also loads of hikes in and around Xela appropriate for independent day trips. See Around Quetzaltenango later in this chapter for more information.

Cycling is a great, efficient way to explore the surrounding countryside or commute to Spanish class. Fuentes Georginas, San Andrés Xecul and the steam vents at Los Vahos (see Around Quetzaltenango) are all attainable in a day by bike. Vrisa Bicicletas (☎ 761-3862), 15a Avenida 0-67, rents mountain and town bikes for US$2.60 a day, US$9.65 a week. They have free maps for self-guided tours and topographical maps of the area for the more gung ho.

Language Courses

In recent years, Xela has become well known for its Spanish-language schools, which attract students from around the world. Unlike Antigua, which has had a similar reputation for quite a bit longer, Xela is not overrun with foreigners, though there is a small student social scene. The Xela Pages Web site, www.xelapages.com/ schools.htm, has information on many of the schools in town.

Xela seems to attract altruistic types, and most of the Spanish schools here are somehow hooked up with social action programs working with the local Quiché Maya, providing opportunities to get involved. Prices for the schools vary a little but not by much; the standard price is US$110/120/130 per week for four/five/six hours of instruction per day, Monday to Friday, including

room and board with a local family, or around US$85 per week without homestay. Some schools charge up to 20% more tuition during the high season from June through August, and many require nonrefundable registration fees. College students may be able to take classes for academic credit. Reputable schools (there are more!) include:

Academia Latinoamericana Mayanse (ALM, ☎ 761-2877), 15a Avenida 6-75, Zona 1 (Apdo Postal 375)

Casa Xelajú (☎ 761-9954, fax 761-5953, ✉ office@ casaxelaju.com, www.casaxelaju.com), Callejón 15, Diagonal 13-02, Zona 1; in the US, PO Box 3275, Austin, TX 78764-3275 (☎ 512-416-6991); classes in Quiché and literature

Celas-Maya (☎/fax 761-4342, ✉ celasmaya@ yahoo.com), 6a Calle 14-55, Zona 1; also offers classes in Quiché

Centro Bilingüe Amerindia (CBA, ☎ 761-1613, fax 761-8773, ✉ cba@guate.net), 7a Avenida 9-05, Zona 1 (Apdo Postal 381); in the US, c/o Martha Holden, 37 Run Hill Rd, Brewster MA 02631-2331 (☎ 508-896-7589); classes in Mayan languages as well

Centro de Estudios de Español Pop Wuj (☎/fax 761-8286, ✉ popwujxel@pronet.net.gt, http:// members.aol.com/popwuj/main.html), 1a Calle 17-72, Zona 1 (Apdo Postal 68); in the US, PO Box 11127, Santa Rosa, CA 95406 (☎/fax 707-869-1116, ✉ popwuj@juno.com)

Centro Maya de Idiomas (CMI, ☎ 767-0352, ✉ info@centromaya.org, www.centromaya.org), 21 Avenida 5-69, Zona 3; classes in Quiché, Mam, Q'anjob'al, and Tz'utuhil

Desarrollo del Pueblo Spanish Language Institute (Progress of the People, ☎/fax 761-4624, Diagonal 12 6-28, Zona 1

English Club International Language School (☎ 763-2198), Diagonal 4 9-71, Zona 9; classes in Spanish, Quiché and Mam

Escuela de Español Sakribal (☎/fax 761-5211), 10a Calle 7-17, Zona 1 (Apdo Postal 164); in the US, c/o Kimberly Mueller, 360 South Pleasant St, No 2, Amherst, MA 01002 (✉ k_mueller@yahoo .com)

Guatemalensis Spanish School (☎/fax 765-1384, ✉ gssxela@infovia.com.gt, www.infovia.com.gt/ gssxela), 19a Avenida 2-14, Zona 1 (Apdo Postal 53)

Instituto de Estudios de Español y Participación en Ayuda Social (INEPAS, ☎ 765-1308, fax 765-

2584, ✉ iximulew@guate.net), 15a Avenida 4-59 at 5a Calle; in the US, Elliott Brown (☎ 607-273-8471); in Germany, Esther Hahn and Frank Noether (☎ 911- 289 113); English, French and Spanish are spoken

Juan Sisay Spanish School (☎ 765-1318, fax 763-2104, ✉ info-sisay@trafficman.com), 15a Avenida 8-38, Zona 1 (Apdo Postal 392); in the US, Stacey Blankenbaker (☎ 650-312-7777, ext 7763, fax 650-312-7779, ✉ sblankenbaker@sfmc.k12 .ca.us)

Kie-Balam Spanish School (☎ 761-1636, fax 761-0391), Diagonal 12 4-46, Zona 1; in the US, c/o Martha Mora, 894 Patricia Dr, Elgin, IL 60120 (☎ 847-888-2514, ✉ moebius@superhighway.net)

Proyecto Lingüístico Quetzalteco de Español (☎/fax 763-1061, ✉ plq@c.net.gt, www.infoserve.net/hermandad/plqe.html), 5a Calle 2-42, Zona 1; in the US, PO Box 452, Manson, WA 98831 (☎ 800-963-9889, ✉ johnsond@telvar.com). This school also runs the Escuela de la Montaña, on an organic coffee finca in the mountains around Xela, where participation in local culture and volunteering are strongly encouraged. Enrollment is limited to eight students

Spanish School Latin Arts (☎/fax 761-0204, contact ✉ latinartsxela@yahoo.com), 10a Avenida C-09, Zona 1

Ulew Tinimit (☎/fax 761-6242, ✉ utinimit@guate.net, www.unet.univie.ac.at/~a9509611/ut.html), 7a Avenida 3-18, Zona 1; Mayan language classes also offered

Utatlán Spanish School (☎ 763-0446, contact ✉ info-utatlan@trafficman.com), 12a Avenida 4-32, Zona 1, Pasaje Enríquez

Organized Tours

Thierry Roquet and the folks at Casa Iximulew and the INEPAS school (☎ 765-1308, fax 765-2584, contact ✉ iximulew@trafficman.com), 15a Avenida 4-59, run several tours to destinations of local intrigue. Half-day tours include Fuentes Georginas, Los Vahos and San Francisco El Alto (US$32 for two people). Plus, they do camping trips of two days or more that visit Lake Atitlán and the Santa María and Santiaguito volcanoes. They also run trips to Flores, Tikal and El Zotz; these start at US$20 a day per person, with a minimum of three people. They have Spanish, English and French speaking guides available.

Mountain Tours (☎ 761-5993, 761-8650, ✉ mountaintours@hotmail.com), Diagonal 13 15-53, Zona 1, has tours to the regularly visited places such as Fuentes Georginas, Zunil and San Francisco El Alto. However, they also have day trips to other, more obscure sites such as Laguna Chicabal, the hot springs at Aguas Amargas and the Mirador Mahermans.

The Guatemalan Birding Resource Center runs recommended birding trips from Xela; see the Organized Tours section in the Getting Around chapter for details.

Special Events

A weekend program promoting the culture and traditions of the area called 'En Tu Xela' was launched to resounding success in 1999. Each Saturday and Sunday, the Parque Centroamérica is given over to marimba bands, folkloric dancers and stalls selling traditional food and handicrafts. At the same time, cultural events are held throughout the city, including dance and theater performances at the Teatro Municipal, art openings and musical recitals. Look for schedules in hotels, restaurants and other places frequented by tourists.

Places to Stay

Budget Most of the cheap hostelries are concentrated at the northern end of the Parque Centroamérica along 12a Avenida and south of the park more or less behind the Casa de la Cultura.

The hot budget choice at the time of this writing is *Casa Argentina* (☎ 761-2470, ✉ casaargentina@trafficman.com, Diagonal 12 8-37), and with good cause. This unpretentious, mellow place is a few minutes' walk from the park, and has big, clean singles/doubles with shared bath for US$4/6 or US$18 by the week. There's a communal kitchen and drinking water for guests. Quetzaltrekkers (see Activities earlier in this section) is also here.

Pensión/Hotel Horiani (☎ 763-5228), officially at 12a Avenida 2-23, though you enter on 2a Calle, is a simple, but clean, little family-run hospedaje with six rooms. Singles/doubles are US$4/6 with shared hot bath. Not as good at this price, but serviceable, is the **Hotel Quetzalteco** on 12a Avenida a half-block from the park. The basic rooms have shared hot bath; go for one upstairs, as those down are dark.

Pensión Casa Suiza (☎ 763-0242, 14a Avenida A 2-36, Zona 1) has 18 basic rooms grouped around a big courtyard. Singles/doubles/triples are US$4/6/7 with shared bath, US$10/13/15 with private bath, and there's a cheap comedor attached. Some readers have complained of noise and brusque management.

Casa Kaehler (☎ 761-2091, 13a Avenida 3-33, Zona 1) is an old-fashioned European-style family pension with seven rooms of various shapes and sizes. Room 7, with private bath, is the biggest and most expensive; it's US$9/11 for one/two people. Otherwise, clean, old rooms with shared hot bath are US$8/10/12 for a single/double/triple. This is an excellent, safe place for women travelers; ring the bell to gain entry. Ask them about tours in the region. Next door, the **Hotel Radar 99** has had mixed reviews. Well-worn rooms with shared bath are US$3/4/6 for singles/doubles/quads. They have a few rooms with private bath.

Across the street, the new **Los Olivos** (☎ 761-0215, 13a Avenida 3-32) is a good, friendly alternative. Clean singles/doubles/triples/quads with private hot bath, cable TV and nice extras such as towels, soap and drinking water are US$13/20/25/28.

Casa Iximulew (☎ 765-1308, fax 765-2584, @ iximulew@trafficman.com, 15a Avenida 4-59) has one clean, spacious room with two beds and shared warm bath for US$5/7or US$6/9 including breakfast at their adjoining restaurant El Rincón de los Antojitos (see Places to Eat). They also rent apartments about a 10-minute walk from the town center for US$70/235 by the week/month; each has two bedrooms, fully equipped kitchen, living room, courtyard and cable TV; unfurnished apartments are US$150 a month. They also arrange homestays with local families and provide tours and other services for travelers. French, English and Spanish are spoken.

The friendly **Hotel Occidental** (☎ 765-4065, 7a Calle 12-23) has a great location right off Parque Centroamérica and is good value. Very clean and quiet singles/doubles with quality beds and shared hot water bath are US$6/7; with private bath they're US$7/11.

The **Hotel Gran Americano** (☎ 761-8118, fax 761-8219) is on the busy 14a Avenida strip at number 3-47. Singles/doubles/triples with hot bath are US$9/12/15. There's a restaurant and parking.

Southwest of the park is the huge old **Hotel Kiktem-Ja** (☎ 761-4304), in the Edificio Fuentes, a colonial-style building at 13a Avenida 7-18. The 20 rooms, all with private bath and eight with fireplace, are on two levels around the courtyard, which also serves as a car park. Rooms hold one to eight people; singles/doubles/triples are US$15/20/25.

Hotel Río Azul (☎ /fax 763-0654, @ cynthia@emailgua.com, 2a Calle 12-15, Zona 1) offers pseudoluxury and cleanliness compared to its neighbors. All rooms have squishy foam beds and private bath. Prices are high for what you get, though: US$9/11/13/15 for a single/double/triple/quad.

For long-term stays, check out the **Hospedaje Tecún** (☎ 765-1203, 761-2382, 4a Calle 10-55, Zona 3), about a 10-minute stroll from the center. This house has several bedrooms, a kitchen, garden and communal space; rooms rent for US$65 a month. Ask at the Bar/Salon Tecún (see Places to Eat later in this chapter) for information. Another option is renting an apartment. Señora Lidia de Mazariegos (☎ 761-2166, 4a Calle 15-34) rents fully furnished apartments with cable TV and free gas for the first month. Read all the fine print before renting an apartment, and know the terms for deposits, gas and electricity charges before plunking down your cash.

Mid-Range If you want to spend a little more for a lot more comfort, head straight for the family-run **Hotel Modelo** (☎ 761-2529, 763-0216, fax 763-1376, 14a Avenida A

2-31, Zona 1). Nice, small rooms with bath, cable TV and phone are US$25/28/31 in the main hotel (three rooms with fireplace are the same price), US$17/20/24 in the equally comfortable **Anexo** (☎ 765-1271). The hotel's good dining room serves breakfast (7:15 to 9:30 am), lunch (noon to 2 pm) and dinner (6 to 9 pm) daily. There's parking here.

Hotel Casa Florencia (☎ 761-2326, 12a Avenida 3-61, Zona 1), just a few steps from the plaza, is run by a pleasant señora who keeps everything spotless. The nine spacious rooms, all with bath, cable TV and carpet, are US$20/25/30 for a single/double/triple. Overpriced breakfast is served in the dining room, and there's parking.

Hotel Villa Real Plaza (☎ 761-4045, 761-6036, fax 761-6780, 4a Calle 12-22, Zona 1), half a block west of the park, is quite comfortable. The 60 large, airy rooms, all with bath, cable TV and phone, are US$32/37/41 for a single/double/triple. There's a restaurant, bar, sauna and parking.

Most tourist towns in Guatemala have at least one hotel fit for honeymooning couples – a quiet place with romantic atmosphere, beautifully and comfortably outfitted rooms, tranquil gardens and a style that distinguishes it. In Xela, this place is the **Casa Mañen** (☎ 765-0786, fax 765-0678, contact ✆ casamannen@xela.net.gt, http://pages.whowhere.lycos.com/travel/hotelcasamannen/, 9a Avenida 4-11). All nine rooms have traditional appointments, hand-carved furniture, tiled floors, TV and private hot bath. Some rooms have fireplaces, and upstairs units have balconies and views. Singles/doubles are US$35/45, and the two suites go for US$50. Breakfast is available and there's a rooftop terrace.

The four-star **Pensión Bonifaz** (☎ 761-2182, 761-2279, fax 761-2850, 4a Calle 10-50, Zona 1), near the northeast corner of Parque Centroamérica, is Xela's best-known hotel. Though it's a bit on the stuffy side, Guatemalans and foreigners have been coming here for years. Some of the 73 comfortably old-fashioned rooms all have cable TV and phone; all have private bathrooms,

some with tubs. Rooms in the original colonial-style building (the one you enter) are preferable to those in the adjoining, modernized building. The hotel has a good dining room, a cheery bar and a car park. Singles/doubles are US$52/64.

The **Hotel del Campo** (☎ 263-1665, fax 263-0074), Km 224, Camino a Cantel, is Xela's largest and most modern hotel. Its 96 rooms have showers and TV and are decorated in natural wood and red brick, and there's an all-weather swimming pool. Rooms on the lowest floor can be dark, so get a room numbered in the 50s. Prices are reasonable: US$25/31/37 for a single/double/triple. The hotel is 4.5km (a 10-minute drive) east of the town center, a short distance off the main road between Quetzaltenango and Cuatro Caminos; watch for signs for the hotel and for the road to Cantel.

Places to Eat

As with hotels, Quetzaltenango has a good selection of places to eat in all price ranges. Cheapest are the food stalls in and around the small market to the left of the Casa de la Cultura, where snacks and substantial main-course plates are sold for US$1 or less.

An excellent place for Guatemalan home cooking is **Café Sagrado Corazón**, on the corner of 9a Avenida and 9a Calle in Zona 1. The gregarious mother-daughter team of Guadalupe and Miriam serves delicious breakfast, lunch and dinner, and there's always a vegetarian option. Lunch plates are US$1.55 or US$2.45, depending if you want the big lunch or the huge one. It's open daily from 9 am to 9 pm, except Sundays, when they close at 3 pm.

Cafe Baviera, at the corner of 13a Avenida and 5a Calle, is a copacetic European-style café. It has good coffee, roasted on the premises, and is a decent place for breakfast. Other meals, pastries, snacks and alcoholic beverages are also served. They sell international cigarettes and tobacco here as well. It's open every day. Across the street, the friendly **Café El Mana** serves hearty, cheap Guatemalan breakfast, lunch and dinner. In the same

HIGHLANDS

vein is the recommended *Café Enano's*, just down the block toward the park.

A terrific place for coffee is the Bazar de Café (☎ 765-4870), on the third floor of the Centro Comercial Mont Blanc at 4a Calle 18-01, Zona 3. They also roast their beans on the premises and have all kinds of java drinks.

A popular spot with good food is the tiny *El Rincón de los Antojitos (15a Avenida at 5a Calle)*. The menu is mostly Guatemalan, with a few concessions to international tastes and a variety of vegetarian dishes. The specialty of the house is *pepian* (chicken in a special sesame sauce), a typical indigenous Guatemalan dish, for US$5. English, Spanish and French are spoken. Nearby, *Giuseppe's Gourmet Pizza (15a Avenida 3-68)* has yummy, filling pizza and pastas at reasonable prices. Locals flock to this place, and it's usually packed by 7 pm. It's open daily from noon to 10 pm. Another place for pizza is the well-regarded *Pizza Rica (13a Avenida 5-42)*.

Cafe La Luna, at the corner of 8a Avenida and 4a Calle, Zona 1, is a comfortable little place to hang out, drink coffee, write letters and socialize with friends. Similar in feel is the *Diego Rivera Café* (☎ 761-2707, 15a Avenida 5-31), a laid-back spot for coffee or a light meal.

Blue Angel Video Cafe (7a Calle 15-22, Zona 1) is popular with Spanish-language students. Prices are very economical, and there's a good variety of excellent, healthy foods to choose from. All the salads and veggies are sterilized. Alcohol is served and there's an awesome tea selection. It's open every day, 2 to 11:30 pm. Nearby, *Café Q (Diagonal 12 4-46)* has a varied menu featuring international flavors, including several interesting vegetarian options like falafel, soy burgers and lentil soup. It's open Monday to Saturday, from 1 pm to 'late.'

The *Bar/Salon Tecún* in Pasaje Enríquez, on the west side of the park, is another popular spot for foreigners to gather in the evening. Good Italian food is served, and there's plenty of drinking and socializing. It's open every day, noon to 3 pm and 5 pm to 1 am.

Pizza Cardinali (14a Avenida 3-41, Zona 1) serves tasty pizza and pasta dishes. In the same block, *Restaurant El Kopetin*, at No 3-51, has red tablecloths, natural wood, a family atmosphere and a long and varied menu ranging from Cuban-style sandwiches to filet mignon. An average full meal costs around US$5; alcohol is served. Both are open every day. A few doors down is *Deli Crepe*, serving big portions of good food at great prices. Tacos, crepes, burritos and *licuados* come in an infinite variety here. Check out this place if you're traveling with children, as the atmosphere and food are very kid-friendly.

A couple of other pleasant restaurants are in the Centro Comercial El Portal at 13a Avenida 5-38, Zona 1. *La Taquería* is a bright, cheerful Mexican restaurant with excellent prices: Full meals are US$2 to US$4. *Bar/Restaurant Scorpio* has lunch specials or burgers for US$2.65, main dishes for US$4. The big fireplace is toasty in the evening. Both have tables inside and out on the patio.

Restaurant Shanghai (4a Calle 12-22, Zona 1) is convenient to the park. The cuisine is Guatemalan Chinese: *pato* (duck), *camarones* (shrimp) and other Chinese specialties for about US$3.35 to US$5 per plate. Hardly gourmet, but passable and cheap Chinese food is also served at *Restaurante Shai Shing (4a Calle 14-25)*, which has no atmosphere but good service.

Pollo Campero, 5a Calle half a block east of the park, serves inexpensive fried chicken, burgers and breakfast every day. Next door, *Xelapan* is a decent bakery open every day from 5:15 am to 8 pm.

The new *Restaurante Las Calas (14a Avenida A 3-21)* was sent from culinary heaven, serving some of the best budget meals anywhere in Guatemala. Satisfying portions of chicken, fish or beef are creatively prepared and served with a unique *salsa picante*; they cost less than US$3 at the time of this writing. This restaurant also features paella and four different types of flan. The service is top-notch, and there's an art gallery through the courtyard. It's open daily from 8 am to 9:30 pm.

Two blocks farther north on 14a Avenida A at number 1-37 is the recommended *Da Valentina*, an authentic Italian place standing out for its pasta dishes and substantial wine list.

The dining room of the *Hotel Modelo* (14a Avenida A 2-31) serves breakfast and has good set-price lunches and dinners (US$5.50). The folks at *Casa Mañen* serve up a mean breakfast, including Belgian waffles, smoked pork chops, fruit and eggs for around US$4.

The dining room of the *Pensión Bonifaz* (☎ 761-2182, 761-2279, fax 761-2850, 4a Calle 10-50, Zona 1), at the northeast corner of the park, is the best in town. This is where the local social set comes to dine and be seen. Food is good, and prices, though high by Guatemalan standards, are low when compared even to those in Mexico. Soup, main course, dessert and drink can run to US$12, but you can spend about half that much if you order only a sandwich and a beer.

La Rueda is a steak house just outside the Terminal Minerva earning high marks from locals. Head out here if you're in the mood for some flesh and a splurge.

Entertainment

It gets chilly when the sun goes down, so you won't want to sit out in the Parque Centroamérica enjoying the balmy breezes – there aren't any. Nevertheless, it's softly lit and still a pleasant place for an evening stroll.

The *Casa Verde* (☎ /fax 763-0271, 12a Avenida 1-40, Zona 1) is a happening venue for concerts, live theater, poetry readings, films, open-mike nights and other evening activities. Wednesday night features salsa dancing. It also has billiards, chess, backgammon and other games and a restaurant/bar. The Casa Verde is open Tuesday to Saturday, 4 pm until around midnight.

Performances and cultural events are also presented at the beautiful *Teatro Municipal* on 1a Calle, and at the *Casa de la Cultura* (☎ 761-6427) on the south side of the park. The *Teatro Roma* (on 14a Avenida A, facing the Teatro Municipal) sometimes screens interesting movies.

The *Alianza Francesa de Quetzaltenango* (☎/fax 761-4076, 15a Avenida 3-64, Zona 1) offers free French films with Spanish subtitles once a week, along with other activities.

Videos are shown every night at 8 pm at the *Blue Angel Video Cafe* (see Places to Eat); the US$1 admission includes a bowl of popcorn. The video schedule is posted on the door, or you can choose a video from the list on the back of the menu and play it before 6 pm. The café here is popular for socializing in the evening. Also showing nightly videos is the *Cinema Café Paraíso* (14a Avenida A 1-04). Admission is US$1.30. For drinking, carousing or to watch a sports event, head to the ever-popular *Bar/Salon Tecún* in Pasaje Enríquez (see Places to Eat). The healthy mix of foreigners and locals here makes for a lively atmosphere.

The bar at the four-star *Pensión Bonifaz* (see Places to Eat) is the place for more high-brow socializing.

Getting There & Around

Quetzaltenango is served by a system of city buses, including those between Parque Centroamérica and Terminal Minerva mentioned in the Orientation and Bus sections. INGUAT has information on city bus routes. There's a taxi stand on the north end of Parque Centroamérica. A taxi from the Terminal Minerva to the city center costs around US$3.

Air There are two daily flights between Xela and Guatemala City. Inter Group Taca flights leave Xela at 8:50 am and 3:10 pm; returning at 8:10 am and 2:30 pm. The 30-minute flight costs US$50 on weekdays and US$35 on weekends. Passengers are restricted to 20 pounds of luggage apiece; you must pay US$0.50 for each pound over the limit.

Bus For 2nd-class buses, head out to the Terminal Minerva on the western outskirts near the Parque Minerva on 6a Calle in Zona 3, next to the market. City buses Nos 2, 6 and 10 run between the terminal and

Parque Centroamérica (look for 'Terminal' and 'Parque' signs in the front window of the bus). You can catch the city bus (US$0.05) to the terminal from 8a Calle at 12a Avenida or 13a Avenida and 4a Calle in the town center.

The city *urbano* bus leaves you a short walk from where the longer distance *extra-urbano* buses depart. To get there, you must cross through the market. Keeping the park and taxis on your left, head toward the bustle and congestion of the market stalls. There's a passageway leading to the other side of the terminal where there are almost hourly buses to many Highland destinations.

As they leave town, buses that depart from Terminal Minerva and head for the Interamericana pick up passengers at bus stops at the corner of 20a Avenida and 7a Calle, at the corner of 14a Avenida and 4a Calle, at the corner of 7a Avenida (Calzada Independencia) and 8a Calle (Calle Cuesta Blanca) and at the Rotunda near the Monumento a la Marimba. You can board them at any of these stops, though you will have a much better chance of getting a seat if you board at the terminal.

Transportes Alamo, Líneas América and Autobuses Galgos, three 1st-class lines operating between Guatemala City and Quetzaltenango, each have their own terminals. Transportes Alamo (☎ 761-2964) is at 14a Avenida 3-76, Zona 3. Líneas América (☎ 761-2063, 761-4587) is at 7a Avenida 13-33, Zona 2. Autobuses Galgos (☎ 761-2248) is at Calle Rodolfo Robles 17-43, Zona 1.

All of the following buses depart from Terminal Minerva, unless otherwise indicated. (It should be noted that several readers have complained about services provided by Autobuses Galgos.)

Almolonga (for Los Vahos) – US$0.35, 10 minutes, 6km; buses every 15 minutes from 5:30 am to 5 pm, with a possible stop for additional passengers in Zona 4 southeast of the park.

Chichicastenango – US$1.50, three hours, 94km; buses at 6, 8:30, 9:30, 10:15 and 11 am, 12:30,

1:30, 2:30 and 4 pm. If you don't get one of these, take any bus heading to Guatemala City and change at Los Encuentros.

Ciudad Tecún Umán (Mexican border) – US$1.95, 2½ hours, 129km; buses every half hour, 5:30 am to 4:30 pm.

El Carmen/Talismán (Mexican border) – take a bus to Coatepeque, and change there to a direct bus to El Carmen. From Coatepeque it's two hours to El Carmen (US$1.65).

Guatemala City – US$3.60, four hours, 206km; 1st-class buses with Transportes Alamo five times daily, with Líneas América six times daily and with Autobuses Galgos eight times daily, each departing from their own terminals (see above). First-class buses stop at Totonicapán, Los Encuentros (change for Chichicastenango or Panajachel) and Chimaltenango (change for Antigua). Second-class buses (US$1.80) depart from Terminal Minerva every half hour, 3 am to 4:30 pm, but they make many stops and so take longer to get there.

Huehuetenango – US$1, two hours, 90km; buses every half hour, 5:30 am to 5:30 pm.

La Mesilla (Mexican border) – US$1.80, 3½ hours, 170km; buses every half hour, 5:30 am to 5:30 pm. Or bus to Huehuetenango and change there.

Momostenango – US$0.45, 45 minutes, 35km; hourly buses, 6:30 am to 5 pm.

Panajachel – US$1.55, 2½ hours, 99km; buses at 5, 6 and 8 am, noon, 3 and 4 pm. Or take any bus bound for Guatemala City and change at Los Encuentros.

Retalhuleu – US$0.80, 1½ hours; 67km, buses every 20 minutes, 4:30 am to 6 pm. (Look for 'Reu' on the bus; 'Retalhuleu' won't be spelled out.) Take this bus for the Xocomil water park (see Around Retalhuleu, in the Pacific Slope chapter).

San Andrés Xequl – US$0.15, 40 minutes; hourly buses from 6 am to 3 pm; or take any bus to San Francisco El Alto or Totonicapán, get out at the Esso station at the Moreiria junction and flag a pickup.

San Bartolo – US$0.65, 1½ hours, 37km; several direct buses daily or take any Aguas Calientes bus to Pologuá and change there to a pickup or another bus; the last return is at 3 pm.

San Francisco El Alto – US$0.25, one hour, 17km; buses every 15 minutes, 6 am to 6 pm.

San Martín Chile Verde (Sacatepéquez) – US$0.25, 45 minutes, 25km; Xelajú buses every

30 minutes from 6:30 am to 4 pm. Placard in the bus window will say 'Colomba' or 'El Rincón.'

Totonicapán – US$0.25, one hour, 30km; buses every 15 minutes, 6 am to 5 pm, departing from the Parque Central Rotonda

Zunil – US$0.25, 15 minutes, 10km; buses every half hour, 7 am to 7 pm, departing from Terminal Minerva, with a possible additional pickup in Zona 4, southeast of the park.

Shuttle Minibus Pana Tours (☎/fax 763-0606), 12a Avenida 12-07, offers shuttle service to Guatemala City, Antigua, Chichi-castenango, Panajachel and other places around Guatemala, including nearby locales such as Fuentes Georginas and Zunil.

Car Rental car companies in Xela include Geo Rental (☎ 763-0267), 13a Avenida 5-38, in the Comercial El Portal, and Tabarini (☎/fax 763-0418), 9a Calle 9-21, Zona 1.

AROUND QUETZALTENANGO

The beautiful volcanic countryside around Quetzaltenango makes for many exciting day trips. The natural steam baths at Los Vahos are primitive, but an outing into the hills surrounding the city can be fascinating whether or not you indulge in a bath. The steam baths at Almolonga are basic but also cheap and accessible. The hot springs at Fuentes Georginas are idyllic.

Market days are great opportunities to check out locals in action. Sunday in Momostenango, Monday in Zunil, Tuesday and Saturday in Totonicapán and Friday in San Francisco El Alto are the days to visit these surrounding towns.

You can feast your eyes and soul on the wild church at San Andrés Xecul, test the potent potables for which Salcajá is famed or hike to the ceremonial shores of Laguna Chicabal from Xela, as well. Or simply hop on a bus and explore the myriad small traditional villages that pepper this part of the Highlands.

Buses from Quetzaltenango to Almolonga, Los Baños and Zunil depart several times per hour from Terminal Minerva; some buses stop at the corner of 9a Avenida and 10a Calle, Zona 1, to take on even more passengers.

Los Vahos

If you're a hiker and the weather is good, you'll enjoy a trip to the rough-and-ready sauna/steam baths at Los Vahos (The Vapors), 3.5km from Parque Centroamérica. Take a bus headed for Almolonga and ask to get out at the road to Los Vahos, which is marked with a small sign reading 'A Los Vahos.' From here it's a 2.3km uphill walk (around 1½ hours) to Los Vahos. Views of the city on a clear day are remarkable.

If you're driving, follow 12a Avenida south from the park to its end, turn left, go two blocks and turn right up the hill; this turn is 1.2km from the park. The remaining 2.3km of unpaved road is steep and rutted, with a thick carpet of dust in the dry season and mud in the rainy season (when you may want a 4WD vehicle). Take the first turn along the dirt road (it's an unmarked sharp right). At the second bear left (this is badly marked).

The road ends at Los Vahos, where you can have a sauna/steam bath and a picnic if you're so inclined. Occasionally, the vents are carpeted with eucalyptus leaves, giving the steam an herbal quality. Los Vahos is open every day, 8 am to 6 pm; admission is US$1.30.

Salcajá

Six kilometers from Xela is this apparently unremarkable town that you pass through en route to all points north. However, beneath all the bustle and dust lurk some special qualities to which Salcajá alone can lay claim.

First, Salcajá's San Jacinto **church** dates from 1496 (construction was completed in 1502). It was the first Catholic church in Guatemala and, indeed, in all of Central America. The façade still retains some color and character, but the real treat is inside, where you'll find several original paintings and a pretty, ornate altar. Salcajá is also famed for its traditional *ikat* style of **textiles**, which are remarkable for the hand-tied and dyed threads that are laid out in the preferred pattern on a loom. Shops selling bolts of this fabric are ubiquitous in Salcajá, and you can usually visit their workshops before purchasing.

Finally, Salcajá is known for its production of two alcoholic beverages that locals consider akin to magic elixirs. *Caldo de frutas* (literally, fruit soup) is like a high octane sangría that will knock your socks off. Made from combining *nances* (cherry-like fruits), apples, peaches, and pears and fermenting them for years, you can purchase fifths of it for US$2.60 after viewing the production process. *Rompopo* is an entirely different type of potent potable, made from rum, egg yolks, sugar and spices. A sickly yellow, rompopo costs around US$4 a fifth. There are little liquor shops all over Salcajá peddling the stuff, but you may like to try the friendly Penjamo at 2a Avenida 4-03, Zona 1. All buses headed north pass through Salcajá, so it's easy to hop off here en route to other destinations.

San Andrés Xecul

Soon after passing through Salcajá, you come to the Moreiria crossroads, where the road branches off to the west. After about 3km on this uphill spur, you'll start seeing rainbow cascades of hand dyed thread drying on the roofs and you'll know you have arrived in San Andrés Xecul. This small town is boxed in by fertile hills and boasts the most bizarre, stunning **church** imaginable. Technicolored saints, angels, flowers and climbing vines fight for space with whimsical tigers and frolicking monkeys on the shocking yellow façade. The red, blue and yellow cones on the bell tower are straight from the circus big top.

Sitting on the wall overlooking the entire Quetzaltenango valley and contemplating this wild combination of Catholic and Mayan iconography, it's hard to believe hallucinogenic substances didn't somehow figure in. Why and how this church came to resemble the inside of a lunatic's mind has

been lost, though the church doors are inscribed 1917. Inside, a carpet of candles illuminate bleeding effigies of Christ. These are unabashedly raffish, with slabs of thick makeup trying to make him look alive and boyish. In one especially campy display, a supine Jesus is surrounded by gold and satin trimmings that hang thick inside his glass coffin. The pews are generally packed with praying indigenous women. The outside of the church was vibrantly refurbished in late 1999.

Continue walking up the hill and you'll come to a smaller (and decidedly more sedate) yellow church. Mayan ceremonies are still held here, and the panoramic view across the valley is phenomenal. The annual festival is November 29 and 30 – a good time to visit this town. There are no facilities; the easiest way to get here is by taking any northbound bus from Xela and alighting at the Esso station at the Moreiria crossroads and hailing a pickup or walking the 3km uphill. Buses returning to Xela line up at the edge of the plaza and make the trip until about 3 pm.

Zunil

• pop 6000 • elevation 2076m

Zunil is a pretty agricultural and market town in a lush valley framed by steep hills and dominated by a towering volcano. As you speed downhill toward Zunil on the road from Quetzaltenango, you will see it framed as if in a picture, with its white colonial church gleaming above the red-tiled and rusted tin roofs of the low houses.

On the way to Zunil the road passes **Almolonga**, a vegetable-growing town known for its fine weaving, 6km from Quetzaltenango. Just over 1km beyond Almolonga, on the left side of the road, is **Los Baños**, an area with natural hot sulfur springs. Several little places along here have bath installations; most are quite decrepit, but if a hot bath at low cost is your desire, you may want to stop. Tomblike enclosed concrete tubs rent for a few quetzals per hour. (Thierry, the Frenchman at the El Rincón de los Antojitos restaurant, likes El Manantial the best.)

Winding down the hill from Los Baños, the road skirts Zunil and its fertile gardens on the right side before intersecting the Cantel to El Zarco road. A bridge crosses a stream to lead into the town; it's 1km from the bridge to the plaza.

Zunil, founded in 1529 as Santa Catarina Zunil, is a typical Guatemalan highland town. The things that make it so beautiful are its setting in the mountains and the traditional indigenous agriculture practiced here. The cultivated plots, divided by stone fences, are irrigated by canals; you'll see the farmers scooping up water from the canals with a shovel-like instrument and throwing it over their plants. Women wash their clothes near the river bridge in pools of hot water that come out of the rocks. In Zunil, the centuries-old life cycle thrives.

Things to See & Do Another attraction of Zunil is its particularly striking **church**. Its ornate facade, with eight pairs of serpentine columns, is echoed inside by a richly worked altar of silver. On market day (Monday) the plaza in front of the church is bright with the predominantly red traditional garb of the local Quiché Maya people buying and selling.

Half a block downhill from the church plaza, the **Cooperativa Santa Ana** is a handicrafts cooperative in which more than 500 local women participate. Handicrafts are displayed and sold here, and weaving lessons are offered. It's open Monday to Saturday from 8:30 am to 5 pm, Sunday 2 to 5 pm.

While you're in Zunil, visit the image of **San Simón**, an effigy of a local Maya hero venerated as a saint (though not of the church) by the local people. The effigy, propped up in a chair, is moved each year to a different house; ask any local where to find San Simón, everyone will know (local children will take you for a small tip). You'll be charged a few quetzals to visit him and US$0.65 for each photograph taken. For more on San Simón, see the boxed text 'A God is a God is A God' in the Santiago Atitlán section of this chapter.

The festival day of San Simón is held each year on October 28, after which he moves to a new house. The festival of Santa Catarina Alejandrí, official patron saint of Zunil, is celebrated on November 25. Almolonga celebrates its annual fair on June 27.

Getting There & Away From Zunil, which is 10km from Quetzaltenango, you can continue to Fuentes Georginas (8km), return to Quetzaltenango via the Cantel road (16km), or alternatively, take the jungle-bound toll road down the mountainside to El Zarco junction and the Carretera al Pacífico. Buses depart every 10 minutes, 6 am to 6:30 pm, for the return trip to Quetzaltenango (US$0.25, one hour).

Fuentes Georginas

Fuentes Georginas is the prettiest, most popular natural spa in Guatemala. Here, four pools of varying temperatures are fed by hot sulfur springs and framed by a steep, high wall of tropical vines, ferns and flowers. Fans of Fuentes Georginas were dismayed when a massive landslide caused by unusually heavy rains in October 1998 destroyed several structures, filled the primary bathing pool with trees, mud and rubble and crushed the angelic Greek goddess that previously gazed upon the pools. Still, after the site was successfully restored, spa regulars realized that the landslide had opened a new vent which feeds the pools. As a result, the water here is hotter than ever. Though the setting is intensely tropical, the mountain air currents keep it deliciously cool through the day.

Besides the restaurant, there are three sheltered picnic tables with cooking grills (bring your own fuel). Down the valley a few dozen meters are seven rustic but cozy cottages for US$5/6/7 for a single/double/triple, plus US$1.55 for each additional person. Each cottage has a shower, a BBQ area and a fireplace to ward off the mountain chill at night (wood and matches are provided). Big-time soakers will want to spend the night: Included in the price of the cottages is all-day, all-night access to the pools, when rules are relaxed.

Trails here lead to two nearby volcanoes: Volcán Zunil (three hours, one way) and

Volcán Santo Tomás (five hours, one way). Going with a guide is essential so you don't get lost. Guides are available (ask at the restaurant) for US$10 for either trip, whatever the number of people in the group.

Fuentes Georginas is open every day from 8 am to 6 pm; admission is US$1.30. Bring a bathing suit, which is required.

Getting There & Away Take any bus to Zunil, where pickup trucks wait to give rides up the hill 8km to the springs, a half-hour away. Negotiate the price for the ride. It's very likely they'll tell you it's US$4 roundtrip, and when you arrive at the top, tell you it's US$4 *each way* – this is an annoying game the pickup drivers play. If there are many people in the group, they may charge US$1 per person. Unless you want to walk back down the hill, arrange a time for the pickup driver to return to pick you up.

You can walk from Zunil to Fuentes Georginas in about two hours. If you're the mountain goat type, you may enjoy this; it's a strenuous climb.

Hitchhiking is not good on the Fuentes Georginas access road, as there are few cars and they are often filled to capacity with large Guatemalan families. The best days to try for a ride are Saturday and Sunday, when the baths are busiest.

If you're driving, walking or hitching, go uphill from Zunil's plaza to the Cantel road (about 60m), turn right and go downhill 100m to a road on the left marked 'Turicentro Fuentes Georginas, 8 km.' (This road is near the bus stop on the Quetzaltenango-Retalhuleu road – note that there are three different bus stops in Zunil.) This road heads off into the mountains; the baths are 8km from Zunil's plaza.

You'll know you're approaching the baths when you smell the sulfur in the air.

San Francisco El Alto
• pop 3000 • elevation 2610m
High on a hilltop overlooking Quetzaltenango (17km away) stands the town of San Francisco El Alto. This whole town is Guatemala's garment district: Every inch is jammed with vendors selling sweaters, socks, blankets, jeans, scarves and more. Bolts of cloth spill from storefronts packed to the ceiling with miles of material, and this is on the quiet days!

On Friday, San Francisco explodes with activity, and the real market action kicks in. The large plaza, surrounded by the requisite church and Municipalidad and centered on a cupola-like mirador, is covered in goods. Stalls are crowded into neighboring streets, and the press of traffic is so great that a special system of one-way roads is established to avoid colossal traffic jams. Vehicles entering the town on market day must pay a small fee, and any bus ride within town is laborious.

San Francisco's market is regarded as the biggest, most authentic market in the country, and it's not nearly as heavy with handicrafts as those in Chichicastenango and Antigua. As in any crowded market, beware of pickpockets and stay alert.

Around mid-morning, when the clouds roll away, panoramic views can be had from throughout town, but especially from the roof of the church. The caretaker will let you go up.

There is a Banco de Commercio on the corner of 2a Calle and 3a Avenida, which changes US cash dollars and traveler's checks. The annual festival day is October 5.

Most people come to San Francisco as a day trip from Quetzaltenango. This is just as well, since the lodging and eating situation in San Francisco is dire. The big, new *Hospedaje Los Altos* at 1a Avenida and 6a Calle is probably your best bet. They charge US$6.45 per person with private bath and there's parking.

Otherwise, you'll have to suffer the *Hotel y Cafetería Vista Hermosa (3a Avenida 2-22, Zona 1)*. Its 25 rooms are ill-kept (though a few on the front enjoy good views), service is nonexistent and the cafeteria rarely has any food to serve. Doubles cost US$5.15 with shared bath, US$7.75 with private shower.

As for eating, you can try the *Comedor San Cristóbal*, near the Hospedaje San Francisco de Assis.

Laguna Chicabal

This magical, sublime lake is nestled in a crater of the Chicabal Volcano (2712m) on the edge of a cloud forest. Laguna Chicabal, is billed as the 'Center of Maya-Mam Cosmovision' on huge signs, both on the path leading out of town and at the crater itself. As such, it is a very sacred place and a hotbed of Mayan ceremonial activity. There are two active Mayan altars on its sandy shores, and Mayan priests and worshippers come from far and wide to perform ceremonies and make offerings here, especially on and around May 3.

Adding to the atmosphere of mystery, a veil of fog dances over the water, alternately revealing and hiding the lake's placid contours. Amidst the thick, pretty vegetation are picnic tables and one of Guatemala's most inviting campsites, right on the lakeshore. Because the lake and grounds have great ceremonial significance, campers and hikers are asked to treat them with the utmost respect. In addition, Laguna Chicabal is pretty much off-limits to tourists during the entire first week of May, so that ceremonial traditions can be observed without interference.

Laguna Chicabal is a two-hour hike from **San Martín Chile Verde** (also known as San Martín Sacatepéquez), a friendly, interesting village about 25km from Xela. This place is notable for the traditional dress worn by the village men. Their elaborate outfit consists of a white tunic with red pinstripes that hangs to mid-shin and has densely embroidered red, pink and orange sleeves. A thick, red sash serves as a belt. The tunic is worn over pants that nearly reach the ankles and are similarly embroidered.

To get to the lake, head down from the highway toward the purple-and-blue church and look for the Laguna Chicabal sign on your right (you can't miss it). Hike 45 minutes uphill through fields and past houses until you crest the hill. Continue hiking, going downhill for 15 minutes until you reach the ranger's station, where you pay the US$1.30 entrance fee. From here, it's another 30 minutes uphill to a mirador and then a whopping 615 steep steps down to the edge of the lake. Start early for best visibility.

Xelajú buses leave Quetzaltenango for San Martín every 30 minutes until 4 pm, but for the return, hailing a pickup is more efficient. There are a few basic cookshacks on the square in San Martín, though you may prefer to hop off in **San Juan Ostuncalco** for a meal. In this interesting town, half-way between San Martín and Xela, the artisans are renowned for their wicker furniture and fine handcrafted instruments. San Juan's market day is Sunday.

Momostenango
• pop 7500

Beyond San Francisco El Alto, 22km from Cuatro Caminos and 35km from Quetzaltenango, this village set in a pretty mountain valley along a fairly smooth country road is Guatemala's famous center for the making of *chamarras*, or thick, heavy woolen blankets. The villagers also make ponchos and other woolen garments. As you enter Momostenango's square, you will see signs inviting you to watch the blankets being made and to purchase the finished products. The best time to do this is on Sunday, which is market day; haggle like mad. A basic good blanket costs around US$13; it's perhaps twice as much for an extra-heavy 'matrimonial.'

Momostenango is also noted for its adherence to the ancient Maya calendar and for its observance of traditional rites. Hills about 2km west of the plaza are the scene of these ceremonies, coordinated with the important dates of the calendar round (see the Facts about Guatemala chapter for details on the Maya calendar). Unfortunately, it's not easy to witness these rites, though Rigoberto Itzep Chanchavac (see Mayan Cosmology later in this section) hosts ceremonial workshops, which can lift the shroud of mystery somewhat.

Picturesque diablo (devil) dances are held here in the plaza a few times a year, notably on Christmas Eve and New Year's Eve. The homemade devil costumes can get quite campy and elaborate: All have masks and cardboard wings, and some go whole hog with fake fur suits and heavily sequined outfits. Dance groups gather in the plaza and dance to a five- to 13-piece band, drinking alcoholic refreshments during the breaks. For entertainment's sake, they are at their best around 3 pm, but the festivities go on late into the night.

Information The Banrural on the south side of the plaza changes US cash dollars and traveler's checks. It's open Monday to Friday from 8:30 am to 5 pm and Saturday from 9 am to 1 pm. The post office is across the plaza on the eastern corner. Medical services are available 24 hours a day at the hospital on 1a Calle and 3a Avenida, near the bus stop.

Due to Momostenango's importance as a center of Mayan ceremonial life, visits during important celestial days such as the summer solstice or the spring equinox can be particularly powerful and rewarding. However, because few Mayan ceremonies are open to outsiders (especially Wajshakib Batz or Maya New Year), don't assume showing up means you'll be able to participate. For Mayan New Year dates, see the Public Holidays & Special Events section in the Facts for the Visitor chapter. Should you be so fortunate as to observe a ceremony, be sure you treat altars and participants with the utmost respect. The annual fair, Octava de Santiago, is celebrated from July 28 to August 2.

Volunteer opportunities are also available here. See Volunteer Work in the Work section of the Facts for the Visitor chapter for more information.

A well-recommended place to pick up some crafts and Momos lore in one shot is at the workshop of Tono Lopez on 2a Avenida, about 200m north of the Church. Tono is an affable, partly mute craftsman who works in wood and papier mâché, fashioning figures, masks and scenes of local interest, including Los Riscos, the Momos Municipalidad and farmers bringing produce to market.

Los Riscos Momostenango has gained some notoriety for these peculiar geological formations on the edge of town. Technically eroded pumice, the bunches of tawny spires rising into the air look like something from Star Trek. To get there, take the left turn that heads you downhill from the bus stop at the Artesanía Palecom; look for the sign that says 'Entrada.' At the first intersection, you'll see another sign hanging from a corner store reading 'A Los Riscos.' Cross the bridge and head uphill about 50m and take the right onto 2a Calle, continuing about 120m to the formations.

Mayan Cosmology The Takliben May (Misión Maya) Wajshakib Batz (contact ℮ ritzep@hotmail.com, www.geocities.com/RainForest/Jungle/9089/Ceremonies.htm), 3a Avenida A 6-85, Zona 3, at the entrance to town, is dedicated to preserving Mayan traditions. Its director, Rigoberto Itzep Chanchavac, is a Sacerdote Maya (priest) responsible for advising the community on when special days of the Mayan calendar fall. Rigoberto also does Mayan horoscopes (US$3.50 to US$7), private consultations and hosts ceremonial workshops. With his facilitation, participants can gain an understanding of customs that usually remain hidden from outsiders. His *tuj*, or traditional Mayan sauna, is open Tuesdays and Thursdays from 2 to 5 pm; advance notice is needed.

Herbal medicines are also an important aspect of the Mayan life cycle or cosmovision. Crecencia Pu at Waqxaqib' B'atz' (☎ 736-5057), Ramasán 3-55, Zona 3, is chock-full of information on the uses of herbs – and she sells them, too.

Hot Springs Roiling with geothermal activity, Momos means hot springs. A 3km hike north of the plaza (take the right hand fork) is Pala Chiquito. It has a cool-water swimming pool, private hot-bath rooms and a nice waterfall; admission is US$0.15. Barranquito is a half-kilometer walk north of the plaza on the Salitre road (take the left-hand fork) where shallow, tepid pools front a 20m high waterfall; admission is free and worth it for the waterfall alone. These are both local places where modesty prevails;

women may feel more comfortable wearing a T-shirt and shorts while bathing. There are many other secluded natural pools for which a local escort is required – something to keep in mind if you'll be in Momos awhile.

Some argue the springs at San Bartolo are better than Fuentes Georginas. San Bartolo boasts clean, hot pools and private cabañas. You can get there from Xela (see the bus information in the Getting There & Around section of Quetzaltenango) or from Momos by getting a pickup (Sunday is easiest) to Pologuá (12km) on the Interamericana and changing there for the town of San Bartolo. Tell the driver to let you off at the spur for the baths, walk downhill and to the left, past the soccer field and a half kilometer to the bridge and the springs just beyond.

Language Courses Kieb Noj Language School (☎ 736-5196), 4a Avenida 4-49, Barrio Santa Isabel, offers classes in Spanish and Quiché. Five hours of instruction for five days a week is US$100; this price includes a homestay with a local family and three meals a day.

Places to Stay & Eat The *Hotel Estiver (1a Calle 4-15, Zona 1)*, four blocks downhill from the bus stop, has eight rooms sharing two large communal bathrooms for US$2.60 per person, plus two large rooms with private bath (one with a shower, the other a tub) for US$3.25 per person.

Other places to stay in Momostenango are very basic. The serviceable *Comedor y Hospedaje Paclom* on 1a Calle just off the plaza, which claims to have hot water, charges US$5.25 for double rooms facing a courtyard crammed with plants and birds. Next door, the *Comedor Santa Isabel* has been recommended for its good home cooking. *Hospedaje Roxana*, on the plaza, charges US$1.45, which may be too much. On the plus side, guests and nonguests can use the hot shower for US$0.65. There are several basic comedores on the plaza, of which *Comedor Aracely*, below the church, receives high marks.

Getting There & Away Catch an early bus from Quetzaltenango's Terminal Minerva, or at Cuatro Caminos, or at San Francisco El Alto. There are five or six buses daily, the last one returning from Momostenango at about 4 pm.

Another bus departs from the west side of the plaza and goes through Pologuá, which might be an advantage to travelers heading for Huehuetenango or La Mesilla. This is also the way to get to San Bartolo.

HUEHUETENANGO
• pop 20,000 • elevation 1902m
Separated from the capital by mountains and a twisting road, Huehuetenango (way-way-tah-nan-go), has that self-sufficient air exuded by many mountain towns. Coffee growing, mining, sheep raising, light manufacturing and agriculture are the main activities in this region.

The lively market is filled daily with traders who come down from the Sierra de los Cuchumatanes, the mountain range (highest in Central America) that dominates the department of Huehuetenango. Surprisingly, the market area is about the only place you'll see colorful traditional costumes in this town, as most of its citizens are ladinos who wear modern clothes.

For travelers, Huehuetenango, or Huehue as it's often called, is usually a leg on the journey to or from Mexico. After leaving San Cristóbal de las Casas or Comitán in Mexico, and then crossing the border, Huehuetenango is the logical place to spend your first night in Guatemala. What with its dusty, crowded streets, Huehue is far from attractive, but it does serve as a perfect staging area for forays deeper into the Cuchumatanes or for backroad travel through the Highlands.

History
Huehuetenango was a Mam Maya region until the 15th century, when the Quiché, expanding from their capital at K'umarcaaj near present-day Santa Cruz del Quiché, pushed them out. Many Mam fled into neighboring Chiapas, which still has a large Mam-speaking population near its border

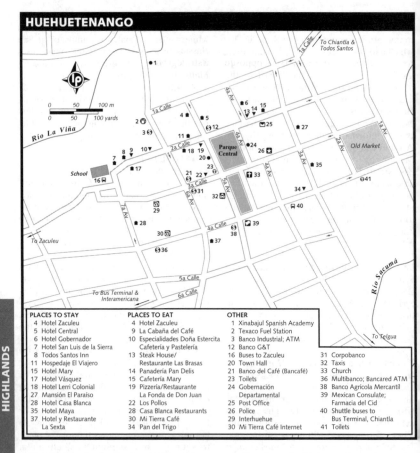

HUEHUETENANGO

To Chiantla &
Todos Santos

Río La Viña

0   50   100 m
0   50   100 yards

Parque
Central

Old Market

School

To Zaculeu

To Bus Terminal &
Interamericana

Río Sacumá

To Telgua

PLACES TO STAY	PLACES TO EAT	OTHER	
4 Hotel Zaculeu	4 Hotel Zaculeu	1 Xinabajul Spanish Academy	31 Corpobanco
5 Hotel Central	9 La Cabaña del Café	2 Texaco Fuel Station	32 Taxis
6 Hotel Gobernador	10 Especialidades Doña Estercita	3 Banco Industrial; ATM	33 Church
7 Hotel San Luis de la Sierra	Cafetería y Pastelería	12 Banco G&T	36 Multibanco; Bancared ATM
8 Todos Santos Inn	13 Steak House/	16 Buses to Zaculeu	38 Banco Agrícola Mercantil
11 Hospedaje El Viajero	Restaurante Las Brasas	20 Town Hall	39 Mexican Consulate;
15 Hotel Mary	14 Panadería Pan Delis	21 Banco del Café (Bancafé)	Farmacia del Cid
17 Hotel Vásquez	15 Cafetería Mary	23 Toilets	40 Shuttle buses to
18 Hotel Lerri Colonial	19 Pizzería/Restaurante	24 Gobernación	Bus Terminal, Chiantla
27 Mansión El Paraíso	La Fonda de Don Juan	Departamental	41 Toilets
28 Hotel Casa Blanca	22 Los Pollos	25 Post Office	
35 Hotel Maya	28 Casa Blanca Restaurants	26 Police	
37 Hotel y Restaurante	30 Mi Tierra Café	29 Interhuehue	
La Sexta	34 Pan del Trigo	30 Mi Tierra Café Internet	

with Guatemala. In the late 15th century, the weakness of Quiché rule brought about civil war, which engulfed the Highlands and provided a chance for Mam independence. The turmoil lasted for decades, coming to an end in the summer of 1525 after the arrival of Gonzalo de Alvarado, brother of Pedro, who conquered the Mam capital of Zaculeu for the king of Spain.

Orientation

The town center is 5km north of the Interamericana. The bus station and new market are 3km from the highway along the road to the town center (6a Calle), on the east side.

Almost every service of interest to tourists is in Zona 1 within a few blocks of the plaza. The old market, bordered by 1a and 2a Avenidas and 3a and 4a Calles in Zona 1, is still the busy one, especially on Wednesday, which is market day. Four blocks west of the market on 5a Avenida between 2a and 3a Calles is the main plaza, called the Parque Central, which is the very center of town and the reference point for finding any other address. Most hotels, restaurants and services are near the park, except for the Telgua telephone office.

Information

The post office is at 2a Calle 3-54, opposite the Hotel Mary, half a block east of the park. The Telgua office is at the Paíz Centro Comercial (known as the Edificio Trián-gulo), at 4a Avenida 6-54, four blocks south of the Parque Central; this is its temporary address while the regular office is being re-modeled (at the time of writing, a four-year project!). More convenient is the Hotel y Restaurante La Sexta (see Places to Stay), where you can make international and long-distance calls.

It is possible to send email from Huehue. There's a small business just inside Mi Tierra Café (see Places to Eat) at 4a Calle 6-46 that has Internet access for US$1.70 for 15 minutes or US$6.45 an hour. It's open Monday to Friday, from 9 am to 12:30 pm and 2:30 to 7 pm and Saturday from 8 am to noon and 3 to 7 pm. Interhuehue, 3a Calle 6-65B, has Internet access for the same price. It's open daily from 8 am to 12:30 pm and 2 to 6 pm.

There is a Bancared ATM accepting Visa cards at the Multibanco branch at 4a Calle 6-81. There are several other banks in Huehue; most are also Western Union agents.

There is a Mexican consulate on 5a Avenida 4-11, near the corner of 4a Calle, in the same building as the Farmacia del Cid; it's open Monday to Friday, 9 am to noon and 3 to 5 pm.

Town-operated *servicios sanitarios* (toilets) are on 3a Calle between 5a and 6a Avenida, only a few steps west of the plaza.

Parque Central

Huehuetenango's main plaza is shaded by big, old trees and surrounded by the town's imposing buildings: on the west side, the Municipalidad (with its band shell on the upper floor) and, on the southeast corner of the main square, the huge colonial church. The plaza has its own little relief map of the department of Huehuetenango.

Zaculeu

Surrounded by natural barriers – ravines and a river – on three sides, the late Post-classic religious center of Zaculeu occupies a strategic defensive location that served its Mam Maya inhabitants well. It finally failed, however, in 1525 when Gonzalo de Al-varado and his conquistadors laid siege to the site. Good natural defenses are no pro-tection against starvation, and it was this that ultimately defeated the Mam. Its name means 'tierra blanca' ('white earth') in the Mam language.

The park-like archaeological zone of Zaculeu is 4km north of Huehuetenango's main plaza. It's open daily from 8 am to 5 pm; admission is free. Cold soft drinks and snacks are available. You're allowed to climb on the restored structures, but it's for-bidden to climb the grassy mounds that await excavation.

From the Parque Central, you can reach Zaculeu by several routes. Jitney trucks and vans depart from in front of the school, on 2a Calle near the corner of 7a Avenida; they depart every 30 minutes (or possibly hourly), 7:30 am to 7:30 pm, and cost US$0.13 for the 20-minute ride to the ruins. Or you can take a taxi from the central plaza for US$5 roundtrip, with a half hour to spend at the ruins. To walk all the way from the main plaza takes about 45 minutes.

Visitors accustomed to seeing ruddy bare stones and grass-covered mounds rather than the tidiness of Zaculeu may find this place unsettling. Restoration has left its pyr-amids, ball courts and ceremonial platforms covered by a thick coat of graying plaster. It's rather stark and clean. Some of the con-struction methods used in the restoration were not authentic to the buildings, but the work goes farther than others in making the site look like it might have to the eyes of Mam priests and worshipers when it was still an active religious center.

When Zaculeu flourished, its buildings were coated with plaster, as they are now. What is missing is the painted decoration, which must have been applied to the wet plaster as in frescoes. The buildings show a

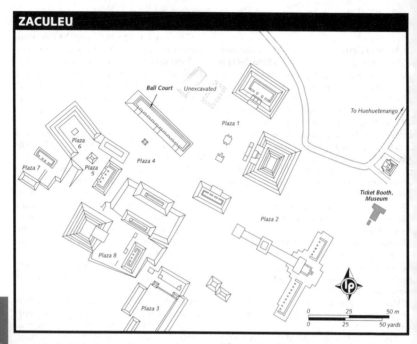

ZACULEU

Ball Court
Unexcavated
Plaza 1
To Huehuetenango
Plaza 6
Plaza 4
Plaza 7
Plaza 5
Ticket Booth, Museum
Plaza 2
Plaza 8
Plaza 3

0   25   50 m
0   25   50 yards

great deal of Mexican influence and were probably designed and built originally with little innovation.

Special Events
Special events include the Fiestas Julias (July 13 to 20), held in honor of La Virgen del Carmen, Huehue's patron saint, and the Fiestas de Concepción (December 5 and 6), honoring the Virgen de Concepción. The Carrera Maratón Ascenso Los Cuchumatanes, a 12km road race that is run from Huehue's central plaza up into the mountains to El Mirador, overlooking the town, is held around October or November each year. The event always attracts hundreds of runners.

Language Courses
The Xinabajul Spanish Academy (☎/fax 964-1518), 6a Avenida 0-69, offers one-on-one Spanish courses and room and board with local families.

Places to Stay
Huehuetenango has a useful selection of places to stay. Your first explorations should be along 2a Calle between 3a and 7a Avenida, just off the plaza; there are several little hotels and eateries in this three-block stretch, and two more hotels half a block off 2a Calle.

Hotel Central (☎ 764-1202, 5a Avenida 1-33), facing the Hotel Zaculeu half a block northwest of the plaza, has 11 largish, simple and well-used rooms with shared bath. Rates are US$3/4/6/7 for a single/double/triple/quad. The hotel's comedor has cheap, hearty meals (US$1.55) daily except Sunday. It opens for breakfast at 7 am.

Hotel Lerri Colonial (☎ 764-1526, 2a Calle 5-49), half a block west of the plaza, has 21 super basic rooms in a convenient location. Rooms are US$3/4 per person with shared/private bath. In the courtyard is a comedor and parking.

HIGHLANDS

Across the street, ***Hospedaje El Viajero*** *(2a Calle 5-30)* is not as good, but it's cheap, with rooms for US$1.95 per person sharing bathrooms with cold showers. The ***Mansión El Paraíso*** (☎ *764-1827, 3a Avenida 2-41)* is a similar place with the same prices.

Hotel y Restaurante La Sexta, on 6a Avenida near 4a Calle, has decent rooms arranged around a courtyard for US$3.90 per person with shared bath and singles/doubles/triples which have hot baths for US$8/10/20. There's a restaurant and parking here, and guests and nonguests can make international phone calls.

Hotel Mary (☎ *764-1618, 2a Calle 3-52)* is a block east of the plaza. It's a cut above the other places: The 25 small rooms have bedspreads and other nice touches. The ground-floor Cafetería Mary is handy, as is the Panadería Pan Delis bakery/café next door. Rooms for one or two people are US$7 with shared bath, or US$7/10/12 for a single/double/triple with private bath and cable TV. Hot water is only available for three hours a day.

Nearby, the friendly ***Hotel Gobernador*** (☎ */fax 769-0765, 4a Avenida 1-45)* is a solid budget choice, with singles/doubles/triples with shared bath featuring an extra-hot and powerful shower for US$4/6/8; rooms with private bath are US$6/9/13. Some rooms are airier and less damp than others. There's also a decent cafeteria here serving breakfast, lunch and dinner.

Hotel Vásquez (☎ *764-1338, 2a Calle 6-67)* has a car park in the front and 20 small, fairly cheerless but very clean rooms at the back. Rates for one or two people are US$4/7 for rooms with shared/private bath.

The ***Hotel Maya*** (☎ *764-1622, fax 764-9246, 3a Avenida 3-55)* is a fairly new place, with clean and comfortable (but generic) singles/doubles/triples, all with private hot bath, for US$12/17/21. Located near the market, this place suffers some from the hustle and bustle of the local scene, which can be at times loud, crowded and trash-strewn.

For a few extra dollars, you'd be better off in the new ***Hotel San Luis de la Sierra*** (☎ *764-9216/7/8, fax 764-9219, 2a Calle 7-00)*. Spotless rooms with private hot bath and cable TV are US$17/24/30. There's a restaurant here (see Places to Eat) and views from the rooftop terrace.

Next door, the ***Todos Santos Inn*** (☎ *764-1241, 2a Calle 7-64)* is among Huehue's best budget hotels. Simple rooms with nice touches such as towels, bedside tables and reading lamps are US$3.25 per person with shared bath or US$5.15 with private bath. There's hot water sometimes, and a few rooms have partial views.

Hotel Zaculeu (☎ *764-1086, fax 764-1575, 5a Avenida 1-14)*, half a block northwest of the plaza, is a colonial-style place with a lovely garden courtyard, a good dining room, laundry service and 37 rooms, all with private bath and cable TV. In the older downstairs section, rooms near the hotel entrance open onto the courtyard and are preferable to those at the back of the hotel; these are US$15/22/30/37 for singles/doubles/triples/quads. Rooms in the newer upstairs section are US$28/37/47 for singles/doubles/triples and may be overpriced at that.

Hotel Casa Blanca (☎ */fax 769-0775 through 0781, 7a Avenida 3-41)* is such a bright, pleasant hotel that it's tempting to say it's the best place in town. The 15 rooms, all with private bath and cable TV, are US$23/30/35 for singles/doubles/triples. There's private parking, and two lovely restaurants are open daily from 6 am to 10 pm.

On the Interamericana, 2km northwest of the turnoff to Huehuetenango and about 8km from the center of town, are several hotels.

Places to Eat

Especialidades Doña Estercita Cafetería y Pastelería, on 2a Calle a block west of the plaza, is a tidy, cheerful place serving pastries as well as more standard dishes. Down the block, ***La Cabaña del Café*** serves Huehue's best fresh roasted coffee and is a popular dinner spot for pasta and other Italian fare. It's open daily from 7 am to 9 pm, though they may be tardy getting open in the morning.

If La Cabaña del Café isn't happening, head straight to the **Hotel San Luis de la Sierra** for an excellent breakfast. Though not the cheapest (around US$2.50), their satisfying breakfasts come with a full pot of coffee and a terrific view of the countryside.

The **Cafetería Mary** and **Panadería Pan Delis** are next to the Hotel Mary, at 2a Calle 3-52. Another good bakery is the **Pan del Trigo** (4a Calle 3-24), which usually has whole-grain breads; the cafeteria here, open every day, offers economical breakfasts and dinners for US$2.

Mi Tierra Café (4a Calle 6-46) is a casual, upbeat place serving tasty food in the Western vein. Breakfast features croissants, omelets, pancakes, juices and good coffee. Dinner borrows heavily from the Tex-Mex realm, with fajitas and tacos sharing the menu with chicken and seafood dishes.

The **Pizzería/Restaurante La Fonda de Don Juan** (2a Calle 5-35), a few steps from the Parque Central, is a clean, reliable place serving pizza and a variety of other dishes. It's open every day.

Los Pollos, 3a Calle between 5a and 6a Avenida, half a block west of the plaza, is open 24 hours a day. Two pieces of chicken with salad, chips and a soft drink cost US$2.85. Burgers and smaller chicken meals are even cheaper.

One of Huehue's best restaurants is the **Steak House/Restaurante Las Brasas**, on 4a Avenida just off 2a Calle, half a block from the Parque Central, where a full meal of Chinese food or steak (the specialties here) should cost no more than US$7 or so. Alcohol is served, and it's open every day.

For lovely surroundings, you can't beat the two restaurants at the **Hotel Casa Blanca** (see Places to Stay), one inside and another outdoors in the garden. Breakfasts are around US$3.35, burgers or sandwiches no more than US$1.65, and steaks (try filet mignon or cordon bleu) are under US$6. Both restaurants are open every day from 6 am to 10 pm.

Getting There & Around

There is one daily flight between Guatemala City and Huehue, via Quiché (US$55, 50 minutes), leaving at 8:50 am and returning to Guatemala City, again via Quiché, at 9:50 am.

The bus terminal is in Zona 4, 2km southeast of the plaza along 6a Calle. To reach Antigua, take any bus going to Guatemala City and change in Chimaltenango; take the same bus and change at Los Encuentros for Lago de Atitlán. Buses serving this terminal include:

Aguacatán – US$0.65, 1½ hours, 22km; a dozen daily departures, starting at 6 am. Take one of these and transfer to a pickup in Aguacatán if you're heading to Cobán but don't want to wait for the 11 am bus to Sacapulas.

Barrillas – US$2.35, seven hours, 139km; daily at 9 am and noon.

Cuatro Caminos – US$1, 1½ hours, 77km. Take any bus heading for Guatemala City or Quetzaltenango.

Guatemala City – US$3.75, five hours, 266km; buses at 2, 3, 8:30, 9:30 and 10 am.

La Mesilla (Mexican border) – US$1.15, two hours, 79km; buses every half hour, 3:30 am to 5 pm.

Nebaj – US$1.70, six hours, 77km; one daily departure at 11:30 am via Aguacatán and Sacapulas.

Nentón – US$1.40, three to four hours, 102km; 5:30 and 9:30 am.

Quetzaltenango – US$1, two hours, 90km; hourly buses, 4 am to 6 pm.

Sacapulas – US$1.05, four hours, 50km; buses at 11 am and 12:30 pm. Sometimes there's a 9:30 am departure, which is convenient if you're going to Cobán via Uspantán.

San Mateo Ixtatán – US$1.95, six hours, 111km; one daily departure.

Soloma – US$1.55, four hours, 69km; Transportes Alicia has departures at 10:15 and 11 am.

Todos Santos Cuchumatán – US$0.90, 2½ hours, 40km; 11:30 am, 12:30, 1 and 4 pm. Sit on the left for views.

Shuttle buses between the terminal and the center of town depart from 4a Calle at the corner of 4a Avenida from 2 am to 11 pm, running every five minutes in the daytime, every half hour at night and before sunrise; cost is US$0.06. Inner-city buses leave you across two covered markets from where the long-distance buses depart; walk through these to get to the other side of the terminal.

A taxi between the bus terminal and the center of town costs US$2.

Tabarini Rent A Car (☎ 764-1951, fax 764-2816) has an office here. Amigos Rent-A-Car (☎ 769-0775, 7a Avenida 3-41) is in the Hotel Casa Blanca. Cars here start at US$52 a day, including unlimited mileage, taxes and insurance.

AROUND HUEHUETENANGO

El Mirador is a lookout point up in the Cuchumatanes, overlooking Huehuetenango, 12km from town. On a sunny day it offers a great view of the entire region and its many volcanoes. A beautiful poem, *A Los Cuchumatanes*, is mounted on plaques here. This is the destination for annual footraces (see Special Events in the Huehuetenango section). Getting to El Mirador is easiest with a private vehicle; a taxi from town costs around US$30 roundtrip.

Fanning out from Huehue are some adventurous and remote routes, where you'll probably be a novelty to the local Mayan folks you meet. Spanish skills and a whole lot of patience will pave the way in these parts. Up toward the northwestern corner of the country, **Nentón** is an area where murder and disappearances were not uncommon during the civil war. Its people have suffered mightily – the war and its aftermath are the primary reasons few tourists have come up this way. At the risk of sounding redundant, visitors should be careful not to take photos without permission.

The road to Nentón wends its way through dense, limestone countryside and is way off the beaten track. There are direct buses from Huehue (see Getting There & Away), or you can take any bus to La Mesilla and get off at the Camojá Grande crossroads and hitch a pickup. Traffic can be extremely light in this area, so you may need to spend the night here. The *Hotel Los Reyes*, on the road to Nentón, is a good choice, or try the *Hotel Solis*, on the road to La Mesilla. There are several serviceable hotels in Nentón as well: The *Hotel y Restaurante las Peñas* has 16 rooms with hot water bath and parking for US$4/7/9 for singles/doubles/triples.

From Nentón you can continue on a very bumpy, unpaved road to **Gracias a Díos**, right on the Mexican border. There are two direct buses a day from Huehuetenango making the 10 hour (or more!) trip. Though there isn't much to do in Gracias a Díos proper, from here you can make the only-for-the-stalwart crossing into Mexico's Lagunas de Montebello region and continue to Comitán. Be forewarned, however, that this isn't an official border post and you must remember to get your entry and exit stamps and pay the US$15 border fee once you get into Mexico. There are many hotels in Gracias a Díos if you get stuck.

Alternatively, the really brazen can head south from Gracias a Díos through Bulej to **San Mateo Ixtatán**, where there a couple of simple hospedajes and the minor archaeological site of Xolcol. From San Mateo you can head east to Barrillas, west to Jacaltenango (an easy hop, skip from Todos Santos) or south to Soloma.

HUEHUETENANGO TO COBÁN

The road from Huehuetenango to Cobán is rarely traveled, often rugged and always inspiring. Starting from high in the Cuchumatanes mountain range, you climb out of Huehuetenango en route to **Aguacatán**, from where you're treated to panoramic views of pine-studded slopes and the fertile valleys below. This leg is best done in the back of a pickup, to afford unimpeded 360° views. There is a Banrural, gas station and other services in Aguacatán. If you get stranded, try the *Hospedaje Nuevo Amanecer*. The last bus to Huehue leaves at 4 pm (US$0.50, 1½ hours).

From Aguacatán, the road snakes down to lower altitudes, through the Río Blanco river valley to Sacapulas along the Río Negro. The road starts climbing again from Sacapulas, wending its way up precipitous (and sadly deforested) slopes until Uspantán. From there, it's a direct shot down through beautifully forested countryside to Cobán. Going in this direction, sit on the

HIGHLANDS

right for views. It takes nearly three days of challenging travel and several bus or pickup transfers to traverse the 150km between Huehue and Cobán, but it's well worth it for the scenery and tableaus of true Highlands life. Adventure types aching for more can continue the odyssey via the off-the-beaten-track Cobán to Poptún route.

Sacapulas

This small, friendly town 50km from Huehue straddles the Río Negro and is a convenient stopover on the Cobán-Huehuetenango route, or if you get stuck coming out of the Cuchumatanes mountain range from Nebaj. There's a Banrural on the plaza (up the hill from the bridge) that changes US dollars but not traveler's checks; it's open weekdays, from 8:30 am to 5 pm and Saturdays from 9 am to 1 pm. There's a Red Cross *Cruz Roja* outpost on the southern bank of the river. Next door is the friendly and clean ***Hotel & Restaurante Río Negro***. The rooms here are basic but comfortable and secure, and cost US$2.60 per person with shared, cold bath. Meals in the restaurant are typical Guatemalan: tasty, filling and cheap (around US$1.50).

Getting There & Away Buses are few and far between in this neck of the woods. There are three daily departures to Quiché (US$1.30, four hours), leaving from the Red Cross side of the river. The first is at 10 am. There is one bus a day to Huehuetenango at 5:30 am (US$1.05, four hours) and two a day to Nebaj (US$0.65, two hours). These last leave from the northern bank of the river; look for the small sign with arrows pointing the way to Huehue and Cobán.

To continue to Cobán via Uspantán, catch the one daily departure at 10 am (US$1, three hours) from the northern bank of the Río Negro.

If you miss your bus, you may be able to catch a pickup, especially in the morning, by waiting at the specified junction. It is nearly unheard of to catch a lift from Sacapulas all the way to Cobán; kudos to your ride karma if you successfully pull this off.

Uspantán

• pop 3413

Uspantán is a small village on the road between Sacapulas and Cobán. Rigoberta Menchú (see the boxed text on Menchú in the Facts for the Visitor chapter) grew up a five-hour walk through the mountains from Uspantán. Travelers who have read her works might be interested to spend some time here. However, Menchú is not universally loved by all her former neighbors, so don't be shocked if you get a chilly reaction on this front.

Uspantán is a benevolent but eerie sort of town, with wide paved avenues and a hush about it that the fog intensifies. It can get very cold here, and you'll be loving that sleeping bag if you brought it and cursing yourself if you didn't. If you're on the Huehuetenango to Cobán route, you'll likely be spending the night here, as the bus leaves before daybreak. There's a Banrural on the plaza that will change US dollars.

Pensión Galindo *(5a Calle 2-09),* about three blocks from the church and the plaza, charges US$2 per person and is a fine place to stay. The new ***Hotel La Uspanteka*** *(4a Calle 5-18),* just off the plaza, has 17 cleanish rooms for US$1.55 per person, and is another good option. It's popular with Guatemalan students and professors. The ***Hotel Casa Blanca***, on the road to Sacapulas, is a bit removed, but is the most modern game in town.

Comedor Central, on 6a Calle one block from the park, is basic but good. ***Comedor Kevin*** *(6a Calle 5-28),* near 6a Avenida two blocks from the plaza, has tasty set lunches for US$1.30.

Getting There & Away Half a dozen buses a day leave Uspantán for Quiché via Sacapulas, at 2, 3, 4, and 5 am and 6 and 9 pm. It's a bad road, and it takes about seven hours to get all the way to Quiché or Huehuetenango (change at Sacapulas) from here.

To continue to Cobán, you need to get the single daily departure at 3 am (US$1.30, 4½ hours). Get there by 2:30 am, as this bus fills up fast with sleepy indigenous men aiming to better their prospects in Cobán.

Along with the Huehue to Sacapulas leg, this is one of the most gorgeous rides in Guatemala. Try to be awake when the sun pushes over the tops of the Cuchumatanes mountains, burning off the fog clinging to the valley below. Sit on the right for views. This epitomizes the Guatemalan chicken bus experience, as it's a difficult ride in an overcrowded, ramshackle bus on terrible roads. You may find yourself praying to higher powers as the bus hydroplanes into space, losing its grip on the muddy mountain passes in the pitch black of night.

LA MESILLA

There is a distance of 4km between the Mexican and Guatemalan immigration posts at La Mesilla/Ciudad Cuauhtémoc, and you must take a collective taxi (US$1). The strip in La Mesilla leading to the border post has a variety of services, including a police station, post office and a Banrural; the bank is also a Western Union agent. There are also moneychangers who will do the deal – at a good rate if you're changing dollars, a terrible one for pesos or quetzales.

If you get marooned in La Mesilla, try *Hotel Mily's*, which has doubles with fan, cable TV and private hot bath for US$13; bargaining may be in order here. Though relatively pricey, this is the best place to bed down between here and Comitán in Mexico, some 85km down the road. Farther down the hill is the super basic cheapie *Hotel El Pobre Simón*. A place to lay your head for the night here is US$1; the comedor attached is very popular with locals.

There are good onward connections from Huehuetenango and Comitán, so just take the next bus from the border post to either of these cities.

SOLOMA

This agricultural town 69km north of Huehuetenango is a good stopover for intrepid travelers venturing farther afield in the province. The Maya here speak Candobal, but most of the ladino cowboys will greet you, startlingly, in English. The town's prosperity and the language skills of its residents can be attributed to the migratory laborers who annually make the arduous trip from this part of Guatemala to the United States, working as cowhands, auto detailers or landscapers. The populace is very gregarious here, and visitors to Soloma will fast make friends.

The cemetery south of town is worth a look, as most of the colorful tombs are bigger than the average Guatemalan home. As cemeteries can be unsafe in Guatemala, this is an opportunity to stroll, photograph and enjoy one at ease. There are good day trips to neighboring villages like San Juan Ixcoy (7km), where the women still wear traditional white huipiles embroidered at the collar and hanging almost to their ankles. There are many comedores in San Juan, affording the opportunity to break for some lunch while you take in the local culture.

In Soloma there is a Banrural on the plaza; next door is the post office. There are many phones sprinkled throughout Soloma that say 'call the US free!' This is a scam (charges range from US$8 to US$20 a minute), and you'd be better off using the international phone services at the Caucaso Hotel (See Places to Stay & Eat). Sunday is market day.

Attesting to the town's prosperity are the fine choices of accommodations. The *Caucaso Hotel*, just beyond the church, is a sweet budget hotel. Clean, simple singles with comfortable beds and shared hot bath are US$3.10; singles/doubles with private bath and cable TV are US$6/10. All rooms come with purified drinking water and complimentary coffee or tea. They have international phone and fax services here too, and there's a nice little patio out back. Also in this price range is the *Hotel San Antonio* (☎ 780-6191), a big architectural anomaly of blue glass at the entrance to town. All the new, clean rooms have private hot bath, cable TV and towels and are US$6/11. Some rooms have views, while others are dark, so check out a few before choosing.

Of the classic cheapies in town, perhaps the best is *Hospedaje Katy*, which has basic rooms with shared bath arranged around a concrete courtyard for US$1.55. Lots of local cowboys hang out here. Similar options are the nearby *Hospedaje San Juan* or the *Hospedaje Viajero*, which is on the south side of the plaza. On Sunday the latter is undesirable, as the location next to the market means voluminous amounts of noise and garbage.

For food, head straight to the *Restaurante Alma Latina*, a sprawling cafeteria on the east side of the plaza serving filling meals for US$1.55. Across the street is the *Restaurante California*, which starts serving breakfast at 7 am; the food is good, the coffee isn't.

Buses leave Soloma for Huehue (US$1.55, four hours) every half hour between 3 and 9 am and hourly from 9 am to 3 pm. There are also buses to Barrillas (five hours), San Mateo Ixtatán and San Miguel Acatán. Minivans serving San Juan Ixcoy and other neighboring villages leave from beside the plaza.

TODOS SANTOS CUCHUMATÁN
• pop 2000 • elevation 2450m

If you're up for a trek into the Cuchumatanes, four buses per day depart from Huehuetenango on the 40km ride to Todos Santos Cuchumatán. The road is rough, the mountain air chilly and the journey slow, but the scenery is spectacular: Goats trot about prodded by their young shepherds, meticulously maintained stone fences mark out plots of land, and everywhere agave plants as big as cars blanket the landscape, along with fiery red hot poker *kniphofia* flowers.

The picturesque town of Todos Santos Cuchumatán is one of the few in which the traditional Maya tzolkin calendar is still remembered and (partially) observed, and where both men and women still wear traditional clothing. Saturday is market day, with a smaller market on Wednesday.

The post office and Banrural are on the central plaza. The bank changes US dollars and traveler's checks, though at worse rates than elsewhere in the country; it's open Monday to Friday from 8 am to 5 pm and Saturday from 9 am to 1 pm.

If you're coming to Todos Santos in winter, bring warm clothes, as it's cold at this high altitude, especially at night. This is a very small town; businesses and sights are either well signposted or known by everyone – so if you can't find something, just ask.

Things to See & Do

Walking around Todos Santos provides superb opportunities to check out the rugged countryside. **Las Letras** on a hillside high above town is a good goal for a morning walk. 'The Letters' spell out Todos Santos, but may be illegible depending on when the stones were last rearranged. Still, it's a hale hike and affords beautiful views, especially in the morning after the fog lifts and before the afternoon cloud cover rolls in. To get there, look for the big yellow tienda called La Hermosa de Occidente on the left hand side of the main street as you head toward Huehue. Alongside the store is a dirt path that bears right and runs parallel to the river; follow this path for 30 minutes to get to Las Letras.

There are also longer hikes to **La Torre** (one hour, plus bus transport), **La Cumbre** (2½ hours) and **Tzichim** (all day), which are facilitated by the Nuevo Amanecer school (see Language Courses). There are usually several trips offered a week, and nonstudents are welcome for a nominal fee.

It's so cold in Todos Santos most of the time, it's a great place to try the traditional **Mayan sauna** called a *chuj*. This is a very small adobe house (traditionally with space for three small people) with wooden boards covering the entrance. A wood fire burns in a stone hearth inside the chuj, and water is sprinkled directly on the stones or heated in a ceramic jug to provide heat and steam. Sometimes herbs are used to create aromatic vapors. A chuj can be very claustrophobic, and the fire burning within the enclosed space is throat-tightening, so it's not an experience everyone will enjoy. Still, if you're into it, check out the new, extra large chuj at the Hospedaje Casa Familiar (see Places to Stay & Eat). They charge US$1 per person; two hour advance notification is required.

Language Courses

La Hermandad Educativa, Proyecto Lingüístico (in Xela call ☎/fax 763-1061, ✉ proylingts@hotmail.com) offers Spanish or Mam classes for US$100 per week, including room and board with a local family. You can just show up (the school is on the main road), or contact them in the US (☎ 800-963-9889, ✉ johnsond@televar.com, P.O. Box 452, Manson, WA 98831).

Another recommended school is Nuevo Amanecer (✉ mitierra@c.net.gt). It offers Spanish, Mam and weaving classes, plus homestays with locals. Language courses are US$115 a week for 25 hours of instruction and homestay; weaving classes are US$85 a week for 25 hours plus homestay or US$1.50 an hour. They host conferences, support local women's cooperatives and lead tours for students and nonstudents alike. The school, 100m west of the plaza on the road to Pajón, has a library and shows films.

Special Events

Todos Santos is famous for the annual horse races held on the morning of November 1 (El Día de Todos los Santos) which are the culmination of a week of festivities and an all-night drinking spree on the eve of the races. Traditional foods are served throughout the day, and there are mask dances. Christmas posadas are held on each of the 10 days leading up to Christmas, with locals making processions through the streets, re-creating the peregrinations of Joseph and Mary, leading up to the birth of Jesus.

Places to Stay & Eat

Hospedaje Casa Familiar, 30m south of the plaza, is a friendly, family-owned place. It's clean but rustic, and there's hot water and a sauna. The rooms have plenty of blankets, windows and a fine view; cost is US$2.60 per person. Breakfast is available – be sure to try the homemade yogurt and banana bread. It's upstairs over a handicrafts shop, which is next door to the Comedor Katy.

The new *Hotelito Todos Santos* is on a road leading east from the plaza. It has three rooms (which face the street and are rather dark and odiferous), with private toilet but no shower. Upstairs rooms share a bath and are better, and some even share a small balcony and partial views; these are US$2.60 per person. There's a casual cafeteria here.

Next door is a classic cheapie, the *Hotel Mam*, with five basic rooms for US$1.55 per person; this place has been reader-recommended.

Otherwise, accommodations consist of two primitive, cheap hospedajes, *Tres Olguitas* and *La Paz*, but treat these as last resorts. There are also rooms in private homes. People with rooms to rent, usually for US$2 per person, will probably solicit your business as you descend from your bus. Try the house attached to the café and shop *Ruinas de Tecumanchun*.

A few small comedores provide food; *Comedor Karin*, next to the Tres Olguitas, serves tasty, wholesome dinners for US$1.30. Other meals are also available. *Comedor Katy* is a decent choice as well. Another comedor, on the plaza, is cheaper than the Katy and is also good.

For gringo-style food, head to the *Restaurant Cuchumatan* on the main road into town; this is a bar as well as a restaurant and a favorite hangout. Nearby, the *Restaurant Tzolkin* is another place serving Western fare such as pancakes, pizza and pasta. It too is a bar.

Getting There & Away

Buses operate between Huehuetenango and Todos Santos four times daily (US$0.90, 2½ hours, 40km). Buses that take villagers into Huehue for shopping and then home again start early in the morning, around 4 am, and the last bus of the day departs in the early afternoon. Ride on top, if you like – the bus goes slow and the views are spectacular.

HIGHLANDS

The Pacific Slope

A lush, humid region of tropical verdure, Guatemala's Pacific Slope is the southeasterly extension of Mexico's Soconusco, the hot, fertile coastal plain of Chiapas. The rich volcanic soil is good for growing coffee at the higher elevations and palm oil seeds and sugarcane at the lower. Vast fincas exploit the land's economic potential by drawing

Highlights

- Visiting the active archaeological dig at Abaj Takalik
- Chilling out and splashing about at Parque Acuático Xocomil, Central America's premier water park
- Exploring the Bilbao, Finca Las Ilusiones and Finca El Baúl archaeological sites tucked away amidst the sugarcane fields near Santa Lucía Cotzumalguapa
- Taking a little beach vacation at Monterrico and ushering baby sea turtles hatched at the Tortugario Monterrico to their new life at sea
- Deep-sea fishing in Iztapa, where the fish are huge and plentiful and many a world record has been set

seasonal workers from the Highland towns and villages, where work is scarce. Along the Pacific shore are endless stretches of spoiled beaches of dark volcanic sand, frighteningly polluted and marred by all manner of human abuse.

Beautiful beaches are not Guatemala's strong suit. The temperature and humidity along the shore are always uncomfortably high, day and night, rainy season and dry. The few small resorts attract mostly local – not foreign – beachgoers.

A fast highway, the Carretera al Pacífico (CA-2), runs from the border crossings at Ciudad Hidalgo/Tecún Umán and Talismán/El Carmen to Guatemala City. The 275km between the Mexican border at Tecún Umán and Guatemala City can be covered in about four hours by car, five by bus – much less than the 342km of the Interamericana through the western Highlands between La Mesilla and Guatemala City, which takes seven hours. If speed is your goal, the Pacific Slope is your route.

Most of the towns along the Carretera al Pacífico are muggy, somewhat chaotic and hold little interest for travelers. The beach villages are worse – unpleasantly hot muggy and dilapidated. There are exceptions, though. Retalhuleu, a logical stopping place if you're coming from the Mexican border, is kick-back and fun to visit. Nearby is the active archaeological dig at Abaj Takalik. The pre-Olmec stone carvings at Santa Lucía Cotzumalguapa, 8km west of Siquinalá, and those at La Democracia, 9km south of Siquinalá, are unique.

The small beach resort village of Monterrico, with its nature reserve and wildlife preservation project, is buzzing with foreigners, who come from Antigua on weekends. Otherwise, the port town of Iztapa and its beach resort of Likín are fine if you simply must get to the beach. South of Guatemala City, Lago de Amatitlán is the citified version of the more beautiful Lago de Atitlán.

PACIFIC SLOPE

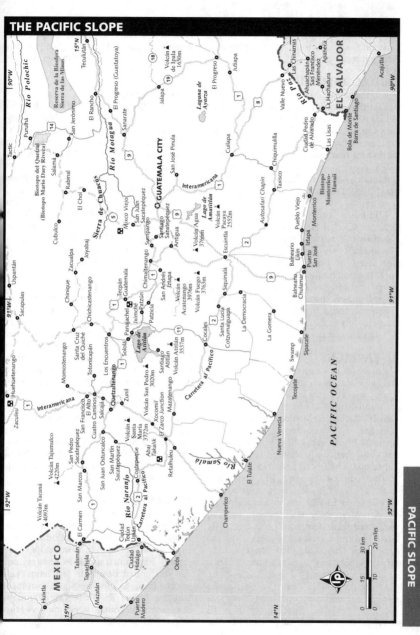

THE PACIFIC SLOPE

Travelers with children will find several fun points of interest on the Pacific Slope, including the Autosafari Chapín and Xocomil water park.

CIUDAD TECÚN UMÁN

This is the preferable and busier of the two Pacific Slope border crossings, with a bridge linking Ciudad Tecún Umán (Guatemala) with Ciudad Hidalgo (Mexico). The border posts are open 24 hours a day, and there are banks here that change US dollars and traveler's checks. Several basic hotels and restaurants are available, but you'll want to get through the border and on your way as soon as possible.

Minibuses and buses run frequently between Ciudad Hidalgo and Tapachula, 38km to the north. From Ciudad Tecún Umán there are frequent buses heading east along the Carretera al Pacífico, stopping at Coatepeque, Retalhuleu, Mazatenango and Escuintla before climbing into the mountains toward Guatemala City. If you don't find a bus to your destination, take any bus to Coatepeque or, better yet, Retalhuleu, and change buses there.

EL CARMEN

Though you can cross at El Carmen, you will encounter much less hassle and expense if you cross at Tecún Umán.

A toll bridge across the Río Suchiate connects Talismán (Mexico) and El Carmen (Guatemala). The border-crossing posts are open 24 hours every day. Minibuses and trucks run frequently between Talismán and Tapachula, a half-hour (20km) away.

There are few services at El Carmen, and those are very basic. There is good bus service from El Carmen to Malacatán on the San Marcos-Quetzaltenango road, and to Ciudad Tecún Umán, 39km to the south. Fairly frequent 1st-class buses run to Guatemala City along the Carretera al Pacífico (US$6, five to six hours, 275km). Transportes Galgos (☎ 232-3661, 253-4868), 7a Avenida 19-44, Zona 1, in Guatemala City, is one company operating along this route. It runs five buses daily from El Carmen, stopping in Ciudad Tecún Umán,

Coatepeque, Retalhuleu, Mazatenango and Escuintla (change for Santa Lucía Cotzumalguapa). Rutas Lima has a daily bus to Quetzaltenango via Retalhuleu and El Zarco junction.

COATEPEQUE

Set on a hill and surrounded by lush coffee plantations, Coatepeque is a brash, fairly ugly and chaotic commercial center, noisy and humid at all times. The town is several kilometers north of the Carretera al Pacífico, and there is no reason to stop here.

Of the town's hotels, the 41-room *Hotel Mansión Residencial* (☎ 775-2018, 0 Avenida 11-49, Zona 2) is about the best, with double rooms with bath for US$15.45. *Hotel Virginia* (☎ /fax 775-1801), Carretera al Pacífico Km 220, has 15 air-con rooms for US$27/35/40 a single/double/triple. Both places have a pool, restaurant and parking.

EL ZARCO JUNCTION

About 40km east of Coatepeque and 9km east of Retalhuleu on the Carretera al Pacífico is El Zarco, the junction with the toll road north to Quetzaltenango. The road wends up from the Pacific Slope, thick with tropical jungle, rising more than 2000m in the 47km from El Zarco to Quetzaltenango. The toll is less than US$1. Just after the upper toll booth, the road divides at Zunil: the left fork goes to Quetzaltenango via Los Baños and Almolonga (the shorter route); the right fork goes via Cantel. For information on these places and the beautiful Fuentes Georginas hot springs near Zunil, see Around Quetzaltenango in the Highlands chapter.

RETALHULEU

• pop 40,000 • elevation 240m

The Pacific Slope is a rich agricultural region, and Retalhuleu is its clean, attractive capital – and proud of it. Most Guatemalans refer to Retalhuleu simply as Reu (ray-oo). As you speed downhill *fast* from Xela toward Reu, the pine trees and corn make way for coffee and bananas, eventually changing to coconuts, heliconia and other tropical flora partial to torrid conditions.

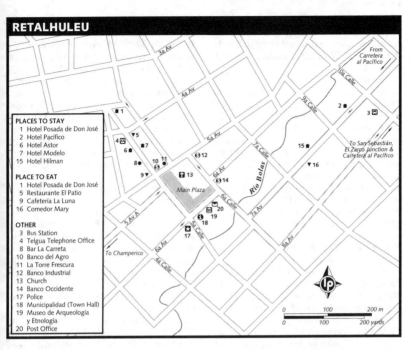

RETALHULEU

PLACES TO STAY
1 Hotel Posada de Don José
2 Hotel Pacífico
6 Hotel Astor
7 Hotel Modelo
15 Hotel Hilman

PLACE TO EAT
1 Hotel Posada de Don José
5 Restaurante El Patio
9 Cafetería La Luna
16 Comedor Mary

OTHER
3 Bus Station
4 Telgua Telephone Office
8 Bar La Carreta
10 Banco del Agro
11 La Torre Frescura
12 Banco Industrial
13 Church
14 Banco Occidente
17 Police
18 Municipalidad (Town Hall)
19 Museo de Arqueología
   y Etnología
20 Post Office

If Coatepeque is where the coffee traders conduct business, Retalhuleu is where they come to relax, splashing in the pool at the Posada de Don José and sipping umbrella drinks in the bar. You'll see their big, expensive 4WD vehicles parked outside. The rest of the citizens get their kicks strolling through the plaza with its whitewashed colonial church and wedding-cake government buildings shaded by royal palms. As you may have already guessed, there isn't too much to do here.

The balmy, tropical air and laid-back attitude are restful. Tourists are something of a curiosity in Reu and are treated very well. The heat is fairly stifling, and if you can splurge for digs with a pool, you'll be happy for it; at the very least, make sure your room has a fan.

Orientation & Information

The town center is 4km southwest of the Carretera al Pacífico, along a grand boulevard lined with towering palm trees. The bus station is on 10a Calle between 7a and 8a Avenidas, Zona 1, northeast of the plaza. To find the plaza, look for the twin church towers and walk toward them.

Most services you may need are within two blocks of the plaza. There is no official tourist office, but people in the Municipalidad (Town Hall), on 6a Avenida facing the east side of the church, will do their best to help.

The post office is on 6a Avenida between 5a and 6a Calles. The Telgua telephone office, at 5a Calle 4-50, is half a block from the plaza.

Banco Occidente, 6a Calle at the corner of 6a Avenida, and Banco Industrial, 6a Calle at the corner of 5a Avenida, both change US dollars cash or traveler's checks and give cash advances on Visa cards. Banco del Agro, on 5a Avenida facing the plaza, changes US dollars cash and traveler's checks and gives cash advances on MasterCard.

Things to See & Do

There's little to see in Retalhuleu proper, but about 30km to the west is the active archaeological dig at Abaj Takalik (see later in this chapter).

The Museo de Arqueología y Etnología, 6a Avenida opposite the south side of the church, is a small museum of archaeological relics. Upstairs are historical photos and a mural showing locations of 33 archaeological sites in the department of Retalhuleu. It's open Tuesday to Sunday 8 am to 1 pm and 2 to 5 pm; admission is US$0.15.

You can swim at the Siboney and Colonial hotels (see Places to Stay & Eat) even if you're not staying there. Cost is US$0.65 at the Siboney and US$1.65 at the Colonial, where there's also a poolside bar.

Places to Stay & Eat

There are a few budget places to stay in Reu and several low-priced, central hotels. Two of the most convenient are just half a block west of the plaza. The better of the two is the newly remodeled *Hotel Astor* (☎ 771-0475, 771-2780, fax 771-2562, 5a Calle 4-60, Zona 1), with a charming courtyard and 27 well-kept rooms, each with ceiling fan, private bath and color cable TV. Singles/doubles are US$13/23, which includes breakfast on weekdays, and there's private parking. The upstairs rooms are new, but the downstairs units around the courtyard have more atmosphere.

Hotel Modelo (☎ 771-0256, 5a Calle 4-53, Zona 1), opposite the Hotel Astor, is a similar place with seven clean rooms on two floors around a central courtyard. The rooms are of varying sizes, with ceiling fans and private bath; singles/doubles are US$8/11, and there's private parking.

For a real cheapie, you could try the very basic and somewhat creepy *Hotel Pacífico* (7a Avenida 9-29), around the corner from the bus station. Rooms are US$2.60 per person, with shared bath; the one room with decrepit private bath is US$6.45 for one or two people. A better budget option is the *Hotel Hilman* (7a Avenida 7-99), which has simple rooms with private bath and fan for US$3.25 per person.

The nicest place in town is the *Hotel Posada de Don José* (☎ 771-0963, 771-0841, ☎/fax 771-1179, 5a Calle 3-67, Zona 1), across the street from the railway station and two blocks northwest of the plaza. On weekends the Don José is often filled with finca owners in town for relaxation; at other times you can get an air-con room with color cable TV, telephone and private bath for US$20/31/38 a single/double/triple; discounts may be available. The 23 rooms are on two levels overlooking the swimming pool, and the café and restaurant tables are beneath an arcade surrounding the pool. They also have an *anexo* with 14 rooms at similar prices.

Out on the Carretera al Pacífico are several other hotels. These tend to be 'tropical motels' by design, with bungalows, swimming pools and restaurants. They are convenient if you have a car, and a hot hike from anywhere if you don't. *Hotel Siboney* (☎ 771-0149, fax 771-0711), Cuatro Caminos, San Sebastian, is 4km east of town where Calzada Las Palmas meets the Carretera al Pacífico. The 25 rooms, all with air-con, cable TV, telephone and private bath, are US$27/29/31 for singles/doubles/triples. *Hotel La Colonia* (☎ 771-0054, fax 771-0191), Carretera al Pacífico Km 178, is 1km east of the Siboney. It has a fairly luxurious layout – bungalows around the swimming pool – with 44 rooms and the same amenities as the Siboney for US$40/50 for singles/doubles.

Several little restaurants facing the plaza provide meals at low prices (under US$3). The *Cafetería La Luna*, on the corner of 5a Calle and 5a Avenida opposite the west corner of the plaza, is a town favorite; it's open every day. The *Restaurante El Patio*, on the corner of 5a Calle and 4a Avenida, is similar. Also around the plaza are several ice cream shops.

Across from the Hotel Hilman (see above) is the *Comedor Mary*, a classic Guatemalan lunch place popular with feasting locals. *La Torre Frescura* is a giant supermarket on 5a Avenida where you can hunt and gather for a picnic; it's also invitingly air conditioned, so browse away.

For the best meal in town, try chilling out at the **Posada de Don José** (see above), where the nice, cool restaurant offers beef and chicken plates for US$4 to US$6 and a big, full meal can be had for US$7 to US$10. Breakfast is served here as well.

Cocktails can be had at the **Bar La Carreta** *(5a Calle 4-50)*, next to the Hotel Astor. This place fancies itself a cowboy watering hole, so it's air conditioned and chummy.

Getting There & Away

Daily flights leave Guatemala City for Reu (US$40, 35 minutes) at 6 am and 3:45 pm. Flights return to Guatemala City daily at 6:45 am (via Coatepeque) and 4:30 pm.

As Reu is the most important town on the Carretera al Pacífico, hooking up with your desired bus is easy. Most buses traveling along the highway stop at the city's bus station, on 10a Calle between 7a and 8a Avenidas, Zona 1, about 400m northeast of the plaza. Long-distance buses include:

Ciudad Tecún Umán – US$1.65, 1½ hours, 78km; buses every 20 minutes, 5 am to 10 pm

Guatemala City – US$3.65, three hours, 186km; buses every 15 minutes, 2 am to 8:30 pm

Quetzaltenango – US$0.80, 1½ hours, 67km; buses every 15 minutes, 3 am to 7 pm

Santa Lucía Cotzumalguapa – US$2.60, two hours, 97km; take any bus headed to Guatemala City

Local buses (see map) depart for Champerico and El Asintal (for Abaj Takalik).

Tabarini Rent A Car (☎/fax 763-0418) has an office at 6a Calle 4-50, Zona 1.

AROUND RETALHULEU

If the heat is making you cranky and torpid, head to the **Parque Acuático Xocomil** (☎ 771-2673), Km 180.5 on the Quetzaltenango road, about 18km north of Reu. This is a gigantic water park in the Disneyland vein, but with a distinct Guatemalan theme. Among the seven water slides, two wave pools and beach are recreations of the temples at Tikal, Copán and the stelae at Quiriguá. Visitors can bob along a river through canyons flanked with ancient temples and Mayan masks spewing water from the nose and mouth, or frolic in a pool with a volcano erupting water. Three real volcanoes – Santiaguito, Zunil and Santa María – can be seen from the grounds.

Xocomil is very well executed and maintained, and kids love it. It is run by a nonprofit agency called IRTRA that administers four fun, free sites throughout Guatemala for workers and their families. Hence, there will be clutches of Guatemalan families at Xocomil when you visit. There are restaurants and swank hotels on the grounds, all of which are expensive for foreigners. A day pass to the park costs US$10. To get to Xocomil, drive through the El Zarco junction north of Reu and toward Zunil for about 10km. By public transportation, take any bus heading to Xela and hop off at Xocomil; all the bus drivers know it.

ABAJ TAKALIK

About 30km west of Retalhuleu is the active archaeological dig at Abaj Takalik (ah-bah tah-kah-leek), which is translated from the Quiché as 'standing stone.' Large 'Olmecoid' stone heads have been discovered, along with many other objects, which date the site as one of the earliest in all of the Mayan realm. The site has yet to be restored and prettified for tourists, so don't expect a Chichén Itzá or Tikal. But if you're fascinated with archaeology and want to witness the discovery as it unfolds, pay a visit. This site is especially important for scholars of pre-Columbian societies because it is believed to be one of the only places where the Olmecs and Maya lived together. More than 70 mounds and 150 structures built using round river rocks have been discovered to date.

It's easiest to reach Abaj Takalik with your own vehicle, but it can be done by public transport. Catch a bus to El Asintal, about 15km west along the Carretera al Pacífico and then 5km down a road heading off to the right. Otherwise, early in the morning take any bus heading west toward Coatepeque, go about 15km west along the

Carretera al Pacífico, and get out at the road on the right that goes to El Asintal. From here it's 5km to El Asintal (you may have some luck hitching). Pickups at El Asintal provide transport to Abaj Takalik, 4km away. Spanish-speaking guides are available at the entrance to the site and are a worthwhile investment for those interested in Mayan archaeology.

CHAMPERICO

Built as a shipping point for coffee during the boom of the late 19th century, Champerico, 38km southwest of Retalhuleu, is a tawdry, sweltering, dilapidated place that sees few tourists. Despite this off-putting but accurate description, it's one of the easiest ocean beaches to get to on a day trip from Quetzaltenango, and beach-starved students still try their luck here. Most beachgoers come only to spend the day, but there are several cheap hotels and restaurants. The *Hotel Mirimar* (☎ 773-7231), at 2a Calle and Avenida Coatepeque, is worth a shot, with singles/doubles/triples for US$4/5/8.

When you get to the beach, walk to the right, go under a pier and keep walking for five more minutes until you get to an estuary. Swimming is pleasant in the warm water at the river mouth, and you'll probably see only a few local families. Swimming can be dangerous in the sea, due to fierce waves and an undertow.

El Tulate, 45km south of the Carretera al Pacífico, is a recommended alternative for a (slightly) better beach and atmosphere than Champerico. Proper facilities are scant, so you can either make it a day trip or rely on the kindness of strangers.

MAZATENANGO

• pop 38,000 • elevation 370m

East of Retalhuleu, about 26km along the Carretera al Pacífico, Mazatenango is the capital of the department of Suchitepéquez. It's a center for the farmers, traders and shippers of the Pacific Slope's agricultural produce. There are a few serviceable hotels if you need to stop in an emergency. Otherwise just keep on keeping on.

SANTA LUCÍA COTZUMALGUAPA

• pop 24,000 • elevation 356m

Going another 71km eastward from Mazatenango brings you to Santa Lucía Cotzumalguapa, an important stop for anyone interested in Mayan art and culture. In the sugarcane fields and fincas near the town stand great stone heads carved with grotesque faces and fine relief scenes. The question of who carved these ritual objects, and why, remains unanswered.

The town itself, though benign enough, is unexciting. The people in town and in the surrounding countryside are descended from the Pipil, an Indian culture known to have historic, linguistic and cultural links with the Nahuatl-speaking peoples of central Mexico. In Early Classic times, the Pipil who lived here grew cacao, the 'money' of the age. They were obsessed with the Mayan/Aztec ball game and with the rites and mysteries of death. Pipil art, unlike the flowery and almost romantic style of the true Maya, is cold, grotesque and severe, but still very finely done. What were these 'Mexicans' doing in the midst of Mayan territory? How did they get here and where did they come from? Archaeologists do not have many answers. There are other concentrations of Pipils, notably in the Motagua Valley of southeastern Guatemala and in western El Salvador. Today these people share a common lifestyle with Guatemala's other indigenous groups, except for their mysterious history.

A visit to Santa Lucía Cotzumalguapa allows you to examine this unique 'lost culture' by visiting a number of its carved stones. Though the sites are accessible to travelers without their own transport, a car certainly simplifies matters. In your explorations you may get to see a Guatemalan sugarcane finca in full operation.

Orientation

Santa Lucía Cotzumalguapa is northwest of the Carretera al Pacífico. In its main square, several blocks from the highway, are copies of some of the famous carved stones found in the region.

There are three main archaeological sites to visit: Bilbao, a finca right on the outskirts of Santa Lucía; Finca El Baúl, a large plantation farther from town at which there are two sites (a hilltop site and the finca headquarters); and Finca Las Ilusiones, which has collected most of its findings into a museum near the finca headquarters. Of these sites, Bilbao and the hilltop site at El Baúl are by far the most interesting. If time and energy are short, head for these.

If you don't have a car and you want to see the sites in a day, haggle with a taxi driver in Santa Lucía's main square for transport. With good negotiating skills, you should be able to secure a ride for around US$12. It's hot and muggy, and the sites are several kilometers apart, so you will really be glad you rode at least part of the way. If you do it all on foot and by bus, pack a lunch so you won't have to return to town. The hilltop site at El Baúl is a perfect place for a picnic.

Warning

In January 1998, near Santa Lucía Cotzumalguapa, a bus full of students from Saint Mary's College in the US was ambushed and robbed, and five women were raped at gunpoint. Although three of the felons were arrested and sentenced to 28 years in prison, in early 2000 several suspects were still being sought in the crime. While attacks like these are random and unpredictable, visitors should ask local travel agents and other travelers as to the current safety situation around Santa Lucía. It is worth noting that the victims were traveling in a rented minivan, a mode of transport favored by tourists and therefore targeted more often than chicken buses by would-be thieves.

Bilbao

This site, no doubt a large ceremonial center, flourished about 600 AD. Plows have unearthed (and damaged) hundreds of stones during the last few centuries; thieves have carted off many others. In 1880 many of the best stones were removed to museums abroad, including nine stones to the Dahlem Museum in Berlin.

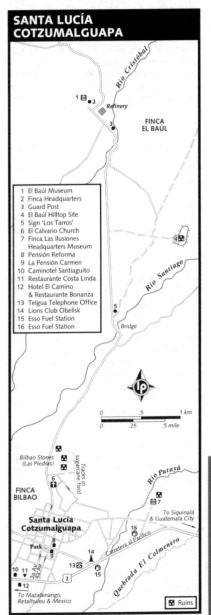

SANTA LUCÍA COTZUMALGUAPA

1 El Baúl Museum
2 Finca Headquarters
3 Guard Post
4 El Baúl Hilltop Site
5 Sign 'Los Tarros'
6 El Calvario Church
7 Finca Las Ilusiones Headquarters Museum
8 Pensión Reforma
9 La Pensión Carmen
10 Caminotel Santiaguito
11 Restaurante Costa Linda
12 Hotel El Camino & Restaurante Bonanza
13 Telgua Telephone Office
14 Lions Club Obelisk
15 Esso Fuel Station
16 Esso Fuel Station

Known locally as simply *las piedras* (the stones), this site actually consists of several separate sites deep within a sugarcane finca. The fields come right to the edge of the town. From Santa Lucía's main square, go north uphill on 3a Avenida to the outskirts of town. Pass El Calvario church on your right, and shortly thereafter turn sharply right. A hundred meters along, the road veers to the right, but an unpaved road continues straight on; follow the unpaved road. The sugarcane fields are on your left, and you will soon see a path cut into the cane.

At times when the cane is high, finding your way around would be very difficult if it weren't for the swarms of local boys that materialize and follow you as you make your way along the edge of the cane fields. At the first sign of bewilderment or indecision they'll yell, '*¿Las piedras? ¿Las piedras?*' You answer '*¡Si!*' and they'll lead you without hesitation into the sea of waving cane along a maze of paths to each site. A tip is expected, of course, but it needn't be large and it needn't be given to every one of the multitude of guides. The boys are in school many days but are dependably at the ready on weekends, holidays and during school vacation time.

One stone is flat with three figures carved in low relief; the middle figure's ribs show prominently, as though he were starving. A predatory bird is in the upper left-hand corner. Holes in the middle-right part of the stone show that thieves have attempted to cut the stone.

Another is an elaborate relief showing players in a ball game, fruit, birds and animals. It also features cacao bean pods, for which this area was famous and which made it rich.

Some of the stones are badly weathered and worn. Some bear Mexican-style circular date glyphs and more mysterious patterns that resemble closely those used by people along the Gulf Coast of Mexico near Villahermosa.

To continue on to El Baúl, you can save time by backtracking to the point where you turned sharply right just beyond El Calvario church. Buses heading out to El Baúl

pass this point every few hours, or you can hitchhike. If you're driving, you'll have to return to the center along 4a Avenida and come back out on 3a Avenida, as these roads are one-way.

A reader wrote the following about his experience finding the stones:

I had a hell of a time finding Las Piedras (the Bilbao stones) – the schoolboy guides must have been at school at 9:30 on a Tuesday. Having found them all (with the help of a local), I wrote these instructions:

From the unpaved road in your instructions, continue as far as the blue house (about 100m). Opposite this there is a path in the sugarcane (you need to climb through the fence) – the first glyph is just up on the left. From there, continue north, and take the second right – the arch-shaped glyph is on the top of the hill. Continue to the end of the path (about 20m), turn left, and left again after 50m up a small path to a very large glyph.

Returning to the previous path and following to the end, take a left turn. Eventually you'll come to the road to Finca El Baúl, cutting the corner.

Of course, these may not be the stones you were describing!

Finca El Baúl

Just as interesting is the hilltop site at El Baúl, which has the additional fascination of being an active place of pagan worship for local people. This is an excellent place for a picnic. Some distance from the hilltop site on another road, next to the finca headquarters, is the El Baúl museum, full of stones that have been uncovered on the property.

The hilltop site at El Baúl is 4.2km northwest of El Calvario church. From the church (or the intersection just beyond it), go 2.7km to a fork in the road just beyond a bridge; the fork is marked by a sign reading Los Tarros. Buses will go as far as this sign. Take the right-hand fork (an unpaved road). From the Los Tarros sign it's 1.5km to the point where a dirt track crosses the road; on your right is a tree-covered 'hill' in the midst of otherwise flat fields. The 'hill' is actually a great ruined temple platform that has not been restored. Make your way across the field and around the south side of the hill, following the track to the top. If you have a car, you can drive to within 50m of the top.

If you visit on a weekend, you may find several worshippers paying their respects to the idols here. They will not mind if you visit as well, and are usually happy to pose with the idols for photographs, in exchange for a small 'contribution.'

Of the two stones here, the great, grotesque, half-buried head is the most striking. The elaborate headdress, 'blind' eyes with big bags underneath, beak-like nose and 'have a nice day' grin seem at odds with the blackened face and its position half-buried in the ancient soil. The head is stained with wax from candles, splashes of liquor and other drinks, and with the smoke and ashes of incense fires built before it, all part of worship. People have been coming here to pay homage for more than 1400 years.

The other stone is a relief carving of a figure surrounded by circular motifs that may be date glyphs. A copy of this stone may be seen in the main square of Santa Lucía Cotzumalguapa.

From the hilltop site, retrace your steps 1.5km to the fork with the Los Tarros sign. Take the other fork this time (what would be the left fork as you come from Santa Lucía), and follow the paved road 3km to the headquarters of Finca El Baúl. (If you're on foot, you can walk from the hilltop site back to the unpaved road and straight across it, continuing on the dirt track. This will eventually bring you to the asphalt road that leads to the finca headquarters. When you reach the road, turn right.) Buses trundle along this road every few hours, shuttling workers between the refinery and the town center.

Approaching the finca headquarters (6km from Santa Lucía's main square), you cross a narrow bridge at a curve. Continue uphill and you will see the entrance on the left, marked by a machine-gun pillbox. Beyond this daunting entrance you pass workers' houses and the sugar refinery on

Mayan counting system

the right and finally come to the headquarters building, guarded by several men with rifles. The smell of molasses is everywhere. Ask permission to visit the museum and a guard will unlock the gate just past the headquarters building.

Within the gates, sheltered by a palapa, are numerous sculpted figures and reliefs which have been found on the plantation, some of which are very fine. Unfortunately, nothing is labeled.

Finca Las Ilusiones

The third site is very close to Bilbao – indeed, this is the finca that controls the Bilbao cane fields – but, paradoxically, access is more difficult. Your reward is the chance to view hundreds of objects, large and small, that have been collected from the finca's fields over the centuries.

Leave the town center by heading east along Calzada 15 de Septiembre, the boulevard that joins the highway at an Esso fuel station. Go northeast for a short distance, and just before another Esso station on the left is an unpaved road that leads, after a little over 1km, to Finca Las Ilusiones and its museum. If the person who holds the museum key is not to be found, you must be satisfied with the many stones collected around the outside of the museum.

Places to Stay & Eat

Hotel pickings in town are slim and very basic. *Pensión Reforma*, Calzada 15 de Septiembre at 4a Avenida, has dark, cell-like rooms (some with hay beds!) for US$3/6 a single/double. The rooms around the courtyard are better, but are only rented by the hour. *La Pensión Carmen*, a block east of the park, is slightly nicer, with basic rooms for US$2.60 per person.

Just a few hundred meters southwest of town, the *Caminotel Santiaguito* (☎ 882-5435/6/7, fax 882-2285, Km 90.4, Carretera al Pacífico) is fairly lavish for Guatemala's Pacific Slope, with spacious tree-shaded grounds, a nice swimming pool and a decent restaurant. The pool is open to nonguests for US$2.60. Motel-style air-con rooms with private bath cost US$24.75/30/34. They're likely to be full on weekends, as the hotel is something of a resort for local people. In the spacious restaurant cooled by ceiling fans, you can order a cheeseburger, fruit salad and soft drink for US$4, or an even bigger meal for US$6.50 to US$8.

Across the highway from the Caminotel is the *Hotel El Camino* (☎ 882-5316), which sports clean rooms with comfortable beds, tiled floors, great showers, and cable TV. Upstairs rooms have lots of light and small balconies; go for one in the back to reduce traffic noise. Singles/doubles/triples with private bath and fan are pretty good values at US$10/16/20; rooms with bath and air-con are US$11/19/24.

The *Restaurante Bonanza*, next to the Hotel El Camino, has been recommended. The *Restaurante Costa Linda*, across the highway and about 50m east, is a friendly place serving tasty ceviche, chicken dishes and burgers at reasonable prices.

Getting There & Away

Esmeralda 2nd-class buses shuttle between Santa Lucía Cotzumalguapa and Guatemala City (4a Avenida and 2a Calle, Zona 9) every half-hour or so from 6 am to 5 pm, charging US$1.50 for the 90km, two-hour ride. You can also catch any bus traveling along the Carretera al Pacífico between Guatemala City and such points as Mazatenango, Retalhuleu or the Mexican border.

To travel between La Democracia and Santa Lucía, catch a bus running along the Carretera al Pacífico toward Siquinalá (8km) and change there for a bus to La Democracia.

Between Santa Lucía and Lago de Atitlán you will probably have to change buses at Cocales junction, 23km west of Santa Lucía and 58km south of Panajachel.

LA DEMOCRACIA
• pop 4200 • elevation 165m

South of Siquinalá, 9.5km along the road to Puerto San José, is La Democracia, a nondescript Pacific Slope town that's hot day and night, rainy season and dry. According to some archaeologists, La Democracia – like Santa Lucía Cotzumalguapa – is in the midst of a region populated from early times by cultures with mysterious connections to Mexico's Gulf Coast.

At the archaeological site called Monte Alto, on the outskirts of the town, huge basalt heads have been found. Though cruder, the heads resemble those carved by the Olmecs near Veracruz several thousand years ago.

Today, these great Olmecoid heads are arranged around La Democracia's main plaza. As you come into town from the highway, follow signs to the museo, which will lead you to bear left, then left and then left again.

Facing the plaza, along with the church and the modest Palacio Municipal, is the small, modern Museo Rubén Chevez Van Dorne, which houses some fascinating archaeological finds. The star of the show is an exquisite jade mask. Smaller figures, 'yokes' used in the ball game, relief carvings and other objects make up the rest of this small but important collection. On the walls are overly dramatic paintings of Olmecoid scenes. A rear room has more dramatic paintings, plus lots of potsherds only an archaeologist could love. The museum is open from 8 am to noon and 2 to 5 pm; admission costs US$0.50.

Places to Stay & Eat

La Democracia has no places to stay and few places to eat. The eateries are very basic and ill-supplied; it's best to bring your own food and buy drinks at one of the tiendas facing the plaza. *Café Maritza*, right next to the museum, is a picture-perfect hot-tropics hangout with a *rockola* (jukebox) blasting music, and a crew of semisomnolent locals doing their thing and sweltering.

Getting There & Away

Chatla Gomerana, Muelle Central, Terminal de Autobuses, Zona 4, Guatemala City, has buses every half-hour, 6 am to 4:30 pm, for the 92km, two-hour ride between the capital and La Democracia. Buses stop at Escuintla, Siquinalá (change for Santa Lucía Cotzumalguapa), La Democracia, La Gomera and Sipacate. The fare is US$1.

AROUND LA DEMOCRACIA

The road south from La Democracia continues 42km to **Sipacate**, a small and very basic beach town. The beach is on the other side of the Canal de Chiquimulilla, an intracoastal waterway. Though there are a few scruffy, very basic places to stay, you'd be better off saving your beach time for Puerto San José, 35km to the east, reached via the road from Escuintla.

ESCUINTLA

Surrounded by rich green foliage, Escuintla should be a tropical idyll where people swing languidly in hammocks and concoct pungent meals of readily available exotic fruits and vegetables. But it's not.

Instead, Escuintla is a hot, dingy, shabby commercial and industrial city that's integral to the Pacific Slope's economy but not at all important to travelers, except for making bus connections. It is an old town, inhabited by Pipils before the conquest but now solidly ladino. It has some marginal hotels and restaurants. If stranded, you might try the *Hotel Costa Sur* (☎ 888-1819, 12a Calle 4-13), two blocks north of the bus terminal. Singles/doubles with private hot bath are US$8/10. There's a restaurant and parking. There is also a branch of the Banco del Ejército with a Visa ATM machine at 1a Calle 1-00, Zona 2.

Most people know Escuintla for its bus terminal. The main bus station is in the southern part of town; this is where you catch the bus to Antigua at 7 am and 1 pm (US$0.65), Puertos San José and Viejo and Iztapa. For Guatemala City, you can catch very frequent buses in the main plaza. Most buses to the border with El Salvador go through Chiquimulilla (see Around Monterrico, later in this chapter).

Autosafari Chapín

Autosafari Chapín (☎ 363-1105, fax 337-1274), Carretera al Pacífico Km 87.5, is a drive-through safari park and animal conservation project earning high marks for its sensitivity and success breeding animals in captivity. Species native to Guatemala here include white-tailed deer, peccaries and macaws. Around the grounds also roam non-native species such as lions, rhinos and leopards. There is a restaurant and pool, and it makes a great day trip if you're traveling with kids; admission is US$4.50. Buses from Guatemala City come here (see the Getting Around chapter), or you can take any bus going from Escuintla to El Salvador. By car, the Autosafari is about 30km from Escuintla on the Carretera al Pacífico toward Taxisco, El Salvador and beyond.

PUERTO SAN JOSÉ & LIKÍN

Guatemala's most important seaside resort leaves a lot to be desired. But if you're eager to get into the Pacific surf, head south from Escuintla 50km to Puerto San José and neighboring settlements.

Puerto San José (population 14,000) was Guatemala's most important Pacific port in the latter half of the 19th century and well into the 20th. Now superseded by the more modern Puerto Quetzal to the east, Puerto San José languishes and slumbers. The beach, inconveniently located across the Canal de Chiquimulilla, is reached by boat.

It's smarter to head west along the coast 5km (by taxi or car) to Balneario Chulamar, which has a nicer beach and also a suitable hotel or two.

About 5km to the east of Puerto San José is **Balneario Likín**, Guatemala's only upmarket Pacific resort. Likín is much beloved by well-to-do families from Guatemala City who have seaside houses on the tidy streets and canals of this planned development.

IZTAPA

About 12km east of Puerto San José is Iztapa, Guatemala's first Pacific port, used by none other than Pedro de Alvarado in the 16th century. When Puerto San José was built in 1853, Iztapa's reign as the port of the capital city came to an end, and it relaxed into a tropical torpor from which it has yet to emerge. Having lain fallow for almost a century and a half, it has not suffered the degradation of Puerto San José.

Iztapa has gained notoriety as one of the world's premier **deep sea fishing** spots. World records have been set here, and en-

thusiasts can go for marlin, sharks and yellowfin tuna, among others. November through June is typically the best time to angle for sailfish. B&B Worldwide Fishing Adventures (☎ 541-296-3962, fax 541-296-9144, in the US 888-479-2277, 🅰 getfishing@ wheretofish.com, www.wheretofish.com/guatemala2.html), 1416 1/2 E 10th Pl., The Dalles, OR 97058; Artmarina (☎ 305-663-3553, fax 305-666-6445, 🅰 fish@artmarina.com, www.artmarina.com), 1390 South Dixie Hwy No 2221, Miami, FL 33146; and Fishing International (☎ 707-542-4242, fax 707-526-3474, in the US ☎ 800-950-4242, 🅰 fishint@fishinginternational.com, www.fishinginternational.com), PO Box 2132, Santa Rosa, CA 95405, run all-inclusive deep sea fishing tours to Iztapa. Guatemala Unlimited can also arrange these trips; see the Organized Tours section of the Getting There & Away chapter.

It is also possible to contract local boat owners for fishing trips, though equipment and comfort may be nonexistent and 'catch-and-release' could prove a foreign concept. The boat owners hang out at the edge of the Canal de Chiquimulilla – head down there to arrange *lancha* services, and bargain hard. Yellowfin tuna will likely be out of reach for the local boats, as these fish habituate the waters some 17km from Iztapa.

Aside from fishing or hiring a lancha to poke around for hidden local beaches, there's not much to do in Iztapa but lounge about, and it's a laid-back enough place to do so. There's a post office here, but no bank.

Places to Stay & Eat

Should you want to stay, check out the *Sol y Playa Tropical* (☎ 881-4365/6, 1a Calle 5-48), which has clean, airy singles/doubles with fans and private bath for US$11/22. Rates are lower in the off-season. There's a pool and a restaurant. There's also the *Hotel Posada María del Mar* (☎ 881-4055), across from the post office, with doubles for US$6.45 without bath or US$11 with private bath. Nearby is the *Brasilia Hotel*, with basic, fanless rooms around a cavernous dance floor for US$4/7 with/without bath. This place is loud when empty – packed with gyrating and rowdy dancers it is sleep-defying.

Getting There & Away

The bonus about Iztapa is that you can catch a Transportes Pacífico bus from the market in Zona 4 in Guatemala City all the way there (four hours), or pick one up at Escuintla (one hour) or Puerto San José. You can also get to Monterrico from Iztapa by catching one of the frequent lanchas across the Canal de Chiquimulilla to Pueblo Viejo (US$0.50) and transferring to one of the several daily buses (US$0.65, one hour).

MONTERRICO

The coastal area around Monterrico is a totally different Guatemala. Life here is steeped with a sultry, tropical flavor – it's a place where hanging out in a hammock is both a major endeavor and goal. Among the main cash crops here is *pachete* (loofa), which get as big as a man's leg. You see them everywhere, growing on trellises and drying in the sun. The architecture, too, is different, with rustic wooden slat and thatched roofed houses instead of the dull cinderblock, corrugated-tin models common elsewhere. Keep your eyes peeled for the awesome Highland volcanoes that shimmer over the hot coastal horizon.

Monterrico itself is a coastal village with a few small, inexpensive hotels right on the beach, a large wildlife reserve and a center for the hatching and release of sea turtles and caimans. The beach here is dramatic, where powerful surf crashes onto black volcanic sand at odd angles. The odd-angled wave-print signals rip tides; deaths have occurred at this beach, so tread with care. Behind the beach, on the other side of town, is a large network of mangrove swamps and canals, part of the 190km Canal de Chiquimulilla.

Monterrico is probably the best spot for a weekend break at the beach if you're staying in Antigua or Guatemala City. It's fast becoming popular with foreigners. On weekdays it's relatively quiet, but on weekends and holidays, it teems with Guatemalan families, and everything seems a bit harried. There is no bank, but there is a post office on Calle Principal.

Things to See & Do

Besides the beach, Monterrico's biggest attraction is the **Biotopo Monterrico-Hawaii**, a 20km-long nature reserve of coast and coastal mangrove swamps bursting with avian and aquatic life. Its most famous denizens are the endangered leatherback and ridley turtles, which lay their eggs on the beach in many places along the coast. The mangrove swamps are a network of 25 lagoons, all connected by mangrove canals.

Boat tours of the reserve, passing through the mangrove swamps and visiting several lagoons, take around 1½ to two hours and cost US$8 for two passengers. It's best to go early in the morning, when you can see the most wildlife. If you have binoculars, bring them for bird-watching. To arrange a boat tour of the canal, stop by the **Tortugario Monterrico** visitor's center on the beach. Local villagers also do boat tours, but the guides who work at the Tortugario are particularly concerned with wildlife. Some travelers have griped about the use of motorboats (as opposed to the paddled varieties), because the sound of the motor scares off the wildlife. If you're under no time crunch, ask about arranging a paddled tour of the canal.

The Tortugario Monterrico is just a short walk east down the beach from the Monterrico hotels (left, if you're facing the sea). Several endangered species of animals are raised here, including leatherback, olive ridley and green sea turtles, caimans and iguanas. There's an interesting interpretive trail and a visitor's center; it's open daily from 8 am to noon and 2 to 5 pm.

The **Reserva Natural Hawaii** is a nature reserve operated by the Asociación de Rescate y Conservación de Vida Silvestre (ARCAS; Association to Rescue and Conserve Wildlife), which has a sea-turtle hatchery 8km east along the beach from Monterrico. Volunteers are welcome all year round, but real sea turtle-nesting season is from June to November, with August and September being the peak

PACIFIC SLOPE

A Race to the Sea

From September to January a delightful ritual takes place every Saturday at sunset in front of Monterrico's beachfront hotels. Workers from the Tortugario Monterrico walk out on the beach carrying big plastic tubs and two long ropes. They lay one rope out along the beach at a certain distance from the waterline, and the second one several yards away, parallel to the first, and tourists from the beach hotels gather around. Come up to see what's going on and you'll find out the plastic tubs are full of baby sea turtles!

Pick a likely looking turtle out of the tub, make a small donation (less than US$2) to support the tortugario (turtle hatchery) and line up behind the rope farthest from the waves. It's an amazing feeling, to hold the baby sea turtle in your hand. When everyone is ready, on the count of three, everyone releases their turtles, which make a frantic scramble toward the sea. Keep an eye on your turtle; if yours is the first to reach the rope closer to the waves, you'll win a free meal for two at one of the Monterrico hotels. Eventually, as the sun is sinking, all the turtles reach the water and are washed away by the waves.

The race is not only a fun chance to win a free dinner, it's also poignant, as you consider the fate of 'your' little sea turtle as you hold it in your hand. All the turtles were hatched within the past two to three days. They're released in a group to give them a better chance of survival. Scientists say that on their race across the sand to the sea, the tiny turtles are being imprinted with the information about their place of birth (the components of the sand, the water, etc) that will enable them to return from the sea to this exact spot to lay eggs when they are adults. Most of them won't make it to adulthood. But the efforts of conservation groups such as the Tortugario are giving this endangered species a better chance.

months. Volunteers are charged US$25 for a room, with optional meals and homestay options with local families. See the Volunteer Work section in the Facts for the Visitor chapter for more about ARCAS.

This part of Guatemala is also treated to awesome **lightning storms** from around November to April.

For studying Spanish, the ALM Language School, based in Antigua and Quetzaltenango, has a branch here in Monterrico.

Places to Stay & Eat

Monterrico has several simple hotels, almost all of which are on the beach; the majority have restaurants attached serving whatever is fresh from the sea that day. From where you alight from the La Avellana boat, it's about a 15-minute walk through the village to reach the beach and the hotels.

Alternatively, if you take the bus from Pueblo Viejo, walk about five minutes toward the beach on Calle Principal. If you've brought a vehicle across on a car ferry, you can park it at any of the hotels. Coming from Calle Principal, head left to reach the cluster of hotels described here, most of which offer discounts for stays of three nights or more.

The **Hotel Baule Beach** (☎ 473-6196) is a ludicrously popular hotel run by former Peace Corps Volunteer Nancy Garver. Throngs of students from Antigua choke the place on weekends, so it's not everyone's cup of tea. However, if you want to party with other travelers, head here. Ragged, sort of clean rooms with private bath, right on the beach, cost US$8/13/17 for singles/doubles/triples; bigger rooms can accommodate up to six. Reasonably priced meals are available, but service can be really slow. Current schedules for every type of transport serving Monterrico are posted here.

The next place over is the new **Hotel El Mangle** (☎ 369-7631). The clean, comfortable rooms here have fans, mosquito nets, private baths, quality beds and towels, and are good value at US$15.45 for two people during high season, US$13 other times. There's a big open space for hanging out, and it's quiet.

A favorite of vacationing Guatemalan families, **Johnny's Lodging** (☎ 337-4191, 633-0321) has clean rooms with fan and private bath for US$7.75 per person. It also has seven bungalows, each with two bedrooms, living room, private bath and fully equipped kitchen for US$50 for four people. Price reductions are available midweek. Two bungalows share a BBQ and small swimming pool. Also here is a second swimming pool and restaurant.

Nearby, the **Kaiman Inn** (☎ 334-6214, ☎/fax 334-6215) has eight rooms, each with fan, mosquito nets and private bath, for US$6.45 per person during the week, US$7.75 on weekends, with rooms holding two to five people. The restaurant, right on the beach, serves excellent Italian cuisine and seafood.

Farther down the beach, the **Hotel Pez de Oro** (☎ 204-5249, ☎/fax 368-3684, contact ✉ laelegancia@guate.net) is Monterrico's most upscale hotel. It has nine clean, pleasant bungalows, each with fan, mosquito nets, private bath and a hammock on the porch. Friday through Sunday, rooms are US$32/44/54 for two/three/four people (singles pay the same as doubles). Rooms are nearly US$10 cheaper on weekdays. There's also a swimming pool and a fine restaurant.

Going in the opposite direction from these hotels, heading right from Calle Principal, are cheaper accommodation options. The first you'll come to is the basic **Hotel El Delfín**. The rooms are nothing fancy and some are moldering a bit, but it's friendly and will do if all else fails. Singles/doubles with mosquito net are US$4/7.

Farther down the beach is the **Hotel La Sirena**, which you'll know by the palm-shaded hammocks and the travelers swinging in them. This is one of Monterrico's best values, with many types of rooms at different prices. Big, bare rooms with private bath, fan and three beds are US$11.60; rooms sleeping four with bath, refrigerator, stove and dining area are US$20; and simple rooms with shared bath are US$5.15 for one or two people. Prices are lower during the week, and you may be able to negotiate. There's a pool, and the restaurant here has the usual fish and pasta dishes that every other beach hotel is serving, but at half the price.

On this same stretch is the **Pig Pen Pub**, an open-air beachfront bar with lots of good music and atmosphere. It's open from 8 pm 'until you're done drinking.' The gregarious owner is an ex-pat who knows the area well. Ask him about birding, mangrove tours and nighttime jaunts to watch local fisherman hauling their catch from the lagoons.

Set back from the beach on the little paths that describe the town of Monterrico proper are two recommended places. The first is the **Guest House**, a fairly new hostel with four cozy and rustic rooms with mosquito nets, fans and shared bath for US$4/6. It's a good value even though it's not directly on the beach. You'll pass it if you're coming from the lanchas from La Avellana; from the beach side, make a left at the first alley after Calle Principal.

On the same inland street, **Restaurant Neptune** garners rave reviews and though it's not the cheapest, it's worth a splash out. There are many simple seafood restaurants on Calle Principal, the one real road in

Monterrico. *El Divino Maestro* on the left as you head away from the beach is a good choice; try their seafood stew for US$3.25.

Getting There & Away

There are two ways to get to Monterrico. First, you can take a bus to Iztapa (four hours from Guatemala City, one hour from Escuintla), catch a lancha across the canal to Pueblo Viejo and switch to another bus for the one-hour ride to Monterrico (US$0.65). This takes longer than the alternative, but it's a pretty journey that allows you to downshift and experience local life at a sane pace.

The second option is getting to La Avellana, from where lanchas and car ferries depart for Monterrico. Direct buses operate between Guatemala City and La Avellana about 10 times daily (US$1.50, four hours, 124km), and hourly between La Avellana and Guatemala City from 4 am to 4:30 pm. Or, change buses at Taxisco, on CA-2 – buses operate hourly between Guatemala City and Taxisco (US$1.65, 3½ hours, 106km) and hourly between Taxisco and La Avellana (US$0.40, 20 minutes, 18km).

Shuttle buses also serve La Avellana. You can take a shuttle bus roundtrip from Antigua, coming on one day and returning the next, for US$25, or one-way for US$12. From Antigua it's a 2½ hour trip. The Adventure Travel Center in Antigua (see the Antigua chapter) comes over every Saturday and returns every Sunday; other shuttle services also make the trip. Shuttle services depart from La Avellana for Antigua at 2:30 pm on Saturdays and Sundays (US$10). If you need to know in advance, phone the Hotel Baule Beach (see above) in Monterrico to check the current schedule for buses and shuttles. During the week, a shuttle to Antigua costs US$15 per person, with a minimum of two people.

From La Avellana, catch a passenger boat or car ferry to Monterrico. The *colectivo* passenger boats charge US$0.35 per passenger for the half-hour trip along the Canal de Chiquimulilla, a long mangrove canal. They start at 4:30 am and run every half hour.

For those wishing to check out the Biotopo Monterrico-Hawaii, there is a new road between Monterrico and the Biotopo, with one bus a day shuttling between the two places.

AROUND MONTERRICO

Surfers found in this part of Guatemala will likely be heading to or from La Libertad in El Salvador. To make this trip, you'll have to change buses and may find yourself spending the night in the friendly cowboy town of **Chiquimullila**. There isn't much going on here, but it's a decent enough place to take care of errands and regroup.

All the buses congregate in a central area of town just off the plaza. Nearby, you'll find a Banrural, Bancafé and Banco G&T. The family-run *Hotel San Juan de Letrán* (☎ 885-0831), on the corner of 2a Avenida and 2a Calle, is a clean place offering good value. Fair-sized rooms with fan and private bath are US$4/7/9. There are also less attractive rooms with shared bath. There are nice plantings, drinking water and parking for guests. The cafeteria attached serves some of the iciest drinks in Guatemala, which are very welcome in this sweltering heat, and big plates of tasty food for cheap. Around the corner is the *Pensión Galicia*, which has dark and basic rooms with shared bath for US$2.60 per person.

Most people shoot straight through Escuintla and Taxisco to Chiquimulilla and on to the Salvadoran border at La Hachadura. This route will take you along the coast of El Salvador for about 110km before it arrives in La Libertad. Buses between Taxisco and Chiquimulilla depart every hour for the 30-minute journey and hourly from Chiquimullila to the border (US$1.30, 45 minutes); the last bus leaves for the border at 6 pm.

There are two serviceable hospedajes in La Hachadura. The other option for getting to El Salvador is to turn north from Chiquimullila and take local buses through Cuilapa and across the border at Las Chinamas, traveling inland before veering south to La Libertad.

LAGO DE AMATITLÁN

A placid lake backed by a looming volcano and situated a mere 25km south of Guatemala City – that's Amatitlán. It should be a pretty and peaceful resort, but unfortunately it's not. The hourglass-shaped lake is divided by a railway line, and the lakeshore is lined with industry along some parts. On weekends, people from Guatemala City come to row boats on the lake (its waters are too polluted for swimming) or to rent a private hot tub for a dip. Many people from the capital own second homes here.

There's little reason for you to spend time here. If you really want to have a look, head for the town of Amatitlán, just off the main Escuintla-Guatemala City highway. Amatitlán has a scruffy public beach area. If you have a car and some spare time, a drive around the lake offers some pretty scenery. Perhaps the lake will one day be restored to its naturally beautiful state.

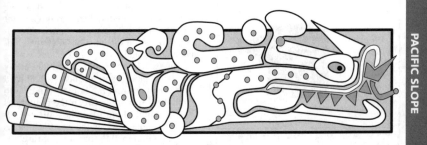

Central & Eastern Guatemala

North and east of Guatemala City is a land of varied topography, from the misty, pine-covered mountains of Alta Verapaz to the hot, dry-tropic climate of the Río Motagua valley. The Carretera al Atlántico (CA-9) climbs northeast out of the capital before descending from the relative cool of the mountains to the dry heat of a valley where dinosaurs once roamed.

Along this highway are many interesting destinations, including the beautiful high-

Highlights

- Experiencing the natural wonders of Semuc Champey and the caves at Lanquín

- Visiting one of the most important Mayan sites at Copán in Honduras

- Kicking back in the Garífuna town of Lívingston on Guatemala's Caribbean coast or in the riverside town of Río Dulce

- Exploring a rarely visited, protected area such as Parque Nacional Laguna Lachuá or the Bocas de Polochic wetlands

- Hitting an off-the-beaten-track route from Cobán to El Petén or from Cobán to Huehuetenango

land scenery around Cobán; the paleontology museum at Estanzuela; the great basilica at Esquipulas, famous throughout Central America; the first-rate Mayan ruins at Copán, just across the border in Honduras; the marvelous Mayan stelae and zoomorphs at Quiriguá; and the tropical lake of Izabal and jungle waterway of Río Dulce. The Carretera al Atlántico ends at Puerto Barrios, Guatemala's derelict Caribbean port, from which you can take a boat to Lívingston, a laid-back hideaway peopled by the Garífuna.

In the time before the Spanish conquest, the mountainous highland regions of the departments of Baja Verapaz and Alta Verapaz were populated by the Rabinal Maya, noted for their warlike habits and merciless victories. They battled the powerful Quiché Maya for a century but were never conquered.

When the conquistadors arrived, they too had trouble defeating the Rabinals. It was Fray Bartolomé de Las Casas who convinced the Spanish authorities to try peace where war had failed. Armed with an edict that forbade Spanish soldiers from entering the region for five years, the friar and his brethren pursued their religious mission and succeeded in pacifying and converting the Rabinals. Their homeland was renamed Verapaz (True Peace) and is now divided into Baja Verapaz, with its capital at Salamá, and Alta Verapaz, centered on Cobán. The Rabinal have remained among the most dedicated and true to the ancient customs, and there are many intriguing villages to visit in this part of Guatemala, including Rabinal itself.

The two departmental capitals are easily accessible along a smooth, fast, asphalt road that winds up from the hot, dry valley into wonderful scenery between the mountains and through long stretches of coffee-growing country. Along the way to Cobán is one of Guatemala's premier nature reserves, the Biotopo del Quetzal. Beyond

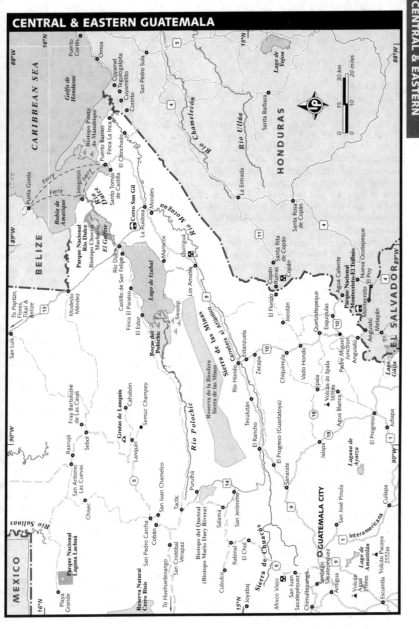

CENTRAL & EASTERN GUATEMALA

Cobán, along rough unpaved roads, are the country's most famous caverns. Still farther afield, on roads left to the whims of nature, are little-used routes to the Petén and other favorite haunts of adventurous types.

SALAMÁ

• pop 11,000 • elevation 940m

Highway 17, also marked CA-14, leaves the Carretera al Atlántico at El Rancho, 84km from Guatemala City. It heads west through a dry, desert-like lowland area, then turns north and starts climbing up into the forested hills. After 47km you come to the turnoff for Salamá. Descending the other side of the ridge, the road winds down into the broad valley of the Río Salamá, and enters the capital of the department of Baja Verapaz, 17km from the Carretera.

Services here of interest to travelers are grouped around or near the plaza. The Bancafé across from the church changes cash and traveler's checks at a poor rate and gives cash advances on Visa cards; it's open Monday to Friday, from 9 am to 5 pm, and Saturday, from 9 am to 1 pm. The Banrural on the plaza may offer better rates. The Telgua telephone office is across the street from the Hotel Tezulutlán (see Places to Stay & Eat) and there is a police station on the corner of 5a Calle and 9a Avenida, Zona 1.

EcoVerapaz (☎/fax 940-0294), 8a Avenida 4-77, Zona 1, has local, trained naturalists offering a variety of interesting tours throughout Baja Verapaz. Caving, birding, hiking, horseback riding and orchid trips are among their specialties. They have English-speaking guides. One-day tours start at US$25 per person for a group of ten or more; US$40 per person for a group half that size.

Things to See & Do

Salamá is an attractive town with some reminders of colonial rule. The main plaza boasts an ornate colonial **church** with gold encrusted altars and a carved pulpit, one of only two in Latin America (the other is in Lima, Peru). Look for it to the left before the altar. Be sure to check out Jesus lying in a glass coffin with cotton bunting in his stig-

mata and droplets of blood seeping from his hairline. His thick mascara and the silver lamé pillow where he rests his head complete the scene. Mass is still held here.

The Salamá **market** is impressive for its colorful, local bustle, particularly on Sunday.

Places to Stay & Eat

Should you want to stay the night, *Hospedaje Juárez* (☎ 940-0055, 10a Avenida 5-55, Zona 1), in the block directly behind the church, is a good, clean, safe and friendly place to stay. All 15 rooms have private hot bath and cost US$5.15 per person. There's no sign out front. The same family runs a cheaper place with the same name on the corner of 5a Calle, just down the block. Rooms here with shared bath are US$3.90 per person.

The *Hotel Tezulutlán* (☎ /fax 940-0141), just off the main square behind the Texaco fuel station, has 15 rooms arranged around a nice garden courtyard. All have cable TV and private bath (four rooms have hot water); they cost US$11/14/17 a single/double/triple. There are also two rooms with shared bath that cost US$6.45 for two people. Next door, the *Restaurant Happy Ranch* does entire roasted chickens for US$3.25. Across the street, *Hotel San Ignacio* (☎ 940-0186) is a clean family-run place where singles/doubles are US$4/5 with shared bath, US$5/8 with private cold bath; the *Cafetería Apolo XI* is in the same building.

The new *Hotel Real Legendario* (☎ 940-0187, 8a Avenida 3-57, Zona 1) offers decent value. Their clean, secure singles/doubles/triples with private hot bath and cable TV cost US$9/14/18. Travelers with children may want to check out the *Turicentro Las Orquídeas* (☎ 940-0142, Carretera a Salamá Km 147). Here, they have rooms flanking a restaurant, pool and open spaces hung with hammocks.

Parking is available at all of the above places to stay.

Near the plaza there are many places to eat. A few doors from the plaza, *Cafe Deli-Donas* is a popular, hospitable café serving light meals, sweets and Salamá's best coffee;

it's open every day. Nearby, the *Cafetería Central* has savory, filling lunches for US$3.25. At the *Restaurante El Ganadero*, a half-block off the plaza on the road out of town, a lunch might cost US$4 to US$6, a sandwich much less. On the plaza, *Pollo to Go* serves burgers and chicken in clean and friendly surroundings; you can take out or eat in. Nearby, *Restaurante Caña Vieja* is also an option.

Getting There & Away

As this is a departmental capital, there are frequent buses to and from Guatemala City, arriving and departing from in front of the Municipalidad. Buses bound for Guatemala City depart hourly between 3 am and 4 pm (US$2, three hours, 151km). Arrive early for a seat. Buses coming from Guatemala City continue west from Salamá to Rabinal (US$1, one hour, 19km) and then 15km farther along to Cubulco. Buses for San Jerónimo leave from in front of the church every half hour from 6 am to 4 pm (US$0.25, 20 minutes).

In Guatemala City, buses to Salamá depart hourly, 5 am to 5 pm, from the office of Transportes Unidos Baja Verapacenses (☎ 253-4618), 17a Calle 11-32, Zona 1.

AROUND SALAMÁ

Ten kilometers along the road to Salamá from the Cobán highway, you come to the turnoff for **San Jerónimo**, which is 5km north of Hwy 5. Behind the town's beautiful church is an old sugar mill now used as a museum displaying a decent collection of artifacts and photographs, though none of the former are labeled; admission is free. The grounds here are immaculate and there's a playground to keep the kids out of trouble. On the plaza are some large stones that were carved in ancient times.

About a five minute walk from the town center are Los Arcos, a series of 124 arches from the 17th century in various states of decay that formed a sophisticated aqueduct system that powered the sugar mill. To get there, take the main road heading east (away from Salamá) and bear right and slightly downhill, where you'll see a sign saying

Coffee is grown near Salamá.

'Barrio El Cavalario.' Keep an eye to your right along this road and you'll start to see the arches. A second set of arches can be seen by going right at the second dirt alley on this road. If you continue straight ahead for about 50m, rather than going right, you'll see more arches through gaps in the trees. Continue straight on this road to reach Finca San Lorenzo, a coffee farm open to the public. The last bus of the day returning to Salamá leaves at 4 pm.

Nine kilometers west of Salamá along Hwy 5 is the village of **San Miguel Chicaj**, known for its weaving and for its traditional fiesta from September 25 to 29. Continue along the same road for another 10km to reach the colonial town of **Rabinal**, founded in 1537 by Fray Bartolomé de Las Casas as a base for his proselytizing. Rabinal has gained fame as a pottery-making center (look especially for the hand-painted chocolate cups), and for its citrus fruit harvest (November and December). Rabinal is also known for its adherence to pre-Columbian traditions, folklore and dance. If you can make it here for the annual fiesta of Saint Peter, between January 19 and 25 (with things reaching a fevered pitch on January 21), or Corpus Cristi, do so. Market day here is Sunday. Two small hotels, the *Pensión Motagua* and the *Hospedaje Caballeros*, can put you up.

It's possible to continue on from Rabinal another 15km to the village of **Cubulco**. Or, from Rabinal you can follow Hwy 5 all the way to Guatemala City, a trip of about 100km on which you pass through several small villages. It's best to traverse this remote stretch only with a 4WD vehicle. Buses do ply this route, albeit very slowly. Along the way you could visit the ruins of Mixco Viejo near **San Juan Sacatepéquez**, about 25km from Guatemala City.

Mixco Viejo, dated to the Late Classic Period (estimates range from the 12th to 13th century), was the active capital of the Pocoman Maya when the Spaniards came and crashed the party. The location of this ceremonial and military center is awesome, wedged between deep ravines, with just one way in and one way out. To further fortify the site, the Pocoman built impressive rock walls around the city. It took Pedro de Alvarado and his troops more than a month of concerted attacks to conquer Mixco Viejo. When they finally succeeded, they furiously laid waste to this city, which scholars believe supported close to 10,000 people at its height. There are several temples and two ball courts here. Self-sufficient campers can overnight here for free.

It's difficult to reach this site by public transportation. By car, take Highway 5 north from Guatemala City, through San Juan Sacatepéquez to the village of Montúfar. Just after crossing the bridge spanning the Pixcayá River, you'll come to the ruins.

BIOTOPO DEL QUETZAL

Along the main highway (CA-14), 34km beyond the turnoff for Salamá, you reach the Biotopo Mario Dary Rivera nature reserve, commonly called the Biotopo del Quetzal, at Km 161, just east of the village of Purulhá (no services). The ride is sobering: Entire hillsides are deforested and covered in huge sheets of black plastic meant to optimize the growing conditions for cultivating *xate*. This green fern, exported for use in floral arrangements, is traditionally harvested from the jungles of the Petén, a laborious and ecologically finite undertaking. Though xaté is still taken from the jungle, commercial growers have discovered they can simulate the Petén's growing conditions here, in the traditional stomping grounds of the quetzal.

If you stop here intent on seeing a quetzal, odds are you'll be disappointed – the birds are rare and elusive and their habitat is all but destroyed. You have the best chance of seeing them from February to September. If you're really intent on seeing Guatemala's national bird in the wild, head to the Proyecto EcoQuetzal in Cobán (see Organized Tours in the Cobán section later in this chapter).

Though your chances of seeing a quetzal are slim to none, it's still well worth a visit to explore and enjoy this lush high-altitude cloud forest ecosystem that is the quetzal's natural habitat.

Trail guide maps in English and Spanish may be purchased for US$0.50 at the visitors' center. They contain a checklist of 87 birds commonly seen here. Other animals

The quetzal

include spider monkeys and *tigrillos*, which are similar to ocelots. Good luck spotting either of these.

Two excellent, well-maintained nature trails wind through the reserve: the 1800m Sendero los Helechos (Fern Trail) and the Sendero los Musgos (Moss Trail), which is twice as long. As you wander through the dense growth, treading on the rich, dense, spongy humus and leaf-mold, you'll see many varieties of epiphytes (air plants), which thrive in the Biotopo's humid jungle atmosphere.

Both trails pass by waterfalls, most of which cascade into small pools where you can take a dip; innumerable streams have their headwaters here, and the Río Colorado pours through the forest along a geological fault. Deep in the forest is Xiu Ua Li Che (Grandfather Tree), some 450 years old, which was alive when the conquistadors fought the Rabinals in these mountains.

The reserve is open every day from 6 am to 4 pm (you must be in by 4 pm, but you can stay longer); admission is US$5. There's a visitors' center, and drinks (but no food) are available at the site.

Camping, once permitted here, is no longer allowed, though this may have changed by the time you read this, so it couldn't hurt to check.

There are two lodging places within a short distance of the reserve. Just beyond it, another 200m up the hill toward Purulhá and Cobán, is the *Hotel y Comedor Ranchito del Quetzal* (☎ 953-9235, 331-3579 in *Guatemala City*), a rustic hospedaje. Simple rooms with shared bath are US$6/7/9 a single/double/triple; rooms with private hot bath are US$8/9/13. Reasonably priced meals are served, and there are vegetarian options.

The more comfortable *Posada Montaña del Quetzal* (☎ 208-5958, 335-1805 in *Guatemala City, Carretera a Cobán Km 156.5), Purulhá, Baja Verapaz*, is 5km back along the road toward the Carretera al Atlántico. This attractive hostelry has 18 white stucco, tile-roofed bungalows, each with a sitting room and fireplace, a bedroom with three beds and a private hot bath, for US$20/34/42/50 a single/double/triple/quad; larger two-bedroom bungalows are US$30/43/51/60. The complex has a restaurant, a large swimming pool and a smaller children's pool. You can usually catch a shuttle between the Biotopo and the posada, or hitch a ride.

A half-kilometer before the Biotopo proper, at CA-14 Km 160.5, is the recommended *Biotopín Restaurant*, with decent meals at good prices.

COBÁN
• pop 20,000 • elevation 1320m

The asphalt road between the Biotopo and Cobán is good, smooth and fast, though curvy, with light traffic. Ascending into the evergreen forests, tropical flowers are still visible here and there. As you enter Cobán, a sign says 'Bienvenidos a Cobán, Ciudad Imperial,' referring to the city charter granted in 1538 by Emperor Charles V.

The town now called Cobán was once the center of Tezulutlán (Tierra de Guerra in Spanish, the Land of War), a stronghold of the Rabinal Maya.

In the 19th century, when German immigrants moved in and founded vast coffee and cardamom fincas, Cobán took on the aspect of a German mountain town as the finca owners built town residences. The era of German cultural and economic domination ended during WWII, when the US prevailed upon the Guatemalan government to deport the powerful finca owners, many of whom actively supported the Nazis.

Today, Cobán is an interesting town to visit, though dreary weather can color your opinion of the place. Most of the year it is either rainy or overcast, dank and chill. You can count on sunny days in Cobán for only about three weeks in April. In the midst of the 'dry' season (January to March) it can be misty and sometimes rainy, or bright and sunny with marvelous clear mountain air – it's kind of hit-or-miss.

Guatemala's most impressive festival of Indian traditions, the folkloric festival of Rabin Ajau with its traditional dance of the Paabanc, takes place in the latter part of

COBÁN

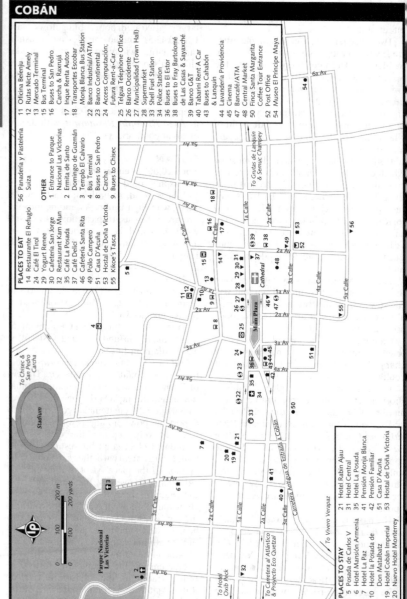

PLACES TO EAT
14 Restaurante El Refugio
24 Café El Tirol
29 Yogurt Renee
30 Cafetería San Jorge
32 Restaurant Kam Mun
35 Café La Posada
37 Café Delici
46 Cafetería Santa Rita
49 Pollo Campero
51 Casa D'Acuña
53 Hostal de Doña Victoria
55 Kikoe's Tasca
56 Panadería y Pastelería Suiza

OTHER
1 Entrance to Parque Nacional Las Victorias
2 Ermita de Santo Domingo de Guzmán
3 Templo El Calvario
4 Bus Terminal
8 Buses to San Pedro Carcha
9 Buses to Chisec
11 Oficina Belenju
12 Rutas Nicte Amely
13 Mercado Terminal
15 Bus Terminal
16 Buses to San Pedro Carcha & Raxrujá
17 Inque Renta Autos
18 Transportes Escobar Monja Blanca Bus Station
22 Banco Industrial/ATM
23 Banco Continental
24 Access Computación; Futura Rent-a-car
25 Telgua Telephone Office
26 Banco Occidente
27 Municipalidad (Town Hall)
28 Supermarket
33 Shell Fuel Station
34 Police Station
36 Buses to El Estor
38 Buses to Fray Bartolomé de Las Casas & Sayaxché
39 Banco G&T
40 Tabarini Rent A Car
43 Buses to Cahabón & Lanquín
44 Lavandería Providencia
45 Cinema
47 Bancafé/ATM
48 Central Market
50 Finca Santa Margarita Coffee Tour Entrance
52 Post Office
54 Museo El Príncipe Maya

PLACES TO STAY
5 Posada de Carlos V
6 Hotel Mansión Armenia
7 Hotel La Paz
10 Hotel la Posada de Don Matalbatz
19 Hotel Cobán Imperial
20 Nuevo Hotel Monterrey
21 Hotel Rabin Ajau
31 Hotel Central
35 Hotel La Posada
41 Pensión Monja Blanca
42 Pensión Familiar
51 Casa D'Acuña
53 Hostal de Doña Victoria

July or in the first week of August. The national orchid show is hosted here every December.

There is not a lot to do in Cobán itself except enjoy the local color and mountain scenery, but the town is a good base for several side trips, including to the nearby Grutas de Lanquín and Cuevas Semuc Champey (see Around Cobán).

Orientation & Information

The main plaza (el parque) features a disconcertingly modern and relatively ugly concrete bandstand. Most of the services you'll need are within a few blocks of the plaza and the cathedral. The shopping district is around and behind the cathedral, and you'll smell the savory cardamom, which vendors come from the mountains to sell, before you see it.

The heart of Cobán is built on a rise, so unless what you're looking for is in the dead center, be ready to walk uphill and down.

Though there's no tourist office here (a shame for such a happening area), the Casa D'Acuña or the Hostal de Doña Victoria (see Places to Stay) can give you loads of information.

The post office is a block from the plaza on the corner of 2a Avenida and 3a Calle. The Telgua telephone office is on the plaza.

At last check, Access Computación (☎ 951-4040, ✉ intercafe@c.net.gt), 1a Calle 3-13, was the only business offering email services in Cobán; it's expensive at US$7.75 an hour, but it's the only game in town. It's in the same complex as the Café El Tirol (see Places to Eat) and is open Monday to Friday from 8 am to noon and 2 to 7 pm, and Saturday from 10 am to noon and 3 to 5 pm.

Banco Occidente, on the plaza, changes US dollars cash and traveler's checks and gives cash advances on Visa cards. Banco G&T, behind the cathedral, also changes money and gives cash advances on Master-Card. Banco Industrial, on 1a Calle, changes money and has a Visa ATM. Bancafé, 1a Avenida 2-66, also has a Visa ATM.

Laundry service is available from Lavandería Providencia on the plaza or from the Casa D'Acuña; the former is a slightly better deal.

Templo El Calvario

You can get a fine view over the town from the Templo El Calvario, a church atop a long flight of stairs at the north end of 7a Avenida. Indigenous people leave offerings at outdoor shrines and crosses in front of the church. You can walk around behind the church to enter the Parque Nacional Las Victorias, though this is not the park's main entrance.

The Ermita de Santo Domingo de Guzmán, a chapel dedicated to Cobán's patron saint, is 150m west of the bottom of the stairs leading to El Calvario.

Cardamom

The world's coffee drinkers know that high-quality coffee is important to Guatemala's export trade, but few know that Guatemala is the world's largest exporter of cardamom. In Alta Verapaz, cardamom is more important to the local economy than coffee, providing livelihood for some 200,000 people. Cardamom (Elettaria cardamomum), a herbaceous perennial of the ginger family native to the Malabar Coast of India, was brought to Alta Verapaz by German coffee-finca owners.

The plants grow to a height of between 1½m and 6m and have coarse leaves up to 76cm long that are hairy on the underside. The flowers are white, and the fruit is a green, three-sided oval capsule holding 15 to 20 dark, hard, reddish-brown to brownish-black seeds. Though the cardamom plant grows readily, it is difficult to cultivate, pick and sort the best grades, so fragrant cardamom commands a high price. That does not seem to bother the people of Saudi Arabia and the Arabian Gulf states, who purchase more than 80% of the world supply. They pulverize the seeds and add the powder to the thick, syrupy, pungent coffee that is a social and personal necessity in that part of the world.

Parque Nacional Las Victorias

This forested 82-hectare national park, right in town, has ponds, BBQ, picnic areas, children's play areas, a lookout point, camping (US$1.30) and kilometers of trails. It's open every day from 8 am to 4:30 pm; admission is US$0.80. The entrance is at 11a Avenida and 3a Calle, Zona 1.

Vivero Verapaz

Orchid lovers mustn't miss a chance to see the many thousands of species at this famous nursery (☎ 952-1133). The rare *monja blanca*, or white nun orchid, Guatemala's national flower, can be seen here; there are also hundreds of species of miniature orchids, so small that you'll need the magnifying glass they will loan you to see them. For US$0.65, the owners will take you on a tour to see all the species. The national orchid show is held here each December, and by all accounts, it's spectacular. Otherwise, try to visit between October and February when many flowers are in bloom.

Vivero Verapaz is on the Carretera Antigua de Entrada a Cobán, about 2km from the center of town. It's a 20-minute walk southwest from the plaza on this road, which is thick with traffic, or you can hire a taxi for around US$1.50. It's open Monday to Saturday, 9 am to noon and 2 to 5 pm.

Finca Santa Margarita

Finca Santa Margarita (☎ 952-1286, 952-1454), 3a Calle 4-12, Zona 2, is a working coffee farm offering stellar guided tours of their operation. From propagation and planting to roasting and exporting, the 45-minute tour will tell you all you ever wanted to know about these powerful beans. At tour's end, you're treated to a cup of coffee and can purchase beans in light, medium or dark varieties straight from the roaster (US$2 to US$4 a pound). Tours are available Monday to Friday, from 8 am to 12:30 and 1:30 to 5 pm and Saturday, from 8 am to noon; admission is US$2 per person, and the talented guide speaks English and Spanish.

Museo El Príncipe Maya

The Museo El Príncipe Maya (☎ 952-1541), 6a Avenida 4-26, Zona 3, is a private museum featuring a collection of pre-Columbian artifacts, with an emphasis on jewelry, other body adornments and pottery. The displays are well designed and maintained; the museum is open Monday to Saturday, from 9 am to 6 pm; admission is US$1.30.

Language Courses

There are two schools offering Spanish instruction in Cobán. The Muq'b'ilb'e School (☎ 951-2459), 6a Avenida 5-39, Zona 3, is run by Oscar Macz and is well recommended by Peace Corp volunteers and other former students for Spanish and Q'eqchi' instruction. There is also the Instituto Internacional Cobán (INCO, ☎/fax 951-3113), 6a Avenida 3-03, Apdo 22, Zona 1, for Spanish classes.

Organized Tours

Aventuras Turísticas (☎ 951-4213, ☎/fax 951-4214), 3a Calle 2-38, Zona 3, in the Hostal de Doña Victoria, leads tours to Laguna Lachuá, the recently discovered caves of Rey

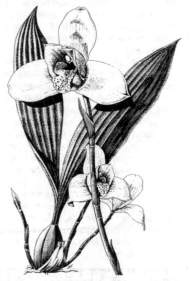

White nun orchid

Marco and Candelaria, Semuc Champey and Lanquín, Tikal, Ceibal and anywhere else you may want to go, as they will customize itineraries. They employ French, English and Spanish-speaking guides.

The Casa D'Acuña (☎ 951-0482, 951-0484, fax 952-1547, @ uisa@infovia.com.gt), 4a Calle 3-11, Zona 2, offers it's own tours to Semuc Champey, the Grutas de Lanquín and other places farther afield.

The folks at Access Computación (see Information earlier in this section) offer day trips and overnight camping excursions to the Río Sachicha and the beautiful lagoon and waterfalls there. The trips are not cheap (US$20 each for a day trip; US$27 for camping), but the river runs through private land and therefore is inaccessible to independent travelers. They lead cave tours and trips to El Salto waterfall as well.

Proyecto EcoQuetzal (☎/fax 952-1047, @ bidaspeq@guate.net, www.granjaguar .com/peq), 2a Calle 14-36, Zona 1, is an innovative project offering ethnotourism trips in which participants hike to nearby villages nestled in the cloud forest and stay with a Q'eqchi' Maya family. To maximize the experience, travelers are encouraged to learn some Q'eqchi' words and stay with their host family for at least two days. For around US$11 a day, you'll receive three meals, lodging and guided hikes to interesting spots. The men of the family are the guides, providing them an alternative, sustainable way to make a living. When given a month's notice, this outfit also offers quetzal-viewing platforms; contact their office for full details.

Reservations are required at least one day in advance. The Proyecto also rents boots, sleeping bags and binoculars at reasonable prices, so you need not worry if you haven't come prepared for such a rugged experience. Their office is open weekdays, from 8:30 am to 1 pm and 2 to 5:30 pm. Participants should speak at least a little Spanish.

Places to Stay

There's camping in town at the Parque Nacional Las Victorias (see previous page).

Water and toilets are available, but no showers. When choosing a room in Cobán, you may want to ensure the showers have hot water because it can be cold in these parts.

Casa D'Acuña (☎ 951-0482, 951-0484, fax 952-1547, @ uisa@infovia.com.gt, 4a Calle 3-11, Zona 2), down a steep hill from the plaza, is a clean, very comfortable European-style hostel. Cost is US$4.50 per bunk, in rooms with two or four beds and shared bath with an incredible hot shower. They have one private double with shared bath for US$9. Also here is a good restaurant, a sitting room, gift shop, laundry service and reasonably priced local tours.

One of the cheapest places in town is the *Pensión Familiar*, at the intersection of 2a Calle and the Carretera de Entrada a Cobán. Basic rooms with saggy beds are US$2.60 per person. The only thing distinguishing it from the other super cheapies are the two caged, often riled toucans at the entrance.

The *Hotel Cobán Imperial* (☎ 952-1131, 6a Avenida 1-12, Zona 1) is 250m from the plaza. It's old but clean, popular with Guatemalan families and has parking in the courtyard. Singles/doubles/triples are US$6/9/13 with private bath. The adjoining *Nuevo Hotel Monterrey* has singles/doubles with shared bath for US$3/4 and singles/doubles with private bath for US$4/6.

Hotel La Paz (☎ 952-1358, 6a Avenida 2-19, Zona 1), 1½ blocks north of the plaza, is cheerful, clean and an excellent deal for the price: Singles/doubles are US$4/7 with shared bath, US$5/9 with private bath. It has many flowers, parking in the courtyard, and a good cafeteria next door. They claim to have hot water.

The old-fashioned *Hotel Rabin Ajau* (☎ 951-4796, fax 951-0808, 1a Calle 5-37, Zona 1) is well located and fairly plain; its disco is noisy. There's a restaurant and parking. Rooms with private bath are US$12/16/20 a single/double/triple. You can rent a TV with cable for US$2.60 per night.

The *Hotel Central* (☎ 952-1118, ☎/fax 951-1442, 1a Calle 1-79, Zona 1) is tidy, with rooms arranged around a flowered courtyard. Singles/doubles/triples are US$7/13/18 without televisions, US$10/15/21 for those with. The Cafetería San Jorge is also here.

Hotel Mansión Armenia (☎ 951-4284, 951-0978, 7a Avenida 2-18, Zona 1), one block from Templo El Calvario, is a comfortable place, clean, quiet and modern, with courtyard parking and a cafeteria. Rooms with private bath and cable TV are US$11/20/28 a single/double/triple. The **Posada de Carlos V** (☎ 952-3502, fax 951-3501, 1a Avenida 3-44, Zona 1) has singles/doubles/triples with private hot bath and cable TV for US$11/20/28. There's parking and a restaurant here.

Hotel Oxib Peck (☎ 951-3224, fax 952-1039, 1a Calle 12-11, Zona 1) is 12 blocks (750m) west of the plaza on the road out of town. The rooms are clean and presentable, and there's a dining room, laundry service and parking. Singles/doubles/triples with private bath and cable TV are US$15/22/29.

Conveniently located for odd-hour bus travel is **Hotel la Posada de Don Matalbatz** (☎ /fax 951-0811, 3a Calle 1-46, Zona 1). This friendly place has a selection of rooms, including big, clean units facing a pretty courtyard and with private hot bath and cable TV for US$8.40 per person. Some are mildewy, so sniff a few out first. Upstairs, the attic room has the most light and character and sleeps five. Rooms with clean, shared bath and little balconies are US$6.20 per person. There's a restaurant, parking and pool table here, and you can make international calls.

The **Pensión Monja Blanca** (☎ 952-1712, 951-0531, fax 951-0533, 2a Calle 6-30, Zona 2) is peaceful despite its location on busy 2a Calle. After walking through two courtyards, you come to a lush garden packed with fruit and hibiscus trees around which the rooms are arranged. Each spotless room, furnished with two good quality single beds, has the light switches on the outside – no hanky panky will be tolerated by the strict señora running the place. Rooms with private hot bath are US$9 per person, those without are US$5.15. This is a good place for solo women travelers.

Hostal de Doña Victoria (☎ 951-4213/4, 3a Calle 2-38, Zona 3) is in a restored

mansion more than 400 years old. Comfortable rooms with private bath surround a central courtyard with plants and a restaurant/bar. Prices are US$17/24/30/33 for one to four people.

Best in town is the **Hotel La Posada** (☎ 952-1495, 951-0588, 1a Calle 4-12, Zona 2), just off the plaza in the very center of town. Colonial in style, its colonnaded porches are dripping with tropical flowers and furnished with easy chairs and hammocks from which to enjoy the mountain views. The rooms have nice old furniture, fireplaces and wall hangings of local weaving; they rent for US$23/29/34 a single/double/triple with private bath.

The **Park Hotel** (☎ 951-3388), in Santa Cruz Verapaz at Km 196.5, 14km from Cobán on the highway to Guatemala City, has modern little bungalows and a restaurant set amid tropical forest and grassy grounds. The 54 regular rooms in prefab duplex bungalows cost US$16/25/33 a single/double/triple. The suites are more attractive, with living room, fireplace and cable TV; these are US$37/43 a single/double. This hotel was for sale at the time of writing.

The **Vivero Verapaz** (☎ 952-1133) orchid nursery also has three fully equipped cabañas for rent. The nice, quiet cabañas for one or two people are US$23 on weekdays or US$45 for an entire weekend.

Places to Eat

Most of Cobán's hotels have their own restaurants. The one at the **Casa D'Acuña** is one of the best in town, with authentic Italian and other European-style dishes served in an attractive setting. Dinners start at around US$5; save some room and budget for dessert. They open at 7 am for breakfast. The restaurant at the **Hostal de Doña Victoria** is also a good bet.

The small, friendly **Café Delicí**, on the corner of 1a Calle and 2a Avenida, just behind the cathedral, serves awesome coffee, espresso and other java drinks. Try some pastries or the wholesome lunch of the day (US$1.30).

Café El Tirol, near the Hotel La Posada, advertises 'the best coffee' (try the specials) and several types of hot chocolate in four languages. It's a cozy little place in which to enjoy pastries and coffee for US$1 to US$2. Breakfast and light meals are served as well. It's closed on Sunday.

Café La Posada, on the west end of the plaza, has tables on a verandah overlooking the square, and a comfortable sitting room inside with couches, coffee tables and a fireplace. All the usual café fare is served. In the same building, *Hotel La Posada* has a pleasant dining room with good food but slow service.

Cafetería Santa Rita, also facing the main plaza, is small, tidy and popular with locals. Good, simple Guatemalan breakfasts, lunches and dinners go for around US$2.

Cafetería San Jorge, 1a Calle between 1a and 2a Avenidas, near the cathedral, has a varied menu and a dining room with views through large windows. Substantial meat dishes are offered (US$3), along with a variety of sandwiches (US$1 to US$2). Next door, *Yogurt Renee* makes delicious fruit yogurts and ice cream.

Pollo Campero has an outlet across from the post office on 2a Avenida at 2a Calle.

Restaurante El Refugio, at the corner of 2a Avenida and 2a Calle, Zona 4, has rustic wooden decor and a menu with lots of meat dishes (grilled steaks are US$3 to US$8), Mexican dishes and burgers. Steer clear of the turtle soup and any other endangered or threatened species they may be serving.

Almost 500m from the plaza on the road out of town is the *Restaurant Kam Mun (1a Calle 8-12, Zona 2)*. Its Chinese fare, served in a nice, clean atmosphere, costs US$5 to US$8 for a full meal.

Kikoe's Tasca, on the southern part of 2a Avenida near the Casa D'Acuña, is a bar in the Bavarian vein. Cocktails, beer and food are served; it opens at 5 pm daily.

In the evening, *food trucks* (kitchens on wheels) park around the plaza and offer some of the cheapest dining in town. Some serve safe food, others don't.

To satisfy even the most nagging chocolate craving, run, don't walk to *Panadería y Pastelería Suiza (5a Calle 2-96, Zona 3)*, where truffles and other quality chocolates are handmade in-house.

Getting There & Away

Air There is one daily flight from Guatemala City to Cobán at 9:50 am (US$45, 30 minutes). That same plane returns to Guatemala City from Cobán at 10:30 am every day.

Bus The highway connecting Cobán with Guatemala City and the Carretera al Atlántico is the most traveled route between Cobán and the outside world, but there are other off-the-beaten-track options, most of which are graced by buses. Give the phenomenal Cobán to Huehuetenango route a try (for details see the Huehuetenango to Cobán section in the Highlands chapter), or head to El Estor from Cobán. Then there's the classic backdoor route to the Petén from Cobán via Fray Bartolomé de Las Casas and on to Poptún (see the Backdoor Petén Routes section later in this chapter). Always double-check bus departure times for these less frequently served destinations.

Many buses depart from Cobán's new bus terminal, southeast of the stadium. Buses to Guatemala City, Salamá, Lanquín and many other destinations leave from completely different terminals and stops. Bus stops are shown on the Cobán map. From Cobán, buses include:

Biotopo del Quetzal – US$1, one hour, 58km. Any bus heading for Guatemala City will drop you at the entrance to the Biotopo.

Cahabón – US$2, 4½ hours, 85km. Same buses as to Lanquín; there are more than a dozen daily.

Chisec – 1½ hours, 66km. Six buses a day leave from the corner of 1a Avenida and 2a Calle between 6 am and 3 pm. The last bus returns to Cobán from Chisec at 12:30.

El Estor – US$2.30, 7½ hours, 166km. Brenda Mercedes and Valenciana buses depart from the bus terminal 12 times daily; the first departure is at 4 am, the last is at 3 pm. This is the bus to take to Tactic (40 minutes).

Fray Bartolomé de Las Casas – US$2, 5½ hours, 101km. Several buses daily, starting at 5 am. You can catch this bus on 2a Avenida near the Banco G&T.

Guatemala City – US$2.20 to US$3.60, four hours, 213km. Transportes Escobar Monja Blanca (☎ 251-1878), 2a Calle 3-77, Zona 4, has buses leaving for Guatemala City every half hour from 2 to 6 am, then hourly from 6 am to 4 pm.

Lanquín – US$1.15, 2½ hours, 61km. Buses depart at 6 am, noon, 1 and 3 pm from Oficina Belenju on 3a Calle. Return buses depart Lanquín at 5 am, 7 am and 3 pm. Rutas Nicte Amely buses leave at 5:15 am and 12:15 pm (and go all the way to El Estor), returning at 4:30 am and 2 pm. You can catch these buses from 2a Calle, across the street from the Lavandería Providencia.

Playa Grande (Laguna Lachuá) – US$3, four hours, 141km. One daily bus leaves from 2a Avenida near the Banco G&T at 4:30 am. This town is sometimes called Cantabal.

Puerto Barrios – 6½ hours, 335km. Take any bus headed to Guatemala City and change at the El Rancho junction. Do the same to get to Río Dulce, but transfer again at La Ruidosa junction, 169km past El Rancho.

Raxrujá – US$2, five hours, 81km. Daily buses at 4, 6 and 8 am.

Salamá – US$1.15, 1 hour, 57km. Frequent minivans leave from 2a Calle, across the street from the Lavandería Providencia.

San Cristóbal Verapaz – US$0.15, 20 minutes, 19km. Buses run every 30 minutes.

San Pedro Carchá – US$0.10, 20 minutes, 6km. There are buses every 10 minutes, 6 am to 7 pm.

Sayaxché – US$5, seven hours, 184km. One daily departure at 4:40 am leaves from 2a Avenida near the Banco G&T; this route goes via Chisec, but you can also take a different adventure via Sebol and Raxrujá (189km). Take any bus headed for Fray and change at Sebol, or take a direct bus to Raxrujá for this option.

Senahú – US$2, three hours. Buses leave the main terminal at 6:30 and 11:30 am and 2:30 pm.

Tactic – See El Estor.

Uspantán – US$1.30, 4½ hours, 94km. Two buses depart daily at 10 am and noon.

Car Because it is such a good base for exploring the surrounding mountains and cave systems, Cobán now has several places that rent cars.

All of these companies are small and may not have every type of vehicle available at every moment. It's a good idea to reserve one in advance. If you want to go to the Grutas de Lanquín or Semuc Champey,

you'll need a vehicle with 4WD. Rental car companies include:

Futura Rent-a-Car (☎ 952-2059), 1a Calle 3-13, Zona 1, in the same building as the Café El Tirol in the rear right corner of the courtyard

Inque Renta Autos (☎ 952-1994, 952-1172), 3a Avenida 1-18, Zona 4

Ochoch Pec Renta Autos (☎ 951-3474, 951-3214), opposite La Carrita el Viaje at the entrance to town

Tabarini Rent A Car (☎ 952-1504, ☎/fax 951-3282), 7a Avenida 2-27, Zona 1

AROUND COBÁN

Cobán, and indeed all of Alta Verapaz, is becoming a magnet for Guatemalan adventure travel of both the independent and organized variety. Not only are there scores of villages where you can experience traditional Mayan culture in some of its purest extant forms, there are also caves running throughout the department, waterfalls, pristine lagoons and many other natural wonders yet to be discovered. Go find them!

San Cristóbal Verapaz is an interesting Pokomchi Maya village set beside Lake Chicoj, 19km east of Cobán. During Semana Santa (Easter Week), San Cristóbal artists design elaborate *alfombras* (carpets) of colored sawdust and flower petals rivaled only by those in Antigua. In addition, San Cristóbal is home to the Centro Comunitario Educativo Pokomchi (CECEP, ☎ 950-4039, contact ✉ cecep@intco.com.gt), an organization dedicated to preserving traditional and modern ways of Pokomchi life. To this end, CECEP recently inaugurated the Katinamit Museum, featuring art, tools and textiles still in daily use; admission is US$0.65 and includes an introduction and orientation on the Pokomchi. CECEP also offers volunteer and ethnotourism opportunities. If you want to spend the night in San Cristóbal, check out the Pokomchi-owned and operated hotel called the ***Portón Real***.

Tactic is a small town 32km south of Cobán which offers myriad opportunities to experience traditional Mayan culture. On the plaza is the Cooperativa de Tejadores, where women demonstrate weaving techniques and sell their wares. On the outskirts of Tactic, atop the hill called Chi Ixhim, is an altar to the God of Maiz; anyone in town can point the direction. There are a few places to stay over, but none as nice as *Country Delight*, Carretera C-14 Km 166.5, where there are hiking trails, camping facilities, rooms and a restaurant. They can supply information on the area and its attractions. Tactic celebrates the fiesta of the Virgen de la Asunción from August 11 to 16.

Balneario Las Islas

At the town of San Pedro Carcha, 6km east of Cobán on the way to Lanquín, is the Balneario Las Islas, with a river coming down past rocks and into a natural pool great for swimming. It's a five- to 10-minute walk from the bus stop in Carcha; anyone can point the way. Buses operate frequently between Cobán and Carcha; the trip takes 20 minutes.

San Juan Chamelco

About 16km southeast of Cobán is the village of San Juan Chamelco, which features swimming at the Balneario Chio. The church here sits on top of a small rise, providing awesome views of the villages below. The church dates back to the colonial period and may have been the first in Alta Verapaz; paintings inside depict the arrival of the conquistadors. Mass is still held here in both Spanish (Sundays at 5 pm) and Q'eqchi' (Sundays at 7 and 9:30 am).

In Aldea Chajaneb, Jerry Makransky (everyone knows him as 'Don Jerónimo,' *@* sbrizuel@c.net.gt) rents comfortable, simple bungalows for US$25 per person (US$45 per couple) per day, which includes three ample, delicious vegetarian meals fresh from the garden. He also offers many activities, including tours to caves and the mountains and inner tubing on the Río Sotzil. Jerry dotes on his guests, and the atmosphere is friendly.

To get there, take a bus from Cobán to San Juan Chamelco. From there, take a bus or pickup toward Chamil and ask the driver to let you off at Don Jerónimo's. Take the

footpath to the left for 300m, cross the bridge and it's the first house on the right. Alternatively, you can hire a taxi from Cobán for about US$6.

Grutas de Lanquín

If you don't mind bumping over bad roads, the best excursion to make from Cobán is to the caves near Lanquín, a pretty village 61km to the east. If you get this far, make sure you visit Semuc Champey.

The Grutas de Lanquín are a short distance northwest of the town, and extend for several kilometers into the earth. You must first stop at the police station in the Municipalidad (Town Hall) in Lanquín, pay the US$1.30 admission fee and ask them to open the cave for you; there is no attendant at the cave otherwise. The cave has lights, but bring a powerful flashlight anyway. You'll also need shoes with good traction, as it's slippery inside with moisture and bat crap.

Though the first few hundred meters of cavern have been equipped with a walkway and are lit by diesel-powered electric lights, most of this subterranean system is untouched. If you are not an experienced spelunker, you should think twice about wandering too far into the caves; the entire extent has yet to be explored, let alone mapped.

Aside from funky stalactites, these caves are crammed with bats; at sunset, they fly out of the mouth of the cave in formations so dense they obscure the sky. For a dazzling display of navigation skills, sit at the entrance while they exit. The river here gushes from the cave in clean, cool and delicious torrents; search out the hot pockets near the shore.

Camping is permitted near the cave entrance, and you can swim in the river, which has some comfortably hot pockets close to shore. Otherwise, there are a few places to stay at Lanquín. In town, *La Divina Providencia* has simple rooms for about US$2 per person. *El Recreo* (*☎* 952-2160), between the town and the caves, is more attractive and more expensive, with singles/doubles for US$15/20. The new *El Retiro* is a recommended place in town popular with the backpacking set. It has four rooms that all share a bath and cost US$2.60 per person. Meals are available for around US$1.50. The *Comedor Shalom* is also good for a meal.

Semuc Champey

Ten kilometers south of Lanquín, along a rough, bumpy, slow road, is Semuc Champey, famed for a natural wonder: a great limestone bridge 300m long, on top of which is a stepped series of pools of cool, flowing river water good for swimming. The water is from the Río Cahabón, and most of it passes underground, beneath the bridge. Though this bit of paradise is difficult to reach, the beauty of its setting and the perfection of the pools, ranging from turquoise to emerald green, make it all worth it. Many people consider this the most beautiful spot in all Guatemala.

It's possible to camp at Semuc Champey, but be sure to pitch a tent only in the upper areas, as flash floods are common down below. It's risky to leave anything unattended, as it might get stolen. Also, solo travelers may feel uncomfortable in such a secluded spot.

Tours to the Grutas de Lanquín and Semuc Champey, offered in Cobán for around US$35 per person, are the easiest way to visit these places. On your own, if you're driving, you'll need a 4WD vehicle.

Buses operate several times daily between Cobán and Lanquín, continuing to Cahabón. Buses leave Lanquín to return to Cobán at 4:30, 5 and 7 am and 2 and 3 pm. Since the last return bus departs so early, you should probably plan to stay the night. There are occasional buses and trucks from Lanquín to Semuc Champey and your chances of catching one are better in the early morning. Otherwise, it's a long, hot walk unless you have your own vehicle, in which case it's a slow, rugged drive. Admission to the site is US$1.

Parque Nacional Laguna Lachuá

This park is renowned for the perfectly round, pristine turquoise lake (220m deep) for which it was named. Until recently, this Guatemalan gem was rarely visited by travelers because it was an active, violent area during the civil war and the road was in pathetic disrepair. The new road means you can get here from Cobán in four hours by bus. Take a bus from Cobán to Playa Grande (Cantabal) and ask the driver to leave you at the park entrance near the village of San Marcos. From here, it's a 5km walk to the park; admission is US$5, a bunk with mosquito net is US$7 per person and camping space costs US$1.50; overnight visitors can use the cooking facilities, so come prepared with food and drink. You can rent canoes for exploring the lake, and there are hiking trails.

BACKDOOR PETÉN ROUTES

One alternative is to go north to Flores via Sayaxché. Unless you take the one daily direct departure from Cobán (see Getting There & Away, earlier in the Cobán section), getting to Sayaxché from Alta Verapaz involves a few bus changes, and you'll have to break up the journey at least once before you get to Flores. One possibility is to take any bus from Cobán to Fray and alight at the Sebol junction, 5km east of Fray Bartolomé de Las Casas, to connect with a bus (or more likely, a pickup) going north. Or you can take a bus directly from Cobán to Raxrujá and connect with a ride north from there. If you get stuck, Raxrujá, 15km beyond Sebol, has serviceable hotels and places to eat. The *Pensión Guiterrez* has been recommended for its rooms with net, fan and shared bath for US$1.95 per person. There are several daily scheduled departures to both Sayaxché and Cobán from Raxrujá.

The Cobán-to-Poptún-via-Fray Bartolomé de Las Casas route used to be a scratch of dirt road with one truck passing a week, if you were lucky. Nowadays, plenty of buses and pickups ply the decent roads leading north from Cobán, before turning east for Poptún. The route is dotted with traditional Mayan villages where only the patriarchs speak Spanish, and then only a little. This is a great opportunity for getting off the Gringo Trail and into the heart of Guatemala. Do it while you still can!

Fray Bartolomé de Las Casas

This town, often referred to as simply Fray (pronounced fry), is pretty substantial for being in the middle of nowhere, but don't let its size fool you. This is a place where the weekly soccer game is the biggest deal in town, chickens languish in the streets and siesta is taken seriously. Since you can't make it from Cobán to Poptún in one shot, you'll be spending the night here.

The town itself is fairly spread out, with the plaza and most tourist facilities on one end and the market and bus terminus on the other. Walking between the two takes about 10 minutes. Coming from Cobán, you'll want to hop off at the central plaza.

There's a Banrural just off the plaza that changes US dollars and traveler's checks. Nearby is the post office and police station. Stop in at the Municipalidad (also on the plaza) for information on getting to the Las Conchas limestone pools near Chahal, which are rumored to be better than those at Semuc Champey.

The friendly *Hotel y Restaurante Diamelas*, near the plaza, is the best place in town and is often full as a result. Here the five rooms with private bath are US$3.25 per person. The cafetería serves a terrific set lunch. Nearby is the *Hosepdaje Ralios*, but it's not as good, with dark, basic rooms around a neglected courtyard for US$2.35. On the road toward the market is the *Hospedaje Lorena*, which has cells for rooms at the same price. The *Hotel & Restaurant Fontana*, farther down this road, is deceptively attractive. Rooms with fan and private bath are US$3 per person; US$2.35 without. A certain solo female traveler was harassed here, so steer clear if you fall into this category.

Helados Kandy, on the park, has ice cream, and the *Panadería Padre las Casas*, between the park and the market, has fresh breads, pies and pastries at 3 pm daily.

One daily bus departs from the plaza at 3 am for Poptún (US$3.90, five hours, 100km). Don't miss it or you'll be resorting to Plan B! The one daily departure for Sayaxché leaves Fray at 10 am (4½ hours, 117km). Buses for Cobán leave at 5, 6, 8, 10 and 11 am (US$2, 5½ hours, 101km).

RÍO HONDO

Río Hondo lies along CA-9 southeast of Cobán, 42km from El Rancho Junction (126km from Guatemala City). Beyond Chiquimula are turnoffs to Copán, just across the Honduran border; to Esquipulas and on to Nueva Ocotepeque (Honduras); and a remote border crossing between Guatemala and El Salvador at Anguiatú, 12km north of Metapán (El Salvador).

The town of Río Hondo (Deep River) is northeast of the junction, but lodging places hereabouts list their address as Río Hondo, Santa Cruz Río Hondo or Santa Cruz Teculután – it's all the same place. Nine kilometers west of the junction are several attractive motels right on CA-9, which provide a good base for explorations of this region if you have your own vehicle. By car, it's an hour from here to Quiriguá, half an hour to Chiquimula or 1½ hours to Esquipulas.

Another big attraction of Río Hondo is the Valle Dorado aquatic park and tourist center (see the next page).

Note that the Río Hondo motels are looked upon as weekend resorts by locals and residents of Guatemala City, so they may be heavily booked on weekends. They're popular as bases for visits to the area in general, to the Valle Dorado aquatic park in particular, and also in their own right – all of them are modern, pleasant places, with well-equipped bungalows (all have color cable TV and private bath), spacious grounds and good restaurants. All except the Hotel Santa Cruz have giant swimming pools. On weekdays they provide lodging for people who work in the area.

The following four motels are all near one another at Km 126 on the Carretera al Atlántico, 126km from Guatemala City.

Cheapest of the four is the *Hotel Santa Cruz* (☎ 934-7112, ☎/fax 934-7075), where rooms in duplex bungalows are US$9.65 per person with fan, US$12 with air-con. The popular restaurant here is cheaper than some of the others. Four apartments with kitchens are also available.

Hotel El Atlántico (☎ 934-7160, fax 934-7041), Carretera al Atlántico Km 126, is probably the most attractive of the four, with a large swimming pool, spacious grounds and a good restaurant. Large, well-equipped bungalows are US$16/27/32 a single/double/triple. It's also probably the most popular; reservations are wise.

Across the highway, on the north side, the *Hotel Nuevo Pasabién* (☎ /fax 934-7201, 934-7073/74) has large rooms for US$20/34 with air-con, less with fan.

Opposite the Hotel Santa Cruz and behind the 24-hour Shell gas station, *Hotel Longarone* (☎ 934-7126, fax 934-7035) is the old standard in this area. Some rooms are in a long row, others are in duplex bungalows. Simple rooms are US$24/30/36 a single/double/triple, or US$30/36/42 with cable TV and fridge; all have air-con. It has two large swimming pools, two smaller ones for children and a tennis court.

The restaurants at all of these hotels are open every day from around 6 am to 10 pm. Along the highway are various other smaller, cheaper eateries.

Nine kilometers east of these places, right at the junction with CA-10 (the road heading south to Chiquimula and Esquipulas), is the *Hotel Río*, Carretera al Atlántico Km 135. It's very beat-up. Rooms with private bath are US$6/7 with two/three beds.

Valle Dorado (☎ 941-2542, 933-1111, fax 941-2543), on the Carretera al Atlántico at Km 149, 14km past the CA-10 junction and 23km from the other Río Hondo hotels, is an enormous complex that includes an aquatic park with giant pools, waterslides, toboggans and other entertainment. Rooms are US$45 for one to four people, or US$72 for six. Make reservations on weekends, when it fills up with families.

Many people prefer to stay at one of the other Río Hondo hotels and come to Valle Dorado for the day. Day use costs for children/adults are US$5/6, US$4/5 during the week. The park is open for day use every day from 8 am to sunset.

ESTANZUELA
• pop 10,000

Traveling south from Río Hondo along CA-10, you are in the midst of the Río Motagua valley, a hot expanse of what is known as 'dry tropic,' which once supported a great number and variety of dinosaurs. Three kilometers south of the Carretera al Atlántico you'll see a small monument on the right-hand (west) side of the road commemorating the earthquake disaster of February 4, 1976.

Less than 2km south of the earthquake monument is the small town of Estanzuela, with its Museo de Paleontología, Arqueología y Geología Ing Roberto Woolfolk Sarvia, an interesting and startling museum filled with dinosaur bones, some reconstructed and menacing looking. The museum is open every day from 8 am to noon and from 1 to 5 pm; admission is free. To find the museum, go west from the highway directly through the town for 1km, following the small blue signs pointing to the *museo*; anyone you see can help point the way. Next door to the museum is a small shop selling cold drinks and snacks.

Within the museum are most of the bones of three big dinosaurs, including those of a giant ground sloth some 30,000 years old and a prehistoric whale. Other exhibits include early Mayan artifacts.

ZACAPA
• pop 18,000 • elevation 230m

Capital of the department of the same name, Zacapa is several kilometers southeast of highway CA-9 just off of CA-10. It offers little to travelers, though the locals do make cheese, cigars and superb rum. The few hotels in town are basic and will do in an emergency, but better accommodations are available in Río Hondo, Esquipulas and Chiquimula.

CHIQUIMULA
• pop 24,000 • elevation 370m

Another departmental capital, this one set in a mining and tobacco-growing region Chiquimula is on CA-10, 32km south of the Carretera al Atlántico. It is a major market

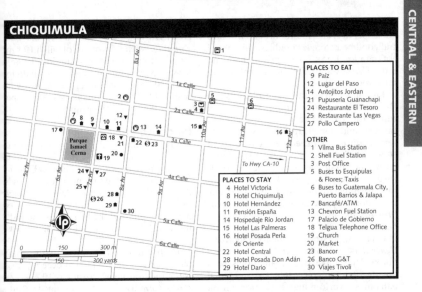

CHIQUIMULA

PLACES TO EAT
9 Paíz
12 Lugar del Paso
14 Antojitos Jordan
21 Pupusería Guanachapi
24 Restaurante El Tesoro
25 Restaurante Las Vegas
27 Pollo Campero

OTHER
1 Vilma Bus Station
2 Shell Fuel Station
3 Post Office
5 Buses to Esquipulas
  & Flores; Taxis
6 Buses to Guatemala City,
  Puerto Barrios & Jalapa
7 Bancafé/ATM
13 Chevron Fuel Station
17 Palacio de Gobierno
18 Telgua Telephone Office
19 Church
20 Market
23 Bancor
26 Banco G&T
30 Viajes Tivoli

PLACES TO STAY
4 Hotel Victoria
8 Hotel Chiquimulja
10 Hotel Hernández
11 Pensión España
14 Hospedaje Río Jordan
15 Hotel Las Palmeras
16 Hotel Posada Perla
   de Oriente
22 Hotel Central
28 Hotel Posada Don Adán
29 Hotel Dario

Parque Ismael Cerna

To Hwy CA-10

town for all of eastern Guatemala, with lots of buying and selling activity every day. It's also a transportation point and overnight stop for those making their way to Copán in Honduras; this is the reason that most travelers stop here. There are also some interesting journeys between Chiquimula and Jalapa 78km to the east (see Jalapa later in this chapter). Among other things, Chiquimula is famous for its sweltering climate and its decent budget hotels.

Orientation & Information
Though hot, Chiquimula is easy to get around on foot.

The post office, on 10a Avenida between 1a and 2a Calle, is in the dirt alley, around to the side of the building opposite the bus station. The Telgua telephone office is on 3a Calle, a few doors downhill from Parque Ismael Cerna. The Hotel Hernández (near the plaza) offers domestic and international telephone services and email for US$0.15 a minute. The Hotel Victoria (near the bus station) has phone service, too. The busy market is in the same block as Telgua.

Many banks will change US dollars cash and traveler's checks. Banco G&T, half a block from the plaza at 7a Avenida 4-75, Zona 1, changes both and also gives cash advances on Visa and MasterCard; it's open Monday to Friday from 9 am to 8 pm, Saturday 10 am to 2 pm. These hours are typical for most of the banks in town. Bancor at 3a Calle 8-30 has longer Saturday hours, from 9 am to 6 pm. Bancafé at 3a Calle and 7a Avenida, Zona 1, has a Visa ATM for quick cash.

There's a Viajes Tivoli office here (☎ 942-4915, 942-4933, fax 942-2258), at 8a Avenida 4-71, Zona 1, should you need to deal with any travel arrangements.

Places to Stay
Hotel Chiquimulja (☎ 942-0387, 3a Calle 6-51) is on the north side of the plaza. It was being remodeled at the time of writing, but was scheduled to reopen, with sporting rooms with private bath and air-con. There's parking here.

A block east of the Chiquimulja, downhill on the same street, are several other hotels. *Hotel Hernández* (☎ 942-0708, 3a Calle 7-41, Zona 1) is a great value, clean, pleasant and friendly; the owner speaks English, Spanish and a little French. There's a sparkling swimming pool, parking, telephone service, and the rooms all have fans and good beds. Singles/doubles with shared hot bath are US$4/7; with private bath and cable TV they are US$8/10. They also have some rooms with air-con.

Just downhill in the same block is the **Pensión España** (3a Calle 7-81, Zona 1), with basic, closet-like rooms – but it has gardens, and it's cheaper at US$2/4 for a single/double. **Hospedaje Río Jordan** (☎ 942-0887, 3a Calle 8-91, Zona 1), a block farther downhill, has parking in the courtyard and charges US$2/4 per person in rooms with shared/private bath – probably better for the price than the España. **Antojitos Jordan**, also here, is a simple place for meals and snacks.

On this same stretch is the friendly **Hotel Central** (☎ 942-6352, 3a Calle 8-30, 2nd floor). They have five clean rooms with private bath, air-con, cable TV and small balconies overlooking the action on 3a Calle for US$8/13/16/19. The beds here are good.

Hotel Victoria (☎ 942-2732, 942-2179), at 2a Calle and 10a Avenida, is convenient to the bus station, which is probably the only reason to stay here. Small rooms with fan, cable TV, telephone and private bath are US$5/8/11/15 a single/double/triple/quad. They also have telephone service, and a good, cheap restaurant with big breakfasts for US$2. Better is the nearby **Hotel Las Palmeras** (☎ 942-4647, fax 942-0763, 10a Avenida 2-00). This clean, family-run place has singles/doubles with private bath, cable TV, air-con and good beds for US$7/13; those with fan are US$4/8.

Hotel Posada Perla de Oriente (☎ 942-0014, fax 942-0534, 12a Avenida 2-30, Zona 1) has a small swimming pool, a children's play area and a restaurant; enter on 2a Calle. Rooms are simple, with private bath, fan and cable TV, and cost US$12/21/30/42 a single/double/triple/quad.

Hotel Posada Don Adán (☎ 942-3924, 8a Avenida 4-30, Zona 1) is spotless. It's run by a friendly, efficient señora who charges US$13/18/22 a single/double/triple for rooms with private bath, telephone, cable TV, fan and air-con. Almost next door is the **Hotel Dario** (☎ 942-0192, 8a Avenida 4-40, Zona 1), with 15 rooms of all different shapes, sizes and levels of comfort. From a darkish room with a fan and shared bath for US$2.60 per person, to an airier unit with bath, cable TV and air-con for US$5.25 per person, they cover the gamut.

Places to Eat

Eating in Chiquimula is easy, as there are lots of cheap little places. Try the **Pupusería Guanachapi**, opposite the Pensión España. You can fill up here for only a few quetzals. Around the corner on 8a Avenida, **Lugar del Paso** serves reasonably priced grilled meats, burgers and chicken dishes and has a full bar. Dining is en plein air in a rocky courtyard.

Restaurante El Tesoro, on the main plaza, serves Chinese food at decent prices. Near the southeast corner of the plaza, **Pollo Campero**, 7a Avenida at 4a Calle, serves up fried chicken, burgers and breakfasts. It's open every day, and its air-con is a treat.

For a step up in quality, try the **Restaurante Las Vegas** (7a Avenida 4-40), half a block from the plaza. It's perhaps Chiquimula's best, with fancy plants, jazzy music, a well-stocked bar and full meals for around US$6 (sandwiches less). It's open every day from 7 am to midnight.

The **Paíz Grocery Store,** 3a Calle on the park, is tremendous and sells close to everything under the sun. Stock up here for a picnic, or stop in to enjoy the air-con. The **panadería** next door to the Hotel Hernández opens at 5:30 am – perfect for that predawn bus departure.

Getting There & Away

Chiquimula is not a destination but a transit point. Your goal is probably the fabulous Mayan ruins at Copán in Honduras, just across the border from El Florido. Travelers exploring the back roads in this area will enjoy the variety of hotels and eateries (and swimming pools!) afforded by a bigger town like Chiquimula and may want to layover here.

Several companies operate buses to Guatemala City and Puerto Barrios; all of them arrive and depart from the bus station area on 11a Avenida, between 1a and 2a Calles. Minivans to Esquipulas and buses to Flores arrive and depart from the bus station area a block away, on 10a Avenida between 1a and 2a Calles. Vilma (☎ 942-2253), which operates buses to El Florido, the border crossing on the way to Copán, has its own bus station a couple of blocks north.

Agua Caliente (Honduran border) – Take a minibus to Esquipulas and change there.

Anguiatú (El Salvador border) – US$1, one hour, 54km. Hourly minibuses, 6 am to 3:30 pm.

El Florido (Honduras border) – US$1, 2½ hours, 58km. Buses depart from the Vilma bus station at 6, 9, 10:30 and 11:30 am, 12:30, 1:30, 2:30 and 3:30 pm. Coming in the opposite direction, they depart hourly from El Florido from 5:30 am to 3:30 pm.

Esquipulas – US$0.80, 45 minutes, 52km. Minibuses run every 10 minutes, 4 am to 8 pm. Sit on the left for the best views of the basilica.

Flores – US$7, 10 hours, 385km. Transportes María Elena buses depart at 6 am and 3 pm.

Guatemala City – US$3, three hours, 169km. Rutas Orientales, Transportes Guerra and Guatesqui operate buses departing every half hour, 3 am to 4:30 pm.

Ipala – See Jalapa.

Jalapa – US$1, 4½ hours, 78km. Hourly buses run from 5 am to 4 pm. Sit on the right for views. Take this bus to Ipala (1½ hours).

Puerto Barrios – US$2.50, 4½ hours, 192km. Buses run every 30 minutes, 4 am to 3 pm; take this bus for Quiriguá (US$1.30, two hours, 103km) and Río Dulce (change at La Ruidosa junction); US$2, three hours, 144km.

Quiriguá – See Puerto Barrios.

Río Dulce – See Puerto Barrios.

Río Hondo – US$1, 35 minutes, 32km. There are minibuses every half-hour, 5 am to 6 pm. Or take any bus heading for Guatemala City, Flores or Puerto Barrios.

AROUND CHIQUIMULA
Volcán de Ipala

Volcán de Ipala is a 1650m volcano, notable for it's beautifully clear crater lake measur-

ing nearly a kilometer around and nestled below the summit at 1493m. The dramatic hike to the top takes you from 800m to 1650m in about two hours, though you can drive halfway up in a car. There are trails, a visitors' center and a campsite on the shores of the lake. To get there, take a bus from Chiquimula (1½ hours) or Jalapa (three hours) to Ipala and transfer to a minivan to Agua Blanca (US$0.25, departures every 15 minutes). The trail head is at El Sauce just before Agua Blanca; look for the blue INGUAT sign. There are several banks and serviceable (but basic) hospedajes in Ipala if you want to overnight in town.

Jalapa

Jalapa is a small, friendly town 78km from Chiquimula, and the route is a stunning one: Verdant gorges choked with banana trees alternate with fog-enveloped valleys. Crossing the rugged mountain passes you'll see waterfalls, rivers and creeks flowing through the growth. Though there isn't much going on in Jalapa proper, it's a good stopover between Chiquimula and Volcán Ipala, and there are plenty of services for travelers.

There are several banks in Jalapa, all clustered around the bus terminal, that change US dollars and traveler's checks. Banco Continental, 1a Calle A 1-03, Zona 2, is open Monday to Friday from 8:30 am to 8 pm and Saturday from 10 am to noon. There is also a Banco G&T nearby. There's a travel agency next to the Pensión Casa del Viajero, if you need to buy, change or confirm plane tickets.

There are many places to stay in Jalapa. The ***Hotel Villa Plaza I*** (☎ 922-5751, *Avenida Chipilapa A 0-64*) has clean singles/doubles/triples around a small courtyard, with private bath and TV, for US$10/16/18. Better is their ***Hotel Villa Plaza II*** (☎ 922-4841, *1a Calle 0-70*), with big rooms with private hot bath and cable TV for the same price. ***Restaurante Casa Real***, next door, is the nicest place to eat in Jalapa.

Hotel Real del Centro (☎ 922-5383, *Avenida Chipilapa B 1-58, Zona 2*) has large, clean rooms with quality beds and private hot bath for US$8/15/18. This is a good value, though rooms in the back are dark. You can't miss the pink and purple monster that is the **Hotel Recinos** (☎ 922-2580), on the west side of the terminal. The clean rooms with fan and shared bath here for US$2.60 per person may be the best deal in town. They have pricier rooms with private bath and cable TV as well.

The **Pensión Casa del Viajero** (1a Avenida 0-64) is four long blocks from the terminal, but is a safe, clean place to stay. Their rooms with private bath and hot shower are US$5.20 per person or US$2.60 per person without bath. Some rooms and beds are better than others. Breakfast is served here from 6:30 am. Otherwise, you can get good bread and pastries sold at either of the two **Vipan** outlets that are near the terminal. **Mr. Pepe's**, across from the Hotel Villa Plaza II, has burgers, sandwiches and a great selection of ice cream.

Buses leave Jalapa for Chiquimula, most continuing to Esquipulas, every hour from 4 am to 5 pm; sit on the left for views. To Guatemala City, there are departures every half hour between 2 am and 3 pm.

PADRE MIGUEL JUNCTION & ANGUIATÚ

Between Chiquimula and Esquipulas (35km from Chiquimula and 14km from Esquipulas), Padre Miguel Junction is the turnoff for Anguiatú, the border of El Salvador, which is 19km away. It takes half an hour to reach the border from this junction. Minibuses pass by frequently, coming from Chiquimula, Quezaltepeque and Esquipulas. There's nothing much here at the crossroads, only a guard house and a bus stop shelter.

The border at Anguiatú is open every day from 6 am to 6 pm, though you might be able to get through on 'extraordinary service' until 9 pm. Across the border there are hourly buses to San Salvador, passing through Metapán, 12km from the border, and Santa Ana, 47km farther along.

ESQUIPULAS

From Chiquimula, CA-10 goes south into the mountains, where it's cooler and a bit more comfortable. After an hour's ride through pretty country, the highway descends into a valley ringed by mountains. Halfway down the slope, about a kilometer from the center of town, there is a mirador from which to get a good view. The reason for a trip to Esquipulas is evident as soon as you catch sight of the place, dominated by the great Basílica de Esquipulas towering above the town, its whiteness shimmering in the sun. The view has changed little in the more than a century and a half since explorer John L Stephens saw it and described it:

Descending, the clouds were lifted, and I looked down upon an almost boundless plain, running from the foot of the Sierra, and afar off saw, standing alone in the wilderness, the great church of Esquipulas, like the Church of the Holy Sepulchre in Jerusalem, and the Caaba in Mecca, the holiest of temples ... I had a long and magnificent descent to the foot of the Sierra.

History

This town may have been a place of pilgrimage even before the Spaniards' conquest. Legend has it that the town takes its name from a noble Mayan lord who ruled this region when the Spanish arrived, and who received them in peace.

With the arrival of the friars, a church was built, and in 1595 an image of Christ carved from black wood was installed behind the altar. The steady flow of pilgrims to Esquipulas became a flood after 1737, when Pedro Pardo de Figueroa, Archbishop of Guatemala, came here on pilgrimage and went away cured of a chronic ailment. Delighted with this development, the prelate commissioned a huge new church to be built on the site. It was finished in 1758, and the pilgrimage trade has been the town's livelihood ever since.

Esquipulas has assured its place in modern history as well: In 1986, President Vinicio Cerezo Arévalo spearheaded a series of meetings here with the other Central American heads of state to negotiate regional agreements on economic cooperation and peaceful conflict resolution. The resulting pact, known as the Esquipulas II Accord, became the seed of the

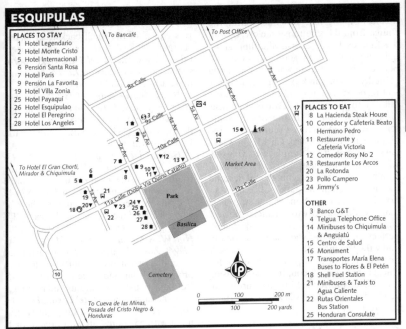

ESQUIPULAS

PLACES TO STAY
1 Hotel Legendario
2 Hotel Monte Cristo
5 Hotel Internacional
6 Pensión Santa Rosa
7 Hotel Paris
9 Pensión La Favorita
19 Hotel Villa Zonia
25 Hotel Payaquí
26 Hotel Esquipulao
27 Hotel El Peregrino
28 Hotel Los Angeles

To Hotel El Gran Chorti,
Mirador & Chiquimula

To Cueva de las Minas,
Posada del Cristo Negro &
Honduras

PLACES TO EAT
8 La Hacienda Steak House
10 Comedor y Cafetería Beato
   Hermano Pedro
11 Restaurante y
   Cafetería Victoria
12 Comedor Rosy No 2
13 Restaurante Los Arcos
20 La Rotonda
23 Pollo Campero
24 Jimmy's

OTHER
3 Banco G&T
4 Telgua Telephone Office
14 Minibuses to Chiquimula
   & Anguiatú
15 Centro de Salud
16 Monument
17 Transportes María Elena
   Buses to Flores & El Petén
18 Shell Fuel Station
21 Minibuses & Taxis to
   Agua Caliente
22 Rutas Orientales
   Bus Station
25 Honduran Consulate

Market Area

Park

Basilica

Cemetery

Guatemalan Peace Accords, which were finally signed in 1996.

Orientation & Information

The basilica is the center of everything. Most of the good cheap hotels are within a block or two of it, as are numerous small restaurants.

The town's only luxury hotel is on the outskirts, along the road to Chiquimula. The highway does not enter town; 11a Calle, also sometimes called Doble Vía Quirio Cataño, comes in from the highway and is the town's 'main drag.'

The post office is at 6a Avenida 2-15, about 10 blocks north of the center. The Telgua telephone office, 5a Avenida at the corner of 9a Calle, is open every day. You can use phone cards in the public telephones here.

A number of banks change US dollars cash and traveler's checks. Bancafé, 3a Avenida 6-68, Zona 1, changes both, gives

cash advances on Visa and MasterCard, and is the town's American Express agent.

There's a Honduran consulate (☎ 943-2027, 943-1547, fax 943-1371) in the Hotel Payaquí, facing the park. It's open Monday to Saturday, 8:30 am to noon and 2 to 5 pm.

January 15 is the annual Cristo de Esquipulas festival, with mobs of devout pilgrims coming from all over the region to worship at the altar of the Black Christ.

Basilica

A massive pile of stone that has resisted the power of earthquakes for almost 2½ centuries, the basilica is approached through a pretty park and up a wide flight of steps. The impressive facade and towers are floodlit at night.

Inside, the devout approach the surprisingly small (with all the fuss, you'd think it was life size) El Cristo Negro with extreme reverence, many on their knees. Incense, murmured prayers and the scuffle of sandaled feet fills the air. When there are throngs of pilgrims, you must enter the church from the side to get a close view of the famous Black Christ. Shuffling along quickly, you may get a good glimpse or two before being shoved onward by the crowd behind you. On Sundays, religious holidays and (especially) during the festival around January 15, the press of devotees is intense. Guatemalan tourist authorities estimate that one million visitors a year come to Esquipulas to see the Black Christ. On weekdays, you may have the place to yourself, which can be very powerful and rewarding.

When you leave the church and descend the steps through the park, notice the vendors who have set up shops, selling straw hats that are decorated with artificial flowers and stitched with the name 'Esquipulas,' perfect for pilgrims who want everyone to know they've made the trip. These are very popular rearview mirror accessories for chicken bus drivers countrywide. Cruising the religious kitsch sold by the throngs of vendors around the basilica is an entertaining diversion.

Cueva de las Minas

The Centro Turístico Cueva de las Minas has a 50-meter-deep cave (bring your own light), grassy picnic areas, and the Río El Milagro, where people come for a dip and say it's miraculous. The cave and river are half a kilometer from the entrance gate, which is behind the Basilica's cemetery, 300m south of the turnoff into town on the road heading toward Honduras. It's open every day, 6:30 am to 4 pm; admission is US$0.35. Refreshments are available.

Places to Stay

Esquipulas has an abundance of places to stay. On holidays and during the annual festival, every hotel in town is filled, whatever the price; weekends are fairly busy as well, with prices substantially higher. On weekdays when there is no festival, ask for a *descuento* (discount) and you'll probably get it.

The best place to search for a cheap room is in the streets to the north of the towering basilica.

The family-run *Pensión Santa Rosa* (☎ 943-2908), 10a Calle at 1a Avenida, Zona 1, is typical of the small backstreet places, charging US$3/4 for rooms with shared/private bath. The *Hotel Paris* next door is similar, as is the *Pensión La Favorita*, and there are several others on this street.

Hotel Monte Cristo (☎ 943-1453, fax 943-1042, 3a Avenida 9-12, Zona 1) is clean and OK, with parking and a restaurant. Singles/doubles are US$7/11 with shared bath, US$13/20 with private bath.

Hotel El Peregrino (☎ 943-1054, 943-1859, 2a Avenida 11-94, Zona 1), on the southwest corner of the park, has simple rooms with private hot bath for US$6.45 per person, plus a new section in the rear where larger, fancier rooms with cable TV are US$23 for two people. Next door, the *Hotel Los Angeles* (☎ 943-1254, 2a Avenida 11-94, Zona 1) has 20 rooms arranged around a bright inner courtyard, all with private bath, fan and cable TV, for US$8/15. Both places have restaurants and parking.

In the same block, *Hotel Payaquí* (☎ 943-2025, fax 943-1371) is a large, attractive hotel with 55 rooms, all with private bath, cable TV, telephone and fridge. Rooms are the same price, with or without air-con: US$20/32 a single/double. It has two restaurants, one in the rear by the swimming pool and one in front, with a view of the park. Next door, the *Hotel Esquipulao* (☎ 943-2023) has singles/doubles with private bath and cable TV for a reasonable US$7.75 per person. There's a pool, restaurant and parking here.

Hotel Villa Zonia (☎ 943-1133, 10a Calle 1-84, Zona 1) is a bright hotel with 15 rooms, all with private bath and cable TV. Rooms are US$22/25 with one/two double beds, and there's parking.

Hotel Internacional (☎ 943-1131, 943-1667, 10a Calle 0-85, Zona 1) is clean and pleasant, with a small swimming pool, sauna, restaurant and parking. The 49 rooms, all with private bath, cable TV and phone, are US$15/20 for singles/doubles with fan, US$20/24 with air-con.

Hotel Legendario (☎ 943-1824/5, ☎/fax 943-1022), at the corner of 3a Avenida and

9a Calle, Zona 1, is modern and quite comfortable. The 40 rooms all have private bath, fan, cable TV and large windows opening onto a nice grassy courtyard with a swimming pool; singles/doubles are US$45/55. There's a restaurant and parking.

Hotel Posada del Cristo Negro (☎ 943-1482, fax 943-1829, Carretera Internacional a Honduras Km 224) is 2km from the church, out of town on the way to Honduras. Broad green lawns, a pretty swimming pool, a large dining room and other services make it elaborate. In the 1960s, this may have been Guatemala's best country-club resort. Comfortable rooms with private bath, fridge and TV cost US$14/20/27/33 a single/double/triple/quad. Two or three children (up to age eight) are free in each room.

Hotel El Gran Chorti (☎ 943-1148, 943-1560, fax 943-1551, Km 222) is 1km west of the church on the road to Chiquimula. The lobby floor is a hectare of black marble; behind it a serpentine swimming pool is set amidst lawns, gardens and umbrella-shaded café tables.

There's a game room and, of course, a good restaurant, bar and cafeteria. The rooms have all the comforts, and the rates reflect it: US$47/52 a single/double, US$66 for a junior suite (sleeps four) and US$81 for a master suite (sleeps six). There may be discounts available mid-week.

Places to Eat

Restaurants are slightly more expensive here than in other parts of Guatemala. Budget restaurants are clustered at the north end of the park, where hungry pilgrims can find them readily. It is very important to ask in advance the price of each food item you order, and to add up your bill carefully.

3a Avenida, the street running north opposite the church, has many small eateries. **Comedor Rosy No 2** is tidy and cheerful, with meals for around US$2.50 and big bottles of pickled chiles on the tables. Across the street, **Restaurante y Cafetería Victoria** is a bit fancier, with tablecloths and plants, but prices are higher.

In the same block, **Comedor y Cafetería Beato Hermano Pedro** advertises '¡Coma bien y pague menos!' ('Eat well and pay less!'). Set prices for full meals are around US$2.

On the west side of the park, **Jimmy's** is a bright and clean cafeteria with big windows looking out onto the park. Prices are reasonable, and there's a good selection. Roast chicken is one of the specialties here; you can get a whole chicken for US$6, or a quarter chicken with fries, salad and tortillas for US$2.

La Rotonda, on 11a Calle opposite the Rutas Orientales bus station, is a round building with chairs arrayed around a circular open-air counter under a big awning. It's a welcoming place, clean and fresh. The menu of the day, with soup, a meat main course, rice, vegetables, dessert, tortillas and coffee or lemonade is US$4, and there are plenty of other selections to choose from, including pizza, pasta and burgers. Nearby, the **comedor** attached to the Pensión Santa Rosa has good set lunches for US$1.55. What Guatemalan town of any standing could be without its beloved **Pollo Campero**? The Esquipulas branch is on 11a Calle and even has a drive-thru.

All of these places are open every day from around 6 or 6:30 am until 9 or 10 pm.

The more expensive **La Hacienda Steak House**, 2a Avenida at the corner of 10a Calle, is an enjoyable place for grilled steaks, chicken and seafood; it's open every day from 8 am to 10 pm. **Restaurante Los Arcos**, on 11a Calle opposite the park, is another more upscale restaurant, open every day from 7 am to 10 pm.

All of the mid-range and top-end hotels have their own dining rooms.

Getting There & Away

Buses to Guatemala City arrive and depart from the Rutas Orientales bus station (☎ 943-1366) on 11a Calle at 1a Avenida, near the entrance to town. Minibuses to Agua Caliente arrive and depart across the street; taxis also wait here, charging the same as the minibuses, once they have five passengers ready to roll.

Minibuses to Chiquimula and to Anguiatú depart from the east end of 11a Calle; you'll probably see them hawking for passengers along the main street. Transportes María Elena operates buses to Flores from the far eastern side of town, beyond the market.

Agua Caliente (Honduras border) – US$0.70, 30 minutes, 10km. Minibuses run every half hour, 6 am to 5 pm.

Anguiatú (El Salvador border) – US$1, one hour, 33km. Minibuses run every half hour, 6 am to 4 pm.

Chiquimula – US$0.80, 45 minutes, 52km. Minibuses run every 10 minutes, 5 am to 5 pm.

Flores – US$7.75, 11 hours, 437km. Transportes María Elena buses depart at 4:20 am and 1:30 pm.

Guatemala City – US$3.10, four hours, 222km. Rutas Orientales *servicio especial* buses depart at 6:30 and 7:30 am, 1:30 and 3:30 pm; ordinary buses depart at 3:30, 5, 6:30, 7:30, 8:15 and 11:30 am, 1, 1:30, 3, 3:30 and 5:30 pm.

COPÁN SITE (HONDURAS)

The ancient city of Copán, 13km from the Guatemalan border in Honduras, is one of the most outstanding Mayan achievements, ranking with Tikal, Chichén Itzá and Uxmal in splendor. To fully appreciate Mayan art and culture, you must visit Copán. This can be done on a long day trip by private car, public bus or organized tour, but it's better to take at least two days, staying the night in the town of Copán Ruinas. This is a sweet town, with good facilities, so unless you're in a huge rush, try to overnight here.

There are two Copáns: the town and the ruins. The town is about 12km east of the Guatemala-Honduras border. Confusingly, the town is named Copán Ruinas, though the actual ruins are just over 1km east of town. Pickup trucks coming from the border will usually take you on to the ruins after a stop in the town. If not, the *sendero peatonal* (footpath) alongside the road makes for a pretty walk, passing several stelae and unexcavated mounds along the way to the Copán ruins and Las Sepulturas archaeological site a couple of kilometers farther.

History

Pre-Columbian People have been living in the Copán valley at least since around 1200 BC and probably before that; ceramic

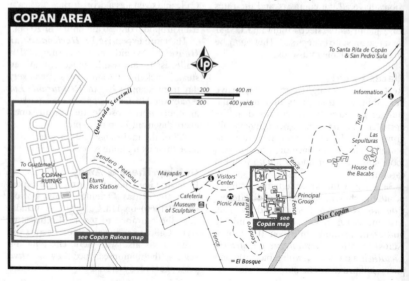

COPÁN AREA

evidence has been found from around that date. Copán must have had significant commercial activity since early times, as graves showing marked Olmec influence have been dated to around 900 to 600 BC.

Around AD 426 one royal family came to rule Copán, led by a mysterious king named Mah K'ina Yax K'uk' Mo' (Great Sun Lord Quetzal Macaw), who ruled from AD 426 to 435. Archaeological evidence indicates that he was a great shaman, and later kings revered him as the semidivine founder of the city. The dynasty ruled throughout Copán's florescence during the Classic period (AD 250–900).

Of the early kings who ruled from about 435 to 628 we know little. Only some of their names have been deciphered: Mat Head, the second king (no relation to Bed Head); Cu Ix, the fourth king; Waterlily Jaguar, the seventh; Moon Jaguar, the 10th; and Butz' Chan, the 11th.

Among the greatest of Copán's kings was Smoke Imix (Smoke Jaguar), the 12th king, who ruled from 628 to 695. Smoke Imix built Copán into a major military and commercial power in the region. He may have taken over the nearby princedom of Quiriguá, as one of the famous stelae at that site bears his name and image. By the time he died in 695, Copán's population had grown substantially.

Smoke Imix was succeeded by Uaxaclahun Ubak K'awil (18 Rabbit) (695–738), the 13th king, who willingly took the reins of power and pursued further military conquest. In a war with his neighbor, King Cauac Sky, 18 Rabbit was captured and beheaded. He was succeeded by Smoke Monkey (738–749), the 14th king, whose short reign left little mark on Copán.

In 749, Smoke Monkey was succeeded by his son Smoke Shell (749–763), one of Copán's greatest builders. He commissioned the construction of the city's most famous and important monument, the great Hieroglyphic Stairway, which immortalizes the achievements of the dynasty from its establishment until 755, when the stairway was dedicated. It is the longest such inscription ever discovered in the Maya lands.

Yax Pac (Sunrise or First Dawn; 763–820), Smoke Shell's successor and the 16th king, continued the beautification of Copán. The final occupant of the throne, U Cit Tok', became ruler in 822, but it is not known when he died.

Until recently, the collapse of the civilization at Copán had been a mystery. Now, archaeologists have begun to surmise that near the end of Copán's heyday the population grew at an unprecedented rate, straining agricultural resources. In the end, Copán was no longer agriculturally self-sufficient and had to import food from other areas. The urban core expanded into the fertile lowlands in the center of the valley, forcing both agricultural and residential areas to spread onto the steep slopes surrounding the valley. Wide areas were deforested, resulting in massive erosion that further decimated food production and resulted in flooding during rainy seasons. Interestingly, this environmental damage of old is not too different from what is happening today – a disturbing trend, but one that meshes with the Mayan belief that life is cyclical and history repeats itself. Skeletal remains of people who died during Copán's final years show marked evidence of malnutrition and infectious diseases, as well as decreased lifespans.

The Copán valley was not abandoned overnight – agriculturists probably continued to live in the ecologically devastated valley for maybe another one or two hundred years. But by the year 1200 or thereabouts, even the farmers had departed, and the royal city of Copán was reclaimed by the jungle.

European Discovery The first known European to see the ruins was a representative of Spanish King Felipe II, Diego García de Palacios, who lived in Guatemala and traveled through the region. On March 8, 1576, he wrote to the king about the ruins he found here. Only about five families were living here at the time, and they knew nothing of the history of the ruins. The discovery was not pursued, and almost three centuries went by until another Spaniard,

Coronel Juan Galindo, visited the ruins and made the first map of them.

It was Galindo's report that stimulated John L Stephens and Frederick Catherwood to come to Copán on their Central American journey in 1839. When Stephens published the book *Incidents of Travel in Central America, Chiapas, and Yucatán* in 1841, illustrated by Catherwood, the ruins first became known to the world at large.

Today The history of Copán continues to unfold today. The remains of 3450 structures have been found in the 24 sq km surrounding the Principal Group, most of them within about half a kilometer of it. In a wider zone, 4509 structures have been detected in 1420 sites within 135 sq km of the ruins. These discoveries indicate that at the peak of civilization here, around the end of the 8th century AD, the valley of Copán had over 20,000 inhabitants – a population figure not reached again until the 1980s.

In addition to examining the area surrounding the Principal Group, archaeologists are continuing to explore the Principal Group itself and making new discoveries. Five separate phases of building on this site have been identified; the final phase, dating from AD 650 to 820, is what we see today. But buried underneath the visible ruins are layers of other ruins, which archaeologists are exploring by means of underground tunnels. This is how the Rosalila temple was found, a replica of which is now in the (closed) Museum of Sculpture; below Rosalila is yet another, earlier temple, Margarita. Two of these excavation tunnels, including Rosalila, are open to the public.

Archaeologists also continue to decipher more of the hieroglyphs, gaining greater understanding of the early Maya in the process. In 1998, a major discovery was made when archaeologists excavated a burial chamber beneath the Acropolis presumed to be that of the great ruler Mah K'ina Yax K'uk' Mo' (Great Sun Lord Quetzal Macaw). To learn more about this excavation, see the December 1997 *National Geographic* article entitled 'The Royal Crypts of Copán.'

Visiting the Ruins

The archaeological site is open every day from 8 am to 4 pm. Admission to the ruins is US$10 and includes entry to Las Sepulturas archaeological site. The two excavation tunnels are open daily from 8 to 11 am and 1 to 3 pm; admission to the tunnels is an additional US$12.

The Museum of Sculpture, also at the site, has been closed since 1999 because the building housing the collection is structurally unsound. How ironic that the ancient Maya successfully erected temples lasting millennia, but the museum designed to hold the artifacts from that great culture threatens to collapse! This is a pity, because many of the original stelae are housed in the museum, as well as the awesome replica of the impressive and colorful Rosalila temple. The museum will be closed indefinitely – a loss for travelers this way.

The visitors' center *(centro de visitantes)* at the entrance to the ruins houses the ticket seller and a small exhibition about the site and its excavation. Nearby are a cafeteria and souvenir and handicrafts shops. There's a picnic area along the path to the Principal Group of ruins. A nature trail *(sendero natural)* entering the forest several hundred meters from the visitors' center passes by a small ball court.

Pick up a copy of the booklet *History Carved in Stone: A guide to the archaeological park of the ruins of Copán* by noted archaeologists William L Fash and Ricardo Agurcia Fasquelle, available at the visitors' center for US$1.65. It will help you to understand and appreciate the ruins. It's also a good idea to go with a guide, who can help to explain the ruins and bring them to life. Guides are US$20 no matter the size of the group; packs of trained guides hang out at the visitors' center.

Visitors should not touch any of the stelae or sit on the altars at Copán.

Principal Group The Principal Group of ruins is about 400m beyond the visitors' center across well-kept lawns, through a gate in a strong fence and down shady avenues of trees. Two resident macaws often

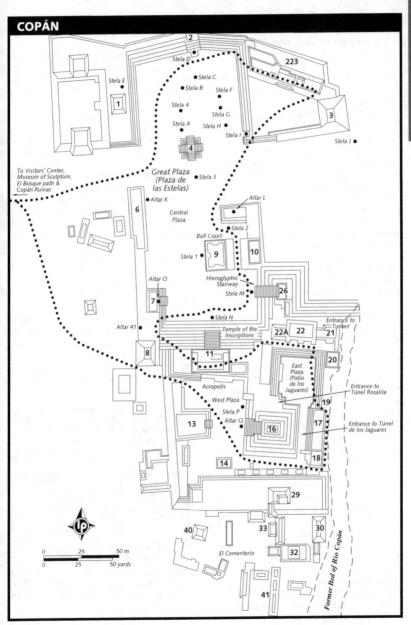

COPÁN

Stela E

1

2

Stela D

Stela C

Stela B

Stela F

Stela 4

Stela G

Stela A

Stela H

Stela I

223

3

Stela J

4

To Visitors' Center,
Museum of Sculpture,
El Bosque path &
Copán Ruinas

*Great Plaza
(Plaza de
las Estelas)*

Stela 3

6

Altar K

Central
Plaza

Altar L

Stela 2

Ball Court

9

10

Stela 1

Altar O

7

Hieroglyphic
Stairway

Stela M

26

Stela N

Altar 41

22A

22

*Temple of the
Inscriptions*

Entrance to
Túnel

21

8

11

20

Acropolis

*East
Plaza
(Patio de
los Jaguares)*

Entrance to
Túnel Rosalila

West Plaza

19

Stela P

Altar Q

16

17

Entrance to Túnel
de los Jaguares

13

18

14

29

40

33

30

El Cementerio

32

41

Former Bed of Río Copán

0   25   50 m

0   25   50 yards

loiter along here. The ruins themselves have been numbered for easy identification and a well-worn path circumscribes the site; see Copán map.

Stelae of the Great Plaza The path leads to the Great Plaza *(Plaza de las Estelas)* and the huge, intricately carved stelae portraying the rulers of Copán. Most of Copán's best stelae date from AD 613 to 738. All seem to have originally been painted; a few traces of red paint survive on Stela C. Many stelae had vaults beneath or beside them in which sacrifices and offerings could be placed.

Many of the stelae on the Great Plaza portray King 18 Rabbit, including stelae A, B, C, D, F, H and 4. Perhaps the most beautiful stela in the Great Plaza is Stela A (AD 731); the original has been moved inside the Museum of Sculpture, and the one outdoors is a reproduction. Nearby and almost equal in beauty are Stela 4 (731); Stela B (731), depicting 18 Rabbit upon his accession to the throne; and Stela C (782) with a turtle-shaped altar in front. This last stela has figures on both sides. Stela E (614), erected on top of Structure 1 on the west side of the Great Plaza, is among the oldest.

At the northern end of the Great Plaza at the base of Structure 2, Stela D (736) also portrays King 18 Rabbit. On its back are two columns of hieroglyphs; at its base is an altar with fearsome representations of Chac, the rain god. In front of the altar is the burial place of Dr John Owen, an archaeologist with an expedition from Harvard's Peabody Museum who died during excavation work in 1893.

On the east side of the plaza is Stela F (721), which has a more lyrical design than other stelae here, with the robes of the main figure flowing around to the other side of the stone, where there are glyphs. Altar G (800), showing twin serpent heads, is among the last monuments carved at Copán. Stela H (730) may depict a queen or princess rather than a king. Stela 1 (692), on the structure that runs along the east side of the plaza, is of a person wearing a mask. Stela J, farther off to the east, resembles the stelae of Quiriguá in that it is covered in glyphs, not human figures.

Ball Court South of the Great Plaza, across what is known as the Central Plaza, is the Juego de Pelota, or ball court (731), the second largest in Central America. The one you see is the third one on this site; the other two smaller courts were buried by this construction. Note the macaw heads carved atop the sloping walls. The central marker in the court is the work of King 18 Rabbit.

Hieroglyphic Stairway South of the ball court is Copán's most famous monument, the Hieroglyphic Stairway (743), the work of King Smoke Shell. Today it's protected from the elements by a roof. The flight of 63 steps bears a history – in several thousand glyphs – of the royal house of Copán; the steps are bordered by ramps inscribed with more reliefs and glyphs. The story told on the inscribed steps is still not completely understood because the stairway was partially ruined and the stones jumbled.

At the base of the Hieroglyphic Stairway is Stela M (756), bearing a figure (probably King Smoke Shell) in a feathered cloak; glyphs tell of the solar eclipse in that year. The altar in front shows a plumed serpent with a human head emerging from its jaws.

Glyphs from the Copán Hieroglyphic Stairway

Beside the stairway, a tunnel leads to the tomb of a nobleman, a royal scribe who may have been the son of King Smoke Imix. The tomb, discovered in June 1989, held a treasure trove of painted pottery and beautiful carved jade objects that are now in Honduran museums.

Acropolis The lofty flight of steps to the south of the Hieroglyphic Stairway is called the Temple of the Inscriptions. On top of the stairway, the walls are carved with groups of hieroglyphs. On the south side of the Temple of the Inscriptions are the East Plaza and West Plaza. In the West Plaza, be sure to see Altar Q (776), among the most famous sculptures here; the original is inside the Museum of Sculpture. Around its sides, carved in superb relief, are the 16 great kings of Copán, ending with its creator, Yax Pac. Behind the altar is a sacrificial vault in which archaeologists discovered the bones of 15 jaguars and several macaws that were probably sacrificed to the glory of Yax Pac and his ancestors.

The East Plaza also contains evidence of Yax Pac – his tomb, beneath Structure 18. Unfortunately, the tomb was discovered and looted long before archaeologists arrived. Both the East and West Plazas hold a variety of fascinating stelae and sculptured heads of humans and animals. To see the most elaborate relief carving, climb Structure 22 on the northern side of the East Plaza. Excavation and restoration is still under way.

If you walk around Structures 17 and 18 you can see mother nature doing her thing: Heavy rain damage and erosion have sent chunks of land and stones tumbling down from the back face. Work crews were toiling furiously to repair it in early 2000, though the back portion of Structure 18 was still threatening to collapse.

Rosalila & Jaguar Tunnels In 1999, exciting new additions were made to the wonders at Copán when two excavation tunnels were opened to the public. The Rosalila tunnel *(Túnel Rosalila)* exposes the Rosalila temple below Structure 16, and

the Jaguar Tunnel *(Túnel de los Jaguares)* shows visitors the Galindo Tomb, below Structure 17 in the southern part of the East Plaza (Patio de los Jaguares).

Descending into these tunnels is exciting (and not just a little claustrophobic), as you bear witness to what archaeologists and the Mayan masses before them saw – a triumph of engineering and craftsmanship coming to life in carved stone. The Rosalila Tunnel reveals the actual temple over which Structure 16 was built, and you can still see traces of the original red paint; the carvings are remarkably crisp and vivid, especially the Sun God mask looming over the doorway. This is considered by some scholars to be the best-preserved stucco edifice in the Mayan world. Everything is behind Plexiglas to protect it from natural and human elements.

The Túnel de los Jaguares is longer and only slightly less dramatic, with its burial tombs and niches for offerings. The Galindo Tomb was one of the first tombs discovered at Copán, in 1834. Bones, obsidian knives and beads were found here, and archaeologists date the tomb's antebase mask to AD 540 . The decorative macaw mask here is incredible. This tunnel is over 700m long, damp, foreboding and just a little eerie.

Though the US$12 price of admission is dear (prohibitive for some), these tunnels will not be open indefinitely and are worth a look for their historical, scientific and cultural significance.

Museum of Sculpture

Copán is unique in the Mayan world for its sculpture. The newest addition to the ruins at Copán is this magnificent museum, opened in August 1996 and closed indefinitely in 1999.

Though you may not get to do it, entering the museum is an impressive experience all by itself: Walking through the mouth of a serpent, you wind through the entrails of the beast, then suddenly emerge into a fantastic world of sculpture and light.

The highlight of the museum is a true-scale replica of the Rosalila temple, discovered in nearly perfect condition by archaeologists in 1989 by means of a tunnel dug into Structure 16, the central building of the Acropolis (see the Rosalila & Jaguar Tunnels section, earlier). Rosalila, dedicated in AD 571 by Copán's 10th ruler, Moon Jaguar, was apparently so sacred that when Structure 16 was built over it, Rosalila was not destroyed but was left completely intact.

The original Rosalila temple is still in the core of Structure 16. Under it is a still earlier temple, Margarita, built 150 years before. Beneath that, there are other even earlier platforms and tombs.

The other displays in the museum are stone carvings, brought here for protection from the elements. Eventually, assuming the museum building can be restored to soundness, all the important stelae may be housed here, with detailed reproductions placed outdoors to show where the stelae originally stood. So far, Altar Q and Stelae A, N, P and 2 have been brought into the museum, and the ones you see outdoors are reproductions.

El Bosque & Las Sepulturas

Excavations at El Bosque and Las Sepulturas have shed light on the daily life of the Maya in Copán during its golden age.

Las Sepulturas, once connected to the Great Plaza by a causeway, may have been the residential area where rich and powerful nobles lived. One huge, luxurious residential compound seems to have housed some 250 people in 40 or 50 buildings arranged around 11 courtyards. The principal structure, called the House of the Bacabs (officials), had outer walls carved with the full-size figures of 10 males in fancy feathered headdresses; inside was a huge hieroglyphic bench.

To get to Las Sepulturas you have to go back to the main road, turn right, then right again at the sign (2km).

The walk to get to El Bosque is the real reason for visiting it, as it is removed from the main ruins. It's a one-hour walk on a well-maintained path through foliage dense with birds, though there isn't much of note at the site itself save for a small ball court. Still, it's a powerful experience to have an

hour-long walk on the thoroughfares of an ancient Mayan city all to yourself. To get to El Bosque, go right at the hut where they stamp your ticket.

COPÁN RUINAS
☎ 504 • pop 6000

The town of Copán Ruinas, oftentimes simply called Copán, is just over 1km from the famous Mayan ruins of the same name. It is a beautiful little village paved in cobblestone and lined with white adobe buildings with red-tile roofs. There's even a lovely colonial church on the plaza. This valley was inhabited by the Maya for around two thousand years, and an aura of timeless harmony permeates the air. Copán has become a primary tourist destination, but this hasn't disrupted the town's integrity to the extent one might fear.

Orientation & Information

Parque Central, with the church on one side, is the heart of town. Copán is very small, and everything is within a few blocks of the plaza. This is fortunate for visitors, since the town doesn't use street signs. The ruins are 2km outside of town, on the road to La Entrada. Las Sepulturas archaeological site is a few kilometers farther along.

Banco de Occidente on the plaza changes US dollars and traveler's checks, Guatemalan quetzales and Salvadoran colones, and it gives cash advances on Visa and MasterCard. Banco Atlántida, also on the plaza, changes US dollars and traveler's checks and gives cash advances on Visa cards.

For US dollars, the banks give a better rate than the money changers at the border, but slightly less than banks elsewhere in Honduras. Both banks are open Monday to Friday from 8 am to noon and 2 to 5 pm, Saturday 8 am to noon. Café ViaVia (see Places to Stay) also changes traveler's checks.

The post office is a few doors from the plaza, and the Hondutel telephone office is around the corner. Next door, the Asociación Copán sells postcards, books and inter-

COPÁN RUINAS

To Agua Caliente / Hot Springs

Staircase

To Guatemala

Bridge

To River

Staircase

Soccer Field

Sendero Peatonal

To Ruins, Copán, Santa Rita de Copán & La Entrada

Parque Central

Quebrada Sesesmil

To River & Los Sapos

PLACES TO STAY
2 Hotel Bella Vista
3 Hotel Calle Real
4 Hotelito Yaxpac
5 Posada del Annie
8 Hotel Paty
11 Hospedaje San José
12 Hotel Marina Copán
14 Hotel Los Jaguares
15 Hotel La Posada
17 Hotel Brisas de Copán
19 Hotel California
20 Hotel Los Gemelos
22 Hotel Posada Honduras
30 Hotel Plaza Copán
32 Hotelito Copán
33 Hotel Yaragua
35 Café ViaVia

42 Hotel Camino Maya
44 Hotel Popol Nah
45 La Casa de Café B&B;
   Hostel Iguana Azul

PLACES TO EAT
7 El Sesteo
12 Glifo's
13 Café Velchez
18 El Jakal Comedor
19 Tres Locos
24 Llama del Bosque
25 Comedor Izabel
34 Tunkul Bar
35 Café ViaVia
39 Vamos A Ver
46 Pizza Rica
48 Carnitas Nia Lola
49 Los Gauchos Restaurant-
   Parrillada Uruguaya

OTHER
1 Mirador El Cuartel
6 Monarcas Travel
8 Cinema El Jaral
9 Police Station
10 Pickup Trucks to the Border
12 Bar Jaguar Venado
16 Banco de Occidente
21 Maya Connections
23 Bus Station
24 Supermarket
27 Post Office
28 Museo de Arqueología
   Maya
29 Palacio Municipal (City Hall);
   Immigration Office
31 Church
34 Tunkul Bar
36 Ixbalanque Spanish School;
   Go Native Tours
37 Macanudo
38 Justo A Tiempo Laundry
   & Book Exchange
40 Hondutel Telephone Office
41 Asociación Copán
43 Banco Atlántida
47 Copán Net

pretive materials about the ruins. Email services are available, but are expensive at around US$6 an hour. Copán Net is across the street from Justo a Tiempo, and Maya Connections is adjacent to Hotel Los Gemelos. The latter has international phone and fax services as well; it's open daily from 7:30 am to 6 pm.

There's an Honduran immigration office inside the Palacio Municipal should you need to deal with any visa issues. It's open weekdays from 7 am to 4:30 pm.

The Justo A Tiempo laundry offers laundry service and a book exchange; it's

closed on Sunday. The family at Hotel Los Gemelos operates a less-expensive laundry service.

Things to See & Do

Of course, the main attraction of the Copán region is the archaeological site, covered previously. There are, however, other fine places to visit in the area and these are covered in the Around Copán Ruinas section later in this chapter.

In town, the **Museo de Arqueología Maya** on the plaza is well worth a visit. It contains the original Stela B, portraying

King 18 Rabbit. Other exhibits of painted pottery, carved jade, Mayan glyphs and a calendar round are also interesting and informative, as is the Tumba del Brujo, the tomb of a shaman or priest who died around AD 700 and was buried with many items under the east corner of the Plaza de los Jaguares. The museum is open every day except Sunday from 8 am to noon and 1 to 4 pm; admission is US$2.

About four blocks north of the plaza is the **Mirador El Cuartel**, the old jail, with a magnificent view over town. The building is now used as a school; you can still go up there to enjoy the view.

A pleasant, easy walk on the road on the south side of town provides a fine view over the corn and tobacco fields surrounding Copán. On this same side of town is an agreeable walk to the river.

You can rent a horse in Copán Ruinas and ride to the ruins or make other, lengthier excursions. Rides can be arranged by any of the town's tour companies and most hotels. Alternatively, you'll likely find a horse for hire by just asking around town and bargaining. The Hotel Hacienda El Jaral (see the Around Copán Ruinas section, later) also offers horseback riding.

A popular horseback excursion is to **Los Sapos**, 5km from town. The *sapos* (toads) are old Mayan stone carvings in a spot with a beautiful view over the town. You can get there by horseback in about half an hour or walk in about an hour, all uphill; admission is US$2. From Los Sapos you can walk to a stela. On top of the hill is the **Hacienda San Lucas**, a century-old farmhouse that has been converted into a restaurant. They have plans to open a hospedaje here and construct hiking trails too.

Language Courses

The Ixbalanque Spanish School (☎/fax 651-4432, 🖂 ixbalan@hn2.com), in the same block as the Tunkul Bar, offers 20 hours of one-on-one instruction in Spanish for US$185 per week, including homestay with a local family that provides three meals a day. Instruction only, for 20 hours a week, costs US$125.

Organized Tours

Go Native Tours (☎ 651-4432, 🖂 ixbalan@hn2.com), sharing an office with Ixbalanque Spanish School, offers local trips and ecological tours farther afield. It also organizes bird-watching trips to Lago de Yojoa, a mountain lake known to birders for reputedly having some 350 species of birds.

Xukpi Tours (☎ 651-4435, 651-4503), operated by Jorge Barraza, also runs several ecological tours both locally and farther afield. His ruins and bird-watching tours are justly famous, and he'll do trips to all parts of Honduras and to Quiriguá (Guatemala). Most days Jorge can be found at the archaeological site.

Samuel of Yaragua Tours (☎ 651-4464, fax 651-4050) in the Hotel Yaragua (see Places to Stay) leads reader-recommended local tours, horseback riding trips and excursions to Lago de Yojoa. Caving trips are another option with this outfit.

Monarcas Travel (☎ 651-4361, contact 🖂 monarcas@conexion.com), a block north of Banco de Occidente, leads tours to almost anywhere in the Mayan world, including Tikal, Ceibal, and Uaxactún. They also operate the shuttle service between Copán and Antigua (see the Getting There & Away section).

Places to Stay

Budget *Hostel Iguana Azul* (☎ 651-4620, fax 651-4623, 🖂 casadecafe@mayanet.hn, www.todomundo.com/ iguanaazul/index .html) is next door to La Casa de Café B&B and operated by the same friendly people. New in 1997, it has 12 comfy bunk beds (US$5 per person) in two rooms with shared hot, hot, terrific bath in a colonial-style ranch home. Three private rooms sleep two and rent for US$11 each. There's a nice garden, and the common area has books, magazines, travel guides and lots of travel information. This is backpacking elegance at its finest.

The *Hotel Los Gemelos* (☎ 651-4077), a long block northeast from the plaza, is a longtime favorite with budget travelers. Operated by a very friendly family, it has a garden patio, a place to wash your clothes (or a laundry service if you prefer) and enclosed parking; coffee is always available. Singles/doubles with shared cold bath are US$5/7.

Across the street, *Hotel California* has four attractive rooms for $US7 apiece, decorated with lots of bamboo and woven mats and all sharing a hot bath.

In the same block, *Hotel Posada Honduras* (☎ 651-4082) has 13 simple rooms encircling a courtyard full of mango, mamey and lemon trees, with enclosed parking out back. Single/double rooms with shared cold bath and fan are US$3/5; with private cold bath they are US$5/7. On the same street, the *Hotelito Copán* was rebuilding at the time of writing.

Tucked away on a residential street a block and a half from the plaza is the congenial *Hospedaje San José* (☎ 651-4195). The six rooms (they're building three more) with shared bath and fan in a familial atmosphere cost US$3/5 for one/two people. The facilities are basic, but loaded with authenticity, and you'll feel a part of the family.

Other simple places include *Hotelito Yaxpac* (☎ 651-4025), with just four plain rooms, all with private hot bath, for US$6/7. The *Hotel La Posada* (☎ 651-4070), half a block from the plaza, has rooms with shared bath for US$3/5/7; those with private bath are US$11/14.

The *Hotel Calle Real* (☎ 651-4230), nearly three blocks uphill from the plaza, is a good value with new, clean and quiet rooms with fan, tiled floors and private hot bath for US$7 per person (the doubles have only one bed); the upstairs rooms are better. The grounds are beautifully landscaped and there's parking. This is not a hangout for travelers (yet!), so if you want to meet and greet, this may not be the place for you.

The new *Café ViaVia* (☎ 651-4652, contact @ jncooman@lenz.unah.hondunet .net), next door to the Tunkul bar, is a great addition to the Copán hotel scene. This small European-style hotel has four spotless rooms with private hot bath, tiled floors and

great beds (2m long for the tall folks reading this!) for US$10/13 for one/two people. There's a café (see Places to Eat, later in this section), hammocks, a small garden and plenty of space to chill out. Inquire about discounts for longer stays. English, French, German and Dutch are spoken.

Another new place, *Posada del Annie* (☎ 942-4020), almost two blocks from the plaza, has rooms with private bath and fan for US$13/17. This may be overpriced for what you get. Also in this price range is the *Hotel Yaragua* (☎ 651-4464, fax 651-4050), a half block from the plaza, which has rooms with private bath and cable TV for US$10/18/25. The dense, tropical courtyard provides the atmosphere that makes this place.

The *Hotel Paty* (☎ 651-4021, fax 651-4019), near the soccer field, has rooms around a courtyard, all with private hot bath, for US$11/13 for singles/doubles. *Hotel Popol Nah* (☎ 651-4095), south of the plaza, is a clean place with seven rooms for US$14/18/21, all with private hot bath and some with air-con.

The *Hotel Bella Vista* (☎ 651-4502, fax 651-4657) is up on a hill overlooking town, four blocks from the plaza. It has a beautiful view; large, comfortable singles/doubles/ triples/quads cost US$11/14/18/24 with private cold bath, cable TV and phone, or US$14/18/21/28 for private hot bath. There's parking in the courtyard.

Mid-Range Copán also has a number of more upmarket places. One of the most attractive is *Hotel Brisas de Copán* (☎ 651-4118), near the soccer field. Comfortable upper rooms with cable TV, fan, shared terraces and plenty of light are US$21; larger rooms with two double beds but no TV are US$16.50. All the rooms have private hot bath.

For B&B accommodations there's the *La Casa de Café* (☎ 651-4620, fax 651-4623, contact @ casadecafe@mayanet.hn, www .todomundo.com/casadecafe), four blocks from the plaza. It's a classy place, with loads of a character in a beautiful setting; an outdoor area with tables and hammocks has a view over cornfields to the mountains of Guatemala. Five rooms with private hot bath and nice touches are US$30/38 for one or two people. All prices include a hearty breakfast.

Right on the plaza is the new and quite lovely *Hotel Plaza Copán* (☎ 651-4274, fax 651-4039). Rooms have all the amenities: private hot bath, air-con and fan, good beds, cable TV and telephone, plus some extras like private balconies and views of the church. Singles/doubles/triples are US$40/45/50; rooms differ, so look at a few. There's a pool, restaurant, a terrace with views and parking.

Other more expensive places in town include *Hotel Los Jaguares* (☎ 651-4451, fax 651-4075), with singles/doubles for US$35/41; *Hotel Camino Maya* (☎ 651-4578/4646, fax 651-4517), with singles/doubles/triples for US$48/54/60; and the large *Hotel Marina Copán* (☎ 651-4070/1/2, fax 651-4477, ✉ hmarinac@netsys.hn), with singles/doubles/triples for US$75/85/95, including a swimming pool and restaurant/bar. Two kids stay free with accompanying adults. All of these places are beautiful, luxurious and right on the plaza.

Hotel Hacienda El Jaral is a lush eco-tourism resort with many activities, 11km from town on the way to La Entrada (see Around Copán Ruinas, later in this chapter).

Places to Eat

The *Tunkul Bar*, two blocks from the plaza, is one of Copán's main gathering spots. It's an attractive covered-patio bar/restaurant with good food, decent music, gregarious clientele and a book exchange. A variety of meat and vegetarian meals all cost around US$2.50. The Tunkul is open every day from 7 am to 11 pm or midnight; happy hour runs from 7 to 8 pm for beer, 8 to 9 pm for mixed drinks.

Next door, the *Café ViaVia* serves breakfast, lunch, dinner and cocktails in a convivial atmosphere, with tables overlooking the street and a replica of Altar Q behind

the bar. The coffee is good and the prices reasonable. They have not-too-dated international newspapers and magazines and can arrange horseback riding trips. ViaVia is open weekdays from 7 am to 10 pm and until midnight on weekends.

Across the street, the *Llama del Bosque* is another popular place to eat, offering a good selection of meals and snacks; their *anafre* (fondue) is especially tasty. In the same block, *Comedor Izabel* is a cheap, basic comedor with decent food. Both are open every day from 6:30 am to 9 pm.

Two simple comedores serving good and cheap Guatemalan eats, with some concessions (like pasta) made for international tastes, are *El Jakal Comedor* and *El Sesteo*. They are across the street from each other, near the soccer field.

Another friendly spot is the *Vamos A Ver* restaurant, half a block from the plaza. It's a cozy little covered-patio place with good, inexpensive foods that you don't always see while traveling in Central America: good homemade breads, a variety of international cheeses, good soups, fruit or vegetable salads, rich coffee, fruit licuados, a wide variety of teas and always something for vegetarians. It's open every day from 7 am to 10 pm.

Farther along, *Carnitas Nia Lola* is an open-air restaurant with a beautiful view toward the mountains over corn and tobacco fields. It's a relaxing place with simple and economical food; the specialties are charcoal-grilled chicken and beef. It's open every day from 10 am to 10 pm.

On the road to the Hostel Iguana Azul is *Pizza Rica*, a new place serving (what else?) pizza, plus pasta dishes for a little variety. It's open daily from 11 am to 11 pm. Also in this vein is *Tres Locos* in the Hotel California, serving simple pasta dishes, salads and pizza. It's open daily from 11:30 am to 8:30 pm.

Los Gauchos Restaurant-Parrillada Uruguaya is one of Copán's fancy restaurants. It's great for meat-eaters; meat and seafood main courses are around US$6.25 to US$11, or you can get the giant Parrillada Especial for four people for US$20. There's a fine view from the tables outside on the verandah and beautiful decor inside.

According to locals, *Glifo's*, in the Hotel Marina Copán, is the best place in town. Expect to pay around US$10 per person for fine, international food in comfortable surroundings; it's open daily from 6:30 am to 9 pm. The *Café Velchez*, next door, has the only cappuccino machine in town and has a cigar bar upstairs.

Entertainment
The *Tunkul Bar* and the bar in *Carnitas Nia Lola* are happening spots in the evening, though they're being rivaled by *Macanudo*, a new bar across the street from Pizza Rica. This place has a robust mix of locals and travelers; it's open daily except Sunday from 5 pm to midnight. Happy hour is from 6 to 8 pm. For drinks, you might also try the bar in the *Café ViaVia*. The *Bar Jaguar Venado*, in the Hotel Marina Copán, though not cheap, has live marimba music on Friday and Saturday nights from 5 to 8 pm. All the other upscale hotels on the plaza have bars in their lobbies as well.

Catching a movie is the only thing to do in Copán after hours, besides taking cocktails. The *Cinema El Jaral* at the Hotel Paty shows typical Hollywood fare daily, which may be just what you're craving.

Getting There & Away
If you need a Honduran visa in advance, you can obtain it at the Honduran consulate in Esquipulas or Guatemala City.

Several Antigua travel agencies offer weekend trips to Copán, which may include stops in other places, including the ruins at Quiriguá. All-inclusive day trips from Antigua to Copán cost around US$100 and are very rushed. Check with the agencies in Antigua for details.

Air Aereo Ruta Maya/Jungle Flying Tours (in Guatemala City ☎ 360-4917/20, fax 331-4995, ✉ jungleflying@guate.net; in Copán ☎ 651-4023) offers round-trip flights from Guatemala City to an airstrip near Copán (US$192, 30 minutes). After landing at the strip, passengers are transferred to a bus

and driven to the ruins. They also offer an all-inclusive tour and transportation package for US$270 per person, and will charter flights to virtually anywhere in the Mayan world.

Bus It's 227km (seven hours) from Guatemala City to El Florido, the Guatemalan village on the Honduran border, but there's no direct bus service. You have to take a bus to Chiquimula, and change there for connecting service to the border. See the Guatemala City and Chiquimula sections for further details about these routes.

If you're coming from Esquipulas, you can get off the bus at Vado Hondo, the junction of CA-10 and the road to El Florido, and wait for a bus there. As the bus will probably fill up before departure, it may be just as well to go the extra 8km into Chiquimula and secure your seat before the bus pulls out.

All the buses serving Copán Ruinas and points farther afield in Honduras depart from the tiny bus station near the soccer field, including the 7 am Casasola (☎/fax 651-4078) departure to San Pedro Sula (US$4.20, three hours). The exceptions are the 6 am and 3 pm GAMA express buses (☎ 651-4421) to San Pedro Sula, which depart from the Hotel Paty.

Shuttle Minibus Monarcas Travel (see Organized Tours, earlier in this section) in Copán Ruinas and Antigua runs a shuttle between those two towns. Scheduled shuttles leave Copán for Antigua daily at 2 pm with a minimum of four passengers (US$29 each) and can stop in Guatemala City en route. Tickets are sold at Monarcas Travel, Asociación Copán and Maya Connections. Shuttles leave Antigua at 4 am and Guatemala City at 5 am.

Car If you travel by organized tour or private car, it's faster than going by bus. You could conceivably visit the ruins as a day trip from Guatemala City, but it's exhausting and far too harried. Starting from Río Hondo, Chiquimula or Esquipulas, it still takes a full day to get to Copán, tour the ruins and return, but it's easier. Still, it's better to spend at least one night in Copán if you can.

Drive south from Chiquimula 10km (or north from Esquipulas 48km) and turn eastward at Vado Hondo (Km 178.5 on CA-10). There's a small motel just opposite the turning, which will do if you need a bed. A sign reading 'Vado Hondo Ruinas de Copán' marks the way on the two-hour, 50km drive from this junction to El Florido.

Twenty kilometers northeast of Vado Hondo are the Chorti Maya villages of Jocotán and Camotán, set in mountainous tropical countryside dotted with thatched huts in lush green valleys. Jocotán has a small Centro de Salud (medical clinic) and the *Hotel Katú Sukuchuje* (☎ 941-2431, fax 942-0139). Rooms with private hot bath are US$4/7/11 for a single/double/triple. There's a restaurant and parking. The road between Camotán and El Florido is pretty terrible.

Along the road, you may have to ford several small streams. This causes no problem unless there has been an unusual amount of rain in the previous days.

Crossing the Border The Guatemalan village of El Florido, which has no services beyond a few soft-drink stands, is 1.2km west of the border. At the border crossing are a Banrural branch, a few snack stands and the very basic *Hospedaje Las Rosas*, which can put you up in an emergency. The border crossing is open every day from 7 am to 7 pm.

Money changers will approach you on both sides of the border anxious to change Guatemalan quetzals for Honduran *lempiras*, or either for US dollars. Usually they're offering a decent rate because there's a Guatemalan bank right there and the current exchange rate is posted in the Honduran immigration office – look for it. Still, if the money changers give you a hard time, change enough at the border to get you into Copán Ruinas and then hit one of the banks there. Of course, if it's Sunday, you're beholden to the money changers – a situation they relish. Though quetzals and US dollars may be accepted at a few establishments in

Copán Ruinas, it's best to change some money into Honduran currency.

You must present your passport to the Guatemalan immigration and customs authorities, pay fees (some of which are unauthorized) of US$2.60, then cross the border and do the same thing with the Honduran authorities. If you just want a short-term permit to enter Honduras and plan to go only as far as Copán, tell this to the Honduran immigration officers and they will charge you a fee of US$1. You'll receive a separate piece of paper with a three day stamp that you have to produce upon crossing back into Guatemala. With such a permit you cannot go farther than the ruins and you must leave Honduras by the same route. If you want to travel farther in Honduras, you'll probably need a tourist card, which costs US$10 and may take a bit more time to secure.

When you return through this border point, you must again pass through both sets of immigration and customs (remitting your temporary permit to the authorities), but pay *no* fees.

If you are driving a rented car, you will have to present the Guatemalan customs authorities at the border with a special letter of permission to enter Honduras, written on the rental company's letterhead and signed and sealed by the appropriate company official. If you do not have such a letter, you'll have to leave your rental car at El Florido and continue to Copán by pickup.

On the Honduran side of the border are several little cookshacks where you can get simple food and cool drinks while waiting for a pickup truck to leave. Pickup trucks depart from the border every 40 minutes throughout the day. They should charge around US$1.50 for the 14km, 45-minute ride to Copán Ruinas, which is payable before you depart.

Don't let the pickup guys bully you: Some try to overcharge tourists on the ride from the border to Copán. Bus service has been suspended since the road between Copán and the border fell into disrepair, and though the road is undergoing repavement, bus service still may have not resumed by the time you arrive. If there is still no bus, stand your ground with the pickup drivers and demand to pay a fair price. Often, the pickup drivers begin by asking for a ridiculous sum, but eventually relent if they see you won't pay more than a reasonable price.

Copán Ruinas to Guatemala Pickups going to the border depart from just before the small bridge and police station on the road to Guatemala. They leave every 40 minutes (or when full), 6 am to 6 pm, and charge around US$1.50. Make sure you are charged the correct price – ask around beforehand to find out what the price should be. On the Guatemala side, buses to Chiquimula (US$1, 2½ hours, 58km) depart from the border hourly from 5:30 am to 3:30 pm.

AROUND COPÁN RUINAS
Hacienda El Jaral
On the highway 11km from town, heading toward La Entrada, *Hotel Hacienda El Jaral* (☎ 552-4457) is an ecotourism resort offering many activities, including birdwatching in a bird sanctuary-lagoon (thousands of herons reside here from November to May), horseback riding, bicycling, hiking, river swimming, inner tubing, canoeing and 'soft rafting' on the Río Copán. Also on the grounds are a swimming pool, a children's play area and two restaurants.

Guests and nonguests alike are welcome to use all the facilities (the exception is the swimming pool, which is for hotel guests only). If you want to stay over, luxurious rooms with air-con, private hot bath, cable TV and fridge, all in duplex cabins with outdoor terraces, are US$50/55 for singles/doubles, with larger rooms available.

Santa Rita de Copán
Nine kilometers from town (20 minutes by bus) on the road toward La Entrada, Santa Rita de Copán is a lovely village built at the confluence of two rivers. Just outside Santa Rita is El Rubí waterfall, with an inviting swimming hole. It's about a half-hour uphill

walk on a trail departing from opposite the Esso gas station beside the bridge on the highway; ask people along the way how to get there.

Agua Caliente
The Agua Caliente hot springs (not to be confused with Agua Caliente in Honduras, not far from Esquipulas) are 23km north of Copán Ruinas via the road running north out of town. Here hot water flows and mingles with a cold river in pretty surroundings. If you ford the river and follow the trail on the other side, you will come to the source of the near-scalding spring. For this reason, soaking is recommended only in places where the hot and cold water mix. There are changing facilities, a basketball court and bathrooms here, but no food or water for sale. The last is very important to prevent dehydration while soaking, so bring your own. To get to the springs, you can drive (45 minutes), hire a pickup (US$20) or hitch, though traffic is light during the week (the best time to go). Fully self-sufficient campers can make an overnight of it. It's open daily from 8 am to 5 pm; admission is US$0.05.

QUIRIGUÁ
From Copán it is only some 50km to Quiriguá as the crow flies, but the lay of the land, the international border and the condition of the roads make it a journey of 175km. Quiriguá is famed for its intricately carved stelae, the gigantic brown sandstone monoliths that rise as high as 10.5m, like ancient sentinels in a quiet tropical park.

A visit to Quiriguá is easy if you have your own transport; it's more difficult but certainly not impossible if you're traveling by bus. From Río Hondo junction it's 67km along the Carretera al Atlántico to the village of Los Amates, where there are a couple of hotels, a restaurant and a bank. The village of Quiriguá is 1.5km east of Los Amates, and the turn-off to the ruins is another 1.5km to the east. Following the access road south from the Carretera al Atlántico, it's 3.4km through banana groves to the archaeological site.

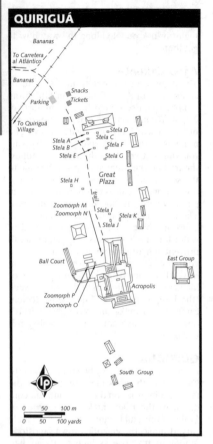

QUIRIGUÁ

Bananas

To Carretera
al Atlántico

Bananas

Parking

Snacks
Tickets

To Quiriguá
Village

Stela A
Stela B
Stela E

Stela D
Stela C
Stela F

Stela G

Stela H

Great
Plaza

Zoomorph M
Zoomorph N

Stela I
Stela K
Stela J

Ball Court

East Group

Acropolis

Zoomorph P
Zoomorph O

South Group

0   50   100 m
0   50   100 yards

History

Quiriguá's history parallels that of Copán, of which it was a dependency during much of the Classic period. Of the three sites in this area, only the present archaeological park is of interest.

Quiriguá's location lent itself to the carving of giant stelae. Beds of brown sandstone in the nearby Río Motagua had cleavage planes suitable for cutting large pieces. Though soft when first cut, the sandstone dried hard in the air. With Copán's expert artisans nearby for guidance, Quiriguá's stonecarvers were ready for greatness. All

they needed was a great leader to inspire them – and to pay for the carving of the huge stelae.

That leader was Cauac Sky (725–84), who decided that Quiriguá should no longer be under the control of Copán. In a war with his former suzerain, Cauac Sky took King 18 Rabbit of Copán prisoner in 737 and later had him beheaded. Independent at last, Cauac Sky commissioned his stonecutters to go to work, and for the next 38 years they turned out giant stelae and zoomorphs dedicated to the glory of King Cauac Sky.

Cauac Sky was followed by his son Sky Xul (784–800), who lost his throne to a usurper, Jade Sky. This last great king of Quiriguá continued the building boom initiated by Cauac Sky, reconstructing Quiriguá's Acropolis on a grander scale.

Quiriguá remained unknown to Europeans until John L Stephens arrived in 1840. Impressed by its great monuments, he lamented the world's lack of interest in them:

Of one thing there is no doubt: a large city once stood there; its name is lost, its history unknown; and … no account of its existence has ever before been published. For centuries it has lain as completely buried as if covered with the lava of Vesuvius. Every traveler from Yzabal to Guatimala has passed within three hours of it; we ourselves had done the same; and yet there it lay, like the rock-built city of Edom, unvisited, unsought, and utterly unknown.

Stephens tried to buy the ruined city in order to have its stelae shipped to New York, but the owner, Sr Payes, naturally assumed that Stephens (being a diplomat) was negotiating on behalf of the US government and that the government would pay. Payes quoted an extravagant price, and the deal was never made.

Between 1881 and 1894, excavations were carried out by Alfred P Maudslay. In the early 1900s all the land around Quiriguá was sold to the United Fruit Company and turned into banana groves. The company is gone, but the bananas and Quiriguá remain. Restoration of the site was carried out by the University of Pennsylvania in the 1930s.

In 1981, UNESCO declared the ruins a World Heritage Site, one of only three in Guatemala, along with Tikal and Antigua.

Ruins

The beautiful park-like archaeological zone is open every day from 7:30 am to 5 pm; admission is US$0.65. A small stand near the entrance sells cold drinks and snacks, but you'll be better off bringing your own picnic.

Despite the sticky heat and (sometimes) bothersome mosquitoes, Quiriguá is a wonderful place. The giant stelae on the Great Plaza are all much more worn than those at Copán. To impede their further deterioration, each has been covered by a thatched roof. The roofs cast shadows that make it difficult to examine the carving closely and almost impossible to get a good photograph, but somehow this does little to inhibit one's sense of awe.

Seven of the stelae, designated A, C, D, E, F, H and J, were built during the reign of Cauac Sky and carved with his image. Stela E is the largest Mayan stela known, standing some 8m above ground, with another 3m or so buried in the earth. It weighs almost 60,000kg. Note the exuberant, elaborate headdresses; the beards on some of the figures (an oddity in Mayan art and life); the staffs of office held in the kings' hands; and the glyphs on the sides of the stela.

At the far end of the plaza is the Acropolis, far less impressive than the one at Copán. At its base are several zoomorphs, blocks of stone carved to resemble real and mythic creatures. Frogs, tortoises, jaguars and serpents were favorite subjects. The low zoomorphs can't compete with the towering stelae in impressiveness, but as works of art, imagination and mythic significance, the zoomorphs are superb.

Places to Stay & Eat

In the center of the village of Quiriguá, 700m south of the Carretera al Atlántico, the **Hotel y Restaurante Royal** is simple, clean and quiet. Rooms with shared bath are US$4/7 a single/double; larger rooms with private bath and five beds are US$6/9/13/17/20 for one to five people. The restaurant serves meat and vegetarian meals. Most guests here are international travelers in town to visit the archaeological site.

At Los Amates, on the Carretera al Atlántico 3km west of Quiriguá village, is a 24-hour Texaco fuel station. Behind the Texaco station, the **Hotel y Restaurante Santa Mónica** has eight rooms with private bath for US$7/9/11 a single/double/triple. About 100m east of the Texaco station is the **Ranchón Chileño**, the best restaurant in the area, where you can get good, filling meals for about US$6 and light meals for half that much.

Comedor y Hospedaje Doña María, Carretera al Atlántico Km 181, is at the east end of the Doña María bridge, 20km west of Los Amates. The 10 rooms here, all with private bath, rent for US$6 per person; they are old but clean, lined up along an open-air walkway beside the river. Across the river there's a large, grassy parklike camping area with coconut palms and fruit trees, covered picnic tables and campsites for US$4 per group, vehicle or tent. Ask at the hotel, and they'll open the gate for you. The en plein air restaurant, open every day from 6 am to 9 pm, has a great view of the river, and there's good swimming here. You're welcome to cross the footbridge for a picnic, just ask permission first.

Getting There & Around

The turnoff to Quiriguá is 205km (four hours) northeast of Guatemala City, 70km northeast of the Río Hondo junction, 43km southwest of the road to Flores in El Petén, and 90km southwest of Puerto Barrios.

Buses running Guatemala City-Puerto Barrios, Guatemala City-Flores, Esquipulas-Flores or Chiquimula-Flores will drop you off or pick you up here. They'll also drop you at the turnoff to the archaeological site if you ask.

The transportation center in this area is Morales, about 40km northeast of Quiriguá. It's not pretty, but this is where the bus for Río Dulce originates. If a guaranteed seat isn't important to you, skip Morales and wait at the La Ruidosa junction for the next Río Dulce bus.

From the turnoff on the highway, it's 3.4km to the archaeological site. Buses and pickups provide transport between the turnoff and the site for US$0.25 each way. If you don't see one, don't fret; it's a pleasant walk on a dirt road running through banana plantations to get there.

If you're staying in the village of Quiriguá or Los Amates and walking to and from the archaeological site, you can take a short cut along the railway branch line that goes from the village through the banana fields, crossing the access road very near the entrance to the archaeological site.

LAGO DE IZABAL

This largest Guatemalan lake, to the northwest of the Carretera al Atlántico, is just starting to register on travelers' radar screens. Most visitors checking out the lake stay at Río Dulce, the village on the north side of the bridge where CA-13, the road heading north to Flores and Tikal, crosses the east end of the lake. East of this bridge are El Golfete and the beautiful Río Dulce, which meets the Caribbean at Lívingston; river trips are a highlight of a visit to eastern Guatemala. Other places to stay around the lake include San Felipe, Mariscos, El Estor and Finca Paraíso.

Other cool spots around the lake include El Castillo de San Felipe (an old Spanish fortress), the Cerro San Gil wildlife refuge and the Bocas del Polochic river delta. There are many undiscovered spots in this area waiting to be explored, so don't limit yourself.

Río Dulce

Head northwest from Morales and La Ruidosa junction (Carretera al Atlántico Km 245) along the road to Flores in El Petén, and after 34km you'll reach the village of Río Dulce, also sometimes called El Relleno or Fronteras. Río Dulce (Fronteras) is the village on the north side of the bridge over the lake, and El Relleno is the village on the south side. In addition to

the locals, Río Dulce has a sizable transient population of foreign yachties.

Orientation & Information Unless you're staying at Hotel Backpacker's (see Places to Stay & Eat, next page) or volunteering at the adjacent Casa Guatemala, get off the bus on the north side of the bridge near the Río Bravo Restaurant. Otherwise you'll find yourself trudging over what is believed to be the longest bridge in Central America – it's a very hot 30-minute bummer of a walk.

Tijax Express, right by the river near where the bus drops you, is Río Dulce's unofficial tourist information center. Bus, *lancha*, hotel and other important travel details are available here. It's open every day and English is spoken. If you need to change cash or traveler's checks, hit the Banrural or Banco de Comercio in town. Cap't Nemo's Communications (☎ 902-0616, ✉ rio@guate.net), beside Bruno's on the river, offers email and international phone and fax services. It's open Monday to Saturday from 8 am to 6 pm and Sundays from 9 am to 5 pm. It caters to contact-starved yachties and so isn't cheap.

The minute you alight from the bus, young men will approach you and try to put you on a motorboat to Lívingston. This may be exactly what you want to do. However, you can spend some relaxing days around the lake if you're so inclined.

For details of the Río Dulce boat trip, see the Lívingston section. If you're looking for lakeside ambiance minus the Río Dulce congestion and pace, head to Denny's Beach (see the Mariscos section, later in this chapter).

If you're up for a diving or snorkeling trip to the Belizean Cayes, ATI Divers (✉ santacruz@guate.net, VHF channel 09) offers seven-day, six-night excursions on their trimaran in the amiable, laid-back style that has made their Iguana Perdida hotel famous on Lago de Atitlán (see the Santa Cruz La Laguna section of the Highlands chapter). Trips include all immigration taxes and full board; snorkeling costs US$370 and scuba diving starts at US$490, with the chance to get PADI certified during the adventure. The ATI office is at Bruno's (see Places to Stay & Eat, below) or contact them via email or VHF.

Places to Stay & Eat

Hacienda Tijax (☎ 902-0858, in Guatemala City 367-5563, ✉ tijax@guate.net, www.tijax.com, VHF channel 09), a 500-acre hacienda two minutes by boat across the cove from the Río Bravo Restaurant or about a kilometer north of the village by road, is a special place to stay. Activities include horseback riding, hiking, bird-watching, sailboat trips and tours around the rubber plantation and medicinal plant gardens.

Small, private rooms over the hacienda's restaurant are US$6/10 for one or two people. New cabañas built over the river with fans, mosquito nets and shared bath sleeping one/two/three people cost US$13/17/22. Thai-style thatch-roofed houses with private hot water bath and kitchens are US$50 for one or two people. There's also a camping area, where you can pitch a tent for US$2 per person. The folks here speak Spanish, English, Dutch, French and Italian. They'll come pick you up from across the river; ask at the Tijax Express. Day passes are US$1.30. Some travelers are uncomfortable with the isolation of this place and the monstrous tab that can accrue as they eat and drink at the restaurant.

Just up from the dock is the *Las Brisas Hotel*. You could do worse than the singles with shared bath here for US$4.50. Rooms with private bath and fans are US$6.45 per person; US$10.75 with air-con.

Just before the bridge, you'll see a path leading to *Bruno's* (☎ /fax 902-0610, ✉ rio@ guate.net), a riverside hangout for yachties needing to get some land under their feet. The four rooms with private hot bath and air-con are comfortable, clean and cost US$23 a double. They have some cheaper (but still clean and comfortable) rooms with a sink, fan and shared bath for US$8/16. There's also an apartment for rent with two bedrooms (sleeps five), a living room, kitchen, and air-con for US$75. There's

plenty of space to kick back here – poolside is highly recommended.

Other places to stay in the village include the *Riverside Motel*, a simple place on the highway with basic rooms with shared bath and fan for US$4 for one or two people. *Hotel Don Paco*, a yellow building with no sign, is another simple place; rooms with shared bath are US$4/7. *Hotel Portal del Río* is among the better hotels in the village (which isn't saying much), with rooms with private bath and fan for US$5.15; those with air-con and cable TV are US$13. Across the street is the similar *Hotel Café Sol*.

Across the bridge is *Hotel Backpacker's* (☎ 208-1779, ✉ casaguatemala@guate.net), a business run by Casa Guatemala and the orphans this non-profit serves. They have a variety of accommodations available, none of it dirt cheap. The location over the river makes it popular with budget travelers, nonetheless. Floppy, foam dorm beds without/with bath are US$4/5 and there are no nets or fans; space to hang your hammock is US$2, plus US$2.60 if you need to rent one. Basic private rooms without/with bath are US$7/10 per person – go for one overlooking the river. There's a restaurant and bar here, and they offer lancha, laundry, phone, fax and email services (US$5.15 an hour). If you're coming by lancha, ask the boatman to let you off here to spare yourself that walk across the bridge.

For dining, the best place is the *Restaurant Rio Bravo*, with its open-air deck over the lake, just on the north side of the bridge. They have a good variety of seafood, ceviche and pasta dishes, and there's a full bar. Simple lunch and dinner plates start at US$4, and they have a good US$1.30 breakfast.

Nearby, *Bruno's*, another open-air place right beside the water, is a restaurant/sports bar with satellite TV and video; its floating dock makes it popular with yachties. *Cafetería La Carreta*, off the highway on the road toward San Felipe, is consistently recommended by locals. *Hacienda Tijax* has a restaurant with a full bar and good coffee.

Several (more expensive) places to stay are on the waterfront farther from town. All have their own restaurants and are accessible only by boat. *Hotel Catamaran* (☎ 947-8361, fax 203-8860, ✉ hcatamaran@guate.net) is an upmarket place with rooms for US$36/41, bungalows for US$45/54/63 and a fancy restaurant and sports bar. Also on the lakeshore, *Mario's Marina* has good food; this is a popular hangout for the sailing set.

Getting There & Away Grupo Taca has flights from Guatemala City to Río Dulce (US$50, one hour) on Friday, Saturday and Sunday at 11:30 am and 4 pm, with an additional morning flight at 6 am on Saturday and Sunday. Flights from Río Dulce to the capital leave on Friday, Saturday and Sunday at 12:45 and 5:10 pm, with an additional weekend morning flight at 7:10 am.

Beginning at 7 am, eight buses a day head north along a paved road to Poptún (US$3.90, three hours, 99km), continuing to Flores (US$6.45, five hours, 208km). The 8:30 and 10:30 pm departures continue all the way to Melchor de Menchos (US$9) on the Belize border. In the other direction, buses go to Guatemala City (US$4.50, five hours, 274km) fifteen times a day. To get to Puerto Barrios, take any bus heading for Guatemala City and change at La Ruidosa.

The Atitlán Shuttle minibus operates from an office on the highway near Tijax Express. Shuttles to Antigua cost around US$35.

Dilapidated Fuentes del Norte buses leave for El Estor (US$1.30, 1½ hours, 43km) from the highway in the middle of town, across from the Restaurant Costa Libre. There are several daily departures between 7:30 am and 4 pm. This bus does *not* go to San Felipe; you need to take one of the nearby colectivo pickup trucks to get there.

Colectivo motorboats go down the Río Dulce to Lívingston whenever a minimum of six to eight people want to go. With plenty of stops, the trip takes about three hours and costs around US$7.75 per person (be sure to bargain for a fair price). Boats usually leave in the morning, but they may leave throughout the day.

The Road to Flores

North across the bridge is the road into El Petén, Guatemala's vast jungle province. It's 208km to Santa Elena and Flores, and another 71km to Tikal.

The entire stretch of road from the Carretera al Atlántico to Santa Elena has been recently paved, so it's a smooth ride all the way from Río Dulce to the ruins of Tikal. You can make it there in a snappy five hours.

The forest here is disappearing at an alarming rate, falling to the machetes of subsistence farmers. Sections of forest are felled and burned off, crops are grown for a few seasons until the fragile jungle soil is exhausted, and then the farmer moves deeper into the forest to slash and burn new fields. Cattle ranchers, slashing and burning the forest to make pasture, have also contributed to the damage, as have resettled refugees and urban Guatemalans moving from the cities to the Petén in their endless effort to make a living.

Mariscos

Mariscos is the principal town on the lake's south side. Since the construction of the road from El Estor to Río Dulce created an alternate link to the Carretera al Atlántico, Mariscos has taken a backseat to those lakeside towns. As a result, *Denny's Beach*, 10 minutes by boat from Mariscos, is a good place to get away from it all. They offer cabañas (US$5 per person), tours, hiking and swimming, and host full moon parties. You can camp here or sling a hammock for US$2 per person. It's operated by Dennis Gulck and his wife, Lupe. When you arrive in Mariscos, you can radio them on VHF channel 63 – many people and businesses in Mariscos use radios, so it isn't hard to find one – and they'll come to pick you up. Otherwise, you can hitch a ride with a *cayuco* (dugout canoe) at the market for US$0.65 or radio from Cap't Nemo's Communications in Río Dulce and they'll send someone to pick you up. *Karlinda's* and *Marinita* are other places to stay in Mariscos; both have restaurants and offer lake tours.

El Estor

The major settlement on the northwestern shore of Lago de Izabal is El Estor. Once a nickel-mining town, it is now growing in popularity as a way station for intrepid travelers on the Cobán-Lago de Izabal route through the beautiful Panzós valley. This is also the jumping-off point for explorations into the Bocas del Polochic, an extremely biodiverse area supporting more than 300 species of birds and many varieties of butterflies and fish. The fall migration in September and October and the spring migration in April and May are supposed to be fantastic. This area is also a favored habitat of the elusive manatee. A visit here before it attains ecotourism mecca status is highly recommended.

Orientation & Information El Estor is a friendly, somnolent town that visitors won't have a hard time negotiating. There's a Banrural on the corner of 3a Calle and 5a Avenida that changes US dollars and there's a branch of Corpobanco across the street; the latter is also a Western Union agent. The police station is on the corner of 1a Calle and 5a Avenida, near the lakeshore. Phone calls can be made from Comedor Dalila No 1, described in the next section.

There's an office of the Fundación Defensores de la Naturaleza (☎ 949-7237, contact ✉ defensores@pronet.net.gt) next to the police station. Visitors interested in exploring the Reserva de la Bíosfera de Sierra de las Minas or the Bocas del Polochic should stop in here. To visit Sierra de las Minas, you need to obtain permission from the Defensores, which may be denied, as they generally work with tour groups, not independent travelers. But they can also assist in contracting guides for birding and other trips around the Bocas del Polochic. Ask for permission to stay at their scientific research station near the Río Zarquito; transport, a bunk and three meals a day cost around US$15 per person.

The Asociación Feminina Q'eqchi' on 5a Avenida across from Hugo's Restaurant sells clothes and accessories made from traditional cloth woven by the association's members. All profits benefit the women involved in the program.

Places to Stay & Eat Overlooking the lake as its name implies, the *Hotel Vista al Lago* (☎ 949-7205, 6a Avenida 1-13, Zona 1) is inviting and clean. Built between 1825 and 1830, the building was once a general store owned by an Englishman and a Dutchman; 'the store' gave the town of El Estor its name. The 21 rooms here, each with private bath and fan, are US$9/11/15 a single/double/triple. The owners can arrange tours and guides.

Hotel Santa Clara (☎ 949-7244, 5a Avenida 2-11) also has clean rooms with private bath on the upper level for US$5/7/8 and not-as-good rooms downstairs without bath for US$1.95 per person. *Hotel Villela* (6a Avenida 2-06) is another recommended place to stay, with clean, simple rooms around a lush courtyard and grassy area with tables and chairs that encourage guests to linger. Rooms with private bath and fan are US$3.25 per person.

Somewhat removed from the other hotels is the *Hotel and Restaurante Marisabel*, on 1a Calle and 8a Avenida, about 80m east of Hotel Vista al Lago along the lakeshore. The seven rooms here are new, clean, airy and arranged around pretty, landscaped grounds. They cost US$10/19 for one/two people. There's a restaurant.

Comedor Dalila No 1, across from Transportes Valenciana, is a good, clean and cheap place serving huge plates of simple food. On the road into town, *Restaurante Centenario* has been locally recommended, as has *Ranchón Tipico Chaabil*, which is probably the best place to eat here. It's across the street from the Fuentes del Norte bus office on the park. *Hugo's Restaurant* serves basic meals, and they have information about tours around the lake and cabañas on the Río Sauce.

For diversion purposes, there's a *billiards parlor* on 2a Calle and 5a Avenida. Then there's *Cine Video Allan*, on the lakeshore east of Hotel Vista al Lago, which shows blockbusters from the US. Sometimes the films are dubbed and other times they have subtitles, though it may be worth the price of admission just to see the likes of Steven Seagal mumbling malapropisms in a Spanish accent.

Getting There & Away Brenda Mercedes and Transportes Valenciana buses operate between El Estor and Cobán (US$2.30, 7½ hours, 166km) several times a day. The first departure is at 5 am. The route is slow going but very beautiful. Fuentes de Polochic has three morning departures to Guatemala City (US$7, four hours, 216km). Fuentes del Norte has several departures for Guatemala City also, plus hourly buses from 6 am to 5 pm to Río Dulce and Puerto Barrios.

There are no public boat services between El Estor and other lake destinations. Private lanchas can be contracted, though this can be pricey, especially for solo travelers. Ask at your hotel or the Defensores office about hiring a boat.

El Boquerón

This beautiful canyon abutting the tiny Cakchiquel Maya settlement of the same name is about 6km east of El Estor. Here, you can hire a guide and canoe for around US$1 to explore the Río Sauce. The refreshing water here is also good for a swim. To get here, take the bus from Río Dulce to El Estor and ask the driver to let you off the bus at El Boquerón, 6km before El Estor. Walk about 100m toward the river (north) and negotiate a canoe ride with one of the families living on its banks. The folks at Hugo's Restaurant in El Estor also offer tours to El Boquerón with English speaking guides (US$10).

Finca El Paraíso

On the north side of the lake, between San Felipe and El Estor, the Finca El Paraíso is a popular destination for day trips coming from Río Dulce and other spots around the lake. At the finca, which is a working ranch, you can walk to an incredibly beautiful spot

in the jungle where a wide, hot waterfall drops about 12m into a clear, deep pool. You can bathe in the hot water, swim in the cool pool or duck under an overhanging promontory and enjoy a jungle-style sauna. Also on the finca are a number of interesting caves and good hiking. Admission is US$0.65 and there are bungalows for rent for US$20 for two people.

To get to the finca, take the El Estor bus from Río Dulce (US$1, one hour). The last bus in either direction passes at around 5 pm, so don't dawdle past then unless you plan on spending the night.

El Castillo de San Felipe

El Castillo de San Felipe (the fortress and castle of San Felipe de Lara), about 3km west of the bridge, was built in 1652 to keep pirates from looting the villages and commercial caravans of Izabal. Though the fortress deterred the buccaneers a bit, a pirate force captured and burned it in 1686. By the end of the next century, pirates had disappeared from the Caribbean, and the fort's sturdy walls served as a prison. Eventually, though, the fortress was abandoned and became a ruin. The present fort was reconstructed in 1956.

Today the castle is protected as a park and is one of the lake's principal tourist attractions. In addition to the fort itself, there are grassy grounds, BBQ and picnic areas and swimming in the lake. It's open every day, 8 am to 5 pm; admission is US$1.

Places to Stay & Eat Near the Castillo the *Hotel Don Humberto* can put you up for US$4/7/11 a single/double/triple in simple but clean rooms with private bath. There's also a restaurant here, or you could try the *Cafetería Selva Tropical* for a meal. Nearby, *Viñas del Lago* (☎ 902-7505, fax 476-3042) is a much fancier hotel with rooms for US$60/70/80.

On the lakeshore, about a 10-minute walk from El Castillo, the *Rancho Escondido* (☎ /fax 369-2681 in Guatemala City) is a nice little hotel and restaurant. Downstairs rooms with shared bath are US$5/9 a single/double; more attractive upstairs

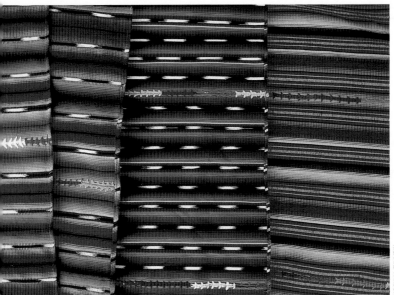

RICHARD I'ANSON

abric detail – Sunday Market, Chichicastenango

LEANNE WALKER & ANDREW MARSHALL

ats for sale – Antigua

TONY WHEELER

Embroidery – Panajachel

KRAIG LIEB

Semana Santa parade – Antigua

ERIC L WHEATER

Palm Sunday procession – Antigua

ERIC L WHEATER

Religious procession – San Rafael Petzal

rooms with private bath are US$7/13, or you can stay in a hammock for US$2.50 per night. There's laundry service, good food, swimming in the lake and other activities. The owners will come to pick you up when you arrive in Río Dulce; ask at the Tijax Express and they'll radio for you.

Getting There & Away San Felipe is on the lakeshore, 3km west of Río Dulce. It's a beautiful 45-minute walk between the two towns, or a colectivo pickup truck, running about every half-hour, provides transport for US$0.35. In Río Dulce it stops on the corner of the highway and road to El Estor, across from the Restaurant Costa Libre; in San Felipe it stops in front of the Hotel Don Humberto, at the entrance to El Castillo.

Boats coming from Lívingston will drop you in San Felipe if you ask. The Río Dulce boat trips usually come to El Castillo, allowing you to get out and visit the castle if you like. Or you can come over from Río Dulce by private launch for US$5.

PUERTO BARRIOS
• pop 35,000

Heading eastward from La Ruidosa junction, the country becomes even more lush, tropical and humid until you arrive at Puerto Barrios – and you'll promptly wish you were anywhere else.

The powerful United Fruit Company once owned vast plantations in the Río Motagua valley and many other parts of the country. The company built railways to ship its produce to the coast, and it built Puerto Barrios early in the 20th century to put that produce onto ships sailing for New Orleans and New York. Laid out as a company town, Puerto Barrios has long, wide streets arranged neatly on a grid plan and lots of Caribbean-style wood-frame houses, many on stilts and most that have seen better days.

When United Fruit's power and influence declined in the 1960s, the Del Monte company became successor to its interests. But the heyday of the imperial foreign firms was past, as was that of Puerto Barrios. A new, modern, efficient port was built a few kilometers to the southwest at Santo Tomás de Castilla, and Puerto Barrios settled into tropical torpor.

For foreign visitors, Puerto Barrios is little more than the jumping-off point for boats to Punta Gorda (Belize) or Lívingston, the fascinating Garífuna enclave on the northwestern shore of the Río Dulce. As the boats for Lívingston leave at odd hours, you may find yourself staying the night in Puerto Barrios. It's a pretty unfriendly place, especially compared to the gregarious, hospitable tenor that typifies most Guatemalan towns. And while the ships and sailors may have left for a new port, the bars, brothels and belligerents that frequent them remain. Given a choice, most travelers opt to move on from here as fast as possible.

Orientation & Information

Because of its spacious layout, you must walk or ride farther in Puerto Barrios to get from place to place. For instance, it's 800m from the bus terminal by the market to the Muelle Municipal (Municipal Boat Dock) at the foot of 12a Calle, from which boats depart for Lívingston and Punta Gorda. You are liable to be in town just to take a boat, so you may want to select a hotel near the dock. However, avoid getting there via 9a Calle, which is crawling with ruffians.

El Muñecón, at the intersection of 8a Avenida, 14a Calle and the Calzada Justo Rufino Barrios, is a statue of a *bananero* (banana worker); it's a favorite monument in the town.

The post office is on the corner of 6a Calle and 6a Avenida. The Telgua telephone office is on 13a Calle, between 5a and 6a Avenidas.

Many banks change US dollars cash and traveler's checks. Banco G&T, 7a Calle between 5a and 6a Avenidas, changes both and gives cash advances on MasterCard and Visa; it's open Monday to Friday from 9 am to 8 pm, Saturday 10 am to 2 pm. The Banco de Quetzal is upstairs over the Litegua bus station. The Bancafé on 13a Calle near 6a Avenida has a Bancared ATM that accepts Visa cards.

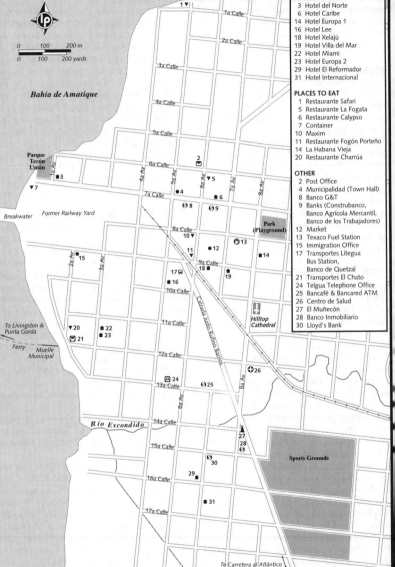

PUERTO BARRIOS

0   100   200 m
0   100   200 yards

Bahía de Amatique

Parque
Tecún
Umán

Breakwater   Former Railway Yard

To Livingston &
Punta Gorda

Ferry   Muelle
Municipal

Río Escondido

Park
(Playground)

Hilltop
Cathedral

Sports Grounds

To Carretera al Atlántico

PLACES TO STAY
3 Hotel del Norte
6 Hotel Caribe
14 Hotel Europa 1
16 Hotel Lee
18 Hotel Xelajú
19 Hotel Villa del Mar
22 Hotel Miami
23 Hotel Europa 2
29 Hotel El Reformador
31 Hotel Internacional

PLACES TO EAT
1 Restaurante Safari
5 Restaurante La Fogata
6 Restaurante Calypso
7 Container
10 Maxim
11 Restaurante Fogón Porteño
14 La Habana Vieja
20 Restaurante Charrúa

OTHER
2 Post Office
4 Municipalidad (Town Hall)
8 Banco G&T
9 Banks (Construbanco,
    Banco Agrícola Mercantil,
    Banco de los Trabajadores)
12 Market
13 Texaco Fuel Station
15 Immigration Office
17 Transportes Litegua
    Bus Station,
    Banco de Quetzal
21 Transportes El Chato
24 Telgua Telephone Office
25 Bancafé & Bancared ATM
26 Centro de Salud
27 El Muñecón
28 Banco Inmobiliario
30 Lloyd's Bank

The immigration office (☎ 948-0802, 948-0327) is at 9a Calle and 2a Avenida, a couple of blocks from the dock. Be sure to get your entry or exit stamp if you're moving on to Belize or Honduras.

In the evening, the noisy bars and brothels along 9a Calle really get going.

Places to Stay

A couple of good, clean hotels are on 3a Avenida between 11a and 12a Calles, one block from the dock. Both have clean rooms with private bath and fan arranged around a central courtyard used as a car park. *Hotel Europa 2* (☎ 948-1292), perhaps the slightly more attractive, has singles/doubles for US$4.65 per person; at the *Hotel Miami* (☎ 948-0537) they are US$6/10, or US$15 with air-con. If you're driving and need a safe place to leave your car while you visit Lívingston, you can park in the courtyard of either place for US$2.50 per day.

The original *Hotel Europa 1* (☎ 948-0127), on 8a Avenida between 8a and 9a Calles, is 1½ blocks from the cathedral (look for the openwork cross on top of the steeple). Fairly clean, comfortable and quiet, it has singles/doubles with bath for US$5/10.

Hotel Xelajú (☎ 948-0482), nearby on 9a Calle between 6a and 7a Avenidas, is a cheaper, more basic place, with brusque management; singles/doubles/triples with shared bath are US$4/5/6. Parking in the courtyard costs US$1.65 extra. Also on 9a Calle is the OK *Hotel Villa del Mar*, with clean rooms and good beds for US$3.25 per person. The shared bath is a little stinky, though.

The *Hotel Lee* (☎ 948-0685), on 5a Avenida around the corner from the Litegua bus terminal, is a friendly, family-owned place offering great value. The rooms are a bit cramped, but have private bath, good beds, fans and purified drinking water, all for US$4.50 per person. There's a restaurant and bar attached.

The *Hotel Caribe* (☎ 948-0494), on 7a Calle between 6a and 7a Avenida, is a sprawling place with 39 rooms. Units with fan and private bath are US$9/14; those with air-con and cable TV are US$12/17. There's a gigantic disco here and you get the feeling the rooms may see their share of drunk, amorous couples just off the dance floor.

In a class by itself, the old *Hotel del Norte* (☎ 948-2116, ☎/fax 948-0087), 7a Calle at 1a Avenida, is at the waterfront end of 7a Calle, 1.2km from the dock (you must walk around the railway yard). In its airy dining room overlooking the Bahía de Amatique, you can almost hear the echoing conversation of turn-of-the-century banana moguls and smell their pungent cigars. Spare, simple and agreeably dilapidated, this is a real museum piece. Rooms with sea view, private bath and air-con are US$13/20/26 a single/double/triple; less agreeable interior rooms with fan are US$9/14. Meals are served in the dining room; there's also a bar, and two swimming pools beside the sea. Service is refined, careful and elegantly old-fashioned, but the food can be otherwise.

East of the streambed and south of the main road, Calzada Justo Rufino Barrios, are two fancier, more comfortable hotels. The 48-room *Hotel El Reformador* (☎ 948-0533, 948-5489, fax 948-1531, 16a Calle and 7a Avenida No 159) is a modern building offering what they call 2nd- class rooms with fan, TV and private bath for US$14/24, or US$24/29 with air-con. Better-located 1st-class rooms with bath, air-con and TV are US$33/51. It has its own restaurant.

Around the corner, *Hotel Internacional* (☎ 948-7719/20), on 7a Avenida between 16a and 17a Calles, has a swimming pool, restaurant and parking. Singles/doubles with private bath and TV are US$9/14 with fan, US$14/25 with air-con.

Puerto Barrios' fanciest is the *Hotel Puerto Libre* (☎ 948-3066, fax 948-3513), at the junction of the Carretera al Atlántico, the road into Puerto Barrios, and the road to Santo Tomás de Castilla, 5km from the boat dock. Rebuilt after a fire in 1992, its 44 rooms come with private bath, air-con, cable TV and phone. It also has a swimming pool, restaurant and parking. Rates are US$51/58 a single/double.

Places to Eat

The town's most enjoyable restaurant is *Restaurante Safari* (☎ *948-0568*), on a thatch-roofed, open-air dock right over the water at the west end of 5a Avenida, about a kilometer from the town center. Locals and visitors alike love to eat here, catching the fresh sea breezes while mariachis stroll from table to table. Seafood meals of all kinds are the specialty, and they go for around US$6 to US$10; burgers, sandwiches and chicken are also served. It's open every day, 10 am to 9 pm.

Restaurante La Fogata, 6a Avenida between 6a and 7a Calle, is another fancy place, specializing in charcoal-grilled steaks and seafood. There's live music most nights, and a set lunch for US$3.50.

Simpler places include the *Restaurante Fogón Porteño*, opposite the bus station, which features charcoal-grilled chicken, steak and seafood. *Maxim* is a funky Chinese place at the corner of 6a Avenida and 8a Calle. *La Habana Vieja*, attached to the Hotel Europa 1, has tasty grilled meats, seafood and pasta dishes at reasonable prices. There's a full bar here.

Perhaps the oddest eatery in town is *Container*, a café and drinks stand at the foot of 7a Calle, near the Hotel del Norte. It's made of two steel shipping containers, and the chairs and tables set out in the street afford a fine view of the bay.

Restaurante Calypso, attached to the Hotel Caribe, is a disco and restaurant in

---

United Fruit Company

As late as 1870, the first year that bananas were imported to the US, few Americans had ever seen a banana, let alone tasted one. By 1898 they were eating 16 million bunches annually.

In 1899 the Boston Fruit Company merged with the interests of the Brooklyn-born Central American railroad baron Minor C Keith to form the United Fruit Company. The aim was to own and cultivate large areas of Central American land by well-organized modern methods, providing predictable harvests of bananas that Keith, who controlled virtually all of the railroads in Central America, would then carry to the coast for shipment to the US.

Central American governments readily granted United Fruit rights at low prices to large tracts of undeveloped jungle, for which they had no other use. The company provided access to the land by road and/or rail, cleared and cultivated it, built extensive port facilities for the export of fruit and offered employment to large numbers of local workers.

By 1930, United Fruit was capitalized at US$215 million and was the largest employer in Central America. The company's Great White Fleet of transport ships was one of the largest private navies in the world. By controlling Puerto Barrios and the railroads serving it, all of which it had built, United Fruit effectively controlled all of Guatemala's international commerce, banana or otherwise.

The company soon came to be referred to as El Pulpo, The Octopus, by local journalists, who accused it of corrupting government officials, exploiting workers and in general exercising influence far beyond its role as a foreign company in Guatemala.

United Fruit's treatment of its workers was paternalistic through and through. Though they worked long and hard for low wages, the workers' wages were higher than those of other farm workers, and they received housing, medical care and in some cases schooling for their children. Still, indigenous Guatemalans were required to give right of way to whites and remove their hats when talking to them. And the company took out of the country far more in profits than it put in: Between 1942 and 1952 the company paid stockholders almost 62 cents in dividends for every dollar invested.

The US government, responding to its rich and powerful constituents, saw its role as one of support for United Fruit and defense of its interests.

one. ***Restaurante Charrúa***, right at the Muelle Municipal, serves filling and cheap (a great combination) breakfasts, lunches and dinners of typical Guatemalan fare.

Getting There & Away

The airport at Puerto Barrios receives a limited number of international flights, but is served often from Guatemala City (US$50, one hour). Daily flights leave the capital at 6 am and 4 pm, with an additional 11:35 am flight on Friday, Saturday and Sunday. Planes return to Guatemala City from Puerto Barrios weekdays at 7:10 am and 5:10 pm and Fridays, Saturdays and Sundays at 1:05 and 5:30 pm. There is also a 7:30 am flight on Saturday and Sunday.

There are also flights between Puerto Barrios and Santa Elena/Flores (US$65, 50 minutes). Planes leave Puerto Barrios for Flores on Monday, Wednesday and Friday at 8:25 am, returning the same day at 1:35 pm.

The Transportes Litegua bus station (☎ 948-1172, 948-1002) is near the corner of 6a Avenida and 9a Calle. This is also the terminal for most other local and long distance buses. Express buses to Guatemala City (US$5.15, five hours, 295km), leave at 1, 1:30, 2, 3, 7, 7:30 and 10 am, noon and 4 pm. Ordinary buses take several hours longer and leave more frequently, though none later than 4 pm.

Buses for Chiquimula (US$2.50, 4½ hours, 192km) leave hourly. Take this bus

United Fruit Company

On October 20, 1944 a liberal military coup paved the way for Guatemala's first-ever free elections. The winner and new president was Dr Juan José Arévalo Bermejo, a professor who, inspired by the New Deal policies of Franklin Roosevelt, sought to remake Guatemala into a democratic, liberal nation guided by 'spiritual socialism.' His successor, Jacobo Arbenz, was even more vigorous in pressing the reform program. Among Arbenz's many supporters was Guatemala's small Communist party.

Free at last from the repression of past military dictators, labor unions clamored for better conditions, with almost constant actions against *la Frutera*, United Fruit. The Guatemalan government, no longer willing to be bought off, demanded more equitable tax payments from the company and divestiture of large tracts of its unused land.

Alarm bells sounded in the company's Boston headquarters and in Washington, where powerful members of Congress and the Eisenhower administration – including Secretary of State John Foster Dulles – were convinced that Arbenz was intent on turning Guatemala Communist. Several high-ranking US officials had close ties to United Fruit, and others were persuaded by the company's effective and expensive public relations and lobbying campaign that Arbenz was a threat.

During the summer of 1954, the CIA planned and carried out an invasion from Honduras by 'anti-Communist' Guatemalan exiles, which resulted in Arbenz's resignation and exile. The CIA's hand-picked 'liberator' was Carlos Castillo Armas, a military man of the old caste, who returned Guatemala to rightist military dictatorship. The tremendous power of the United Fruit Company had set back democratic development in Guatemala by at least half a century.

A few years after the coup, the US Department of Justice brought suit against United Fruit for operating monopolistically in restraint of trade. In 1958 the company signed a consent decree, and in the years following it surrendered some of its trade in Guatemala to local companies and some of its land to local owners. It yielded its monopoly on the railroads as well.

Caught up in the 'merger mania' of the 1960s, United Fruit merged with United Brands, which collapsed as the financial climate worsened in the early 1970s. In 1972 the company sold all of its remaining land in Guatemala to the Del Monte corporation.

for Quiriguá and Río Dulce. You have to transfer at La Ruidosa.

You can store your luggage at the terminal for about US$0.25 per piece per day.

Boats depart from the Muelle Municipal at the foot of 12a Calle. Get to the dock from 30 to 45 minutes prior to departure for a decent seat; otherwise you could end up standing.

A ferry departs for Lívingston every day at 10 am and 5 pm; the trip takes 1½ hours and costs US$1.35. On the Lívingston side, it returns to Puerto Barrios every day at 5 am and 2 pm. *Colectivo lanchas* (collective launches) depart from both sides whenever there are 12 people ready to go; they take 30 minutes and cost US$2.60.

Most of the movement from Lívingston to Puerto Barrios is in the morning, returning in the afternoon. From Lívingston, your last chance of the day to come by boat may be on the 2 pm ferry, especially during the low season when fewer travelers are shuttling back and forth. After that, it might be the next morning before 12 people get together for the colectivo. If everything goes according to plan, the ferry will arrive in Puerto Barrios at 3:30 pm, but remember that the last express bus to Guatemala City leaves at 4 pm, so you'll have to run from the dock to the bus station. Good luck.

Small *lanchas* depart from Puerto Barrios for Punta Gorda in Belize on Monday, Wednesday, Thursday and Saturday at 10 am and on Tuesday and Friday at 8 am. Boats return from Punta Gorda every day except Sunday at 4 pm; these take 50 minutes and charge US$7.75. Transportes El Chato (☎ 948-5525), at the Muelle Municipal in Puerto Barrios, is one company offering this service. You may also be able to contract a colectivo going to Punta Manabique, which is north of Puerto Barrios.

The boats to Punta Gorda no longer stop in Lívingston. If you take one of these boats, you must pass through Guatemalan customs and immigration before boarding the boat. Allow some time, and have your passport and tourist card handy.

Overland Route Information on this route from Puerto Barrios to Puerto Cortés (Honduras) is based on letters from Camille Geels and Anja Boye (Denmark), Peter Kügerl (Austria) and Matthew Willson (UK) and conversations with Gunther Blauth (Germany).

Whereas this route used to be off-limits to all but the most adventurous travelers, new roads and bridges make it a fairly easy crossing and you can make it from Lívingston to Puerto Cortés in one day. With the wind at your back and a bit of genuine hustle, you can make it to La Ceiba, the gateway to the Honduran Bay Islands, in one long day. Some people to prefer to break the journey at Omoa, where there's the well-recommended ***Roli's & Bernie's Place*** (☎/fax 658-9082, contact ✉ r&b@yaxpactours.com).

The trip to Puerto Cortés takes about four hours, so get an early start. The first thing you need to do is to get your Guatemalan exit stamp from the immigration office in Puerto Barrios. You may want to get it the day before, so you don't have to spend the time on the day of travel. The trade-off here is that you have to overnight in Puerto Barrios. Otherwise, you can take the 5 am ferry from Lívingston to Puerto Barrios and cool your heels until the immigration office opens.

Take the bus from the market in Puerto Barrios to Finca La Inca (US$0.50), the last station on the bus line; the buses depart hourly, starting at 7 am. At Finca La Inca, get off the bus and switch to a pickup that will take you over a new bridge spanning the Río Motagua and into Honduras. Here you get your passport stamped, pay US$2 and continue on the pickup to Tegulcigalpita (US $1, one hour). From Tegulcigalpita, there are buses going to Omoa, Puerto Cortés and beyond. If you miss the chance to get your passport stamped before Tegulcigalpita, be sure to take care of that piece of business at the immigration office in Puerto Cortés or Omoa.

Presumably, the same thing can be done in reverse if you're coming to Guatemala from the Honduran side.

LÍVINGSTON
• pop 5500

As you come ashore in Lívingston, which is only reachable by boat, you will be surprised to meet black Guatemalans who speak Spanish as well as their traditional Garífuna language; some also speak the musical English of Belize and the islands. The town of Lívingston is an interesting anomaly, with a laid-back, very Belizean way of life (including a bit of reefer madness), groves of coconut palms, gaily painted wooden buildings, and an economy based on fishing and tourism.

The Garífuna (Garinagu, or Black Carib) people of Lívingston and southern Belize are the descendants of Africans brought to the New World as slaves. They trace their roots to the Honduran island of Roatán, where they were settled by the British after the Garífuna revolt of 1795 on the Caribbean island of St Vincent. From Roatán, the Garífuna people have spread out along the Caribbean Coast of Central America all the way from Belize to Nicaragua. Since arriving in Central America, they have intermarried with Carib Indians in St Vincent as well as with Guatemalan Maya and shipwrecked

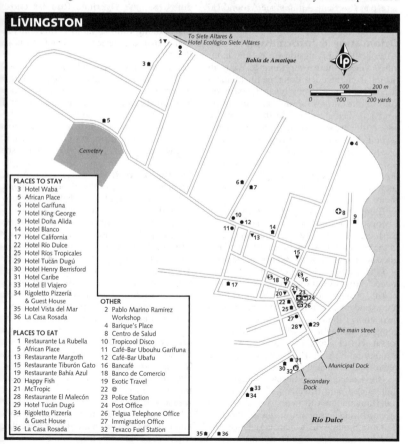

LÍVINGSTON

To Siete Altares &
Hotel Ecológico Siete Altares

Bahía de Amatique

Cemetery

the main street

Municipal Dock

Secondary Dock

Río Dulce

PLACES TO STAY
3 Hotel Waba
5 African Place
6 Hotel Garifuna
7 Hotel King George
9 Hotel Doña Alida
14 Hotel Blanco
17 Hotel California
22 Hotel Río Dulce
25 Hotel Ríos Tropicales
29 Hotel Tucán Dugú
30 Hotel Henry Berrisford
31 Hotel Caribe
33 Hotel El Viajero
34 Rigoletto Pizzería
   & Guest House
35 Hotel Vista del Mar
36 La Casa Rosada

PLACES TO EAT
1 Restaurante La Rubella
5 African Place
13 Restaurante Margoth
15 Restaurante Tiburón Gato
19 Restaurante Bahía Azul
20 Happy Fish
21 McTropic
28 Restaurante El Malecón
29 Hotel Tucán Dugú
34 Rigoletto Pizzería
   & Guest House
36 La Casa Rosada

OTHER
2 Pablo Marino Ramírez
   Workshop
4 Barique's Place
8 Centro de Salud
10 Tropicool Disco
11 Café-Bar Ubouhu Garífuna
12 Café-Bar Ubafu
16 Bancafé
18 Banco de Comercio
19 Exotic Travel
22 @
23 Police Station
24 Post Office
26 Telgua Telephone Office
27 Immigration Office
32 Texaco Fuel Station

sailors of other races, thus developing a distinctive culture and language incorporating African, Indian and European elements.

Other people in Lívingston include the indigenous Q'eqchi' Maya, who have their own community a kilometer or so upriver from the main dock, ladinos and a smattering of international travelers.

Beaches in Lívingston are generally disappointing, as the jungle comes right down to the water's edge in most places. Those beaches that do exist are often clogged with vegetation and are unsafe for swimming because of contaminated water. Swimming is safe at Los Siete Altares; see Around Lívingston, near the end of this chapter.

Orientation & Information

After being in Lívingston for half an hour, you'll know where everything is. Walk up the hill from the dock along the town's main street. The fancy Hotel Tucán Dugú is on your right, with several small restaurants on your left. The street off to the left at the base of the hill goes to the Casa Rosada and several other hotels, and continues on to a Q'eqchi' Maya community. At the top of the hill another street goes left to several hotels and restaurants. Though technically there are street names here, no one uses them.

There's no tourist information office in Lívingston, but Exotic Travel, based at the Restaurante Bahía Azul on the main street in the center of town, has free maps and is a good source of information about the town and the things to do in the area (see Organized Tours, later in this section).

The post office is half a block off the main road and the Telgua telephone office is next door. Email services are offered by a company calling itself '@,' located adjacent to the Hotel Río Dulce, and also at the Restaurant El Malecón. The former is more reliable and expensive.

The Banco de Comercio changes US dollars cash and traveler's checks, as does the Bancafé on the main street. Several private businesses do too, including the Restaurante Bahía Azul, which also changes the currencies of Belize and Honduras.

Laundry service is available at the Rigoletto Pizzería & Guest House (more economical) and at the Hotel La Casa Rosada. It's difficult to get laundry sufficiently dry in the rainy season, as most of the laundry is line dried here. Check if they have a dryer where you're washing your clothes, or you may be returned a heap of clammy laundry.

The immigration office is on the main street coming up from the dock. It's open every day, 7 am to 9 pm. Although they claim they will not administer exit stamps for travelers taking the overland route from Puerto Barrios to Puerto Cortés in Honduras (see the Overland Route section, earlier in this chapter), it's worth asking, since getting your stamp in Lívingston will spare you the experience of hanging out in Puerto Barrios.

Use mosquito repellent and other sensible precautions, especially if you go out into the jungle; remember that the mosquitoes here on the coast carry both malaria and dengue fever.

Pablo Marino Ramírez has a workshop by the sea where he makes Garífuna drums and woodcarvings. You're welcome to visit.

Special Events

Lívingston is packed with merrymakers during Semana Santa. The day of San Isidro Labrador, who was a cultivator, is celebrated on May 15 with people bringing their agricultural products to a mass in the morning, followed by a procession through the streets carrying an image of the saint. The national day of the Garífuna is celebrated on November 26 with a variety of Garífuna cultural events. The day of the Virgin of Guadalupe, Mexico's patron saint, is celebrated on December 12.

Organized Tours

Exotic Travel (☎ 947-0049/51, fax 947-0136, ✉ kjchew@hotmail.com), based at the Restaurante Bahía Azul, offers various tours that let you get out and see the natural wonders of the area. Their Ecological Tour takes you for a walk through town, up to a lookout spot and on to the Río Quehüeche, where you take a half-hour canoe trip down the river and then a jungle walk to Los Siete Altares (the Seven Altars). From there you walk down to the beach, hang out for a while, then walk along the beach back to Lívingston. The trip leaves from the Bahía Azul restaurant every day at 9 am and arrives back around 4 pm; the cost is US$7.75 and includes a box lunch. This is a great way to see the area, and the friendly local guides can also give you a good introduction to the Garífuna people who live here.

The Playa Blanca tour goes by boat first to the Seven Altars, then to the Río Cocolí where you can swim, and then on to Playa Blanca for two or three hours at the best beach in the area. The trip goes with a minimum of six people and costs US$7.75. The Casa Rosada hotel offers the same trip for US$12.50, and includes a picnic lunch.

Exotic Travel also offers day trips to the Cayos Sapodillas, well off the coast in southern Belize, where there is great snorkeling and fishing. Cost is divided among the number of people going (if eight people go, it's US$19.50 each), plus US$10 to enter the cayos.

Exotic Travel also offers trips to the Punta de Manabique biological reserve for US$13 per person, with a minimum of six people. Smaller groups can do any of these tours if they're willing to pay the difference. Also ask about a new mountain biking tour being offered by Exotic Travel.

Tours are also organized to the Finca El Paraíso on Lago de Izabal (see the Lago de Izabal section, earlier in this chapter). It's a long day trip from Lívingston, leaving at around 6 am and returning by around 7 pm. Hotel La Casa Rosada offers this trip for US$20 per person, maximum nine people. Lunch is included. The folks at Rigoletto Pizzería & Guest House also run tours that stop in eight different, super-picturesque spots, including the Castillo de San Felipe on Lago de Izabal. It's an all-day trip and costs US$15 per person for groups of three or more.

Trips duplicating all of the above itineraries are also organized by the Happy Fish restaurant (☎ 902-7143), but not on any fixed schedule.

Places to Stay

When you arrive by boat, you may be met by local boys who will offer to take you to a hotel, helping you carry your luggage if you like (there are no taxis in Lívingston). They'll take you to one place after another until you find one you like. They'll expect a small tip from you and also will get a commission from the hotel.

Don't sleep on the beach in Lívingston – it isn't safe.

Budget Several places to stay are right beside the river, to the left of the boat dock. *Hotel Caribe (☎ 947-0053),* a minute's walk along the shore, is one of the cheapest places in town: Singles/doubles are US$3/5 with shared bath or US$4/7 with private bath. Look before you rent. *Hotel El Viajero* is another basic place along here, with rooms for US$3/4 with shared/private bath.

Even cheaper is the scruffy *Hotel Blanco*, which has basic rooms on two floors, all with shared bath. Upstairs units are US$2.60 per person; downstairs they're US$1.95. This place is uphill, past the center of town, and is popular with hard-core budget travelers hanging out and on.

Hotel Río Dulce, an authentic Caribbean two-story wood-frame place up the hill from the dock on the main street, is another cheapie. Upstairs rooms are US$3.25, with shared bathrooms out in the back yard; three rooms with private bath are US$6.50. The rooms here are none too clean, and you may hear mice at night. Still, many shoestring travelers like this funky old place. The wide balcony overlooking the street catches the breeze and is great for people-watching.

Next door, the *Hotel Ríos Tropicales (☎ 947-0158)* is a good deal, with big, clean rooms with private bath and fan around a patio for US$5.80 per person. Rooms with shared bath are US$4.50. There are hammocks for chilling here, a restaurant, and you can hand wash clothes.

Hotel California is a fine, clean place with 10 simple rooms with private bath for

US$5/8 a single/double. The owners are friendly.

A few blocks from the center of town, the *Hotel King George* (☎ 947-0326) is a simple but clean place, if a little rough around the edges. Singles/doubles are US$5/7 with private bath. Across the street, the *Hotel Garífuna* (☎ 947-0183, fax 947-0184) is more presentable, with rooms with private bath for US$6/8/11 a single/double/triple. They have international phone and fax service here, too.

The *African Place* (☎ 948-0218/0221), a large white building with Moorish arches, is an old favorite in Lívingston. The 25 rooms are clean and pleasant, and there's a big garden in the rear with lots of space and flowers. Rooms with shared bath are US$4/6/7 a single/double/triple; with private bath they are US$6/10/13. There's also a good restaurant here.

The African Place does present some possible problems, though. It's a longish walk from town (10 or 15 minutes), and also there were reports a few years back of items missing from some travelers' rooms.

Turn right at the African Place and you come to the *Hotel Waba* (☎ 947-0193), where clean rooms with private bath are US$6/8 a single/double. Two rooms with shared bath are US$2.60 per person. The balcony has a sea view, and there's an open-air palapa restaurant in the yard serving affordable breakfast, lunch and dinner.

For homey, friendly atmosphere, you can't beat the *Rigoletto Pizzería & Guest House*, beside the river 300m southwest of the dock. Comfortable guestrooms sharing a clean bathroom are US$10.50 a double. All three meals are served (the owner is a great cook),and there's laundry service and a rear garden with tables and chairs right beside the river. Boats will drop you off here if you ask.

Hotel Henry Berrisford (☎/fax 948-1568), beside the river, has decent, clean rooms with private bath and TV. Beware, though: it often runs out of water, and the swimming pool is not always clean. Rooms with fan are US$7.50 per person, or US$10 per person with breakfast; with air-con and

breakfast they are US$14 per person. There's live music downstairs on weekends.

Hotel Doña Alida (☎ /fax 947-0027), beside the sea a few blocks from the center of town, has a beautiful beach, a restaurant and terraces with a sea view. Doubles are US$13 with shared bath, extra-large triple rooms are US$39 with private bath, some with a sea view. A double bungalow is US$28. Breakfast is available.

La Casa Rosada (☎ 947-0303, fax 947-0304) is a groovy, attractive place to stay. It's right on the river, 800m to the left of the dock; boats will drop you here if you ask. Ample riverside gardens, a dock with a gazebo, and refreshments available anytime all contribute to the relaxed, friendly ambiance. For US$8 a person you can enjoy one of ten pleasant, free-standing, thatch-roofed bungalows with fans, screens and mosquito nets. There are three clean shared bathrooms. Also available are a laundry service, daily trips and tours and one of the best restaurants in town.

Just down the street is the family-owned *Hotel Vista al Mar* (☎ 947-0131). They have three very basic bungalows for US$8/11. The singles are overpriced for what you get, but there's one decent room with a double bed. They accept credit cards, and there's a restaurant. The stagnant water that sometimes laps at the back of this place is worrisome, however. Next door are basic rooms for rent by the month.

The *Hotel Ecológico Siete Altares* (☎ 332-7107, fax 478-2159, ❷ sietealtares@hotmail.com) is a welcoming cluster of riverside bungalows about an hour's walk from Lívingston. The rustic thatched bungalows have fans and sleep two, four or six people and cost US$10 per person. You can take a lancha from the dock in Lívingston (five minutes) or follow the shore northwards toward Siete Altares for an hour. There's a restaurant nearby.

Top End Among all these laid-back, low-priced Caribbean lodgings, the 45-room *Hotel Tucán Dugú* (☎/fax 948-1588, in Guatemala City 334-7813, fax 334-5242, ❷ tukansa@guate.net), just up the hill from the dock, is a luxurious anomaly. Modern but still Caribbean in style, it has many conveniences and comforts, including tropical gardens, a swimming pool and a jungle bar where you might expect to see Hemingway or Bogart. Rooms are fairly large, with modern bathrooms, ceiling fans and little balconies overlooking the pool and gardens. Singles/doubles/triples are US$60/66/90, more during Semana Santa and New Year's.

Places to Eat

Food in Lívingston is more expensive than in the rest of Guatemala because most of it (except fish and coconuts) must be brought across from the mainland. *Tapado*, a rich stew made from fish, shrimp, crab, other seafood, coconut, and plantain, spiced with coriander, is the special local dish. A local potent potable is made by slicing off the top of a green coconut and mixing in a healthy dose of rum. These *coco locos* hit the spot and are sold in shacks along the main street.

The main street is also lined with little comedores. Your best plan may be to choose the place that is currently the most popular. At the time of writing, *Restaurante Tiburón Gato* was the title holder and may still be hopping when you get to Lívingston.

Restaurante Margoth has filling fish, meat and ceviche dishes at reasonable prices. The meals are well prepared and there's a full bar, but service can be slow.

The *Restaurante Bahía Azul* is a popular gathering spot in relaxed surroundings, with good food and prices and live music some evenings. It's open every day, 7 am to 10 pm.

Other popular places on the main street include the *Restaurante El Malecón*, just up the hill from the dock, on the left. It's airy and rustic, with a loyal local clientele and good views of the water; a full meal of Caribbean-inspired fare can be had for US$4 to US$7. A bit farther up the hill, the *McTropic*, on the right-hand side, is half restaurant and half shop; it's favored by the thriftiest crowd. The *Happy Fish* on the main street is also good.

The *African Place*, a few blocks from the center of town (see Places to Stay, earlier in this section), serves a variety of exotic and local dishes. Full meals, including delicious tapado, are available for US$6 or less.

On the road beside the river are a couple of other good restaurants. The *Rigoletto Pizzería* (see Places to Stay), operated by the talented cook María, who has lived in several countries, has an international menu of Italian, east Indian, Chinese and other dishes, with many meat and vegetarian selections. Her pizzas are made with real mozzarella cheese imported all the way from Guatemala City (as she likes to boast) and baked in an authentic pizza oven; they're also available for take-out.

Farther along, the restaurant at *La Casa Rosada* is another very enjoyable riverside spot. All three meals are served. Dinners are ample and good, costing US$6 to US$8; reservations are advisable. The coffee here is probably the best in town.

On the northern shore is the very simple *Restaurante La Rubella*, but don't let the name deter you. They serve chilly drinks and snacks, and the view is fine.

The dining room of the *Hotel Tucán Dugú* is Lívingston's most expensive spot; a good, complete dinner with drinks goes for around US$15.

Entertainment

The Garífuna have a distinctive form of music and dance. The traditional Garífuna band is composed of three large drums, a turtle shell, some maracas and a big conch shell, producing throbbing, haunting rhythms and melodies. The chanted words are like a litany, with responses often taken up by the audience. The *punta* is the Garífuna dance, and it's got a lot of gyrating hip movements.

Lívingston is about the only place in Guatemala where Garífuna music and dance are easily accessible for visitors. The *Restaurante Bahía Azul* has live Garífuna music on weekends and sometimes on other evenings. The *Café-Bar Ubafu* has live Garífuna music and dancing most nights; it's liveliest on weekends. Across the street, the *Café-Bar Ubouhu Garífuna* is another popular night spot.

The disco called **Barique's Place**, by the sea on the north side of town, is open on weekends. This is a moonlit, beachy place, thick with locals, where the liquor flows freely and things can get rough. It might not be the most comfortable place for travelers, especially solo women. The **Tropicool Disco**, on the other hand, is usually packed with foreigners getting down to disco beats. It's next to the Café-Bar Ubafu and a real party most weekends.

Some nights of the week, the busiest place in town, with the loudest music, is the Templo Evangélico Iglesia del Nazareno (Evangelical Church of the Nazarene).

Getting There & Away

The only way to get to Lívingston is by boat. Frequent boats come downriver from Río Dulce and across the bay from Puerto Barrios; see those sections, earlier in this chapter, for details. There are also international boats coming from Honduras and Belize.

Exotic Travel (☎ 947-0049/51, fax 947-0136, ✉ kjchew@hotmail.com) operates international boat routes to Omoa (Honduras) and Punta Gorda (Belize). They run on a schedule, but will also go at any other time there are a minimum of six people. Be sure to get your entry and exit stamps entered into your passport at the immigration offices on both ends of the journey.

The boats to Omoa depart from Lívingston at 7 am on Tuesday and Friday, arriving at about 10 am. In Omoa, the boat docks near the bus stop where you can catch a bus to Puerto Cortés, San Pedro Sula or La Ceiba (cheapest gateway to the Bay Islands). The boat leaves Omoa for the return trip around noon or 1 pm, arriving back in Lívingston around 3:30 pm. Cost is US$35 from Lívingston to Omoa, US$25 from Omoa to Lívingston. The captain will take you to get your passport exit and entry stamps on both ends of the journey.

The boats to Punta Gorda (Belize) also leave Lívingston at 7 am on Tuesday and Friday. This is a shorter trip, taking just 45 minutes; cost is US$13 each way. The boats depart Punta Gorda for the return trip at 9 am. Get your own exit stamp from the immigration office in Lívingston; the captain will take you to get your entry stamp in Punta Gorda.

Trips to Punta Gorda, Omoa and other places can also be arranged at the Happy Fish restaurant (☎ 902-7143).

AROUND LÍVINGSTON
Río Dulce Cruises

Lívingston is the starting point for boat rides on the Río Dulce. Passengers enjoy the tropical jungle scenery, have a swim and a picnic and explore the Biotopo Chocón Machacas, 12km west along the river.

There are several ways to make the voyage up the Río Dulce. Almost anyone in Lívingston can tell you who's currently organizing trips. Exotic Travel, at the Restaurante Bahía Azul, makes trips daily, as do the Hotel La Casa Rosada and the Happy Fish restaurant (see previous page). Or you can simply walk down to the dock and arrange a trip – many local boatmen hang out there, and it's good to support them.

Shortly after you leave Lívingston, the river enters a steep-walled gorge called **Cueva de la Vaca**, its walls hung with great tangles of jungle foliage and bromeliads and the humid air noisy with the cries of tropical birds, including cormorants and herons. Just beyond that is **La Pintada**, a rock escarpment covered with graffiti. Local legend says people have been tagging this spot since the 1700s, though the oldest in evidence is from the 1950s. If you're lucky, you may be able to spot a freshwater dolphin in these parts. Farther on, a thermal spring forces sulfurous water out of the base of the cliff, providing a delightful place for a swim.

Emerging from the gorge, the river eventually widens into **El Golfete**, a lake-like body of water that presages the even vaster expanse of Lago de Izabal.

On the northern shore of El Golfete is the **Biotopo Chocón Machacas**, a 7600-hectare reserve established to protect the beautiful river landscape, the valuable mangrove swamps and, especially, the manatees that inhabit the waters (both salt and fresh).

A network of 'water trails' (boat routes around several jungle lagoons) provide ways to see the bird, animal and plant life of the reserve. A nature trail begins at the visitors' center and winds its way through forests of mahogany, palms and rich tropical foliage. Jaguars and tapirs live in the reserve, though your chances of seeing either are nil. The walrus-like manatees are even more elusive. These huge mammals can weigh up to a ton, yet they glide effortlessly beneath the calm surface of the river.

From El Golfete and the nature reserve, the boats continue upriver to the village of Río Dulce, where the road into El Petén crosses the river, and to El Castillo de San Felipe on Lago de Izabal (see the Lago de Izabal section).

A manatee can weigh up to a ton.

The trip is also offered from Río Dulce; ask at the Tijax Express office.

From whichever end you begin, you can make it one-way (US$7.75) or round-trip (US$13) between Lívingston and Río Dulce. Trips organized by the Hotel La Casa Rosada and the Rigoletto Pizzería & Guest House cost a bit more, but may be worth it because they stop at more places. The tours offered by Exotic Travel are little more than speedy transportation between Lívingston and Río Dulce with few stops or interpretations of the surroundings.

Los Siete Altares

The Seven Altars is a series of freshwater falls and pools about 5km (1½-hour walk) northwest of Lívingston along the shore of the Bahía de Amatique. It's a pleasant goal for a walk along the beach and a good place for a picnic and a swim. Follow the shore northward to the mouth of a river. Ford the river and walk along the beach until it meets the path into the woods (about 30 minutes). Follow this path all the way to the falls. If you'd rather not do the ford, boats at the mouth of the river will ferry you across for a few quetzals.

Boat trips go to the Seven Altars, but it's better to walk there, because you get to see the pure nature and also the Garífuna people who live along the way. Although robberies on this walk were common in the past, Lívingston has beefed up its police force, quadrupling the number of officers on the beat, so you should have an enjoyable, safe walk. The falls can be disappointing in the dry season, however.

Finca Tatin

This is a wonderful B&B, Spanish school and sustainable development project at the confluence of the Ríos Dulce and Tatin. Finca Tatin (☎ 902-0831, contact ✉ fincatatin@centramerica.com, www.centramerica.com/fincatatin) was built by husband and wife team Carlos and Claudia Simonini after they tired of sailing around the world. They run Finca Tatin with contagious care and enthusiasm, and you may find yourself staying awhile.

Claudia teaches the Spanish classes and is eminently qualified, as she holds a BA in language and literature. A program of 20 hours of instruction in an open thatch bungalow overlooking the river, including room, is US$120 a week. Crash courses of four hours of instruction, plus room for US$22 a day, are also available. Guests can use the kitchen or have meals prepared for US$2.60, with cheaper vegetarian options available. If your Spanish is up to snuff and you just want to chill here, basic rooms in thatched bungalows with shared bath are US$5 a day. There are trails, waterfalls and endless river tributaries that you can explore with one of the *cayucos* available for guest use. Or, ask for camping suggestions in the area. There's good birding here, and dense rainforest. For the most part, the Simoninis have let the forest go natural, so this is not a place for phobics of bugs or creeping fauna. Finca Tatin is easiest to reach by lancha from Lívingston (30 minutes). Hire a *lanchero* or call the Finca and they'll come pick you up (US$3.90). Spanish, English, French and Italian are spoken.

Proyecto Ak'Tenamit

Not far from the mouth of the Río Tatin on the Río Dulce, about 10km from Lívingston, is the Proyecto Ak'Tenamit (☎ 902-0608, VHF channel 88, www.mayaparadise.com/aktename.htm), an organization working with the local Q'eqchi' Maya population to improve their quality of life. To this end, they run a school and a medical clinic, as well as a floating dental clinic on their catamaran moored in the Río Dulce. They welcome visitors and volunteers (see the Volunteer Work section of the Facts for the Visitor chapter).

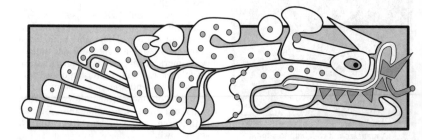

El Petén

In the dense jungle cover of Guatemala's vast northeastern department of El Petén, you may hear the squawk of parrots, the chatter of monkeys and the rustlings of strange animals moving through the bush. The landscape here is completely different from that of Guatemala's cool mountainous Highlands or its steamy Pacific Slope. Your usual means of perception will prove inadequate for your Petén adventures, which may seem supernatural at times – and

Highlights

- Experiencing the imperial, inspiring ruins set deep in the lush jungle at Tikal
- Heading off the trodden path to visit ruins buried in the forest at Sayaxché; continuing by back roads to Cobán
- Taking a river or road route to ancient sites in nearby Mexico, including Yaxchilán, Bonampak and Palenque
- Venturing far into the Petén jungle to remote Mayan sites such as El Perú, El Zotz and El Mirador
- Hanging out in Poptún, horseback riding, caving or just swinging in a hammock

you should have plenty of bug repellent at the ready!

The monumental ceremonial center at Tikal is among the most impressive Mayan archaeological sites. The ruins of Uaxactún and Ceibal, though not so easily accessible, are perhaps more exciting to visit for that reason. The remains of several dozen other great cities hidden in El Petén's jungles that were previously only accessible to archaeologists with aircraft (or to artifact poachers) are now open for limited tourism. This access is a good thing and a not so good thing.

On the plus side, determined travelers can now visit a variety of Mayan sites hidden deep in the jungle, and many of the treks are led by guides from local communities. The guides can have an alternative source of income in what is designed to be an ecologically low-impact activity. However (and this is where the good news turns bad), simply taking people into these dangerously fragile ecosystems can have a negative effect on these areas. The situation worsens when guides and their charges neglect to observe simple rules of ecotourism, such as carrying out garbage. See Responsible Tourism, later in this section, for more on penetrating the jungle depths in a sane and sustainable manner.

In 1990, the Guatemalan government established the one million-hectare Maya biosphere reserve, which includes most of northern El Petén. The Guatemalan reserve adjoins the vast Calakmul biosphere reserve in Mexico and the Río Bravo Conservation Area in Belize, forming a huge multinational reserve totaling more than two million hectares. If you have the gumption and desire, you can venture into areas in the core of the reserve and explore the myriad wonders there.

There are three main reasons a person would want to venture into the forests of El Petén: first, to visit Tikal (the greatest Mayan religious center yet excavated) and other important archaeological sites; second, to enjoy the great abundance and variety of animal and bird life; and third, to see the Guatemala of small farming villages and jungle hamlets, without paved roads or colonial architecture. Many travelers also linger in Poptún, a small town 113km southeast of Santa Elena and a popular backpacker layover for decades.

Though it is possible to visit Tikal on a single-day excursion by plane from Guatemala City, travelers are strongly encouraged to stay over at least one night, whether in Flores, El Remate or Tikal itself.

There is a great deal to see and experience, and a day trip simply cannot do it justice.

Getting Around

The roads leading into El Petén – from the Carretera al Pacífico and from Belize – have all been paved. With El Petén's forests already falling to the machete at an alarming rate, these good, new roads have encouraged migration of farmers and ranchers from other areas of the country, leading to even more marked deforestation. Further compounding the problem are refugee resettlement programs that are logically

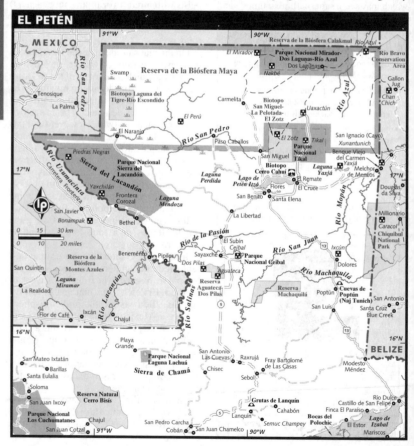

EL PETÉN

looking toward the Petén frontier to provide plots for the landless, homeless refugees forced from their villages during the civil war. Although travel in this area is now fast and smooth, there's a lot less forest to behold.

In years past, incidents of robbery of luxury and tourist buses were a concern, especially those traveling between Río Dulce and Flores and the Belizean border at Melchor de Mencos/Benque Viejo del Carmen. Fortunately, things have quieted down considerably since then and the overwhelming majority of foreigners now enjoy safe visits to El Petén. Still, contacting your embassy or consulate in Guatemala City for current information on the safety of these roads is a good idea; query other travelers as to the latest road and robbery conditions as well.

The road connecting Flores-Santa Elena and Tikal is also a good, fast, paved road. The Guatemalan government long ago decided to develop the adjoining towns of Flores, Santa Elena and San Benito, on the shores of Lago de Petén Itzá, into the region's tourism base. The airport, hotels and other services are here. Though there are a few small hotels and restaurants at Tikal, other services will remain limited.

POPTÚN
• pop 8000 • elevation 540m

The small town of Poptún is about halfway between Río Dulce and Flores. The reason most travelers come here is to visit Finca Ixobel (see boxed text about Michael DeVine, next page). There are also a couple of other places to stay and eat, and it makes a good stopover en route to Tikal, especially if you're coming over the rough road via Fray Bartolomé de Las Casas. In this case, you'll need a break, and Poptún is the perfect place for it.

There are several banks strung along 5a Calle in the town of Poptún that will change US dollars cash and traveler's checks. Bancafé gives cash advances on Visa cards, but there's nowhere to use MasterCard here. The Telgua telephone office is behind the police station near the market and the Municipalidad. Barring technical difficulties, email services are available at the Fonda Ixobel II restaurant daily from 11 am to 1 pm for US$2.60 a half hour.

Places to Stay & Eat

The best facilities are at the 400-acre *Finca Ixobel* (☎/fax 927-7363, @ fincaixobel@ conexion.com.gt, Web site, http://fincaixobel .conexion.com/). For several decades Carole DeVine has offered travelers tent sites, palapas for hanging hammocks, beds and lip-smacking homemade meals, with veggie options galore. Finca Ixobel is a special place, famous for its camaraderie – it's friendly and relaxed, a great place for meeting other travelers from all parts of the globe. It's also renowned for its food and its activities. Swimming, horseback riding, camping trips, inner-tubing on the river and a famous cave trip are all organized on a daily basis, for a reasonable charge. Visitors interested in the painted caves of Naj Tunich should ask at the finca if the site has reopened.

Camping or hammock space costs US$2.10 per person. Beds are US$3 in dormitories or US$6/7 for one/two people in tree houses, or you can pay US$7/9/11 for a single/double/triple private room with shared bath, or US$12/16/21 for a bungalow with private bath. A big, private villa with bath is US$15/20/24. Meals offer stellar value, particularly the eat-all-you-like buffet dinner for US$4.50. Or you can cook in the campground; if you do, you must bring all your own food, as there is no store on the finca.

Everything here is on the honor system: Guests keep an account of the potables they drink (wine and beer are sold here), the food they eat and services they use. Watch your budget and don't neglect the tip box for the staff when you settle up! There are often volunteer opportunities for fluent bilingual English-Spanish speakers in exchange for room and board. If the finca suits your style and you want to help/ hang out for a month minimum, ask about volunteering.

EL PETÉN

The Murder of Michael DeVine

Poptún is a sleepy, dusty town on the fringe of the vast jungle region of El Petén, where there's little happening for mainstream visitors except Finca Ixobel. This bohemian hideaway has been going strong for decades, offering weary travelers a little R&R in a rustic, friendly atmosphere with great folks and even better food. These days you can zip to the Finca from Guatemala City over a smooth, fast road in the most luxurious of coaches in six hours.

Things weren't always so rosy in this corner of Guatemala, however. Indeed, up until the early 1990s and the signing of the Peace Accords, Poptún was a training ground for the vicious anti-guerrilla forces called Kaibiles, and a place where locals habitually looked over their shoulders and kept their opinions to themselves for fear of reprisals. Like most places in Guatemala during the civil war, murders and 'disappearances' also struck Poptún, and on June 8, 1990, the American-born Michael DeVine, cofounder of Finca Ixobel, was found dead by the side of the road. A machete had been taken to his neck.

A protracted investigation into this heinous abuse of human rights revealed a sordid tale of murder, impunity and CIA involvement. Finally, in 1995, Guatemalan colonel (and paid CIA informant) Julio Roberto Alpirez was implicated in covering up the murder of both Michael DeVine and Efraín Bámaca Velásquez, Guatemalan guerrilla leader and husband of American lawyer Jennifer Harbury. Roberto was suspended, US aid to the Guatemalan military was temporarily withheld (but ultimately restored) and two CIA officials were fired, providing overdue, but still insufficient, closure for friends and families of the victims.

Amidst rolling green expanses and trails, horses romping wild and a refreshing swimming pool, Carole DeVine, Mike's widow, continues to run Finca Ixobel with a passion. You wouldn't think such a tragedy could befall such an idyllic place, but then again, that holds true for all of Guatemala, not just Poptún and the finca.

Finca Ixobel also owns the *Tierra Grande* protected area and sanctuary, 16km from Poptún. This patch of rainforest supports a variety of tropical plants and animals, and trips here are a valuable introduction to the jungle. Visitors sleep in hammocks, cook on an open fire and bathe in the river. The finca folks run good-value trekking and camping trips of 3/4/5 days (US$65/84/103 per person), including transportation, guide, food and equipment. Horses are available for an additional US$32 a day. Tours are arranged at the finca or you can call ahead. Volunteers are also needed to work with the Tierra Grande program reintroducing captive animals into the wild. A two week minimum commitment is required.

The turn-off for the finca is marked on the highway, 5km south of town. In the daytime, you can ask the bus driver to let you off there; it's a 15-minute walk to the finca. At night, or if you don't feel like making the walk, get off the bus in town and go to the *Fonda Ixobel II* restaurant, near the bus stop. They will radio for a taxi, which costs US$1 per person to the finca. It's important not to walk to the finca at night, as it's an isolated spot and robberies have been known to occur on the way. Indeed, robberies have also been attempted in broad daylight, so solo travelers might want to avail themselves of the taxi service.

In Poptún the town, there are several serviceable hotels. The good *Hotel Posada de los Castellanos* (☎ 927-7222) is owned and operated by the same family that has the Hotel Ecológico (see below). Clean rooms with fan and private bath, arranged around a leafy courtyard, are US$5/6/8/10. Some rooms are dark. Near the market are the *Pensión Isabelita* and the better *Pensión Izalco*, which has rooms with shared bath for US$3/4 without/with fans. Splurge for the fan!

There are also a couple of other places to stay in **Machaquila**, several kilometers beyond Poptún. *Camping Cocay (☎ 927-7024, ✉ birgitleistner@compuserve.com, http://ourworld.compuserve.com/homepages/birgitleistner)*, 7km north of town and then 700m from the highway, is a very primitive campground in the forest beside the river, good for swimming, inner-tubing and fishing. The prices of US$2.60 per person in a tent or hammock or US$3.25 in a dorm include breakfast; dinner is available for US$3.25. They, too, offer activities in the area, and the owner speaks German, English and Spanish. This place is primitive, remote and right in the jungle. Bring ample mosquito repellent; you'll need it.

The more upmarket *Hotel Ecológico Villa de los Castellanos (☎ 927-7541/42, fax 927-7307)* is just off the highway in Machaquila, 7km north of Poptún. It, too, is right beside the river and is great for swimming and inner tubing. Thatch-roofed cabins with electricity, private hot bath and two or three double beds are US$30/40/50 a single/double/triple. There's a restaurant here and acres of gardens with many edible and/or medicinal plants. Both these places are well sign-posted.

Getting There & Away

Bus All the Guatemala City-Flores buses stop in Poptún; see the section on Flores in this chapter and the Getting Around chapter for bus details.

Buses also travel the remote route between Poptún and Fray Bartolomé de Las Casas (usually called simply Fray or Las Casas), on the way to Cobán. From Poptún it's five hours to Fray, and then a further 5½ hours to Cobán.

Flores – US$2.60, two hours, 113km. Several buses run daily. The first departures, at 8 and 10:30 am, do not pass Finca Ixobel, so guests there must travel into the town of Poptún to make those early buses. A taxi from the finca is US$1 per person and easily arranged.

Fray Bartolomé de Las Casas – US$3.90, five hours, 100km. One bus departs at 11:30 am daily.

Guatemala City – US$7.75, eight hours, 373km. Daily buses run at 9 and 10:30 am, noon, 1 and 4 pm, with an additional deluxe departure at 10 pm (US$16.75).

Melchor de Mencos (Belize border) – US$3.90, four hours, 199km. Transportes Rosita buses (☎ 927-7413) leave at midnight, 2 and 4 am.

Río Dulce – US$3.90, three hours, 99km. Take any bus heading for Guatemala City.

Car If you're driving, fill your fuel tank before leaving Flores or Río Dulce, take some food and drink and a spare tire, and get an early start. The road is good in both directions, so drivers should have no problem driving between the major tourist destinations in El Petén. As in all of Guatemala, driving at night in this region is best avoided.

FLORES & SANTA ELENA

The town of Flores (population 2000) is built on an island in Lago de Petén Itzá. A 500m causeway connects Flores to her sister town of Santa Elena (population 17,000, elevation 110m) on the lakeshore. Adjoining Santa Elena to the west is the town of San Benito (population 22,000).

Flores, the departmental capital, is the more dignified town, with its church, small government building and municipal basketball court arranged around the main plaza atop the hill in the center of the island. The narrow streets are paved in cement blocks and flanked by charming houses with red adobe roofs, many of which are small hotels and restaurants.

Santa Elena is a rumpled town of dusty, unpaved streets, with many hotels and restaurants. San Benito is even less attractive, but its honky-tonk bars keep it lively.

The three towns actually form one large settlement, usually referred to simply as Flores.

History

Flores was founded on an island *(petén)* by the Itzáes after their expulsion from Chichén Itzá, and it was named Tayasal. Cortés dropped in on King Canek of Tayasal in 1524 while on his way to Honduras, but the meeting was, amazingly, peaceable. Only in March 1697 did the

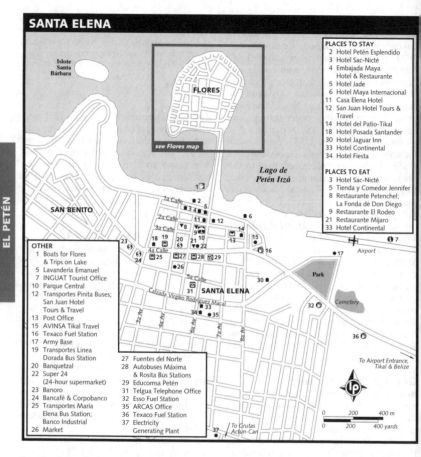

SANTA ELENA

Islote
Santa
Bárbara

FLORES

see Flores map

Lago de
Petén Itzá

SAN BENITO

1a Calle
2a Calle
3a Calle
4a Calle
5a Calle

SANTA ELENA

Calzada Virgilio Rodriguez Macal

3a Av
5a Av
7a Av
8a Av

Airport

Park

Cemetery

To Airport Entrance,
Tikal & Belize

To Grutas
Actun-Can

PLACES TO STAY
2 Hotel Petén Esplendido
3 Hotel Sac-Nicté
4 Embajada Maya
   Hotel & Restaurante
5 Hotel Jade
6 Hotel Maya Internacional
11 Casa Elena Hotel
12 San Juan Hotel Tours &
   Travel
14 Hotel del Patio-Tikal
18 Hotel Posada Santander
30 Hotel Jaguar Inn
33 Hotel Continental
34 Hotel Fiesta

PLACES TO EAT
3 Hotel Sac-Nicté
5 Tienda y Comedor Jennifer
8 Restaurante Petenchel;
   La Fonda de Don Diego
9 Restaurante El Rodeo
21 Restaurante Mijaro
33 Hotel Continental

OTHER
1 Boats for Flores
   & Trips on Lake
5 Lavandería Emanuel
7 INGUAT Tourist Office
10 Parque Central
12 Transportes Pinita Buses;
   San Juan Hotel
   Tours & Travel
13 Post Office
15 AVINSA Tikal Travel
16 Texaco Fuel Station
17 Army Base
19 Transportes Linea
   Dorada Bus Station
20 Banquetzal
22 Super 24
   (24-hour supermarket)
23 Banoro
24 Bancafé & Corpobanco
25 Transportes María
   Elena Bus Station;
   Banco Industrial
26 Market

27 Fuentes del Norte
28 Autobuses Máxima
   & Rosita Bus Stations
29 Educomsa Petén
31 Telgua Telephone Office
32 Esso Fuel Station
35 ARCAS Office
36 Texaco Fuel Station
37 Electricity
   Generating Plant

0   200   400 m
0   200   400 yards

Spaniards finally bring the Maya of Tayasal forcibly under their control.

At the time of its conquest, Flores was perhaps the last major functioning Mayan ceremonial center, covered in pyramids and temples, with idols everywhere. The God-fearing Spanish soldiers destroyed these 'pagan' buildings. Today when you visit Flores you won't see a trace of them, although the modern town is doubtless built on the ruins and foundations of Mayan Tayasal.

Tayasal's Mayan citizens fled into the jungle, giving rise to the myth of a 'lost'

Mayan city. Some scholars believe the Itzáes relocated to the magnificent El Mirador site near the Guatemalan-Mexican border, their sudden absence from Flores thus fueling the lost city myth.

Orientation

The airport is on the eastern outskirts of Santa Elena, 2km from the causeway connecting Santa Elena and Flores. Each bus company has its own terminal, jumbled cheek by jowl in Santa Elena. All long distance buses drop passengers in Santa Elena, so if you want to stay in Flores, you'll have to walk or hire a taxi across the causeway. Alternatively, you can hop onto a local lancha to make the quick lake crossing.

Santa Elena's 'main drag' is 4a Calle. All the important hotels, restaurants and banks are on this street or just off it. Opening hours in Flores seem relative. Don't be surprised if you show up someplace during normal hours to find it locked up tight.

Information

Tourist Offices INGUAT has a tourist information desk at the airport (☎ 926-0533) and on the plaza in Flores (☎ 926-0669). Both are open every day from 7:30 to 10 am and from 3 to 6 pm.

Money Some hotels and travel agencies in Flores will change US dollars cash and traveler's checks, but at a pretty terrible rate; most people head to Santa Elena to do their banking.

Banks in Santa Elena line 4a Calle. Banco Industrial has a 24-hour ATM and gives cash advances on Visa cards. Bancafé changes cash and traveler's checks and also gives cash advances on Visa cards. It's open Monday to Friday, 8:30 am to 7 pm, Saturday 9 am to 1 pm. Banoro changes cash and traveler's checks. It's open weekdays 8:30 am to 8 pm, Saturday 9 am to 4 pm. Banquetzal has good rates and gives cash advances on MasterCard. San Juan Travel at the San Juan Hotel gives cash advances on Visa, MasterCard and American Express cards, as does EcoMaya in Flores (see Travel Agencies, later in this section).

Besides the US exchange, currencies of the US, Mexico and Belize can be changed at the Banquetzal at the airport, which also gives cash advances on MasterCard. It's supposedly open seven days a week from 8 am to noon and 2 to 5 pm.

Post & Communications In Flores, the post office is just off the plaza to the southeast. Martsam Travel Agency, EcoMaya and Cahuí International Services offer domestic and international telephone and fax services. Wired folks will be stoked to learn that email businesses have recently hit Flores.

TikalNet on Calle Centroamérica and café .net on Avenida Barrios both have reasonably priced Internet services.

In Santa Elena, the post office is on the corner of 2a Calle and 7a Avenida. The Telgua telephone office on 5a Calle is open every day. Educomsa Petén (☎ 926-0765), 4a Calle 6-76, Local B, Zona 1, has email and computer services.

Travel Agencies Several travel agencies in Flores offer a range of services for visitors. Martsam Travel Agency (☎/fax 926-0493), next to the Hotel Petén, and Cahuí International Services (☎/fax 926-0494), next to the Hotel Santana, offer travel agency and telephone/fax services, tours, currency exchange and bicycle rental. EcoMaya has similar services, plus a newsstand with international newspapers and magazines, a small book exchange and message board. They also run organized tours to several archaeological sites in the jungle (see ProPetén and Organized Tours, later in this section).

Most of the travel agencies in Flores lead trips to the more accessible sites, including Tikal, Uaxactún and Ceibal. For example, the Hotel Guayacán (see the Places to Stay section) has trips to Ceibal (US$25) with an Aguateca option (US$60). Martsam offers transportation to sites such as Yaxjá for US$15 per person (great for independent travelers), or you can take a guided tour for US$40 per person, with a minimum of four people. There are other places offering tours and special deals, so shop and ask around.

San Juan Hotel Tours & Travel in Santa Elena and the San Juan de Isla Hotel & Travel Agency in Flores (see Places to Stay) offer direct minishuttle services to destinations of interest to travelers, including Belize City, Chetumal near the border of Mexico, Belize and Palenque, among others. (See Getting There & Away at the end of this section for details.) These shuttles are efficient and convenient, if spendy.

Laundry In Flores, try Lavandería Petenchel, open Monday to Saturday 8 am to 8 pm. In Santa Elena, Lavandería Emanuel

EL PETÉN

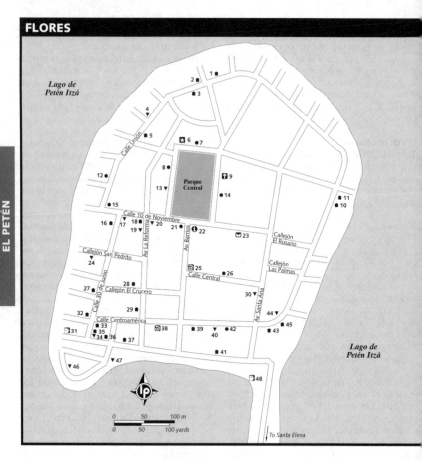

FLORES

Lago de Petén Itzá

Lago de Petén Itzá

To Santa Elena

on 6a Avenida near the causeway does a good job and the laundry is ready in an hour. It's open Monday to Saturday, 8 am to 7 pm.

Emergency The national police can be reached at ☎ 926-1365, and the national hospital is at ☎ 926-1333.

Responsible Tourism
Visitors to any of the sites deep in the Petén forest should be very conscious of traveling responsibly, as a continued human presence here will have a negative

impact on the ecological balance. Indeed, the Reserva de la Biosfera Maya is split into three (theoretical) zones in an effort to spare further degradation of the forest: The multiple use zone permits agriculture, including slash and burn, homesteading and harvesting of chicle and *xate*; a buffer zone permits chicle and xate harvesting only; and the core zone allows none of the above, but permits limited tourism. Observing the following basic guidelines and insisting your guides do the same will help protect this area: All non-organic garbage should be carried out, human waste and

EL PETÉN

toilet paper should be buried in a pit at least 15cm deep and 100m from a water source, and only dead wood should be used to build fires.

One issue of particular concern is the use of pack animals on these trips. Generally, a four-person expedition (two tourists, a guide and a cook) requires four mules. The problem is these animals eat copious amounts of sapodilla tree leaves; nearly an entire mature tree will be stripped of its branches to feed four mules for one day. Multiply this over a three-day trip with four paying participants, and you

begin to see the scope of the problem. This is disturbing. If you can avoid using mules on your trip, do so. Otherwise, inquire about alternative food sources for the animals.

Another nagging problem is mud. There's lots of it between May and November (halfway up a mule's leg is the norm), and machete-wielding guides hacking trails around mud patches kills new growth on the forest floor. Walking around a mud patch also makes it bigger, setting off an endless cycle of widening destruction. Hiking in these muddy conditions is no treat anyway, so try to arrange your trip for the dry season.

Trekking through the Petén in a responsible way gets really tricky when tourists contract freelance guides. Whereas the *Comite* guides are required to attend classes and complete coursework pertaining to responsible tourism, independent guides won't necessarily adhere to the ideals inherent to ecotourism. Indeed, oftentimes they're unaware of rudimentary, low-impact travel concepts. In this case, it is up to you, the traveler, to ensure basic tenets of responsible tourism are respected.

Grutas Actun-Can

The caves of Actun-Can, also called La Cueva de la Serpiente (The Cave of the Serpent), are of standard limestone. No serpents are in evidence, but the cave-keeper will turn on the lights for you after you've paid the US$1.15 admission fee (8 am to 5 pm daily) and may give you the rundown on the cave formations, which suggest animals, humans and various scenes. Bring a flashlight if you have one and adequate shoes – it can be slippery. Explorations take about 30 to 45 minutes.

At the cave entrance is a shady picnic area. Actun-Can makes a good goal for a long walk from Santa Elena. To find it, walk south on 6a Avenida past the Telgua office. About 1km from the center of Santa Elena, turn left, go 300m and turn right at the electricity generating plant. Go another 1km to the site. A taxi from Santa Elena costs US$2.

Useful Organizations

CINCAP The Centro de Información sobre la Naturaleza, Cultura y Artesanía del Petén, on the north side of the plaza in Flores, sells handicrafts of the region and has exhibits about the natural resources and forest conservation efforts of the Petén. It's open Tuesday to Saturday 9 am to 1 pm and 2 to 7 pm. In the same space is the Asociación Alianza Verde (☎/fax 926-0718, contact ✆ alianzaverde@conservation.org.gt), an organization dedicated to responsible tourism in El Petén. It's open weekdays from 9 am to noon and 2 to 6 pm and Saturdays 9 am to noon.

ARCAS The Asociación de Rescate y Conservación de Vida Silvestre (ARCAS) has a wildlife rescue center about 2km from the Hotel Villa Maya, which is about 10km east of Santa Elena. Animals here include macaws, green and yellow parrots, jaguars, howler and spider monkeys, kinkajous and coatimundis (pizotes) that have been rescued from smugglers and the illegal pet trade. At the center, the animals are rehabilitated for release back into the wild. You are welcome to visit, but you should ask permission first (☎/fax in Guatemala City 591-4731).

Volunteers are welcome to stay here, paying US$50 per week for room and board and volunteering any amount of time. Contact ARCAS for volunteer details (see Volunteer Work in the Facts for the Visitor chapter).

ProPetén The Proyecto Petenero para un Bosque Sostenible (ProPetén, ☎ 926-1370, fax 926-0495, ✆ propeten@guate.net, www.conservation.org) on Calle Central in Flores is the Guatemalan arm of Conservation International. ProPetén works with forest communities to promote tourism and other alternative uses of the Petén's natural resources. To this end, they've organized and trained special *Comites Comunitarios de Ecoturismo* (Community Ecotourism Committees) that take tourists into the jungle. Comite guides are usually *xateros* (collectors of xate, a palm used in flower

bouquets) or *chicleros* (collectors of chicle, used to make chewing gum) who know the forest very well, but may be light on the archaeological significance of the sites.

In conjunction with ProPetén, the committees offer tours to El Zotz (with an optional Tikal leg), El Perú near the Laguna del Tigre national park and El Mirador, the crown jewel of Mayan cities. While none of these trips can be made independently, due to the lack of potable water in the forest and the tangle of confusing trails, travelers wishing to arrange for Comite guides directly (rather than a travel agency) should head to ProPetén. Working directly with the Comites will save you about 30% on the price of a trip, but may be more time-consuming; all arrangements, including the trip itself, will be conducted in Spanish.

Organized Tours

Land Tours Travel agencies in Flores offer a number of interesting tours around the remote parts of the Petén region. EcoMaya (☎ 926-1363, 926-3321, fax 926-3322, ✆ ecomaya@guate.net, www.ecomaya.com), on Calle 30 de Junio, has some of the most authentic, demanding trips available. Cooperating with ProPetén and the Comites Comunitarios de Ecoturismo, EcoMaya has trips to El Perú (aka the Scarlet Macaw Trail), El Mirador and El Zotz. Nothing luxurious here; participants should be in good shape mentally and physically, as they'll sleep in hammocks, hike for long stretches through thick jungle, eat what's fed them and be constantly munched by the ants, mosquitoes and ticks swarming about. Trips start at around US$110 for a three-day, two-night excursion, including food, water, sleeping gear and Spanish-speaking guide. EcoMaya also administers two area Spanish schools (see the Around Lago de Petén Itzá section, later in this chapter) and sells alternative rainforest products such as cohune oil, potpourri and botanicals.

AVINSA Tikal Travel (☎ 926-0808, fax 926-0807, ✆ info@tikaltravel.com, www .tikaltravel.com), 4a Calle, Santa Elena, offers well-recommended trips to several sites, including Yaxjá and Nakum, with an optional Tikal extension. Horseback riding, lots of hiking and excellent wildlife viewing opportunities are highlights of this tour, as are the archaeological sites themselves. Guides are available in English or Spanish, and they'll also customize tours.

Monkey Eco Tours (☎ 201-0759, fax 926-0808, in the US fax 978-945-6486, ✉ nitun@nitun.com, www.nitun.com), based at the Ni'tun Ecolodge on the northwest side of the lake, specializes in lux adventure camping trips. Transport is via Land Cruisers. Portable showers, inflatable mattresses and crystalware are provided, and they employ specialized guides such as birders, archaeologists and biologists. They offer tours to El Mirador, Río Azul, Ceibal, Dos Pilas and Tikal, among other sites.

Lago de Petén Itzá As you stroll around town, particularly in Flores, locals will present themselves and offer boat rides around the lake. Many are freelance agents who get a commission; it's better (by that I mean; cheaper) to talk with the boat owner directly.

You should bargain over the price and inspect the boat. Or ask at the Restaurante/Bar Las Puertas in Flores; Carlos, the owner, offers boat trips around the lake and across to the other side, where he has land and a private dock for swimming and sunning. The travel agencies may also be able to arrange boat trips.

There's good bird-watching on the Río Ixpop, which feeds into the east side of the lake. Boat trips start from El Remate, on the

EL PETÉN

Chicle & Chewing Gum

Chicle, a pinkish to reddish-brown gum, is actually the coagulated milky sap, or latex, of the sapodilla tree (*Achras zapota*), a tropical evergreen native to the Yucatán Peninsula and Central America. *Chicleros* (chicle workers) enter the forests and cut large gashes in the sapodillas' trunks, making a pattern of V-shaped cuts as high up as 9m. The sap runs from the wounds and down the trunk to be collected in a container at the base. After being boiled, it is shaped into blocks for shipping. The cuts often kill the tree, and thus chicle harvesting tends to result in the serious depletion of sapodilla forests. Even if the tree survives the first round of cuts, a typical tree used for harvesting chicle has a life span of just 10 years.

First used as a substitute for natural rubber (to which the sapodilla is related), by about 1890 chicle was best known as the main ingredient in chewing gum.

As a result of war research for a rubber substitute during the 1940s, synthetic substitutes were developed for chicle. Now chewing gum is made mostly from these synthetic substitutes. However, in the northern reaches of the Petén, chicleros still live in the forest for months at a time harvesting the sap for gum. To check out some real chicle gum, visit www.junglegum.com.

east side of the lake (see the El Remate section later in this chapter).

Places to Stay
Santa Elena *Hotel Posada Santander* (☎ 926-0574) on 4a Calle is a simple, spotless and friendly family-run hostelry in a convenient but loud location. Ample rooms with private bath and two good double beds are US$6/7 a single/double. Rooms with shared bath are US$4/5. The family also operates Transportes Inter Petén, with economical minibus service to Tikal and other places.

Nearer the lake, *Hotel Sac-Nicté* (☎ 926-0092) has clean, large upstairs rooms with private bath, balcony and views across the lake to Flores for US$10.50. Downstairs rooms have no view and cost US$7.75. The hotel has a restaurant, parking and transportation service.

Hotel Continental (☎ 926-0095), on 6a Avenida at Calzada Virgilio Rodríguez Macal, is a large hotel, fairly far removed from everything. Rooms are US$2.60 per person with shared bath or US$3.90 with private bath. There's a restaurant here, and parking in the courtyard. Better is the *Hotel Fiesta*, next door, which also has a restaurant.

Santa Elena has other cheap but less attractive hotels, including the *Hotel Jade*, with rooms for US$2.50 per person, and *San Juan Hotel Tours & Travel* (☎ 926-0041/2, 926-2011/3), which charges US$4/6 for rooms with shared bath, US$10/12/14 with private bath and fan and US$22/24/30 with bath and air-con. Nearby, the brand-new *Embajada Maya Hotel y Restaurante* is another alternative.

Hotel del Patio-Tikal (☎ 926-0104, in Guatemala City ☎ 331-5720) looks severe from the outside but is actually a nice colonial-style hotel with a pretty central courtyard. Its 22 rooms, all with air-con and ceiling fan, cable TV, telephone and private bath, are US$48 for one or two people, US$51 for three. There's a bar, restaurant, pool and small gym here.

Hotel Maya Internacional (in Guatemala ☎ 334-8136/9, fax 334-8134,

@ stpvillas@pronet.net.gt), directly lakeside, has singles/doubles/triples for US$60/67/70.

Right on the water is the sparkling new *Hotel Petén Esplendido* (☎ 926-0880, fax 926-0866, in Guatemala City ☎ 360-8140, fax 332-3232, @ hpesplen@guate.net), which boasts the only elevator in all of El Petén. This is a luxury hotel with every amenity, including a swank poolside bar, conference room and two restaurants. The 62 rooms are modern, spotless, have little balconies and are wheelchair accessible. Rates are US$75/85/95. English, Italian and German are spoken.

Hotel Villa Maya (☎/fax 926-0086, in Guatemala City ☎ 334-8136, fax 334-8134, @ stpvillas@pronet.net.gt), on Laguna Petenchel about 10km east of Santa Elena, has 40 double rooms in bungalows with private bath, ceiling fan, hot water, beautiful views of the lake and blissful quiet. There's a patio restaurant, three tennis courts, two swimming pools, two private lagoons and a wildlife refuge. Prices are US$77/85/93 a single/double/triple.

Flores The cheerful, family-run *Hotel Villa del Lago* (☎/fax 926-0629), beside the lake on the east side of the island, is a fine, clean place to stay, much nicer inside than its appearance would suggest. Simple double rooms with private bath are US$6.45. Bigger, more comfortable units with bath, fan and TV are US$15.50 for two people; US$19.50 with air-con. Next door, *Restaurante/Bar Posada El Tucán* has forgettable rooms with shared bath for US$2 per person. These are off to one side of the restaurant.

Facing the causeway is the new *Petenchel Hotel* (☎ 926-3359). This is a solid value, with clean rooms with private hot bath and comfortable beds for US$7/9. Providing atmosphere is a small courtyard jammed with plants; some rooms are dark, however.

Next door is an entrance to the friendly *Hotel y Restaurante La Canoa* (☎ 926-0852/53). Rooms with private hot bath are US$3.90 per person. Upstairs rooms are airier, and downstairs triples can be crowded. The two rooms with shared bath are US$2.60 per person. There's a good, popular restaurant here.

San Juan de Isla Hotel & Travel Agency (☎ 926-0041/42) has beat-up, overpriced rooms with private bath and fan for US$10/12 a single/double. From the rooftop there is a view across the lake to Santa Elena. They accept Visa, MasterCard and American Express. Nearby, the **Hotel Guayacán** (☎ 926-0351) has basic, but serviceable rooms with shared bath for US$2.60 per person.

Hospedaje Doña Goya (☎ 926-3538) is one of the best budget choices in town and often full as a result. Secure, spotless rooms with comfortable beds and shared hot bath are US$4/7; doubles with private bath are US$7.75. Some rooms have small balconies overlooking the street, which can be loud. There's a rooftop terrace with hammocks and lounge chairs from which to enjoy lake views. Breakfast is available here from 6 am, and there's a safe for valuables. Solo women travelers will do well to head here first.

The **Hotel Posada Tayazal** (☎ 926-0568), on Calle Unión, has decent, cleanish doubles with private hot bath and fan for US$7.75. The upstairs rooms are hot and close, but have partial lake views.

The simple but clean **Posada Tucán No 2** (☎ 926-1467) is OK. Singles/doubles are US$5/6 with shared bath, and some rooms have lake views. Next door, the **Mirador del Lago** is a good value, with doubles with private hot bath and good beds for US$7.75. There's a roof terrace with lake views, and you can buy cold drinks in the lobby.

Hotel Santa Rita (☎ 926-0710) is clean, friendly and family-run; it's an excellent value at US$6/9 a single/double with private bath. The adjacent **Restaurante y Hotel La Jungla** (☎ 926-0634) has clean, generic rooms with private cold bath for US$10/14/18. This place will do in a pinch and they accept credit cards.

The **Hotel y Restaurante Posada El Peregrino** on Avenida La Reforma has reasonable doubles with shared bath for US$6.45; US$9 with private hot bath and TV. The restaurant here is terrific.

Hotel y Restaurante La Mesa de los Mayas (☎/fax 926-1240) is a lovely place, very clean and well-kept. Doubles with private bath and fan/air-con are US$15/20 or US$20/25 for a triple/quad with private bath and fan. They accept Visa and Master-Card.

The **Hotel Jaguar Inn** (☎ 926-0002, Calzada Virgilio Rodríguez Macal 8-79, Zona 1) is comfortable without being fancy, but slightly inconveniently located 150m off the main road near the airport. It's good if you have a vehicle. Rooms with private bath are US$18/24 a single/double with fan, US$24/30 with air-con.

The new **Casa Elena Hotel** (☎ 926-2238/9, fax 926-0097, in Guatemala ☎ 472-4045, fax 472-1633), on the first block over the causeway, has nice, clean rooms that are short on character but long on comfort. Each is equipped with private hot bath, cable TV and telephone, and costs US$35/45. Some rooms have park views, others overlook the swimming pool. There's a bar, restaurant and roof terrace.

Hotel Sabana (☎/fax 926-1248), on the north side of the island, has a restaurant and sun deck over the water. Rooms with private bath, fan, air-con and cable TV are US$20/30/40 a single/double/triple.

Hotel Casona de la Isla (☎ 926-0523, fax 926-0593, ✉ lacasona@guate.net) is a romantic place with a lakeside Jacuzzi and swimming pool with a waterfall and an open-air bar/restaurant. All 27 rooms have private bath, cable TV, phone, air-con and chairs on the balcony outside the room. Singles/doubles/triples are US$33/37/47.

Hotel Petén (☎/fax 926-0692, contact ✉ lacasona@guate.net) has a small courtyard with tropical plants, a pleasant lakeside terrace and restaurant, plus an indoor swimming pool. The 19 comfy-if-plain rooms, all with private bath, air-con and fan, are US$25/30/40 a single/double/triple from April to June and September to November; all other times they're US$30/35/45. Try to get a room on the top floor with a view of the lake.

The new **Casa Azul Guest House** (☎ 926-1138, fax 926-0593, ✉ lacasona@guate.net), on the northern shore, is a comfortable and quiet place with quirky rooms. (Note that the Casona de la Isla, the Hotel Petén and the Casa Azul all share the same email address.) All the rooms are different, but spotless, and have private hot bath, cable TV, refrigerator, telephone, air-con and balcony for US$30/35 a single/double. The ones facing the water are most desirable.

At the **Hotel Santana** (☎ 926-0491, ☎/fax 926-0662), most of the rooms have great lake views, with large private balconies with chairs. Singles/doubles/triples/quads with private bath, cable TV, air-con and fan are US$30/45/55/65. There's a restaurant with a lakeside terrace.

Hotel Isla de Flores (☎ 926-0614, in Guatemala City ☎ 476-8775, fax 476-0294, @ reservaciones@junglelodge.guate.com, www.junglelodge.guate.com) is clean and attractive. The rooms are large and well-equipped, with cable TV, air-con, ceiling fan, telephone and private bath with tub. Many rooms have private balconies with a view of the lake. Singles/doubles are US$35/40.

Places to Eat

As with hotels, the restaurants in Santa Elena tend to be cheaper than those in Flores. All are fairly simple and open long hours. Beer, drinks and sometimes even wine are served. Also on the menu at most places are a variety of local game, including tepezcuintle (a rabbit-sized jungle rodent known in English as the paca, or cavy), venado (deer), armadillo, pavo silvestre (wild turkey) and pescado blanco (white fish). As local game becomes ever more scarce, travelers will have to check their conscience before indulging in dishes that may soon jump from the menu to the endangered species list.

Santa Elena Hotel Sac-Nicté, Hotel Fiesta, the Hotel Continental, the Embajada Maya and the Casa Elena Hotel have restaurants. For a real splurge, try one of the two fancy restaurants overlooking the water at the Hotel Petén Esplendido.

Restaurante El Rodeo, at the corner of 2a Calle and 5a Avenida, is often recom-

mended by locals. It's open every day from 11 am to 9 pm. In the same block, **Super 24** is a 24-hour supermarket. Load up here if you're heading on a multiday jungle trek, and bring enough goodies to share with your guides and any people living in the forest you may encounter. In the next block of 2a Calle, **Restaurante Petenchel** and **La Fonda de Don Diego** are also popular. **Restaurante Mijaro**, a simple comedor on the main road, is another place recommended by locals; it's open every day 7 am to 9 pm.

The **Tienda y Comedor Jennifer** is a really simple place just over the causeway (near the Hotel Jade) with only a few tables and chairs, great people watching, good food and cold beer. A big plate of fried chicken with French fries will run you US$2.

Flores **Restaurante/Bar Las Puertas** is a popular restaurant and bar with decent, if pricey, food. It's a good spot for friendly conversation, as this is the hangout for an interesting mix of people. This is one of only a handful of places where you can get a real cup of coffee in Flores. There's live music on weekends. It's open Monday to Saturday, 9 am to 1 am.

Restaurante Chal-tun-ha is small and congenial, with an open and fresh decor, a terrace right over the water and a fine view across the lake. The menu offers a good selection of inexpensive dishes. It's open every day 9 am to 7:30 pm. **Restaurante**

Don Quijote, another cool little place, is on a small boat docked on the southern shore.

Restaurante/Bar Posada El Tucán, next to the Villa del Lago, has a thatched roof and a lakeside terrace that catches any breezes. Set breakfasts cost US$2 to US$3, lunches and dinners US$5 to US$8. Across the street is the good *Restaurante & Pizzería Picasso*, offering pizza, pasta and salads at fair prices.

Restaurante La Canoa is cheaper and plainer, but its dark, high-ceilinged dining room appeals to budget travelers, as does the decent food at low prices. Don't miss the killer tortillas here. A few doors down on Calle Centroamérica is a no-name *frozen yogurt shop* that's actually the front room of someone's house. There's only one flavor a week, but this stuff is *good,* even at a steep US$0.50 a cone.

Restaurante La Jungla has a tiny street-side terrace. Nearby, *La Hacienda del Rey* has a huge terrace, invitingly adorned with white lights strung from the rafters. This place specializes in meat: Mixed grill, sirloin, porterhouse and T-bone steaks are all on offer. It isn't cheap (US$11 for a hefty porterhouse), but has a nice atmosphere and is open at 5 am for breakfast – perfect for a nip of coffee before the early shuttle to Tikal.

Hotel y Restaurante La Mesa de los Mayas is a popular restaurant serving good traditional foods as well as local game. A mixed plate goes for US$9, a vegetarian plate is US$5 and chicken costs even less. It's open every day, 7 am to 11 pm.

The *Restaurante Gran Jaguar* is good for a meal, though big tour groups turn up here from time to time. It has a variety of inexpensive dishes, attractive decor and bar service. It's open Monday to Saturday 11 am to 10 pm.

Restaurante La Unión, on the northwestern bend of the island, has reasonably priced chicken, pasta and seafood dishes. The real reason to come here is the location, which is right on the water, with terrific views.

The *Mayan Princess Café, Bar & Cinema*, on the corner of Calle 10 de Noviembre and Avenida La Reforma, serves western food along the lines of chicken Florentine and ravioli with pesto. They do it surprisingly well, and the prices are reasonable (around US$4 a plate) despite the smallish portions and spotty service. Across the street is the very local, very friendly *Sala Maya*, serving set and à la carte meals at rock bottom (for Flores!) prices. Try their *limonada con soda,* which will cure what ails you on a hot day.

A place serving delicious comfort food at great prices is the *Hotel y Restaurante Posada el Peregrino*. For US$3.25 you can dine on a big plate of succulent roasted chicken accompanied by french fries, salad and rice – highly recommended.

A similar place – weaker on the food but stronger on the atmosphere – is *El Mirador*, on the west side of the plaza. Here you can dine on a large, set lunch for US$1.50, while enjoying lake views. The cook shacks nearby are a good place to get *refacciones,* simple snacks like tacos and fries.

Then there's *La Luna*, in a class by itself. This very popular restaurant and bar cultivates a classic tropical ambiance, with overhead fans that whirl away while smooth music wafts about and potted palms catch the breeze. The food is continental and delectable, with innovative chicken, fish and beef dishes the likes of which you'll be hard pressed to find anywhere else in Guatemala. Drinks come with complimentary peanuts, and the coffee is real; expect to pay around US$8 for a meal, excluding cocktails. It's open for lunch and dinner every day but Monday. It's on the corner of Calle 30 de Junio and Calle 10 de Noviembre.

Entertainment

Flores is pretty dead at night, but there are a couple of places to hang out if you need to escape your hotel room. *Kayuko's* is a co-pacetic bar with a pool table on Calle Unión. They serve light meals at tables overlooking the lake, and the satellite dish means sports fans can catch a game. It's closed Monday.

El **Balcón del Cielo** is a bar with awesome views of the lake off to the west and the church across the plaza to the east, and is a great place to take a cocktail while watching the sunset. The music is decent and the peanuts are free. They also serve light meals. The bar at **La Luna** is popular, as well.

The **Mayan Princess Café, Bar & Cinema** shows free movies (some of dubious quality) at 4 and 9 pm in its dining room. There are comfy chairs and imported beers available, but the later showings can be a bit of a drag if you're trying to carry on a dinner conversation.

Getting There & Away

Air The airport at Santa Elena (usually called 'the airport at Flores') is quite busy these days. International flights include those to/from Belize City with Tropic Air, Island Air, Grupo Taca, Racsa, Tapsa and Aerovías; flights to/from Palenque, Chetumal, Cancún and Havana with Aerocaribe; and a flight to/from Cancún four times a week with Aviateca and daily with Grupo Taca.

There's quite a variation in flight prices between Flores and Guatemala City, ranging from around US$50 to US$85. Package tours including airfare and accommodations may work out to be cheaper, and are available at many travel agencies. See the Tikal section, later in this chapter, for more on this.

There are also flights between Flores-Santa Elena and Puerto Barrios (US$65, 50 minutes) on Monday, Wednesday and Friday at 1:35 pm.

More regional airlines will be opening up routes to and from Flores in the near future, though your travel agent at home may not be able to get up-to-date information on some of these small, regional carriers. Travel agents in Flores and Antigua will have current information, but may charge more for a ticket than you would pay by buying it at the airport.

When you arrive at the airport in Flores, you may be subjected to a cursory customs and immigration check, as this is a special customs and immigration district. You have to pay a US$20 departure tax if you're leaving Guatemala, US$0.65 if you're flying within the country.

Bus Travel by bus to or from Flores is now fast and comfortable over new roads. The exception are the Bethel and the Sayaxché routes, which remain riddled with potholes and rough patches.

Each bus company has its own bus station. Transportes Pinita buses depart from the San Juan Hotel in Santa Elena (☎ 926-0041/2). Transportes María Elena buses go from the Hotel Santander in Santa Elena (☎ 926-0574). Other bus companies in Santa Elena include Fuentes del Norte (☎ 926-0517), Linea Dorada (☎ 926-0070 926-1817, ✉ lineadorada@intelnet.net.gt), Autobuses Máxima (☎ 926-0676) and Transportes Rosío. For several destinations, you will have the choice of taking a tourist mini-shuttle or a local 'chicken bus.' The latter will always be slower and cheaper – and probably more memorable.

Belize City – US$20, five hours, 222km. The San Juan Hotel runs a daily shuttle, picking up passengers at their hotel at 5 am, arriving in Belize City around 10 am, connecting with the boat to Caye Caulker and San Pedro, Ambergris Caye. Or take local buses from Santa Elena to Melchor de Mencos and change there (see Melchor de Mencos, below).

Bethel (Mexico border) – US$3.25, four hours, 127km. Transportes Pinita buses run at 5 and 8 am and 1 pm; this is a rough road.

Carmelita – US$3.90, five hours, 80km. Transportes Pinita has a daily departure at 1 pm. It returns from Carmelita daily at 5 am.

Ceibal – See Sayaxché.

Chetumal (Mexico) – US$35, seven hours, 350km. A special direct 1st-class Servicio San Juan bus departs from the San Juan Hotel and Hotel Continental in Santa Elena every day at 5 am, bypasses Belize City and goes straight to Chetumal. At Chetumal it connects with buses heading north along the coast to Tulum, Playa del Carmen and Cancún. In the opposite direction, the bus to Flores departs from the main bus terminal in Chetumal at 2:30 pm. Cheaper are Rosita buses leaving Santa Elena for Melchor de

Mencos on the Belize border (see below), with a connection at the border to Chetumal.

El Naranjo – See the From El Petén to Chiapas section, later in this chapter.

El Remate/Puente Ixlú – 40 minutes, 35km. Tikal-bound buses and minibuses will drop you here. Buses to/from Melchor de Mencos will drop you at Puente Ixlú/El Cruce, less than 2km south of El Remate.

Esquipulas – US$7.75, 11 hours, 437km. There are two daily Transportes Santa Elena departures, at 6 am and 2 pm. This bus goes via Chiquimula (US$6.45, 10 hours).

Guatemala City – US$10.30, 12 hours, 488km. Fuentes del Norte operates buses all day from 7:30 am to 9:30 pm. Linea Dorada luxury buses (US$30, eight hours) depart at 10 am, 8 and 10 pm. Autobuses Máxima runs Pullman buses at 7 and 8 pm.

La Ruidosa (crossroads to Puerto Barrios) – US$6, eight hours, 242km. Take any bus bound for Guatemala City.

Melchor de Mencos (Belize border) – US$2, two hours, 100km. There are 2nd-class Transportes Pinita buses at 5, 8 and 10:30 am and Rosita buses at 5, 7:30 and 11 am and 2, 4 and 6 pm. On the Belize side, buses (US$0.50) and share-taxis (US$2) take you to Benque Viejo and San Ignacio (30 minutes) every hour or so.

Palenque (Mexico) – See From El Petén to Chiapas, later in this chapter.

Poptún – US$2.60, two hours, 113km. Take any bus heading for Guatemala City.

Río Dulce – US$6.45, five hours, 208km. Take any bus heading for Guatemala City.

San Andrés (around the lake) – US$0.65, one hour, 20km. Transportes Pinita buses run at 5:30 am and noon. They depart San Andrés for the return trip at 7 am and 1:30 pm. Boats make this trip more frequently (US$0.40, 30 minutes), departing from San Benito on the west side of Santa Elena and from Flores beside the Hotel Santana.

Sayaxché – US$1.30, two hours, 61km. There are 2nd-class Transportes Pinita buses at 5:30, 7, 8, 9 and 10:30 am and 1 and 3:30 pm. There are also tours from Santa Elena via Sayaxché to the Mayan ruins at Ceibal, departing from the San Juan Hotel and Hotel Continental at 8 am and returning to Santa Elena at 4 pm (US$30).

Tikal – US$1.30, two hours, 71km. Transportes Pinita bus runs daily at 1 pm, continuing to Uaxactún. It departs Tikal for the return trip at 6 am.

It's quicker and more convenient to take a shuttle minibus to Tikal (see below).

Uaxactún – US$2.50, three hours, 94km. A Transportes Pinita bus leaves at 1 pm. It departs from Uaxactún for the return trip at 5 am.

Shuttle Minibus Minibuses bound for Tikal pick up passengers in front of their hotel (5, 6, 8 and 10 am) and from the airport (meeting all flights). Any hotel can arrange a trip for you. The fare is US$5.15 per person round-trip; the trip takes one to 1½ hours.

Return trips generally depart from Tikal at 2, 4 and 5 pm. Drivers will anticipate that you'll want to return to Flores that same afternoon; if you know which return trip you plan to be on, they'll hold a seat for you or arrange a seat in a colleague's minibus. If you stay overnight in Tikal and want to return to Flores by minibus, it's a good idea to reserve a seat with one of the minibus drivers when they arrive in the morning. Don't wait until departure time and expect to find a seat. You may also have success hitching a ride with other tourists with their own transport.

A taxi (for up to four people) from Flores-Santa Elena to Tikal costs US$40 round-trip.

Getting Around

Buses and minibuses bound for the small villages around the lake and in the immediate vicinity depart from the market area in Santa Elena.

Several hotels, car rental companies and travel agencies offer rentals, including cars, 4WDs, pickup trucks and minibuses. Rental car companies are in the arrivals hall at Flores airport. They include:

Garrido	☎ 926-0092
Hertz	☎ 926-0332, 926-0415
Koka	☎ 926-0526, 926-1233
Los Compadres	☎ 926-0444
Los Jades	☎ 926-0734
Nesa	☎ 926-0082
Tabirini	☎/fax 302-5900

EL PETÉN

A basic car with unlimited *kilometraje* (distance allowance) costs a minimum of around US$50 per day. The travel agency at the San Juan Hotel in Santa Elena (☎ 926-0041/2, fax 926-0514) also has rental cars, and there is a Hertz office in the lobby of the Hotel Camino Real Tikal (☎ 929-0206, ext 2).

Cahuí International Services in Flores (☎/fax 926-0494) rents bicycles for US$0.85 per hour or US$6.65 per day. The Hotel Guayacán (☎ 926-0351) rents bicycles for US$0.65 an hour. Around the lake in El Remate, Casa Mobego (☎ 926-0269) rents bicycles too.

Lanchas ferrying passengers between Santa Elena and Flores depart from either end of the causeway (US$0.15, five minutes). Motorboats making tours around Lago de Petén Itzá depart from the Santa Elena end of the causeway. Colectivo boats to San Andrés and San José, villages across the lake, depart from San Benito on the west side of Santa Elena and from alongside the Hotel Santana in Flores (US$0.40 if the boat is full, or US$7.75 for one passenger). You can also contract lancheros here for tours around the lake, but you'll need to bargain hard.

EL REMATE

Once little more than a few thatched huts 35km northeast of Santa Elena on the Tikal road, the village of El Remate keeps on growing, thanks to the tourist trade. Right on the lakeshore, El Remate is becoming a tertiary tourist center, after Flores and Tikal. Halfway between the two places, it allows you to be closer to Tikal than Flores, but still be on the lake.

El Remate is known for its wood carving. Several handicrafts shops on the lakeshore opposite La Mansión del Pájaro Serpiente sell local handicrafts and rent canoes, rafts and kayaks.

From El Remate an unpaved road snakes its way around the northeast shore of the lake to the Biotopo Cerro Cahuí, the luxury Hotel Camino Real Tikal and on to the villages of San José and San Andrés on the northwest side of the lake. It's possible to go all the way around the lake by road.

With their newfound prosperity, Rematecos have built a *balneario municipal* (municipal beach) just off the highway; several cheap pensions and small hotels have opened here as well.

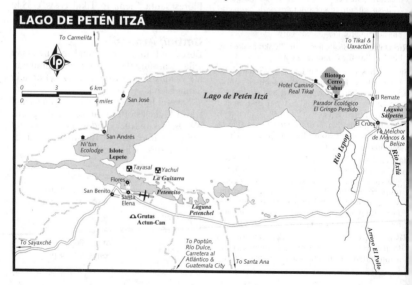

KRAIG LIEB

Volcano & clouds – Eastern Guatemala

ALFREDO MAIGUEZ

Canoe on Río Dulce

Pyramid at Tikal

Stone bas relief at Tikal

Ruins at Tikal

Biotopo Cerro Cahuí

At the northeast end of Lago de Petén Itzá, about 43km from Santa Elena and 3km from the Flores-Tikal road, the Biotopo Cerro Cahuí covers 651 hectares of sub-tropical forest. Within the reserve are mahogany, cedar, ramón, broom, sapodilla and cohune palm trees, as well as many species of lianas (climbing plants) and epiphytes (air plants), including bromeliads, ferns and orchids. The hard wood of the sapodilla was used in Mayan temple door lintels, which have survived from the Classic period to our own time. This is also the tree from which chicle is sapped.

Animals roaming the reserve include spider and howler monkeys, ocelots, white-tailed deer, raccoons, armadillos and some 21 other species. More than 24 maritime species found here include fish, turtles and snakes, as well as the *Crocodylus moreletti*, the Petén crocodile. The bird life, of course, is rich and varied. Depending upon the season and migration patterns, you might see kingfishers, ducks, herons, hawks, parrots, toucans, woodpeckers and the famous ocellated (or Petén) turkey, a beautiful big bird resembling a peacock.

A network of loop trails starts at the road and goes up the hill, affording a view of the whole lake and of Laguna Salpetén and Laguna Petenchel. A trail map is at the entrance.

Entrance to the reserve costs US$2.60 per person. You may find the gate always open, or it may be open only from 6 am to 4 pm (once in, you can stay as late as you like). If you want to enter earlier but find the gate closed, go to the administration center and they'll let you in. You can camp here for an additional US$2.60; there are toilets and showers, but nowhere to buy food or other necessities closer than El Remate, some 3km away.

Places to Stay & Eat

El Remate has several small hotels and pensions, and more are opening all the time.

La Casa de Don David (☎ 306-2190), on the lakeshore about 10m from the Flores-Tikal road, is operated by American-born David Kuhn (the original 'gringo perdido') and his friendly Guatemalan wife. Bland rooms with private bath in free-standing bungalows are US$15/20/25. Nowadays, this place is more the haunt of organized tour groups than world travelers. Disappointing meals are served on the wide upstairs terrace overlooking the lake. There's horse-back riding, and in the early mornings and evenings they do a two-hour boat ride, crossing the lake and entering the Río Ixpop to see the crocodiles, birds and other wildlife (US$5.15 per person). Daily tours to Ceibal are also available here for US$35, including lunch and bus and boat transport to the site. A shuttle to Tikal from here costs US$5 round-trip.

There are a few cheaper places on the Flores-Tikal road worth a look. Offering terrific value is *Casa de Don Luis*, on the east side of the road. This friendly, family-owned place has two spotless rooms with comfortable beds, fan and shared bath for US$7/8/9. They may have a few more rooms built by the time you get there. There's no sign, but look for the slatted gate just before the *Casa de Juan*, which itself has super-basic rooms with walls reaching only partially to the ceiling for US$1.95 per person. Rooms do have fan and nets, however.

Nearby, on the path leading to the lake, is the *Hotel Sun Breeze*. Here, they offer simple, clean cement block rooms with shared bath for US$2.60 per person. There are one or two simple *comedores* nearby for meals; try the Casa de Juan.

There are a couple of other pleasant places with great lake views on the Flores-Tikal road. At the *Mirador del Duende* (☎ 926-0269, fax 926-0397), you can camp with your own hammock or tent for US$1.30 a person, sleep in a shelter (like a permanent tent) for US$2.60 per person or stay in a bungalow for US$4.50 per person. Healthy, economical vegetarian food is served. The owner boasts that this is a 'mosquito-free zone,' thanks to the breezes coming off the lake. Forest hiking tours are offered, and you can rent horses (US$10 a day) and canoes (US$4 a day) here.

EL PETÉN

Next door, **La Mansión del Pájaro Serpiente** (☎ /fax 926-0065) has 10 very attractive rooms with private hot bath for US$75, plus lovely gardens, a swimming pool and a reasonably priced restaurant/bar. Deep discounts may be available if you just drop in.

A couple of other good places are about 3km west of El Remate on the road around the north side of the lake, near the Biotopo Cerro Cahuí. First you'll come to a few budget places, most with lake views and all very laid-back. The **Casa de Doña Tonita** has six beds in a thatched *rancho* for US$3.25 per person. This is communal living in simple conditions (there are no fans or nets), but it could be a blast for a group. There is a restaurant.

Nearby, **Casa Mobego** (☎ 926-0269), across the road from the lake, has simple camping bungalows with outside bathrooms for US$4 per person. It's cheaper if you get meals here: US$9 per person covers accommodations, dinner and breakfast. A swimming dock is in front, and they rent mountain bikes.

Farther along this road, right on the lakeshore, is the **Parador Ecológico El Gringo Perdido** – the Lost Gringo Ecological Inn (☎ /fax in Guatemala City 334-2305). Shady, rustic hillside gardens hold a restaurant, a bucolic camping area, and simple but pleasant bungalows and dormitories. Per person rates are US$3 for a campsite, US$6 for a camping bungalow with roof, beds and mosquito netting, US$10 for a dorm bunk and US$14 for rooms with private bath. Four-person bungalows, each with its own patio, hammocks and chairs and a small private dock for swimming and sunning on the lake, are US$25 per person, breakfast and dinner included. Two luxury bungalows with air-con are US$50. Overall cost is cheaper if you get a room-and-meals package. Activities include swimming, fishing, windsurfing, volleyball, basketball, boat trips on the lake, and bicycling.

Farther around the lake is the luxury **Hotel Camino Real Tikal** (☎ 926-0207, @ caminor@infovia.com.gt), the fanciest hotel in the Petén. Located adjacent to the Biotopo Cerro Cahuí 5km west of El Remate, the Camino Real has 120 air-con rooms with all the comforts. Two restaurants and two bars keep guests happy, as do tennis courts, a swimming pools, water sports on the lake, a gym and all the other top-class services. Rates are US$100/110 a single/double, meals extra. (This hotel is rather remote, especially if you don't have your own wheels.)

Getting There & Away

Any bus or minibus going north from Santa Elena to Tikal can drop you at El Remate. Taxis from Santa Elena or the airport will take you for US$20. Once you are in El Remate, you can hail any passing bus or minibus on the Flores-Tikal road to take you to Tikal or Flores, but traffic is light after mid-morning.

AROUND LAGO DE PETÉN ITZÁ

San Andrés, a small town on the northwest side of the lake, is home to the Eco-Escuela de Español (☎/fax 928-8106, in the US ☎ 800-429-5660, ext 264, contact @ ecoescuela@conservation.org, www.conservation.org/ecoescuela), a Spanish language school that comes highly recommended by alumni. Cost is US$200/220 per week for four/six hours of daily instruction, including room and board with a local family. The volunteer opportunities, class trips and total immersion offered by this school are particularly rich and focus heavily on cultural and ecological issues.

A few kilometers farther west, **Ni'tun Ecolodge** (☎ 201-0759, fax 926-0807, @ nitun@nitun.com) is a beautiful place on the lakeshore with 30 hectares of grounds. Four spacious, attractive houses, each with three double beds, thatched roof, stone walls and private patio, are US$40/60/80 for a single/double/triple. The restaurant here is also very beautiful; a package of airport transfers, accommodations and three meals a day is US$55 per person. Bernie, who built and operates the hotel, is an adventurer who also operates Monkey Eco Tours (see Organized Tours in the Flores & Santa Elena section, earlier in this chapter).

San José, a town of about 3000 on the northwest shore of the lake, supports the Bio-Itzá Spanish School (contact EcoMaya in Flores, ☎ 926-1363, 926-3321, fax 926-3322, ✆ ecomaya@guate.net, www.ecomaya .com; in the US ☎ 800-429-5660), another consistently recommended program. The school offers 20 hours of study a week and a homestay with a local family for US$200 a week, or 20 hours of instruction and camping facilities (including hammock and mosquito net, shared kitchen and bathroom use) for US$125 a week. Students work closely with the Itzá community on projects such as their 36km nature reserve, medicinal plant gardens and Itzá language academy.

San José is a special place to be on Halloween, the eve of All Saint's Day (November 1), when perfectly preserved human skulls that are housed in the church are paraded around town on a velvet pillow. The skulls make visits to predetermined houses, where blessings are sought, offerings made, and a huge feast caps off the rite. The procession lasts throughout the night, with many houses visited and feasts shared by participants. Frequent boats shuttle people between San José and Flores-Santa Elena for this event.

San Andrés and San José are most easily reached by boat from Flores or San Benito. When full, lanchas leave for San Andrés (US$0.40, 30 minutes) and San José (US$0.65, 45 minutes), or you can bargain for a private boat. Buses also leave twice daily for these towns (at 5:30 am and noon), but it's a long, laborious ride and not nearly as enjoyable as the boat passage.

TIKAL

Towering pyramids poke above the jungle's green canopy to catch the sun. Howler monkeys swing noisily through the branches of ancient trees as brightly colored parrots and toucans dart from perch to perch in a cacophony of squawks. When the complex warbling song of some mysterious jungle bird tapers off, the buzz of tree frogs provides background noise and it will dawn on you that this is indeed hallowed ground.

Certainly the most striking feature of Tikal is its steep-sided temples, rising to heights of more than 44m. But Tikal is different from Chichén Itzá, Uxmal, Copán and most other great Mayan sites because it is fairly deep in the jungle. Its many plazas have been cleared of trees and vines, its temples uncovered and partially restored, but as you walk from one building to another you pass beneath the dense canopy of the rain forest. Rich, loamy smells of earth and vegetation, a peaceful air and animal noises all contribute to an experience not offered by other, readily accessible Mayan sites.

If you visit from December to February, expect some cool nights and mornings. March and April are the hottest and driest months. The rains begin in May or June, and with them come the mosquitoes – bring rain gear, repellent and, if you plan on slinging a hammock, a mosquito net. July to September is muggy and buggy. October and November see the end of the occasional rains and a return to cooler temperatures; this may be the best time – weatherwise – for a Tikal visit.

Day trips by air from Guatemala City to Tikal (landing in Flores/Santa Elena) are popular, as they allow you to get a glimpse of this spectacular site in the shortest possible time. Still, the site is so big that you need at least two days to see even the major parts thoroughly.

History

Tikal is set on a low hill, which becomes evident as you walk up to the Great Plaza from the entry road. The hill, affording relief from the surrounding low-lying swampy ground, may be why the Maya settled here around 700 BC. Another reason was the abundance of flint, the valuable stone used by the ancients to make clubs, spear points, arrowheads and knives. The wealth of flint meant good tools could be made, and flint could be exported in exchange for other goods. Within 200 years the Maya of Tikal had begun to build stone ceremonial structures, and by 200 BC there was a complex of buildings on the site of the North Acropolis.

EL PETÉN

TIKAL

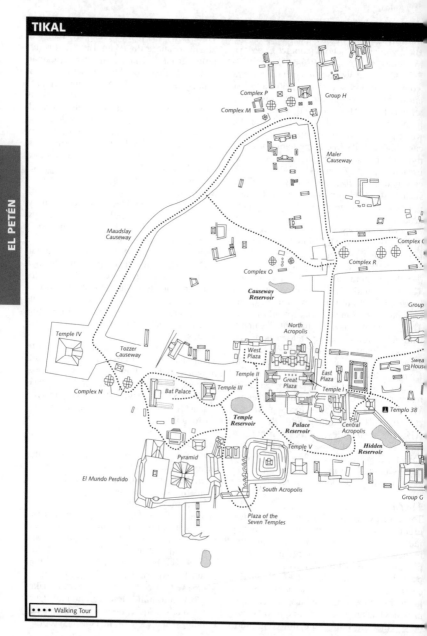

Complex P

Complex M

Group H

Maler Causeway

Maudslay Causeway

Complex O

Complex R

Complex C

Causeway Reservoir

Temple IV

Tozzer Causeway

North Acropolis

West Plaza

Group

Swea House

Complex N

Bat Palace

Temple III

Temple II

Great Plaza

East Plaza

Temple I

Templo 38

Temple Reservoir

Palace Reservoir

Central Acropolis

Hidden Reservoir

Temple V

Pyramid

El Mundo Perdido

South Acropolis

Group G

Plaza of the Seven Temples

•••• Walking Tour

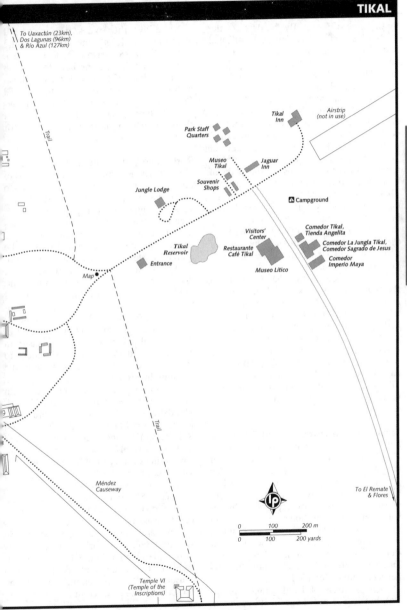

Classic Period The Great Plaza was beginning to assume its present shape and extent by the time of Christ. By the dawn of the Early Classic period, around AD 250, Tikal had become an important religious, cultural and commercial city with a large population. King Yax Moch Xoc, in power about AD 230, is looked upon as the founder of the dynasty that ruled Tikal thereafter.

Under Yax Moch Xoc's successor, King Great Jaguar Paw, who ruled in the mid-4th century, Tikal adopted a new and brutal method of warfare used by the rulers of Teotihuacán in central Mexico. Rather than meeting their adversaries on the plain of battle in hand-to-hand combat, the army of Tikal used auxiliary units to encircle the enemy and throw spears to kill them from a distance. This first use of 'air power' among the Maya of Petén enabled Smoking Frog, the Tikal general, to conquer the army of Uaxactún; thus Tikal became the dominant kingdom in Petén.

By the middle of the Classic period, in the mid-6th century, Tikal's military prowess and its alliance with Teotihuacán allowed it to grow until it sprawled over 30 sq km and had a population of perhaps 100,000. In 553, Lord Water came to the throne of Caracol (in southwestern Belize), and by 562, using warfare methods learned from Tikal, had conquered Tikal's king and sacrificed him. Tikal and other Petén kingdoms suffered under Caracol's rule until the late 7th century.

Tikal's Renaissance Around 700 a new and powerful king named Moon Double Comb (682-734), also called Ah Cacau (Lord Chocolate), 26th successor of Yax Moch Xoc, ascended the throne of Tikal. He restored not only the military strength of Tikal, but also its primacy as the most resplendent city in the Mayan world. He and his successors were responsible for building most of the great temples around the Great Plaza that survive today. King Moon Double Comb was buried beneath the staggering height of Temple I.

The greatness of Tikal waned around 900, but it was not alone in its downfall,

which was part of the mysterious general collapse of lowland Mayan civilization.

No doubt the Itzáes, who occupied Tayasal (now Flores), knew of Tikal in the Late Postclassic period (1200 to 1530). Perhaps they even came here to worship at the shrines of their old gods. Spanish missionary friars who moved through El Petén after the conquest left brief references to these junglebound structures, but their writings moldered in libraries for centuries.

Rediscovery It wasn't until 1848 that the Guatemalan government sent out an expedition, under the leadership of Modesto Méndez and Ambrosio Tut, to visit the site. This may have been inspired by John L Stephens' bestselling accounts of fabulous Mayan ruins, published in 1841 and 1843 (though Stephens never visited Tikal). Like Stephens, Méndez and Tut took an artist, Eusebio Lara, to record their archaeological discoveries. An account of their findings was published by the Berlin Academy of Science.

In 1877, the Swiss Dr Gustav Bernoulli visited Tikal. His explorations resulted in the removal of carved wooden lintels from Temples I and IV and their shipment to Basel, where they are still on view in the Museum für Völkerkunde.

Scientific exploration of Tikal began with the arrival of English archaeologist Alfred P Maudslay in 1881. Others continued his work: Teobert Maler, Alfred M Tozzer and RE Merwin among them. Tozzer worked tirelessly at Tikal on and off from the beginning of the century until his death in 1954. The inscriptions at Tikal were studied and deciphered by Sylvanus G Morley.

Since 1956, archaeological research and restoration has been carried out by the University Museum of the University of Pennsylvania and the Guatemalan Instituto de Antropología y Historia. Further efforts were undertaken in 1991, when the governments of Guatemala and Spain agreed to conserve and restore Temples I and V; the project was nearing completion in early 2000.

In the mid-1950s, an airstrip was built at Tikal to make access easier. In the early 1980s, the road between Tikal and Flores was improved and paved, and direct flights to Tikal were abandoned (flights now land in Flores/Santa Elena). Tikal National Park was declared a UNESCO World Heritage Site in 1979.

Orientation & Information

Tikal is located in the vast Parque Nacional Tikal, a 576-sq-km preserve containing thousands of separate ruined structures. The central area of the city occupied about 16 sq km, with more than 4000 structures.

The road from Flores enters the national park boundaries about 15km south of the ruins. When you enter the park you must pay a fee of US$6.45 for the day; if you enter after about 3 pm, you can have your ticket validated for the following day as well. Multilingual guides are available at the visitors' center (US$20 for a half-day tour).

The area around the visitors' center includes three hotels, a camping area, a few small comedores, a tiny post office, a police post, two museums and a disused airstrip. From the visitors' center it's a 20- to 30-minute walk southwest to the Great Plaza.

The walk from the Great Plaza to the Temple of the Inscriptions is over 1km; from the Great Plaza to Complex P, it's 1km in the opposite direction. To visit all of the major building complexes, you must walk at least 10km, probably more, so wear comfortable shoes.

For complete information on the monuments at Tikal, pick up a copy of *Tikal – A Handbook of the Ancient Maya Ruins* by William R Coe. The guide is widely available and on sale in Flores and at Tikal. *The Birds of Tikal* by Frank B Smithe (Natural History Press, 1966), available at the Tikal museums, is a good resource for birdwatchers. For tips on birding in Tikal see Birding, later in this chapter.

The ruins are open from 6 am to 5 pm. You may be able to get permission to stay until 8 pm by applying to the Inspectorería to the west of the visitors' center. Carry a flashlight if you stay after sunset or arrive before dawn, though this may be advice that is not necessary, as park authorities have been cracking down on after-hours visitors. Crime against foreigners at Tikal, though relatively rare, is part of the reason for these stricter regulations, as are falling accidents, which are more common after dark.

Visitors should wear shoes with good rubber treads that grip well. The ruins here can be very slick from rain and organic material, especially during the wet season. Also, bring lots of water, as dehydration is a real danger if you're walking around all day in this heat. There is overpriced water for sale at the ruins. Please don't feed the pizotes that wander about the site.

Great Plaza

Follow the signs to reach the Great Plaza. The path comes into the Great Plaza around Temple I, the Temple of the Grand Jaguar. This was built to honor – and bury – King Moon Double Comb. The king may have worked out the plans for the building himself, but it was actually erected above his tomb by his son, who succeeded to the throne in 734. The king's rich burial goods included stingray spines, which were used for ritual bloodletting, 180 beautiful jade objects, pearls and 90 pieces of bone carved with hieroglyphs. At the top of the 44m-high temple is a small enclosure of three rooms covered by a corbelled arch. The sapodilla-wood lintels over the doors were richly carved; one of them was removed and is now in a Basel museum. The lofty roofcomb that crowned the temple was originally adorned with reliefs and bright paint. It may have symbolized the 13 realms of the Mayan heaven.

It used to be that visitors could make the dangerous climb to the top, but since (at least) two people tumbled to their deaths, the stairs have been closed. Don't fret, though, the views from Temple II just across the way are nearly as awe-inspiring. Temple II, also known as the Temple of the Masks, was at one time almost as high as Temple I, but it now measures 38m without its roofcomb.

Nearby, the North Acropolis, while not as immediately impressive as the twin temples, is of great significance. Archaeologists have uncovered about 100 different structures, the oldest of which dates from before the time of Christ, with evidence of occupation as far back as 400 BC. The Maya built and rebuilt on top of older structures, and the many layers, combined with the elaborate burials, added sanctity and power to their temples. Look especially for the two huge, powerful wall masks, uncovered from an earlier structure and now protected by roofs. The final version of the Acropolis, as it stood around AD 800, had more than 12 temples atop a vast platform, many of them the work of King Moon Double Comb.

On the plaza side of the North Acropolis are two rows of stelae. Though hardly as bowl-you-over as the magnificent stelae at Copán or Quiriguá, these served the same purposes: to record the great deeds of the kings, to sanctify their memory and to add 'power' to the temples and plazas that surrounded them.

Central Acropolis

South and east of the Great Plaza, this maze of courtyards, little rooms and small temples is thought by many to have been a palace where Tikal's nobles lived. Others think the tiny rooms may have been used for sacred rites and ceremonies, as graffiti found within them suggest. Over the centuries the configuration of the rooms was repeatedly changed, suggesting that perhaps this 'palace' was in fact a noble or royal family's residence changed to accommodate different groups of relatives. A hundred years ago, one part of the acropolis, called Maler's Palace, provided lodgings for archaeologist Teobert Maler when he worked at Tikal.

West Plaza

The West Plaza is north of Temple II. On its north side is a large Late Classic temple. To the south, across the Tozzer Causeway, is Temple III, 55m high. Yet to be uncovered, it allows you to see a temple the way the last Tikal Maya and first white explorers saw

them. The causeway leading to Temple IV was one of several sacred byways built in the temple complexes of Tikal, no doubt for astronomical as well as aesthetic purposes.

South Acropolis & Temple V

Due south of the Great Plaza is the South Acropolis. Excavation has hardly even begun on this huge mass of masonry covering two hectares. The palaces on top are from Late Classic times (the time of King Moon Double Comb), but earlier constructions probably go back 1000 years.

Temple V, just east of the South Acropolis, is 58m high and was built around AD 700. Unlike the other great temples, this one has rounded corners, and one very tiny room at the top. The room is less than a meter deep, but its walls are up to 4.5m thick. The view (as usual) is wonderful, giving you a 'profile' of the temples on the Great Plaza. The restoration of this temple by a team of Guatemalan and Spanish archaeologists and historians was nearly complete in 2000.

Plaza of the Seven Temples

On the west side of the South Acropolis is the Plaza of the Seven Temples. The little temples, all quite close together, were built in Late Classic times, though the structures beneath must go back at least a millennium. Note the skull and crossbones on the central temple (the one with the stela and altar in front). On the north side of the plaza is an unusual triple ball court; another, larger version in the same design stands just south of Temple I.

El Mundo Perdido

About 400m southwest of the Great Plaza is El Mundo Perdido (the Lost World), a large complex of 38 structures with a huge pyramid in its midst. Unlike the rest of Tikal, where Late Classic construction overlays work of earlier periods, El Mundo Perdido exhibits buildings of many different periods: the large pyramid is thought to be essentially Preclassic (with some later repairs and renovations); the Talud-Tablero Temple (or Temple of the Three Rooms),

Early Classic; and the Temple of the Skulls, Late Classic.

The pyramid, 32m high and 80m along the base, has a stairway on each side, and had huge masks flanking each stairway, but no temple structure at its top. Each side of the pyramid displays a slightly different architectural style. Tunnels dug into the pyramid by archaeologists reveal four similar pyramids beneath the outer face; the earliest (Structure 5C-54 Sub 2B) dates from 700 BC, making this pyramid the oldest Mayan structure at Tikal.

There are great views from the central pyramid, and it's flat top makes a great place for a picnic, weather permitting. Loads of birds flock around the Lost World and you can watch packs of pizotes hunting and gathering in the ruins' midst.

Temple IV & Complex N

Complex N, near Temple IV, is an example of the 'twin-temple' complexes popular with Tikal's rulers during the Late Classic period. These complexes are thought to have commemorated the completion of a katun, or 20-year cycle in the Mayan calendar. This one was built in 711 by King Moon Double Comb to mark the 14th katun of Baktun 9. The king himself is portrayed on Stela 16, one of the finest stelae at Tikal.

Temple IV, at 64m, is the highest building at Tikal and the second highest pre-Columbian building known in the Western Hemisphere, after El Tigre at El Mirador (see the Remote Mayan Sites section at the end of this chapter). It was completed about 741, in the reign of King Moon Double Comb's son. From the base it looks like a precipitous little hill. A series of steep wooden steps and ladders will take you to the top. The view is almost as good as from a helicopter – a panorama across the jungle canopy. If you stay up here for the sunset, climb down immediately thereafter, as it gets dark on the path very quickly.

Temple of the Inscriptions (Temple VI)

Compared to Copán or Quiriguá, there are relatively few inscriptions on buildings at Tikal. The exception is this temple, 1.2km southeast of the Great Plaza. On the rear of the 12m-high roofcomb is a long inscription; the sides and cornice of the roofcomb bear glyphs as well. The inscriptions give us the date AD 766. Stela 21 and Altar 9, standing before the temple, date from 736. The stela had been badly damaged (part of it was converted into a *metate* for grinding corn!) but has now been repaired.

Warning Note that the Temple of the Inscriptions is remote from the other complexes, and there have been incidents of robbery and rape of single travelers and couples in the past. Though safety has been greatly improved at Tikal, ask a guard before you make the trek out here, or come in a group.

Northern Complexes

About 1km north of the Great Plaza is Complex P. Like Complex N, it's a Late Classic twin-temple complex that probably commemorated the end of a katun. Complex M, next to it, was partially torn down by the Late Classic Maya to provide building materials for a causeway, now named after Alfred Maudslay, which runs southwest to Temple IV. Group H, to the northeast of Complex P and M, had some interesting graffiti within its temples.

Complexes Q and R, about 300m due north of the Great Plaza, are very Late Classic twin-pyramid complexes with stelae and altars standing before the temples. Complex Q is perhaps the best example of the twin-temple type, as it has been mostly restored. Stela 22 and Altar 10 are excellent examples of Late Classic Tikal relief carving, dated 771.

Complex O, due west of these complexes on the western side of the Maler Causeway, has an uncarved stela and altar in its north enclosure. An uncarved stela? The whole point of stelae was to record great happenings. Why did this one remain uncarved?

Museums

Tikal has two museums. **Museo Lítico**, the larger museum, is in the visitors' center. It houses a number of stelae and carved stones from the ruins. Outside is a large relief map showing how Tikal would have looked during the Late Classic period, around AD 800 AD. The photographs taken by Alfred P Maudslay of the jungle-covered temples in various stages of discovery are particularly striking. Admission is free.

The **Museo Tikal**, which is smaller, is near the Jungle Lodge. It has some fascinating exhibits, including the burial goods of King Moon Double Comb, carved jade, inscribed bones, shells, stelae, ceramics and other items recovered from the excavations. Admission is US$1.30.

Both museums are open Monday to Friday from 9 am to 5 pm, Saturday and Sunday 9 am to 4 pm.

Birding

Sure there are howler and spider monkeys romping throughout Tikal, but visitors will be equally impressed by the plethora of birds flitting through the canopy and across the green expanses of the plazas. Around 300 bird species (migratory and endemic) have been recorded at Tikal. Early morning is the best time to go birding, and even amateur bird-watchers will have their share of sightings here. Bring binoculars if you have them, tread quietly and be patient, and you will probably see some of the following birds in the areas specified:

- tody motmots, four trogon species and royal flycatchers around the Temple of the Inscriptions
- two oriole species, keel-billed toucans and collared aracaris in El Mundo Perdido
- great curassows, three species of woodpecker, crested guans, plain chachalacas and three tanager species around Complex P
- three kingfisher species, jacanas, blue herons, two species of sandpiper and great kiskadees at the Tikal Reservoir near the entrance. Tiger herons sometimes nest in the huge Ceiba tree along the entrance path
- red capped and white collared manakins near Complex Q; Emerald toucanets near Complex R

In addition, look for several hawk species near the reservoirs, hummingbirds through-out the park, several parrot species (brown hooded, white-fronted, mealy and red-lored) and Aztec parakeets while exploring the ruins.

Ask at the visitors' center about early morning and late afternoon tours led by accomplished birder Luis Antonio Oliveros.

Trails

The Sendero Benilj'a'a, a 3km trail with three sections, begins in front of the Jungle Lodge. Ruta Monte Medio and Ruta Monte Medio Alto (both one hour) are accessible all year round. Ruta Monte Bajo (35 minutes) is accessible only in summer. There is also a short interpretive trail called *El Misterio de la Vida Maya* (The Mystery of Mayan Life) that leads to the Great Plaza.

Organized Tours

All the hotels can arrange guided tours of the ruins, plus trips to other places in the region, including Uaxactún, Ceibal, Yaxjá and Nakum. The Jungle Lodge is a good place to ask about these tours.

Places to Stay

Intrepid visitors used to convince park guards (with a US$5 'tip') to let them sleep atop Temple IV, but this is an extremely rare deal these days, as safety is a major concern. If you are caught in the ruins after hours, you're likely to be escorted out. Your best bet to catch some solitude at the ruins and get an early glimpse of the wildlife in the park is to camp at the entrance and rise with the sun.

Other than camping, there are only three places to stay at Tikal. Most are booked in advance by tour groups, even though most groups (and individuals as well) stay near Lago de Petén Itzá and shuttle up to Tikal for the day. In recent years, travelers have lodged numerous complaints of price gouging, unacceptable accommodations and 'lost' reservations at Tikal hotels. And the value you get at these places compared to hotels in the rest of the country is laughable. It may be best to stay in Flores or El Remate and visit Tikal on day trips.

On the other hand, staying at Tikal enables you to relax and savor the dawn and dusk, when most of the jungle birds and animals can be seen and heard (especially the howler monkeys). If you'd like the thrill of staying overnight at Tikal, the easiest way is to forget about making reservations (which can be frustrating) and take a tour. Any travel agency can arrange one including lodging, a meal or two, a guided tour of the ruins and airfare. The Adventure Travel Center (☎/fax 832-0162, ✆ viareal@guate .net), 5a Avenida Norte No 25-B, near the arch in Antigua, is one place arranging these trips, and there are plenty of others. There's no need to make reservations if you just want to camp in the camping area.

Cheapest of Tikal's lodgings is the *official camping area* by the entrance road and the disused airstrip. Set in a large, open lawn of lush grass with some trees for shade, it has tent spaces on the grass and also on concrete platforms under palapa roofs; you can hang your hammock here, too. Water for the toilets and showers is more dependable than it has been in previous years, since it's now brought in. Camping is US$4.50 per person. The Restaurant Café Tikal, across the way near the museum, rents camping equipment at reasonable rates, so you can camp here even if you don't have your own gear.

The Jaguar Inn has a smaller camping area with bathroom and shower facilities. Camping is US$3.25 per person with your own tent or hammock; they don't rent camping equipment, however.

Largest and most attractive of these middling hotels is the *Jungle Lodge (in Guatemala City ☎ 476-8775, 477-0754, fax 476-0294, ✆ reservaciones@junglelodge .guate.com, www.junglelodge.guate.com)*, built originally to house the archaeologists excavating and restoring Tikal. It has 34 decent rooms in duplex bungalows, each room with private hot bath and two double beds, for US$48/60/70/80 a single/double/triple/quad. In an older section are 12 much less attractive rooms with shared bath for US$20/25 a single/double. There's a swimming pool, large garden grounds, and a restaurant/bar with breakfast for US$5 and lunch or dinner for US$10.

Tikal Inn (☎/fax 594-6944, 926-0065 – both numbers work for voice or fax), past the Jaguar Inn as you walk away from the small museum down toward the old airstrip, is the next most attractive. It has 17 rooms in the main building, as well as bungalows, which are slightly nicer, plus gardens, a swimming pool and restaurant. The rooms are quite simple and clean, all with private hot bath and ceiling fan, but have walls that extend only partway up to the roof and thus afford little conversational privacy. Singles/doubles are US$27/35 in the main building, US$55/82 in the bungalows. The electricity only operates from 11 am to 10 pm.

The *Jaguar Inn (☎ 926-0002, ✆ solis@ quetzal.net)*, to the right of the museum as you approach on the access road, has nine bungalow rooms with private bath and ceiling fan for US$30/48/66/78 a single/double/triple/quad in the high season; US$20/32/44/52 in low. Dorm beds are available for US$10 per person. The restaurant serves breakfast for US$3, lunch and dinner for US$6.

Places to Eat

As you arrive in Tikal, look on the right-hand side of the road to find the little comedores: *Comedor Imperio Maya, Comedor La Jungla Tikal, Comedor Tikal, Comedor Sagrado de Jesus* and *Tienda Angelita*. The Comedor Imperio Maya, first on the way into the site, seems to be the favored one. You can buy cold drinks and snacks in the adjoining shop. The comedores offer simple comfort in rustic and agreeable surroundings and are run by local people serving huge plates of fairly tasty food at low prices. The meal of the day is almost always a piece of roast chicken, rice, salad, fruit and a soft drink for around US$4, which can easily feed two hungry people. Simpler plates of rice, beans and eggs can be had for a fraction of this price if you ask. All of these places are open every day from around 5 am to 9 pm.

Picnic tables beneath shelters are located just off Tikal's Great Plaza, with itinerant soft-drink peddlers standing by, but no food is sold. If you want to spend all day at the ruins without having to make the 20- to 30-minute walk back to the comedores, carry food and water with you.

The **Restaurant Café Tikal**, in the visitors' center, across the street from the comedores, serves fancier food at fancier prices. Lomito (tenderloin of beef) is featured, as are other steaks, at US$10 a portion. Plates of fruit cost less. All the hotels also have restaurants.

Getting There & Away

For details of transport to and from Flores and Santa Elena, see the Flores & Santa Elena section earlier in this chapter. Coming from Belize, you can get off the bus at El Cruce/Puente Ixlú a northbound bus or minibus – or hitch a ride with an obliging tourist – to take you the remaining 35km to Tikal. Note that there is very little northbound traffic after lunch. If you come to Puente Ixlú in the afternoon, it's probably best to continue to Flores or El Remate for the night rather than risk being stranded at El Cruce.

You don't need a car to get to Tikal, but a 4WD vehicle of your own can be useful for visiting Uaxactún. If you're driving, fill your fuel tank in Flores; there is no fuel available at Tikal or Uaxactún.

UAXACTÚN

Uaxactún (wah-shahk-toon), 23km north of Tikal along a poor, unpaved road through the jungle, was Tikal's political and military rival in Late Preclassic times. It was conquered by Tikal's King Great Jaguar Paw in the mid-4th century, and was subservient to its great sister to the south for centuries thereafter.

When you arrive at Uaxactún, sign your name in the register at the guard post (at the edge of the disused airstrip, which now serves as pasture for cattle). About halfway down the airstrip, roads go off to the left and to the right to the ruins.

Villagers in Uaxactún live in houses lined up on either side of the disused airstrip, making a living by collecting chicle, *pimienta*

(allspice) and xate from the surrounding forest.

Ruins

The pyramids at Uaxactún were uncovered and put in a stabilized condition so that no further deterioration would result, but they were not restored. White mortar is the mark of the repair crews, who patched cracks in the stone to prevent water and roots from entering. Much of the work on the famous Temple E-VII-Sub was done by Earthwatch volunteers in 1974.

Turn right from the airstrip to reach Group E and Group H, a 10- to 15-minute walk. Perhaps the most significant temple here is E-VII-Sub, among the earliest intact temples excavated, with foundations going back perhaps to 2000 BC. It lay beneath much larger structures, which have been stripped away. On its flat top are holes, or sockets, for the poles that would have supported a wood-and-thatch temple.

About a 20-minute walk to the northwest of the runway are Group A and Group B. At Group A, early excavators sponsored by Andrew Carnegie simply cut into the sides of the temples indiscriminately, looking for graves. Sometimes they used dynamite. This unfortunate work destroyed many of the temples, which are now in the process of being reconstructed.

The ruins are always open and accessible, and no admission is charged. However, the turnoff onto the Uaxactún road is inside the gate to Tikal, so you must pay the US$6.45 admission fee there before proceeding.

Organized Tours

Tours to Uaxactún can be arranged at the hotels in Tikal. The Jungle Lodge, for example, offers a trip to Uaxactún departing daily at 8 am and returning at 1 pm, in time to meet the 2 pm buses back to Flores. The trip costs US$60 for one to four people, split among the number of people going, or US$15 per person for more than four people.

Places to Stay & Eat

If you have your own camping gear, there are several places to camp. **Eco Camping**, at the entrance to the larger group of ruins, is an organized campground with basic cabins.

Posada y Restaurante Campamento El Chiclero, on the left side of the airstrip, is a primitive place with seven musty thatch-roofed rooms with walls going only part way up and screen the rest of the way. Rooms are US$4.50 per person, or you can pitch a tent. Bathrooms are shared, and there's no electricity. It's a 10-minute walk from the ruins. Trips can be arranged here to other places in the area, including Parque Nacional El Mirador-Dos Lagunas-Río Azul, La Muralla, Nakbé and Manantial.

Getting There & Away

During the rainy season (from May to October, sometimes extending into November), you may find it difficult to get to Uaxactún. At other times of the year, be sure to ask in Flores or Tikal about the condition of the road. You may be advised it's only possible to make the hour-long drive in a 4WD vehicle.

A bus operates daily between Santa Elena and Uaxactún, stopping at Tikal on the way. The cost is US$2.50 for the three-hour ride from Santa Elena, or US$1 for the one-hour ride from Tikal. The bus departs

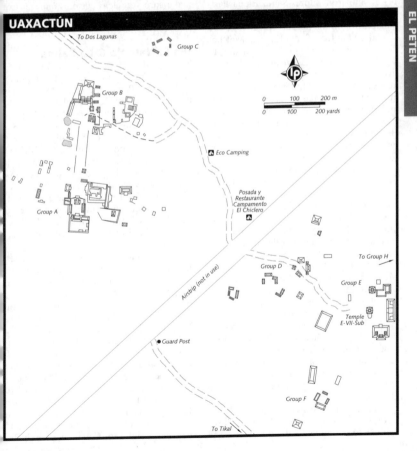

UAXACTÚN

To Dos Lagunas

Group C

Group B

0   100   200 m
0   100   200 yards

Eco Camping

Group A

Posada y Restaurante Campamento El Chiclero

To Group H

Group D

Group E

Airstrip (not in use)

Temple E-VII-Sub

Guard Post

Group F

To Tikal

Uaxactún daily at 6 am and departs Santa Elena at 1 pm for the return trip.

If you're driving, fill your fuel tank in Flores; there is no fuel available at Tikal or Uaxactún. You might also want to pack some food and drink, though drinks and a few snacks are available in the village at Uaxactún. You can hire a taxi from Flores to Uaxactún for about US$50; bargain hard.

From Uaxactún, it's 104km farther to the Río Azul ruins, or 88km to the lakeside village of San Andrés.

EASTWARD TO BELIZE

It's 100km from Flores-Santa Elena eastward to Melchor de Mencos, the Guatemalan town on the border with Belize. You can take a bus from Santa Elena to Melchor de Mencos, where you can transfer to another bus on the Belizean side. Alternatively, there's a San Juan Hotel shuttle bus at 5 am that goes all the way to Belize City and connects with the boat to Caye Caulker and Ambergris Caye. This shuttle enables travelers to avoid spending the night in Belize City – a seedy city if there ever was one. See the Flores & Santa Elena section for details on these shuttle buses.

The road from Flores to El Cruce and Puente Ixlú is good, fast asphalt. If you're coming from Tikal, start early in the morning and get off at El Cruce to catch a bus or hitch a ride eastward. For the fastest, most reliable service, however, it's best to be on that 5 am San Juan shuttle bus; it should pass the crossroads at about 6 am.

East of El Cruce the road goes to Melchor de Mencos; the trip takes two hours. In the past, there was guerrilla and bandit activity along this road, and there's an extremely remote chance that your bus could be stopped and its passengers relieved of their valuables. (It's been a long time since this has happened.)

At the border you must hand in your Guatemalan tourist card and pay a small fee (around US$1.30) before proceeding to Benque Viejo in Belize, about 3km from the border. At the border, there are Batty Brothers, Novelo's and Shaw's buses waiting to continue to Benque Viejo, San Ignacio, Belmopan and Belize City. If you arrive in Benque Viejo early enough in the day, you may have sufficient time to visit the Mayan ruins of Xunantunich on your way to San Ignacio. There are many serviceable hotels and interesting things to do around San Ignacio.

FROM EL PETÉN TO CHIAPAS (MEXICO)

There are currently three official routes through the jungle from Flores, in Guatemala, to Palenque, in the Mexican state of Chiapas. Whichever way you go, make sure you clear customs and get exit and entry stamps in your passport on both sides of the border.

Via El Naranjo & La Palma

The traditional route is via bus to El Naranjo, then by boat down the Río San Pedro to La Palma and finally by colectivo and bus to Tenosique and Palenque.

Transportes Pinita buses to El Naranjo (on the Río San Pedro) depart from the San Juan Hotel in Santa Elena daily at 5, 7, 8, 9 and 11 am, 1 and 3:30 pm; cost is US$2.60 for the rough, bumpy five-hour ride (125km). Rosío buses depart for the same trip at 4:45, 8 and 10:30 am and 1:30 pm. The San Juan Hotel offers an inclusive Santa Elena to Palenque transportation package via El Naranjo and La Palma for US$30 per person. These cater to tourists and leave daily at 5 am.

El Naranjo is a hamlet with a few thatched huts, large military barracks, an immigration post and a few basic lodging places. From El Naranjo you must catch a boat on the river around midday for the four-hour cruise to the border town of La Palma (US$20, bargain *hard*). From La Palma you can go by colectivo or bus to Tenosique (1½ hours), then by bus or *combi* to Emiliano Zapata (one hour, 40km), and from there by bus or combi to Palenque.

Going in the reverse direction, travel agencies in Palenque offer to get you from Palenque to La Palma by minibus in time to catch the boat to El Naranjo, which departs between 8 and 9 am. You then catch the bus or the dreadful five-hour ride to Flores, arriving there around 7 pm the same day. The cost is about US$55 per person. However, you can do it yourself by taking the 4:30 am bus from the ADO terminal to Tenosique, then a taxi (US$10) to La Palma to catch the 8 am boat. If you catch a later bus, there are basic, cheap hotels in Tenosique, or you can find a place to hang your hammock and rough it in La Palma.

Via Bethel & Frontera Corozal

A faster route is by early morning bus on the terrible road from Flores via La Libertad and the El Subín crossroads to the co-op hamlet of Bethel (US$3, four hours), on the Río Usumacinta, which forms the border between Guatemala and Mexico.

The early bus should get you to Bethel before noon, but if you're stuck you can spend the night at the *Posada Maya*, beside the river in the tropical forest 1km from Bethel. Lodging and meals are available here, and it's not expensive; you can rent a cabin, or sling a hammock. Food is grown in the organic garden. Activities include swimming in the river and tours to nearby places such as Yaxchilán, a natural spring and a lookout point. The owners are friendly and helpful to travelers, and they can arrange transport, including boats and horses.

Frequent boats make the half-hour trip downriver from Bethel to Frontera Corozal on the Mexico side, charging from US$4 to US$12 for the voyage, depending to some extent on your bargaining power and how many passengers are going.

At Frontera Corozal (formerly Frontera Echeverría) there's a restaurant and primitive accommodations, but you're better off taking one of the colectivos (shared taximinibuses) that wait for passengers to Palenque. The last colectivo tends to leave around 2 or 3 pm. The San Juan Hotel in Santa Elena also offers this as an all-inclusive transportation package for US$30, departing daily at 5 am and arriving in Palenque in the early afternoon.

From Frontera Corozal, a chartered boat to the Yaxchilán archaeological site might cost US$60, but sometimes you can hitch a ride with a group for US$10 or so; this is difficult in the off-season. Buses from Frontera Corozal take four to 4½ hours to reach Palenque; the fare is US$5.

Coming from Palenque, you can bus to Frontera Corozal (US$4, two or three hours), take a boat upstream (25 minutes to the Posada Maya, 35 minutes to the village of Bethel), and either stay overnight at the Posada Maya or continue on the bus to Flores.

In Palenque, travel agencies may insist that you can't do the trip on your own, that you must sign up for their US$30 trip, and that there is no place to stay overnight at the border. Not so! These organized trips save you some hassle, but you can do the same thing yourself for half the price. Just be sure to hit the road as early as possible in the morning.

Via Sayaxché, Pipiles & Benemérito

From Sayaxché, you can negotiate a ride on one of the cargo boats for the eight-hour trip (US$6.45) down the Río de la Pasión via Pipiles (the Guatemalan border post) to Benemérito, in Chiapas. These cargo boats leave when there's enough cargo and people to go, so it could take a day or several to arrange passage. From Benemérito, proceed by bus or boat to the ruins at Yaxchilán and Bonampak, and then onward to Palenque. There are also buses that run directly between Benemérito and Palenque (US$12, 10 hours).

SAYAXCHÉ AREA

The town of Sayaxché, 61km south of Flores through the jungle, is the closest settlement to a half-dozen Mayan archaeological sites, including Aguateca, Altar de Sacrificios, Ceibal, Dos Pilas, El Caribe, Itzán, La Amelia and Tamarindito. Of these, Ceibal, on the Río de la Pasión, is currently the best restored and most interesting, partly because of its Mayan monuments and partly because of the river voyage and jungle walk necessary to reach it. In the bone dry months (March, April and May), Ceibal can be reached with a 4WD.

Dos Pilas, under excavation at present, is not equipped to receive overnight visitors without their own camping gear. However, in good weather, you can make the trek in four hours on foot. From Dos Pilas, the minor sites of Tamarindito and Aguateca can be reached on foot and by boat, but they are unrestored, covered in jungle and of interest only to the very intrepid. There are campgrounds at all these sites.

Sayaxché itself is of little interest, but its few basic services allow you to eat and stay overnight in this region before pushing on.

Orientation & Information

The bus from Santa Elena drops you on the north bank of the Río de la Pasión. The main part of town is on the south bank. Frequent ferries carry you over the river for US$0.15.

The Banoro on the corner of the main street changes US dollars cash and traveler's checks, but at a weak rate. A block up the hill and to your right is also a Banrural that will change money. There's a post office way off the main drag near the radio station; head for the radio tower and ask passersby to steer you in the right direction.

Organized Tours

Viajes Don Pedro (☎/fax 928-6109), right on the riverbank, is run by the affable Pedro Mendéz, who is part boatman, part harbormaster and part social director. He can arrange transportation and guides to any of the area sites. Half-day trips for one to three passengers to Ceibal or Dos Pilas are US$33; to Aguateca it's US$40. These prices are for transport only, but guides can be contracted here too. Longer camping trips can be arranged, as can journeys to the Altar de Sacrificios, Yaxchilán and Bonampak sites near the Mexican border.

Viajes Turísticos & Restaurant La Montaña (☎ 928-6169, 928-6114, fax 928-6168), just up from Banoro, is another outfit running local tours. The friendly folks here run day trips to Ceibal (US$60 for up to five passengers) and Aguateca (US$70 for up to eight passengers), including guide. All-inclusive four-day, three-night camping

trips taking in Ceibal, Dos Pilas and Aguateca are also offered here for US$300 per person, minimum four people. Bookings can be made here for the Hotel Ecológico Posada Caribe as well (see Places to Stay & Eat, later in this chapter).

Ceibal

Unimportant during the Classic Period, Ceibal grew rapidly thereafter, attaining a population of perhaps 10,000 by AD 900. Much of the population growth may have been due to immigration from what is now Chiapas, in Mexico, because the art and culture of Ceibal seems to have changed markedly during the same period. The Postclassic Period saw the decline of Ceibal, after which its low, ruined temples were quickly covered by a thick carpet of jungle.

Today, Ceibal is not one of the most impressive Mayan sites, but the journey to Ceibal is among the most memorable. A two-hour voyage on the jungle-bound Río de la Pasión brings you to a primitive dock. After landing, you clamber up a narrow rocky path beneath gigantic ceiba trees and ganglions of jungle vines to reach the archaeological zone.

Smallish temples, many of them still (or again) covered with jungle, surround two principal plazas. In front of a few temples and standing seemingly alone on paths deeply shaded by the jungle canopy, are magnificent stelae, their intricate carving still in excellent condition. It takes about two hours to explore the site.

Dos Pilas

Dos Pilas (Two Stelae) usually refers to several sites lying within a 32km protected area 17km southwest of Sayaxché, including Arroyo de Piedra, La Amelia and Tamarindito. Dos Pilas itself was a military base from which the Maya fanned out to conquer their neighbors, and so is compact in design and features some of the only defensive walls ever found at a lowland Guatemalan site. Glyphs deciphered at Dos Pilas suggest that the founders may have come from Tikal, as the motifs are so similar as to belie coincidence.

The majority of the ruins at this site are unexcavated, so you may find yourself standing around looking at a bunch of grassy mounds while getting gnawed on by mosquitoes. In the case of Dos Pilas, as in much of life, the thrill is not in the destination itself, but in the journey. Trips running from Sayaxché to Dos Pilas can be arranged; camping overnight is highly recommended.

Aguateca, nearby, is almost an exact replica of Dos Pilas. Dates on the carved stela at Aguateca span from about AD 700 to the beginning of the 9th century.

Places to Stay & Eat

Hotel Guayacán (☎ 926-6111), right near the dock on the south side of the river in Sayaxché, is basic and serviceable. Rooms for one or two people cost US$13/16 with shared/private bath. There's a patio overlooking the river. The *Hotel Mayapán*, up the street to the left, has cell-like rooms for US$2 per person. Upstairs rooms are much better, cleanish and have private bath and fan for US$6/9.

The *Hotel Posada Segura* is the best budget option in town. Clean rooms with good beds, fan and shared bath are US$3.90

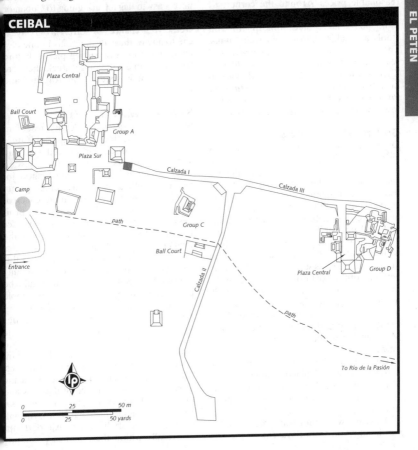

CEIBAL

per person; those with private bath are US$7.75. To get there, take your first right up from the river and follow this road until it dead ends, then hook a left. The nice folks running this place are building a cafeteria here.

The ***Hotel Ecológico Posada Caribe*** (☎ *928-6114, 928-6169, fax 928-6168, in Guatemala City ☎/fax 230-6588)*, on Laguna Petexbatún, has rooms for US$22 per person with kitchen privileges or US$54 per person with three meals a day.

Restaurant La Montaña serves tasty roasted chicken and other simple dishes at reasonable prices. Around the corner, ***El Botanero Restaurant Café-Bar*** is a dark, funky place chock full of atmosphere, with stools and tables hewn from tree trunks. They serve a variety of beef, chicken and seafood dishes starting at around US$3.25. There's a full bar, and it's a good place to kick back and have a beer. ***Restaurant Yaxkin*** is typical of the other few eateries in town: basic, family-run and inexpensive.

Getting There & Away

Day trips to Ceibal are organized by various agencies and drivers in Santa Elena, Flores and Tikal for about US$30 per person round-trip. It can be done cheaper on your own, but this is significantly less convenient.

Transportes Pinita buses depart from Santa Elena at 5:30, 7, 8, 9 and 10:30 am, 1 and 3:30 pm for Sayaxché (US$1.30, two hours). From here you can arrange a tour with one of the agencies (see Organized Tours earlier in this section) or strike a deal with one of the boat drivers hanging out by the river. From the river, it's less than 30 minutes' walk to the Ceibal site. You should hire a guide to see the site, as some of the finest stelae are off the plazas in the jungle. Most lancheros, conveniently, also serve as guides.

Buses leave Sayaxché for Flores from across the river at 5, 6 and 11 am and 1 pm. There is also one Fuentes del Norte departure to Guatemala City at 11 am (US$9, 14 hours).

Travelers wistful for some rugged travel can head south from Sayaxché to the San Antonio Las Cuevas crossroads near Raxrujá, and then east to Fray Bartolomé de Las Casas, west to Playa Grande and Parque Nacional Laguna Lachuá or south to Cobán. This last route is over rutted, mountainous road, and though treacherous, is very pretty.

One daily bus leaves Sayaxché at 8 am for Raxrujá via the San Antonio crossroads (US$2.60, 2½ hours, 81km). From the crossroads there is a 10:30 am bus to Playa Grande and a 10 am bus to Cobán via Chisec (US$2.60, 4½ hours, 94km), which you'll probably just miss. Fortunately, it's fairly easy to flag a truck going to Cobán or Fray if the day is still fairly young. To increase your chances of getting from Sayaxché to any of these destinations in one day, try jumping on a departing pickup before that first 8 am bus. If you get stuck, there are a couple of hospedajes in Raxrujá and Chisec.

REMOTE MAYAN SITES

Several sites buried in the Petén forest of interest to archaeology buffs and adventure travelers are open for limited tourism. While few of these sites can be visited without a guide because of their remote location, the difficult, uncharted jungle terrain you must brave to get there and the lack of water (potable or otherwise), many businesses in Flores and Santa Elena now offer trips to sites deep in the jungle (see the ProPetén and the Organized Tours sections under Flores & Santa Elena, earlier in this chapter). Few of these tours offer anything approaching comfort, and you should be prepared for buggy, basic conditions. People reluctant to use a mosquito repellent containing DEET may want to reconsider taking one of these trips.

Freelance guides can lead tourists to some of these sites, which will save you some money, but there are drawbacks. These guides usually know little about the archaeological significance of the sites and even less about responsible tourism. Also, there is no assurance that your trip will come off successfully or at all. Aborted trips are totally within the realm of possibility.

given the difficulty of these treks and the logistics involved (for example, all potable water must be packed in). In this case, you'll have no claim to any money you may have paid up front.

Yaxjá

This important ceremonial site on the lake of the same name is about 48km east of El Remate. A road goes most of the way, but the last few kilometers must be covered on foot. Yaxjá means 'green water' and scholars believe this site may have served as a vacation spot for the Maya nobility during the Classic period. There are several sets of ruins here (including a large plaza and two temples), which are connected by a network of causeways. On Topoxté island in the middle of the lake are the ruins of an observatory. Trips here usually continue to Tikal on foot and may include a visit to the Nakum site 17km north of Yaxjá by dirt road and/or a visit to El Naranjo, another impressive site with several large structures and stelae, 15km west of the Belize border.

El Perú

This site 62km northwest from Flores is located along the Scarlet Macaw Trail, so called because much of the route passes through the natural habitat of these impressive birds. Visitors to El Perú have a very good chance of seeing macaws nesting. The trek starts in Paso Caballos, where there are some smaller ruins, and continues by boat along the Río San Pedro to El Perú. There are several important structures here, which have been dated from 300 to 900, including the *El Mirador de los Monos* (The Monkey Lookout). Because of its proximity to Tikal and its location on the Río San Pedro, archaeologists believe El Perú was an important commercial center.

El Zotz

Zotz means bat in many Mayan languages, and you'll interact with plenty of them on a trek to this archaeological site, 23km east of Tikal as the crow flies. So many bats pour from the cave here at dusk they blacken the sky. Among the many unexcavated mounds

and ruins here is the Devil's Pyramid, which is so tall you can see clear over the canopy to the temples of Tikal. Trips to El Zotz can be extended to include an incredible backdoor trek to Tikal through dense forest and the communities nestled within it.

Río Azul

These small, important ruins are just over 80km northeast of Tikal, very near the tripartite border formed by Guatemala, Belize and Mexico. Scholars surmise Río Azul was a military base abandoned around AD 535. There are some 350 buildings and several temples here, but the real attractions are the vibrant cave paintings that adorn tombs sprinkled throughout the site. Unfortunately, widespread looting has severely compromised the integrity of Río Azul, facilitated by the nearby airstrip that services the *campamento chiclero* (chicle camp) very close to this site. Treaties banning the trafficking in Mayan artifacts were precipitated, in part, by the volume of ceramics being flown out of Río Azul. A trip here can be combined with visits to Tikal and Uaxactún.

El Mirador

This archaeological site is buried within the farthest reaches of the Petén jungle, just 7km south of the Mexican border. A visit here involves an arduous jungle trek of six days and five nights (60km round-trip), with no facilities or amenities aside from what you carry in and what can be rustled from the forest. The trip departs from a cluster of houses called Carmelita – the end of the line.

The metropolis at El Mirador, dated to 150 BC to AD 150 (perhaps the first Mayan city ever built and abandoned for mysterious reasons), contains the largest cluster of buildings in one single site, among which is the biggest pyramid ever built in the Mayan world: El Tigre measures 18 stories high (more than 60m) and its base covers 18,000 sq meters. Its twin, La Danta (The Tapir), though technically smaller, soars higher because it's built on a rise. From atop La Danta pyramid, some 105m above the forest floor, virgin canopy stretches into the distance as far as your eye can see. The green bumps hovering on the horizon are other pyramids still buried under dense jungle. There are hundreds of buildings at El Mirador, but a major ongoing excavation has never been tackled, so almost everything is still hidden beneath the jungle. You'll have to use your imagination to picture this city that at its height spread over 16 sq km and supported tens of thousands of citizens.

Scholars are still figuring out why and how El Mirador thrived (there are few natural resources and no water sources save for the reservoirs built by ingenious, ancient engineers) and what led to its abandonment. Some archaeologists argue that the roots of the Mayan hieroglyph system developed at El Mirador and spread to other parts of the Mayan world, challenging theories of long standing.

Trips here also visit the site of El Tintal en route to El Mirador and can include a couple of extra days to see the site at Nakbé. This trip is not for the faint of heart. Conditions are rudimentary: There are no toilets, beds, cold beverages or baths. The ants, ticks and mosquitoes never relent, the mud is knee-deep and the hiking is strenuous and dirty. That said, folks who make this journey will never forget it.

For more on this incredible site, see the September 1987 *National Geographic* article 'An Early Maya Metropolis Uncovered: El Mirador.' This is the most thorough, mainstream investigative report ever written on the site and sheds lots of light on the mystery of this great city.

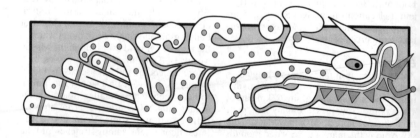

Language

There are 20 Mayan indigenous languages still used throughout Guatemala, but Spanish is still the most commonly spoken language and the one visitors will encounter on a daily basis. If you're anxious to try out some Mayan dialects, see the short and sweet Mam and Quiché sections at the end of this phrasebook.

For more Spanish words and phrases, get a copy of Lonely Planet's *Latin American Spanish phrasebook*.

For information on Spanish language courses, see Language Courses in the Facts for the Visitor chapter.

Pronunciation

Most of the sounds in Spanish have equivalents in English, and written Spanish is mostly phonetic.

Stress

Usually the stress is on the second to last syllable of a word. Words ending in an 'r' (usually verbs) have the stress on the last syllable. If there is an accent on any vowel, the stress is on that syllable.

amigo – a-MI-go   *comer* - com-ER   *aquí* – a-QUI

Greetings & Civilities

Greetings are used frequently. Saying *por favor* (please) and *gracias* (thank you) are second nature to most Guatemalans and a recommended tool in your travel kit. The first three greetings that follow are often shortened to *buenos/as*.

Good morning.	*Buenos días.*
Good afternoon.	*Buenas tardes.*
Good evening/night.	*Buenas noches.*
Hello	*Hola.*
How are you?	*¿Cómo está?* (formal), *¿Cómo estás?* (informal)
How are things going?	*¿Qué tal?*
Well, thanks.	*Bien, gracias.*
Very well.	*Muy bien.*
Very badly.	*Muy mal.*
Goodbye.	*Adiós.* (rarely used)
Bye, see you soon.	*Hasta luego.* ('sta luego')
Please.	*Por favor.*
Thank you.	*Gracias.*
Many thanks.	*Muchas gracias.*
You're welcome.	*De nada.*
Excuse me.	*Permiso.* (used when in a crowd)
Sorry.	*Perdón.*
Excuse me/Forgive me.	*Disculpe, Discúlpame.*
Good luck!	*¡Buena suerte!*
Mister, Sir	*Señor* (formal)
Mrs, Madam	*Señora* (formal)
unmarried woman	*Señorita*
pal, friend	*compañero/a, amigo/a*

LANGUAGE

More Useful Words & Phrases

The following brief guide should help you cope during your Guatemalan adventures.

I'd like to introduce you to…
  Le presento a…

A pleasure (to meet you).
  Mucho gusto.

What is your name?
  ¿Cómo se llama usted? (formal)
  ¿Cómo te llamas? (informal)

My name is…   *Me llamo…*

Where are you from?
  ¿De dónde es usted? (formal)
  ¿De dónde vienes? (familiar)

I am from…   *Soy de…*
  Australia   *Australia*
  Canada   *Canadá*
  England   *Inglaterra*
  France   *Francia*
  Germany   *Alemania*
  Israel   *Israel*
  Italy   *Italia*
  Japan   *Japón*
  New Zealand   *Nueva Zelanda*
  Norway   *Noruega*
  Scotland   *Escocia*
  South Africa *África del Sur*
  Sweden   *Suecia*
  Switzerland   *Suiza*
  the US   *los Estados Unidos*

Can I take a photo?
  ¿Puedo sacar una foto?

Of course/Why not/Sure.
  Por supuesto/Cómo no/Claro.

How old are you?
  ¿Cuántos años tiene?

Do you speak English?
  ¿Habla inglés?

I speak a little Spanish.
  Hablo un poquito de español.

I don't understand.
  No entiendo.

Could you repeat that?
  ¿Puede repetirlo?

Could you speak more slowly please?
  ¿Puede hablar más despacio por favor?

How does one say…?
  ¿Cómo se dice…?

What does…mean?
  ¿Qué significa…?

Where is…?   *¿Dónde hay…?*
  a hotel   *un hotel*
  a boarding house   *una pensión*
  a guesthouse   *un hospedaje*

I am looking for…   *Estoy buscando…*
  a cheap hotel   *un hotel barato*
  a good hotel   *un hotel bueno*
  a nearby hotel   *un hotel cercano*
  a clean hotel   *un hotel limpio*

Are there any rooms available?
  ¿Hay habitaciones libres?

Where are the toilets?
  ¿Dónde están los servicios/baños?

I would like a…   *Quisiera un…*
  single room   *cuarto sencillo*
  double room   *cuarto doble*
  room with a bath   *cuarto con baño*

Can I see it?   *¿Puedo verlo?*
Are there others?   *¿Hay otros?*
How much is it?   *¿Cuánto cuesta?*
It's too expensive.   *Es demasiado*
                         caro.

your name   *su nombre*
your surname   *su apellido*
your room number   *el número de*
                         su cuarto

Where is…?   *¿Dónde está…?*
  the central bus   *la estación central*
    station   *de autobuses*
  the railway station   *la estación*
                                 de trenes
  the airport   *el aeropuerto*
  the ticket office   *la boletería*
  bus   *autobús/camión*
  bus (long distance)   *flota/bus/*
                                 camioneta

When does the bus/train/plane leave?
¿Cuándo sale el autobus/tren/avión?

I want to go to...
Quiero ir a...

What time do they leave?
¿A qué hora salen?

Can you take me to...?
¿Puede llevarme a...?

Could you tell me where...is?
¿Podría decirme dónde está...?

Is it far?
¿Está lejos?

Is it close to here?
¿Está cerca de aquí?

I'm looking for...	*Estoy buscando...*
the post office	*el correo*
the embassy	*la embajada de...*
the museum	*el museo*
the police	*la policía*
the market	*el mercado*
the bank	*el banco*

Stop!   *¡Pare!*

Wait!   *¡Espera!*

I want to change some money.
Quiero cambiar dinero.

I want to change travelers' checks.
Quiero cambiar cheques viajeros.

What is the exchange rate?
¿Cuál es el tipo de cambio?

How many quetzales per dollar?
¿Cuántos quetzales por dólar?

Is there an ATM around here?
¿Está una cajera automática cerca de aquí?

cashier	*caja*
automated teller machine (ATM)	*cajera automática*
credit card	*tarjeta de crédito*
the black market	*el mercado negro*
bank notes	*billetes de banco*
exchange houses	*casas de cambio*
Watch out!	*¡Cuidado!*
Help!	*¡Socorro! ¡Auxilio!*
Fire!	*¡Fuego!*
Thief!	*¡Ladrón!*
I've been robbed.	*Me han robado.*
They took...	*Se llevaron...*
my money	*mi dinero*
my passport	*mi pasaporte*
my bag	*mi bolsa*
my backpack	*mi mochila*
Where is...?	*¿Dónde hay...?*
a policeman	*un policía*
a doctor	*un doctor*
a hospital	*un hospital*

Leave me alone!	*¡Déjeme!*
Don't bother me!	*¡No me moleste!*
Get lost!	*¡Váyase!*
today	*hoy*
this morning	*esta mañana*
this afternoon	*esta tarde*
tonight	*esta noche*
yesterday	*ayer*
tomorrow	*mañana*
week/month/year	*semana/mes/año*
last week	*la semana pasada*
next month	*el próximo mes*
always	*siempre*
it's early/late	*es temprano/tarde*
now	*ahora*
right now	*ahorita*
before/after	*antes/después*
What time is it?	*¿Qué hora es?*
It is 1 o'clock.	*Es la una.*
It is 7 o'clock.	*Son las siete.*

Numbers

0	*cero*	7	*siete*	14	*catorce*
1	*uno, una*	8	*ocho*	15	*quince*
2	*dos*	9	*nueve*	16	*dieciséis*
3	*tres*	10	*diez*	17	*diecisiete*
4	*cuatro*	11	*once*	18	*dieciocho*
5	*cinco*	12	*doce*	19	*diecinueve*
6	*seis*	13	*trece*	20	*veinte*

21	*veintiuno*	101	*ciento uno*
22	*veintidós*	102	*ciento dos*
30	*treinta*	200	*doscientos*
31	*treinta y uno*	300	*trescientos*
40	*cuarenta*	500	*quinientos*
50	*cincuenta*	600	*seiscientos*
60	*sesenta*	900	*novecientos*
70	*setenta*	1000	*mil*
80	*ochenta*	2000	*dos mil*
90	*noventa*	100,000	*cien mil*
100	*cien* (when followed by a noun, *ciento*)	1,000,000	*un millón*
		2,000,000	*dos millones*

Ordinals

first	*primero*	eighth	*octavo*
second	*segundo*	ninth	*noveno, nono*
third	*tercero*	tenth	*décimo*
fourth	*cuarto*	eleventh	*undécimo*
fifth	*quinto*	twelfth	*duodécimo*
sixth	*sexto*	twentieth	*vigésimo*
seventh	*séptimo*		

Modern Mayan

Since the Classic period, the two ancient Mayan languages, Yucatecan and Cholan, have subdivided into 35 separate Mayan languages (Yucatec, Chol, Chorti, Tzeltal, Tzotzil, Lacandon, Mam, Quiché, Cakchiquel etc), some of them unintelligible to speakers of others. Writing today is in the Latin alphabet brought by the conquistadors – what writing there is. Most literate Maya are literate in Spanish, the language of the government, the school, the church, radio, TV and the newspapers; they may not be literate in Mayan.

Pronunciation

There are several rules to remember when pronouncing Mayan words and place names. Mayan vowels are pretty straightforward; it's the consonants that give problems. Remember:

c is always hard, like 'k'

j is always an aspirated 'h' sound. So *jipi-japa* is pronounced hee-pee-haa-pah and *abaj* is pronounced ah-bahh; to get the 'HH' sound, take the 'h' sound from 'half' and put it at the end of ah-bahh

u is 'oo' except when it begins or ends a word, in which case it is like English 'w'; thus *baktun* is 'bahk-toon,' but *Uaxactún* is 'wah-shahk-toon' and *ahau* is 'ah-haw'

x is like English 'sh,' a shushing sound

Mayan glottalized consonants, those followed by an apostrophe (b', ch', k', p', t'), are similar to normal consonants, but pronounced more forcefully and 'explosively.' An apostrophe following a *vowel* signifies a glottal stop, *not* a more forceful vowel.

Another rule to remember is that in most Mayan words the stress falls on the last syllable. Sometimes this is indicated by an acute accent, sometimes not. Here are some pronunciation examples:

Abaj Takalik	ah-BAHH tah-kah leek	Pacal	pah-KAHL
Acanceh	ah-kahn-KEH	Pop	pope
Ahau	ah-HAW	Tikal	tee-KAHL
Dzibilchaltún	dzee-beel-chahl-TOON	Uaxactún	wah-shahk-TOON
Kaminaljuyú	kah-mee-nahl-hoo-YOO	Xcaret	sh-kah-REHT
Oxcutzkab	ohsh-kootz-KAHB	Yaxchilán	yahsh-chee-LAHN

Quiché

Quiché is widely spoken throughout the Guatemalan Highlands, from the area around Santa Cruz del Quiché to the area adjacent to Lake Atitlán and around Quetzaltenango. There are an estimated 1,806,000 Quiché Mayans living in Guatemala, giving you plenty of opportunity to practice some of the common terms and phrases listed below.

Greetings & Civilities These are great icebreakers, and even if you're not completely and accurately understood, there will be goodwill and smiles all around if you try some of these sayings.

Good morning.	*Saqarik.*	Bye. See you soon.	*Kimpetik ri.*
Good afternoon.	*Xb'eqij.*	Thank you.	*Uts awech?*
Good evening/night.	*Xokaq'ab'.*	Excuse me.	*Kyunala.*
Goodbye.	*Chab'ej.*		

More Useful Words & Phrases

What is your name?	*Su ra'b'i?*	vegetables	*ichaj*
My name is…	*Nu b'i…*	blanket	*k'ul*
		soap	*ch'ipaq*
Where are you from?	*Ja kat pewi?*	good	*utz*
I am from…	*Ch'qap ja'kin pewi…*	bad	*itzel*
Where is a…?	*Ja k'uichi' ri…?*	open	*teb'am*
bathroom?	*b'anb'al chuluj?*	closed	*tzapilik*
hotel?	*jun worib'al?*	hard	*ko*
police station?	*ajchajil re tinamit?*	soft	*ch'uch'uj*
doctor?	*ajkun?*	hot	*miq'in*
bus stop?	*tek'lib'al?*	cold	*joron*
		sick	*yiwab'*
Do you have…?	*K'olik…?*	north (white)	*saq*
coffee?	*kab'e?*	south (yellow)	*k'an*
boiled water?	*saq'li?*	east (red)	*kaq*
copal?	*kach'?*	west (black)	*k'eq*
a machete?	*choyib'al?*		
rooms?	*k'plib'al?*		
We have it.	*K'olik.*		
We don't have it.	*K'otaj.*		

Numbers

1	*jun*	5	*job'*	9	*b'elejeb'*
2	*keb'*	6	*waq'ib'*	10	*lajuj*
3	*oxib'*	7	*wuqub'*	11	*julajuj*
4	*kijeb'*	8	*wajxakib'*	12	*kab'lajuj*

13	*oxlajuj*	19	*b'elejlajuj*	70	*lajuj re waqk'al*
14	*kajlajuj*	20	*juwinak*	80	*waqk'al*
15	*o'lajuj*	30	*lajuj re kawinak*	90	*lajuj re o'k'al*
16	*waklajuj*	40	*kawinak*	100	*o'k'al*
17	*wuklajuj*	50	*lajuj re oxk'al*	200	*lajuj k'al*
18	*wajxaklajuj*	60	*oxk'al*	400	*omuch'*

Mam

Mam is spoken in the department of Huehuetenango, in the western portion of the country. This is the indigenous language you'll hear in Todos Santos, nestled among the Cuchumatanes mountains.

Greetings & Civilities Luckily, in Mam you need only know two phrases for greeting folks, no matter the time of day:

Good morning/afternoon/evening.	*Chin q'olb'el teya.* (informal singular)
	Chin q'olb'el kyeyea. (informal plural)
Goodbye.	*Chi nej.*
Bye. See you soon.	*Chi nej. Ak qli qib'.*
Thank you.	*Chonte teya.*
How are you?	*Tzen ta'ya?*
Excuse me.	*Naq samy.*

More Useful Words & Phrases

What is your name?	*Tit biya?*	Where is a...?	*Ja at...?*
My name is...	*Luan bi...*	bathroom?	*bano?*
Where are you from?	*Jaa'tzajnia?*	hotel?	*hospedaje?*
I am from...	*Ac tzajni...*	police?	*policia?*
		doctor?	*medico/doctor?*

Many words in Mam have been in disuse for so long that the Spanish equivalent is now used almost exclusively.

Where is the bus stop?		good	*banex* or *g'lan*
Ja nue camioneta? (literally, where does the bus stop?)		bad	*k'ab'ex* or *nia g'lan*
		open	*jqo'n*
Do you have...?	*At...?*	closed	*jpu'n*
coffee?	*café?*	hard	*kuj*
boiled water?	*kqa'?*	soft	*xb'une*
a machete?	*machete?*	hot	*kyaq*
rooms?	*cuartos?*	I am...	*At...*
Is there somewhere we can sleep?		cold	*xb'a'j* or *choj*
Ja tun kqta'n?		sick	*yab'*
We have it.	*At.*	north (white)	*okan*
We don't have it.	*Nti'.*	south (yellow)	*eln*
How much is the...?	*Je te ti...?*	east (red)	*jawl*
fruits and vegetables	*lobj*	west (black)	*kub'el*
blanket	*ponch* (short for poncho)	white	*saq*
		yellow	*q'an*
a covering of whatever sort	*qtxowaj*	red	*txa'x* (also the word for raw)
soap	*jabon*	black	*q'aq*

Numbers

1	*jun*	6	*waq'ib'*
2	*keb'*	7	*wuqub'*
3	*oxib'*	8	*wajxakib'*
4	*kijeb'*	9	*b'elejeb'*
5	*job'*	10	*lajuj*

The numbers from one to 10 are the same as in Quiché. For numbers higher than 10, Mam speakers use the Spanish equivalent.

Menu Translator

Antojitos & Refacciones

Many dishes fall under the heading of *antojitos* ('little whims'), savory or spicy concoctions that delight the palate. Many of these same snacks are called *refacciones*.

burrito – any combination of beans, cheese, meat, chicken or seafood, seasoned with salsa or chile and wrapped in a wheat-flour tortilla

chile relleno – *poblano* chile stuffed with cheese, meat or other foods, dipped in egg whites, fried and baked in sauce

chuchitos – steamed corn dough stuffed with spicy meat and served in a corn husk

elote – grilled corn on the cob, served with salt and lime

quesadilla – flour tortilla topped or filled with cheese and occasionally other ingredients and then heated

queso relleno – 'stuffed cheese,' mild yellow cheese stuffed with minced meat and spices

taco – a soft or crisp corn tortilla wrapped or folded around the same filling as a burrito

tamale – steamed corn dough stuffed with meat, beans, chiles or nothing at all, wrapped in corn husks

tostada – flat, crisp tortilla topped with meat or cheese, tomatoes, beans and lettuce

Sopas (Soups)

caldo – broth, most usually meat-based

chipilín – cheese and cream soup on a maize base

pozole – hominy soup with meat and vegetables (can be spicy)

sopa de arroz – not a soup at all but just a plate of rice; commonly served with lunch

sopa de lentejas – lentil soup

sopa de pollo – bits of chicken in a thin chicken broth

sopa de verduras – vegetable soup

Huevos (Eggs)

You can order eggs over easy by saying 'dar un vuelta'; literally, give them a turn.

huevos estrellados – fried eggs

huevos fritos – fried eggs

huevos rancheros – ranch-style eggs: fried, laid on a tortilla and smothered with spicy tomato sauce

huevos revueltos – scrambled eggs; *con tomate y cebolla,* with chopped up bits of tomato and onion (the most common way fried eggs are served)

Pescado, Mariscos (Seafood)

Obviously, you'll find the best seafood on the Pacific and Caribbean coasts. Ceviche is available almost everywhere, including the Highlands. Fish and seafood cooked 'a la plancha' means sauteed and put 'on the plate' (can be applied to meats too). The following types of seafood are available in seafood restaurants most of the year.

almejas – clams

atún – tuna

cabrilla – sea bass

camarones – shrimp

camarones gigantes – prawns

cangrejo – large crab

ceviche – raw seafood marinated in lime juice and mixed with onions, chiles, garlic, tomatoes and *cilantro* (fresh coriander leaf)

dorado – dolphin

filete de pescado – fish fillet

huachinango – red snapper

jaiba – small crab

jurel – yellowtail

langosta – lobster

lenguado – flounder or sole

mariscos – shellfish

ostiones – oysters

pargo – red snapper

pescado – fish after it has been caught (see *pez*)

pescado al mojo de ajo – fish fried in butter and garlic

pez – fish that is alive in the water (see *pescado*)

pez espada – swordfish

sierra – mackerel
tiburón – shark
tortuga or *caguama* – turtle
trucha de mar – sea trout

Carnes y Aves (Meat & Poultry)
The simplest meat dishes are served 'a la plancha' (sauteed) or 'a la parrilla' (grilled).

arroz con pollo – a mound of rice mixed with chopped up bits of chicken
asado – roast
barbacoa – literally 'barbecued', but by a process whereby the meat or fish is covered and placed under hot coals
bistec – beefsteak; sometimes any cut of meat, fish or poultry
bistec de res – beefsteak
birria – barbecued on a spit
borrego – sheep
cabro – goat
carne al carbón – charcoal-grilled meat
carne asada – tough but tasty grilled beef
chicharrones – deep-fried pork skin
chorizo – pork sausage
chuletas de puerco – pork chops
cochinita – suckling pig
codorniz, la chaquaca – quail
conejo – rabbit
cordero – lamb
costillas de puerco – pork ribs or chops
guajolote – turkey
hígado – liver
jamón – ham
milanesa – crumbed, breaded
milanesa de res – crumbed beefsteak
parrilla mixta – mixed grill; several types of grilled meats
patas de puerco – pig's feet
pato – duck
pavo – turkey
pepián – a Guatemalan specialty made with chicken and vegetables in a piquant sesame and pumpkin seed sauce
pollo – chicken
pollo asado – grilled (not roast) chicken
pollo frito – fried chicken
puerco – pork
salchichas – sausages similar to hot dogs
tepezcuintle – jungle rodent the size of a rabbit; most often seen in the Petén

tocino – bacon or salt pork
venado – venison

Frutas (Fruit)
anona – custard apple or chirimoya; when ripe it's foul smelling but tasty
coco – coconut
dátil – date
fresas – strawberries; any berries
guayaba – guava
higo – fig
hocote – a small fruit, looks like a dimunitive avocado, ranges from green to orange, eaten with lime and nutmeg
limón – lime or lemon
mango – mango
melón – melon
melocoton – peach
naranja – orange
papaya – papaya
piña – pineapple
plátano – green banana, edible when cooked
toronja – grapefruit
uva – grape

Legumbres, Verduras (Vegetables)
Vegetables are rarely served as separate dishes, but are often mixed into salads, soups and sauces.

aceitunas – olives
ajillo – a small onion akin to a scallion
calabaza – squash, marrow or pumpkin
cebolla – onion
champiñones – mushrooms; also called *hongos*
chícharos – peas
ejotes – green beans
elote – corn on the cob; commonly served with salt and a slice of lime from street grills
jícama – a popular root vegetable that resembles a potato crossed with an apple; eaten fresh with a sprinkling of lime, chile and salt or cooked like a potato
lechuga – lettuce
pacaya – a squash-like staple among the highland Maya
papa – potato
tomate – tomato
zanahoria – carrot

Dulces (Desserts, Sweets)

choco bananos – chocolate covered bananas; also sold with chocolate and peanuts (*maní*)
flan – custard, crème caramel
helado – ice cream
paleta – flavored ice on a stick
pan dulce – sweet rolls, usually eaten for breakfast
pastel – cake
postre – dessert, after-meal sweet

Other Foods

atole – a hot gruel made with maize and milk, cinammon and sugar
azúcar – sugar
bolillo – French-style bread rolls
crema – cream, akin to sour cream, but sweeter; usually served with eggs
fiambre – a traditional salad-type dish eaten on All Saint's Day, made from an assortment of meats, seafood and vegetables (most notably beets) mixed together in a vinegar base
fideos – noodles
guacamole – mashed avocados mixed with onion, chile sauce, lemon, tomato and other ingredients
leche – milk
mantequilla – butter; more often you'll eat *margarina*, margarine
miel – honey
mosh – a hot oat concoction, similar to oatmeal or porridge, served at breakfast in parts of Guatemala; also popular fodder in street food stalls
pimienta negra – black pepper
ponche – a potent potable made from pineapple or coconut juice and rum and served hot
poporopo – neon-colored popcorn balls
queso – cheese
salsa – sauce made with chiles, onion, tomato, lemon or lime juice and spices
sal – salt
tapado – a fish and plantain stew served on the Caribbean coast

At the Table

almuerzo – lunch, but also the midday fixed-priced meal
copa – glass
cuchara – spoon
cuchillo – knife
cuenta – bill
lista – menu (short for *lista de precios*); see *menú*
menú – fixed price meal, as in *menú del día*; sometimes menu
plato – plate
propina – the tip, 10% to 15% of the bill
servilleta – table napkin
taza – cup
tenedor – fork
vaso – drinking glass

Café (Coffee)

café sin azúcar – coffee without sugar; saying this keeps the waiter from adding heaps of sugar to your cup. But it doesn't mean your coffee won't taste sweet; sugar is often processed with the beans.
café negro or *café americano* – black coffee with nothing added except sugar, unless it's made with sugar-coated coffee beans
café con crema – coffee with cream served separately
café con leche – coffee with hot milk
nescafé – instant coffee; *café instantaneo*

Bebidas (Drinks)

aguardiente – super potent sugarcane liquor
aguas – sodas
cerveza – beer
cuxa – fermented corn beer
jugo – juice
licuados – milkshakes made with fresh fruit, sugar and milk or water
limonada – refreshing drink made from lime juice; also *limonada con soda*, made with fizzy soda water
naranjada – orange juice and soda water
ron – rum
rosa de jamaica – hibiscus juice; sometimes called simply *jamaica*

Glossary

abrazo – embrace, hug; in particular, the formal, ceremonial hug between political leaders

alux, aluxes – Mayan for gremlin, leprechaun, benevolent 'little people'

Apartado Postal – post office box, abbreviated *Apdo Postal*

Ayuntamiento – often seen as *H Ayuntamiento (Honorable Ayuntamiento)* on the front of Town Hall buildings, it translates as 'Municipal Government'

barrio – district, neighborhood

billete – bank note (unlike in Spain, where it's a ticket)

boleto – ticket (bus, train, museum, etc)

bolo – colloquial term for drunk (noun)

caballeros – literally 'horsemen,' but corresponds to 'gentlemen' in English; look for it on toilet doors

cacique – Indian chief; also used to describe provincial warlord or strongman

cafetería – literally 'coffee-shop,' it refers to any informal restaurant with waiter service; not usually a cafeteria in the North American sense of a self-service restaurant

cajero automático – automated bank teller machine (ATM)

callejón – alley or small, narrow or very short street

camión – truck; bus

camioneta – bus or pickup truck

cardamomo – cardamom; a spice grown extensively in the Verapaces and used as a flavor enhancer for coffee, particularly in the Middle East

casa de cambio – currency exchange office; offers exchange rates comparable to banks and is much faster to use (uncommon in Guatemala)

cazuela – clay cooking pot, usually sold in a nested set

cenote – large, natural limestone cave used for water storage (or ceremonial purposes)

cerveza – beer

Chac – Mayan god of rain

chac-mool – Mayan sacrificial stone sculpture

chapín – a citizen of Guatemala; Guatemalan

charro – cowboy

chicle – sap of the sapodilla tree, used to manufacture chewing gum

chicleros – men who collect chicle

chingar – literally 'to rape' but in practice a word with a wide range of colloquial meanings similar to the use of 'to screw' in English

chuchitos – corn dough filled with spicy meat and served in a corn husk

chuj – a traditional Mayan sauna; see also *tuj*

chultún – artificial Mayan cistern

cigarro – cigarette

cocina – cookshop (literally 'kitchen'), a small, basic restaurant usually run by one woman, often located in or near a municipal market; also seen as *cocina económica* (economical kitchen) or *cocina familiar* (family kitchen)

cofradía – religious brotherhood, most often found in the highlands

colectivo – jitney taxi or minibus (usually a *combi*, or minibus) which picks up and drops off passengers along its route

comal – hot griddle or surface used to cook tortillas

comedor – a basic and cheap eatery, usually with a limited menu

completo – full up, a sign you may see on hotel desks in crowded cities

conquistador – explorer-conqueror of Latin America from Spain

copal – a tree resin used as incense in Mayan ceremonies

correos – post office

cruce – a crossroads, usually where you make bus connections; see also *tronque*

curandero – traditional indigenous healer

351

damas – ladies, the usual sign on toilet doors
dzul, dzules – Mayan for foreigners or 'townfolk'

encomienda – Spanish colonial practice of putting Indians under the 'guardianship' of landowners, practically akin to medieval serfdom
estación ferrocarril – train station

ferrocarril – railroad
finca – ranch; farm

galón, galones – US gallons (fluid measure of 3.79 liters; sometimes used in Guatemala)
glyph – a symbolic character or figure, usually engraved or carved in relief
gringo/a – a mild pejorative term applied to a male/female North American visitor; sometimes applied to any visitor of European heritage
gruta – cave
guayabera – man's thin fabric shirt with pockets and appliquéd designs on the front, over the shoulders and down the back; often worn in place of a jacket and tie on formal occasions

hacienda – estate; also 'treasury,' as in *Departamento de Hacienda*, Treasury Department
hay – pronounced like 'eye,' meaning 'there is,' 'there are.' You're equally likely to hear *no hay*, 'there isn't' or 'there aren't.'
hombre/s – man/men
huipil – woven white dress from the Mayan regions with intricate, colorful embroidery

IVA – the *impuesto al valor agregado* or 'ee-vah' is a value-added tax, which can be as high as 20%

Kukulcán – Mayan name for the Aztec-Toltec plumed serpent Quetzalcóatl

ladino – a person of mixed Indian and European race; see also *mestizo*
lancha – motor boats used to transport passengers; they're driven by *lancheros*

larga distancia – long-distance telephone
lavadero – a cement sink for washing clothes; see also *pila*
lavandería – laundry; a *lavandería automática* is a coin-operated laundry
leng – colloquial Mayan term for coins in the highlands
libras – pounds (weight measurement of 0.45 kilogram; sometimes used in Guatemala)
lleno – full (fuel tank)

machismo – maleness, masculine virility
malecon – waterfront boulevard
manglar – mangrove
manzana – apple; also a city block. A *supermanzana* is a large group of city blocks bounded by major avenues.
mariachi – ensemble of street musicians featuring a guitar, accordion and bass; often performs in restaurants
mestizo – a person of mixed Indian and European blood; the word *ladino* is more common in Guatemala.
metate – flattish stone on which corn is ground with a cylindrical stone roller
millas – miles (distance of 1.61 km; sometimes used in Guatemala)
mirador – lookout, vista point
mordida – 'bite,' or small bribe paid to keep the wheels of bureaucracy turning. Giving a *mordida* to a traffic cop may ensure that you won't receive a bigger fine.
mudéjar – Moorish architectural style
mujer/es – woman/women

onza(s) – ounce(s) (weight of 28.35 grams; sometimes used in Guatemala)

pachete – loofa; a squash-type vegetable used as shower scrubbies
Palacio de Gobierno – building housing the executive offices of a state or regional government
Palacio Municipal – City Hall, seat of the corporation or municipal government
palapa – thatched palm-leaf roof shelter with open sides
parada – bus stop, usually for city buses
pie, pies – foot, feet (measure of 0.30 meters)

pila – a sink for washing clothes; see also *lavadero*

pinchazo – automobile tire repair shop

pisto – colloquial Mayan term for money, quetzals

propino, propina – a tip, different from a *mordida,* which is really a bribe

punta – sexually suggestive dance enjoyed by the Garífuna of the Caribbean coast

puro – cigar

Quetzalcóatl – plumed serpent god of the Aztecs and Toltecs

rebozo – long woolen or linen scarf covering the head or shoulders

refacciones – simple snacks; literally refreshments

retablo – ornate gilded, carved decoration of wood in a church

retorno – 'return'; used on traffic signs to signify a U-turn or turn around

roofcomb – a decorative stonework lattice atop a Mayan pyramid or temple

rutelero – jitney

sacbé, sacbeob – ceremonial limestone avenue or path between great Mayan cities

sacerdote – priest

sanatorio – hospital, particularly a small private one

sanitario – literally 'sanitary'; usually means toilet

secadora – clothes dryer

Semana Santa – Holy Week preceding Easter

stela, stelae – standing stone monument(s), usually carved

supermercado – supermarket, ranging from a corner store to a large, US-style supermarket

taller – shop or workshop. A *taller mecánico* is a mechanic's shop, usually for cars.

tapado – a hearty seafood stew made on the Caribbean coast

teléfono comunitario – community telephone, found in the smallest towns

teléfono monedero – coin-operated telephone

tepezcuintle – edible jungle rodent the size of a rabbit

tequila – clear, distilled liquor produced, like pulque and mezcal, from the maguey cactus

tienda – small store that may sell anything from candles and chickens to aspirin and bread

típico – typical or characteristic of a region; particularly used to describe food

traje – the traditional clothing worn by the Maya

tronque – a crossroads where you make bus connections; see also *cruce*

tuj – a traditional Mayan sauna; see also *chuj*

tumulos – speed bumps found in many towns, sometimes indicated by a highway sign bearing a row of little bumps

viajero – traveler

vulcanizadora – automobile tire repair shop; see also *pinchazo*

xate – a low growing fern native to the Petén region and exported for use in floral arrangements particularly in the US.

xateros – men who collect xate

Xinca – a small, non-Maya indigenous group living on the Pacific Slope.

zotz – bat, the mammal, in many Mayan languages

LONELY PLANET

Guides by Region

Lonely Planet is known worldwide for publishing practical, reliable and no-nonsense information in our guides and on our Web site. The Lonely Planet list covers just about every accessible part of the world. Currently there are 16 series: Travel guides, Shoestring guides, Condensed guides, Watching Wildlife guides, Pisces Diving & Snorkeling guides, City Maps, Road Atlases, Out to Eat, World Food, Journeys travel literature and Pictorials.

AFRICA Africa on a shoestring • Cairo • Cape Town • Cape Town City Map • East Africa • Egypt • Egyptian Arabic phrasebook • Ethiopia, Eritrea & Djibouti • Ethiopian (Amharic) phrasebook • The Gambia & Senegal • Healthy Travel Africa • Kenya • Malawi • Morocco • Moroccan Arabic phrasebook • Mozambique • Read This First: Africa • South Africa, Lesotho & Swaziland • Southern Africa • Southern Africa Road Atlas • Swahili phrasebook • Tanzania, Zanzibar & Pemba • Trekking in East Africa • Tunisia • Watching Wildlife East Africa • Watching Wildlife Southern Africa • West Africa • World Food Morocco • Zimbabwe, Botswana & Namibia
Travel Literature: Mali Blues: Traveling to an African Beat • The Rainbird: A Central African Journey • Songs to an African Sunset: A Zimbabwean Story

AUSTRALIA & THE PACIFIC Auckland • Australia • Australian phrasebook • Australia Road Atlas • Bushwalking in Australia • Cycling New Zealand • Fiji • Fijian phrasebook • Healthy Travel Australia, NZ and the Pacific • Islands of Australia's Great Barrier Reef • Melbourne • Melbourne City Map • Micronesia • New Caledonia • New South Wales & the ACT • New Zealand • Northern Territory • Outback Australia • Out to Eat – Melbourne • Out to Eat – Sydney • Papua New Guinea • Pidgin phrasebook • Queensland • Rarotonga & the Cook Islands • Samoa • Solomon Islands • South Australia • South Pacific • South Pacific phrasebook • Sydney • Sydney City Map • Sydney Condensed • Tahiti & French Polynesia • Tasmania • Tonga • Tramping in New Zealand • Vanuatu • Victoria • Watching Wildlife Australia • Western Australia
Travel Literature: Islands in the Clouds: Travel in the Highlands of New Guinea • Kiwi Tracks: A New Zealand Journey • Sean & David's Long Drive

CENTRAL AMERICA & THE CARIBBEAN Bahamas, Turks & Caicos • Baja California • Bermuda • Central America on a shoestring • Costa Rica • Costa Rica Spanish phrasebook • Cuba • Dominican Republic & Haiti • Eastern Caribbean • Guatemala • Belize, Guatemala & Yucatán: La Ruta Maya • Healthy Travel Central & South America • Jamaica • Mexico • Mexico City • Panama • Puerto Rico • Read This First: Central & South America • World Food Mexico • Yucatán
Travel Literature: Green Dreams: Travels in Central America

EUROPE Amsterdam • Amsterdam City Map • Amsterdam Condensed • Andalucía • Austria • Baltic States phrasebook • Barcelona • Barcelona City Map • Berlin • Berlin City Map• Britain • British phrasebook • Brussels, Bruges & Antwerp • Budapest • Budapest City Map • Canary Islands • Central Europe • Central Europe phrasebook • Corfu & the Ionians • Corsica • Crete • Crete Condensed • Croatia • Cycling Britain • Cycling France • Cyprus • Czech & Slovak Republics • Denmark • Dublin • Dublin City Map • Eastern Europe • Eastern Europe phrasebook • Edinburgh • Estonia, Latvia & Lithuania • Europe on a shoestring • Finland • Florence • France • Frankfurt Condensed • French phrasebook • Georgia, Armenia & Azerbaijan • Germany • German phrasebook • Greece • Greek Islands • Greek phrasebook • Hungary • Iceland, Greenland & the Faroe Islands • Ireland • Istanbul • Italian phrasebook • Italy • Krakow • Lisbon • The Loire • London • London City Map • London Condensed • Madrid • Malta • Mediterranean Europe • Mediterranean Europe phrasebook • Moscow • Munich • Norway • Out to Eat – London • Paris • Paris City Map • Paris Condensed • Poland • Portugal • Portuguese phrasebook • Prague • Prague City Map • Provence & the Côte d'Azur • Read This First: Europe • Romania & Moldova • Rome • Russia, Ukraine & Belarus • Russian phrasebook • Scandinavian & Baltic Europe • Scandinavian Europe phrasebook • Scotland • Sicily • Slovenia • South-West France • Spain • Spanish phrasebook • St Petersburg • St Petersburg City Map • Sweden • Switzerland • Trekking in Spain • Tuscany • Ukrainian phrasebook • Venice • Vienna • Walking in Britain • Walking in France • Walking in Ireland • Walking in Italy • Walking in Spain • Walking in Switzerland • Western Europe • Western Europe phrasebook • World Food France • World Food Ireland • World Food Italy • World Food Spain
Travel Literature: Love and War in the Apennines • The Olive Grove: Travels in Greece • On the Shores of the Mediterranean • Round Ireland in Low Gear • A Small Place in Italy

INDIAN SUBCONTINENT Bangladesh • Bengali phrasebook • Bhutan • Delhi • Goa • Healthy Travel Asia & India • Hindi/Urdu phrasebook • India • Indian Himalaya • Karakoram Highway • Kerala • Mumbai (Bombay) •

LONELY PLANET

Mail Order

Lonely Planet products are distributed worldwide. They are also available by mail order from Lonely Planet, so if you have difficulty finding a title please write to us. North and South American residents should write to 150 Linden St, Oakland, CA 94607, USA; European and African residents should write to 10a Spring Place, London NW5 38H, UK; and residents of other countries to Locked Bag 1, Footscray, Victoria 3011, Australia.

Nepal • Nepali phrasebook • Pakistan • Rajasthan • Read This First: Asia & India • South India • Sri Lanka • Sri Lanka phrasebook • Tibet • Trekking in the Indian Himalaya • Trekking in the Karakoram & Hindukush • Trekking in the Nepal Himalaya
Travel Literature: The Age of Kali: Indian Travels and Encounters • Hello Goodnight: A Life of Goa • In Rajasthan • A Season in Heaven: True Tales from the Road to Kathmandu • Shopping for Buddhas • A Short Walk in the Hindu Kush • Slowly Down the Ganges

ISLANDS OF THE INDIAN OCEAN Madagascar & Comoros • Maldives • Mauritius, Réunion & Seychelles

MIDDLE EAST & CENTRAL ASIA Bahrain, Kuwait & Qatar • Central Asia • Central Asia phrasebook • Dubai • Hebrew phrasebook • Iran • Israel & the Palestinian Territories • Istanbul • Istanbul City Map • Istanbul to Cairo on a shoestring • Jerusalem • Jerusalem City Map • Jordan • Lebanon • Middle East • Oman & the United Arab Emirates • Syria • Turkey • Turkish phrasebook • World Food Turkey • Yemen
Travel Literature: Black on Black: Iran Revisited • The Gates of Damascus • Kingdom of the Film Stars: Journey into Jordan

NORTH AMERICA Alaska • Boston • Boston City Map • California & Nevada • California Condensed • Canada • Chicago • Chicago City Map • Louisiana & the Deep South • Florida • Hawaii • Hiking in Alaska • Hiking in the USA • Las Vegas • Los Angeles • Miami • Miami City Map • New England • New Orleans • New York City • New York City City Map • New York City Condensed • New York, New Jersey & Pennsylvania • Oahu • Pacific Northwest • Puerto Rico • Rocky Mountains • San Francisco • San Francisco City Map • Seattle • Southwest • Texas • USA • USA phrasebook • Vancouver • Virginia & the Capital Region • Washington, DC • Washington, DC City Map • World Food Deep South, USA
Travel Literature: Caught Inside: A Surfer's Year on the California Coast • Drive Thru America

NORTH-EAST ASIA Beijing • Cantonese phrasebook • China • Hiking in Japan • Hong Kong • Hong Kong City Map • Hong Kong Condensed • Hong Kong, Macau & Guangzhou • Japan • Japanese phrasebook • Korea • Korean phrasebook • Kyoto • Mandarin phrasebook • Mongolia • Mongolian phrasebook • Seoul • South-West China • Taiwan • Tokyo
Travel Literature: In Xanadu: A Quest • Lost Japan

SOUTH AMERICA Argentina, Uruguay & Paraguay • Bolivia • Brazil • Brazilian phrasebook • Buenos Aires • Chile & Easter Island • Colombia • Ecuador & the Galapagos Islands • Healthy Travel Central & South America • Latin American Spanish phrasebook • Peru • Quechua phrasebook • Read This First: Central & South America • Rio de Janeiro • Rio de Janeiro City Map • Santiago de Chile • South America on a shoestring • Trekking in the Patagonian Andes • Venezuela
Travel Literature: Full Circle: A South American Journey

SOUTH-EAST ASIA Bali & Lombok • Bangkok • Bangkok City Map • Burmese phrasebook • Cambodia • Hanoi • Healthy Travel Asia & India • Hill Tribes phrasebook • Ho Chi Minh City • Indonesia • Indonesian phrasebook • Indonesia's Eastern Islands • Jakarta • Java • Lao phrasebook • Laos • Malay phrasebook • Malaysia, Singapore & Brunei • Myanmar (Burma) • Philippines • Pilipino (Tagalog) phrasebook • Read This First: Asia & India • Singapore • Singapore City Map • South-East Asia on a shoestring • South-East Asia phrasebook • Thailand • Thailand's Islands & Beaches • Thailand, Vietnam, Laos & Cambodia Road Atlas • Thai phrasebook • Vietnam • Vietnamese phrasebook • World Food Thailand • World Food Vietnam

ALSO AVAILABLE: Antarctica • The Arctic • The Blue Man: Tales of Travel, Love and Coffee • Brief Encounters: Stories of Love, Sex & Travel • Chasing Rickshaws • The Last Grain Race • Lonely Planet Unpacked • Not the Only Planet: Science Fiction Travel Stories • On the Edge: Extreme Travel • Sacred India • Travel with Children • Travel Photography: A Guide to Taking Better Pictures

LONELY PLANET

You already know that Lonely Planet produces more than this one guidebook, but you might not be aware of the other products we have on this region. Here is a selection of titles which you may want to check out as well:

Central America on a shoestring
ISBN 1 86450 186 3
US$21.99 • UK£13.99 • 159FF

Mexico
ISBN 1 86450 089 1
US$24.99 • UK£14.99 • 179FF

Yucatán
ISBN 1 86450 103 0
US$17.99 • UK£11.99 • 139FF

Latin American Spanish phrasebook
ISBN 0 86442 558 9
US$6.95 • UK£4.50 • 50FF

Available wherever books are sold.

LONELY PLANET

ON THE ROAD

Travel Guides explore cities, regions and countries, and supply information on transport, restaurants and accommodation, covering all budgets. They come with reliable, easy-to-use maps, practical advice, cultural and historical facts and a rundown on attractions both on and off the beaten track. There are over 200 titles in this classic series, covering nearly every country in the world.

Lonely Planet Upgrades extend the shelf life of existing travel guides by detailing any changes that may affect travel in a region since a book has been published. Upgrades can be downloaded for free from **www.lonelyplanet.com/upgrades**

For travelers with more time than money, **Shoestring** guides offer dependable, first-hand information with hundreds of detailed maps, plus insider tips for stretching money as far as possible. Covering entire continents in most cases, the six-volume Shoestring guides are known around the world as 'backpackers' bibles.'

For the discerning short-term visitor, **Condensed** guides highlight the best a destination has to offer in a full-color, pocket-sized format designed for quick access. They include everything from top sights and walking tours to opinionated reviews of where to eat, stay, shop and have fun.

CitySync lets travelers use their Palm™ or Visor™ handheld computers to guide them through a city with handy tips on transport, history, cultural life, major sights, and shopping and entertainment options. It can also quickly search and sort hundreds of reviews of hotels, restaurants and attractions, and pinpoint their location on scrollable street maps. CitySync can be downloaded from **www.citysync.com**

MAPS & ATLASES

Lonely Planet's **City Maps** feature downtown and metropolitan maps, as well as transit routes and walking tours. The maps come complete with an index of streets, a listing of sights and a plastic coat for extra durability.

Road Atlases are an essential navigation tool for serious travelers. Cross-referenced with the guidebooks, they also feature distance and climate charts and a complete site index.

LONELY PLANET

ESSENTIALS

Read This First books help new travelers to hit the road with confidence. These invaluable predeparture guides give step-by-step advice on preparing for a trip, budgeting, arranging a visa, planning an itinerary and staying safe while still getting off the beaten track.

Healthy Travel pocket guides offer a regional rundown on disease hot spots and practical advice on predeparture health measures, staying well on the road and what to do in emergencies. The guides come with a user-friendly design and helpful diagrams and tables.

Lonely Planet's **Phrasebooks** cover the essential words and phrases travelers need when they're strangers in a strange land. They come in a pocket-sized format with color tabs for quick reference, extensive vocabulary lists, easy-to-follow pronunciation keys and two-way dictionaries.

Miffed by blurry photos of the Taj Mahal? Tired of the classic 'top of the head cut off' shot? **Travel Photography: A Guide to Taking Better Pictures** will help you turn ordinary holiday snaps into striking images and give you the know-how to capture every scene, from frenetic festivals to peaceful beach sunrises.

Lonely Planet's **Travel Journal** is a lightweight but sturdy travel diary for jotting down all those on the road observations and significant travel moments. It comes with a handy time zone wheel, world maps and useful travel information.

Lonely Planet's eKno is an all-in-one communication service developed especially for travelers, with low-cost international calls, free email and voicemail so that you can keep in touch while on the road. Check it out on **www.ekno.lonelyplanet.com**

FOOD & RESTAURANT GUIDES

Lonely Planet's **Out to Eat** guides recommend the brightest and best places to eat and drink in the top international cities. These gourmet companions are arranged by neighborhood, packed with dependable maps, garnished with scene-setting photos and served with quirky features.

For people who live to eat, drink and travel, **World Food** guides explore the culinary culture of each country. Entertaining and adventurous, each guide is packed with details on staples and specialties, regional cuisine and local markets, as well as sumptuous recipes, comprehensive culinary dictionaries and lavish photos good enough to eat.

Index

Bold indicates maps.

Boxed Text

MAP LEGEND

ROUTES

City Regional

.... Freeway
.... Toll Freeway
.... Primary Road
.... Secondary Road
.... Tertiary Road
.... Dirt Road

.... Pedestrian Mall
.... Steps
.... Tunnel
.... Trail
.... Walking Tour
.... Path

TRANSPORTATION

.... Train
.... Metro

.... Bus Route
.... Ferry

HYDROGRAPHY

...... River; Creek
.... Canal
.... Lake

.... Spring; Rapids
.... Waterfalls
.... Dry; Salt Lake

ROUTE SHIELDS

[1] Carretera Interamericana
[9] Carretera Nacional
[5] Carretera Departamental

BOUNDARIES

...... International
.... State

.... County
.... Disputed

AREAS

.... Beach
.... Building
.... Campus

.... Cemetery
.... Forest
.... Garden; Zoo

.... Golf Course
.... Park
.... Plaza

.... Reservation
.... Sports Field
.... Swamp; Mangrove

POPULATION SYMBOLS

◎ NATIONAL CAPITAL ...... National Capital
◉ State Capital .... State Capital

● Large City .... Large City
● Medium City .... Medium City

● Small City .... Small City
● Town; Village .... Town; Village

MAP SYMBOLS

■ .... Place to Stay
▼ .... Place to Eat
● .... Point of Interest

.... Airfield
.... Airport
...... Archeological Site; Ruin
.... Bank
.... Baseball Diamond
.... Battlefield
.... Bike Trail
.... Border Crossing
.... Bus Station; Terminal
...... Cable Car; Chairlift
.... Café
.... Campground
.... Castle
.... Cathedral
.... Cave

.... Church
.... Cinema
...... Embassy; Consulate
.... Ferry Terminal
.... Footbridge
.... Garden
.... Gas Station
.... Hospital
.... Information
.... Internet Café
.... Lighthouse
.... Lookout
.... Mission
.... Monument
.... Mountain

.... Museum
.... Observatory
.... Park
.... Parking Area
.... Pass
.... Picnic Area
.... Police Station
.... Pool
.... Post Office
.... Pub; Bar
.... RV Park
.... Shelter
.... Shipwreck
.... Shopping Mall
...... Skiing - Cross Country

.... Skiing - Downhill
.... Stately Home
.... Surfing
.... Synagogue
.... Tao Temple
.... Taxi
.... Telephone
.... Theater
.... Toilet - Public
.... Tomb
.... Trailhead
.... Tram Stop
.... Transportation
.... Volcano
.... Zoo

Note: not all symbols displayed above appear in this book

LONELY PLANET OFFICES

Australia
PO Box 617, Hawthorn 3122, Victoria
☎ 03 9819 1877 fax 03 9819 6459
email talk2us@lonelyplanet.com.au

USA
150 Linden Street, Oakland, California 94607
☎ 510 893 8555, TOLL FREE 800 275 8555
fax 510 893 8572
email info@lonelyplanet.com

UK
10A Spring Place, London NW5 3BH
☎ 020 7428 4800 fax 020 7428 4828
email go@lonelyplanet.co.uk

France
1 rue du Dahomey, 75011 Paris
☎ 01 55 25 33 00 fax 01 55 25 33 01
www.lonelyplanet.fr

World Wide Web: www.lonelyplanet.com *or* AOL keyword: lp
Lonely Planet Images: lpi@lonelyplanet.com.au